Dalhuisen on Transnational Comparative, Commercial, Financial and Trade Law, Volume 1

This is the fifth edition of the leading work on transnational and comparative commercial and financial law, covering a wide range of complex topics in the modern law of international commerce, finance and trade. As a guide for students and practitioners it has proven to be unrivalled. Since the fourth edition, the work is now divided into three volumes, each of which can be used independently or as part of the complete work.

Volume one covers the roots and foundations of private law; the different orientations and structure of civil and common law; the concept, forces, and theoretical basis of the transnationalisation of the law in the professional sphere; the autonomous sources of the new law merchant or modern *lex mercatoria*, its largely finance-driven impulses; and its relationship to domestic public policy and public order requirements.

Volume two deals with transnational contract, moveable and intangible property law.

Volume three deals with financial products and financial services, with the structure and operation of modern commercial and investment banks, and with financial risk, stability and regulation, including the fall-out from the recent financial crisis and regulatory responses in the US and Europe.

All three volumes may be purchased separately or as a single set.

Dalhuisen on Transnational Comparative, Commercial, Financial and Trade Law

Volume 1

Introduction—The New *Lex Mercatoria* and its Sources

Jan H Dalhuisen, PhD, LLM, FCI Arb

Professor of Law, Dickson Poon School of Law
King's College London

Miranda Chair in Transnational Financial Law
Catholic University Lisbon

Visiting Professor UC Berkeley

Corresponding Member
Netherlands Royal Academy of Arts and Sciences

Member New York Bar

ICSID Arbitrator

·HART·
PUBLISHING
OXFORD AND PORTLAND, OREGON
2013

Published in the United Kingdom by Hart Publishing Ltd
16C Worcester Place, Oxford, OX1 2JW
Telephone: +44 (0)1865 517530
Fax: +44 (0)1865 510710
E-mail: mail@hartpub.co.uk
Website: http://www.hartpub.co.uk

Published in North America (US and Canada) by
Hart Publishing
c/o International Specialized Book Services
920 NE 58th Avenue, Suite 300
Portland, OR 97213-3786
USA
Tel: +1 503 287 3093 or toll-free: (1) 800 944 6190
Fax: +1 503 280 8832
E-mail: orders@isbs.com
Website: http://www.isbs.com

British Library Cataloguing in Publication Data
Data Available

ISBN: 978-1-84946-451-2

Typeset by Compuscript Ltd, Shannon
Printed and bound in Great Britain by
MPG Printgroup Ltd

Contents

Table of Cases

France

Germany

International Cases

Netherlands

Switzerland

United Kingdom

United States

Table of Legislation and Related Documents

France

Germany

International

Italy

Netherlands

Poland

Portugal

Switzerland

United Kingdom

United States

Part I   The Transnationalisation of Commercial and Financial Law. The Law Concerning Professional Dealings

1.1 Introduction

1.1.1 The Place and Evolution of Modern Commercial and Financial Law in Civil and Common Law. The Concept of Transnationalisation

Commercial law, including financial and trade law, has long had a somewhat different status in civil and common law. This has, first, to do with the different attitudes towards the role of legislation and particularly towards systematic legal thinking, but it is also a matter of coverage and practice and ultimately one of the recognition (or not) of the special place that commercial and financial law may have in either legal system. This discussion has acquired renewed relevance in modern times and is increasingly influenced or matched by the idea or realisation that, at least in international dealings or professional cross-border activities however defined, the relevant commercial and financial law might not emanate from states at all, either in the civil or common law tradition, but rather from *a legal order of its own* and may then be considered *transnationalised*. This goes back to an era when commercial law was indeed not national and did not belong to any particular legal order except its own.

To the extent that commercial and financial law must still be considered national, the evolution of the civil and common law, their origins and their differences, remain very relevant in discussing the nature and application of this law as we shall see. It is of special importance and may create particular problems if these national laws are applied in international cases by courts in other countries or by international arbitrators. Even if commercial and financial law were to become fully transnationalised, consideration should still be given to whether the common law or civil law approach and methodology should be followed or favoured or whether a different approach altogether should prevail. The differences between the two systems will be discussed in greater detail below in sections 1.2 and 1.3.[1] Here it is sufficient to note that in *civil law countries* the codification ethos

---

[1] As far as civil law is concerned (as will be discussed in greater detail below), its history is largely Roman; its method is largely that of the natural law school of Grotius and his followers; and the nationalistic statutory approach is largely due to nineteenth-century political imperatives and developments. Roman law and the common law are the only truly original Western legal systems of private law. The natural law school may suggest a third development in Western Europe, but it is usually associated with the development of the Roman law into the modern civil law. It is, in any event, highly important for a proper understanding of the civil law as we know it today. For valuable discussions of this development see the classic treatises of Paul Koschaker, *Europa und das römische Recht* (1947, reprinted 1953) and of Franz Wieacker, *Privatrechtsgeschichte der Neuzeit*, 2nd edn (1967, reprinted 1996).

looks primarily for legislation and (often) assumes in that connection that private law, including commercial and financial law, is *one* intellectually coherent *national system* that is essentially statutory or codified. This suggests that private law is imposed from above as an internally consistent system that is complete, explainable from within, and capable of finding solutions for all eventualities, present and future, on the basis of the proper application of its rules or otherwise the principles underlying it.[2]

This attitude is rule-oriented and formal. In essence, it waits for the state to effectuate change through legislation when there is a need to adapt the law, which is thus nationalised as to its formation, and territorial. Since the system and its coherence are here considered of primary importance, in private law codification, states will rely on academic advice to preserve intellectual rigour and consistency—at least that is the idea. The application of this law is subsequently seen mainly as a technique which has logic as its core and automatically correct solutions are expected if this intellectual system of rules is properly applied. Extraneous sources of law are irrelevant. That applies especially to fundamental and general principles but also to custom and party autonomy unless the statutory texts specifically refer to them and allow them to operate. There is no other source of law.

This approach was the result of three nineteenth-century paradigm shifts that changed the private law on the European Continent completely and also fundamentally affected commercial and financial law. The result was the modern civil law differentiating it henceforth from the earlier universal Roman law and also from the approach of the common law. The idea is then that a) all law, including private law, is national; b) it issues from states, hence the dominance of legislative texts; and c) these texts present or should aspire to present an intellectual system which is internally coherent and complete, and reflects per definition the reality of human relationships. As we shall see, in the European Union (EU) projects for private law unification there is an unarticulated combination of these various views, as there is in UNCITRAL and UNIDROIT, the sum total of which is the continuation of a top-down statist approach to private law formation. It claims exclusivity for its texts which control all private law, including, in principle, the contractual content. There are no overriding values and party autonomy operates only by licence of the state.[3] Private law is nationalised. Treaty law is no more than national law adopted by the contracting states.

---

[2] As we shall see below in s 1.2.9, this was particularly a German intellectual ideal that, combined with the early nineteenth century Romantic emphasis on nationality and creativity and the subsequent notion of the creation of society according to preconceived intellectual or academic models (but always by country), also began to dominate civil law thinking outside Germany during the nineteenth and twentieth centuries. For German orthodoxy in this respect, see K Larenz, *Methodenlehre der Rechtswissenschaft*, 6th edn (1991) 6, 437 and the student version, revised by CW Canaris, 3rd edn (1995) 263.

[3] A dynamic forward-moving force in the law is not denied here, but it is not autonomous and depends on a liberal interpretation within this more static, abstract system. *cf* n 185 below for other (minority) views in Germany. This situation is very different from the one in the US under the Uniform Commercial Code (UCC) which, as we shall see, encourages the common law, equity and custom or the law merchant to operate besides it (Sec 1-103), accepts and favours bottom-up law formation and is in that sense not a European-style codification at all. See also text at n 26 below. It is further imbued by realism as the Americans perceive it, see ss 1.3.4-5 below, that is guided by practical need and a continuous search for operational sufficiency which requires and allows constant adaptation in the practice of the law, here commercial law in particular, and permits its continued expansion 'through custom, usage and the agreement between the parties.' There is true party autonomy and respect for the contract and its content as such, subject only to public order and policy requirements, as indeed there was on the European Continent before the nineteenth century.

This is also reminiscent of the old common-law tradition, although the English may now be somewhere in the middle. See text at n 17 below. They do not require legislative texts and a top-down approach to pervade all law formation although legislation became increasingly important in private law as well. The Law Commission

This remains the basic approach in modern private law unification to which the Draft Common Frame of Reference (DCFR) and its progeny as models for codification at the level of the EU also testify.[4] It follows that there is no real need for empirical research and this law is not questioned, for example, as to its fairness, efficiency or responsiveness to social or economic needs.[5] They are assumed to result from the system itself, and because it is the law, it must as such be accepted as correct, never mind how far from practical realities it may be, and whatever unexpected and undesirable side effects it may have, or indeed how poor the intellectual back-up may prove to be or to have become. This is the civil law expression of legal positivism (and formalism) and still the mainstream of its thinking.[6] In this approach, it is explicit that commercial (and financial) law is an inextricable part of the national codification (whether or not contained in a separate code) and subject to its method and way of application. It is thus equally national and intellectual, and must be made to fit. It is not independent, merely *lex specialis* or refinement. In this approach, even international commercial transactions are covered by and must find a solution for their problems in these national laws, the proper one then being found through conflict rules or rules of private international law.

It follows, *first*, that the further development of the law, even private law, is perceived primarily as an activity of the state and as such is centralised and monopolised at state level. Law, even commercial and financial law, is thus deemed made and imposed, not found, even if it is based on an analysis of prior experiences. In particular, it denies the autonomous law creation impulses that may emanate from other groupings, for example, in commercial and financial practices or custom unless specially admitted by the state system which always has the last word.

Second, this law, even though commercial and financial, is academic and maintains in civil law countries an aura of self-evidence that derives from the pretence of intellectual consistency and completeness of the codified private law system as a whole. Its true legitimacy is not then in the democratic process, which in any event was often wanting when this law was first codified, or even in economic rationality, but in its systemic consistency and conceptual unity which claims by definition to be close enough to reality—even commercial and financial reality—to guide it and, if necessary, to redirect and control it for the greater benefit of all participants and the public at large.

---

in particular favours texts of this nature. The English courts so far remain pragmatic, have always dealt with fragmented legal sources, and are comfortable with them but some closing of the gap between Continental and English legal thinking has been noticed and at least English academia does not necessarily follow in the American footsteps: see PS Atiyah and RS Summers, *Form and Substance in Anglo-American Law: A Comparative Study of Legal Reasoning, Legal Theory, and Legal Institutions* (Oxford, Clarendon Press, 1987). No doubt there is greater Scottish comfort with civil-law thinking which trickled through in particular into the Draft Common Frame of Reference (DCFR) as a model for EU codification, where Scottish academics have been more active, but, as will be discussed in greater detail below in ss 1.4.1-2, the tolerance for other sources of law and especially the respect for party autonomy, the lack of systemic thinking, and the absence of a belief in the sufficiency of the academic model remain probably the key distinguishing elements between common and civil law (of the German variety in particular).

[4] See s 1.4.19 below.

[5] Although the question of whether morality in particular would be automatically served in this manner remained important in nineteenth-century German philosophical thinking: see Roscoe Pound, vol II *Jurisprudence* (1959) 223; it became much less of an issue in the run up to the German Codification in 1900 and in subsequent philosophical discourse in Germany.

[6] For the modern form of legal positivism in private law formation and application, see s 1.4.15 below.

Third, as in codification countries, the national private law regime is thus perceived as one intellectual statist system that monopolises the field, it follows that commercial and financial law is considered part of, and captured in, that system. It is not perceived to be independent from it but is merely *lex specialis* as just mentioned. These specialised areas have, therefore, no separate place in the law and cannot evolve independently. Commercial and financial law must fit the system and is then confined in its evolution.

Fourth, this monopolisation of the law formation function at the level of the state confirms that there is little room for the operation of other sources of law, such as commercial and financial practice and custom, or for general principles (other than those underlying the codes), whether or not commercial, national or transnational; or for efficiency considerations or considerations of economic growth; or for any cost benefit analysis, unless expressly admitted or tolerated by the codes or their systems themselves. It was already said that in this approach, even party autonomy setting forth the terms of a deal only operates by government licence and is therefore constrained to what the codified system will allow and it is not respected per se.[7] This approach to party autonomy goes far beyond the ordinary constraints derived from public order and public policy requirements which parties must respect. It concerns here the validity of their agreement itself, which thus depends on statist fiat. There is in fact no party autonomy as source of law.

Fifth, the result is that this law is static and without a dynamic forward-moving force except through legislation or case law which raises the question of interpretational powers and freedom in the state courts. It was secondary as the legislative approach supported by system thinking and a policy-oriented nationalistic outlook remained the focus and assumed for its further development foremost governmental insight (through its academies) into what was necessary in terms of updating and adaptation. Commercial and financial law shows, however—as does regulation—that such insight may not be forthcoming and that autonomous law-creating forces therefore remain necessary to keep private law up to date and functional. Thus fundamental and general principle, custom and practices, and party autonomy may still have to be included, although not openly but rather hidden in a *liberal* interpretation technique of a domestic nature; in contract, in modern times often operating behind the notion of good faith.

Sixth, in case of doubt or when situations were not explicitly covered or were new, and thus where the formal law lagged behind, it is true that even in civil law there had always been some interpretational flexibility largely based on an extrapolation of rules from existing legislation and its system or implementing case law. It could also mean inductive or otherwise analogical reasoning, but, although in this approach in modern times a more liberal teleological interpretation technique was allowed to provide greater flexibility, whilst even pressing ethical, social, and efficiency considerations might be admitted in the interpretation process, this was still mainly done to support and complete the national system, its tenets and especially its credibility. In essence, this method of interpretation continued to be subservient to the system rather than to society or to the community this law served, which system was thus perceived as remaining formal and closed in principle.

---

[7] Note that in pre-codification times, this autonomy was subject only to public policy constraints which were at first expressed mainly in the notion of a just cause (*iusta causa*), see vol II, ch 1, s 1.2.6. The approach in modern codification is quite different: party autonomy itself is licensed and not merely made subject to public policy and public order requirements.

Seventh, this attitude also fundamentally affected *international* transactions, even those in commerce and finance. Although these transactions were likely to be outside the immediate scope and concern of local codifications which were seldom written for them, they had to fit into *national* laws as there was (in this way of thinking) no other. It thus became necessary to search for the more appropriate but always *national* law in the above sense under applicable *conflicts of law* (or private international law) rules in international cases leading to the application of the domestic law considered the most closely connected with the case in question, even if, as we shall see, it became increasingly difficult and artificial to define or identify.

Eighth, as a more liberal interpretation technique created some flexibility at the edges, this could have led to the extrapolation and expansion of the *lex fori* into international cases, especially taking into account the foreign elements of the case and increasingly also other more transnational sources of law so that a form of transnationalisation would result in the interpretation of domestic laws. It is an approach that gained some ground in the US also (interstate) as we shall see[8] but not so far in Europe. The problem is that each legal system then creates its own form of transnationalisation.

Ninth, quite apart from the problems of identifying the closest connection, particularly in factual situations with many contacts, there naturally arose, in this approach, ever greater problems when considerations (or values) that surpassed national concerns, it being implicit in the codification approach that all moral, social and economic ordering as well as an adequate level of legal certainty, were expected from and had to be provided by a national legislator in international cases as well. This was hardly any longer feasible in an ever more globalised world and economy, nor was it rational to continue to expect it.

Tenth, regulation which remained mostly domestic also became increasingly a problem in international transactions as it had to be established which governmental interests prevailed in this connection and in what aspects if they were conflicting. This raised the issue of the proper jurisdiction to prescribe, as the Americans call it, as well as the question of the operation of international minimum standards.

At a more philosophical level, the civil law approach assumes above all that in matters of private law we live with an account of human behaviour that can be clarified scientifically and is orderly, in essence based on repetition. That is the neo-classical view in macroeconomics which is often believed to have failed us, but we struggle with the same problem in the law, where it is further complicated by nationalistic thinking. Indeed, the codification approach in its purest form does not consider or accept that the future is different from the past and that it cannot be systematically captured nor that international transactions may require their own transnationalised legal regime that might operate quite differently.

It means that in considering better (private) law, the inclination is always to remedy the shortcomings of the past in a national context, the idea being that new or ever evolving patterns, even if transnational, can still be satisfactorily covered in this manner. Proper and ever better analysis of past experiences is here the ultimate guide in law formation, completed by intellectual extrapolation and systematisation. The idea is that 'truth' can be established in this manner and that the reality of human relations can thus be discovered and formulated in an academic model and can hence be correctly guided, for which the

---

[8] See s 2.2.3 below. Even in the traditional conflicts of law approach, this may well reflect what actually happens in practice.

state with its power of rule imposition is the superior channel. For those who think in this manner, the only alternative to national codification for international dealings is treaty law, which is, in this view—as has been mentioned before—upon ratification still considered the expression of national law; retains its territorial limitations; and always remains a super-imposed statist formal legal facility.[9]

Nevertheless, in the application of codified law or of treaty law of this nature, inconsistencies and inadequacies could not be avoided. The subsequent need for a liberal interpretation technique meant indeed that other sources of law—which in a globalising world were also not necessarily territorial—revived, not least in international dealings. Thus fundamental and general principle, custom or industry practices, as well as expanded notions of party autonomy resumed their traditional roles to sort out contradictions and inadequacies and to make better sense, although in civil law academia this development remains in essence largely ignored even for international dealings.

Domestic statutory texts and their logical coherence thus remain the centre of attention, even if some uniform transnational law may now be considered if expressed in treaty texts whilst liberal interpretation is further admitted to save the system and its credibility, but law, including private law, remains here in essence a pre-existing national system of formal rules. There are no other admissible sources of law. They would only confuse and deviate from the proper state-ordained path.

In the EU, the DCFR, mentioned above, which since 2008/2009 has been presented as a model for European codification, even though it has as yet no official status, except for its sale carve out in the 2011 EU Commission's proposal for a Regulation concerning a Common European Sales Law (CESL), is the latest expression of this attitude. In that sense the DCFR and CESL are concerned mainly with remaking the past in a territorial manner, now at the level of the EU. See section 1.4.19 below and more particularly Volume II, chapter 1, section 1.6 and chapter 2, section 1.11. Thus the approach remains academic, systematic, legislative, and nationalistic, albeit at the expanded EU level but in the traditional civil law, mainly German, codification manner.

To repeat: in civil law orthodoxy, there is little room here for an autonomous commercial and financial law at the national level, let alone transnationally. Newer globalising tendencies and needs thus continue to be ignored, even in commerce and finance. The DCFR and its progeny are in fact, a product not of transnationalisation but of national codification thinking, now at EU level. In particular, there is little understanding of the emergence of a transnational commercial and financial legal order with its own law and its own public order requirements, the result of which is now usually referred to as the new or modern *lex mercatoria* or international law merchant.[10] This new law merchant is not based on,

---

[9] This attitude is not limited to civil law, as we shall see. Thus Roy Goode, 'Rule, Practice, and Pragmatism in International Commercial Law' (2005) 54 *ICLQ* 539, 549 limits transnational law to treaty law. That seems extreme precisely because of treaty law's territorial aspects.

[10] In the following, the word 'international' will be reserved largely for transborder *public* law and 'transnational' for transborder *private* law. As we shall see, recognition of other sources of law, especially customary law, general principle and party autonomy as original sources of law, was never as problematic in public international law as was expressed in Art 38(1) of the Statute of the International Court of Justice. This reflects the older Grotian approach which, until the nineteenth century, also prevailed in private law and of which there may remain more in the common law approach. The revival of the same approach for transnational private law formation is the preferred one in this book. See also JH Dalhuisen, 'Legal Orders and their Manifestation: The Operation of the International Commercial and Financial Legal Order and its *Lex Mercatoria*' (2006) 24 *Berkeley Journal of International Law* 129.

and does not adhere to, the civil law codification idea but allows various sources of law to operate and establishes a hierarchy between them. As we shall see, this suggests at least in part a bottom up, dynamic process of law formation and application and in method goes back to pre-codification days.

As just mentioned, the lack of newer thinking is also reflected in the CESL (see for a critique Volume II, section 1.6.13) and covers a subject (sale of goods) that in common law traditionally belongs to the area of commercial law. Indeed, there is no whiff of a transnational approach. Worse, the methodology was never properly considered; the civil law codification approach was assumed to be natural and uncontentious. Although limited to cross-border dealings within the EU, the operation of the modern *lex mercatoria* is ignored; as an opt-in instrument, the only alternative remains here national law. There are still no other sources of law admissible in international professional dealings, at least that is the approach, although it may be questioned whether there is sufficient authority to exclude them. As a minimum, this should have been part of the discussion. The idea that there might be a separate legal order for professional dealings altogether, which develops a law that is not primarily state controlled, is dynamic and also applies within the EU, remains here inconceivable, but it is the real issue.

Quite apart from its other defects and pretentions, nationalistic system thinking of this nature around pre-existing hard and fast local rules has a tendency to stultify the law whatever the reach of more liberal interpretation techniques may be. In fact, this more static statist civil law approach to law formation has a problem with all innovation, even domestic, thus not only in international commercial and financial dealings. In more modern terms, it has particular difficulty with the legal response to a globalising world and cannot cope with its dynamism. See also section 1.1.4 below. This is not without consequence and it may be posited that nationalistic system thinking in the above manner is the reason why modern civil law has been particularly wanting in international commerce and finance, has increased legal risk in these areas, and may well be driving vital markets away. One may think here particularly of international finance and the operation of the financial markets, which are increasingly globalised and for which civil law thinking can give little support.[11] This will be demonstrated throughout this book. As just mentioned, a more liberal interpretation might be used to save the system but the techniques mostly remain national-system-bound and are in any event, contentious in property law. This will be further explained in Volume II. For the reason why, at least in commerce and finance, this civil law approach as a national model or system must now be more fundamentally revisited, see more particularly the discussion in section 1.4 below.

It was not always thus, and may no longer be the way of the future, but it is the nineteenth-century inheritance of the civil law, often closely associated with the emergence of the modern state in Continental Europe. On the European Continent it superseded the received Roman law that had been customary and was supported by the secular natural

---

[11] We shall see, however, that there is significant acceptance of a more transnational approach, particularly in France where it is demonstrated in particular in the attitude to international arbitration, recently perhaps best represented before the Hague Academy by Emanuel Gaillard, 'Aspects Philosophiques du Droit de l'Arbitrage International' (2008) 329 *Receuil des Cours* 49; see further *Cour de Cass Civ* 1, 29 June 2007 in *Ste PT Putrabali Adyamulia v Societe Rena Holding et Societe Mnugotia Est Epices*, Arret n 1021, 207 *Revue de l'Arbitrage*, 507. As we shall also see in the text at n 29 below, it may be less strong in other codification countries.

law of those days. It was not statist or territorial and had been more universal,[12] although particularly in commerce and finance it was supplemented by a myriad of local laws and practices.[13] In fact, there were multiple sources of law that could compete.

It is also relevant, especially in commerce, that there was at the time a variety of judges,[14] the judicial function often being private, and they would use their own knowledge of custom and practices, as specialised arbitrators may still do today.[15] Enforcement was also mostly private and therefore conducted within the commercial communities themselves. Law formation was not then the natural province of states, most certainly not in commerce, unless public order was engaged, as was often considered the case in bankruptcy but was otherwise exceptional. Where statutes were produced, they were even then normally regional or city compilations of existing customs gathered mainly to provide greater transparency and to promote trade more generally (in which local government often had a taxation interest, which also explains the eagerness to provide order in market places and to protect trade routes as far as possible). Thus the purpose was not to preempt or prevent

---

[12] This earlier law had never been officially promulgated but was basically found, not imposed. Long considered the best expression of rationality, this Roman law was given a high customary status, see ss 1.2.4–1.2.5 below, and was considered universal, although subject to competing local laws. Fundamental and general principles, custom and industry practices supplemented it and, especially since Grotius, guided the natural law schools, see s 1.2.7 below. Moreover, parties could freely legislate amongst themselves (subject to the requirement of a valid cause or similar public policy constraints which were then minor) and there was true party autonomy in the legal sense. For the history and remnants in France and present day revival see s 1.4.9 below.

Civil law codification wiped them out as independent sources of law. See B Cremades and S Plehn, 'The New Lex Mercatoria and the Harmonisation of the Laws of International Commercial Transactions' (1984) 2 *Boston University International Law Journal*, 324. At first for obvious efficiency and transparency reasons—therefore as a product of enlightenment or rationalism, which also entailed the centralisation and nationalisation of the judicial function. It is substantially the background of the French *Code Civil*, as we shall see in s 1.2.8. below, but the codification drive was later joined and became dominated by forces of pure nationalism in the Romantic Rousseauian and German (Hegelian) variant of the codification theme, in which the state became the expression of the general will or even the true embodiment of the human condition—the individual and its law being considered nothing by themselves. See also section 1.2.9 below.

Ultimately states of this nature took charge of what they then believed to be a society in which they saw themselves as the originator and enforcer of all rules per country. Commerce and finance were not excluded and their international reach was ignored. Legal orders different from states were denied existence. There is no place here for international law either, except as some ultimate, unreachable ideal (in terms of world nationality).

Whether these state absolutist notions in law formation helped or distracted from modern capitalism, is less clear. The initial idea was in any event not to redirect and censure trade and commerce, but the commercial law was henceforth *lex specialis* to the national, state-created, system of private law as there was no longer anything else. Whatever international legal unity there still was depended on the old traditions being recognised to some extent in the new laws (although transformed to fit the general private law system per country) and otherwise on treaty law.

[13] This is often referred to as the older *lex mercatoria*. However, it should be understood that its rules were not the same everywhere but developed in answer to practical needs. Only to the extent that these needs were felt everywhere, did the rules show some innate uniformity but there were significant differences. See FR Sanborn, *Origins of the Early English and Maritime and Commercial Laws* 126. The laws of admiralty, for example, were not the same in the English Channel/French coast and offshore Italy (The Amalfian Table). The bankruptcy laws also varied widely. See JH Dalhuisen, *Dalhuisen on International Insolvency and Bankruptcy* (1986) 1–25ff.

[14] See WC Jones, 'An Inquiry into the History of the Adjudication of Mercantile Disputes in Great Britain and the United States' (1958) 25 *University of Chicago Law Review*, 445.

[15] It is well understood that modern arbitrators find on the basis of laws and facts pleaded by the parties and are not free to use or rely on their own knowledge without a proper hearing and argument, unless they may state as *amiable compositeurs* or the arbitration is specialised and depends on peer knowledge in arbitrators, not unusual in quality issues, which are largely factual. This is a different type of arbitration, however, based not on law but on expertise in arbitrators and presents an older type of dispute resolution which left decisions to senior experts trusted in the particular trade and often not requiring any reasoning.

further development by the commercial communities themselves (which were not united except by the needs of their various trades which could be very local).

In the *common law*, the situation was and still is different from the one we find in modern civil law. In its formation and further evolution, common law was often helped, but never monopolised, by legislation. System thinking and the search for and application of one coherent system of private law are here not major issues either, at least not traditionally. By its very nature, the common law moves from case to case, is factual and result-oriented, and in principle leaves room for other sources of law, in trade, commerce and finance especially for industry practices or customs, supported by party autonomy, and therefore by the order that participants create amongst themselves.

This should not be idealised but it is clear that the common law has, at least in principle, the tools and willingness to be more responsive to practical needs. It has avoided the grip of the academic model. As a consequence, commercial law was also able to retain a more independent status and role in common law countries, although especially in England, nationalism and the tightening grip of the common law itself also impacted on a more decentralised approach to commercial law and on the reach of party autonomy, custom and commercial practices, as we shall see.[16] This also affected the commercial law's international status in England. It became there also substantially territorial.

In fact, in England by the eighteenth century the commercial law had already been incorporated into the common law and had lost its independence,[17] although it was not

---

[16] As to the other source of law: general principle, the common law had always been wary of it, as on the whole it dislikes generalisation, see s 1.4.6 below. Worse perhaps, was that custom became subject to the law of precedent, depending as such on court recognition, see text at n 21 below.

[17] In England, there was already some statutory law and a Statute of Merchants (Acton Burnell) of 1283, in an effort to attract foreign traders to England, promoted the speedy settlement of disputes between all merchants, while an Act of 1303 (*Carta Mercatoria*) had recognised the law merchant as an independent source of law amongst all traders, exempted foreign traders from local taxes, and gave them freedom to trade throughout England.

The old commercial courts did the rest and their laws were originally more particularly connected with fairs and the maritime activities in the Channel ports, where participants were peripatetic merchants or maritime transporters, including foreigners, which required prompt justice to be enforced either against the person of the debtor, if still present at the fair, or, particularly in his absence, against his goods before they left the court's jurisdiction. See F Pollock, "The Early History of the Law Merchant in England' (1901) 67(3) *Law Quarterly Review*.

The courts in the staple markets, which also attracted foreigners, were the Staple Courts which were statutory from 1354 onwards. The Staple Courts often consisted of the mayor and two constables or merchants, who could be foreign if a foreign merchant was involved. At more local fairs, on the other hand, there often operated Borough- or Pie Powder Courts, used especially for civil and criminal litigation between the participants in these markets, who were mostly locals. These courts often only operated during the fairs with a process 'from hour to hour and day to day'.

In all these courts, judges and juries of merchants were used to discover the applicable customs, although there were some written sources of the applicable commercial law also, such as the Red Book in Bristol and the Black Book of Admiralty in London. There were others in maritime law, notably the laws of Visby and the laws of Oleron, a small island off the French coast of Aquitaine, which were highly regarded and often consulted elsewhere.

Special maritime courts began to operate after 1360, at first competent mainly in criminal cases (piracy), later also in civil cases with the emphasis on charters, ship mortgages, maritime insurance, early forms of bills of lading and the earlier forms of negotiable instruments such as bills of exchange and cheques. To appear before these courts, the plaintiff had to prove that the defendant was a merchant and establish the applicability of commercial law or custom, but the presence of the defendant was not strictly necessary as long as some of his goods were in the jurisdiction. It should be emphasised that the law merchant of those early days was *not* as a consequence a uniform law in any sense and that its content varied with the markets and products covered—and it could be very local—but the common outstanding feature was that both this law and the courts that administered it were

completely subsumed and retained some special place in particular through the endeavours of Lord Mansfield.[18] But as its courts were similarly overtaken by the common law jurisdiction, this restricted the further independent development of commercial law.[19] Moreover, in the nineteenth century, the notion gained ground, in England too, that all law issued from a sovereign, although it did *not* depend on legislation. That is the school of Bentham and Austin, which became dominant as we shall see in section 1.3.3 below. Nationalism thus entered and further eroded the support for other sources of private law, especially customary law, all the more so when international, although the common law itself was often still considered of 'immemorial usage', but that was then deemed a kind of overriding higher custom[20] and in any event always national.

In the meantime, in common law countries, the emerging rule of precedent confined the role of custom or market practices further (see section 1.3.3 below,) and to a large extent

autonomous. Others have noted as other common features the customary nature of these courts, their summary jurisdiction, and spirit of equity and common sense that was not concerned with technicalities. See, eg W Mitchell, *An Essay on the Early History of the Law Merchant* (Cambridge University Press, 1904). Jealousy eventually manifested itself in the common law courts, especially in the Court of Admiralty in London. The common law judges eventually took the view that the older commercial and admiralty courts only operated by franchise and could, therefore, be controlled by the common law courts. Consequently, these older courts started to disappear, although they were never formally abolished; after the middle of the eighteenth century only the Court of Tolzey in Bristol survived. The overriding influence of Chief Justice Sir Edward Coke is often mentioned in this connection. Eventually the requirements that the defendant had to be a merchant and that commercial law or custom was applicable disappeared. After 1765, the common law courts considered that 'the law of merchants and the law of the land are the same: a witness cannot be admitted to prove the law of merchants'. See *Pillans v Van Mierop* [1765] 97 ER 1035 [1765] 3 Burr 1663, 1669. This appears to have concluded the trend.

[18] Although this integration of commercial law into the common law is generally considered to have been completed under Chief Justice Coke, Lord Mansfield in particular subsequently tried to develop commercial law alongside commercial practice but always within the confines of the common law and its courts. As we shall see, this left at least some room for commercial custom and practices as independent sources of law but it did not reestablish independence. In *Pillans v Van Mierop*, see n 17 above, Lord Mansfield accepted that the rules of the law merchant had become part of the common law and were no longer autonomous custom. He accepted the jurisdiction of the common law courts but added that the common law and its courts had to recognise the *dynamics of international business* so that commercial law was to evolve alongside commercial practice. Yet the law merchant as an independent legal order governing the legal relationship between merchants had ceased to be recognised and the national common law sustained the international character of commerce to only a limited extent, more in the nature of courtesy or *comitas*. *cf* C Schmitthoff, 'International Business Law: A New Law Merchant' (1961) *Current Law and Social Problems* 129, 138. This nevertheless proved particularly important for negotiable instruments (although the first time the promissory note was declared a negotiable instrument in England was earlier in 1680, in the case of *Sheldon v Hently* [1681] 2 Show 160 involving bills of lading, and (later) documentary sales, such as the FOB and CIF sales, ship mortgages, the stoppage of goods in transit and in the concept of bailment, therefore the protection of the physical possession of goods, in agency, partnership and joint ownership where commercial principle continued to be closely followed.

However, once having lost the autonomy of its courts, the commercial law never recovered a truly independent role in common law countries, and the same may now also be said of its modern branch of financial law. Nevertheless, it is not incidental or mere *lex specialis*, and it clearly covers whole areas of the common law in full.

[19] However, commercial law was poorly administered by the common law courts, and this is an important reason why in common law the law of chattels long remained, and probably still remains, underdeveloped. The greater speed and flexibility of the older proceedings, not bogged down by procedural and evidential formalities, had fostered trade and proved especially important for foreigners and their protection. These benefits were lost when the common law judges became the commercial judges, most with experience only in land law and some in tort. Even today this is reflected in high costs and inefficiencies.

The further result was that much commercial expertise and flexibility were lost in this part of the law. By the end of the nineteenth century, the international connection had also been neglected, so that commercial law became a domestic affair in England, a situation further promoted by the preponderant impact of British colonial trade.

[20] Not, therefore, very different from the Roman law on the European Continent, see s 1.2.5 below.

they lost their status as a dynamic source of law.[21] As we shall see, this also affected equity that until then had functioned as another more flexible corrective or supplement of the law, particularly important in commerce and now also in finance, a facility in the meantime often taken over by legislation, although the equitable jurisdiction is not completely exhausted as we shall also see.

More recently, especially in England, academia has become more active in the law and has subsequently started to look for a more coherent system of rules distilled from disparate case law and statutory texts. Although the English courts have remained pragmatic, there thus also entered a measure of *nationalistic system thinking*, at least at academic level in England,[22] more so than in the US where this struggle is now often cast in terms of legal realism versus legal formalism as we shall see.[23] This may also affect the commercial and financial law and integrate it further into the common law.

The consequence of the integration of commercial law into the common law is, however, that the distinction between commercial and other private law is no longer fundamental in common law either, except that no systemic unity is assumed. As already mentioned, the distinction between *law* and *equity*, discussed in section 1.3.1 below, at first each with their own courts, may remain here more important, and also cuts through what may still be considered commercial and modern financial law, equity notions having become a particularly important support for commercial and financial law (despite the confining nature of the rule of precedent). Here we find company and bankruptcy law, the law of trusts, including related structures—now mostly statutory—and floating charges and conditional or finance sales, assignments and set-off, indirect agency and fiduciary duties.

Indeed, in all common law countries, there is now also substantial legislation in the field of private law, which may also extend into commercial and financial law. To a large extent it superseded the corrective power of the equity judges. Whilst the equity judges had often looked for inspiration abroad, especially in the Roman law, statutory law is by definition nationalistic or at least territorial. Even so, in common law countries statutory intervention is generally still different from the civil law approach in that it tends to be corrective or remedial and therefore incidental, except perhaps in typical equity areas such as company and bankruptcy law, where legislation is more comprehensive. However, even then it does not aspire to systematic thinking or overarching intellectual conceptualisation that seeks automaticity in its application and eliminates in the process other more spontaneous sources of law.

---

[21] It set customary law in concrete and it thus lost much of its dynamic character; it was thought that this prevented courts from becoming confused, a somewhat strange argument. See JH Baker, *An Introduction to English Legal History*, 3rd edn 1990) 418; see also RW Aske, *The Law Relating to Custom and the Usages of Trade* (1909) 23; and HJ Berman and C Kaufman, 'The Law of International Transactions (Lex Mercatoria)' (1978) 19 *Harvard International Law Journal* 221, 227.

[22] Especially in the 20th century, when the academic study of law became more established and valued in England. See ss 1.3.2 and 1.3.3.below for the role of the Law Commission in this process and for early codification ideas in England. A more formalistic approach is adopted here but it is not the traditional common law attitude that was fact-, rather than rule-oriented, and moved from case to case.

[23] See more particularly s 1.3.4 .below and for the UCC approach, also n 3 above.

Legal formalism is the opposite of legal realism and rests on the idea of the self-sufficiency of the legal system as a set of pre-existing, often hard and fast, black-letter rules that can be more or less mechanically applied and that are considered to produce acceptable results in a more objective manner. In doing so, legal formalism is inclined to disregard the original purposes which a particular norm was meant to serve and does not test its practical effects.

In the US, the Uniform Commercial Code (UCC) in section 1-103 clearly expresses the view that the statutory texts are to be interpreted so as to leave as much room as possible for the common law, equity, custom, the law merchant and party autonomy.[24] Even though it calls itself a 'code', it is therefore not a code in the civil law sense because it does not seek to monopolise the field and eliminate other sources of law,[25] and, although undoubtedly looking for structure, it is also not systemic in the civil law manner.[26]

This represents the more traditional common law approach, which still finds an equivalent in England in the mostly literal and therefore restrictive interpretation of statutory private law texts,[27] again to leave as much room as possible for the more traditional sources of law, especially the common law and equity (although, as we have already seen this may now be less true for the custom), even if increasingly construed and perceived academically as one national coherent system.

On the other hand, the predominantly nationalistic approach to private law formation and operation, although still different from the civil law approach, has also led in common law countries to the extension of *domestic* law to *international* transactions and consequently to an embrace of Continental European conflicts of law or private international law notions pointing to the proper connection, therefore to the idea that *only* domestic laws could apply to international transactions, even in international commerce and finance. This is not, therefore, transnational law. Although private international law as a system of hard-and-fast conflict rules has long been reconsidered in the US, as we shall see in sections 2.2.2 to 2.2.3 below, this has not been the case in England.

In fact, as we shall also see, the more robust resistance against the alternative of transnationalisation of private law, including the rejection of other autonomous transnational sources of law in the modern *lex mercatoria*, often comes from England, even though it would benefit English practitioners most and appears to fit the common law tradition much better than the civil law.[28] It is more welcome in France where greater transnationalism is now accepted in these matters.[29]

---

[24] In s 1-103 UCC it is further stated that the principles of law and equity, including the law merchant and the law relative to the capacity to contract, principal and agent, estoppel, fraud, misrepresentation, duress, coercion, mistake, bankruptcy, or other validating or invalidating cause, shall supplement the UCC, unless displaced by particular (mandatory) provisions of it.

[25] It is also practical and misses the typical nationalistic element. See RM Buxbaum, 'Is the Uniform Commercial Code a Code?' in U Drobnig and M Rehbinder, *Rechtsreaklismus, multikulturelle Gesellschaft und Handelsrecht* (Berlin, 1994) 197; and J Gordley, 'European Codes and American Restatements: Some Difficulties' (1981) 81 *Columbia Law Review* 140; see further s 1.3.3 below for earlier American attempts at codification.

[26] The UCC does not, for example, maintain a uniform concept of property law for all the chapters or Articles. In Art 2 on the sale of goods it maintains a more general notion of ownership and its transfer that also exists between non-professionals, but in Art 2A on equipment leases and Art 8 on the trading and holding of modern investment securities entitlements, proprietary rights are only defined incidentally, that is for each specific structure without resorting to general proprietary principles or a unitary system of proprietary rights. That is also true in Art 9 on secured transactions.

[27] See s 1.3.3 below.

[28] This has been pointed out by others, see notably AF Lowenfeld, 'Lex Mercatoria: an Arbitrator's View' (1990) 6 *Arbitration International* 133 in reply to English nationalism and positivism represented by Lord Mustill 'Contemporary Problems in International Commercial Arbitration' (1989) 17 *International Business Lawyer* 161ff, who even considered as absolutely void a contract in which transnational law is chosen as the controlling law. This has now officially been denied in the EU Regulation, (EC) No 593/2008, on the Law Applicable to Contractual Obligations (Rome I, Preamble 13).

[29] See n 11 above.

1.1.2 The Transnationalisation of Commercial and Financial Law. Common or Civil Law Approach? Methodology

Whatever the aims of nineteenth-century nationalism in private law may have been, both in civil and common law, commercial law formation through an autonomous process of transnationalisation, mainly through the force of principles and practices, was never entirely eradicated in international dealings even in civil law countries. One may think of the law concerning bills of lading; negotiable instruments especially eurobonds and euro-market practices including clearing and settlement; the law of assignment, of set-off and netting in international finance, and of letters of credit (UCP) and trade terms (Incoterms). It may also concern the important and connected issue of finality of title transfers and payments. For more detailed references see section 1.4.4 below.

It is clear that it concerns here the key *legal infrastructure of the international markets*, which can no longer be suitably covered by domestic laws. Where a generation ago the international markets might still have been peripheral to domestic markets and domestic legal systems, they have now moved to the centre, their size being far greater than that of the largest domestic markets.

If we think of the form this new transnational law takes, or should take, and how it compares to the more traditional common or civil law concepts of private law, it should be repeated that it is ultimately system thinking and the technical or mechanical approach to law and its application that truly distinguishes civil law from common law. That also affects our perception of commercial and financial law in common and civil law, more so than the statist or nationalistic and legislative approach per se, which to some extent both now share.

It is indeed this issue of domestic system thinking that may particularly affect our views of the place of commercial and financial law. If we mean to go forward with globalisation in a more coordinated manner, from a legal point of view, this presents a fundamental *methodological issue*, which needs to be resolved and also affects the appropriateness of codification in the civil law manner (through treaty law or, in the EU, possibly through regulation) of private law at the transnational level, especially in its elimination of all other sources of law.

It may be repeated in this connection that the informal formation of transnational law with reference to a number of autonomous sources of law is traditionally more suited to a common law rather than civil law environment; common law being 'bottom up' and going from case to case. If a more formal approach is taken, notably through treaty law, we may on the other hand come closer to the civil law technique, top-down, through an intellectual, government-endorsed framework or system. It has been said before that this appears to be the approach of UNCITRAL and UNIDROIT. Such a system may not easily admit other competing independent sources of law, especially of overarching fundamental principle, custom and general principle, or party autonomy, even if the good faith notion may *indirectly* reintroduce them at least in contract. A more liberal interpretation technique may generally do so in other areas as well, such as, for example, in the structures of movable property, as we shall see in section 1.4.3, although a liberal interpretation technique is traditionally much less common in this area of civil law.

This may all be considered to have a special relevance in the EU where attempts are now being made towards a kind of codification at the transnational level in Europe, in which connection the 2008–2009 DCFR and the 2011 draft Regulation on a Common European Sales Law (CESL) have already been mentioned. They also cover, by way of their unitary approach, professional dealings (although limited in the CESL to transactions that involve at least one SME), and thus also the areas of international commerce and finance and the operation of the international market place to the extent operating in the EU. The fuller implementation of the DCFR (and CESL) would then also affect its centre in London, and may result in a version of commercial and financial law which is very different from the one that currently obtains there. In the EU, this approach through legislation (treaty law or regulation) would at the same time fundamentally affect and curtail the more informal transnationalisation drive in the modern *lex mercatoria* with its spontaneous revival of the different autonomous transnational sources of law as we shall see.

In the view presented in this book, the new, immanent *lex mercatoria* is preferred for professional dealings and is indeed considered to be substantially based on fundamental and general principles, industry practices or custom, and party autonomy as independent sources of law: see section 1.4 below for a more detailed description of these sources of law. Treaty law (assuming it is widely adopted), although in principle still territorial and limited to activities in contracting states, may also figure, but is then only one of the sources of this law, not the dominant source, and must find its place amongst the others and even if mandatory may yield to a higher mandatory international fundamental principle or public order requirements and mandatory international custom.

This *lex mercatoria* or new transnational law merchant is as a consequence not, or not necessarily, systemic, intellectual and abstract in the traditional civil law codification sense, but may be closer to traditional common law in its development and operation, and not altogether different from public international law and its sources, as they function in the law between states, recognised as such in Article 38(1) of the Statute of the International Court of Justice (ICJ). In recent times, the best operation of this multiple source type of law can be seen in foreign investment arbitral awards, which may represent the most vivid expression of this approach.

As we shall see in section 1.4.13,[30] rather than the formation of one coherent, comprehensive system, the result is a *hierarchy* in these various sources of law that become potentially applicable. Domestic law may still remain the residual rule (although itself then also transnationalised).[31] As we shall also see, this transnational private law is *deferential* to public policy, normally of a domestic regulatory nature including domestic tax and environmental laws, assuming that there is sufficient conduct or effect of the transaction on the territory of the state which wants its policies enforced in this respect in the international transaction in question. This may also be the case for fundamental domestic values and may then be encapsulated in public order requirements.

---

[30] See also JH Dalhuisen, 'Legal Orders and their Manifestation: The Operation of the International Commercial and Financial Legal Order and its *Lex Mercatoria*' (2006) 24 *Berkeley Journal of International Law* 129 and JH Dalhuisen, 'The Operation of the International Commercial and Financial legal order: The Lex Mercatoria and Its Application' (2008) 19 *European Business Law Review* 985.

[31] See ss 1.4.12–1.4.13ff below. For the residual rule of domestic law in particular, see JH Dalhuisen, 'What could the Selection by Parties of English Law in a Civil Law Contract in Commerce and Finance Truly Mean?' in M Andenas and D Fairgrieve (eds) *Tom Bingham and the Transformation of the Law* (2009) 619.

As the new transnational law itself is private law, as such it does not mean to circumvent relevant domestic public policy of this nature (although between the parties it may still seek to rearrange the risks and financial consequences), and also respects domestic public order requirements as overarching if a sufficiently similar contact can be shown, but it is subject at the same time to the very *transnational* public-order considerations obtaining in the transnational commercial and financial legal order itself from which the modern *lex mercatoria* issues and in which it fundamentally operates.[32] In international transactions, domestic concepts of public order may then increasingly be tested against the concept of transnational public order in terms of internationally accepted *minimum* standards. This is an important development and is then outside the new *lex mercatoria* proper.

In the area of professional dealings, the formation and operation of this transnational private law—a de-nationalised law, shedding its statist and territorial nature—may be considered the natural and unavoidable consequence of globalisation and the internationalisation of the flows of persons, goods, services, knowledge, capital and payments. This is the perspective of this book. It introduces legal structures particularly made for and suited to these international dealings, which need not then be borrowed from local laws.

This transnationalising law between professionals should be *distinguished* in particular from *consumer law*, which remains by its very nature more domestic and protection-oriented, as well as more subject to special domestic (regulatory or policy) concerns. This may have immediate repercussions, for example, in the way concepts of reliance or good faith are applied in contract law. The protection they bring may be less proper and necessary, or may play out very differently for professionals in their international dealings. Relationship thinking thus takes over. As we shall see in section 1.1.4 below and later in Volume II, chapter 2 and Volume III, chapter 1, this may also be relevant for financial structures involving movable assets of professional parties seeking funding in more creative ways internationally, which structures may be much less suitable for consumers domestically.

The distinction between professional and consumer dealings becomes here fundamental (see further section 1.1.8 below); the former being legally increasingly transnationalised, the latter remaining domestic in a legal sense; the former being subject to immanent law creation forces, the latter being essentially regulated and therefore increasingly statutory, based on repeat transactions and need for public protection of weaker participants under national laws.[33] The result is, at least conceptually, an ever-increasing fracturing of the traditional systemic approach of the civil law even domestically according to the *nature of the relationship* of participants. This is a crucial departure in civil law thinking and is more familiar to common law.

---

[32] In American terms, the issue here is the jurisdiction to prescribe the law in international cases, and depends largely on an analysis of the facts and the circumstances of each case. This is also the approach adopted in Art 9 of the EU Regulation, (EC) No 593/2008 on the Law Applicable to Contractual Obligations, (Rome I) and in a more refined way in the American Restatements (Restatement (Second) of Conflict of Laws, s 6 and Restatement (Third) of Foreign Relations, ss 402–403).

[33] The EU has legislated fairly extensively in the area of consumer law, see n 443 below, and, since the 1992 Maastricht Treaty, considers it a legitimate preoccupation, although the Maastricht Treaty did not give the EU special legislative powers in private law formation. All such powers are still based on, and confined by, the promotion of the internal market. It means that in the consumer area, this is still primarily a question of setting uniform consumer standards to facilitate cross-border business rather than to protect consumers.

It may well be that in the EU, the DCFR with its codification approach and generally more prescriptive statist attitude, is relatively suitable in the area of consumer law from which it comes, and this may also be borne out in the CESL, but its fundamental problem is its lack of distinction in this regard with the result that consumer law concepts and domestic notions of protection in this area constantly spill over into the professional sphere. This is also demonstrated in the CESL and is wholly improper.

It has already been suggested that at least the general attitude in international dealings, therefore in the professional area, is becoming more like that of the traditional common law at least if the move towards a new *lex mercatoria* for these dealings is properly understood. That is not surprising because of the traditionally more pragmatic attitude and gradual approach of the common law to law formation and its bottom-up nature. Common law influence is apparent first in a greater reliance on practices, custom and party autonomy. It is further promoted by the fact that it has always been more result- and practitioner-oriented, is used to operating from case to case, is more sensitive to the facts—and perhaps therefore more used to supporting new business structures and their needs from a legal perspective (and not unduly encumbered by pre-existing legal notions, models or systems) and were comfortable with multiple legal sources.

The common law is in any event not given to confining system thinking, whatever the modern academic tendencies in England. It can therefore look with more confidence to new developments, at least in business. Particularly in equity, it also has a number of facilities such as trusts, floating charges and conditional or temporary proprietary interests that the civil law lacks. In fact, the common law's traditional mistrust of intellectual sophistication (although less so in the US) gives it flexibility, in the US through legal realism, which the civil law may now also need if it wants to progress. It is in any event more called for in the transnationalisation process of private professional law. A further important contributing factor is that the English language has become the lingua franca of the commercial and financial world. Its legal terminology is naturally geared more towards the common law than to any other system.

As already mentioned, the EU idea of codification (if the DCFR may be considered representative) runs counter to these modern developments at the transnational level and remains inspired by the concept of a system-driven unitary set of rules that is statist and territorial, the same in principle for consumers and professionals. It also poses the question of the status of the other sources of law.

In professional dealings, it further excludes the views and needs of all other countries. The USA and Japan, but also modern emerging countries, may have an interest as well and a view on how to proceed at least with regard to commercial and financial transactions which affect or play out on their territories or in which their businesses are involved when operating in the EU. The DCFR approach presents not only a statist but also an inward-looking mentality that seems distrustful of and unfriendly towards international business and the outside world more generally, even in international trade, commerce and finance on which the EU, like others, wholly depends.

In the meantime, it should be noted that there is no demand from practitioners for transnational codification in this formal manner, and that the DCFR and its progeny are driven purely by a particular strand of academic opinion, especially in Germany. Here policy dominates over quality, which compares poorly with what the UCC achieved in the US. In fact, it appears to be mainly an updating effort of the German Civil Code or BGB, now extended to all dealings within the EU, even if, according to more profound German academic and practitioners opinion, it is as such not of sufficient quality as a new model. See more particularly Volume II, chapter 1, section 1.6 and chapter 2, section 1.11.

As a minimum, such an effort at EU level would appear to require a much more extensive discussion of the true underlying issues and methodology. Earlier, UNIDROIT and UNCITRAL initiatives ran along similar lines, although in narrower areas (including the Vienna Convention on the International Sale of Goods); they were never particularly successful; neither had they been asked for by the business community.[34] In Europe, only the work of the ICC, particularly in Incoterms and UCP,[35] driven by the business community itself, has been a major success. This participation appears to be a key element in more formal law formation efforts of this nature cross-border, at least if the result is to apply to international professional dealings and relationships. It is that participation in the American Law Institute that has made the UCC a success.

1.1.3 The Coverage of Domestic and Transnational Commercial and Financial Law

In commercial and financial law, other differences between the common and civil law approach derive from its coverage. In common law countries, commercial law is traditionally associated with the sale and transportation of goods (which in the English terminology are tangible movable assets only) and with the related shipping or other forms of transportation, insurance, and payment methods and therefore traditionally with the contract for the sale of goods, with specialised trade terms such as FOB and CIF, and with bills of lading, bills of exchange, promissory notes, and other methods of payment. It has already been said, that commercial law in a common law sense still allows for a considerable independence from the general system.

---

[34] Even the best known of these treaties, the 1980 Vienna Convention on the International Sale of Goods, see vol II, ch 1, s 2.3, although now ratified by 74 countries, has not been accepted by the UK and Brazil, nor by some smaller trading countries such as Portugal. More importantly, it was substantially rejected by the international commercial practice that commonly excludes its application. The UNIDROIT Mobile Equipment Convention (see vol III, ch 1, s 2.1.9) may hold some greater promise and there may also be some reasonable prospect for the UNIDROIT 2009 Geneva Convention on Substantive Rules Regarding Intermediated Securities, see vol II, ch 2, s 3.2.4, but it is altogether not a great harvest.

Again, the reason is probably that UNCITRAL and UNIDROIT seldom managed to respond to true needs, and the results were generally not asked for by commercial practice, nor were they sufficiently pace-setting; rather they were product of compromises between domestic notions, often formulated by academics with insufficient practical knowledge, or by practitioners with an insufficient conceptual grasp of newer developments. This may have applied in particular to the potentially significant 2001 UNCITRAL Convention on the Assignment of Receivables in International Trade. It provided an important opportunity to move forward, but in the end proved a disappointment. See vol II, ch 2, s 1.5.13 and vol III, s 2.4.5ff.

In practice, more important were the UNCITRAL Model Law on International Commercial Arbitration (1985) and the UNCITRAL Model Law on Cross-border Insolvency (1997). Perhaps the greater success of these model laws derived from the fact that they did not mean to impose a uniform system but were content with more modest forms of harmonisation. They did not seek to impose from above through treaty law but were rather meant to guide domestic reform legislation.

[35] See text preceding n 337 below.

Thus certain features of the ordinary common law of contract, such as the concept of consideration, never affected the agreement to transfer negotiable instruments, implemented through delivery or endorsement. Also, contrary to the more normal *nemo dat* rule, bona fide purchasers or holders of these instruments are generally protected. Indeed, this type of protection is better supported in commercial law than in the rest of the common law (equity excepted),[36] and underscores the point that integration between common law and commercial law does not fully exist in common law countries.

Commercial law in a common law sense is then likely to cover the entire area, that is to say the *contractual* as well as *proprietary* aspects of the trade in goods, therefore also the transfer of ownership and any secured interests in these assets, for example to protect payment or raise finance, and the protection of bona fide purchasers as a matter of transactional finality. Thus in common law, the transfer of property in goods is seen as essentially a commercial law issue and not as a matter that is dealt with primarily by a general system of property law (on which the common law traditionally lays less stress anyway).

This has led to a tendency to treat the *entire* law of chattels and intangible assets as a distinct commercial law matter within the common law. This more fractured approach to property law is also borne out by the operation of equitable proprietary interests as more incidental rights, which in commercial and financial law is especially relevant in the area of asset-backed financing, leading in movable property to floating charges, conditional or temporary ownership rights, and in the area of the assignment and payment of receivables to bulk assignments of present and future claims, and in the payment area to liberal set-off and netting facilities as we have seen.[37]

In fact, it has already been noted that in common law countries important features of commercial law derive from equity, a facility civil law crucially missed. Indeed, it suggests a more incidental approach and brings with it greater judicial discretion, activism and direction, especially in trust, company and bankruptcy law, even though this law is now largely statutory. Equity in this manner conferred a flexibility on commercial law that is still important and might otherwise have been lost in common law countries as well.

---

[36] Sale of goods, transportation and insurance law, considered the typical commercial law subjects in common law, developed from the trade between England and the European Continent and acquired some distinguishing features from that contact, in which there may still be some faint remnants of a Roman law orientation. As the common law mainly developed in connection with land law, it at first possessed more scope for the persuasive force of other law in these commercial areas. In fact, the treatment of the sale of goods, transportation and insurance as especially defined contract types was itself due to continental influence: traditionally the common law does not define different types of contract and does not endow each with its own special contractual regime.

Interestingly, English maritime law developed in this way the continental concept of the ship master based on the *patria potestas* of Roman law. However, as we have seen, this history no longer sets maritime contracts and maritime concepts apart as commercial law on the European Continent. In fact, in the nineteenth and twentieth centuries, these areas of law developed more strongly and separately in England as a trading nation than they did on the European Continent.

[37] It should be noted that in England, commercial law as such is also referred to as trade law. There is a terminology issue here within the common law family. In the US, trade law is first and foremost associated with tariffs and international trade restrictions and agreements, now centred on the operation of the World Trade Organization (WTO). The result is that trade law in English terms is private law and therefore more properly part of commercial and financial law, but it is in American terms rather public or regulatory law and thus the result of governmental involvement and international arrangements between states designed to facilitate trade or investments.

In civil law, the coverage of commercial law is traditionally different, being much broader in one way and narrower in another. It is broader in that it is not unusual, for example, to find company law and insolvency law and much of financial law and therefore also services, covered by commercial law. This is especially the case in the French tradition, which is more service- than sales-oriented. But the civil law notion of commercial law is also narrower, as its coverage is only partial, as already mentioned in terms of *lex specialis*, and major topics in the commercial law area remain part of the general law or legal system.

This particularly concerns the proprietary aspects (such as transfer of ownership in goods and investments and the creation of any security interests therein, even if connected with the sale of goods) and their operation in bankruptcy, and brings with it the civil law restriction to only a small number of internally closely connected property rights (the *numerus clausus* notion of proprietary right). But it also concerns the general notions of contract law and of partnerships and even corporate associations, which in the commercial law area are equally derived from the general private law system.

If we accept for the moment globalising or transnationalising forces in the private law, especially in commerce and finance and thus in professional dealings, in the manner as discussed in the previous sections, and then turn to what may now be considered more particularly *transnational* substantive commercial and financial law or the new law merchant or modern *lex mercatoria*, we see that not only in as far as method (see previous section) but also in as far as *coverage* is concerned, the common law approach provides the starting point.

This means that the sale of goods, or rather the operation of international market place especially in commoditised goods or physical movable assets remains central, as is demonstrated by the 1980 Vienna Convention on the International Sale of Goods (CISG) and by the other work of the United Nations Commission for International Trade Law (UNCITRAL), whatever its success, particularly in the areas of bills of lading, negotiable instruments, payments and receivables financing. It is also evident in the area of shipping and maritime law. In other words, this new law is primarily oriented towards the international market place.

While the *sale of goods* and the operation of the international market are thus the major starting points of transnational commercial law, it is also true that more recently *financing* and *financial instruments* have become an important part of transnational law and are increasingly driving it. Here we also move into the coverage of certain classes of intangible assets such as receivables. Euromarket products and practices are here especially indicative[38] but no less relevant are transnationalised assignment, payment, set-off and netting notions. Although the international market place remains here at the centre of developments, there is also an important move towards *services*, and therefore towards the French commercial law tradition. This suggests a broadening approach in terms of coverage, but also confirms a more incidental approach in terms of products.

There is here a clear shift, partly because the typical older mercantile function of commercial law instruments, like bills of lading and negotiable instruments, are losing much of their importance in trading environments that are increasingly paperless and electronic,

---

[38] See, for the autonomy of the international capital markets and for the operation of the eurobonds market vol III, ch 2, ss 2.1.1–2.1.2.

and that are, especially for payments and investment securities, closely connected with clearing, settlement and netting notions, now more commonly the subject of financial law as we shall see in Volume III.

Thus, in so far as shares and bonds are concerned, the traditional (bearer and other) investment securities are increasingly being replaced by securities entitlements in paperless book-entry systems, see Volume II, chapter 2, section 3.1, and are no longer transferred through physical delivery but rather through a system of debits and credits in securities accounts, a system that resembles to a large extent modern payments through bank transfers which move here to the centre and will be extensively discussed in Volume III, chapter 1, section 3.1. Even domestically, the greater impact of modern finance on commercial law is increasingly clear. In this connection, it may be noted that the direction of modern company law development in both common and civil law is also in the same financial (capital markets and corporate finance) direction.

These developments explain why this book pays close attention to financial products and services including their regulation, to the financial markets and their operation, and to the creation of ever-more sophisticated financial instruments and payment facilities internationally that have not only affected and transnationalised the way capital is raised (particularly in the eurobond markets) and payments are made, but also the manner in which investments are held, transferred and protected. This is the subject of Volume III.

It is clear that in this updated realm of international commerce and finance, the more important features of the new transnational law or modern *lex mercatoria* can no longer be predominantly the law of the sale of goods and related laws concerning commodity trading and shipping or indeed the mercantile law. Financial law becomes here the core of commercial law. As already mentioned, this also means a move in the direction of services and ever newer proprietary structures especially in asset backed financing, including those using intangible assets, notably receivables.

1.1.4 Legal Dynamism as a Key Notion in Transnational Commercial and Financial Law. Law as a Dynamic Concept in Modern Contract and Movable Property

In fact, more important than its precise coverage, is the nature of this new professional law which is dynamic. Indeed, through its different sources, method and coverage, another significant aspect of this new transnational commercial and financial law, or new *lex mercatoria*, is that it embraces a more *dynamic concept* of law that operates, it is submitted, around a more objective but also more powerful concept of *party autonomy* that is itself transnationalised when operating amongst professionals and is here an original source of law.[39]

This modern 'privatisation' of private law at the transnational level is thus particularly connected with a reinforcement and extension of party autonomy in the international

---

[39] See for this concept and its autonomy s 1.4.9 below.

market place, which may subsequently fold into practices commonly accepted amongst professionals in their business, an approach that was largely lost in civil law countries when commercial and financial law was domesticated and incorporated into more formal and intellectual local legal frameworks that were mostly statutory. It has already been pointed out in the previous section that this more modern transnational attitude combines a more dynamic approach to law formation, which recognises different sources of law, with a more pragmatic approach to coverage, although it remains centred on the operation of the international market place now extended in the direction of international finance and professional services more generally.

In the law of personal or movable property, stronger party autonomy at the transnational level may do away with the civil law notion of a limited number of proprietary rights (the idea of the *numerus clausus*).[40] To the uninitiated, it might seem extraordinary that parties may in this way expand their rights against third parties, who in the nature of all proprietary rights would have to respect them, but it is less objectionable where there is a stronger protection of bona fide purchasers at the same time (as there always was in the common law approach in equity which has this flexibility) or even of purchasers in the ordinary course of business of commoditised products (who need not then be bona fide and in any event do not have a search duty). Proprietary rights are

---

[40] As will be discussed more extensively in vol II, ch 2 and vol III, ch 1, s 1.1.9, civil law has traditionally been opposed to an open system of proprietary rights, sees this as a public policy issue, and recognises only a limited number of these rights. This is the notion of the *numerus clausus* of proprietary rights that, however, has only operated since the nineteenth century and was formulated and discovered not much before the seventeenth century as we shall see. It goes into the fundamental distinction between the law of property and obligations in civil law at the level of the system.

In equity, in common law countries, the system is in essence open, important in modern finance especially in the law of chattels and intangibles. It means that third parties must respect the rights so created and acquire the assets as transferees subject to the rights of others, but only to the extent that they knew of them. It follows that in that (equitable) system, bona fide purchasers or assignees are generally protected. This is now commonly extended to transferees of commoditised products acquired in the ordinary course of business. There is here no search duty either, except for insiders such as banks and professional suppliers who should and can know better.

This means that the ordinary commercial flows are always protected against this type of proprietary interests which cannot be traced in them. A more open system of proprietary rights in this manner, allows for stronger risk management tools amongst insiders as we shall see.

Surprisingly, the idea of a *numerus clausus* of proprietary rights is now sometimes also advocated for common law by proponents of the law and economics school which favour standardisation; see TM Merrill and HE Smith, 'Optimal Standardization in the Law of Property: The *Numerus Clausus* Principle' (2000) 110 *Yale Law Journal* 1; see also H Hansman and R Kraakman, 'Property, Contract, and Verification: The *Numerus Clausus* Problem and The Divisibility of Rights' (2002) 31 *Journal of Legal Studies* 373. See for common law writers on the subject of the *numerus clausus*, B Rudden, 'Economic Theory v Property Law: The *Numerus Clausus* Problem' in *Oxford Essays in Jurisprudence*, 3rd Series (1987) 239. See further A Fusaro, 'The *Numerus Clausus* of Property Rights' in E Cooke (ed), *Modern Studies in Property Law, vol 1 Property 2000* (2001) 307.

As we shall see, it denies the strong risk management element inherent in party autonomy in the creation of (equitable) proprietary rights in modern finance, particularly in new forms of asset backed funding. Nevertheless, there is increasingly strong evidence of a more flexible use of proprietary rights in international finance. For the idea of contractualisation of proprietary rights in common law, see JH Langbein, 'The Contractarian Basis of the Law of Trusts' (1995) 105 *Yale Law Journal* 624; see further vol II, ch 2, s 1.10.

It may be noted in this respect that German case law opened up the system through its concept of floating charge or *Sicherungsuebereignung*, see vol III, ch 1, s 1.4, and at one stage also went the way of recognising proprietary expectancies or conditional ownership rights (or the *dingliche Anwartschaft*), see BGH, 22 February 1956, BGHZ 20, 88, although this important concept was not developed further and remains largely confined to the area of reservation of title; as it does in the Netherlands, see vol III, ch 1, s 1.2. An insufficient insight into the nature of the commercial flows and fear of breaking the *numerus clausus* notion (which is itself not expressed in the BGB) were here important contributing factors.

here not cut off at their creation but only at the level of their operation; see further the discussion in Volume II, chapter 2, section 1.10.

This may be considered as increasingly customary in professional circles and reflects equity in a common law sense. That suggests first a strong but also more objective notion of party autonomy in this area. Not everything goes and transnational public order restrictions may impose themselves, but there is the legitimisation through evolving transnational practice. Public order in particular protects here the *commercial flows* in the international market place against the effects thereon of greater freedom in the creation of proprietary rights. To repeat, they then only operate amongst a group of professional insiders such as banks and suppliers who are or become used to these newer techniques. The ordinary course of business is thus freed from the impact of adverse interests so created.

That is a crucial departure and denotes the limit of greater party autonomy in this area allowing property law nevertheless to become a *prime risk management tool*, especially clear in asset-backed funding where floating charges and conditional or temporary ownership rights freely operate side by side and next to more traditional security interests. It is indeed submitted that this is becoming a key facility in the modernisation of personal or movable property law at the transnational level. See again more particularly, Volume II, chapter 2, section 1.10.

If one keeps in mind the autonomous development of negotiable instruments and documents of title in the older *lex mercatoria*, this more modern development related to the operation of the international marketplace and its proprietary structures may be less surprising. It is now more especially relevant in modern financial transactions, even at the domestic level. In civil law countries, this is generally not yet identified and analysed, although it is even now sometimes found in the area of finance leasing and repo financing and in the area of receivables and their transfer, and in the interests[41] that may be created in them.[42]

---

[41] For assignments of receivables, greater latitude is now sometimes assumed in civil law, and parties might at least be able contractually to choose different domestic laws of assignment. See the discussion in vol II, ch 2, s 1.9.2 and vol III, ch 1, s 1.1.10.

In Dutch case law, for example, in proprietary aspects of assignments, the law of the underlying claim and in other cases the law of the assignment have sometimes been upheld as applicable following Art 12(1) and (2) of the 1980 Rome Convention on the Law Applicable to Contractual Obligations, now Art 14(1) and (2) of the 2008 EU Regulation (EC) No 593/2008 on the Law Applicable to Contractual Obligations (Rome I), rather than on the law of the debtor or that of the assignor. See for the legal nature of finance leasing, vol III, ch 1, s 2.4, and of repo financing, s 4.2.

[42] See for the bona fides requirement in England allowing the collecting younger assignee to retain its collections, which was only implicit in *Dearle v Hall* (1828) 3 Russ 1, *Rhodes v Allied Dunbar Pension Services Ltd* [1987] 1 WLR 1703. There is no investigation duty and acquiring knowledge of the earlier assignment after the second assignment but before notice is given thereunder is irrelevant for the entitlement to the collection. If there is a registered charge, there may be constructive or implied notice, although this is not automatically the case in England and in particular does not apply to any restrictive assignment covenants in a floating charge as these covenants need no filing. See further vol III, ch 1, s 1.5.9.

In this connection, it should be noted that especially the English equity rule protecting the first *collecting bona fide* assignee is not proposed to be adopted in the DCFR (it protects the bona fide assignee but forgets to require collection, see Art III-5:121 (1)), which would appear to be the necessary corollary of a more open system of assignment, see vol II, ch 2, s 1.11.3.

The 2001 UNCITRAL Convention on the Assignment of Receivables in International Trade suffered here from a lack of conceptual clarity and innovative spirit, see vol III, ch 1, s 2.4.5ff, which led to its failure. Its main problem is that it could not assimilate the receivable with the promissory note. The measure to which this is done determines the success of conventions of this nature. *cf* also s 2-110 UCC in the US.

Its major achievement was nevertheless a liberal identification requirement, which allowed the inclusion of future claims, but *major shortcomings* of the Convention were in its failure (not immediately clear from Art 8) to

For assets located in different countries, the technique is increasingly to locate them all at the place of the owner, now already often favoured for receivables, so that they can be transferred in bulk under one regime. That is important but may still suggest the application of a (reformed) national law although subject to fundamental adjustment of more traditional conflicts of law notions (here the *lex situs* rule for the applicable property rules). It still requires recognition of such interests at the place of their location or collection, however. In a more advanced legal environment, the owner's law could be transnationalised or formulated by the parties at the transnational level regardless of location in the manner just explained,[43] again subject to proper protection of the commercial flows as a public order requirement of the transnational commercial and financial legal order itself. This would result in an informal uniform regime, applicable everywhere, including in local bankruptcies.

It is the force of transnational practice that makes the difference here whilst imposing its own logic, ultimately entering, as we shall see, domestic legal regimes, even in bankruptcy where it is especially important, in this area buffeted by evolving *mandatory* transnational custom and general principle,[44] or even by the transnational public order itself.

provide for a uniform notification regime (or its waiver) and in its documentation or formalities regime (or their waiver). This was unfortunate, especially in the context of bulk assignments, all the more so as under Art 27 it is unclear which local law might be applicable. The reliance in these aspects on domestic law destroyed any notion of an international bulk assignment which was the true focus of the Convention. The DCFR also deals with the subject but does not manage to move it forward either, especially because of its lack of insight into the asset nature of claims and the operation and significance of bulk assignments.

Closely related was the UNCITRAL Convention's failure to establish a uniform regime for priorities. It concerns here the right of the assignee in the receivables over the right of a competing claimant. Instead, the Convention refers the matter to the law of the assignor (Arts 22 and 30), or leaves it to the Contracting States to opt for one of the systems set out in the Annex to the Convention (Art 42). Inspired by the UCC filing system, the Annex itself prefers a system based on registration of an assignment (Arts 1ff of the Annex). But states may also opt for a *prior tempore* rule based on the time of the contract of assignment (Arts 6ff of the Annex), which conforms to the German approach. Finally, they may also opt for a priority rule based on the time of the notification of the assignment (Arts 9ff of the Annex), which is wholly unconducive to bulk assignments and rather reflects old French law.

[43] See for receivables, n 42 above. See for this technique more generally vol III, ch 1, s 1.1.10.

[44] Indeed, the final test of such newer (prospectively internationalised) proprietary structures is in bankruptcy. Precisely because bankruptcy has hitherto been purely a matter of domestic law, this area is likely to encounter the greatest problems with transnationalised property rights and other new structures.

The idea of autonomy requires that in this area too, transnational law must increasingly demand recognition in domestic bankruptcy courts as customary law. In an earlier work, I dealt extensively with international bankruptcy from the perspective of recognition and enforcement in other countries and the internationalisation of concepts that exist in that connection, see *Dalhuisen on International Insolvency and Bankruptcy*, vol I (1986) 3.266.3ff. I shall revert to this in a fourth volume to this series.

Note in this connection also the Australian (Victoria) cases in *IATA v Ansett* [2005] VSC 113, [2006] VSCA 242, and [2008] HCA38, in which the Australian High Court ultimately accepted that, at least in a non-financial CCP (central counterparty, see also vol III, ch 1, s 2.6.4) in respect of mutual airline claims resulting from passenger cancellations and ticket changes, this transnational form of clearing and settlement and set-off trumped the Australian bankruptcy laws. This was and important precedent, see further C Chamorro-Courtland, "The Legal Aspects of Non-Financial Market Central Counter Parties", (2012) 27.4 *Banking and Finance Law Review*, and an advance notably on *British Eagle International Airlines Ltd v Compagnie Nationale Air France* [1975] 2 All ER 390, discussed in vol III, ch 1, s 3.2.3 in connection with novation netting and its limitations in bankruptcy in England.

In the meantime international bankruptcy principles are developing and are being written down. See IMF, *Orderly & Effective Insolvency Procedures* (1999) and World Bank, *Principles and Guidelines for Effective Insolvency and Creditors Rights Systems* May 2001 available at www.worldbank.org/ifa/ipg_eng.pdf. For another compilation, see also Koopman *et al* (eds), *Principles of European Insolvency Law* (2003).

If we concentrate on transnational commercial and financial law, we may note that a more diverse and fractured system of proprietary rights is evolving at that level, with different proprietary notions for different areas of the law or for different (financial) products and this system may eventually also be followed or recognised domestically in terms of transnational practice or custom. Again, it assumes and confirms a higher degree of party autonomy, even in proprietary matters, but it may also be more objective, that is, fenced in by the practices evolving at that level and the need of protection of the commercial flows as a transnational public order requirement.

This may affect in particular modern forms of (electronic) payment, securities entitlements and their transfer; the treatment of conditional and temporary ownership rights in finance leases and repurchase agreements; the (bulk) assignment of payment obligations, receivables financing and securitisations; the development of security interests in the form of non-possessory floating charges; the notion of agency (and the transfer of ownership in indirect or undisclosed agency); the evolution of fiduciary duties; and the important principle of segregation of assets in formal, resulting or constructive trusts and the facility of tracing. In this connection no less important are the modern notions of set-off and netting.

To repeat, one recognises here transnationally the innovative pull and challenge of *equity* in a common law sense, where, because civil law did not have this facility, the greatest differences between common and civil law resulted. It will be discussed more extensively in Volume II, chapter 2, section 1.3.1. Domestically, the more incidental and fractured attitude to proprietary rights and the absence of systemic thinking in this area have in more modern times been fundamentally supported by the different chapters or Articles of the UCC in the US, which are often particularly enlightening in these areas.

The French alone amongst major civil law countries, in their *Code Monetaire et Financier* of 1999 show here, largely for financial services purposes, a willingness to adjust. In the process they also acquired a level of comfort with different proprietary structures for different financial products leading to significant innovations in France in the laws concerning repos, securitisations, assignments and reservation of title, whilst in the French *Code Civil*, through more recent amendment, floating charges and trust structures have also been introduced. However, French law, although having become pragmatic in these areas,[45] still lacks the detail and also a clear academic support as to what

However, their usefulness will be limited if they do not manage to deal with the very concepts of proprietary or priority/separation or segregation rights, and their operation and acceptance in the international sphere. The same applies to the modern set-off and netting facilities in terms of preferences as we shall see in vol III, ch 1, s 3.2.7.

[45] See vol III, ch 1, s 1.3. The French, at least in commerce and finance, ultimately proved to be pragmatic by introducing in the last 25 years through amendments to their Bankruptcy Act, amendments to their *Code Civil* (CC), and the introduction of a new Monetary and Financial Code (CMF). It resulted in the following facilities: (1) the *reservation of title*, now in Arts 2367–2372 of the French CC (*Ordonnance* no 2006–346 of 23 March 2006) as a true payment protection devise (abandoning in the process the fundamental concept of '*solvabilite apparente*', see vol III, ch 1, s 1.1.9); (2) the *bulk assignment* for financial purposes (*Loi Dailly*) now in Arts L 313-23–L 313-35 CMF; (3) *securitisation* or *titrisation* through the creation or facilitation of *fonds communs de créances* (FCCs), now contained in Arts L 214-43–L 214-49 CMF; (4) *repos* or *pension livree* in Arts L 432-12–L 432-19 CMF; (5) *finance leases* (already earlier regulated by Law 66-455 of 2 July 1966 on the *credit-bail*), now in Arts L 313-7–L 313-11 CMF; (6) the *floating charge* since 2006 in Arts 2333–2366 CC, *Ordonnance* no 2006-346 *relative aux Sûretés* of 23 March 2006, see also *Rapport au Président de la République relative à l'ordonnance no 2006–346 du 23 Mars 2006 relative aux Sûretés*, JO no 71 of March 24 2006 (it was followed by a short Decree No 2007–404 of 22

is necessary to make such a system operate, notably in terms of party autonomy and the protection of the commercial flows.[46] Rather, it still captures these newer developments in static laws or formal legislation, not merely in a facilitating manner but in a limited and prescriptive way.

These adjustments are basically pragmatic and an instant reply to market pressure, also in terms of Paris keeping up with London as an international financial centre, and they are not necessarily more fundamental in terms of a new paradigm in respect of the system of private law property rights as a whole. They are nevertheless important indications of a less dogmatic approach in civil law. It should be noted in this respect that the Germans have made no such attempt so far, mainly for fear of destroying the unity of their system. This also transfers into the DCFR, which maintains a similar unworldly approach and even tries to undo whatever case law had achieved in Germany in terms of floating charges and bulk transfers of future (replacement) assets as we shall see.

Conceptually, at least at the transnational level, the result of newer thinking in this area is a more dynamic law of movable property in modern transnational commercial and financial dealings. However, legal dynamism and a less static approach to private law and its rules are *not* confined to personal property and are at least as necessary and demonstrable in *contract* law, where so far the modern notion of good faith has been used in major civil law countries domestically to create greater flexibility, behind which even other sources of law may re-emerge. That is likely to become ever more apparent at the transnational level, it is submitted, where in this area there are no pre-conceived system constraints either. Even pressing moral, social and especially efficiency considerations may then find readier acceptance in a more modern interpretation technique. That is indicative, although these considerations, except those concerning efficiency, may not always be highly relevant in international trade, commerce and finance and in any event may not always give more protection. It may even give less, as we shall see.

But a truly dynamic concept of contract law goes further and is more fundamental. One may think here especially of the infrastructure of modern contract requiring a more dynamic approach to contract formation, during which, depending on the phase of the negotiations,

---

March 2007 concerning some aspects of real estate mortgages); and now even (7) the *trust* or *fiducie* since 2007 in Arts 2011–2031 CC. See also P Matthews, 'The French Fiducie: and now for something completely different?' (2007) 22 *Trust Law International* 1.

It was followed in 2009 by the introduction of (8) the *fiducie-surete*, in Arts 2372-1–2372-6 (*mobiliere*) and Arts 2488-1–2488-6 (*immobiliere*) CC. It allows the setting apart of property with a trustee for the benefit of funding parties subject to the conditions of the arrangement. Appropriation is possible as an alternative to security interests, still subject, however, to the return of any overvalue but in the case of natural persons only, Art 2372-3 CC.

The introduction of these new facilities completely destroyed any idea of one system of proprietary rights in France (although this author is not aware of any study explaining the impact on the *Code Civil* and its proprietary system), whose 200-year anniversary was nonetheless celebrated in some style in 2004. Under the circumstances, one wondered why.

[46] No less 'damage' to traditional civil law system thinking in this area came with the EU Collateral Directive, see vol III, ch 1, s 1.1.8, which pulled the rug from under most Continental orthodoxy in the law of personal property in the context of finance. The Dutch and Germans were no longer able to integrate it into their 'systems' and the Directive's contents figure as a special section to their Codes.

pre-contractual duties emerge and parties assume steadily increasing obligations. They no longer depend on a ritual kind of mating dance in the offer and acceptance language, traditionally resulting in a fixed moment of contract formation.[47] This more recent approach accepts a progression in commitment during the entire contract period,[48] in which conduct and reliance,[49]

---

[47] As to the more traditional offer and acceptance notion, it is seldom recognised that it is relatively recent. On the European Continent, the natural law school of Grotius and Pufendorf in the seventeenth and eighteenth centuries had completed the theoretical structure of the law of contract based on consensus as we know it today in civil law. See Grotius, *De Iure Belli ac Pacis*, Lib II, Cap XI, iv.1, emphasising the mutuality of promises rather than the consensus idea itself or the more modern model and process of offer and acceptance, but *cf* also Cap XI, xiv and his *Inleidinge* or *Jurisprudence of Holland* (RW Lee trl 1953) III.10, where Grotius noted that by contract we mean a voluntary act whereby the one party promises something to the other with the intention that the other party should accept it and thereby acquire a right against the first party. *cf* also Pufendorf, *De Iure Naturae et Gentium* 1674, Lib III, Cap IV, s 2.7.
This resulted in the general applicability of the famous maxim *pacta sunt servanda*, itself derived from the early Canon law heading of the relevant chapter in the *Decretales* of Pope Gregory IX of 1234 which had been at the beginning of this development ('*Pacta quantumque nuda servanda sunt*'). Through the seventeenth-century works of the French jurist Domat, *Les Lois Civiles dans leur Ordre Naturel, Livre I Introduction* (Paris, 1777), the concept of consensus entered the French Codes.
One key is that it captured the contract and the rights and obligations arising thereunder at the moment of its formation, the determination of which then became a separate but prime issue. The other great French jurist, Pothier, formulated the notion of offer and acceptance in the eighteenth century more precisely, see *Traité des Obligations*, no 4, although the question of acceptance had already been raised by Bartolus in connection with the use of agents: *Commentaria* D.15.4.1.2. Only in the nineteenth century, was this insight described in terms of the will of the parties, see vol II, ch 1, s 1.2.1 which led to more refined offer and acceptance theories.
In common law, as we shall see in vol II, ch 1, s 1.2.2, there is no similar emphasis on consensus or a meeting of minds and the parties' will or intent relates there rather to the individual promises they make. In common law, it is the more objective doctrine of consideration, which is the notion of exchange or bargain (or sometimes the notion of sufficient reason), that still provides the main basis for the validity of contracts. Offer and acceptance language dates here only from the nineteenth century, imported from the Continent.

[48] It means amongst other things that the moment a contract is concluded or formed may not be as clear as it used to be and the conclusion may show a progression. More formal notions of offer and acceptance also recede into the background, both in common and civil law, replaced as they are by a longer drawn out negotiation or formation process especially in respect of larger duration contracts. Rights and obligations appear here more gradually, depending on the stage reached in the negotiations.
A closely related aspect is the credit that must now more generally be given to the *raising of expectations* and any *detrimental reliance* on them by others. It is also clear that the way one party chooses to *organise* itself may itself give rise to these expectations. Thus the buying of a ticket on the bus and the purchase of groceries in a supermarket can often best be explained by reliance on the organisation that the seller of these service or of the goods has put in place and the choice and selection power that is in this manner given to the buyer rather than in terms of offer and acceptance or of bargain and consensus. The way the seller has *organised* itself in these situations does not, for example, allow the ticket seller or cash attendant discretion in refusing the travel service or the taking away of the groceries if the correct price is offered unless there are special reasons which the ticket seller or cash attendant would then have the burden of explaining. Intent of the ticket seller or cash attendant is here largely irrelevant.
It more generally poses the question of when reliance by others becomes justified and starts binding that party having given rise to the expectation. This will often depend on the circumstances and is therefore a factual issue, in which the type of parties may be significant and a beginning of performance may be required.

[49] Indeed, in the newer approaches, *reliance* on reasonable expectations (which again suggests the relevance of the circumstances and type of parties), is the basic issue in *contract formation* and its timing, whilst *culpable breach of reasonable expectations and duties* is the prime ground for actions for damages. It is clear that such actions may then be more closely related to tort than to more traditional, subjective concepts of contract. Conduct and reliance become here key in terms of contract formation and are themselves dynamic in determining the emerging rights and obligations of the parties and therefore the content of their contract. They do not merely operate besides offer and acceptance, but the latter become a subcategory of the former.

disclosure duties,[50] a beginning of performance,[51] and acceptance of risk of future developments[52] also figure.[53]

It is possible to move even further and put the whole emphasis (not just in terms of formation) on justified expectations, detrimental reliance, duties of care and co-operation, of disclosure, investigation and loyalty, and on the contractual purpose and consider them to be the basic source and *essence* of modern contractual rights and obligations, *only the details* of which would then depend on the more specific objectives of the parties. At least professionals may be able to do that. In this connection, they may also insist on a more literal interpretation of their contract if not already implied in a good faith approach, especially where the contract functions as a road map and risk management tool between them.[54]

This newer contractual approach or model will be discussed more extensively under modern contract theory in Volume II, chapter 1. It involves a process of *objectivation* of norms in which in a largely corporate modern environment traditional will theories and

---

[50] In later phases of the contract too, new rights and obligations emerge, although, as for pre-contractual disclosure duties, perhaps less between professionals than between professionals and weaker unsuspecting parties. The European and UNIDROIT Contract Principles simply accept consumer notions and do not distinguish between consumer and professional dealings. That is also the basic approach of the DCFR, see more particularly vol II, ch 1, s 1.6.

As for these contractual negotiation duties, see vol II, ch 1, ss 1.3.12ff. Modern contract theory differentiating between the types of parties in this instance may explain the English case *Walford v Miles* [1992] 2 WLR 174, and the denial in it of the duties of pre-contractual negotiation and co-operation between professionals, although it did not rule out claims in negligence for costs incurred unnecessarily.

[51] In particular, reliance might need a response in some *beginning of performance* by the relying party and cannot be merely in the mind or on a piece of paper. It is an aspect of reliance having to be detrimental. See for this requirement PS Atiyah, 'Contract, Promises and the Law of Obligations' (1978) *LQR* 193. In the early *droit coutumier* in France, where the promise itself became binding, this extra requirement (besides that of a lawful cause) was not unknown either, at least in the law of sales. See A Esmein, *Etudes sur les contrats dans les tres ancien droit francais* 5, 29 (1883). The codification dropped it and may therefore be considered to have a lesser requirement for contract enforceability than the immanent transnational law may have.

[52] Another key modern insight is that *entering into a relationship* of whatever nature implies acceptance of much of what follows and for which one may not have bargained, and in any event much may happen which could not have been foreseen. That is risk acceptance. When signing a contract, parties thus take a risk which may be considerable especially between professionals. It will not give them a way out of the contract on the mere basis of lack of original intent except in extreme cases (when holding a party to the contract would become manifestly unreasonable). In such relationships, much unknown risk must be considered discounted. See further vol II, ch 1, s 1.3.14. Any detriment falls where it falls and that must be accepted as a risk one took.

The European and UNIDROIT Contract Principles and DCFR appear to be little aware of this and the Vienna Convention in Art 79 only operates with a broadened *force majeure* concept, which, as it concerns here professional sales, may, still have to be interpreted narrowly.

[53] Yet another aspect of modern contract theory is the importance of the *demonstrable contractual purpose* in determining the contract's content and effect, again as some objective standard regardless of what the original intent of one of the parties may or may not have been. This is the essence of *teleological* interpretation.

[54] As we have seen, in a more objective contract interpretation, parties may also face pressing external *ethical, social and efficiency* standards in the implementation of their transaction, although the impact will again depend on the situation, including the type of parties and taking into account the standards they may have set amongst themselves. This is sometimes called the *normative* interpretation technique which goes well beyond a mere teleological one.

The term 'normative' when used in this connection, does not refer to any ideal type or to ethical aspirations per se, as it usually is in the positivist tradition, but rather refers to to legally or objectively binding considerations or correctives which may have an extralegal origin in moral, social, cultural or economic considerations. It could also simply relate to rationality or common sense. Again, it is more than a merely purposive or teleological interpretation, which looks for the objective of the agreement in terms of its interpretation (although this is also important in this context). See also s 1.2.14 below.

an anthropomorphic attitude to private law[55] and to contract formation in particular are abandoned, and at least duration contracts may be seen as a form of partnership or a framework in which new obligations emerge in a continuous process of law formation that is not solely guided by the parties' will at a fixed moment in time but rather by conduct, reliance and acceptance of risk, especially of ever changing circumstances. It may still give rise to post-contractual renegotiation duties, although in professional dealings, short of a contractual hardship clause, only when the risk of new developments becomes manifestly unreasonable for one party to bear,[56] which in professional dealings is not likely to occur soon.

It has already been said that good faith but also market practices now often operate as a front behind which legal dynamism is rekindled, at least in contract. A liberal interpretation technique is soon accompanied by the revival of other autonomous sources of law.[57] Good faith case law can often be analysed in this manner in civil law countries[58] and the more

---

[55] The strong emphasis on the will is a typical nineteenth-century Continental European idea, connected with romantic philosophy, and suggests a thoroughly anthropomorphic attitude to contract law that is now out of place for professional dealings in a largely corporate environment. See also n 196 below. See for the more modern idea of party autonomy and present day meaning and operation, s 1.4.9 below.

[56] In the case of hardship due to intervening unforeseeable, unavoidable and undiscounted circumstances, re-negotiations may be sought under the UNIDROIT Contract Principles (written for professional contracts) as soon as the contractual equilibrium is disturbed, whilst there need not even be severe financial consequences (Art 6.2). This is hard for professionals to understand. One may wonder whether this rule is also considered to be related to good faith and therefore mandatory. Again this could at most be so in clear cases. This is consumer thinking. At least the DCFR avoids good faith language, Art III.-1:110.

In a similar vein, surprising (standard) terms must be expressly accepted even amongst professionals (Art 2.19), whilst Arts 7.1.6 and 7.4.13 limit their freedom with respect to exemption clauses and agreements to pay fixed sums for non-performance. These rules also seem to be mandatory amongst professionals. This is also the attitude in the DCFR. The question is why? Who needs protection here, and against what? See further vol II, ch 2, s 1.6.

[57] In countries such as Germany, Austria, Switzerland and the Netherlands, in contract law, the modern, more dynamic approach is now closely associated with the good faith notion in the interpretation and supplementation of contracts. In its extreme form, it may even lead to contractual adjustments on the basis of what may be considered fair and reasonable in objective terms, or even rational and common sense, or what may be required in a social sense in terms of (re)distribution or is morally demanded in an advanced society. In Germany in particular, that plays a role in terms of pre-contractual disclosure duties as it had earlier in the case of profound changes of circumstances. This has been an area of statutory law since 2002. The problem is that consumer law thinking quickly spills over into professional dealings. This is also true of the DCFR as we shall see.

[58] Although in civil law, the notion of good faith is often considered just one (other, open but mandatory) norm that supplements the codes (but is only in interpretation authorised by them to do so), it has in truth acquired a *multifaceted* character and is by no means always mandatory. It (a) supplements the contract; but may sometimes (b) also derogate from it if the result would be manifestly unreasonable; (c) may activate other sources of law; and (d) stretches existing norms to new situations by selecting new facts as being legally relevant.

In operating in these ways, 'good faith' is sometimes judicial discretion and sometimes judicial limitation. It may be legal principle or a more precise legal rule. It is sometimes the highest norm (if morally, socially or economically sufficiently pressing, and may then be mandatory), sometimes practical norm (if promoting good sense, co-operation and reasonable care, and is then directory). It is sometimes legal refinement and differentiation, sometimes generalisation and system building. It may be rule formulation, or rule application, selecting and weighing the relevant facts and defining the legal consequences (*Konkretisierung*). It may even be subjective, although it is mostly objective. It sometimes looks at the nature of legal relationships of the parties and their special interests and sometimes at the nature of their transaction and its particular features. At one time it may set rules for judicial decision making but at other times provides only judicial direction and guidance. It looks for fairness, particularly in consumer and small company cases, and for what makes sense and is practical, particularly in business cases. It is sometimes structure, but mostly movement. It is always inter-relational but is probably more important in human relationships than in business dealings. See further vol II, ch 1, s 1.3.4.

modern civil law literature is aware of these developments.[59] Some of these ideas can also be identified in England[60] although they are expressed differently.[61] They are clearer in the US, where they are closely connected with legal realism.[62] As already noted, they receive insufficient

---

[59] Misuse of the notion of good faith is not excluded, however, and intellectual prejudice may be as rampant in its application as in the application of the legal model good faith is meant to correct or expand, eg by referring to certain behaviour as *obviously* contrary to good faith, see also J Vranken, *Exploring the Jurist's Mind* (2006).

[60] See Lord Hoffmann in *ICS Ltd v West Bromwich BS* [1998] 1 WLR 896, 912, referring to the reasonable man approach, with a preference for contextual interpretation to abstract literalism, but also in *BCCI v Ali* [2001] 2 WLR 735, 749 restating the principle of literal interpretation on the basis of a narrow view of the parties' intent, at least as a starting point. Similarly, Lord Steyn in *Total Gas Marketing Ltd v Arco British Ltd* [1998] 2 Lloyd's Rep 209 alluded to the contractual language, the contractual scheme, the commercial context and the reasonable expectations of the parties.

This is relationship thinking. The path finding approach of Lord Bingham in terms of relationship thinking in formation of contracts was demonstrated in *Interfoto Picture Library Ltd v Stiletto Visual Programmes Ltd* [1989] 1 QB 433, 439. English case law is careful to avoid broad concepts, however, such as the one to teleological interpretation (of statutes), and prefers to use the term 'purposive' instead, which may denote a more limited concept. See further the comment of Lord Denning in *Bulmer v Bollinger* [1974] Ch 401, s 1.3.3 below.

[61] The common law's emphasis on the nature of the relationship between the parties means that it needs the notion of good faith *much less* than civil law in this connection. Implied terms, fiduciary duties, notions of reliance, and sometimes resort to natural justice do the rest. Protection of small investors against their brokers may present here a case in point. Good faith notions in civil law do not reach as far as fiduciary duties traditionally do in common law. Moreover, the common law is less unfriendly to other sources of law, as we have seen. The often heard proposition on the European Continent that English contract law is primitive, because it does not even accept the notion of good faith, is therefore ill informed and imperceptive. See further vol II, ch.1, s 1.3.7.

[62] See MA Eisenberg, 'The Emergence of Dynamic Contract Law' (2000) 88 *California Law Review* 1747.

In the USA, the notion of good faith now operates more directly than in England: see for a fuller discussion vol II, ch 1, s 1.3.7. In the UCC under German influence, a general reference to good faith was inserted in s 1-304. It imposes an obligation of good faith in the performance or enforcement of every contract or duty under the UCC, but strictly speaking *not* in the formation. Interestingly, s 1-201(b)(20) UCC defines the concept as 'honesty in fact in the conduct or transactions concerned'. The 'in fact' language suggested a subjective approach ('empty head, pure heart'), but has gradually acquired a more normative or objective meaning, see s 1-201(19) (old), whilst s 1–201(a)(20) (new) now adds after 'honesty in fact' a reference to 'the observance of reasonable commercial standards of fair dealing'.

Indeed, for sales, s 2-103(1)(b) UCC had done so earlier, now repeated in its new version (s 2-103 (1)(j)); see also s 3-103(a)(6) UCC (for negotiable instruments), s 5–102(a)(7) UCC (for letters of credit) and s 9-102 (a)(43) UCC (when used in the area of secured transactions. See for a more limited use of the concept in this area of proprietary rights, Comment 10 to s 8-102 UCC (for adverse claims in security entitlements).

There are several other references to good faith in the UCC, eg for the sale of goods, in ss 2-603 and 2-615. It remains exceptional in the common law of contract, however, and is substantially statutory and even then, as in the UCC, incidental, as the many individual references to it show. At least in the UCC, good faith does *not* cover pre-contractual duties or strictly speaking even gap-filling but *only* the performance or enforcement of the contract, here joined by a general provision on the unenforceability of *unconscionable clauses* in contracts for the sale of goods, see s 2-302 UCC, particularly (but not only) relevant in sales to consumers.

On the other hand, in the US, the non-binding Restatement (Second) of Contracts of 1981 s 205, stated for the first time more generally that every contract imposes upon each party a duty of good faith and fair dealing in its performance and its enforcement. This was then followed by the 1990 revision of s 3-103(a)(4) UCC (for negotiable instruments) which, as far as the UCC is concerned, was first in accepting the idea that good faith could also means the observance of reasonable commercial standards of fair dealing, but good faith remained here also a matter of performance and enforcement of the contract only. This is now the general UCC approach.

It follows that in the interpretation of intent, the normative approach is now increasingly followed in the USA. Australia and New Zealand also have abandoned the narrow common law approach in this area. More limited notions of foreseeability and reasonableness may, however, commonly still be found in most legal systems as possible correctives to the parties' exposure in this connection when it comes to any assessment of damages even where the requirements of good faith are deemed violated in a more objective sense.

For the US see also EA Farnsworth, 'Good Faith in Contract Performance' in J Beatson and D Friedmann (eds), *Good Faith and Fault in Contract Law* (1995) 153. See for a case that could more readily be explained as covering a pre-contractual situation, *Teacher's Ins & Annuity Ass'n v Butler* 626 F Supp 1229 (SDNY 1986) in which a developer refused to close a loan deal whilst objecting to a pre-payment fee in the closing documents. The court recognised a duty of good faith and fair dealing in every commercial transaction and found a breach of this duty

acknowledgement in the DCFR (and earlier in the Principles of Contract Law (PECL)) which now stands for the latest, more classical, example of codification thinking in Europe. The reason for this is its anthropomorphic idea of contract and a prescriptive consumer law ethos which makes these texts unsuitable for professional dealings.

For professionals, the contract itself is likely to be primarily a road map and prime risk-management tool. Good faith interpretation does not then always provide more rights; it can also be restrictive, especially when predictability requires it. Proper risk management through contract is an overriding aim in all professional dealings. Particularly in this respect, the initiative of the parties remains paramount whilst good faith notions or corrections recede in importance, although it has already been observed that in civil law the notion of good faith is often still perceived as unitary, therefore operating for both professionals and consumers in a similar manner. This is a serious mistake. On the other hand, it can easily be maintained that good faith underlies all contract interpretation, including professional contracts as long as it is understood that it may work out very differently in consumer and business dealings. Again, proper relationship thinking is the key here and should move to the centre of the good faith concept itself. Civil law has still some way to go in this respect.

Indeed in modern contract theory, the notion of party autonomy is recast primarily in terms of initiative and organisation.[63] It is no longer psychological and is therefore more objective, locked in, in particular, by conduct and reliance notions and supplemented (and sometimes corrected) by other sources of law. The modern notion of good faith, if properly understood, supports this and may thus extend as well as limit the protections of the parties depending on the nature of their relationship (different in professional and consumer dealings) and on the type of their deal (different therefore in duration contracts and sale of individual goods). In this vein, the commercial contract will often be interpreted literally, especially if operating as a road map and risk management tool. Good faith itself requires it; it may mean fewer rights, not more.

Thus modern contract theory[64] generally underwrites a dynamic concept of contract law, see Volume II, chapter 1, section 1.1.4, often accepted in more ambitious domestic

---

on the basis of commercial practice which accepted pre-payment fees in loan agreements even if not normally included in a bank's commitment letter. The court, therefore, rejected the borrower's argument as a pretext for getting out of the deal also taking into account that the draft loan agreement had included the fee and that the problem had never been raised until the eve of closing. The case can, however, also be seen in the context of performance pursuant to the commitment letter.

[63] Especially in terms of risk allocation, including the risk of unforeseeable events, particularly in duration contracts, *party autonomy* thus remains an important concept, fully recognised by modern contract theory, especially between professionals including their right to set standards or even eliminate adjustment possibilities except in extreme cases. Only if the situation gets totally out of hand will there be redress under more objective good faith notions, which may include termination of the agreement, but again it is unlikely to be an issue of lack of intent. Parties retain here a sense of *initiative* and *imagination* and will use their contract as a tool of risk management in as far as they can foresee these risks, but intent is here no longer central as a notion in itself.

[64] For modern contract theory, see esp Eisenberg, n 62 above, 1743, 1747 and earlier S Macauley, 'Non contractual Relationships in Business', (1963) *American Sociological Review* 55 and 'Contract Law and Contract Techniques; Past, Present and Future' (1967) *Wisconsin Law Review* 805; G Gilmore *The Death of Contract* (1974); PS Atiyah, *The Rise and Fall of Freedom of Contract* (Oxford, 1979) and *Essays on Contract* (Oxford, 1986); RA Hillman, 'The Crisis in Modern Contract Theory' (1988–89) 67 *Texas Law Reporter* 103 (1988/89) and 'The Richness of Contract Law: an Analysis and Critique of Contemporary Theories of Contract Law' (1999) *Michigan Law Review*; J Beatson and D Friedman, 'Introduction: From 'Classical' to 'Modern' Contract Law', in J Beatson and D Friedman (eds) *Good Faith and Fault in Contract Law* (Oxford, 1994); S Styles, 'Good Faith:

academic writing, although in practice the notion of good faith is by no means everywhere similarly extended or unchallenged as we shall also see, but it is true that under pressure of circumstances, domestic courts have often been forced to implement it in a liberal manner in order to remain credible and responsive, although even then in the civil law way of system thinking, at least in academia, there also remains an urge to use the new case law to complete or reinvent the system through extrapolation and reinterpretation.[65] Again, transnational commercial and financial law is here more likely to be responsive and ultimately to lead. It takes in *both* contract and movable property law the *risk management perspective*, which connects both the contractual and proprietary examples of legal dynamism given above. It should be noted, in this connection, that at the more formal level, even for contract law, the CISG is not up to date but this is no less true for the UNIDROIT and European Principles of Contract Law and the more recent DCFR as model for a uniform European (EU) private law, followed in 2011 by CESL, all of which will be more extensively discussed in Volume II, chapter 1, section 1.6 for contract and chapter 2, section 1.11 for movable property, including receivables.

In summary, in terms of modern legal dynamism, it could perhaps be said for modern commerce and finance that what the civil law concept of good faith is doing for contract as a transforming concept, making the (civil) law in this area adapt to modern realities, ultimately allowing for different types of relationships to be taken more significantly into account and, therefore, at least in professional dealings, accepting a continuous process of law formation, is at the transnational level increasingly matched by some similar transforming force in respect of movable proprietary structures, which allows for a degree of

A Principled Matter' in ADM Forte, *Good Faith in Contract and Property Law* 157 (1999); R Brownsword, *Contract Law: Themes for the Twenty-first Century* (London, 2000); Hugh Collins, *The Law of Contract*, 4th edn (London, 2003); E McKendrick, *Contract Law*, 6th edn (Basingstoke, 2005).

[65] Thus German academics typically look for system everywhere, even in more open textured provisions and often talk in this connection, for example, of the inner system (*Binnensystematik*) of the good faith notion, referring in particular to the reliance notion, pre-contractual duties, normative interpretation, supplementation and correction techniques, the (continued) validity of the contract, the performance obligations and excuses of the parties, and, in appropriate cases, to their re-negotiation duties, all originally developed on the basis of the concept of good faith.

In German doctrine, see the major commentary of Palandt/Heinrichs, *Bürgerliches Gesetzbuch* (2011), at s 242, nos 2 and 13, there follows then some attempt at classification of the functions of good faith (*Funktionkreisen*), like interpretation, supplementation and correction of duties or adjustment in case of a profound change of circumstances, functions which are by no means new and are now expressed in specific provisions of the BGB: ss 241(2), 280, 311(2) and (3), 313. They had already appeared in the *Justinian Digests*, in connection with the definition of the powers of the Roman praetor in contract law (D.1.1.7 Papinianus). See also F Wieacker, *Zur Rechtstheoretischen Präzisierung des sec 242, Recht und Staat in Geschichte und Gegenwart* (Tübingen, 1956) 20. Within these good faith functions, there is a further effort to distinguish classes of cases (*Fallgrupen*), like, in the supplementation function, the development of pre-contractual and post-contractual rights and duties and of consumer or workers' rights (not necessarily, however, along the lines of altogether clear rules or new contract types), and, in the correction function, the emphasis on estoppel, abuse of rights, own co-operation duties, and on the manner in which rights were acquired or are invoked like in the case of standard terms.

But only some clear notions were identified in this manner, such as the abuse of rights (*exceptio doli*), the notion of clean hands, of own misbehaviour and of lack of co-operation; none very original. Also the loss of a right to performance became accepted if there was contrary conduct or if there were declarations on which the other party could rely as an excuse. Another development was the loss of rights whilst not timely invoking them (*Verwirkung*). All are of limited application, however, and it is altogether not a large crop. The search for rules in the above manner ignores not only the dynamic character of the concept of good faith but also good faith's modern multifaceted nature, see n 58 above.

party autonomy in proprietary matters creating room in particular, for typical asset backed financial products, a development more akin to that of equity in common law.[66]

1.1.5. Legal Pragmatism at the Transnational Level. Notions of Certainty, Finality and Predictability. The Need to Find Structure, Not System

Altogether the emerging new transnational law merchant or modern *lex mercatoria*, based on its various sources and the hierarchy of norms deriving from them, that is the law of international professional dealings, is less systemic and more pragmatic, particularly in its method, coverage and responsiveness, which all go to legal dynamism, especially in contract and movable property as submitted in the previous section. The resulting law is less concrete and cannot avoid some flux if only because it is still in its formative era and is particularly geared to respond to new situations. It embodies a way of thinking and presents an environment in which existing rules are foremost *guidelines* (unless the situation is fully repetitive) and subject to a good deal of party autonomy, but the new *lex mercatoria* also espouses firm notions of finality especially for payments and title transfers as we shall see. It should be noted, however, that even domestically, a similar state of fluidity is becoming clearer in respect of much black-letter private law except perhaps in the few areas where the law remains absolutely settled, such as in the area of conveyancing of real estate or where mandatory law is imposed especially through regulation. Even then, texts are seldom fully clear, policies poorly expressed or unattainable, and their meaning evolves in any event in interpretation.

In private law, greater fluidity is the unavoidable consequence of factual patterns becoming ever more diverse and complex, and of practical needs evolving ever more quickly. In the area of what we might term 'directory law' (or default rules), where the legal system has a mere support function, this may be more easily accepted and can also be more easily handled through the use of party autonomy in choosing or amending the applicable rules, but it is also unavoidable in the law's application in areas where it is (semi-)mandatory, even in private law, as in personal property law or even in contract, when the contractual infrastructure is an issue, for example, in terms of legal capacity to contract, in issues of validity and legality, or in matters of the continued existence of the agreement and obligations thereunder.

There is now more movement and this is also more readily understood, especially by the so-called 'legal realists' in the US, already mentioned,[67] who present the view that the private law is only legitimate in its operational adequacy and ethical, social and economic sufficiency. Thus, pressing ethical, economic, efficiency, utilitarian and social factors had to be

---

[66] It may also be said that, although this good-faith concept has (except in the US) so far met with less favour in common law countries (which, as noted in n 61 above, have other techniques that may lead to similar results, especially the emphasis on the nature of the relationship of the parties, fiduciary duties, implied terms, and the notion of estoppels and reliance), in movable property on the other hand this equitable transformation process has not yet been recognised in civil law countries, with the exception perhaps at the formal level of modern developments in France, as demonstrated in n 45 above, whilst in particular the EU Collateral Directive of 2002, discussed more fully in vol II, ch 2, Part III, may give some indication of what is to come. So may the 2001 UNIDROIT Mobile Equipment Convention, see vol III, ch 1, s 2.1.8.

[67] See n 23 above.

accepted as having an impact on private law, affecting the application of both statute and precedent. Ever evolving values, policies and needs then become key issues in the interpretation process (of statute, property law and contract), even if in commerce and finance, and therefore in the law between professionals, value considerations may often be less relevant, but issues of efficiency and utility or abuse and fraud may still be overriding. Cost/benefit considerations may then also become more relevant in the operation of this law.

Although this perspective was first articulated in the US in the 1930s (see section 1.3.4 below), it has also been accepted (albeit often reluctantly) in one form or another in countries such as Germany, Austria and the Netherlands, which, in the civilian law tradition, still work in essence with a statutory text and its system. This is so at least in the law of obligations as applied by the courts. The ensuing flexibility is therefore clearer in contract (especially because of the good-faith concept) than in movable property law.

Indeed, it is manifested foremost in a *liberal interpretation technique* in respect of codified texts, especially in the law of obligations, that could otherwise no longer be considered complete, nor operate as such. But the re-systemising tendencies in academia at the domestic level were also noted,[68] and at least in civil law countries nationalistic system thinking remains a prime academic preoccupation. There is here considerable tension in civil law as there continues to operate a belief in national academic models adequately capturing and guiding reality,[69] even for international transactions in respect of future fact patterns. As we have seen, this attitude has also spilled over into countries like England, where, especially in circles around the Law Commission which means to articulate law reform, statutory law, and thus legal texts, are also popular and a system mentality has been cultivated.

Greater fluidity in the rules raises everywhere the issue of *legal certainty* or lack thereof, and predictability. In modern international transactions (given their ever greater frequency and value), this problem is aggravated by the fact that legal certainty can no longer come from domestic laws that were never written for them and often operate at the cost of limited sophistication. The traditional conflict rules of private international law, always pointing to the applicability of a national law, here reach their useful end or suggest a certainty that may be of such a low quality that it may destabilise the relevant commercial and financial transactions for solely dogmatic reasons, often being no more than pure nationalism supported by domestic system thinking.

Certainty of this nature is often supported by the notion of law as pure technique or a logical framework that, when properly applied, always arrives at the correct answers. It has already been said that codification in the civil law manner was its culmination. To repeat, the idea is here that human behaviour can be systematically captured for the present and the future—a particular academic ideal and preoccupation in Germany—but for the social sciences this attitude and its idea of certainty have been fundamentally questioned, not only by Popper and his followers.[70] One may also recall in this connection the reference of Jerome Frank to the childish dread of uncertainty and unwillingness to face legal realities.[71] In fact, a search for certainty of this nature may hold everything back.

Rather, it is for professional parties through extended notions of party autonomy to chart a course through the risks of their international transactions, on both the contractual

---

[68] See n 65 above.
[69] For the connected problems see section.1.2.12 below.
[70] See n 208 below.
[71] J Frank, *Law and the Modern Mind* (1930) 41 and 159.

and proprietary side, in the manner that was discussed in the previous section, where it was also noted that their contract is likely to become a road map and may need literal interpretation. Even good faith may require that. It was further pointed out that their proprietary structures, especially in international finance in asset-backed finance, also become in this way tools of risk management that could be extended trans-border, supported by industry practices and subject to a more sophisticated protection of the ordinary course of business against hidden charges. There are of course also the tax and regulatory complications to be considered.

In the absence of a proper supranational legislator, and given the insufficient and often backward-looking spirit of much existing local black-letter law or even treaty law, we may instead have to get used to the idea that the certainty that commercial (or more generally professional) law requires must in a modern internationalised environment in private law increasingly come from the understanding, discipline, and practices of the participants themselves, helped by fundamental and more general legal principles that transcend national laws. As we have seen, this suggests in particular, a greater role for industry practices or custom and party autonomy, even in proprietary matters, always subject to the requirements of the commercial flows and their promotion and to legitimate public order concerns, particularly in terms of market abuse, which concept itself is likely to be transnationalised in professional dealings. That is the future if globalisation holds and should be better understood by all.

Instead of certainty of this nationalistic nature, which may now often only be obtained at too low a level in terms of quality, it is submitted that the emphasis should be on *finality* of title transfers and payments, therefore on transactional certainty,[72] which is a much narrower (proprietary) concept,[73] and on *predictability* for the rest. Finality is a key issue

---

[72] Only in terms of the narrower issue of the *finality* of their transactions, especially in respect of title transfers and payments, is there an overriding need for certainty which the law merchant was always prone to provide, *viz* the law of negotiable instruments and bills of lading.

Certainty of this nature has traditionally been stressed in English case law ever since Lord Mansfield, especially in mercantile transactions; see *Vallejo v Wheeler* [1774] 1 Cowp 143, 153 (KB); see more recently *Homburg Houtimport BV v Agrosin Private Ltd, The Starsin* [2003] 1 Lloyd's Rep 571, 577 (Lord Bingham of Cornhill) and *Compania de Neviera Nedelka SA v Tradex Internacional SA, The Tres Flores* [1974] QB 264, 278 (Roskill LJ). For the US, see *Mc Carthy, Kenney & Reidy, PC v First National Bank of Boston* 524 NE 2d 390 (Mass 1988). Again, it should be noted that it concerns here often negotiable instruments and letters of credit, all related to payments, or bills of lading, therefore a narrower strand of commercial law where *finality* is indeed of special importance. See also *Pero's Steak and Spaghetti House v Lee* 90 SW 3d (Tenn 2002).

In this context, emphasis on finality is not incompatible with the transnationalisation of commercial and financial law, see also JH Sommer, 'A Law of Financial Accounts: Modern Payment and Securities Transfer Law', (1998) 53 *Business Law* 1181. It is submitted that the concept of finality may be enhanced by it. It would also seem misconceived to ask in this context for clearer rules of conflicts of laws and be satisfied even with arbitrary rules and therefore an arbitrary choice of some domestic law whatever its quality and responsiveness. That is a step backwards and contrary to the basic tenants, history and true needs of international commerce and finance. They are nationalistic academic fabrications. The recent and new references in this connection to 'certainty' in the Preamble (6 and 16) of the EU Regulation (EC) No 593/2008 on the Law Applicable to Contractual Obligations (Rome I) are misconceived and disappointing, but typical for traditional conflicts of law thinking.

[73] In terms of the legal characterisation of transfers and their *finality*, important issues arise in securities transfers and in payments, especially those through the banking system. They centre on fraudulent or defective instructions, the meaning of acceptance of the transfer or payment, the question of capacity and intent, and the transfer and its formalities (eg, in terms of existence, identification and delivery of the assets) and acceptance.

In terms of *transnational general principle*, which may well be in the process of becoming customary in a *mandatory* manner, the necessary *finality* may here be underpinned by: (a) de-emphasising the role and subjectivity of capacity and intent whilst giving these notions an objective meaning; (b) the abstract nature of all transfers in the German tradition (separating them from any underlying contractual or instruction defects); (c) the indepen-

in transactions, including payment, as we shall see throughout this book, and is therefore a central theme and concern of the new *lex mercatoria* besides, and closely connected with, the protection of the ordinary commercial and financial flows against adverse interests. It is a proprietary issue. The concept of predictability on the other hand, is less absolute and assumes rationality and sensibility. It rests on the idea of law as sufficient guidance for parties to determine their behaviour and for arbitrators and judges to reach a conclusion in dispute resolution. It is a different concept from certainty, which as just mentioned sees law as pure technique with inbuilt automaticity in result. This is unrealistic, even undesirable. One could argue that it is also anti-social. Predictability assumes, on the other hand, movement, and can deal with legal dynamism. Some degree of legal uncertainty is a fact of life and not necessarily to the detriment of the legal profession. It is unavoidable in incongruent factual patterns or in newer situations,. It is increased by the ever greater internationalisation of trade and commerce, itself mostly seen as an important and irreversible process. It is also enhanced by the uncertain grip of domestic regulation in international transactions.[74]

Yet the lack of certainty in a technical sense should not be more destabilising than absolutely necessary. It is one reason why the professional community may prefer to live with its own rules to the extent it can. Again, it suggests a measure of spontaneous transnationalisation and a larger reliance on (transnational) custom and practices and, further, a greater degree of party autonomy at that level. Aiming at better risk management tools, it is for this community to decide what it prefers (unless there are major public order or public policy issues involved) and it is likely to find it better to operate under more flexible rules than under the wrong rules. At least professionals come from a community that is used to taking and managing risks and they may be better able to deal with greater uncertainty than with the wrong rule.[75]

Indeed, it appears that professionals can normally handle these risks, aided by an ability to devise better structuring and protection schemes amongst themselves. It is also the essence of enhanced party autonomy in the law of movable property, as we have seen, and it is much of the international transaction lawyers' activity promoted by their clients':

(a)   understanding of the trade, the market infrastructure, and the requirements of the commercial flows, whilst developing and formulating custom and practices in these areas and enforcing them amongst themselves;

(b)   access to the international commercial arbitration practice in the case of disputes between them; and

(c)   being better positioned to ask for help, when needed, from states in the form of supporting treaty law (or within the EU in the form of Directives or Regulations, of

---

dence of the transfer or payment obligation and of the transfer and payment itself, as derived from the negotiable instrument and the letter of credit practice; (d) the *bona fides* of transferees once they have been credited or have received the assets in respect of any defect that may attach to the title, in other words the underlying assets (securities and cash) may assumed to be clean; and (e) justified reliance of transferees and especially payees who were owed the relevant assets or moneys and received them.

Thus it may be shown that transnationalisation may provide a considerable support function especially in this key aspect of finality of international transactions, see more particularly vol II, ch 2, s 1.4.6.

[74] In international situations, uncertainty may be compounded by the question of how far domestic mandatory *regulatory* laws or public policy may still impact on international transactions, see also n 32 above. It creates uncertainty of a different kind and raises issues of relevant contact, conduct and effect that, at present, are only capable of resolution on a case by case basis. See more particularly ss 1.5.6 and 2.2.6ff below.

[75] For the notion of professional, see s 1.1.8 below.

which the Settlement Finality and more particularly the Collateral Directives were prime examples).[76] Organisations like UNCITRAL, UNIDROIT and especially the ICC may provide a useful supporting function in this connection as well, but only if activated upon such requests.

It is a situation that has, in fact, been in practice for quite some time, has not led to disaster, and is unlikely to do so in the near future. This evolution should therefore be approached with confidence and imagination.

In truth, at least at the transnational level in the private law amongst professionals, the search is on for a new legal framework that is closer to present-day international reality, to how society works for them, and is thus capable of supporting their transactions in a more responsive and imaginative manner for the benefit of all participants. It has already been said that, theoretically, the formation, operation and application of the new transnational law merchant or *lex mercatoria* in the professional sphere in this manner takes its cue from the development and application of public international law. It is about how commercial (and financial) law is escaping the grip of domestic systems and is being transformed to better support international transactions and to provide a reasonable degree of predictability and finality where it matters, particularly in title transfers and payments. The limit is the public policy and public order which themselves may be transnationalised.

In private law, this takes us back to the time before the great nineteenth-century codifications when lawyers like Grotius accepted many sources of law and sought to find *structure* in them, not *system*. This is an important distinction. Finding structure is a dynamic forward-moving process. Finding system, on the other hand, is based on the idea that the system represents or can find reality and has in it all answers. In this way it seeks to set present-day law in concrete and is retrospective by definition. At best, it means to extrapolate newer law from past experiences but always assumes an existing intellectual model, framework or system that can handle all eventualities. It assumes that life is basically repetition.

The new law merchant rejects this approach and is dynamic and forward-looking, but it will also be shown that it is not averse to structure, and even seeks it by type of relationship, subject or product. The law of assignment or set-off and netting may be a prime example. It follows that the content and operation of the modern *lex mercatoria*, if properly understood, is by no means as vague, novel, uncertain or incomplete as is sometimes argued. As we shall also see, its hierarchy of sources and norms, with local law remaining the residual rule, presents a full operative legal system (for those who still wish to see one), no less than any domestic one: see section 1.4.13 below. But even then it does not claim to have all the answers.

1.1.6 Social, Economic, Intellectual or Democratic Legitimacy

A recurrent theme in discussing immanent law formation in the manner attempted here, and the operation of the modern *lex mercatoria* is the question of its legitimacy. In this connection it is often thought that statist law is more legitimate because it is democratic, at

---

[76] See also n 46 above.

least in democracies. This underpins in the minds of some the argument for codification, an issue that will be further discussed in section 1.2.13 below. It must be doubted, however, whether this is the correct perspective. In any event, the major modern civil codes—those of France and Germany—did not come about through a democratic process. The common law emanating principally from the courts could not possibly be so characterised. Where through legislation social values are incorporated into private law, there is clearly much to be said for democratic support, but social values enter through case law just as much and that has proven to be very necessary.

Rather, codification in the German manner had intellectual coherence and system thinking at its core, the idea being that in this manner society could operate better, but there was also a more transcendental aspect: states having the deeper insights in society and how it works. As has already been said, in this view, the state speaks here primarily through its academies and rubber-stamps their efforts, which derive their legitimacy from the academic effort itself and its search for 'truth' in that sense and its models to represent it. Legitimacy does not come, in this approach, primarily from the democratic process.

Other strong claims to legitimacy may derive from law as a community product and therefore, especially in customary law, from being more truly participatory. Efficiency considerations may also underpin this type of law. Although in the academic perceptions custom and practices are often declared inferior or primitive, nothing suggests that they are so in their operation. They have much to do with the infrasructure of the market place and stand for a more diverse society and for a multifaceted and more dynamic system of law.

The view has already been expressed that the modern *lex mercatoria* is in essence based on a number of non-territorial autonomous sources of law, notably fundamental and general principle, custom and practices and party autonomy, sometimes joined by uniform treaty law, whilst the residual rule remains territorial local law. This will be elaborated below in section 1.5 on the operation of the international commercial and financial legal order and its autonomy. It may thus be seen that some of the rules as well as the structure of this new law, are based on fundamental values or on more universal public order requirements; others on societal and efficiency forces; and yet others on statist action either through a legislature or through the court system. That is the simple consequence of having different sources of law and legal diversity in that sense, a theme that will be elaborated throughout this book and about which there is nothing per se undemocratic or illegitimate.

1.1.7 The Traditional Civil and Common Law Notions of Commercial Law. The Notion of Commerciality

The previous sections have looked at the different notions and coverage of commercial law in both civil and common law, and at this type of law formation at the transnational level, its reaction to system thinking, its need for more dynamic law, and its legitimacy. Its expanding international coverage was also considered.

This may merit some further consideration and a discussion of the more traditional theoretical notions that are still used in domestic laws to set commercial law apart even if, as we have seen, its independence in both civil and common law countries is in question, although for different reasons. As we shall also see, these more traditional notions do not best serve the transnationalisation concept, which depends rather on the concept of professionalism (see section 1.1.8 below).

However, these more traditional notions cannot yet be completely discarded. If one starts by looking at some civil law commercial codes, for example at the French *Code de Commerce* (CdC) of 1807 (redrafted in 2000) and the German *Handelsgesetzbuch* (HGB) of 1900, as well as at a common law commercial code like the US UCC of 1962, one may see considerable differences even between civil law countries.

As regards the *coverage* of commercial law, which even differs markedly between the CdC in France and the HGB in Germany, in civil law it is always related to commerce, in which connection a notion of *commerciality* is used, which may, as compared to common law, produce limitations; as a consequence the concept of commercial law may be narrower and more *service*-oriented in civil law. In France, there is particular importance in the distinction, as commercial disputes are still brought before separate commercial courts.

On the other hand, in the absence of a clear *commerciality notion* or concept, in the modern *common law*, there is *no single overriding criterion* that determines the coverage of commercial law. Importantly, non-merchants engaged in the sale of goods, using cheques, and yielding security interests in their personal property are covered as much by commercial law as are merchants and this is borne out by the UCC in the US.[77]

In common law, there is still a difference in the approach to custom which has a broader and more independent meaning in commercial law going conceivably beyond mere contract term and therefore also operating in other areas. It has already been said that in documents of title and negotiable instruments there is no need for consideration for their trading whilst bona fide purchasers of these instruments are protected. Here again, one detects special concern with the commercial flows and finality, but beyond this, in common law, it is now often tradition or statutory convenience that determines whether a matter is considered part of commercial law. There are hardly any particular consequences or special features left in the law deriving from the mere commercial law qualification. There are none in the type of courts before which commercial cases are brought, although, as in England, there may be commercial law divisions in the ordinary courts.

In the USA, the modern UCC (1962, but frequently revised since), which applies as uniform law (exceptionally) in all states of the USA (civil and commercial law being state

---

[77] Within the US, the UCC from the beginning separately defined the notion of merchants and dealings between merchants in s 2-104, but *only* in the context of the law of the sale of goods and not in any broader sense. However, the UCC did not eliminate consumer sales from Art 2 UCC, but only has some special rules concerning merchants.

A merchant is here defined as a person who normally deals in goods of the kind or otherwise holds himself out by his occupation as having knowledge or skill peculiar to the practices or goods involved in the transaction or to whom such knowledge or skill may be attributed by his employment as an agent or broker or other intermediary who by his occupation holds himself out as having such knowledge or skill. Dealings between merchants are transactions with respect to which both parties are chargeable with the knowledge and skills of merchants.

In earlier versions of Art 2 UCC, a broader distinction between consumer and professional sales was proposed: see ZB Wiseman, 'The Limits of Vision: Karl Llewellyn and the Merchant Rules' (1987) 100 *Harvard Law Review* 465. Art 2 UCC is therefore less professional-oriented than originally planned, reflecting the reality that in domestic sales professional dealings have so far acquired fewer distinctive features. Consumers have in the meantime obtained special protection under broader consumer laws, often at the federal level. In this manner, commercial law has indirectly regained a place of its own.

matters),[78] covers in this connection only a number of products, specifically negotiable instruments, bills of lading and warehouse receipts, and letters of credit as well as the sale of goods. It also deals with secured transactions in moveable property (including intangibles) and now even with finance (equipment) leases, which were eventually distinguished from secured transactions, and with payment systems and investment securities. On the other hand, it does not cover transportation, either on land or by sea, nor the related insurance. Company law and bankruptcy were never part of commercial law in the common law sense.[79]

As mentioned, in civil law countries that still have a separate commercial law, there is usually a *more substantive criterion of commerciality* and therefore at least in theory a clearer view of what is commercial. In France this is provided by the notion of the 'commercial act'; in Germany by the idea of 'dealings with merchants'. These definitions form the intellectual basis of the coverage by the commercial codes of these countries as we shall see in the next section, but fundamental distinctions have become much less important here also, and the coverage by the commercial codes is in both France and Germany often incidental, if not erratic. Non-merchants may sometimes also find themselves covered by these codes, for instance in writing cheques. Again, there is no doubt that in France the most important factor is not coverage by the commercial code itself, but rather the jurisdiction of the commercial courts in mercantile matters still with lay judges, and an accelerated procedure. These courts no longer exist in Germany. There are still commercial sections in the lower courts of that country, with some lay input, but they otherwise operate much like normal courts.

In view of the limited modern impact of the distinction between commercial and civil law, some civil law countries such as the Netherlands, Switzerland, Italy, and Brazil have done away with it altogether. However, as has already been mentioned several times, and as we shall see in the following sections, in the modern internationalised market place, the

---

[78] It means that the UCC was promulgated separately in each state of the Union and that the text may still vary between states. Also amendments are not always introduced simultaneously in all states. Some have repealed part of it (especially Art 6 on Bulk Transfers), but others have not. The UCC was itself a joint project of the American Law Institute and the National Conference of Commissioners on Uniform State Laws, started in 1942. The American Law Institute is a private body, since 1923 devoted to the harmonisation of legal concepts among the various states of the USA, especially through producing Restatements of the law as it has done in various areas such as tort, contract, agency and (interstate) conflicts of law. The Restatements are non-binding, but have nevertheless had a considerable impact on the further development of the law in the relevant areas and serve as guidelines for the courts.

The National Conference of Commissioners on Uniform State Laws, on the other hand, which has existed since the end of the nineteenth century, has drafted a number of Uniform Laws for adoption in the different states. The UCC is by far the most important of these Uniform Laws and is now accepted (with certain modifications) in all 50 states of the Union.

The UCC uses the term 'Article' in the sense of chapter or book. Each is divided into individual sections. Besides the chapter on sales (Art 2); there is the one on Bills of Exchange and similar types of payment instruments (Art 3); on Bank Deposits and Collections (Art 4); on Letters of Credit (Art 5); on Bulk Transfers (Art 6); on Documents of Title including Bills of Lading and Warehouse Receipts (Art 7); on Shares, Bonds and similar types of investment securities (Art 8); and on Secured Transactions (Art 9). Art 1 contains definitions. It is no exaggeration to say that Art 2 and especially Art 9 were at the time of their first publication (1952) original pieces of legislation. They were substantially introduced in the various states of the USA after 1962 and are regularly updated. Some new chapters have been added, particularly Art 2A on the Equipment Lease (a form of leasing) and Art 4A on Fund Transfers (payments).

[79] The UCC is in fact often considered bipolar with on the one extreme the sale of goods in Art 2 and on the other the security interests in Art 9, although the sale of goods remains here at the centre of commercial law itself; see also K Llewellyn, 'Problems of Codifying Security Law' (1948) 13 *Law and Contemporary Problems* 687.

distinction between professional and consumer dealings may have become more apt, with the former essentially being covered by a transnationalised legal regime or order and the latter remaining in essence subject to more prescriptive domestic laws.

Obviously, if there is to be any true meaning in distinguishing legally between commercial and other matters, it must be in some special legal regime applying to merchants and the dealings between them. At the very least, the commercial law regime should be more informal and custom-oriented, if not also more international. No less important would be the competence of special courts to hear commercial cases with simplified proceedings. They would be more specialised, less formal and speedier or be replaced by international commercial arbitration. Yet little is left of this in local laws.

As we have seen, in common law, the major difference is now in the role of commercial custom as an independent (although in England in practice often limited) source of law. There are no longer any autonomous courts. In the USA, the UCC reflects at least an accommodating approach to custom. To repeat, in, section 1-103(a)(2), the UCC envisages that the Code, for the areas it covers, is to be liberally construed to promote its underlying purposes and policies, one of them being to permit the continued expansion of commercial practices through custom, usage and agreement of the parties.

As just mentioned, France looks in this connection at *acts of commerce* and Germany at the dealing with and therefore *status of merchant*. Even in France, the German approach is often considered the more logical one, but at the time of the French codifications at the beginning of the nineteenth century, it was not considered proper to create a special class of people—in this case merchants—with different rights, even if these rights did not imply privileges but sometimes a less refined and harsher regime of enforcement. Nevertheless, treating merchants differently was considered counter to the then new notion of equality. The result was that the basic French concept of commercial law became tied to commercial acts or *actes de commerce* engaged in by otherwise equal people—at least that was the idea. There is no conceptual definition, however, and these acts are merely enumerated; compare Articles L 121-1 and L 110-1 (old Articles 1 and 632) CdC. They concern mainly the purchase of assets for resale and the intermediary services rendered in this connection, the renting of property, manufacturing activity, transportation and banking business.

Even though the basis was therefore *not* the concept of *merchants* or *commercants*, who are people or entities who habitually engage in commerce, the acts of commerce, as enumerated, are only covered by the CdC if they occur between merchants, except in so far as bills of exchange and cheques are concerned, which are commercial between all persons (except in a procedural sense). In France the result is that in their dealing merchants may not always be engaged in commercial acts as defined (even if they operate as merchants). On the other hand, persons not normally engaged in commerce may still engage in commercial acts but are not then covered in their activities by the CdC (except for bills of exchange and cheques). They are in any event sued in the ordinary courts.

In practice, the substantive relevance of the doctrine of commercial acts in France is modest, even in the law of sales. The most important aspects of commercial sales are that testimonial evidence against commercial contracts is admitted, which is unlike the situation under the *Code Civil* (Article 1341 CC). Furthermore case law[80] established that registered mail notice rather than court action is sufficient to put a party to a commercial contract in

---

[80] *Cour de Cass Req* 28 Oct 1903, DP 1.14 (1904).

default, thus creating the condition in which the remedies of rescission of the contract and/ or damages become available. Another point is that joint and several liability of commercial debtors is presumed, thus derogating from the rule in Article 1202 CC. Since 1925, Article 631 CdC (old) has provided further that agreements to arbitrate future disputes are valid and enforceable in matters in which the commercial courts are otherwise competent.

Tying commercial law to acts of commerce (as enumerated) is often presented as the *objective* approach, as distinguished from the *subjective* approach, to commercial law—in France, *droit réel* versus *droit personnel*. This latter approach ties commercial law to the activities of merchants. France has opted for the objective approach (enumeration of the acts of commerce) with a subjective twist and limitation (in the indirect reference to these acts having to take place between merchants). In Germany it was the reverse: all merchants are governed in principle by the commercial code, but only of course for the activities it covers. Here, the term 'merchant' remains largely undefined, however, though case law looks for an element of independence, of business activity, and of repetitiveness of the activity.

Thus in Germany the coverage of the commercial code is primarily based on the activities of merchants as such (if both parties are merchants or at least the party making commitments), but only in those areas covered by the commercial code, which also in Germany is somewhat haphazard. It follows that commercial law does not cover activities between merchants which are not commercial in terms of that code. So, even in Germany, a definition of commercial acts (*Handelsgeschäfte*) comes in, although some activity is considered commercial per se. On the other hand, some commercial activity may also be engaged in by non-merchants, such as the writing of cheques or the drawing of bills of exchange, which is now covered by a separate statute. Where non-merchants engage in commercial activity that activity may still be covered by the commercial code, but the activity is then considered commercial only in a more generic or wider sense. In fact, many provisions of the HGB do not cover specific commercial matters at all and apply equally to non-merchants. The distinctions are therefore not so clean and clear in Germany either. Much is historical accident, not fully cleared up in 1897 when the current German civil and commercial codes were put in place. There are many voices in Germany arguing for an abandonment of the distinction between civil and commercial law altogether.[81]

In Germany, as in France, the substantive law effect of commercial acts between merchants is thus also limited and incidental. Of particular interest, however, is that the transfer of a business activity implies the liability of the transferee for all its outstanding debt (section 25 HGB). This is a much contested rule. Another interesting feature is that interest and fees are implied in business activity and need not expressly be agreed (section 354 HGB).

The *real problem* in all this, in both France and Germany and in all countries that still maintain similar abstract criteria for the application of commercial law, is that merchants are not only engaging in commercial activity but also in non-commercial acts. On the other hand, non-merchants also engage from time to time in commercial activities. The consequence is that neither the concept of merchant nor the concept of commercial activity can be defined exclusively in terms of the other. Hence the confusion.

---

[81] See CW Canaris, *Handelsrecht*, 22nd edn (1995) 8ff, *cf* also K Schmidt, *Handelsrecht* (1999) 5.

Another notable aspect of commercial law in France and Germany is the absence of any general reference to the status and impact of custom and industry practices, even in commerce. As we have already seen, this is entirely in line with codification thinking that is suspicious of, and uncomfortable with other sources of law, and particularly with an internationalist approach. But beyond pure system thinking, especially in commerce, this attitude was always curious.

It has already been said that in France, commercial law as a separate body of law remains more important than elsewhere because of the special court system. Historically, French commercial law originated on two fronts: in trade with England, through the Channel ports, leading to maritime and insurance law; and in trade with Italy, through the fairs of Brie and Champagne, later moved to Lyons, in the East, leading to laws concerning transportation on land, bills of exchange and bankruptcy.[82] These were codified in the *Réglements de la Place de Change de la Ville de Lyon* of 1667, largely copied in the first all-French commercial code (*Ordonnance de Commerce de Terre*) of 1673, promulgated by Louis XIV and amended in 1716 and 1739. It was the result of an initiative of Minister Colbert who also ordered an *Ordonnance sur la Marine*, which was promulgated in 1681. They served as main sources for the French CdC of 1807.

As a consequence, the French Commercial Code still maintains the distinction between land and sea transportation law (in Books I and II old), although maritime law is now the subject of many different statutes. In the meantime, company law was put in a separate statute in 1966, bankruptcy in 1967 and banking in 1984. Many other provisions were repealed and the CdC was, as a consequence, much depleted, but it still covered commercial intermediaries and exchanges, negotiable instruments and the jurisdiction of the commercial courts. These subjects have recently been regrouped in the new French CdC of 2000, which again also covers company and bankruptcy law.

As for the specialised French commercial courts, there are many commercial courts throughout the country. Their presidents are elected by the local business community and they have lay judges. These courts have their origin in an Edict of Charles IX of 1563, which established in Paris an elected lay commercial court to decide the smaller commercial cases. This set-up was subsequently copied in many provincial towns. The commercial courts hear the commercial cases, including matters of company and bankruptcy law regarding merchants. The proceedings are informal and geared to speed. Parties need not be represented by counsel. The system has worked well and traditionally had a good reputation, although in modern times it has not remained free from scandal and accusations of rigging.

Belgium also has a system of commercial courts, but they were abandoned in the Netherlands. As in Switzerland and Italy, which took the step earlier, there is no longer a separate commercial code. Some of the content of the former commercial codes has been shifted to the civil codes or otherwise to separate statutes.

As regards the history of commercial law in Germany, there was enormous diversity in civil and commercial law between the different German States and Northern German (Hanseatic) towns, well into the nineteenth century. After 1848 there was at least a Bill of Exchange Act as a uniform law, therefore promulgated per state and not at national level. From 1861, there was a General German Commercial Code, itself at first a uniform law, but

---

[82] See, for the history of French bankruptcy, *Dalhuisen on International Insolvency and Bankruptcy*, vol 1 (1986) 1–60.

it acquired federal status in the North German Bund in 1869 and became the all-German Commercial Code after Germany's unification in 1871. A commercial Supreme Court was established in Leipzig in 1871. After 1879 it was converted into the German Supreme Court or *Reichsgerichtshof* (now *Bundesgerichtshof* in Karlsruhe) and the separate commercial court system disappeared. Thus in Germany there are no longer special commercial courts but there are special commercial chambers within the courts. They deal with commercial cases pursuant to the *Gerichtsverfassungsgesetz* of 1877. Each contains two lay judges who need not be lawyers. They are appointed for a term of four years, which may be extended.

As already mentioned, the German Commercial Code was adapted in 1897 at the time of the general German private law codification (*Bürgerliches Gesetzbuch* or BGB), without a fundamental re-orientation, and was then called the *Handelsgesetzbuch* or HGB. Both entered into force on 1 January 1900. In 1937, company law (the AG but not the GmbH) was put in a separate statute. In Germany, bankruptcy law had always been separate.[83]

1.1.8 Old and New Commercial and Financial Law. Transnational Notion of Professionality, a Separate Legal Order for Professional Dealings

We saw that the contract for the sale of moveable tangible assets (or goods in a common law sense) is often still considered to be at the heart of commercial law in common law countries where this law is trade-oriented. In civil law, there are only some limited special rules for sales in the commercial codes which otherwise have a bias towards the commercial rendering of services but also cover other subjects like (sometimes) company, insurance, banking and bankruptcy law.

Professionality of the contracting parties is *not* a feature per se of traditional commercial law of this type, especially not in common law, but if, as in France and Germany, special commercial law rules are sometimes still applied to these contracts, it is because in essence they are concluded between merchants, therefore in more modern terminology between professionals in their trade. Whatever the traditional differences between the French and German approaches in this respect (see the previous section), this suggests *greater expertise, business contact, and regular activity for financial gain* and therefore an activity between professionals or businessmen, even if sales may also be concluded between private persons under the normal private law rules, and cheques drawn, and services of transportation and insurance contracted for under the same commercial code.

For *domestic* activities, one may conclude, however, as many have, that the distinction between business (or professional) and private (or non-professional) activity as such has gradually become *less* important for the law. This is reflected in commercial law having become less significant as a different branch of the law everywhere, even if France still

---

[83] For a history of German commercial law, see Goldschmidt, 'Universalgeschichte des Handelsrechts' in his *Handbuch des Handelsrechts*, 3rd edn (1891). See, for the nineteenth-century discussions on the relationship between BGB and HGB, P Raisch, *Die Abgrenzung des Handelsrechts vom bürgerlichen Recht als Kodifikationsproblem im 19 Jahrhundert* (1962). The first more theoretical treatises on commercial law appeared from the sixteenth and seventeenth centuries, notably in Italy: see Straccha, *Tractatus de Conturbatonibus sive Decoctoribus* (1553), and Casaregis, *Discursus Legales de Commercio* (1740). See, for older French commercial law, J Savary (who largely drafted the *Ordonnance* of 1673), *Du Parfait Negociant* (1695).

maintains a separate court system for commercial disputes. It has already been noted that some civil law countries, such as Italy, Switzerland, the Netherlands and Brazil have therefore abandoned any such distinction and there is no longer a separate commercial code in these countries. Many writers in Germany also argue for this, as noted above. In modern times, domestically, special treatment has often become relevant, *not* for business dealings, but rather for consumers or non-professionals in their dealings with each other and particularly with professionals—therefore outside commerce. The result is that professionals and their dealings are again differently treated, although that is now not so much by design on the basis of special commercial or customary considerations, but rather by default, on the basis of special needs for others, especially consumers.

This may be relevant for instance in the application of modern notions of good faith to determine the rights and duties of the parties to a contract, when expertise and reasonable expectations may be taken into account, compare in particular sections 157 and 242 of the German BGB. This was considered especially important for the protection of weaker parties but may even now be much less relevant for professional dealings, see section 1.1.4 above and in particular Volume II, chapter 1, section 1.3.3. In civil law, the good faith notion may thus result in the nature of the relationship of the parties and the legal effect thereof on their dealings becoming a distinctive feature, as it is in common law where this was done, however, without using the doctrine of good faith; see Volume II, chapter 1, section 1.1.1. As we have seen, the result may be *less* protection for professionals all around. The notion of good faith in civil law is here only at its beginning as we shall see and there is commonly still a serious danger of a spill-over effect of consumer protections into professional dealings.

It was already been noted (in section 1.1.3) that in recent times financial rather than trade or mercantile considerations emphasise the special nature of modern commercial law and is introducing new notions not only of contract but also of proprietary law. Again, this is particularly relevant for professionals. In the financial world, leases, repos, secured transactions (including floating charges), and investment securities entitlements, have thus given rise to new notions of proprietary rights, which are alien particularly to traditional civil-law thinking and its systematic unitary approach and which pay no regard to the traditionally closed nature of its proprietary system. In section 1.1.4 above, the dynamic nature of modern contract and movable property law in the professional sphere was further introduced as another major modern development typical for professional dealings.

To repeat, at this stage, this is mostly relevant for professionals, with commercial law merely the likely conduit, but it is another reason why modern commercial law as a separate part of private law is once more in the ascendant. The additional reason is *transnationalisation*. Under the pressures of financial innovation and internationalisation, not only is a transnationalised system of substantive law being created, but this system is at the same time acting as a laboratory in which experimentation is taking place separated from the rest of private law in its domestic variants. This is the new *lex mercatoria* or law merchant; a law for international professional dealings whose features are legal transnationalisation, dynamism and, unavoidably at this stage also, experimentation.

As will be discussed in greater detail below, this law and its new structures are indeed largely meant to operate between *professionals* who are more likely to be able to deal with them and to fashion them. They are also able better to deal with risk and manage it, even legal risk. It reinforces the emphasis on *professional* dealings as the essence of *all* commercial law and of its separateness from the rest of private law and may be connected also with the operation for them increasingly of a distinct new commercial and financial legal order which is transnationalised, see section 1.5.5 below.

In any event, special (but not necessarily better) treatment of professionals has always remained more important in *international* dealings, of which the international sale of goods is perhaps still the best example, even if financial dealings may have exceeded them in importance or at least in legal attention. Even if the new 2011 EU proposal for a Regulation on the Law of Sales (CESL) may well now have a different approach to cross-border sales within the EU, international sales present a clear instance of a situation where extra risks and complications gave rise to a different legal regime. In a *technical sense*, international sales have indeed always been considered to be contracts between *professional* parties only, therefore between parties who are both knowledgeable in the area of their sale and its risks, are likely and able to make the special arrangements necessary in this connection and are aware of and able to develop *special industry practices* to this end, for which in international sales one should always be on the look-out (compare Volume II, chapter 1, sections 2.1.4 to 2.1.5). Furthermore, in the additional arrangements completing an international sale, such as transportation and insurance, one may also see differences in treatment as compared to domestic dealings which are now likely to be more consumer-influenced.[84]

Unlike domestic sales, the subject of *international* sales in this sense is indeed not commonly thought to cover consumer sales at all, or even sales of goods concerning which an otherwise professional party does not have special knowledge. To the extent that a distinct pattern has developed, the international sale is further limited in scope in that, as a term of art, it is not believed to cover the sale of real estate, negotiable instruments, other documents of title, bonds and shares, or assignments of intangible property (like receivables) either. This is clearly reflected in the 1980 (UNCITRAL) CISG, Article 2, which offers a part-codification of the applicable directory law and is meant as a uniform law. As we shall see (in Volume II, chapter 1, section 2.3.1) it has been adopted by many countries, even if in practice it is often still expressly excluded by the parties to these sales, meaning that the larger actors remain sceptical of the result. One particular reason is the subjective nature of the concept of fundamental breach in Article 25 and of force majeure in Article 79. Another is the unilateral right of the buyer to reduce the price under Article 50. The smaller seller is here particularly at risk. But there is also the confusion about the relationship of the text to other sources of law, evidenced in Articles 4, 7 and 9, the old fashioned offer and acceptance language in Part II which is still directed towards spot sales between private individuals, and the partial coverage of the subject of sales in the text which does not deal with the title transfer and key notion of transactional finality.

Other types of sales may, of course, also be the subject of international sales contracts, including consumer sales (which may require a whole set of other safeguards, increasingly important in cross-border internet transactions) and the rendering of connected cross-border services. However, they are not commonly included in a reference to international sales in a *technical* sense, which, as to subject matter, is therefore limited to tangible *moveable assets sold between professionals located in different states*. In such sales, there are traditionally different rules as to delivery and passing of risk. In view of the distance, there may also result some special *duties of care* of the buyer to protect the goods upon arrival should disputes arise and

---

[84] See for the concept of merchant and its importance in Art 2 of the UCC, n 77 above. As just mentioned, domestically its importance is now often de-emphasised, but internationally it revives.

goods be rejected. On the other hand, the seller might have a special duty of care if the buyer delays taking delivery in order to preserve the assets, even if the risk has passed to the latter (for example, upon tender of delivery); compare Article 85ff of the CISG. The subject of international sales will be dealt with more extensively in Volume II, chapter 1, Part II.

As just mentioned, much more obvious is the professionalisation in connection with modern financial dealings, even domestically, which is particularly reflected in the law of movable property. If one takes the UCC as an example, it is clear that Article 2 on the sale of goods still maintains a general notion of ownership and its transfer that also obtains between non-professionals, but in Article 2A on equipment leases and in Article 8 on the trading and holding of modern investment securities entitlements, the emphasis is on professional activities (of intermediaries and on the relationship of investors with them). Proprietary rights are then only defined incidentally, that is, for each structure specifically without any resort to general proprietary principles or a unitary system of proprietary rights. That is also true in Article 9 on secured transactions that in its latest text tends to address itself more particularly to professionals (thus excluding consumer transactions; compare, for example, section 9-109(d)(13)). Again, this is all about finance. In Article 4A (section 4A-108) on electronic payment, consumers are explicitly excluded. They are also excluded in Article 5 from the practice of issuing letters of credit (section 5-102 (9)(b)). It confirms the assumption that because of the specialised nature of these financial arrangements, they cannot be handled or are less suitable or even dangerous for non-professionals.

In the meantime, separating out international professional dealings has become increasingly common, even outside finance. Sensitivity to the special nature of activities of *professionals* operating internationally is, for example, suggested in the 1995 UNIDROIT Principles of Contract Law. According to the Preamble, they apply only to international commercial contracts, a restriction not contained in the 1998 European (Lando) PECL, which also apply to consumer dealings but are otherwise quite similar. In the UNIDROIT Principles, internationality and commerciality are not defined but the idea is clear, even though many of the rules seem to come straight from domestic consumer laws. This explains the similarity with the European Principles. Both sets of Principles will be analysed in greater detail in chapter 2, section 1.6.

Thus, in these various areas, the distinction between professional and other dealings has become important, at least transnationally.[85] A *more radical* approach altogether is the *distinction in general* between the *professional sphere* on the one hand and the *private or consumer sphere* on the other with emphasis therefore on: (a) the types of parties rather than

---

[85] The notion of commerciality has also been defined in the context of sovereign immunity in terms of the distinctions between acts *de jure imperii* and *de jure gestionis*, but the aim is then to distinguish public and commercial acts of sovereigns and their agencies, not to distinguish between (international) commercial and other private law acts.

In the EU, the notion of consumer is of considerable importance, notably in the protection of consumers through consumer contract law. The ECJ has defined 'consumers' as natural persons acting outside the range of professional activity: see Case 361/89 *De Pinto* [1991] ECR I-1189. Problems may arise where individuals also act professionally, raising the question whether such activities may still benefit from consumer protection. Protection is not afforded unless the professional activity was insubstantial: see Case C-464/01 *Gruber* [2005] ECR I-439. The counterparty may here rely on his good faith when an individual contracts for his business. It is also relevant whether the goods are or could be used for professional purposes, require delivery at a business address, or there is VAT registration. This suggests that the buyer may have raised wrong expectations and accordingly bears the risk, but in internet transactions it may be simply the nature of the goods and the likelihood of professional use that will determine the issue.

on the nature of their dealings; and (b) the qualification of the one as essentially globalised and legally transnationalised, and of the other as remaining in essence domestic.

Modern commercial law is then typically tied to *all* flows of goods, services, knowledge, and money *between professionals*, who increasingly conform here to internationally established patterns. This may become relevant even if on occasion they may still be operating purely domestically, yet under internationalised standards. There is here no basic other limitation in scope. This is the preferred approach in this book and ties the new transnational law to the emergence of a *new legal order* for all professional dealings, whether or not playing out domestically or transborder. See further the discussion in section 1.5 below.

The result in so far as the applicable law is concerned, is the application of transnationalised legal concepts to *all* dealings of professionals to support their legitimate needs (which are needs that do not offend public order and policy in the place of operation). That is the modern concept of the *lex mercatoria* as here defended, in which, as we shall see, there are several sources of law amongst which local laws may still play the residual role, but, crucially, these local laws are then transnationalised and may accordingly be adjusted and transformed to fulfill their role in that context and at that level.[86]

Professional dealings are here considered to be all dealings in the international flows of goods, services, capital and technology between individuals or entities that:

(a)   make it their business to do so;
(b)   regularly engage in that activity; and
(c)   are sufficiently expert in it.[87]

The direct consequence is a less subtle legal attitude to these professionals who are used to dealing in risk. It may also mean specialised proprietary structures not used in other parts of private law, and a more dynamic approach to contract as summarised in section 1.1.4 above and as will be more extensively the subject of Volume II. In sales, this leads to the basic distinction between professional and consumer sales, with the legal regime applicable to professionals being considered increasingly transnationalised. Importantly, this would be so even on those occasions when the relevant transaction may not have any international aspects; again, in this approach, it would be unrealistic to consider local professional dealings to remain subject to different rules if they concern the same business and are similarly structured. Economically speaking, there is indeed ever less justification to subject professional dealings to a different legal regime depending on the origin of the parties and their location in one or more countries. The result of the underlying flows being internationalised is thus a unitary legal approach for all operations in the professional sphere in which *internationality* need no longer be defined. Neither needs commerciality. Arbitrary distinctions in this connection may thus be avoided.[88]

---

[86] See JH Dalhuisen, 'What Could the Selection by the Parties of English Law in a Civil Law Contract in Commerce and Finance Truly Mean?' in M Andenas and D Fairgrieve, *Tom Bingham and the Transformation of the Law* (2009) 619.

[87] Another feature is here that only companies are likely to be involved in international dealings (therefore not individuals, certainly not consumers), whose business requires some expertise, is on some scale, whilst the interests to be defended are considerable but it also means that these issues primarily arise between parties that are aware of and used to taking some risk and apt to handle it professionally.

[88] The considerable confusion that is here arising in the EU in the context of its Draft Common Frame of Reference (DCFR) as a proposal for the codification of private law in EU and the more recent carve out for the law of sales in the Oct 2011 EU proposal for a Regulation in this area, will be discussed in nol II, ch 1, s 1.6. It may suffice here to say that in these texts no proper distinctions are made between consumer and professional dealings

It should be clear that these transactions are no longer confined to the sale of goods or other forms of trading or even financial transactions, but may also include agreements between, for example, large law firms and accounting firms in the realm of services even within the same country.

In summary, the consequence of a transaction being in the professional sphere, or rather in the transnational commercial and financial legal order, is the increased likelihood of it being taken out of the domestic law context altogether, both on the contractual and proprietary side (for movable property). It will be governed by its own set of transnational legal concepts in a unified cross-border legal framework, even if within that new law the contractual and proprietary structures may not yet form a single coherent or closed system of rights and obligations. This precisely defines the scope and challenge of the new *lex mercatoria*, but it was argued before that the professional community is likely to be well able to deal with this challenge and devise the necessary protections and make good use of the flexibility it entails within the larger room for party autonomy it is being given. Indeed, this has become the major task of structuring or transaction lawyers in international commerce and finance and is supported in international commercial arbitrations.

1.1.9 The Role and Status of International Commercial Arbitration

Not only are international commercial and financial dealings increasingly taken out of a domestic legal environment, but their operation within the transnational commercial and financial legal order with its own *lex mercatoria*, is also proving to have a profound effect on the dispute resolution in that order. It is common still to domesticate international commercial arbitrations in the place of the seat, which continues to nationalise all arbitrations even if international,[89] Although these issues may remain contentious, in the laws of *arbitration* a special approach to international professional dealings is now commonly

---

and between domestic dealings and transnational dealings, all dealings within the EU for these purposes now being considered domestic. There is thus no room either for a separate transnational legal order also operating within the EU. The consequence is that consumer protection issues spill over into professional dealings, also where they are transnational within the EU, eg between Portugal and Finland. This is another world, however, with very different ideas of risk. Not recognising this makes these EU proposals untenable in the professional sphere.

[89] The notion of the 'seat' of an arbitration in the place where it is conducted (making its *lex arbitri* applicable and, in the view of many, founding the award in it also, that is always in a national law), is in itself a strange one and hardly rational. It corresponds with the Savignian notion that all legal relationships have a seat or *Sitz* in a national law and that notion is then expanded to all legal action. This became the mantra in a time of extreme nationalism but it was always axiomatic, no more than political philosophy where 50 years earlier people had held exactly the opposite view. Furthermore, extraterritoriality of this law is then automatically assumed, governing the international arbitration in all its effects. This is an expression of statutist thinking, see s 2.1.2 below, commonly limited, however, to status and real estate matters.

Seat notions also emerged later in company law, but there it remained uncertain whether it was completely formalised at the place of the registration of a company or whether the place of its real activity had to be considered instead. This remains internationally an unresolved issue till this day and there are two different views. It is also reflected in international bankruptcy, although there seat language is not commonly used, rather the notions of primary and secondary bankruptcy depending on the intensity of activity in the country concerned.

taken.[90] It is, in fact, implied in the reference to international commercial arbitration itself, but the true consequences remain disputed.

It is generally accepted, however, that different arbitration rules apply and that there is a special internationalised arbitration regime when the (professional) parties come from different countries; when the subject matter is of an international nature; or when the arbitration takes place in an unrelated country. Compare the French Decrees Numbers 80-345 and 81-500 (1981) and the new Decree Number 2011-48 (2011), setting international commercial arbitration fundamentally apart; see also Article 1(3) of the UNCITRAL Model Arbitration Law of 1985, updated in 2006.[91] This Model Law (which does not as yet dispense with the notion of the seat), although not a treaty text, is important in the furthering of a special regime for international arbitrations. It is now accepted in several common law countries including some states of the USA, in Scotland, and in some East European countries including Russia, and is much used as guidance elsewhere, even in countries like England and Germany that did not follow it literally but have new arbitration acts, although especially the English Act 1996 still does not maintain here a fundamental distinction between domestic and international arbitrations either.

The distinction leads increasingly to the application of additional or different arbitration rules for international commercial or professional disputes. In this connection the following special features of international commercial arbitration may be noted:

(a)   the separability of the arbitration clause, which finds its true legal base in transnational law or in the international commercial and financial legal order and its public order, as does ultimately the jurisdiction of arbitrators, activated to that effect by the arbitration clause but not created thereby. This activation itself is then also a matter of transnational law;

(b)   the same may be said for the foundation of the related concept of arbitrability, which now also covers competition, securities, and other public policy issues;

(c)   the status and role of international arbitrators is equally founded in the international legal order itself and may compare more particularly to the role of equity judges in common law jurisdictions;[92]

---

[90]   See for this internationalisation or delocalisation of international commercial arbitration J Lew, 'Achieving the Dream: Autonomous Arbitration', (2006) 22 *Arbitration Internationa'l*, 179(Freshfield Lecture, 2005); and earlier J Paulsson, 'Delocalisation of International Arbitration: When and Why it Matters' 22 (1981) *ICLQ*, 53, and more recently J Paulsson, 'Arbitration in Three Dimensions', (2011) 60 *ICLQ* 291, see further also n 95 below. See for the leading defence of legal nationalism in international arbitration, the denial of the latter's existence, and the belief in the dominance of the seat and its *lex arbitri*, FA Mann, 'Lex Facit Arbitrum', 2 *Arbitration International* (1986) 245. Yet the development has been steadily away from localisation ever since the 1958 New York Convention on the Recognition and Enforcement of Foreign Arbitral Awards did away with the double exequatur, meaning that recognition of awards elsewhere no longer depended on the prior sanction of the courts of the seat.

[91]   The UNCITRAL Model Arbitration Law accepts that an arbitration is international when the parties (at the time of the conclusion of the arbitration agreement) have their places of business in different countries, or the place (or seat) of the arbitration or the place of (a substantial part) of the performance is outside the country of the parties. Parties may also expressly agree that the arbitration shall be international. As to 'commerciality', the Model Law states in a footnote to Art 1(1) that it should be given a wide interpretation so as to cover matters arising from all relationships of a commercial nature whether or not contractual. It then gives a number of non-exclusive examples. The idea clearly is that all international business is covered.

[92]   It is posited in this connection that, ever since Roman law—the praetorian law or *ius honorarium*—this extra facility has proved to be a necessary institutional pre-requisite to the adequate operation of private law, especially in order to prevent it from stultifying and to underpin private law's dynamic character. Ordinary courts cannot

(d)   this international status is also the cause of the procedural flexibility and discretion of international arbitrators in matters of admission of evidence and applicability of private international law rules;[93]

(e)   it is equally the platform for the acceptance of multiple sources of law and the hierarchy of the new law merchant or the modern *lex mercatoria* in matters of substantive law application in international arbitrations;

(f)   it leads further to the *limitation* as a matter of transnational public *order* of the impact of *lex arbitri* of the seat;

(g)   similarly, it leads to a limitation of the review by the domestic courts, either when the awards are challenged in the country where they are rendered (of their seat or any other) or in the context of their recognition and enforcement in other countries; and

(h)   notably the sanction of the courts of the seat is no longer required for the international standing of these awards and is no precondition to their enforcement elsewhere. It also follows that their annulment at the seat is no longer dispositive in recognition and enforcement elsewhere either.[94]

properly take this on, never mind how liberal they may be in their interpretation technique and legislators cannot adequately handle it—it would require a continuous process of updating which is beyond their purview. At the level of transnationalisation, there is in any event no formal legislator.

The special position of international commercial arbitrators in this regard is underlined by the opinion often expressed in the sense that at least international commercial arbitrators may rely on notions of the *lex mercatoria* whilst ordinary courts remain beholden to the application of national laws. This is a grave error which would in particular exclude resort to international custom and general principle in domestic courts unless authorised by a national law and thus seriously compromise the role of commercial courts in international commerce and finance, but the sentiment is correct in so far that international commercial arbitrators may have extra powers, which, as is here suggested, are institutionally founded in the international commercial and financial legal order itself and rely on their conscience, knowledge, and sensibility, as equity judges did: see further JH Dalhuisen, 'International Arbitrators as Equity Judges' in PH Becker, R Dolzer and M Waibel (eds), *Making Transnational Law Work in the Global Economy: Essays in Honour of Detlev Vagts* (210) 510.

In this connection, Preamble 13 of the EU Regulation of 2008 on the Law Applicable to Contractual Obligations (Rome I which replaced the earlier Rome Convention in this area) makes it at least clear that parties may now opt for non-state law as the law applicable to their contract, which state courts would then have to apply, but short of such an election, this could still be doubtful. International arbitration agreements and arbitrators are outside the scope of the Regulation and are not therefore subject to similar constraints and may not therefore depend here solely on a parties' choice of law to the effect in their contract.

[93] Importantly, this freedom may also concern the method of reasoning in the award. Unfortunately these awards are becoming longer and longer. One reason is that arbitrators seem to feel that they must answer each point raised by the parties. Judges operate differently: they identify the relevant facts and relevant laws and deem the rest of the arguments immaterial and irrelevant and leave them as they are. Arbitrators seem less confident.

It may matter in particular where the reasoning may give rise to annulmentas under Art 52(1)(e) of the ICSID Convention, which of all the grounds for annulment under this Article looks most like an ordinary appeal ground: 'the award has failed to state the reasons on which it is based'.

In *International Centre for Settlement of Investment Disputes Washington, DC Compañía de Aguas del Aconquija SA and Vivendi Universal SA v Argentine Republic* (ICSID Case No ARB/97/3, Annulment Proceeding), 10 August 2010, the Ad Hoc Committee found that the standard is that the 'reasoning used by the Tribunal must have been plausible, that means adequate to understand how the Tribunal reached its decisions, it being given the benefit of the doubt if there is room for a difference of opinion in the matter'. Nevertheless, the question of reasoning remains problematic in international arbitrations and seems to become ever more so.

[94] This is the French position culminating in the *Putrabali* decision of the French Cour de Cassation, n 11 above, but it is also the American position, see *Chromalloy Airoservieces Inc v Arab Republic of Egypt*, 937 F Supp 907 (DDC 1996) although the reasoning is different. In the US, it is considered a matter of domestic US public

Thus on a better view, these awards and the arbitration agreements on which they are based, as well as the power and status of international arbitrators, are founded in the international commercial and financial legal order itself from which they derive their legitimacy and the awards derive their international currency.[95] International arbitration is not then merely based on party autonomy which would limit the jurisdiction of international arbitrators. It follows that the arbitration clause activates but does not found the arbitration. Or at least, that would now appear to be the more satisfactory academic model to explain and clarify what is happening and to guide the process of international arbitration in respect of commercial and financial dealings between professionals in our times. Globalisation of commerce and finance goes together with transnationalisation of its legal regime and of its dispute resolution, review, and enforcement facilities.

In fact, there is little point in being a nationalist in an internationalist world. It produces ever more unsatisfactory or contradictory answers. We see here a historical trend: law, even commercial law, was nationalised in the nineteenth century and became territorial. That was the model and political philosophy of those days. This trend is now reversed, the movements of the international flows of goods, services, information, payments, and money (if not also of people) and their scale require it.

It earlier led in Europe to the conditions that made the EU in its present much extended form, possible and necessary and is also at the heart of its openly declared existence as a separate legal order. But the trend goes much beyond it. That is in international arbitration also the drift of French case law up to the Cour de Cassation which introduced the concept of an international arbitral order. It is much the same as the transnational and commercial legal order in respect of all professional dealings as proposed in this book,

---

policy that favours arbitration whether a foreign annulled award can still be recognised and enforced in the US and US courts exercise their discretion under the New York Convention in this manner.

The key is, however, that annulment by the court of the seat is not dispositive in the US either and that is more and more the international attitude and in fact the consequence of the NY Convention having abandoned the double exequatur of the 1927 Geneva Convention and having rendered annulment at the seat no more than a ground for refusal of recognition and enforcement elsewhere as a matter of discretion of the recognising court.

However, there is often still considerable confusion here. The need for support at the place of the arbitration from the courts of the seat is often confused with the question of where the arbitration and the award are founded. Support may be necessary in many countries. In fact, recognition and execution is only one example of it. Like the latter, this support is usually not necessary in the country of the seat where there are mostly no relevant asserts or activities. The seat will be chosen for its neutrality in this respect. Provisional measures and preservation matters equally do not normally concern the country of the seat but must be demanded wherever relevant. Many countries may thus have to support and the *lex arbitri* of any of them is then relevant, not merely and certainly not exclusively, the one of the seat.

It may be that the courts of the seat and their laws are the more appropriate when it comes to appointing arbitrators and dismissing them, if the applicable arbitration rules chosen by the parties do not provide for such eventualities, but even such measures have no force outside the countries of the seat. Extraterritoriality of the laws of the seat in this regard may not be assumed and it is quite possible—even if undesirable—that other arbitrators emerge elsewhere and that they, or dismissed arbitrators, proceed to an award. It will ultimately all be a matter for review and recognition in recognition countries, where indeed the true control is, not therefore in the country of the seat.

[95] See for the *Putrabali* case, n 11 above. In the literature, see Paulsson n 90 above. The idea has been defended that party autonomy itself carries the delocalisation, it then being seen as a legal order of its own. The pre-existence of an international commercial and financial legal order that sanctifies party autonomy of this nature and also founds the status and powers of the arbitrators, which are merely activated by the arbitration clause, is here preferred. See further the discussion in s 1.5.5 below.

even if the new French Arbitration Act of 2011 hesitates to draw the conclusion and still seems to think that international arbitration to the extent it operates in France remains a French product. The more modern trend is no longer concerned with definitions like 'internationality' and 'commerciality' (see the discussion in the previous section), but rather with professional dealings per se.

The special arbitration regime for professionals in their international dealings is indirectly, even if incompletely, confirmed in the 1958 New York Convention on the Recognition and Enforcement of Foreign Arbitral Awards (Article 1.3). First, there is the reference to 'foreign' awards and abolition of the double exequatur. It also allows states to limit the application of the Convention to commercial awards (the 'commercial reservation'). Even if they do *not* do so, the common view is that disputes between states on boundary and similar political issues, perhaps including disputes with foreign investors (unless further treaties allow it in which connection bilateral investment treaties or BITs may be important), are excluded and so too are employment and family law issues unless incidental to the main dispute. The New York Convention thus limits itself to international (commercial) arbitral disputes, although expressed in the (imperfect) language of 1958 which could not have foreseen the direction international commerce and finance was to take, nor its modern scale and its ever more justified claim to constituting a legal order of its own as it did well into the eighteenth century, an approach to be explored further below in sections 1.4 and 1.5.

1.1.10 International Arbitration and International Commercial Courts

As has already been noted in the previous section, in international arbitrations, the transnationalisation of modern commercial law is often dealt with informally. International arbitrators tend to enjoy greater freedom in conducting these proceedings and in finding the applicable law. Accordingly, they commonly assume greater freedom in fashioning the rules of procedure and evidence and the applicable private international law rules wherever they may still be relevant. In finding or developing the applicable substantive law, they may then also more freely rely on transnational custom or principle where necessary or appropriate and operate with a different concept of party autonomy that may even extend into the proprietary area, as we have seen.

This is the area of the modern *lex mercatoria* with its various legal sources and their hierarchy, which then also covers the role and powers of international arbitrators. It was suggested in this connection that the role of international arbitrators is becoming here more akin to that of equity judges in a common law sense before the latters' role became much curtailed in England after the eighteenth century when legislation took over as the more normal corrective of the common law.[96]

---

[96] See n 92 above.

In international commercial cases, it is submitted, national courts should assume the same freedoms, but often hesitate.[97] This is also an issue of powers.[98] To support the new transnational law in the professional sphere, it would therefore not be a bad idea, nor too far-fetched a proposition,[99] to set up an international court system for professional dealings operating in a similar manner as the commercial courts once did in regionally divided countries.

[97] It is worth noting in this connection that there may be a formal attempt at approximation when parties choose a local court for the resolution of their international commercial disputes. This is the subject of the 2005 Hague Convention on Choice of Law Agreements which facilitates international recognition and enforcement of ensuing judgments in all Member States of the Convention, along the simplified ways of the New York Convention for international arbitration awards. This is considerable progress. The Convention has so far only been ratified by Mexico but has been signed by the US and the EU.

The difference remains, however, in the attitude to the applicable law, where arbitrators are likely to exercise greater freedom. It is submitted that ordinary courts chosen by the parties should do the same so that a real alternative results, the distinction then being only in the possibility of appeals in the ordinary courts, a facility, it is further submitted, the parties should be allowed to exclude (an issue with which the Convention unfortunately does not deal—such an exclusion is still against public order in many countries).

[98] Note also in this connection Judge Wilkey speaking for the majority in the Court of Appeals in the American case, *Laker Airways Ltd v Sabena Belgian World Airlines* 731 F2d 909 (DC Circuit 1984), at the same time as the English judiciary in *Amin Rasheed Shipping Corporation v Kuwait Insurance Company* [1983] 1 WLR 228, 241, see n 100 below: 'Despite the real obligations of courts to apply international law and foster comity, domestic courts do not sit as internationally constituted tribunals. Domestic courts are created by national constitutions and statutes to enforce primarily national laws. The courts of most developed nations follow international law to the extent it is not overridden by national law. Thus, courts inherently find it difficult neutrally to balance competing foreign interests'.

Note that this statement came within the explicit rejection of the balancing test of para 403 of the Restatement (Third) of the Foreign Relations Law of the United States (1987), even though a reasonable link between forum and controversy was considered to be an important limitation on US jurisdiction. This Restatement was in preparation at the time and is now more commonly accepted, cf the US Supreme Court in *Hartford Fire Insurance Co v California* 509 US 764 (1993), in which both the majority and the dissenting minority relied on it. See for a further and more particular discussion, the dissent of Justice Scalia in that case. To the extent this Restatement is now accepted, it puts the status of the courts in dealing with international commercial cases in a different light.

Note also that by using a forum selection clause, it is normally accepted (unless the forum selection would work out to be unfair or utterly unreasonable for one of the parties in the circumstances of a case) that parties may choose a court that balances the potentially involved governmental interests better or more neutrally, like an international commercial arbitration panel would do that has undoubtedly an international status, see further s 2.2.6 below. To the extent national courts are increasingly willing to do the same, again it is not illogical to impute to them a similar status. It would certainly seem fair to say that, especially under the influence of much increased internationalisation and globalisation since 1984, matters have moved on.

It should also be noted in this connection that, within the EU, domestic courts in EU matters sit as European courts subject to the guidance of the European Court of Justice, from which prejudicial opinions may be and frequently are asked. The notion of national courts sitting as international courts is therefore by no means new. Another issue that could be raised in this connection is whether domestic courts would have to be more conservative in developing international law than international courts or international arbitrators would have to be. In this connection the observation of Lord Slynn in the first *Pinochet* case [2000] 1 AC 61, which implied that the House of Lords in a case like this one did *not* sit as an international court and would therefore be more restricted in developing international law, may be of interest. The majority clearly did not see it this way, although it did not argue the point explicitly. Cf also L Collins, 'Foreign Relations and the Judiciary' (2002) *ICLQ* 509 with reference to the Court of Appeal in *Kuwait Airways Corp v Iraqi Airways Co* [2001] 3 WLR 1117, 1207 in which the further development by the English courts of international law as to what was justiciable or not was also not considered impeded.

[99] See in favour of such an international court to operate as an appellate court in the supervision and recognition of arbitral awards internationally Mauro Rubino-Sammartano, *International Arbitration Law and Practice* (2001) 980, and JH Dalhuisen, 'The Case for an International Commercial Court' in KP Berger et al (eds), *Festschrift Norbert Horn* (2006) 893. See further HM Holtzmann, 'A Task for the 21st Century: Creating a New International Court for Resolving Disputes on the Enforceability of Arbitral Awards', and SM Schwebel, 'The Creation and Operation of an International Court of Arbitral Awards', both in M Hunter et al (eds), *The Internationalisation of International Arbitration*, The LCIA Centenary Conference (1995) at 109 and 115.

The concern of these last two authors is the recognition of foreign awards under the New York Convention of 1958 and the possible bias of local judges. The idea is to replace their involvement with that of an international court, which would acquire exclusive jurisdiction in the matter. Enforcement of recognition orders of such an

One possibility in this context would be to accept that domestic courts in international commercial matters sit as international commercial courts.[100] Judgments of these courts should then become universally enforceable, much as international arbitration awards are

international court would, of course, remain a domestic affair. It would be logical that such a court would also become solely competent for challenges or setting aside petitions, which are now normally brought in the domestic courts of the place of the arbitration. Other forms of ancillary proceedings could be added, such as interim protection measures and compelling the attendance of witnesses, see also M Hunter et al (above) at 157. The proposal is important though more limited than what is proposed here.

[100]   See for the idea of local courts operating as international courts in this connection, the English case of *Amin Rasheed Shipping Corporation v Kuwait Insurance Company* [1983] 1 WLR 228, 241. The case is of special interest in view of the important cast of judges expressing their (minority) views in the lower courts with the House of Lords ultimately re-establishing orthodoxy. The facts in this case are not of great import. There was an insurance contract concerning an insurer in Kuwait, drafted much along the lines of the relevant standard English policy, yet without a choice of law and competent forum clause. There thus arose concern about the applicable law and about the jurisdiction of the English courts.
In the lower courts, Judge (as he then was) Bingham [1982] 1 WLR 961, thought that the contract could be covered by an international regime inspired along English lines (although not so in this case), so that under the applicable English rules of international jurisdiction the competency of the English courts could be established on the basis of the application of English law. In the Court of Appeal, the Master of the Rolls Sir John Donaldson thought that English courts could have jurisdiction over an unwilling defendant because the English courts could, in cases like these, function as *international commercial courts*.
In the House of Lords [1984] 3 WLR 241, Lord Diplock thought, however, that contracts could not operate in a vacuum as they would then be only scraps of paper. International law was clearly considered vacuous in this connection and the implication was that only a domestic law could apply, which in this case was eventually thought to be English law, a view supported by Lord Wilberforce. Lord Diplock further thought that English courts could not operate as international commercial courts and thus force themselves on unwilling defendants. Also, for English jurisdiction in cases like these, there would have to be a solid basis, which could be, but need not be, and was in this case was *not*, found to be in the application of English law, especially since in this case there was a Kuwaiti court available.
In a later unrelated case, *EI du Pont de Nemours v Agnew* [1987] 2 Lloyd's Rep 585, Lord Bingham, then in the Court of Appeal, borrowed some of the 'legal vacuum' language but seemed to leave open the question whether that vacuum could be filled by international law, including international general principles or custom, while in the same year in the *Deutsche Schachtbau- und Tiefbohrgesellschaft* case [1987] 3 WLR 1023, the Court of Appeal under Sir John Donaldson held unanimously that at least international arbitrators could rely for the applicable law on internationally accepted principles, thus accepting not only general principle as a source of law but allowing *international* principles and customs to operate in that connection also. Notably, this was not considered to be against English public order. See further the discussion in section 3.3.1 below.
It is sometimes submitted that this could only be so in international arbitrations and that at least the 1980 Rome Convention on the Law Applicable to Contractual Obligations did not allow it in ordinary courts: cf *Dicey and Morris on the Conflict of Laws*, 13th edn (2000) 1216 and 15th edn (2012) 1223, but in truth the text is inconclusive and the point seems never to have been considered. So much is clear, however, that, even in England, no true principle is involved any longer as it is inconceivable that there is any fundamental difference between the applicable law in courts of law and in arbitrations. As far as the 1980 Rome Convention on the Law Applicable to Contractual Obligations was concerned, it was a matter of interpretation on which there was much contrary opinion in the rest of Europe. In any event, where more substantive rules are introduced, as in Arts 5, 6 and 7, more general principles of protection or balance were used. The replacement of the Convention by an EU Regulation in 2008, has not clarified the issue, except that under its Preamble, parties may choose a non-statist law even though the relevant text was ultimately deleted from the body of the regulation itself. It left also open the question whether judges may do so in appropriate cases if no such choice has been made by the parties.
In the US, opinion also moves in the direction of accepting international principle as the applicable law, see eg DW Rivkin, 'Enforceability of Arbitral Awards based on *Lex Mercatoria*' (1993) 9 *Arbitration International* 67.
In connection with international arbitrations, the question has further arisen whether they themselves could operate in a legal vacuum, therefore, in this terminology, separate from a domestic law or legal system (or local arbitration Act), often perceived to be the domestic law of the seat of the arbitration: see also n 94. above and accompanying text; also A Redfern and M Hunter, *Law and Practice of International Commercial Arbitration*, 5th edn (2009) 188ff. ICSID arbitrations notably do not operate in a national arbitration framework. Again, the more significant issue would appear to be whether the vacuum may be filled in another manner, eg by transnational law emanating from the transnational commercial and financial legal order as the new law merchant setting also common international arbitration standards.

under the New York Convention of 1958 on the Recognition and Enforcement of Foreign Arbitral Awards or as *in rem* judgments are habitually enforced in admiralty worldwide.

The difference with international arbitrations is that there might be more stability in such a court system and there would also be the possibility of appeal. On the other hand, local courts might still be predisposed to apply their own regulatory laws even in international cases that have little contact with their own territory and may also not attain the status of equity judges that arbitrators may now have in the development of transnational law. See the previous section 1.1.8.

Such an international court system comprised of domestic courts sitting in international commercial cases (they could have some lay judges) could have a central highest international appeal court to test points of law (thus forgoing national layers of appeal). That would not apply to international commercial arbitrations, which normally do not provide for an appeal in this sense.

This International Commercial Court could also be enabled to give preliminary opinions on points of transnational private law or the modern international *lex mercatoria*, and on such issues as the reach of domestic mandatory and other regulatory laws in international cases and on matters of international procedure or public order, if the relevant court or arbitration tribunal or the parties in agreement on such a request so wished. In principle, this would follow the EU example of preliminary opinions under Article 267 TFEU.

This highest court could also deal with international enforcement of commercial judgments and arbitral awards if contested in the domestic courts of the place of enforcement (on the limited grounds set out in the New York Convention but substituting international public policy considerations for domestic ones) and take over the adjudicatory challenges and supervision of the arbitral process in the courts of the place of the arbitration (seat), although these courts could still function in support subject to a similar system of preliminary opinions which could also be requested by the arbitration tribunal if it considered its authority to be undermined in this manner. Interim measures, especially involving attachments or similar preservation orders, might also be sought from such an International Commercial Court, especially if assets were located outside the country of the seat of the

---

One thing is clear, there is in these international cases a close connection between the law applied and the status of the tribunal. If the law is transnational, it is not strange to assume that courts applying such law (be they national courts or arbitration panels) thereby acquire an international status as well. Thus when in *Amin Rasheed* [1983] 1 WLR 228, 241, there was a discussion of English law being applicable as common currency or lingua franca, this implied internationalisation of both the applicable law and the courts applying it. Seen from this perspective, it was not at all so strange that the commercial courts in London, in the minority opinion, were considered to operate as international commercial courts. Of course, commercial courts in other countries could then claim a similar status.

Neither is it strange that this may affect unwilling defendants assuming an adequate rule of jurisdiction could be formulated for these courts under international (customary) law or on the basis of general principles. The jurisdictional limits could then be found in a vibrant *forum non conveniens* approach in the courts asked to exercise this jurisdiction and in a broad concept of *lis pendens* operated in other international commercial courts subsequently petitioned and asked to intervene, or in an intelligent handling of subject-matter jurisdiction and comity requirements in the American manner. See also s 2.2.6 below.

One consequence which is often overlooked is that the ensuing judgment could then hardly be qualified as a domestic judgment and be asked to be enforced as such. In fact, judgments of this nature should be enforced in the manner of arbitral awards under the New York Convention or now also in the manner of the 2005 Hague Convention on Choice of Court Agreements. Ideally, the principles behind these Conventions should be extended to them, in which connection the question of proper (judicial) jurisdiction would also have to be further considered. Another idea would be to allow the parties to select the regime of these Conventions for the international recognition of commercial judgments.

arbitration. It would not be the idea, however, for this Court to operate otherwise as an appeals or review court, certainly not in the substance of the decision, except, as just mentioned, in respect of local commercial courts acting like international courts in international commercial disputes.

This International Commercial Court should have exclusive jurisdiction in the areas of its competence and be allowed to base its decisions on transnational or international principle and practice much as the ICJ does for public international law disputes under Article 38(1) of its Statute.

In terms of this book, it would be best to introduce here, in respect of substantive private law issues, the hierarchy of norms of the *lex mercatoria* (see sections 1.4.13 and 3.1.2 below) supplemented by a balancing facility or minimum international standards in respect of governmental interests (or regulatory issues) as an international public order requirement. A similar system could be envisaged in matters of procedure and evidence where any domestic *lex arbitri* would thus be preceded by other rules, especially by the practices and customs of international arbitration. It is conceivable that such an approach to procedural issues could also be accepted in domestic commercial courts dealing with international cases. As just mentioned, this system of rules should be supplemented by a uniform notion of international public order for challenges and recognition disputes.

The creation and operation of this International Commercial Court would require treaty status. Its findings should be accepted as final and be directly enforceable in all Contracting States, therefore in all states participating in this scheme. It follows that commercial judgments or arbitral awards ignoring such decisions would not be effective or would be remedied accordingly.

This new Court could thus become an important aid to the development of transnational commercial and financial law and its creation would at this stage probably be more important than codifying transnational law itself for which there is no sufficient direction in practice and theory and no sufficient platform amongst legal practitioners.[101] Although, as has already been noted, a number of eminent authors have given their support to the idea of creating an International Commercial Court for the supervision of international commercial arbitrations and the enforcement of international commercial arbitration awards under the New York Convention of 1958, the subject needs renewed attention. The extension of its jurisdiction to recognition problems in all commercial judgments worldwide (on similar grounds to those contained in the New York Convention) is a further possibility. Decisions would be published in principle (even though parts might still have to be anonymised to protect confidentiality). This jurisdiction could of course, still be expressly excluded by the parties in their agreements.[102]

---

[101] See for practitioners' input in limited areas the UNIDROIT Mobile Equipment Convention of 2002, vol III, ch 1, s 2.1.8 and the EU Financial Collateral Directive, vol II, ch 2, s 3.2.4. See for the lack of this input in the DCFR and CESL and their uncritically following of the established civil law codification ethos, s 1.4.19 below.

[102] There is some kind of example in the WIPO procedure concerning domain names conflicts. Under the classic rules of private international law great differences could arise, encouraging forum shopping. The WIPO procedure allows everyone to ask on line to be entitled to use a domain name registered in the name of someone else. The WIPO then appoints an arbitrator, who decides within six weeks. If he finds in favour of the claimant, the respondent may appeal to the normal state courts to get his domain name back. The first cases were decided on general principles and on those derived from national laws, but are now increasingly determined on the basis of the (transnationalised) case law of these arbitrators, which can be accessed online.

1.1.11 Structure of this Volume

Before the emergence and development of the new *lex mercatoria* is discussed in greater detail, it may be useful for those particularly interested to dwell a little longer on the traditional sources of private law in civil and common law countries, on the development of the codification approach and its significance in this regard, and the survival and significance of other sources of law. This is the subject of the next two main sections (section 1.2 for civil law and section 1.3 for common law), where a further explanation will also be offered for the limited room traditionally left in civil law for the application of fundamental and more general principles and custom. It will also seek to explain and compare attitudes in this regard in the common law and in the modern American variety.

In section 1.4, the sources of law will be discussed more extensively in their operation in civil, common and transnational law. In section 1.5, the discussion will move to the operation of international legal orders and the abandonment of an exclusively statist and territorial view of modern private law creation in favour of a more modern sociological and economic approach leading to greater universalism (at least in international business cases).

This will lead to a fuller introduction to the concept and operation of the hierarchy of principles and norms in the modern *lex mercatoria*. which theme will be further developed in Part III after the traditional conflicts of law approach and its problems have been more fully analysed in Part II, including the problems arising internationally (and therefore also in the application of the modern *lex mercatoria* as a hierarchy of norms) with governmental interests as expressed notably in domestic regulation and similar domestic public policy directives. It concerns here the competition and possible clashes with (domestic) regulatory laws or legal orders.

For the internationally-oriented student interested in the development and operation of different (commercial) legal systems, this lengthy excursion may also serve as an explanation for much of what may, at first glance, look unfamiliar or strange in other legal systems, which she or he has not previously encountered. In particular the different approaches in civil and common law to the sources of the law, statist attitudes and system thinking should be better understood by all.

The approach taken throughout this book is to identify a number of legal constructs, such as in contract the notion of offer and acceptance, *force majeure* and change of circumstances, or otherwise the special rules pertaining to the sale of goods and contractual agency (in Volume II, chapter 1), or in personal property the rules pertaining to assignments (in connection with receivables financing and securitisations), leases and repos (as example of modern finance sales), or floating charges in secured transactions (in Volume III, chapter 1). This is done first to highlight the intrinsic aims and problems in these constructs and their use, then to see what local laws have done with them, and ultimately to consider the requirements of and developments in the transnational practice, where in modern movable property, for example, party autonomy (therefore contractual clauses) is the beginning but where broader practices and fundamental and general principle may need to be demonstrated to underpin newer proprietary structures operating at the transnational level but also public order requirements at that level to protect the international flows of commerce against all kinds of unknown changes or other proprietary interests.

In a comparative sense (therefore in respect of the examples used as illustration and guidance and in identifying a trend), I confine myself in this book largely to the laws and practices of the major countries of the common and civil law, therefore to the laws of England and the USA on the one hand, and of France and Germany on the other. This is not done out of disrespect for any other, but not all can be covered and what is covered should, in my view, be covered in some considerable depth to have meaning. The focus is therefore on the laws in the major industrial, even post-industrial, nations, the development of whose legal systems has been of prime importance for the evolution of commercial and financial law so far.

These legal systems are also likely to provide the natural starting point for the globalised transnational legal structures developing in the international commercial and financial sphere, therefore for professional dealings worldwide, but it will also be shown that it is necessary to move well beyond what the laws of these countries can contribute to arrive at the *new lex mercatoria* which crucially depends on various other sources of law (see section 1.4 below).

1.2 The Origin of Civil Law. Its Traditional Approach to Law Formation and to the Operation of Private Law especially Commercial and Financial Law

1.2.1 The Evolution of Modern Private Law and its Sources

The development of modern international commercial and financial law as an autonomous transnational non-statist phenomenon and the problems it encounters in that connection may be better understood when greater light is shed on the development of the various sources of private law and their autonomy in the course of time.

Although we have become used to the idea that the law, even private law, comes from states—in civil law through codification, in common law of the English variety through the idea that all law ultimately emanates from sovereigns who would only accept and enforce their own laws (and those of others only to the extent incorporated in their own or recognised by them)—it was not always thus and is in fact a typical nineteenth-century nationalistic perception whose prevalence may now be ending, at least in international commerce and finance. As we shall see, it had found important support earlier, among eighteenth-century philosophers, but it is a more recent attitude that became connected with the emergence of the modern state. In England, by that time, it had already led to the absorption of the autonomous commercial (and church) laws into the common law, being the law of the King's courts,[103] even though in common law, the commercial law is, to this day, as we have already seen, not as completely integrated into the general body of the private law as it is in civil law.

---

[103] See n 18 above.

On the European Continent, the *Ius Commune*, which was the pre-codification universal private law of those days derived from Roman law as such never promulgated but operating as a superior form of customary law. It supported but did not interfere with commercial law. As a consequence, commercial law developed mainly from practice and local supporting statutes. It retained greater independence longer than in England, which it took the nineteenth-century codifications to eliminate. This may well prove to have been an exceptional situation and the statist, nationalistic, nineteenth-century view of commercial and financial law may abate, and, it is posited, could now be coming to an end. Globalisation is here the driving force at least in commercial and financial law.

In that sense, a situation more akin to the one that existed under the *Ius Commune* may revive for cross-border transactions and international dealings of that nature. It is in essence a return to the method of Grotius that allowed for multiple sources of law and was never abandoned in public international law where it is still preserved in Article 38(1) of the Statute of the International Court of Justice in respect of the sources of public international law, as already noted. Room is thus created for the revival of a non-territorial transnational *lex mercatoria* as the substantive private law for dealings between professionals, albeit in a much updated form. It has been mentioned before that this may lead to, and require, a fundamental separation from consumer law that is likely to remain purely domestic much longer and is more public policy oriented.

It is obvious that this development is connected with newer economic and social undercurrents of the law and its globalisation in the professional sphere. It is posited that that law is or may be immanent, a product of bottom-up law formation. It presents a view of private law formation and operation that has in the meantime received renewed attention in modern American academia, particularly in the 'law and economics' and 'law and sociology' variants of 'legal realism', even if as yet American legal scholarship has not devoted much attention to the development of these ideas in the context of the modern evolution of a transnational commercial and financial law.[104] It is nevertheless particularly revealing to consider modern American attitudes in this regard which will be briefly summarised in sections 1.3.5 to 1.3.6 below.

But first, to set the scene, the development of the legal systems and sources of law in Western Europe will be covered in some detail for those who may be interested in it. It is only possible to offer here the briefest of sketches of the intellectual, cultural and social evolution of law, especially private law in the two major Western manifestations: civil and common law. Much of this is now ignored in modern legal scholarship, and for many the materials may no longer be easily accessible, but I hope that the overview that follows may provide both insights into the past and a basis for further exploration of what may come in the future.

The evolution of the civil law is the subject of section 1.2. The evolution of the common law will be discussed in section 1.3.

---

[104] See, however, RD Cooter, 'Structural Adjudication and the New Law Merchant: A Model for Decentralisation' (1994) 14 *International Review of Law and Economics* 215, and JH Dalhuisen, 'Legal Orders and their Manifestation: The Operation of the International Commercial and Financial Legal Order and its *Lex Mercatoria*' (2006) 24 *Berkeley Journal of International Law* 129, and s 1.5.5 below.

1.2.2 The Early Developments on the European Continent. Roman Law

In the western world, Roman law was the first legal system to develop into something that went beyond the basics[105] and still has meaning today.[106]

Early Roman law is understood to have developed substantially from the law of the XII Tables (*lex duodecum tabularum*) of around 450 BC—which were lost when Rome was invaded in 390 BC.[107] According to some they never really existed. However, there are many precise references to them in the later literature. Reconstituted but fragmentary and often speculative texts have been produced since the sixteenth century.[108] They show that the Tables contained the basic, largely administrative rules and criminal laws of early Rome as well as the rules of procedure in force in those days.[109]

---

[105] See F de Zulueta, *The Institutes of Gaius*, Pt 1 (Oxford, 1946, reprint 1991), Pt 2 (Oxford, 1953); Fritz Schulz, *History of Roman Legal Science* (Oxford, 1946) and earlier *Principles of Roman Law* (Oxford, 1936); B Nicholas, *An Introduction to Roman Law* (Oxford, 1962); D Daube, *Roman Law* (Edinburgh, 1969); W Kunkel, *Römische Rechtsgeschichte* (1964); M Kaser, *Römisches Privatrecht*, 14th edn (1986); WJ Zwalve, *Hoofdstukken uit de Geschiedenis van het Europese Privaatrecht* [Chapters on the History of European Private Law] (Groningen, 1993).

[106] According to the writer Livy (or Livius), Rome was founded in 754 BC. At first it was under the leadership of Etruscan kings who could exercise all powers (or *imperium*) in this small community of probably not many more than 10,000–20,000 people. *Imperium* included the judicial function which was exercised on the basis of the king's insights, some customary law, edicts decreed by the king, and some laws (*leges*) issued by popular acclaim through a people's assembly or *Comitia*, which was later subdivided into 30 groups or *curiae* when Rome became bigger, each of which would sent representatives and also provide military personnel for the defence of the City. Even then there was already a Senate, which, however, could only give advice (*senatus consulta*).

This system continued after the last king, Tarquinius Superbus, was ousted in 509 BC, following—according to the story—the outcry caused by his son Sextus raping the famous Lucretia, who then killed herself. Henceforth, two consuls were appointed for a term of one year, during which they each exercised the *imperium* in full, including the judicial and legislative functions, although it became established that they were subject to the *leges* of the *Comitia*, which were considered higher than their *edicta*. Eventually the lower classes (*plebs*) obtained a veto right on all the activity of the consuls through the *tribunus plebis* after threatening to leave Rome and create a separate city which supposedly would have fatally undermined Rome's infrastructure and depleted the ranks of its footsoldiers.

From 367 BC, they were allowed to appoint one of the consuls. Eighty years later under the *Lex Hortensia* of 286 BC, after further strike action by the *plebs*, they were allowed to create their own laws by plebiscites (*plebiscita*), which laws were subsequently given the status of *leges*, applicable to all (D.1.2.2.8).

[107] According to the story, the Tables were produced in order to better protect the *plebs* who had objected to the uncertainty of their predicament and to this effect had managed to have the *imperium* transferred for one year to ten lawmakers (the so-called *decemviri de legibus scribundis*). They started to record the laws, but also abused their *imperium* and extended it in time. The consular system was firmly re-established, however, after one of them, Appius Claudius, set eyes on the beautiful Verginia and indirectly made her his slave. She was killed by her father to avenge her honour and to 're-establish her freedom'. Their legislative work was, however, enacted. This is all reported with some relish in the much later Digest Part of the *Corpus Iuris Civilis* of the Emperor Justinian (D.1.2.2.24).

[108] The most widely used is Schoell, *Legis XII tabularum reliquiae* (1866).

[109] According to Livy, the XII Tables were in their time considered the true source of public and private law (*fons omnis iuris publici atque privati*). From early on, they established a number of important principles. Legal equality was accepted, especially after the lifting of the prohibition on marriages between the patriciate and the plebs. There was no primogeniture, nor legal incapacity of women; no privileges in penal law, and no penalties without a judgment, even though they could still be harsh, but the death penalty itself became subject to some important safeguards. Apparently slavery barely existed in Rome's early days, but not paying one's debts could lead to slavery by the sale of the debtor to the surrounding tribes. Slavery could also arise from war; in fact the institution of slavery is often thought to have had its real origin among prisoners of war (*ius servitutis bello introductum*).

There were soon interpretation questions concerning the XII Tables. New actions (*legis actiones*) were increasingly deduced from them, but these were kept secret by the caste of priests that had started to occupy itself with the judicial function. This situation is reported in the much later *Digests*, in an excerpt of the Enchiridion of Pomponius (D.1.2.2). A secretary, Gnaeus Flavius, let out the secret, however, for which the population greatly venerated him (D.1.2.2.7). The published practices showed an advanced interpretation technique in which the literal meaning of words had often been abandoned and the few original actions had been broadened to provide better protection, although there remained a great deal of formalism: the right formula still had to be used and a mistake would lead to the loss of the case which could not be restarted (D.1.2.2.6).[110]

Around the same time (367 BC), the important office of the *praetor* was created. This introduced a new and important phase in the development of the Roman law. The *praetor* was meant especially to focus on the judicial function by granting actions. As he also had the *imperium*, he had original law-creating powers and could thus issue his own *edicta* as well. From then on, for the most part, Roman private law no longer developed through the *leges* or *plebiscita* but rather through the office of the *praetor* because by edict his role was to add to the actions which derived from the XII Tables or from the *leges* and *plebiscita* (D.1.2.2.10). His office was a high one but lasted only one year, at the beginning of which he had to say which actions he would allow; he could not then deviate from this programme, although he could extend it. The *praetor* was free in principle, but normally continued the previous practice. As a jurist of repute, he became confined by the practices elaborated by his predecessors, by his training and reputation, and by the view of his fellow jurists.

Eventually, this led to a standard text, which became known as the *Edictum Perpetuum*. It was lost in history, but reconstructed by the German scholar Otto Lenel in the late nineteenth century (third and last edition, 1927) and proved a very important document, also because large parts of it were later incorporated in the *Corpus Iuris* (see next section).[111] It all shows that, as the later English common law, Roman law was essentially an *action-based* law and developed accordingly. These actions were either *in rem* if intended to recover an asset, or *in personam* if intended to force someone to give or do something or to abstain from action.

The Edict and its interpretation created the so-called praetorian law or the *Ius Praetorium*, also called the *Ius Honorarium* (D.1.2.2.10). This *Ius* was technically different from the *Ius Civile* which remained the normal law prevailing amongst the Roman citizens. It was narrower, could be changed rapidly and was in principle only valid for one year. As a *decretum*, it was subject to the higher XII Tables, to the *leges* and to the *plebiscita*, which were themselves the real basis of the *Ius Civile*, for which the *Ius Honorarium* was only

---

[110] The importance of Flavius's intervention was that it opened the law and its enforcement to outsiders, therefore to lawyers outside the priestly circle, which had tried to monopolise the judicial function through secrecy. The legal actions so revealed are referred to in the Digests as the civil Flavian law (*ius civile Flavianum*), later extended by Sextus Aelius as the Aelian civil law.

[111] The *praetors* would not themselves adjudicate cases, but would in each instance indicate to the parties the *action* on the basis of which they could argue before a privately appointed judge (*iudex privatus*), often supported by lawyers (*iuris consulti*), in the nature of a modern arbitration, the decision in which would be enforced. The *praetors* could also formulate *exceptions* if the basic claim was admitted but special circumstances were pleaded in defence. They could also issue so-called *interdicts* as orders or prohibitions in obvious cases, eg where there was unjustified appropriation of someone else's goods. If litigation was necessary but the defendant did not want to submit to private judges, the *praetor* could declare him *indefensus*, so that he lost his case, although he could reasonably object to the proposed judges.

meant as support (D.1.1.7.1), but at times the *praetor* did not hesitate in his function of allowing or denying actions on the basis of his Edict to intervene and aid, supplement or amend the civil law on the basis of the public interest (*propter utilitatem publicam*).

As such, he was effectively considered to be the living voice of the Roman *Ius Civile* (*viva vox Iuris Civilis*, D.1.1.8). In this respect, there is also a parallel with the later common law, where, in a wholly unrelated development, the Lord Chancellor could intervene in a similar manner through equity, although, it would appear, only in a more restrained and incidental manner (see section 1.3.1 below). The office of the *praetor* demonstrated, as equity later did in England, that private law may need a facility of this nature to move forward, and that, in the absence of ready statutory intervention and amendment, without this facility private law has a tendency to lag behind practical needs and expectations. It may ossify. The absence of such a facility in civil law may have accounted and may still account for extra difficulty in updating itself. It is then left to the interpretation technique of the judges.

Eventually a *special praetor* was appointed for foreigners (*perigrini*), the so-called *praetor perigrinus* operating alongside the *praetor urbanus* (D.1.2.2.28). This became necessary as foreigners did not benefit from the protection of the Roman *Ius Civile*, which was only intended for its citizens but needed some protection in their relationship with Roman citizens and among themselves when in Rome or its provinces. This protection was in Rome provided by the *Ius Gentium*,[112] henceforth further developed by the *praetor perigrinus* much as the *Ius Civile* was by the *praetor urbanus*. The *Ius Gentium* could thus be part of the *Ius Honorarium* when formed by the praetor but applied in principle to different people. In other respects, foreigners remained subject to their own laws, for instance in matters of marriage.

In fact, in those times, the law was considered *personal and not territorial*, each tribe having its own, as Roman citizens had in the form of the *Ius Civile*. But as the *Ius Gentium* was law that was considered primarily based on *natural reason* and as such considered common to all of mankind (*quod naturalis ratio inter homines constitutit*, D.1.1.9), it became applicable *also* to dealings between Romans as supplementary law. Ultimately, it became the *universal* law in the tradition and philosophy of the Stoa, as we shall see. It is this law that was restated in the later *Corpus Iuris* (see next section) and became the foundation of the *Ius Commune* on the Continent of Europe, meant to apply to all. In this environment it may be seen that there was not much need for a conflicts of law doctrine in the modern sense.

Earlier, for Roman citizens in Rome, the *Ius Gentium* proved important because it allowed for the development alongside the *legis actiones* of a different form of proceedings, allowing the plaintiff to describe the relief sought in the complaint itself. This was the procedure *per formulam*, which was to become the normal manner for the commencement of all civil legal proceedings. The *Ius Gentium* also proved crucial for Roman citizens in other respects.

---

[112] This *Ius Gentium* should be clearly distinguished from the law that later became the law between nations for which the term '*Ius Gentium*' is now used.

As it was much concerned with trade and commerce, it made the consensual contracts (*bona fidei iudicia*)[113] of sale, rental, deposit and loan legally binding (D.2.14.7).[114]

1.2.3 Classical Roman Law and the *Corpus Iuris Civilis*

After a period of strife culminating in the murder of Julius Caesar in 44 BC, his nephew Octavius, in 27 BC, under the name of Augustus, assumed the consulate and *imperium* for life and at the same time the right of veto of the *tribunus plebis*. There was no more second consul.

This is considered the beginning of the Roman Empire, although officially the Republic continued with all its laws and the Octavian succession was explained rather as a return to older values. It started, however, an important new phase in Roman history, which also had an effect on its laws. The Senate substantially assumed the legislative function of the *Comitia*, which had become unwieldy (D.1.2.2.9). The *senatu consulta* thus acquired the force of law but the Senate in practice exerted only a rubber stamping role. This meant that all *leges* were made subject to the *imperium* of the Emperor (*constitutiones principis*, D.1.4.1). The further development of the *praetor*'s Edict came to an end and was, by the middle of the second century AD, overtaken by imperial constitutions. The procedure *per formulam* and the private nature of the proceedings were also abandoned, and by the third century law suits were brought before imperial judges (*cognitio*). It is often thought that this centralisation seriously weakened the intellectual advance of Roman law.

But first there developed a special class of lawyers, who could give official opinions (*responsa*), not unlike Queen's Counsels (QCs) in modern England. Some of them were very highly regarded and acquired an official status and their *responsa* the force of law (D.1.2.2.49). In Rome, the law was rightly a matter of great pride to its citizens and, alongside literature, was seen as a most important intellectual and cultural manifestation. A selection of these *responsa*, especially of Papinianus, Ulpianus, Paulus and Gaius, are found in the later Justinian *Digests* as part of the *Corpus Iuris* (to be discussed shortly), and earlier had been ranked in the case of conflict (in the *Lex Citandi* of 426 AD). They became the true source of classical Roman law and operated beside the imperial constitutions. It is at this time, in the second century AD, that Roman law is generally thought to have reached its high point. This is considered best reflected in Gaius' legal treatise of that time (the *Institutiones*), which was long lost but a copy was found in Palympsest in Verona in 1816.

The subsequent centralisation of the judicial function included the possibility of addressing questions directly to the Emperor who would answer in published *rescripta*. These did not, on the whole, aspire to the intellectual heights of the *responsa*. Many of them are still known; they illustrate the mature period of Roman law and a more political, verbose and often less precise style, especially since the Emperor Constantine the Great (306–37 AD), when religious and ethical overtones were sometimes also introduced (in a

---

[113] In the *Ius Civile*, consensus itself had never been sufficient to create a contract and it gave binding force only to a small number of specially defined contract types and for sales had only developed a special type of formal transfer for certain assets (*mancipatio*).

[114] The *Ius Gentium* was also the law covering slavery and freeing of slaves (*manumissus* D.1.1.4). It confirms that slavery was originally only known in respect of or amongst the *perigrini*.

Christianised Empire, especially in the East). There was also loss of effectiveness. True, all foreigners in the Empire became citizens after 212 AD, but many kept their own customary laws, leading to fragmentation. This is clear especially from the legal texts found in modern times in Egypt (the *papyri*).

With the expansion of the Empire, it became vulnerable and more difficult to rule, particularly at the fringes. In 330 AD, a second capital was created by the Emperor Constantine, who earlier introduced freedom of religious worship. It was located in Byzantium (subsequently Constantinople, now Istanbul). After Theodosius the Great (379–95 AD), who made the Christian church the state church (C.1.1.1), there were always two Emperors, often more. Each had the *imperium* and therefore remained fully competent throughout the whole Empire, even if the one resided in the West in Rome, or later also in Milan or Ravenna, and the other in the East in Constantinople. Constitutions were issued together, at least that was the idea, and when one died the other was fully in charge and could block a successor, in practice especially the Emperor in the East, although it often required force.

The centre of the Empire was gradually shifting eastwards, driven also by economic forces, while after 395 AD the so-called Dark Ages started to dawn in the West. Upon the demise of the Roman Empire in the West in 476 AD following the attacks of the Vandals under Odoacer, the Emperor of the East in theory regained sole powers throughout the Empire, as these had never been surrendered[115] but his powers in the West were in truth at an end.

It follows that Roman law continued to develop largely in the East, in Byzantium, culminating in a kind of codification under the Emperor Justinian, which was achieved between 529 and 534 AD upon the direction of his minister Tribonianus and the law teachers Theophilus and Doretheus. This was the *Corpus Iuris Civilis*.[116] It had been preceded by a *Codex* of Theodosius II of 438 AD, meant to establish some order in the Constitutions and Rescripts of the Christian Emperors, and earlier by private selections of them in the *Codices* of Gregorianus and Hermogenianus. The new *Corpus Iuris* was much more comprehensive and (in the Digest part) also included the opinions of major jurists (*iuris consulti*) which

---

[115] Odoacer accepted this and wanted to become an officer of the Empire or rather 'a patrician in charge of the diocese of Italy' under the Emperor Zeno, as indeed requested by the Roman Senate, which declared the continuation of the imperial succession in the West inopportune and asked Zeno to re-establish unity. The Emperor, resuming full powers, refused to recognise Odoacer. Instead, he allowed the Ostrogoths under Theodoric to take over, but Theodoric soon became an independent ruler. Some of the Eastern Emperors, in particular Justinian (after 527 AD), later managed to re-establish an important presence in Italy, but this proved only temporary.

Indeed, at first, the Germanic usurpers of Italy continued to see themselves mostly as kings, consuls or patricians under the Byzantine Emperor and were soon accepted as such. The structure of the old Empire thus remained basically intact in Rome, under the Senate (although by now not much more than a local administrative body), but the West was de facto dominated by the newly established northern tribes: the Ostrogoths in Northern and Middle Italy, later followed there by the Lombards; the Visigoths in Southern France and even Spain; the Burgundians in the Rhone valley; the Francs in Northern France; the Saxons in Northern Germany, in parts of the Netherlands, and eventually in England.

Nevertheless, officially, the *imperium* of the Emperor of the East over the West lasted until the age of Charlemagne, around 800 AD, when this artificial situation was ended and the Emperor of the East accepted the existence of a new Empire in the West (much later called the Holy Roman Empire), which became effectively a German empire until its demise in 1806, although it considered itself a continuation of the Roman Empire in name, which also proved important for the status of Roman law.

[116] The most used English translation of the *Corpus Iuris* (Digests) is Alan Watson, *Digests* (University of Pennsylvania, 1985).

ultimately proved more significant as they formed the basis for the later revival of Roman law in Western Europe. The *Corpus* represented the result of around 1,000 years of legal development and has rightly been identified as a mark of great civilisation, even though some of the best work of the great classical jurists might have been missed out or may have been corrupted in the final texts.

The *Corpus Iuris* was not guided by any set of overriding legal principles,[117] was not systematic, recites scattered cases, opinions and statutory texts, and continues to reflect a casuistic and fractured approach to the law. It even contains long historical tracts. It also struggled with definitions and with the different sources of law, which it did not mean to supersede but it gathered them in one text.[118] In that sense, it was not a modern European style codification or an example for it. Although there was no clear intellectual system or methodology, there emerged a number of broader ideas. In particular, it confirmed the notion that each free man was part of a society founded on respect for the law; that the empire and not individuals would defend the person and his property, enforce binding contracts, and guard against wrongdoing; and that the empire was in this respect one trained hierarchy of functionaries, including judges, who answered to the emperor alone. Much of it is still fairly easily understandable.

This is so also because until the twentieth century the *Corpus Iuris* managed to retain legal force at least in some parts of Europe, especially in Germany, and was in any event never completely forgotten. Even now the *Corpus* has residual importance in Scotland,

---

[117] At one stage, it was widely accepted that this Roman law fostered lifeless rationalism and property absolutism. It was then even suggested that, upon its reception in Western Europe, it not only proved devoid of values (except mercenary ones), but that it was morally menacing, especially in commerce: see for a discussion JQ Whitman, 'The Moral Menace of Roman Law and the Making of Commerce: Some Dutch Evidence' (1996) 105 *Yale Law Journal* 1841. In the twentieth century, it created an anti-Roman law sentiment especially in Germany, where Roman law teaching had in any event been abandoned since the Nazi era (because it was not Germanic).

Left-wing thinkers inclined to a similar attitude. This severe view is now largely discredited. More positively, it can be said that the reception of Roman law did not stand in the way of modern commerce that often required a more dynamic approach. In the meantime, natural law principles, increasingly secularised since Grotius as we shall see, developed important new perceptions and values, notably in the seventeenth-century Dutch school of jurisprudence.

[118] It is true that in the first Title of the *Digests* there are a number of more general remarks and even definitions. Thus, invoking Celsus, the law was considered the art of what is good and fair (*ius est ars boni et aequi*, D.1.1.1). Invoking Ulpianus, justice was considered a constant, unfailing disposition to give everyone his due (*iustitia est constans et perpetua voluntas ius suum cuique tribuendi*, D.1.1.10). In addition, the basic principles of the law were said to be: to live honourably, to injure no one and to give everyone his due, while being learned in the law was to know what was just and unjust.

In D.1.1.1.2, public law was distinguished from private law as it was observed by Ulpianus that some things were good from the point of view of the state and others from the point of view of the individual. Thus, there were public and private interests recognised and protected by the law. Private law was considered to be deduced from natural law (which obtained between all living creatures, even animals), from the *Ius Gentium* (which was the natural law applying to human beings such as the rights of parents over children and the right to repel violence and wrongs), and from the *Ius Civile* (which was the law for citizens of a particular state and could go beyond the *Ius Gentium* in more specific rules, which may or may not be in writing). Then follows a definition of all three in D.1.1.1.3/4 and D.1.1.6/7, and subsequently also of the *Ius Honorarium* in D.1.1.8 and of the *Ius Gentium* again in D.1.1.9.

These definitions, which struggle with the differences between ethics, laws, and instincts, were hardly perfect and were not of much consequence for the rest. Indeed at the very end in D.50.17.202 it was rightly said that all definitions in the law are dangerous (*omnis definitio in iure periculosa est*). The importance was that the *Corpus Iuris* remained comfortable with different sources of law (subject always to the emperor's amending powers) and it did not intend to present one integrated system.

South Africa and Sri Lanka,[119] although it is mainly followed there through the works of the seventeenth- and eighteenth-century Dutch writers like Grotius, Voet, Vinnius, Huber, Groenewegen, Van Leeuwen and Van Bynckershoek.

The *Corpus Iuris* consisted of four parts: the *Digests* or Pandects (50 books), the *Codex* (12 books), the *Institutes* (four books), and the *Novellae*, which contained imperial decisions added later. The *Digests* contained opinions, scholarly excerpts, and case law.[120] The fiction was that there was no contradiction in them and that it presented a working system, although much of it might never have had practical meaning. Moreover, it was in Latin whilst Byzantium spoke Greek. It could in any event be accessed only through experts.[121] Yet one still finds in the *Digests* the basics of modern Continental European private law, including the notions of ownership, possession, holdership; and of contract law (although this was less developed in Roman law as was the law of torts and unjust enrichment).

The *Codex*[122] contained the imperial constitutions and rescripts to the extent that they were still considered relevant. Those that were not included lost the force of law. Those included were not reissued. This meant that they retained their order in the sense that, in the case of conflict, the newer prevailed over the older. Here we find, for example, some of the Roman laws of insolvency. The *Novellae* were added later after the death of the Emperor in 575 AD and contained his newer constitutions. Constitutions of later Emperors were henceforth also called *novellae*, although not officially made part of the *Corpus Iuris*. They were in the Greek language.

The *Institutes* were a textbook written for students but also obtained the force of law and summarised and explained the basics of the law as it then stood. In this respect it followed very closely the earlier example of Gaius, who, as we have seen, had written a similar book in the second century AD.

In classical times, Roman law had been action-based. It seems to have remained so, even though litigation solely based on actions disappeared together with the proceedings based on the *formulae*, later replaced by *cognitio* proceedings in the imperial courts. No system of purely subjective rights based on more general rules followed, however. Thus, a contractual right could not be generally maintained, and an action based on a particular type

---

[119] In these countries, there was unavoidable English influence in the law, but differences with the common law are still significant, especially in property law, in the binding force of contracts regardless of consideration, in the possibility of third parties deriving benefits from a contract, in the possibility of specific performance as a contractual remedy, and in the unitary law of torts based on the *Lex Aquilia*, etc. In trust, company and bankruptcy matters, these countries have substantially adopted common law (equity) notions, and this is clearly seen in commercial law.

For an early authoritative description of Scots law, see James Dalrymple of Stair, *The Institutions of the Law of Scotland* (1681) and for a later one Bell's *Commentaries* (1820). Since the Act of Union the UK Parliament has been empowered to enact legislation for all of the UK, but as far as the Scots are concerned only 'if for the evident utility of the subjects within Scotland'.

[120] The *Digests*, which had gained the force of a constitution eliminating all other opinions, contained in particular a selection of the most important *iuris consulta* amongst the great Roman lawyers on particular issues. It reflected through them also much of the contents of the *Edictum Perpetuum*.

These materials were to some extent categorised and harmonised into a more coherent whole in order to eliminate contradictions or the resurrection of long-abolished practices, but there was no clear underlying unified system as one would find in modern codifications. These textual changes necessary to get some cohesion are now called *interpolations*, and have mostly been traced, but it was unavoidable that in this way older practices were connected with newer ones and made for imperfection and lack of coherence.

[121] See Koschaker, n 1 above, 128.

[122] The term 'codex' suggests a codification in the modern sense, but in fact means 'tree cork'; it became the Latin word for a book with proper pages rather than a scroll.

of recognised contract had to be brought. Only later, in medieval studies of Justinian law and particularly in those of the secular natural law school of Grotius did a more general concept of rules and rights emerge (see section 1.2.7 below).

In the *Constitutio Tanta*, by which the *Corpus Iuris* was promulgated, the Emperor Justinian attributed the prompt accomplishment of this enormous task to the aid and grace of God, considered it sacred and an eternal oracle, and forbade any additions to it of any commentary (see paragraph 29, but of course he did not forbid newer *novellae*; he could not and did not mean to bind his successors). In the case of doubt or need for supplementation, resort should be to the Emperor alone in the nature of the practice of the Rescripts,[123] who in this sense had replaced the praetor already much earlier, as we have seen.

1.2.4 The Revival of Roman Law in Western Europe: The *Ius Commune*

As was pointed out in the previous section, the fall of the Western Roman Empire in 476 AD led to a general decline in the influence of Roman law and its legal institutions in Western Europe. It had to make way for new tribal or local laws if it had not already done so, but it never disappeared completely. First, some territory in Italy remained for a considerable time under the influence of the Emperor of the East and in 554 AD the Emperor Justinian, through his *sanctio pragmatica*, declared the *Corpus Iuris* applicable even in Italy, which country was as such expressly mentioned (rather than the whole Empire of the West).

Secondly, the Frankish tribes in Northern France, the Burgundian tribe in the Rhone valley, the Visigoths in Southern France and in Spain, and the Longobards or Lombards in Northern Italy, permitted the Romans and Gallo-Romans in their territory to retain their Roman laws and even codified these in so-called *Leges Romanae*. The best known of these was the *Lex Romana Visigothorum*, also called *Breviarium Alaricianum* or *Alarici* as it was compiled by their king Alaric II in Toulouse in 506 AD. It was particularly important as it included the *Codex Theodosianus*, which would otherwise have been lost, and also parts of the *Institutes* of Gaius, themselves only rediscovered in full in 1816. Then there was the *Lex Romana Burgundiorum*, from their King Gundobad, and the *Edictum Theodorici* from the Ostrogoth Theodoric in Italy, both from the beginning of the sixth century AD.

Thirdly, these tribes also codified their own laws in the *Leges Barbarorum*, as they came to be called, which showed some Roman law influence, although mainly concerned with criminal law. Of these, the *Lex Barbara Visigothorum* of the Visigoths (641–701) in Southern France and Spain (there the *Fuero Juzgo*), the *Lex Ribuaria* of the Ribuaric Franks (around

---

[123] The *Corpus Iuris* was restated and revised in Greek under the Emperor Basil of Macedonia and his son Leo the Philosopher in the tenth century and was then called the *Basilica*. In fact, it had always been curious that the *Corpus Iuris* had been in Latin, as it was directed at people who spoke Greek (as the West was already lost) and could therefore not read it. The reason was that the old Roman law had such prestige and legitimacy that at first nothing could detract from its texts, whilst the language of the court administration also remained Latin for some considerable time.

The *Basilica* combined the relevant *Digest, Codex* and *Novellae* according to subject matter, resulting in a single document of 60 books. The Latin text remained at first controlling, and was added in the margin (the *scholia*). After 1175, the Basilica was considered to have obtained the force of law and remained as such effective until the end of the Eastern Empire, when it fell to the Turks in 1453 AD.

700) and the *Leges Longobardorum* of the Lombards (seventh to ninth century, starting with the *Edictum Rothari*) were the most important, but similar laws existed amongst the Frisians, Saxons, Bavarians and other Germanic tribes in Germany. Most importantly, as early as the fifth century AD the Salian Franks in Northern France produced the *Lex Salica*. It is still known today for the hereditary nature of the kingdom it reposed in the male line only (LXII (5) or (6), depending on the known texts), although not coupled with a right of primogeniture, as became the more modern variant.

These laws were based on the *personality principle*, as has already been mentioned and was the same principle found in Roman law. This meant that different tribes or groups of citizens in the *same* territory were governed by separate laws. In Rome this had necessitated the development of the *Ius Gentium* for dealings with foreigners, eventually creating a supplementary natural or uniform law for all, as we have seen, whilst the personality principle was virtually abandoned when all inhabitants of the Roman Empire were declared citizens in 212 AD. However, it did not drive out all local laws.

By this time, the Empire had become too big and diverse, and with the invasions of the newer tribes that did not wish to surrender their own laws, the personality principle was *revived* after the Empire disappeared in the West, though notably the Lombards in Italy also started to impose some of their own laws on foreigners in their territory, as the other tribes must also have done for their organisational and more policy-oriented decrees.[124]

The relationship between both local and Roman law often remained tenuous, as we shall see in the next section, especially after Roman law revived more generally. Its status was challenged in France in particular; it posed the question of the hierarchy of the various sources of law. Yet it is clear that the general decline in civilisation, although less so in Italy, southern France and Spain led to a lesser degree of sophistication in the laws of most parts of Western Europe at that time. In fact, there may have remained little need for them until (as in earlier Roman times) the breakdown of the tribal system; the increase in private commercial dealings; the subsequent reinforcement of private property rights and of the right of individuals freely to enter into binding contracts; and the re-emergence of some stronger form of statehood with more centralised enforcement powers. In many parts of Europe, these developments did not take place much before the thirteenth and fourteenth centuries, and then at first only in small regions or cities.[125]

---

[124] In any event, intermarriage changed tribal divides, and rulers naturally became interested in the effect of their politically inspired measures on those living under their rule. Thus, from the eighth century onwards there are clear signs of territorial laws in the so-called *capitularia*, applicable to all in the various tribal territories, at first especially those of the Visigoths. These *capitularia* were mostly purely organisational, but when touching on private law they often showed Roman law influence, as had the *Leges Barbarorum* in a similar way.

In private law, the *capitularia* became the basis of what were later considered regional or local laws, especially in Northern France. They were there often referred to as customary law or the *droit coutumier* (to some extent a misnomer, as they also included local statutory law), later written up in regional or city law books like the *Coutumes de Beauvais* at first and later still in the most important sixteenth-century *Coutumes de Paris*. These local laws were usually drafted by people who were also versed in Roman law.

Roman law itself, which remained more influential in the Southern Parts of France and in Spain and Italy, was then referred to as the *droit écrit*, but in the absence of any promulgation it was only binding because of custom and therefore in reality only another kind of customary or traditional law.

[125] Even the Empire of Charlemagne of around 800 AD did not provide such an environment and did not make much difference for the development of private law, although the administration of justice was improved through the reorganisation of the judiciary.

Only when the Holy Roman Empire itself developed further in what became Germany did it start to favour the older Roman laws, not only to confirm its own legitimacy but also to provide greater legal support and unity on

Thus at first there was not much need for the more sophisticated parts of the Roman law contained in the *Corpus Iuris*. In this situation, only some knowledge of the simpler and more direct *Codex* and *Novellae* survived. In the absence of any formal legal education, the *Institutes* were not widely known either, and the *Digests* were lost altogether, although a copy of them was found in Pisa in the eleventh century (around 1050 AD). This led to a revival of the study of the Justinian Roman law, first in the new University of Bologna where the great Irnerius (in German often referred to as Wernerius) taught on the basis of it.[126]

This happened at a time when society began to feel the need for better laws. The impact of the *Corpus Iuris*, especially the refound *Digests*, which concerned itself mainly with private law, was enormous, although at first only at the academic level; indeed Irnerius came to be called the *lucerna iuris*, the lantern of the law.[127] What the Bible was for theology, the *Corpus Iuris* soon became for legal studies. Its influence on legal practice grew steadily, at first particularly in the Church or *Canon law* which had limited coverage but universal reach. It was imposed in the manner of modern legislation as, unlike the newly revived Roman law, it was officially promulgated (by the Pope). This Canon law was mainly concerned with typical church organisational matters, however, and with the law of marriage, but eventually came to cover some patrimonial law as well, especially the areas of church property and contracts. Parties could also agree to submit disputes to church courts when Canon law would be applied or otherwise Roman law. Gradually, however, the old Roman law moved beyond this limited remit and entered everyday life more generally.

This resulted in what was later called the *Ius Commune* (a term derived from the definition of the *Ius Gentium* in D.1.1.19). This was therefore Roman law as revived in Western Europe on the basis of the *Corpus Iuris*. As already mentioned, it was not promulgated anywhere (except much earlier in 554 AD in some parts of Italy) and since there was in any event no single legislator (or any at all) competent to enact Roman law, it was not possible for it to develop through legislation. Its further development was thus largely left to legal scholars and to a lesser extent to educated judges.

This was also a result of its more complex nature. Its force derived from its greater sophistication; from its status as the law of the Roman Empire (itself being revitalised by the German Emperors); from its unifying nature (there were bits and pieces of it everywhere except in England beyond the Canon law); and from the fact that, in an intellectual sense, it came to be considered the *ratio scripta* or the rational law, and as such an expression of the natural law supplementing, if not also correcting, all other law.

Hence the importance of academic legal studies and of the professors, who were largely responsible for the further evolution of the *Ius Commune*. This was also true of the later civil law that was in the nineteenth century substantially derived from the *Ius Commune*,

---

the basis of a proven model. Even in Southern France for example, the *Breviarium Alarici* was, for the reasons just given, pushed aside in favour of purer Roman law but only after the twelfth century, as were the *Leges Romanae* in the Italian cities.

[126] This university was organised and run by an association of students. Legal studies became so popular that it is said that the university soon had 10,000 students from all over Europe. It was located in what was then part of the territory of the German Emperor, who supported this education as a unifying force. He provided special protection to foreign students and in particular broke with the rule that persons from the same region were jointly and severally liable for each other's debt!

[127] See Odefredus, *Lectura super digesto veteri* at D.1.1.6.

until in the twentieth century the civil law courts became more activist and started to take over.

After the seventeenth century, the *Ius Commune* was eclipsed by the secular natural law school and the subsequent civil law codifications of the nineteenth century, as we shall see. In the twentieth century, Roman law lost any remaining unifying tenor and became truly part of history except in certain smaller legal pockets such as South Africa, Scotland and Sri Lanka as already mentioned.[128]

1.2.5 The *Ius Commune* and its Relationship to Local Law, Including Newer Commercial Law

The revival of Roman law in Western Europe from the eleventh century AD onwards, which had a profound effect on the development of private law on the European Continent (and to some limited extent even in England as we shall see) is a long story but can only be recounted here in a nutshell. It is common to distinguish between a number of successive phases, which played themselves out in different countries and in different ways.[129]

---

[128] See text at n 119 above.

[129] The earliest school was that of the *Glossators* under Irnerius in Bologna, also active in Montpellier in France (Placentinus) and as far north as Oxford (Vacarius). Another famous name in this school was Azo in Bologna, who wrote excerpts for students, especially of the Codex (*Summa Codicis*). Their method was to make remarks (*glossae*) in the margin of the *Corpus Iuris*, which at first mainly took the form of grammatical comments and explanations and cross references, but later also indicated similarities and contradictions and identified those rules, mainly of a Roman organisational nature, which obviously no longer had much current application. These Glossators, as they became known, span the period 1100–1250 AD and their work on the *Corpus Iuris* was selected and combined in the great *glosse* of Accursius, also at Bologna (*Glossa Ordinaria*). This was the end and apotheosis of the first phase.

Their successors tended to elaborate further on these *glossae*, most notably a more critical group that flourished in Orléans in France between 1250 and 1350 AD, the so-called *Ultramontani* under de Revigny. How much of this early work had practical significance other than through Canon law and legal education, can only be guessed. Later followers, mainly in Italy, took a keener interest in the practical side and searched in a scholastic manner for general principles. This allowed for an influx of Christian morality, already found in Canon law at that time, with its divine or natural law (see also s 1.2.6 below).

These commentators and practitioners are called the Post-glossators or Commentators and produced what came to be known as the *mos italicus*, of importance especially in the newly semi-independent cities of Northern Italy where oriental trade and local commerce started to thrive and where there was a corresponding need for better laws in a geographical area that also prided itself on its Roman ancestry and where the Roman laws, especially the *Codex* of Justinian, had never completely lost its validity. In this school, which roughly spans the period between 1250 and 1500 AD, we find the great medieval Italian jurists Bartolus and Baldus.

It is in this period that a better insight into more general rules and subjective rights under them started to emerge. These Commentators no longer thought exclusively in terms of actions and procedural law, as Roman law had been prone to do even in its Justinian variant, or inductively on the basis of existing actions and case law. This allowed for the beginning of more systematic thinking, which was further developed in the natural deductive law school of Grotius, therefore by the seventeenth century, and perhaps a little earlier by Donellus, see s 1.2.7 below. Canon law and local law influence was probably also conducive to it.

The sixteenth-century *School of Bourges* in France, also called the school of the Humanists, among whose number were Donellus (also in Leyden), Cuiacius and Antonius Faber, concerned itself more with the Justinian texts themselves and tried to discover the various interpolations from classical Roman law. It is also referred to as the *mos gallicus*. It was not interested in the *glossae* or the practical application of the Roman law and had a considerable influence on the seventeenth-century *Dutch School* of Grotius, Voet and Vinnius. The latter, however, never lost sight of the practice of the law. It can be said that developments since Accursius were best summarised towards

Again it should always be remembered that this revived Roman law was never officially promulgated but was only considered a higher form of custom. As a consequence, the theoretical basis for its application was always in some doubt and its force in relation to local law uncertain.[130] It is true that the *Digests* themselves (D.1.1.9) had stated that all nations partly made use of laws that were particular to them (in Roman terms the *Ius Civile*) and partly made use of such laws that were common to all (in Roman terms the *Ius Gentium*). In the Middle Ages, this was interpreted as meaning that the law common to all mankind was in fact Roman law as passed down through the *Corpus Iuris*, which was then considered the *ratio scripta* or *ius commune omnium hominum*, to use the wording of D.1.1.9. Hence the term *Ius Commune*, which was the written (Justinian) law or *lex scripta* (or in France the *droit ecrit*).

However, the *Ius Commune* also had to be seen in the light of local law, under D.1.1.9 called *ius proprium*, which the *lex scripta* or Roman law could not ignore. This posed amongst others the question of the true relationship between the *Ius Commune* and local law, therefore the problem of priority of the various sources of law.[131] This still has meaning today when we consider the modern *lex mercatoria* and its relationship to domestic law. It became a fundamental issue at the time, as not only local customs but also local statutes or similar edicts competed. In D.1.3.32.1, there was a first complicating provision which said that custom could invalidate the law (*leges*) as it was simply a later demonstration of the people's will. However, in the case of the *Ius Commune*, this was not necessarily believed to apply to new statutory law[132] except perhaps to city ordinances (or *statuta* in Northern Italy).

It was even thought that the rule of D.1.3.32.1 could mean that the *lex scripta*, therefore Roman (private) law itself, was not merely set aside by new custom but more generally by all local laws, and especially in Northern France no distinction was made in this respect between local custom and statutory law (combined in the *droit coutumier*). On the other hand, Canon law, wary of pagan and secular influences, was inclined to reach the opposite conclusion and insisted that bad local law must always be ignored.[133] That became the rule

the end of the seventeenth century by the work of the Dutch scholar Voet (1647–1713) in his *Commentarius ad Pandectas* which acquired a status similar to that which the *Glossa Ordinaria* had had earlier.

The school of the *Usus Modernus Pandectarum* (Modern Use of the Digests) 1500–1800 AD, mainly in Germany, but also in Italy and Spain, was more a continuation of the *mos italicus*, but it studied non-Roman sources as well. This school was represented by scholars like Carpzovius, Brunnemannus, Bachovius, the Hubers, Berlichius and Mevius. It is not mere chance that this later school was also the most practical in view of increased practical needs.

These writings all tended to be in the nature of what we now call restatements, and had only persuasive force.

[130] See Koschaker, n 1 above, 191.

[131] Priority was claimed explicitly by feudal law: see *Libri Feudorum* 2.1, but also by the Canon law, *Decretum of Gratianus* (which contained an early compilation of the canon laws), *Distinctio* 1.

[132] There was a problem in that originally the Emperor, who was German, was thought to have sole legislative authority over Roman law and the power to amend it, and not, for example, the King of France. This issue was resolved in the fourteenth century in the sense that in this respect, in his own lands, a king was considered to have the status of the Emperor: *princeps imperator in regno suo*: see Koschaker, n 1 above, 141. This maxim belongs with another: *quod principi placuit vigorem legis habet*. It is the idea that any sovereign can make law.

[133] Canon law thus wished to reduce the pagan influences of local or tribal laws on the argumentation of Decr Grat, Dist 8 c 5, which saw Christ as the truth and therefore not custom. The *Decretum of Gratianus* relied here on the *ius naturalis* or natural law, meaning biblical law as expressed by human beings: see more particularly s 1.2.6 below, which could sometimes also be seen in Roman law as *ratio scripta* and was then also higher law, besides the *mores* meaning local customary law, which, technically, could also include the received Roman law, but was then considered lower. However, Canon law itself had to give precedence to the natural law in that sense also.

even beyond the reach of the Canon law in most parts of Europe and continued also after the Reformation, when in the Protestant countries Canon and Roman law were separated. What was more rational and reasonable (*ratio scripta*) therefore prevailed,[134] and that was normally considered to be the Roman law rule (*quidquid non agnoscit glossa, nec agnoscit curia*).

But the practical relationship between Roman and local law was not perceived in the same manner everywhere, and this may be seen as an early expression of tension between positive laws and more fundamental principle or higher and more universal demands of rationality, fairness or justice, or efficiency. As just mentioned, in France it was clear that the kings wished to promote the local laws (*droit coutumier*), including their own decrees at the expense of the Roman law (*droit écrit*), which they saw as the inimical imperial or German usurper's law. This law was therefore considered applicable only if local law did not provide a solution. In Northern France—that is, the part of France north of the Loire river, including notably the Paris area—Roman law thus largely disappeared, and its study was even forbidden in the University of Paris from as early as 1219 AD (officially by a Pope who was also not interested in furthering German imperial ambitions at the time) until well into the seventeenth century, but in Southern France it always remained more powerful. Even in the North, as we have seen, Roman law influence subsisted indirectly in the written-up *droit coutumier,* especially in property and contract law.

In Germany, the rule became the opposite, probably more as a consequence of the weakness of the Emperor than his strength. To counteract the effects of the lack of centralised power and the ensuing diversity of the various German regions, Roman law acted there as unifier and became the preferred law, especially after the setting up of a central court for all of Germany, the *Reichskammergericht* of 1495 AD with its seat in Wetzlar, north of Frankfurt.[135] Before it, local laws had to be proven as a fact and, until they were, the Roman law prevailed as the law best known to the court. That was also the approach in Italy.[136]

The implication was that the *ratio*, which was rapidly associated with all Roman law or *Ius Commune*, prevailed over bad law: *parvum usum ratio vincat,* see also Zwalve, n 105 above, 46. However, the *Ius Commune* itself eventually became subject to the same requirements of the *ratio* rather than being equated with it. This development occurred in the seventeenth to eighteenth centuries, when what was rational was separated from the Roman law, which thus no longer automatically qualified as the *ratio iuris.* That was the achievement of the *natural law school* of Grotius in Holland and more so of the *Vernunftrecht* of his followers Pufendorf and especially Wolff in Germany, as we shall see in s 1.2.7 below. It suggested a new hierarchy under which the secular natural law as developed in this school took precedence.

[134] See also Instruction Court of Holland, 20 August 1531, GPB II, 703, Art 81.

[135] The German writer and philosopher Goethe, *Dichtung und Wahrheit*, 3.12, reports, however, on its large business but very limited number of decisions: according to him, in 1772 there were 20,000 cases pending, of which the 17 judges managed to decide only 60.

[136] In Spain, between 1256 and 1265, Alfonso X El Sabio of Castille compiled a code of law for his territories called the *Siete Partidas*, which was promulgated in 1348. It was a very full code in seven parts, as the title says, covering the laws in general, including a restatement of much organisational church law, governmental law, procedure and property, domestic relations, sales, succession, crimes and general principles. At the same time as it was promulgated (in the *Ordenamiento de Alcala*), it was made clear, however, that royal decrees and local laws retained precedence.

The *Siete Partidas* were in turn much influenced by Roman and Canon law, which was also used in their interpretation, and was studied with great intensity in Spain in the scholastic manner of the Commentators. Some of these studies, which, although scholastic, showed independence of mind, were also used by Grotius to build a rational secular natural law system in his *De Iure Belli ac Pacis*, see n 143 below. Like Bartolus, they started to look at specific legal structures such as contract and property, as such followed by Donellus before Grotius.

There was another aspect to this development. Even where local law prevailed, at least as long as it was reasonable, it was often interpreted in a restrictive way to leave as much room as possible for Roman law. This approach was deduced by Bartolus from D.1.3.14, which required that all that was counter to the *ratio iuris* should not be extensively interpreted and should in any event not be considered a legal rule under D.1.3.15. In this vein, the reach of Roman law was further expanded through analogous and extensive interpretation (D.1.3.12 and D.1.3.13). The result was that in the *Ius Commune* local law was often restrictively, and Roman law extensively, interpreted. Thus only when local law was clearly different, as was normally the case in personal and family law and sometimes in inheritance questions, would Roman law have no effect.

This approach nevertheless left room for the development of city laws, especially in Northern Italy, as in Pisa, Bologna and Milan, relevant also in commercial law where there were many city ordinances. It also happened elsewhere, especially in the trading cities of the Hansa in Northern Germany and the Baltic and later in towns like Antwerp, Rotterdam and Amsterdam. In the view of Bartolus, there was always room for such law as custom, and city councils were able to accelerate the pace through written city laws and regulations which were considered to have similar status (*paris potentiae*), although, again, all such local law was to be restrictively interpreted in the face of Roman law on the subject.

In France, again the opposite approach became accepted, supported by Molinaeus (1500–66), especially after the *Coutume* of Paris was published in 1510. This was liberally interpreted and the Roman law restrictively.[137] But, as we have seen, there remained room for the Roman law, even in Northern France, particularly in the law concerning personal property and obligations, as was later also shown in these areas in the works of Domat and especially of Pothier, which eventually formed the basis for much of the *Code Civil* in these areas.[138]

As for these local laws, they were enforced in France by the so-called *parlements* of which the Parisian one was the most important. These *parlements* were regional bodies, which grew out of the *Curia Regis*. They therefore developed originally not as representations of the people, but as courts, in which the nobility and later also established lawyers (then called the *noblesse de robe*) exercised a judicial function, often on a hereditary basis. As early as 1277, the *Parlement* of Paris was ordered by the King to apply local law before Roman law, whilst much at the same time, as has already been mentioned, the study of Roman law was forbidden in Paris University by a Pope unwilling to promote German influence. Eventually these *parlements* also obtained a legislative function when judges started to interpret the law by issuing general dispositions (*arrêts de règlements*).

In a later phase, the *parlements* even acquired the power to promulgate the king's laws, which had no force and would not be enforced by these *parlements* without it (*droit d'enregistrement*). Both powers made the *parlements* considerable forces in the land, sometimes even directed against the king. From the reign of Louis XIV in the later seventeenth century onwards, there was a constant struggle to at least suppress the promulgation powers of the *parlements* which effectively gave them a veto over Royal laws and their application

---

[137] See also the practical eighteenth-century treatise of Bourjon, *Le Droit Commun de la France et la Coutume de Paris Réduit en Principes*.

[138] See n 154 below.

in an era where legislative intervention at state level was still believed to be exceptional and only remedial.

It was the French Revolution which eventually led to the abolition of the *parlements*, while the new French Civil Code of 1804 (Article 1) was quick to decree that laws entered into force only through promulgation by the sovereign and that there was also no longer any power for judges to decide by general disposition (Article 5).

1.2.6 The Early Evolution of the Notion of Natural Law in Europe

It has been said before that after Grotius natural law in its secular form became a new legal current besides the *Ius Commune*. To some extent, it became integrated in it; in other aspects it was a kind of parallel law. It was always more intellectual and sought structure rather than pretending to be the positive law, which it nevertheless meant to support and explain.

The notion of natural law itself has a long history before it acquired the more modern secular form of fundamental and general principle, see more particularly section 1.4.14 below. As noted above, according to the *Digests* (D.1.1.1.3), the Romans saw natural law as in essence instinct, the law that ruled animals and people alike, expressing itself in the attraction between the sexes and the love of and care for one's offspring. This was the Greek view of the pre-Socratic society. It did not explain nor was it concerned with any relationship with the positive law, which for the Greeks of those days was always the law of the *polis* or city-state.[139]

It is known that in Rome around 50 BC Cicero tried to write up or construct a natural-law code but it was mostly lost. Natural law was here still nature itself, seen as unchangeable, but Cicero broadened the concept, clear from his work *De Legibus*, in that he considered *pure reason* the true law, as such part of all mankind. As natural law, it had direct legal force and effect, could not be abrogated, and was thought especially to result in respect for *freedom, equality and fairness* as they were believed to have existed in the original and true human condition. These were considered the most precious social goods, best protected within a state, which was no less considered a product of nature in this rational

---

[139] The sophists only believed in positive law as created by the *polis* and equated the natural laws with more primitive notions of revenge and self-help remedies. In the subsequent teachings of Socrates, however, pure reason becomes the anchor of all law which then acquires a divine meaning in terms of beauty and goodness of which there was intuitive knowledge, although it was still best expressed in the *polis*. It required and directed knowledge of oneself ('know yourself'), which resulted in a good and practical life style of which freedom, equality and fairness were the expression.

Only in Plato's philosophy do beauty and goodness rise to the notion of a metaphysical idea of reality which represents an ideal world that can only be glimpsed through contemplation and of which the world that we see and its laws are merely a confused reflection. Natural law is then part of metaphysics and applies to the whole cosmos. In daily reality, it remains, however, the *polis* that is the expression of this higher idea and presents a way of life outside which there can hardly be virtue.

The concept of *polis* rises here to a religion or an all life experience that had in this view a tendency to decline in chaos. It must save what can be saved in order to maximise virtue in its citizens. Private law also has that function and does not then primarily denote respect for individual rights. There are here no ideas of democracy or inalienable rights either. They cannot exist separately from the *polis* (and its exigencies), which always came first and had the last word.

sense. To give everyone what belonged to him (as may still be found in D.1.1.10) was the most profound expression of this philosophy in private law.

This had already been the essence of the Greek philosophy of the Stoa, which was the first to abandon the central idea of *polis* and expounded the notion of rationality of Socrates.[140] It was pantheistic and universal or internationalist and saw the acceptance of this state of affairs as the highest human endeavour leading to the greatest harmony and happiness. In this view, states or organisations were not considered to play a different role from individuals and were subject to the same rational imperatives. Morality acquired here a social function; impulsive and emotional behaviour was to be controlled. Evil was an aberration not compatible with true nature or reason, had to be fought, and would eventually lose. After Cicero, Seneca around 50 AD and later the Emperor Marcus Aurelius around 160 AD were important Roman followers of this philosophy.

The philosophy of the Stoa was substantially different from the other (older) great philosophy of Aristotle, which was less idealistic and perhaps more optimistic. It saw creation and achievement rather than self-control and endurance as the essence of human happiness, and true virtue as keeping a balance between extremes such as avarice and generosity. The highest emotional state was intellectual, in which reason could change habits and bring them under control leading to balance and virtue. But not all could attain this state even if it were better. The ethics of Aristotle are therefore less demanding and oppressive than those of the Stoa, but also less idealistic and universal.

Natural law was in the Aristotelian perception the law of physics with its causality independent from human judgment or behaviour ruling everywhere. Positive law was different (the relationship was not yet made clear) and involved human judgement and could therefore vary and lead to inequality and lack of freedom. That was the choice of a state or community dictated by utility. This kind of law was seen as, in essence, a human artifact. So was the state or *polis* in which it was considered that human beings could only truly develop. In this view, the state was a local reality, not a universal condition or expression of pure reason. Private law had to be seen in that context as well and still took the perspective of the *polis* or community rather than of the protection of personal rights. Justice was whatever brought most happiness and balance in such a state. All depended on the environment and the situation; there was less of a moral perspective.

There was, however, agreement with the Stoa in so far that the world order was considered *a given*, subject to immutable or causal laws of nature. But in the Aristotelian view, men had freedom to deviate and make alternative arrangements in areas where the laws of strict causality did not obtain, for example in arranging one's personal and social life, or states imposing their own order. For the later Stoa, this was rather an aberration and demonstrated an improper use of abilities and a denial of nature, which was more fundamental in character.

In Roman times, there had been several more basic ideas as noted in section 1.2.3 above, but one dominant religious force had never been present at the intellectual level to deeply influence the positive law as it developed at the height of the classical period. Although different considerations and attitudes naturally had an impact on the formulation and interpretation of laws, they appear not to have had great significance in the distribution of justice and in the legal activities. This is the reason why these issues were not raised in the

---

[140] See the previous footnote.

previous sections. As just mentioned, in Ulpianus' definition of law in D.1.1.10, the accent is on giving everyone his or her due, much in the tradition of the Stoa, but it did not carry any deeper message for the entire *Corpus Iuris*. Nor apparently did the Christian religion which was by then universally accepted in the Roman Empire, although it did inspire many imperial constitutions.

It has already been mentioned that in the Justinian *Digests*, the *Ius Gentium* becomes the universal (private) law and is then seen as the positive elaboration of the natural law (D1.1.1), expressed for example in respect for one's parents and the acceptance of the gods and of the state (D.1.1.2.). In Rome the *Ius Gentium*, it may be recalled, was originally the law for foreigners but was later considered to have been laid down for mankind more generally, largely based on rationality and common sense and, in the Roman view, *not* always immutable, even though expressive of a certain intrinsic order (the idea in D.1.1.9). The more fundamental notion of natural law was then used to broaden and develop this *Ius Gentium* as universal law further, was considered superior, and believed to be itself incapable of amendment by legislation (D.1.2.11 and D.7.5.2). In this sense, the *Ius Gentium* as described in the Justinian compilation floated on the natural law, which came first but was, as we have seen, a limited concept described rather as a force of nature. Although it was meant to influence the *Ius Gentium*, it was never completely clear how far this went and to what extent it had an effect on the law in its daily operation.

At the time of the renewed study of the Roman law in the late Middle Ages, the situation was quite different. It was the time when the study of theology also took a great leap forward and began to impose its views on the law. The study of both theology and law became *scholastic* in that each unquestioningly accepted the authority of the Bible on the one hand and of the *Corpus Iuris* on the other and did not then consider the world from any other perspective. At the same time—given the overriding authority of the Church—the practice, if not also the study, of the law became subject to the theology of the Church, which in turn became connected with philosophy, in particular with the works of Aristotle. This conditioned the attitude of Thomas Aquinas, the greatest thinker of the time, who addressed the law in his *Summa Theologica*. Once Thomism became the official line of the Catholic Church, it was bound to have an immediate impact on Canon law, which was naturally infused by church morality and philosophy. Eventually, it also had an impact on the rest of the law, and particularly on legal studies.

In the Thomist scheme, there were Divine and Human Laws. The first was either written law, derived from the Bible and its interpretation, mainly in the uncompromising North African manner of St Augustine, or Natural Law, which was its elaboration in the formulation of which humans, as reasonable beings, could participate. Biblical commands to love one's neighbour and to honour one's promises could thus be elaborated into a set of rules concerning interhuman relationships and into a law of contract and property. Aquinas's Human Law was the rest, including Canon Law and the *Corpus Iuris*, as well as domestic laws.[141]

---

[141] From early on it was thought that the will of the state could impose this Human Law in the same way as the Pope imposed his will through Canon law although this was still believed to be exceptional, most certainly in what is now considered private law. The Divine Law, including its Natural Law, was *always* superior because it was supposed to direct mankind towards its salvation. With the Church in command of interpretation of the Divine Law, including Natural Law, all law thus became subject to the prevailing higher norm of Christian morality, at least in its more ethical or policy-oriented aspects.

Natural Law thus became closely related to the biblical commandments of the Old and in particular the New Testament. As a consequence, this law, being religious, had a universal pretence, was directly effective, and could not be overruled by the positive human laws. Under it, in the style of St Augustine, there was no basic freedom or equality, as there was none in the distribution of grace and salvation. In the style of Aristotle, in the Human Law uneven distribution of ownership or even slavery could be condoned (by the Divine Law) on the basis of utility, although equity should guide it. As Human Law was subject to Natural Law of this kind, it was foremost considered an aid to the perfect Christian community, which was, incidentally, an improvement on the view of St Augustine, who had viewed the state and its laws as in essence evil or at least a response to evil and therefore motivated by it. It was also a nod in the direction of the Stoa.

1.2.7 The Emergence of the Secular Natural Law School: Grotius's *De Iure Belli ac Pacis*, its Approach and Impact

As far as Grotius (1585–1645) is concerned, it is possible to read almost anything into his works, so prolific and eclectic was he on such a broad range of subjects during a long life of writing. He was knowledgeable in theology, moral philosophy, history, and the classics, and knew the writers of his day. Yet he may be best understood as a lawyer and is best known for his initiation of the secularisation of natural law as it had developed until that time under strong religious influence.

The essence of his legal thought, derived from the philosophy of the Stoa, was that the law was not limited in its effects by time and space. It transcended borders and jurisdictions and depended for its force on fundamental principles, which were universal and could be directly invoked regardless of their further clarification in a system of positive law. Thus in Grotius's view, there was in essence only one law and one community of mankind, whilst the laws applicable between individuals were in essence the same as those between organisations and between nations. These were views already expressed by Seneca and Cicero, again in the tradition of the Stoa, but had also received strong support in some scholastic writings, especially in Spain, although then driven by religious fervour.[142]

Although these basic principles were immutable, in Grotius's view they did *not* depend on divine inspiration, but relied for their expression and implementation on rationality and utility in the affairs of this world. So the key was: (a) principles; (b) rationality;

---

[142] It has become fashionable to emphasise the Spanish roots of the secular natural law school, and Grotius himself referred at times to the Spanish writers of the sixteenth century, but used their insights mainly to separate himself further from scholastic thinking. See, nevertheless, on these roots Otto von Gierke, *Johannes Althusius und die Entwicklung der naturrechtlichen Staatstheorien*, 3rd edn (1913) 157; J Kohler, 'Die spanishen Naturrechtslehrer des 16 und 17 Jahrhunderts' (1916–17) 10 *Archiv für Rechts- und Wissenschaftsphilosophie* 235, later especially also M Diesselhorst, *Die Lehre des Hugo Grotius vom Versprechen* (1959); F Wieacker, 'Die vertragliche Obligation bei den Klassikern des Vernunftsrechts', in *Festschrift Hans Welzel zum 70 Geburtstag* (1963); and R Feenstra, 'L'Influence de la scolatisque espagnole sur Grotius en droit privé' in Grossi (ed), *La seconda scolastica nella formazione del diritto privato moderno* (Milan, 1973) 377; and 'Les Sources Espagnoles de la Pensée juridique de Grotius' in *Historia del Pensament Juridic, Festschrift Francisco Tomas y Valiente* (1999) 137.

(c) utility; and (d) their interconnection as fundamentals of the law and of all legal systems. This remains the essence of all modern natural-law philosophy. Even though natural law, which is now mostly expressed as a directly applicable fundamental and general legal principle (see section 1.4.14 below), may no longer be perceived as immutable, even in its fundamental principles, for example in terms of human rights, it remains key in all more fundamental legal redirection and therefore also in the understanding of the present transnationalisation process of private law; and this is the reason why this theme is further explored here.

It raises some important issues, notably: (a) the relationship between principle and positive law and the possibility (or not) for the positive law to deviate from principle that is fundamental; (b) the identification of the substantive rights and the method of finding structure in them; and (c) the intervention of states in the law-making process and impact of public policy or reasons of state on law formation. In view of the basic notion of universality, this statist aspect became particularly problematic and will be further discussed in the next section.

Grotius's prime importance is that he had a different view of natural law from the one previously prevailing and began its secularisation. The essence of it as explained in his main work, *De Iure Belli ac Pacis* of 1625,[143] was that all people had a similar inner understanding of what was good or evil[144] and that this distinction, although of divine origin, was *rational* (I.1.10.1) and as such held true for all, even for God, who could not change it, and it would even hold true if God did not exist (I.1.10.5). This is probably the most provocative statement of the whole work, although it was not new and was also held by the Spanish scholastics.[145]

Its true message was that mankind had to strive for the good it knew and to subject its inclinations to the natural law that emerged in this manner and to its principles of peace, freedom, equality, and fairness, which were understood to be universal.[146] It led to a preference

---

[143] This book exists in an English translation by FW Kelsey (Oxford, 1925) reprinted by WS Hein & Co (Buffalo, New York, 1995) and in a French translation of 1867 by Pradier Fodore, reprinted in 1999.

[144] Of the natural law, therefore of the innate distinction between good and evil and of the basic rights and obligations resulting from it, the Old Testament's Ten Commandments were considered an important manifestation, as was the New Testament's Sermon on the Mount, and even the Roman law as *ratio scripta*, but only to the extent that they were rational, and therefore able to distinguish good and evil in the above sense. Rationality acquired *independence* and was *not*, or was no longer considered, inherent in any of these sets of laws. Where there was no such rationality, these laws could only be binding on those for whom they were made; therefore the Old Testament with its many derivative rules only for the Jews, the Roman laws only for the Romans, and the New Testament's commandments only for Christians.

[145] See n 142 above.

[146] The practical effect was that, where the Augustinian/Aristotelian principle had sought to explain and accept human inequality, Grotius insisted on their equality, certainly before the (natural) law. Thus the emphasis turned to peace, freedom, equality and fairness as it must have existed in mankind's original state. This led in essence to four key legal principles: (a) the principle of respect for others and their assets (*alieni abstinentia*); (b) the principle of respect for commitments voluntarily made (*pacta sunt servanda*); (c) the principle of repair of damages culpably inflicted on others (*damni culpa dati reparatio*); and (d) the principle that infringement of this natural law must be punished (*poena inter homines meritum*).

The basic proposition was that these principles could be found in the study of the laws of all civilised peoples (I.1.12) and had to be carefully distinguished from positive law elaborations, therefore from their subsequent detailed implementation and remained valid regardless.

These were therefore the guiding principles of his natural law, which were considered invariable, aprioristic but rational, much in the style of Cicero. They remain the basis, it is submitted, of all natural private law in a modern sense. All the rest, including the State, its organisation, the status of the individuals as free citizens, captives or even slaves, and ownership and the way in which it was held, did not belong to this natural law (or the principles deduced from it). It was so-called voluntary law or *ius voluntarium*. Here the ideas of the Stoa were

for the Greek philosophical school of the Stoa rather than the Aristotelian/Thomist school that had dominated theology and the law until then. This secular natural law was further supported by mankind's presumed natural instinct for peaceful co-existence (*appetitus societatis, Prol* 6). It did not exclude the existence of Divine Law, but it was considered another form of positive law, which had to express the basic tenets of the natural law in this sense.

This allowed Grotius to separate the law from: (a) the theology of St Augustine; (b) the philosophy of Aristotle; (c) Thomism; (d) Canon law; and (e) their influence on the Roman law revival. He did not abandon the old philosophy categorically, and in fact praised Aristotle as philosopher (but not his work on ethics and the law, *Prol* 42, 43). Neither did he separate the law fundamentally from the teachings of Christianity itself or from its morality, or in fact from philosophy, only from the philosophical and theological views that had become traditional. The separation from the Roman law revival also did not entail its rejection but it allowed independent study and criticism plus, eventually, the addition of general principle found in domestic laws.

The separation from theology altogether was achieved in this school by Pufendorf in Germany, who came 50 years later; the separation from philosophy and ultimately even from Roman law or the *Ius Commune* came in this school later still, through people like Wolff, who sought to build the law on the pure *ratio* as it was understood in the eighteenth century in Europe at the time of rationalism or *Enlightenment*.[147] This was the time of the *Vernunftrecht*, the logical–mathematical deduction or *mos geometricus* of the law. It achieved a degree of abstraction in rule formulation that was systematic but also speculative, yet made codification in the modern civil law sense possible although it had not been its objective.[148]

The natural law contained henceforth the fundamental universal principles of the law (*naturae principia*) but also the principles that could be deduced from them (*Prol* 8, 15, 39, 40). There is, in this approach, a fundamental difference with the *ius gentium* which was here considered based on *utility*, could be changed and appeared through *communis opinio*

---

abandoned. They were only there to improve the human lot after mankind had lost its innocence, but they were not its ultimate state.

It meant that by no means all subjective rights were an expression of natural law. Yet the key subjective rights (the *suum*) could be deduced from them and were: (a) the right over oneself or the right to liberty; (b) the right over some others, such as a wife and children; (c) the right over one's property; and (d) the right to claim against others. Even so, the right to private property itself was *not* considered an original natural right but a human invention dependent on the human will which natural law could only protect in that manner (I.1.10.4 and 7).

[147] See Koschaker, n 1 above, 249.

[148] The key message that followed was that natural law was *not* monopolised by any religious or philosophical current, although Christians like Grotius himself would in a Christian society elaborate the positive laws in a Christian way and seek in that manner the fulfillment of natural law ideals: peace, freedom, equality and fairness. There follows a strong ethical and irenic inclination, which, although in Grotius's case closely related to his protestant religion, needed not be religious. He thus argues (even contrary to the views of Cicero) that vows may not be broken, even if made to criminals and tyrants, and that the requirements of good faith must also be maintained in respect of them. On the other hand, one must also not always insist on one's rights, certainly not on the right of war (even in the case of self-defence), of retrieval of possessions, of enforcement of obligations, or on justified punishment. In this approach, Roman law was often criticised, for example, in its requirement of delivery for the transfer of title in movable corporeal assets. Transfer at the time of the conclusion of the contract was thought more natural.

This attitude to freedom has been called a Copernican revolution in the law: see JHA Lokin and WJ Zwalve, *Europese Codificatiegeschiedenis* [History of the Codification in Europe] (Groningen, 1992) 32. See also J Gordley, *The Philosophical Origins of Modern Contract Doctrine* (Oxford, 1991), 112ff for the (weak) relationship with the new (and later) ideas of Descartes, Hobbes and Locke.

or common sense (*aliquis communis consensus, Prol* 40), even though in appearances that difference would not always be great, and when reference to the natural law school was made, they were often considered together. This *ius gentium* was, however, now part of the changeable, *voluntary* law or *ius voluntarium*. In this view, all national or domestic laws were subject to natural law and to the principles deduced from it, *but also* to this *ius gentium* or commonsense law, and this was true for the laws concerning individuals, organisations as well as states. In this way, this natural law acquired the highest rank in the hierarchy of norms.[149]

It was typical for this approach therefore that the *ius gentium* was not only interstate law as it is now often still thought to be (neither had it been in Roman law). Rather, like the natural law, it was considered universal, being based on logic and rationality, on more universal notions of utility, and common sense for all, as such always subject, however, to the fundamental universal natural law principles of which it was considered an expansion.

In finding and further developing structure in this law, *not* system per se, Grotius strove for coherence and support in what he found in terms of substantive rights in Roman and Canon law, in the earlier substantive law searches of Bartolus and Donellus,[150] but also in local laws.[151] This proved a vital departure and allowed for the development of an intellectual coherent framework, especially of private law, that left the action orientation and therefore procedural tenor of the private law behind. His *Introduction to Roman-Dutch Law*,[152] published in 1631 but written (in Dutch) during his captivity around 1620, was the first major manifestation. It had a lesser impact than *De Iure Belli ac Pacis* (1625), but is no less significant because of its greater detail in demonstrating the method.

In *De Iure Belli ac Pacis*, which deals with the law concerning war and peace, there are large tracts on private law in Book 2 (chapters 2 to 19), particularly on the behaviour between individuals and on contract as being the basis for the behaviour and agreements also amongst nations, which, as mentioned above, Grotius thought similar, in the manner of the Stoa. The further elaboration of the private natural law on this basis was done by later writers, especially by Pufendorf in Germany,[153] Domat and Pothier in France[154] and by German rationalists like Wolff, who, as just mentioned, increasingly espoused a logical mathematical approach.[155]

The price was ever-increasing differences in the details of the law, which in the end much discredited this method, the rational and internationalist aims of which were finally destroyed by nineteenth-century legal nationalism and statist perceptions of all law formation. Its substantive rule-finding orientation was ultimately eclipsed by pure intellectual system thinking, as we shall see, but then at the national level. It had already opened the road to the early modern codifications of civil law, first in France in 1804, then in Austria in 1811, whilst the Pandectist offshoot eventually led to the German Code of 1900 (the BGB). However, by that time universalism had gone and all of them were nationalistic.

---

[149] But it posed the problem of the ranking of state imposed law: see s 1.2.8 below.

[150] See also n 129 above.

[151] This applies, for example, to the notion of good faith acquisition in movable property law. Grotius first spotted these developments in Holland and noted them in the margin of the Lund manuscript of his *Introduction to Roman-Dutch Law*, 2nd edn (Dovring, Fisher and Meijers, 1965) 50–55, later also noted in Northern Germany by Mevius, *Commentarii in Ius Lubecense Libri Quinque* (Frankfurt, 1700).

[152] RW Lee (tr), *Inleidinge tot de Romeins-Hollandsche Rechtsgeleerdheid*, 2nd edn (Oxford, 1953).

[153] S Pufendorf, *Ius naturale et gentium*.

[154] J Domat, *Les lois civiles dans leur ordre naturel*, and R-J Pothier, *Traité des obligations*.

[155] C Wolff, *Ius naturae, methodo scientifica pertractum*, see also text at n 148 above.

The natural law school's method of substantive law finding still stands out as having freed the study and development of the law from its historical (religious and philosophical) clutches. Natural law revival of this nature tends to stand at the beginning of any new age when a reappraisal of fundamental principle and the deduction of new rules from new needs overtake the established order. In our day and age, it is for a new transnational law or *lex mercatoria* to facilitate the globalisation of trade, commerce and finance by breaking the grip of domestic laws and showing that there is law beyond it.

Even if there has always been some such source in new principle and in custom, and rational behaviour has been the essence of most rules, the true challenge, at least in international trade and commerce, is now to create or identify a more than incidental set of legally enforceable rights and obligations at global level. This is the subject of much of this book, which in this respect goes back to pre-nineteenth-century perceptions of law formation and legal effectiveness, although not to pre-nineteenth-century law or the old *Ius Commune*.

The term 'natural law' itself continues to give rise to problems of definition.[156] In this book the term 'fundamental and general principle' is often used instead. It is a more modern terminology but can be seen as the continuation of natural law's secular expression: see further section 1.4.14 below.

Another particular achievement of the natural law school, which remains valid today, was its understanding that there is no fundamental difference between the abstractly formulated rule and the legal rules that are applied in each case, and that in respect of the latter there is in any event never a clear line between law as rule and law as principle, or even between the law that *is* (*lex lata*) and the law that *should be* (*lex ferenda*), or between rule and guideline. There is, in other words, never an absolute pre-set system of precise norms (or black-letter law) for each case, but in each instance the legally relevant norm must be found and articulated, no less than the legally relevant facts.

In this articulation of the norm, the configuration of the facts themselves plays an important role. In analysing and formulating the applicable norm, the method thus becomes inductive as well as deductive (for a fuller discussion of these methods, see sections 1.2.13 and 1.4.3 below). From this point of view the law, in particular private law, is always moving and can never be entirely predetermined in a set of pre-existing written rules. Or to put it in the terms of Cardozo: 'Law never is, but is always about to be.'[157]

1.2.8 The Status of State Law in the Philosophies of Grotius, Hobbes, Locke, Kant and Hegel. The Impact of the Age of Enlightenment and the Road to Codification of Private Law in France

The concept of secular natural law requires finally some discussion of the ascent of state power in private law formation, first to achieve specific political objectives, but ultimately on the European Continent to nationalise all private law formation.

---

[156] See also n 414 below.
[157] See *Respectfully Quoted, A Dictionary of Quotations Requested from the Congressional Research Service of Congress* (1989) 191 (from a Yale lecture of 1921).

As mentioned in the previous sections, in the approach of Grotius, who wrote his major works when the devastating Thirty Years War was waged in Germany (from 1618 to 1648), all law was in essence non-statist, universal, therefore not confined in time or space, an approach supported by the philosophy of the Stoa—the political correctness of seventeenth- and eighteenth-century thought. It applied to private citizens and states alike and did not therefore fundamentally distinguish between public and private law. Natural law contained the basic principles. In Grotius's approach, positive law could be more confined but also more expansive than natural law. That was the area of the *ius gentium* or voluntary law based on rationality and utility meant to support the natural law. Both were considered directly effective and enforceable in the sense that they did not need the intervention of a state to become positive. Other spokesmen could be just as authoritative, like judges and commentators. Again, it very much reminds of present day public international law (Article 38(1) of the Statute of the International Court of Justice and in the approach of this book of modern *lex mercatoria* law formation.

It posed, however, the question to what extent the state could override the *ius gentium* or even the natural law.[158] We may think here also of local laws and custom. The latter were in principle subject to this higher natural or rational law, as we have seen, but state law especially could go against it and it was further likely to be localised. This raised the issue of its true legal status and effect. This can also be expressed in terms of the impact of public policy or the '*raison d'etat*' or the *state's command* on the law, its formation and application. Here there are considerable tensions in Grotius's work (and that of his successors), and in this respect it is less clear-cut.

Ever since, this has been an important issue in the study of the relevant sources of private law in national and internationalised legal orders. It is closely connected with the extent of state power, nationalism, and territorialism in the law, and then also affects the status of other sources of law. In institutional terms, at least some hierarchy would have to be considered. In this connection, state absolutist tendencies became increasingly clear as the drift of eighteenth- and nineteenth-century thinking on the European Continent, connected with the emergence of the modern state as an organisational entity concerning itself with an ever greater multitude of facets of daily life. This kind of modern state sees itself as a central force, therefore not merely as a facilitating or correcting entity, even if its power may still be balanced by more objective notions of decentralisation or subsidiarity, of democracy, rule of law, and human rights. It meant that the law not only became the state's main tool to enforce its public policies—directly backed up by its coercive powers—but that all law formation was increasingly considered the sovereign's preserve, including the formation of private law.

We are then in nineteenth-century Continental European legal thinking. The law that private parties produce themselves in custom or practices or in contract is then only accepted if authorised by the state. They are *no longer autonomous* sources of law and this kind of participatory law making, for example, in custom is then deemed inferior. That became part of the codification ethos.[159] Fundamental principles (international or other),

---

[158] It has already been said that the secular natural law considered itself superior in the hierarchy of norms, it being the better expression of rationality: see also the text at n 149 above.

[159] In private law, it became to be supported by an abstract or theoretical/academic model of the reality of human behaviour, believed to be potentially close enough to that reality to serve as a guide and framework that could predict the desired outcome: see more particularly the discussion in s 1.2.9 below. It was the inheritance of

custom and practice, and general core principles have to overcome any statist claims to exclusive law making in order to remain effective. Any international legal order in order to re-establish itself has to deal with these statist ambitions also.

In Grotius's time, there existed no concept of a state being the fountain of all law. Originally it was assumed that the German emperor had power over the Roman law as the Roman Emperors of the East had before, although this power was ultimately thought to reside in all sovereigns, as we have seen.[160] But in private law, such intervention of the state was thought only to be facilitating or dictated by public policy or order requirements, and was relatively rare at the level of the sovereign, but there were city ordinances of all sorts especially also in commerce as noted before. In criminal law, there was always more state intervention, even though criminal law did not depend on legislation either. That is still the situation in common law countries, but in civil law countries it wholly disappeared.

One original idea, already held in the Middle Ages was that the sovereign was anointed, and able to exercise divine right. Such a sovereign could also impose law, but could not go against the divine or natural law, only support and enunciate it. For intervention in private law, there also had to be a just cause or good reason. This confined a sovereign's power in law making considerably, although there was even then the idea that in truth only sovereigns could validate laws, precisely because of their divine right.[161] Others, like Bartolus, had thought that the law-making power truly resided in the people, in the *consensus populi*, of which notably custom and local commercial laws were the expression, although the people could transfer this power, revocably, to the sovereign.

But there was also the issue of state intervention for public policy reasons and objectives more precisely, which as a concept was at first not fully developed. In Grotius's view, the state depended on the will of the people and was therefore a utilitarian construct of the voluntary law or *ius gentium* and not itself dictated by natural law, as we have seen, although natural law fundamentally supported all that was agreed. In that context, there were no fundamental or inalienable human rights either. To the extent they existed, they could always be surrendered (to the state).

In fact, in Grotius's approach, there was already an implicit but full subjugation of the individual to the state through the theoretical construction of the social contract (borrowed from Aristotle) by which state law (*ius civile*) could conceivably become superior to all other sources of law (including therefore the natural law and *ius gentium*) if so required by public policy or reasons of state. But it would somehow have to be so intended by its people and the state was not anointed.

Following this approach, the state remained in principle subject to the fundamental natural law principles itself, but that was only so: (a) barring the agreement of the subjects to

the *Vernunftrecht* and its search for a logical mathematical model, see text at nn 148 and 155 above, but it became a more fundamental scientific German academic ideal in the nineteenth century and ultimately a political issue. It ignored all other law formation and sources of law or considered them inferior.

As we shall see, through their academies, states are assumed to have some superior or at least better insight into what is needed in society, in law formation even to balance the rights and duties between private citizens: see also the discussion in s 1.2.10 below. Only subsequently did democratic legitimacy also become an issue here: see s 1.2.13 below.

[160] See n 132 above. Even in medieval thinking, states could impose the Human Law, see n 141 above, although they seldom did.

[161] *Cf* W Ullmann, *The Medieval Idea of Law as represented by Lucas de Penna* (London, 1946).

the contrary in areas where natural law was not mandatory but permissory (*cf De Iure Belli ac Pacis* II, 2.5); and more importantly (b) unless the public interest required otherwise. In that case, there was *no* sanction against a state that behaved contrary to natural law (*cf De Iure Belli ac Pacis* II.14.6.2). As the public interest is hardly a clear concept, it in fact gave states a free hand, even in the philosophy of Grotius. They defined the public interest.

Inalienable rights against such a state emerged later and remained fragile. Only then did it become possible to talk again of value systems with a normativity that ultimately did not depend on states. It is clear in this connection that, in the end, Grotius's concept of natural law could not resist the increasing power of the modern state, and allowed for the prevalence of domestic imperatives, and therefore of national laws imposed in the public interest, however defined. Ultimately, and somewhat surprisingly, there was here also no beginning of an overriding concept of the rule of law as the basis for the exercise of all power in conformity with natural law. But there was certainly the continuing notion that the law did not depend for its validity on state sanction alone.

Any restraining influence of universal natural law concepts on state action increasingly disappeared after Grotius. This is clear in the work of Thomas Hobbes (1588–1679) in England, but also in that of Grotius's successor in the natural law school: the German writer Samuel Pufendorf (1632–94).[162] In Hobbes' view, rather than there being a natural instinct of people wherever they were or came from to live together in peace (*appetitus societatis*) in the style of Grotius, the human condition was considered to be one of all against all (*bellum omnium in omnes*).[163] To constrain the right of the strongest, people had to impose laws upon themselves. These became the sole sources of justice, which could only operate through a state (after the natural condition had been abandoned).[164] There follows no less the construct of a social contract under which individuals in order to live in peace abandon their personal rights (except those to life and limb).

The accent shifts here entirely to the modern state, which decrees the laws, ultimately even private law, and also sanctions customary law. This had nothing to do with modern ideas of democracy, rather the opposite: state absolutist tendencies. In this system, the sovereign does not owe obedience to its own laws and natural laws are at best a matter of conscience for the sovereign. They do not have a normativity of their own. Pufendorf follows in essence this reasoning also. Natural law has a meaning only if it has become positive law upon the order of the sovereign.[165] International law, as the law between states, has no autonomous place in this system either. Hence its struggle for legitimacy ever since the nineteenth-century ascent of the nation state.

Whilst towards the middle of the seventeenth century in England through John Locke, under strong Dutch republican influence,[166] the concept of inalienable rights against a sovereign emerged as a protection against the all-powerful sovereign under the social contract, at that stage of jurisprudential thought the effect was mainly in private and criminal law, centred on notions of freedom or autonomy, equality, and ownership. Even in Locke's case, this was all seen within the context of the modern state, which, on the basis of the public

---

[162] *De Iure Naturae et Gentium* (*Libro Octo*).
[163] *De Cive I.12*, with the accent on each man being allowed to use his power as he will to preserve himself, T Hobbes, *Leviathan* ch 14.
[164] *De Homine* X.5.
[165] See n 162 above, at VIII.9.5
[166] J Locke, *Two Treatises of Civil Government* (1690).

good, through legislation, could even affect the inalienable rights, although ultimately the people retained the supreme power to remove the legislature. Only in the teachings of Rousseau did these inalienable rights acquire a human-rights flavour and internationalist status, but even in his view these rights were given back to the state so as to re-emerge as state-protected private rights, which could as such be *ius gentium*.

Immanuel Kant (1727–1804), accepting the existence of rational legal principles, did not give them any autonomous legal status either.[167] All depended on their incorporation in the positive law by a state which could ignore them. The rational legal principles (as distinguished from moral principles) were no more than guidelines, and had no legal force of their own. The other dominant nineteenth-century philosopher, Hegel (1770–1831),[168] confirmed this view, in which law could be no more than positive (statist) law.[169] It always had a local character, as it was the expression of a national spirit and depended for its force on a sovereign and for its contents on the will of a people but only as expressed at the level of the state. Here enters an *irrational* element and nationalism starts to prevail which leads into the discussion of the nineteenth-century German Historical School and the impact of the Romantic movement, see the discussion below in section 1.2.9.

Again it should be noted that there is here a progression from the *raison d'etat* prevailing over natural law to the notion that, ultimately, all law emanates from a state, including private law. It may be of interest to show some of the emerging opinions in this connection, leading up to the later ideas of codification of private law in France. Although Francois Quesnay (1694–1774) had said that men do not make law, but only discover those laws that conform to 'the supreme reason that governs the universe'—a typical Enlightenment view that presumes an innate order in human relationships—it was even then thought that this law was more readily discovered by a state.[170] Montesquieu (1689–1755) had still thought that private law was connected with regions, climate and customs,[171] but the *Philosophes* of that time, who were at the heart of the French enlightenment (and *Encyclopedie*)

---

[167] I Kant, *Metaphysik der Sitten* (1797) 340, 341; Mary Gregor (trans), *The Metaphysics of Morals* (Cambridge, 1991) 148.

[168] G Hegel, *Grundlinien der Philosophie des Rechts* (1821) para 211ff; TM Knox (trans), *Hegel's Philosophy of Right* (1967) 136. It should be noted, however, that Hegel was no supporter of von Savigny and in the same book repeatedly rejected the teachings of the Historical School as atavistic, unworldly and ignorant of present day needs and interests; see also H Klenner, 'Savigny's Research Program of the Historical School of Law and its Intellectual Impact in 19th Century Berlin' (1989) 37 *American Journal of Comparative Law* 67, 77, who notes the conservative, mystical and even reactionary traits in the Historical School and in the work of von Savigny in particular, in this respect thought to have been entirely in line with the Prussian politics of those days. Much the same concerns have been expressed, however, about Hegel's work.

[169] Vattel, writing in 1758, ultimately considered the state not bound by the will of anyone else or by any universal laws, but acting only in its own interest. Even customary international law is then reduced to a form of implied consent of states. See in this connection for the development of the notion of positivism in legal terminology, s 1.4.15 below.

[170] See G Bruun, *The Englightened Despots* (1967) 32, see further also G Himmelfarb, *The Roads to Modernity* (2005) 181ff.

[171] *Spirit of the Laws*, XIX, s 4. It is interesting that a historical or cultural element is introduced here that goes against the more mathematical and universalist notions of natural law. This was also the approach of his contemporary Giovanni Batista Vico, as such precursor of the nineteenth-century idea of law as a national product that found its defenders in Germany particularly in the Historial School as we shall see in the next section, and in England in the philosophy of Burke, Bentham and Austin.

movement thought differently and supported the search for universal (intellectual) principle.[172]

Subsequently the issue was from whom this law, therefore also private law, emanated. In this connection the *abbé* Sieyes (1748–1836) declared that the nation was prior to everything. 'Its will is always legal; indeed it is the law itself',[173] although such states were to be guided by reason preferably through the intervention of enlightened despots or an elite, who would then also formulate the law.

These ideas may be seen as the background to the French codification and to the nationalisation of private law formation in France. Others, like Rousseau, preferred the idea of the general will, more in the style of Grotius,[174] defined by the social contract which made citizens outside it anti-social.[175] In truth, even in the Enlightenment movement, law started to stand for the state and its insights and organisational talents, rather than for rationality. Thus, the idea of the radical reshaping of society through state law took hold, ultimately extolled in the Republic of Virtue of Robespierre, in which states were paramount in all things; individuals were nothing. All was policy. There was no natural or other immanent law or balancing principle left.[176] This is Romanticism, of which Rousseau was the true originator, but which got its real chance in Germany.

Whilst summarising the views of these thinkers on the sources of the positive law, it should be realised that (with the exception of Rousseau and Robespierre) they were foremost philosophers and not political theorists. They are therefore less explicit than modern thinkers on law and state would be. Nevertheless, the drift in their ideas is clear and had undoubtedly to do with the emergence of the modern state in an increasingly nationalistic environment in which the law, even private law, was ultimately thought to be at the will of legislators, therefore of the state, or at least that became the idea. The law is here *made*, subject of written texts, and even in private law—that is in the law between individuals or private citizens—in essence no longer found in moral, social, rationality or efficiency needs, but prescribed by the organisational talents and insights of the modern state.

1.2.9 The German Historical and Romantic Schools. German Idealism and the Road to Private Law Codification in Germany

In the previous section, a number of eighteenth-century ideas on the law, and private law in particular, its origin and nature were discussed. They always return, and modern thought about the law, and private law in particular, seems not to have moved forward a great deal.

---

[172] Condorcet (1743–94) opined in this connection that a good law was for all, just as any true proposition is valid for all; see A Goldhammer (trans), F Furet and M Ozouf, *A Critical Dictionary of the French Revolution* (Cambridge, Mass, 1989) 729.

[173] Sieyes, *Qu'est-ce que le tiers etat?* (1789, republished New York, 1979) 10.

[174] It came to the *Encyclopedie* through Diderot's article on 'Natural Law', where it was still connected with the idea of true rationality or reason, and as such always paramount. Rousseau no longer saw it that way. Law and its creation became the policy of the sovereign.

[175] Cole (trans), *The Social Contract*, vol IV (Chicago, Great Books, 1952) ch 8, 439.

[176] *Lettres a ses commettans* (Paris, 1792) II, 55.

The previous discussion also introduced the subject of codification of private law in civil law countries, especially in France. Before finally coming to this topic more broadly, also in its German variant, the German Historical School of the nineteenth century must be mentioned. It preceded the codification in Germany that came in 1900, about 100 years after the French one. During this period, the *Ius Commune* continued to hold sway in Germany, besides the law of a multitude of German states and cities, and was further developed. This was done by the so-called *Pandektists* who managed to give an important further stimulus to this law.

The Historical School overlapped but was separate. It was the school of FC von Savigny, Professor at the Humboldt University in Berlin from its foundation in 1810. He rose to fame as the result of a pamphlet written in 1814,[177] in which he attacked in extravagant terms the suggestion of FJ Thibaut, Professor in Heidelberg for an all-German civil code to counter the enormous diversities of laws in the different states within the Germany of those days (Germany being united only after 1870),[178] the need for which could hardly be denied, although it left room for legitimate disagreement on the method.

In the course of this diatribe, the French *Code Civil* of 1804 was sharply criticised, even called a cancer that had spread into Germany (where it was in force in areas that had been occupied by the French), in which context Savigny condemned its system as well as the works of Pothier on which it was partly based. Later (in the largely rewritten second edition of 1828, followed by a third one in 1840), he accepted the unfairness of this attack.

His main thrust, which he did not later weaken, was in fact against the natural law school because of its abstractions, and especially its universalist pretensions and its perceived lack of respect for the historical development of peoples, although the basic approach of the natural law school had in the meantime already led to the *national* Prussian, French and Austrian codifications. Although they were undeniably expressions of individual states, and in that sense nationalistic, von Savigny considered them unscientific, by which he meant that they did not properly reflect the natural development of the laws of these countries. In this connection, he showed a marked, rather modern, preference for a more flexible and dynamic concept of the law and also became concerned about the static nature of legislation and of codification in particular. That part of his thinking was, however, soon forgotten.

It suggested a practical down-to-earth approach based on local laws and their dynamics, but the truth was that von Savigny was not a practitioner and was only interested in Roman law that he admired, and this was not the *Ius Commune* version either[179]—it was probably considered too diverse and by many not sufficiently enlightened—but rather the classical Roman law in as far as it could be known or reconstructed, or otherwise the *Corpus Iuris*.[180] The rediscovery of the Institutes of Gaius in 1816 clearly helped in this connection.

---

[177] FC von Savigny, *Vom Beruf unsrer Zeit für Gesetzgebung und Rechtswissenschaft* (1814).

[178] FJ Thibaut, *Über die Notwendigkeit eines allgemeinen bürgerlichen Rechts für Deutschland* (1814).

[179] To which he nevertheless devoted much of his earlier research published in his *Geschichte des römischen Rechts im Mittelalter* (1815–31) six vols.

[180] To which he devoted his second main work, the *System des heutigen römischen Rechts*, published in eight volumes between 1840 and 1849, supplemented by another two volumes on *Obigationenrecht* in 1851 and 1852, in the parts concerning the different contract types never completed. These books were ultimately neither treatises on Roman law nor on the use made of it in nineteenth-century Germany but presented rather a more abstract legal theory of private law. Much of it was translated into English.

There were thus some glaring contradictions from the beginning. First, this effort was hardly Germanic or nationalistic.[181] Rather, the true aim appeared increasingly to be the formulation of an intellectually coherent system of law derived from an analysis of the old Roman casuistry. Indeed, intellectualisation along *national* lines seemed to become the true aim rather than substance, which was therefore not to reconstruct the original Roman texts either. This led to a second contradiction in that the intellectual method of the natural law school, which was so vividly rejected for its universal claims, was in this respect fully embraced and continued, ultimately descending in pure academic system thinking of a domestic kind.[182]

It follows that there was a strong intellectual overlay in the German historical school from the beginning, and ultimately this approach became indeed a German intellectual exercise in system thinking as prelude to the *Bürgerliches Gesetzbuch* or German Civil Code (BGB) of 1900. The science of the law of this type thus became considered as a source of law itself and came to embody another typical nineteenth-century German ideal of law as science and technique, even if also product of nationalism. This may also be seen as a typical product of German Idealism,[183] ultimately descending into the idea (not, however,

---

[181] There developed, however, in Germany also a Germanic wing in this movement, led by Beseler, *Volksgeist under Juristenrecht* (1843), and later by Gierke, *Die historische Rechtsschule und die Germanisten* (1903). Their argument ultimately centred on the quality of the *Ius Commune* and its further progress. It was ridiculed by Savigny and Puchta, but in the Germanistic wing the *Ius Commune* and the local laws were thought to provide a better basis for German codification than Roman law casuistry.

[182] This became the true successor of the *Vernunftrecht*, see text at n 155 above, and raises important epistemological questions in terms of a-prioristic knowledge, abstraction, and social control through intellectual system thinking which also poses the question of empirical verification and validity, and truth in that sense.

The philosophical concept of *realism* assumes here that these a-prioristic abstractions reflect nature, also in the social sciences, meaning in particular that all order that is so found was already there and is intrinsic. In this view, academic endeavour brings it out and empirical research is not truly necessary; there is a claim to scientific truth.

This discussion was not new and had gone on since medieval philosophy under the name of *nominalism*, which had held the opposite. Although in this view a-prioristic rules could still exert some control over nature or reality whatever that was, all was ultimately definitional and a true insight into the creation was not considered to be within human bounds.

This led to the idea—even for Kant—that the laws of Newton were not laws found in nature, but were mere human abstractions that nevertheless could explain nature (better). But the true relationship was not clear and it was conceivable in this approach that in due course an entirely different theory could emerge that explained nature better. In fact, we might never know the real truth (the noumena). If this were to be so in the natural sciences, it would be all the more so in the social sciences, including the law.

These issues are relevant but cannot be discussed here much further. See, however, for an interesting contribution and the damage the scientific idea of law in this sense may have done, the work of G Samuel, 'Can Legal Reasoning Be Demystified?' (2009) 29 *Legal Studies* 181. See, for a more fundamental criticism of framework thinking of this kind, K Popper, n 208 below.

[183] German idealism is often referred to in this context but is hard to describe or define; see also K Americs (ed), *The Cambridge Compendium to German Idealism* (2000). In a narrower sense, it is often associated with the speculative philosophy of Fichte, Hegel and Schelling, but it may be seen as a more comprehensive German intellectual attitude. It sought to understand all our most basic intellectual concerns and was in origin a scientific method based on introspection that allowed for other tools than pure reason to reach levels of reality believed to exist beyond mere common sense observation.

In this connection, it was concerned, in particular, with the development and impact of modern science and its insights, its effects on our understanding and on our capability of steering newer realities which might, however, never be fully known (in Kantian parlance the world of the *noumena*). Much behind this was the thought, however, that there were universal concepts that held this world together which world could be improved by searching for them even if they might never be fully discovered. This then became the scientific ideal. It put intellectual endeavour or *Bildung* at the centre of modern development.

universally held but much followed) that through a scientific model akin to that of the natural sciences, a set of legal rules could be distilled that had validity, reflected reality, and held in it the solution to all legal problems. A similar approach was then also advocated for the other social sciences.[184]

It is this intellectual thinking and model creation that is still at the heart of the German private law codification, which system, it was thought, when properly understood and explained, would then be able to tailor for all eventualities. The emphasis is here first on intellectual or abstract system building and subsequently on logic and technique in its application to produce the right answers.[185] This became much of the codification philosophy and interpretation based on it not only in Germany but even in countries

In art, the result was (confusingly) called naturalism, meaning a scientific or academic depicting of reality, see A Hauser, *The Social History of Art*, vol 4 (1951) 60ff. Indeed, reality itself becomes here an academic concept, in the criticism of Nietzsche pure fiction even if necessary to organise life and for it to continue, *Nietzsche Werke*, 1895ff, XVI, 19. In this view, only music had a more direct but only fleeting connection with an inner world or deeper reality.

This type of idealism can only be mentioned here but, like nominalism see n 182 above, and Romanticism see n 191 below, this is not the place further to elaborate on these important ideas or current thinking, except to say that these searches became central to German thought and scientific endeavour in the nineteenth century.

They ultimately crystallised around the very question whether there were innate structures in our thinking and in reality as our thinking perceived it, whether they could be spotted or whether all was merely in the mind or psyche even if some structure could sometimes still be detected, *Wille und Vorstelling* in Schoppenhauer's more sceptical philosophy. Can we know reality through scientific endeavour, through religious revelation, or through searching our inner self for hidden truths (revealed through intuition or perhaps common sense)?

It may be observed in this connection that modern philosophy since World War II has largely separated from the German nineteenth-century tradition and no longer seeks for inner, more universal structures. It is as such much more diversified but also, it could be argued, much more disjointed and its objectives are much less clear, its impact much less obvious, also in the study of the law, especially in Germany, where students now commonly know nothing of all this.

[184] Although scepticism appeared, especially in the works of Dilthey (besides Nietsche and earlier Schoppenhauer), which suggested complete relativism, this did not mean the end of system thinking in the social sciences and especially in the law, but only that it was not based on any inherent normativity but rather on models that identified and were based on some more durable structures in past experiences which these models then strung together into a more coherent intellectual framework for the present. The concepts behind this intellectually highly developed private law were then thought to be based on quantitative and qualitative simplification that made their application possible and led to an intellectual system that claimed no less than to have all legal answers and to solve all problems. This was later also called *Begriffsjurisprudenz*, see also s 1.2.13 below. For the law, this system thinking or search for system in this comprehensive and exclusive sense survived in Germany even in the important works of Eugen Ehrlich on law and sociology, following the sociologist Max Weber.

The message in this book is that we look for or should be looking for structures, see s 1.1.5 above, not for system in this all domineering sense of holding in itself the answer to all legal problems and laying claim to absolute truth.

[185] Thus in law, the nature of the system and legal system thinking became a more particularly German concern, especially vivid in the early parts of Von Jhering's *Geist des roemischen Rechts (auf den verschiedenene Stufen seiner Entwicklung)* (1818–92).

The idea is here that in law formation the state follows the insights of its academies, and then claims superior knowledge (not democracy) for its authority to nationalise all law creation and rubber-stamps the academic proposals. Interestingly, it led from the beginning to Jhering's rejection of the purely national character of private law. The fact that Roman law at its most developed was received in Germany showed, in his view, its more universal character. This makes a great deal of sense, goes back to natural law thinking, but could not break the strong and irrational undercurrent in the nationalisation of all private law in Europe since the nineteenth century.

Nationalistic system thinking remains a strong German conviction that may still be considered dominant today; see also the reference to Karl Larenz in n 2 above, although in a later phase of his life, von Jhering himself started to question not only nationalism but even system thinking of this nature, in what became to be called *Interessenjurisprudenz*. See also the work of Kantorowicz, referred to in s 1.2.13 below. It puts emphasis on justified practical need and a more dynamic approach to private law and its formation and application. It had particular relevance in matters of interpretation.

like France[186] and Austria that had codified much earlier, the idea therefore being (as it were, retroactively) that all these codes presented or were based on a sufficiently clear idea of the reality of human behaviour and endeavour that could control and guide it completely and thus produce the right answers in terms of justice, social peace, efficiency and growth.[187]

Since, as there was no proper all-German legal science, the required analysis and system (and, even more the ability to create it) was lacking in Germany in the early nineteenth century, the moment for a German codification was not then considered to have come. System thinking and analysis, and the creation of a proper German intel-

Currents of this so-called *Freirechtslehre* survive in Germany, but they became more incidental and weaker. See, however, J Koendgen, *Selbstbindung ohne Vertrag* (1981), and earlier J Esser, *Vorverstandnis und Methodenwahl* (1970) and J Esser, *Grundsatz und Norm in der richterlichen Fortbildung des Privatrechts*, 4th edn (Tübingen, Mohr Siebeck, 1990). See further the father of legal hermeneutics (*juristische Hermeneutik*) in Germany H-G Gadamer, *Wahrheit und Methode, Grundzüge einer philisophischen Hermeneutik*, 6th edn (Tübingen, Mohr Siebeck, 1990); K Engisch, *Einführung in das juristische Denken*, 9th edn (Stuttgart, Berlin, Köln, Kohlhammer, 1997) 80; R Zippelius, *Juristische Methodenlehre*, 10th edn (München, Beck, 2006) 99; W Fikentscher, *Methoden des Rechts in vergleichender Darstellung*, Band IV: Dogmatischer Teil (Tübingen, Mohr Siebeck, 1977) 191ff; F Müller and R Christensen, *Juristische Methodik*, 9th edn, Band I, Grundlagen, Öffentliches Recht (Berlin, Duncker/Humblodt, 2004) 250ff; A Kaufmann, *Analogie und 'Natur der Sache'*, 2nd edn (Heidelberg, CF Müller, 1982) 37ff.

It no longer seems to affect the systematic tradition to which most modern German PhDs, theses for professorships, handbooks, and articles testify, but *cf* also M Schillig, *Konkretisierungskompetenz und Konkretisierungsmethoden im Europaeischen Privatrecht* (Berlin, de Gruyter, 2010) ch 8. They tend to be descriptive of the German rules and its system, and of the way it operates, and can be (better) used to cover newer eventualities. Indeed the German legal professorate is itself often considered a bar to renewal as it dominates the younger scholars. As a result, 'law and economics', for example, is in Germany often studied in Economics faculties.

In such an atmosphere, it is not surprising that in searches for European rules of private law, like in the Draft Common Frame of Reference (DCFR), see s 1.4.19 below and vol II, ch 1 ss 1.6.4ff and ch 2, s 1.11, there is no enquiry into true needs nor a review of method and objective. The intellectual model (here derived from the German BGB) is not fundamentally questioned and assumed automatically to produce justice, social peace, efficiency, and economic growth, now through statist intervention of this narure at the EU level. There is no empirical verification of its validity and responsiveness, which are assumed to follow from the intellectual coherence of the system itself.

This remains accepted dogma in much of civil law, but is fundamentally questioned by transnational law formation in the modern *lex mercatoria*, which is here a competing and very different force to attain unification, at least in international or cross-border professional dealings (even within the EU) where it assumes at the philosophical and institutional level a different (non-statist) legal order of its own.

[186] See even now eg G-G Granger, *La science et les sciences*, 2nd edn (1995) 70, still extolling this kind of scientific ideal for the law, in which abstract models of the real world, built on practical experience, are applied through logic and mathematics to new fact situations. Creating these models is considered real legal science, meant to find the missing links in legal normativity and able to predict and regulate behaviour.

The idea is then that ultimately one great universal model of rules can be found that covers all, nature as well as human relationships. Short of such an ultimate triumph, the question remains, however, how such models can be tested for their (continued) validity, especially in law and other social sciences, whether they are self-contained, autonomous, and closed, and what place innovation has in such an approach and how it can come about; see also the text at n 207 below.

This is not to deny the importance of academic models but they are more in the nature of tools of ordering and critique of what we have than in representing ultimate truths. At best, they could lay claim to greater or better truth, but it all remains to be seen and one can never be sure.

[187] This at first led to simplistic uncritical commentaries on the new codes, such as, in France, the commentaries of Aubry and Rau, but it is also at the heart of many subsequent commentaries which are then seldom more than descriptive and mere practitioners' manuals. They do not fundamentally critique the system but accept it as basic and follow it in the scholastic fashion. University studies in the law are then mostly similarly scholastic, uncritical, and not innovative, therefore hardly academic.

lectual analytical ability to arrive at it, became von Savigny's programme, undertaken by himself and his students, amongst whom could be counted in particular Puchta (his successor in Berlin), Dernberg, Vangarow, and Windscheid (in Leipzig).[188] At the same time, the German Theodor Mommsen unraveled the Roman constitutional and criminal laws, and sought nineteenth-century conceptual inspiration in them, at least for Germany. In the area of criminal law, codification had already started, however, especially after 1813 in Bavaria, through the work of Feuerbach, followed in 1851 by a new Prussian Criminal Code.

As already mentioned, it could not be avoided that in von Savigny's search for system in the Roman law, the reference to Roman law seemed to contradict the national spirit or *Volksgeist* which, in the theories of Fichte with his glorification of the active, dynamic and imaginative (Germanic) self (ultimately best realised within a state outside of which individuals could not achieve their purpose or attain their aspirations and freedom),[189] came to be seen to be behind any proper legal system, which thus became national. Indeed under Puchta, the *Volksgeist* idea soon became a belief in *national* laws, which was then translated into national legislation and therefore codification for a modern centralised and civil service-dominated state and judiciary. The *Volksgeist* thus started to be concerned with form rather than substance.[190]

In such a state, the idea of the autonomy of private law was abandoned in favour of state formulation of the basic tenets of all law, even of private law, and individual rights and powers became less important, and in fact depended on state license. This is the nineteenth-century Romantic[191] and German idealist inheritance and overlay, which

---

[188] Of their books, Windscheid's commentary was the most important: *Lehrbuch des Pandektenrechts*, which was reprinted even after the BGB was promulgated and at that time updated by Kipp (1900 and 1906).

[189] JG Fichte, *Saemtliche Werke* iii 47/8, and vi 306.

[190] It had nothing to do with modern democratic notions, as the legislature of those times did not function in that manner. The question then became whether the *Volksgeist* was the national spirit (or perhaps an assortment of national spirits) that prevailed autonomously, or was rather the ordering technique of a modern state that determined the shape of the new codified law. Was it therefore national custom-oriented, or was it state action-driven? In other words, was the concern an immanent law (even if Roman) or was it about strategy and policy? Was the new law to be embedded in social cultures or values, in economic realities, or propelled by the *raison d'etat* or public policy? Or was it mainly an intellectual exercise—private law as icon of German legal thought and intellectual culture—or all of this and more?

In the meantime, the *Volksgeist* itself appeared to be a Romantic notion that proved to be largely anti-industrial, anti-capitalist, anti-big city, and in that context sometimes even anti-Semitic.

[191] Romanticism itself may perhaps best be defined as mankind's efforts to come to grips with its own irrationalities. It is as such a reaction against the Enlightenment which, in line with the classical tradition, proceeded from the idea that all had its given place and that also applied to human action which therefore, if properly understood, was in truth rational; see for an introduction Isaiah Berlin, *The Roots of Romanticism* (Mellon Lectures 1965–66, edited by Henry Hardy and first published in 1999). Romanticism reacted against this.

Naturally, there is here considerable tension in legal matters as all law, as well as legislation, is based on or assumes some sense of order even if it redirects it. To repeat, the key would always appear to be in the true knowledge of reality and how its works and whether such knowledge can be reliably attained. See also the comment at the end of the previous section and in the footnotes above.

In Romanticism, the true accent is rather on will or creation, not primarily on knowledge, therefore on the idea that everyone creates their own universe including its values and that is it. It means that there is no structure in our experiences beyond what people have managed to create for themselves. There is no limit to freedom in that sense, nor is there any form to the unceasing flow of human experiences. Reality is an amalgam of dark forces that can at best be understood in terms of myth and symbolism or metaphor, but we never really know for what they stand. In this mindset, the state also becomes a mystical institution, and so is the law that it creates, but it can do so at will and there is, at least as far as human behaviour is concerned, nothing beyond its control and there are

often overlapped and in which the *Volksgeist* itself becomes superfluous, except for its nationalism, whilst all law, including private law, becomes subservient to modernity and its aims, and therefore political in a nationalistic sense. The most significant formulation and intellectual underpinning of this result may be found in Hegel's *Philosophy of Rights* (1821).[192]

In Germany, these notions and feelings ultimately came together with those of the German Historical School even though balanced at first by a *laissez faire* attitude, which did not aim at transformation but rather at reform. That was the background of the German codification in the *Bürgerliches Gesetzbuch* or BGB of 1900.[193]

In this connection, especially after the unification of Germany in 1870, the need for a national German codification was more strongly felt and the systemic scientific basis for it was then considered to exist, although von Jhering in his later work had already criticised this intellectual exercise in favour of a more practical (German) and less academically abstract (Roman) approach. Indeed, when the first drafts of the new Code (or BGB) appeared, they were attacked for their dogmatic and high professorial tone and for their lack of interest in social and practical problems, although the result was ultimately rather

no innate rules or limitations. Soon it was thought that there was no other source of law or rationality outside it, nor was there any freedom beyond it. Man can only live in society.

The origin of these ideas are already in the Aristotelian view that man could only achieve its true fulfillment in the *polis*, as we have seen in s 1.2.6 above, but the more extreme modern version may be found especially in JG Fichte, see n 189 above, and in Hegel, see n 168 above, where the state becomes the true expression of the human condition and its laws the only laws that count, seen here as an ongoing process of positivation in the self-realisation of man and of its freedom in that sense, that is, always through the state.

In this view, the invisible hand of the market can also be manipulated, and so can the rest, either in a conservative or progressive manner or in any other. The creation can be improved and that becomes the true task of humanity. The action is not then primarily on knowing society but on recreating it, with the state as the ultimate modern re-creating force. Law formation becomes here a tool in this process, which is organised by each individual state in its own image or inexorable march into history.

Late nineteenth century private law codification may be seen in that context, especially in Germany, and is not then strictly confined in its reach by innate, pre-existing principles or realities. The idea becomes rather that an intellectual construct of this nature, although based on some past structures, can be recast and systemised at will. As such, it can fully control social realities (whatever they may be) for now and the future. The system of law is then the one we make, and its values are the ones we give it. This is a strongly Romantic notion and remains another dominant strand in codification thinking besides pure system thinking, probably more truly the aim of German idealism, see n 183 above.

Ultimately, the combination of Romanticism and idealism was given over and made subservient to the hubris of the modern super-state in what was believed to be a makeable society that could be recast at will by states and in which the law was used to impose and enforce their aims.

[192] See also n 168 above for Hegel's criticism of the early Romantics. However, some basic human rights were guaranteed. That had been the achievement of the French Revolution and its *Déclaration des droits de l'homme (et du citoyen)* and the inheritance of John Locke. Yet they often could not be directly invoked and meant in any event little in private law. In the meantime, the more universal or pan-European spirit of the *Ius Commune* was lost.

[193] Moves to a more radical social approach came later, during the Weimar Republic after World War I, but led to nothing, see KW Noerr, *Zwischen den Muehlsteinen, Eine Privatrechtsgeschichre der Weimarer Republik* (1988), although case law and more incidental legislation had already started to protect workers, consumers and later also small investors. Later amendments to the BGB further destroyed any idea of one particular leading concept but the approach remained unitary, one system for all.

conventional[194] and, following Pandektist thinking, not always considered to have been a great improvement.[195]

In practice, the approach was here twofold. First, a general basic structure or general part of the (private) law was developed in which notions of subjective rights and legal act or *Rechtsgeschaft* and *Willenserklaerung* figured large.[196] These general notions were in fact thought to operate in all legal institutions, subsequently to be developed as a second tier in family, property, contract and tort law, and to be interpreted in the light of the essence of these institutions. Together they formed the 'system', which was considered scientific and without which there was not supposed to be any correct legal reasoning. Again, this was evidence of a more general typical nineteenth-century scientific urge in Germany, see text at n 165 above and also section 1.2.13 below. Legal dynamism was not considered to be able to operate outside such a system, never mind what the national development of a people suggested or business required.

Thus the system became everything.[197] This is not objectionable as long as it is empirically tested for its continued self-sufficiency and has some appreciation of the incompatibilities, contradictions and insufficiencies where the law meets the facts in their ever evolving

---

[194] More by default than by design, built on Roman law, but there was much borrowing also from the French CC. This had already been recognised from early on by B Winscheid, *Die geschichtliche Schule in der Rechtswissenschaft* (1878). Clearly, no more was considered necessary until the upheavals after World War I and the need for workers and consumer protection began to be felt, but it did not even then fundamentally transform private law. In particular, it did not lead to a whole 'socialising' or other transformation, although it was tried in Germany in the 1920s and is entirely compatible with codification thinking, based as it is on the notion of the makeability of the law and its system, including private law, and its total severability (it was believed) from any underlying principle (no natural law ideas) and complete surrender (if needs be) to politics: see further KW Noer, cited in n 193 above.

[195] In fact, following Pandektist thinking, there was at the practical level a significant break with the *Ius Commune* and its forward development. It was not always considered with favour, see H Coing, 'German "Pandektistik" in its Relationship to the former "Ius Commune"' (1989) 37 *American Journal of Comparative Law* 9, noting in particular the regressive attitude in respect of some of the major achievements of the *Ius Commune* like the unification of the law of contract; the abandonment of the distinction between *stipulatio* and the contracts *consensus*; the overcoming of the rule '*alteri stipulari non potest*' with the development of agency (which the Pandektists exceptionally accepted, however); and the third party beneficiary concept, the assignment of claims and the abandonment of the construction of the *procurator in rem suam*, the development of a general tort action based on an extended *actio legis Aquiliae*; and the transformation of the *actio de rem inverso* into an unjust enrichment action.

Commercial law concepts, developed in the *Ius Commune*, were also ignored. They were left to a different branch of the law (so-called *Deutsches Privatrecht*). It created an academic attitude in the Pandektists that had little to do with the practice of the law, notably with subjects like company, patent and bankruptcy laws.

[196] The strong accent on the will in this connection is also a typical nineteenth-century idea, connected with Romantic philosophy in which the creative force of mankind took centre stage. Although the general will embodied in the state was supreme, individuals in the space left to them could equally create in any way they wanted. So von Savigny, see Vol 3 *System des heutigen römischen Rechts* (1840) 257.

The emphasis on the *will* (rather than *ratio*), often in a personal anthropomorphic sense, derives here from Kantian and Romantic philosophy with its emphasis on freedom and creation, in private law especially in contract and offer and acceptance theories.

It suggests, however, a thoroughly *anthropomorphic* attitude to contract law. The subjective interpretation technique that follows from this notion of 'will' subsequently had to be tempered, however, first by a more literal interpretation based on mere declarations and later by a more normative approach to interpretation of the contractual rights and obligations of the parties, originally in purposive and teleological interpretation techniques and ultimately especially through good faith notions or a more normative and objective approach in terms of conduct and reliance, but this newer approach has still not fully played out. See for modern contract theory s 1.1.4 above and further vol II, ch 1, s 1.1.4.

[197] See also n 185 above and n 208 below and s 1.2.13 below. In n 65 above, it has already been stated that German academics typically still look for system everywhere, even in more open-textured concepts like good faith.

appearances and unexpected configurations. This is where the problem starts; see further the broader discussion on the codification idea in section 1.2.13 below. Rather than as an academic model only, the system was here perceived as a given societal truth, even if ultimately merely a political fabrication, and therefore basically static, although subject to some interpretational flexibility but always within its own ground rules (until formally amended).[198] In this world, empirical testing was neither necessary nor relevant; it was only the will of the state that counted. To repeat, the pretence was that this law was at the same time complete and covered all eventualities including newer situations. Again, it was by definition considered close enough to reality to continue to lead and guide it. By definition it was just, promoted social peace, and led to efficiency, never mind how out of date it might have become—it remained the pretence. It will be argued later that this type of law formation and application may be subject to severe intellectual (and political) prejudice and, in its statist, formal, and technical attitude and rigidity, is likely to be confining and the enemy of a dynamic forward-moving society.

Whatever the early objections to this system thinking that eliminated all other sources of law may have been, the new German Code entered into force in 1900 after some minor revisions. The new Commercial Code (*Handelsgesetzbuch* or HGB) of 1897, largely a recast of the Commercial Code of 1861 (see section 1.1.7 above), entered into force at the same time.

1.2.10 The Civil Law National Codifications and their Coverage

As noted before, the abandonment of the procedural and often incidental nature of private rights under the *Ius Commune*, and the progressive development of subjective rights under more general rules that were deduced from Roman and natural law principles, rationalist notions, utility, and from case law, or sometimes from local laws, was a long process on the Continent of Western Europe. This law was only delivered from its Roman and later religious (Canon) law overtones through Grotius and his followers, and was then able to find a more articulate expression.

By the eighteenth century it had allowed for the creation of a legal framework of private law that was substantially considered rational, in its basics universal and intrinsically coherent, capable of being comprehensively written down. Although it subsequently became intertwined with nineteenth-century nationalism and later typical academic system thinking that pretended to be able to capture reality and singularly be able to steer it, increasingly supported by newer ideas about the makeability of society through political action, this secular natural law school, which was then found to be inadequate and in its universalism inappropriate, nevertheless provided the basic method and material for the modern civil law codifications, therefore for the French *Code Civil* of 1804, but also for the German BGB of 1900, and all the others.[199]

---

[198] See also text at n 182 above for the early tensions this created, even in Germany.
[199] Codification in the UCC sense should here be distinguished as it was never meant to cover the whole ground and left ample room for other sources of law, as we have seen.

Codification was itself not a natural law school idea. We have already seen at the end of section 1.2.8 above that it was at first more properly product of the Enlightenment in the age of Voltaire, and therefore of French philosophical thought, with which the more German search for an intellectual system and the idea that it could only emanate from a state eventually fused. In section 1.2.9 above, it was already noted that, in Germany, codification was at first rejected by von Savigny, but later more particularly underpinned by German idealism supported by the notion of society creation at the national level and subsequently in private law more particularly by rigorous system thinking (always of a nationalistic academic flavour). Indeed, it may still be maintained that the French Civil Code is primarily a product of the Enlightenment, an exercise in clearing up and rationalisation, the German Civil Code of Romanticism and German idealism in which first intellectual systematisation and subsequently the makeability of society through its laws, even private law, took centre-stage, the state acting here essentially through its academies but also claiming superior societal insights into what was truly needed.

In practical terms, after the French Revolution in 1789, the *Déclaration des droits de l'homme* began to insist on a national codification of at least criminal law (Article 8); henceforth it would be the same for all residents (Article 6). From the first French Constitution of 1791, codification of the civil laws throughout France was demanded. Still, it was not necessarily out of a nationalistic spirit but rather out of a desire for equality and certainty for all, also in private law. Only in the German Historical School did the nationalistic spirit (*Volksgeist*) take centre-stage from the beginning and (whatever the contradictions in this School, which was fascinated by classical Roman law), after Fichte, Hegel and Puchta, the idea that the law could only be expressed through legislation at the level of the state as an imposed order.

The French and German Codes were not the only ones. The elaborate Prussian *Landrecht* of 1794, prepared by Karl Gottlieb Schwarz, who also called himself Svarez, had preceded the German Code in Prussia. It remained effective there until 1900 (and in some of its organisational and administrative law provisions even until the official end of the Prussian state in 1947). Austria produced a more important work in 1811, the *Allgemeines Bürgerliches Gesetzbuch* or ABGB, prepared by Franz Aloys von Zeiller and still in force today. In section 1.1.3 above, it was shown how the impact of the French and German Codes spread, whilst whole new Codes were introduced even in the twentieth century: in Switzerland in 1912 (prepared by Eugen Huber),[200] in Italy in 1942, in Portugal in 1967, in the Netherlands as late as 1992, and in Brazil in 2002. These latter five codes were greatly inspired by the German example. French influence substantially waned as a consequence, but it remains important, especially in Belgium and Luxembourg, and also in Spain and in many countries of Latin America.

The Prussian *Landrecht* ('*Land*' in the sense of 'country', not of immovable property) was a code of more than 19,000 articles, which also covered criminal law and much organisational, procedural and administrative law, and was indeed meant to contain all the law that was to be in force in all of Prussia at that time.[201] It was all quite different from the later French approach in drafting the *Code Civil*, where there was an effort to be concise,

---

[200] The Law of Obligations was in fact already codified in 1883 and remained separate from the Code but was substantially amended in 1912.

[201] Prussia then spread from some possessions in the west, through the north into Berlin and its surroundings and into the very east of Germany, to what is now Poland, whilst there were also some possessions in the south.

whilst the impossibility of covering every eventuality was understood and accepted from the beginning. It is an important insight in modern codification that is nevertheless often presumed to be complete (leading to and requiring a liberal interpretation approach). In France at first only private law was covered (1804); it was later followed by a commercial code (1807); a penal code (1810); and procedural codes for the civil, commercial and criminal courts (1806 and 1810). A similarly concise approach was taken by the Austrians in their codification of 1811.

In France, it was the practitioner Portalis who ultimately managed to provide the necessary direction after four false starts under Cambaceres, later Consul together with Napoleon. Napoleon himself took an interest after 1800,[202] although his true impact has never been properly established and was probably exaggerated later. Crucially, Portalis stressed that a code of this sort could not foresee everything but had to stick to a broader view and should not go into detail. That was the task of judges imbued with its general spirit. Unlike Justinian and Frederick the Great, there was here no fear of comment and interpretation, except if done through the courts by general disposition (as the old *parlements* had done in France, see section 1.2.5 above).

On the narrower subject of codification coverage—as may already be clear from the foregoing—modern civil law codes never had a pre-set content. Thus, some countries included in their codes company law and bankruptcy law, but they could also be covered by different statutes. In this connection, it should be appreciated that the term 'code' itself means nothing, and that all civil law private law statutes have a similar approach and status and are imbued with the same philosophy. The form is therefore not important and nothing should be read into the term 'code' itself. It is the method that counts, especially the intellectual unity of the system and the subordination of all other sources of law.

Although in civil law countries, the idea no doubt was always to cover substantially all of the civil and commercial law in comprehensive codes, it is ultimately a question of convenience whether they do, or whether parts of it are enacted in separate statutes. The enactment procedure and requirements are no different, and convenience is the reason that the contents of the various codes may differ considerably from country to country whilst some parts of the law are left to be covered by more specific statutes. The key is that in a codification country they are all systematically connected into one system of private law that, in its purest version, is considered complete, exclusive as source of law, superseding all prior enactments, and to be explained from within, assuming a single rational framework that is to provide all the answers.

In this large area, the *Landrecht* was only meant to replace the supplementary, mainly general Roman and Saxon laws, and as such still remained supplementary to local laws where in force. Only in some Prussian areas, where, at the beginning of the nineteenth century, French law had been introduced under French occupation and had abolished the local laws, did the *Landrecht* become the prime source of the law. On the other hand, in large areas that became Prussian only after 1815, French codified law continued into force until 1900, especially in the Rhineland.

The Prussian King, Frederick the Great, who ordered this early codification and had been wary of lawyers and of the poor state of the knowledge and administration of the laws in his scattered kingdom, insisted on detail and thought that the judicial function could thus be reduced to the pure administration of the law. Hence its bulkiness which he ultimately also disliked.

[202] The history of the new CC is told by FA Fenet, *Receuil complet des travaux préparatoires du Code Civil* (1827) 15 vols. The new commission of 1800 managed to make a proposal in four months(!) which was preceded by the famous *Discours préliminaire* of Portalis.

As mentioned before, France and Germany also have Commercial Codes as well as Civil Codes, but their contents differ considerably (see section 1.1.7 above). On the other hand, Switzerland, Italy, the Netherlands and Brazil no longer have different Commercial Codes. Their content substantially merged into the Civil Codes, although some may now also be contained in separate statutes, such as company and insurance laws. Bankruptcy is another case in point: in most countries on the Continent, bankruptcy law started as part of the Commercial Codes, at least in countries that reserved this remedy for merchants, as France in essence still does. Yet even in France, bankruptcy law was taken out of the Commercial Code of 1806, as was company law, and was only reintegrated in the new Commercial Code of 2000.

In Germany, bankruptcy never was part of the Commercial Code and company law (in as far as the AG type of public company is concerned) is no longer; in the Netherlands, after the demise of the Commercial Code, company law was transferred to the Civil Code. In the Netherlands bankruptcy law was part of the old Commercial Code at first, but had long been a separate statute (since 1896) and remains so after the new Civil Code became effective in 1992. In truth, bankruptcy is not properly a subject of private law at all. It is regulatory.

As has already been observed, the consequence of nationalism has been that civil law as we know it today is not one single law or even one system. It stands for the codified private law obtaining on the European Continent as it was *nationalised by country*. Decisions in one country have not even persuasive force in the others. Naturally, as a point of comparative law, the laws in other countries may be held up as examples, but so also could the laws of non-civil law countries. Not even shared origin in Roman law and in secular natural law school thinking makes a difference here, whilst general principle or custom also do not bind them closer together. In any event, and as noted before, they are in many civil law countries contested as independent sources of law.

This situation is different between the countries of the Common Law, which still have a basic communality in their laws and have in that way remained closer: see section 1.3.2 below. It is not at all uncommon therefore to see English and American cases cited at least for their persuasive force in other common law jurisdictions. This would be very unusual in civil law countries.

1.2.11 Nationalism and System Thinking. The Question of the Continued Relevance of the Civil Law Codification Idea

Although all three early civil law codes (Prussia, France and Austria) were in essence based on the method of the natural law school and aspired to rationality, as we have seen, their status and approaches were different. The Prussian Code was intended to cover everything, and as a consequence did not mean to leave much room for interpretation but was at first only a subsidiary source of law. The French and Austrian Civil Codes were on the other hand relatively short, were primary sources of law, stuck to the main topics and left the rest to interpretation, which consequently acquired a pivotal role. Only the Austrian Code, in its Article 7, allowed in this connection for recourse to natural law if there were neither precedent nor other related statutes to resolve the issue.

The French Code was in this respect considered *self-contained*. That proved an important feature, which at first seemed to follow from the explicit abolition of all customary local laws in Article 7 of the Introduction Statute. It came about after Cambaceres had insisted on the continuing relevance of those laws and of the Roman law, if not conflicting with the new Code. One recognises here the attitude still present in common law countries which in principle allows case law, equity and custom to operate besides statutory law. In view of the great regional diversity in these laws in France at the time, others insisted, however, on their abolition. In fact, Portalis thought this abolition the most essential part of the whole project,[203] although in the discussions it had been observed that Roman law would always continue to have the persuasive force of the *raison écrite*.

The much later Swiss Civil Code has a well-known special approach to its coverage in Article 1. It establishes that the Code answers all questions in the areas it covers but in the absence of a specific provision, it allows judges to have regard to custom and otherwise formulate the rule as if they were legislators. This approach is unique, although ostensibly limited to gap filling, assuming here a fundamental difference with interpretation. But this facility is seldom used in Switzerland and has not lead to a more dynamic approach to private law formulation. The concept of civil law codification being *self-contained* and complete, and as such capable of covering all eventualities, remains in the minds of many one of its essential features.

Even today, civil law largely cultivates this concept of codification as being exclusive in the areas it covers, also in the sense of later statutory law having absolute precedence over all prior laws in these areas. It had, or acquired, that pretence even in countries like Austria and Switzerland, which had broader interpretation and supplementation provisions. In a more extreme form, one finds this philosophy, centered around system thinking and logic, particularly expressed in the German Civil Code (BGB) and now in the Draft Common Frame of Reference (DCFR) and its progeny in the EU, as we have seen. Again, one sees here the pull of academia, which started to believe in the codified system being an adequate, if not also a true, expression of reality that could be so guided and controlled for the greater benefit of all.

However, only by moving interpretation and therefore the judge to centre stage was it able to work with that fiction and this attitude. In fact, the civil law codification idea suggests and implies a substantial measure of interpretational freedom for the judiciary, more so where the codification is less comprehensive and becomes older when especially reasoning by analogy becomes the main tool to cover newer fact situations that could never have been considered by the older texts. Yet this judicial liberty remains system-bound and contained in that sense. All must be explained from within.

It is this academic ideal and pretence that has become the main distinguishing feature of all civil law, even if it was hardly the original codification idea in France. To repeat, in this way of thinking, there are no other sources of law, whilst the updating of the model is primarily left to academic research, at best based on an extrapolation of past experiences embodied in the system. Parliament must rubber-stamp these academic efforts in legislation lest it destroys the coherence of the system. Any political input would be tantamount to interfering with the laws of Newton. The needs of the practice of the law take second place. Logic is at the heart of this endeavour and will fill the gaps or missing links. The outcome is not questioned—it is just, promotes social peace and efficiency per se—and

---

[203] See Fenet, n 202 above, xcii–xciii.

empirical testing of the results is not considered decisive. This became the civil law version of legal positivism and formalism—law as technique—which in international transactions at least may now be nearing its end: see section 1.4.15 below.

It follows that all civil law codification tends to be highly ambitious but may ultimately prove to be unrealistically pretentious. In modern times, especially in the area of personal property and the law of contract, it may have fallen far short of what is now required, see section 1.1.4 above, at least at the international professional level, and it may be questioned whether codification of this sort and its system thinking remain here the proper answer. It may be posited that, as such, they could become socially and economically destabilising.[204]

Rather, it could be argued that the challenge of modernity and its progression is constant renewal and innovation, also in private law and that the existing codified systems, at least for professional dealings, are hardly likely to be able to cope. It may thus be necessary to revisit the whole concept of civil law codification, especially now that a form of unified private law is considered for the entire EU, including England, even for transnational professional dealings where the operation of other autonomous sources of law has become evident in the international practice as well as the existence of a separate commercial and financial legal order, seen here as the essential aspects of the operation of the modern *lex mercatoria*. As mentioned before, the 2008–2009 DCFR is the latest expression of the codification ambition. Completeness, statism and staticism remain its philosophy. Within the EU, transnationalisation is then pre-empted by a nationalistic, statist law-formation ethos. It has already been said that this is very different from the approach of the UCC in the US which promotes legal dynamism and diversity and respects the other sources of law. Regardless of its name, it is not a civil law style codification at all.

But the rejection of other more dynamic non-statist sources of private law was never fully accepted, even in civil law,[205] to which, in their interpretation paragraphs, the Austrian and Swiss Codes already testified. In any event, as will be discussed more in detail in the next sections, in the area of interpretation, adherence to the system often became a question of semantics when general principle, good faith notions, custom and policy considerations connected with ethical, social and efficiency concerns, entered the equation. The need for considerable freedom of interpretation to maintain the civil law pretence to completeness led to making use of all these sources, whether or not considered independent or autonomous, regardless of how legal scholarship reacted.[206] Secular natural law tendencies thus also survived, but it was seldom admitted that this could happen and

---

[204] It has already been suggested in the text at n 11 above, that there may be a price to pay for the sense of confinement in coverage that results from system thinking in the above civil law manner and from a codification ethos of this kind, for its inflexibility and its atavism, and for its in-built intellectual prejudice. It is arguable that it is exactly this attitude that has contributed, for example, to the financial practice disappearing from civil law countries towards New York, London, Singapore and Hong Kong, all common law jurisdictions, therefore to a serious Continental decline in a strategic industry and its intellectual back-up. It appears that the legal risk in respect of newer financial products is too high for this business to stay on the European Continent. As for EU efforts along these lines, London should beware.

[205] See also text at n 223 below.

[206] There is still a more technical aspect to this when it comes to the possibilities of appeal on points of law, which was originally often considered confined to an appeal of *statutory* interpretation only, in which context an appeal on points of law derived from other sources was not possible: this was the area of fact. Another view was that, if there were other sources of law to be considered, they could become relevant only if the statutory source was fully exhausted, assuming that moment could be truly determined.

system thinking remains paramount, at least in the German tradition and so does the idea that law remains pure technique. However, there is a problem here not only with updating but more generally with newer social and other values. It may also be said that there may be clear intellectual bias.

One proper role of academia is—it is submitted—indeed to formulate hypothetical models,[207] foremost to order the mass of information that comes to us in terms of legislation, cases, reform proposals and writings all the time, and to clarify and simplify but no less to test and critique in this manner the law that derives from more formal sources such as legislation and cases or from immanent sources such as fundamental and general principle, custom and party autonomy.[208] This activity may at the same time provide better guidance for practitioners, in which connection another legitimate academic activity is

[207] By what the search for these academic models should be guided is a key problem. Extrapolation of past experiences, existing case law, and statutory texts, became the usual approach in private law, but *new paradigms* or ways of looking at things or new pictures of reality may also guide, like in the present the struggle between nationalism and globalisation in the formulation of private (transnational) law in the professional sphere. These paradigms need clear identification, and seem to be the vehicles by which the science of the law can progress. Imagination and innovation, then become the centre of academic activity.

The teaching of the positive law or the law as it is, is here not considered a proper academic subject but a high school activity. The writing of practitioners' handbooks is then equally considered unacademic and must be left to the practice of the law. That is indeed the attitude in the top American law schools, which will not engage in that kind of activity. Innovation is here the key, and therefore the law of tomorrow, not teaching and expanding the existing 'system'.

[208] See for the relationship with reality, the text at n 182 above and for new paradigms and their importance see the text at n 307 below.

It was submitted above that the law is an autonomous social force largely there to promote order, better if it promotes in that context justice, social peace, economic efficiency and growth. In doing so, participants including scholars who study this process are likely to be guided by all kind of ideas, axiomas or metaphysical 'truths' and other paradigms or mantras of which they may be little aware and which are often cultural but also generational. Even for academics, these are often not the subject of empirical study.

Hence the often biased, (semi) religious, atavistic, and conventional or purely wishful thinking even in academic findings or proposals. There is little that is truly objective in this. With present insights, it is probably not possible to do better, but it demonstrates and confirms that scientific truth hardly exists, neither in law formation nor operation, and it may also explain the haphazard way some academics opt for one approach, others for another. The effects can hardly be predicted and are in any event muddied by unforeseen consequences. It is another way of saying that academics may search for 'truth' but are unlikely to find it. But one can test and discuss these prejudices or paradigms and certain outcomes can be empirically shown to be more 'truthful' than others.

It is sometimes said in this connection that academically there are no facts without a system and no system without facts. It suggests a dialectic environment, but a key point is that all academic thinking is abstraction in which only certain perspectives are taken or angles (eg ethical, social, or economic perspectives or models or, in legal formalism, a purely legal one) are considered, so that it can as such never cover the totality of life (or reality) and its experiences, let alone their ongoing evolution. Facts in an academic sense thus become contextual fictions. It may be argued that only transcending philosophy might capture them as they are or at least may be able to demonstrate why we must beware.

In the law, one particular tension arises here between fact and norm. One may say that there are no legal norms without legally relevant facts and no legally relevant facts without legal norms. However, in academic system thinking, we work foremost on the norm side and devise models of norms that allow us to determine the legal relevance of facts (from an academic point of view), but whether that is satisfactory at the practical level is an entirely different matter. It may be argued that, in civil law, we constantly confuse here the academic with the practical or assume them to be congruous per se.

For further thought on these important issues and particularly on the method and relevance of theoretical constructions or models in the social sciences (although never elaborated for the law), reference may be made to the scepticism of KR Popper (1902–92), *The Open Society and its Enemies* (1945), *The Poverty of Historicism* (1957), and *The Myth of the Framework* (1994). Here the idea is indeed that we can study the predisposition in academic thinking through 'critical rationalism', possibly empirically. There is no scientific certainty. The academic framework is no more than an abstraction and we can still choose, which choice then becomes a moral issue and a matter of individual responsibility.

finding more structure (but not imposing system in the above manner) in the positive law, see section 1.1.5 above.

Models of this nature may also generate renewed interest in the more doctrinal aspects of the established law, where the better understanding of new paradigms should lead to academically induced innovation, but it is no less a task of academia everywhere to test its newer models for their usefulness or otherwise improve them. This is mostly not happening in civil law, academics largely missing the practical insights into what is going on and what is needed.

The true question is whether, in its application to the real world, all of this can be served by one model or perspective only. That is still the codification idea and the concept behind its system. Indeed, in civil law, the academic models as contained in the old codes aspire here to be the sole practical guides. This is a doubtful proposition that diminishes the true role of academia at the same time: academics writing practitioners' handbooks and taking pride in it!

This is not to suggest that this activity is not important, only that it is not academic. It is also not to say that it is inferior—but it is steeped in the past, at best able to fill in gaps in the system on the basis of legal reasoning that depends on the established canons of interpretation. A true academic approach on the other hand looks for new models all the time that may better capture realities as they evolve, and can more clearly explain and simplify. It is geared to innovation without which it is nothing. These newer models often require a jump or new paradigm as just mentioned. They may not be purely rational either and there is no guarantee that they will be superior. We do not have the insights to properly propel the law. But they may be better and give more guidance than the experiences of the past or what religion or mystique or intuition may otherwise suggest.

Much of it may be speculative and may upon proper empirical testing for its operational validity and efficiency lead to nothing, but at least in terms of this book, in international dealings, it enables us to contemplate alternatives to nationalist codifications, especially the revival of the *lex mercatoria* as transnational law in the professional sphere, and to suggest its structure and operation. In that context, it is also possible to find room for a more dynamic contract and even movable property law, at least for professional dealings; see section 1.1.4 above. In finding structure in, for example, the law of assignment, this may also give us new tools to respond better to present-day needs and requirements. That is here perceived as the key of academic endeavour in law and remains the attitude in the best American law schools, lost, unfortunately, for the most part in Europe, particularly in civil law countries and their universities.

1.2.12   Modern Policy Arguments in Favour of a Statist and Static Attitude towards the Formation of Private Law. Deficiency in System Thinking. Misunderstandings concerning Democratic Legitimacy and Certainty

As was explained before, the original idea of codification of private law, both in France and Germany, had to do with the emergence of the modern state and its organisational powers. It had nothing to do with more modern democratic notions, rather the opposite: state absolutist tendencies which were suspicious of civil society. In this vein, these codes or their derivatives have mostly proved willing to serve any kind of regime since.

In more modern times, in conclusion it may be said that four concepts in particular support the statist and static or rule-based approach to private law formation, and therefore the civil law codification approach: (a) the idea that through an intellectual system we can fully capture human relationships and activity and subsequently guide and control it; (b) that the state through its academies has here the deeper insights and should promulgate the result and centralise this law; (c) that this is also better democracy (assuming that we now have a properly elected legislature) as all rules are then ultimately seen as policy requiring validation by a democratic process; and (d) the idea that this approach provides greater legal certainty, which is then valued as a special good in its own right. These latter two points have already been discussed in section 1.1.5 above and will not be here extensively revisited but only summarised.

Much has also already been said on legal system thinking in private law. The key question for practitioners, legislators and judges is here the same: extrapolation of past experiences, or developing instead a view of what is needed in an ever-changing world and moving forward with it? To repeat: do we live with an account of human behaviour that can scientifically be clarified and is in essence based on repetition? That is the neoclassical view in macro-economics, often believed to have failed us, but we struggle with the same problem in the law. Or must we accept that the future is different from the past and cannot be systematically captured. In this latter view, we need to become more comfortable with dynamic law that at least in the private relationships, therefore in private law, *develops itself* all the time through its different sources, therefore in essence autonomously, although aided by legislation or treaty law if there is an obvious and useful need (as well as the required insight). It is cut down by clear public policy or public order considerations. Preserving the existing system is not then itself one of these considerations.

These insights are all the more relevant now that domestic systems have ever greater difficulty updating themselves and dealing with globalisation. In any event, they have proved in practice to be riddled with contradictions and inconsistencies; it must be admitted that even the new Dutch Civil Code of 1992 or the Brazilian one of 2002 could hardly catch up. In fact, it has already been said that the whole notion of codification in the civil law sense is in the balance.

The democratic argument is superficially understandable, but in democracies, even now, private law legislation, at least in civil law countries, is mostly formal democracy only, and not therefore participatory, not much political choosing, but largely parliamentary rubberstamping of academic models. It may in fact be one of the reasons of legislative inertia and lack of interest in this activity. It may lead to much delegation to the executive branch. In any event, many civil law countries still have much private law that did not come through a democratic process at all. More importantly, neither did the common law. It never affected national or even international acceptance, for example in private international law.

Of course, in Europe, legislative inertia could now be reversed, notably at EU level, but that does not necessarily produce a true democratic back-up either, or promote technical and operational insight. How democratic and insightful, for example, the DCFR, which since 2008–2009 has been circulating as a model for a European civil code, and more particularly, the Draft EU Regulation on a European Sales Law (CESL), is or would be if stamped into law at the EU level, may be seriously questioned, see section 1.4.19 below. The project is academic and still proceeds on the basis that academia has the answers and politicians must follow. In any event, there is no sufficient authority in the EU for such a project that could only be justified on the basis of the dubious ground that the completion of the internal market requires it.[209] At least professionals do not want that kind of law.

The further argument that all law is policy or values, and therefore needs democratic validation, may also require some greater elucidation, as these policies and values are then thought to be for the political process alone to select and determine and are in that approach considered legitimate only if made or imposed through the formal legislative process of a state, preferably democratic, but it would be a sad day indeed if they could only emerge in the law in this manner.

That all law is public policy in this sense was nevertheless also one of the tenets of legal realism in the US or at least one strand in its thinking, see sections 1.3.3 and 1.3.6 below. This view no less inclined to some form of statism in private law formation and application, but it was never universally held nor widely followed and states were hardly seen as monopolists of social values.[210] Indeed, although policy considerations are often crucial in the formulation and interpretation of the law, at least in the United States it is now better understood that not all is *public* policy. Social policy is as important[211] and is continuously expressed more in particular through case law, also of a private law nature, and in fact no less in the way the law is explained and applied between practitioners. Economic consideration and efficiency notions may be no less relevant in this connection.

It may thus be seen that in an advanced decentralised social and political environment, policies and values emerge more freely and move the law forward. As such, they are expressed and find respect in many different ways and are *not* solely articulated through the political process whether or not supported by academic models. Especially in democracies, these policies should not be considered the sole preserve of legislators, and this argument is not valid in support of all law, including private law, having to be exclusively statist and being nationalised in that sense.

Much of the development of consumer law was, for example, based on a better appreciation of the difference in the relationship between consumers and professionals, and therefore resulted from more sophisticated relationship thinking in private law and emerged

---

[209] In this connection, it should also be noted that, in the US, private law remained state law and there has never been a move to federalise it. Not even the UCC is federal law, but it is true that American students in the major law schools are used from the beginning to 50 jurisdictions operating side by side and there is as a consequence some 'national' private law in terms of a general common overlay besides the federal legal order. It also stimulates an understanding of, comfort with, and respect for legal diversity from the beginning. That is a great advantage as compared to the background of most European students.

[210] Subsequently, there even started to result a denial of the difference between public and private law: see JH Merryman, 'The Public Law–Private Law Distinction in European and American Law' (1963) 17 *Journal of Public Law* 3; EJ Weinrib, *The Idea of Private Law* (1995); JL Coleman, *The Practice of Principle* (2001) 3ff.

See for a more recent discussion N Jansen and R Michaels, 'Private Law beyond the State? Europeanisation, Globalisation, Privatization' (2006) 54 *American Journal of Comparative Law* 843, and, by the same authors, 'Private Law and the State' (2007) 71 *RabelsZ* 346, 352. See further MJ Horwitz, 'The History of the Public/Private Law Distinction' (1982) 130 *University of Pennsylvania Law Review* 1423.

The true difference is in the cause of action and remedies. In private law, even if reinforced by mandatory state intervention, eg in the area of consumer law, the recourse remains damages (or specific performance). In public law, there will be enforcement by governmental agencies, whilst private parties do not have redress unless they have specifically been given so. In this respect the distinction remains of major significance and also operates at the transnational level. The modern *lex mercatoria* will be respectful of domestic public law in this sense if it has a sufficiently close connection to the case in question. See also ss 2.2.6ff below.

[211] MA Eisenberg, *The Nature of the Common Law* (1988) 28.

through case law,[212] often long before legislators became active in this field. The same was often true for workers' protection, and this is a process of law formation that continues all the time.

On the other hand, it should also be considered that dealings between professional participants do not normally produce great moral issues or problems of (re)distribution. The economic system and how it works, is known to, accepted, and depended upon by them,[213] and special protections, like those now often necessary in consumer dealings, would not normally be applicable amongst professionals. Between professionals, notions of good faith, which are often invoked as public order concepts, as we have already seen, may in fact mean less protection, a more literal approach to contract interpretation, fewer disclosure duties, and renegotiation in the case of changed circumstances only in extreme situations. This cannot be repeated often enough, and fundamentally also goes against a unitary approach.

The more important conclusion is that, however intermingled public and private law intervention may now be, there is a compelling need, and full legitimacy for private law formation beyond the reach of states. In fact, true democracy is respectful of diversity in law formation and of the operation of different communities under different rules unless legitimate public policy or a public order issue are at stake. So is the rule of law. Again, nothing supports the idea either that states have here the deeper insights in the reality of human relationships, in the needs of society, or in anything else. Typical nineteenth-century German thinking about private law and its formation comes here to an end.

1.2.13 Interpretation and System Thinking in Civil Law: *Begriffs-* and *Interessenjurisprudenz*. Modern Hermeneutics

The *Ius Commune* had not been able to develop a coherent vision of interpretation. It accepted multiple sources of law. In its treatment of formal (written) legal texts, it did not incline to literal interpretation either, especially not of the *glossae*, and it may even have veered to what we now call teleological interpretation. The idea inherent in the law was considered dominant, and finding it the most urgent activity, which was certainly also true for the *Corpus Iuris*. Sophistry and hair-splitting were avoided. Natural law undercurrents could not be ignored. A mathematical approach based on pure deduction or syllogism never seems to have gained much ground, but analogy was popular and proceeded on the basis that if the originators of the relevant legal texts had thought of it, the particular facts would have been similarly covered.[214] In contract, as we shall see in Volume II, section 1.3.2, there did not develop a coherent approach to interpretation either, but the literal interpretation was here also avoided whilst writers like Grotius started to think in terms 'aequitas'.

---

[212] Lord Bingham in *Interfoto Picture Library Ltd v Stiletto Visual Programmes Ltd* [1989] 1 QB 433.
[213] See for a definition of professionals in this connection, s 1.1.8 above.
[214] See more particularly Baldus at C 6.50.1 under 1, and Lucas de Penna, *Tres Libri Codicis* (C 10–12) at C 12.15.1.

After the codification, there was at first much emphasis on literal interpretation.[215] It was indeed supported by the use of syllogism in which a black-letter rule (which could also be derived from case law) operated as the *major* and the facts of the case as the *minor*. For example, if it were decreed that everyone must drive his or her vehicle on the right, then that would be the rule or the major. You happened to drive your car on the left: that would be the fact or the minor. The result is a violation of the law (in this case often the criminal law narrowly interpreted anywhere, but it could also lead to an action in negligence). This is also called *deductive reasoning* and is quite simple on its face.

Logic is here at the heart of the legal interpretation process, in which the rule is taken as literally as possible (whilst historical interpretation is never accepted). Clearly, the weakness is in the choice of the major and the minor: ultimately this technique only deals with form not substance. It creates problems especially where, in our example, the person in question used a bicycle, which might not have been a 'vehicle' in a literal sense. Interpretation through *induction*[216] in which the higher category is 'all that moves on wheels or mechanically', or finally through analogy[217] could then follow. Here reliance on *the system* as a whole could provide further 'certainty'.

Whatever the appearances, and however logical and perfect the system may have looked, this type of inductive or analogical reasoning was thus not necessarily automatic in its results or even objective, and implied in fact much discretion and variation which posed the question of the institutional power of the judiciary. However limited this power may have been perceived to be originally, if it did not work in the sense that it did not yield a reasonable or sensible result, formalism of this nature had to be abandoned. Interpretation on the basis of the purpose of the rule or the policy behind it (*purposive* or *teleological* interpretation) would then appear unavoidable, assuming the purpose could be clearly established, which in the present example could be either limitation of bodily harm of others or the efficiency of traffic movement, but was at first not favoured. Depending on

---

[215] See also the reference to Aubry and Rau in n 187 above. The original French idea of the role of the judge was indeed that of '*bouche de la loi*'. There was no interpretional freedom, interpretation in essence also being left to the legislator. This also affected the activity of the *Cour de Cassation* which was to preserve this system and guard against judicial interpretational freedom. It was considered as such part of the legislative branch and would quash offending judgments and refer the matter to another court for decision. But as of 1837, the *Cour de Cassation* started to take the lead in interpretation and it is now generally considered part of the judicial branch and supervises the interpretation activity in the lower courts.

[216] This technique is also referred to as *per genus proximum et differentia specifica*, leading to a logical *Begriffspyramide*. In civil law, it is a commonly used method for analysing case law. By removing extraneous facts one may find the higher rule and by adding others one may find the new lower rule. In consumer and worker protection, for instance, one may conclude that the protection of weaker parties is the higher rule; adding in small investors one may then conclude that they are also protected under a lower rule, and so on. So much seems clear, but considerable problems arise where, for example, civil delicts are compared with more narrowly defined criminal acts, or where legal structures that may at one level seem comparable, have in law a very different function (such as security interests and conditional sales and transfers, see vol III, ch 1, ss 1.1.3 and 2.1).

The inductive method is therefore by no means objective, and is always dependent on structural characterisations and policy issues or objectives. In civil law, the method may have to be restrained to fit within the overall system of the applicable code and will not then produce any rules which become too remote from the larger codified framework.

[217] From the point of view of logic, analogy is a problematic concept that nevertheless has great importance in legal reasoning. It is about the relationship between norm and fact in one situation to be applied to another, eg, if cars are subject to the rule that they must be driven on the right, by analogy this requirement could be considered to exist in respect of bikes. But similarly the situation for bikes might be compared to that obtaining in respect of mopeds which in many countries may be used on pavements moving in any direction. Again, there is nothing objective per se in these choices either.

the purpose the rule was given if not clearly expressed in the rule itself, this approach was no less subjective.

Another obvious and probably even more immediate problem was what to do with clear contradictions which arise in any formal system of rules and what with extra-judicial considerations, like those of justice, social peace, and efficiency, especially when they themselves were contradictory as policy objectives. It is clear that logic is not here the answer either or that as a minimum it must be accepted that the law practices an own notion of logic in legal reasoning. It was thus not surprising that, in Continental Europe, the codification notion with its pre-set intellectual system of rules and its addiction to logic, became increasingly dependent on more liberal interpretation techniques, at least to support its claim of completeness and of being able satisfactorily to cover all eventualities, including newer fact situations and modern societal developments. This became all the more necessary in the absence of regular formal amendment which proved to be politically unrealistic to expect. Judges were increasingly left to engage in elaborating and adjusting the system.

In civil law, legal thought in the twentieth century particularly started to concentrate on this question of interpretation. This translated into the continuing importance, first of systemic and analogical reasoning in dispute resolution, but subsequently also of teleological interpretation and then even into the appreciation of extra-legal considerations, especially pressing ethical, social, and efficiency considerations. As mentioned before, it moved the judge to centre-stage, even in civil law, which originally had been much more concerned with creating a model or system in the law that would work better especially in the daily practice and lead to a better life for all. It had been much less concerned with dispute resolution which was correctly perceived as an imperfect art. See also the discussion in section 1.4.16 below.

Extra-legal considerations could then also come in and concern in particular these ethical, social and efficiency considerations or practicalities. In Germany, this led early to the theory of *Interessenjurisprudenz*, which accepted that such considerations, when sufficiently pressing, could be taken into account in the judicial function and adjudication, as against that of the *Begriffsjurisprudenz*, which in its interpretation technique continued to rely foremost on the text of the law and its system. This is not to say that it was without merit, as it managed further to develop, in an intellectual manner, large areas of the law and attained in case law often greater clarity and order, but it became too restrictive.

Hence the *Interessenjurisprudenz*, which had its intellectual base in the later work of von Jhering, as we have seen[218] and which received a more sociological expression in the so-called 'free law finding' movement (*Freirechtslehre*) often associated with the work of Hermann Kantorowicz[219] (a student of Max Weber) and Eugen Ehrlich.[220] Both approaches led ultimately to adjudication and dispute resolution becoming the centre of academic attention, even in civil law, whilst there was henceforth less interest in the adequacy and efficiency of the law as a whole and of private law more particularly in its daily application

---

[218] See R von Jhering, *Scherz und Ernst in der Jurisprudenz* (1884) and *Der Zweck im Recht* (1887), see also n 165 above and accompanying text. Koschaker, n 1 above, 279 attributed system thinking to eighteenth-century thinkers like Wolff, but considered the idea abandoned since the free law finding movement in early twentieth-century Germany. This may have been premature, see also n 65 above for the desperate search for system in all case law analysis in Germany. See for the attitude of Portalis in France, s 1.2.10 above.

[219] H Kantorowicz, *Der Kampf um die Rechtswissenschaft* (1906).

[220] E Ehrlich, *Grundlegung der Soziologie des Rechts* (1913).

in ordinary life. All became dispute resolution. In the emphasis on litigation or the law's role in dispute resolution, there is here a move from *macro-* to *micro*-thinking, in case law much as there had long been in common law. It is submitted that this also presented a major shift in the academic approach to law in civil law countries. By the later part of the twentieth century, original system thinking acquired a further narrowing perspective and became system perfection through case law.

Given this perspective, from earlier on it became an important issue whether a freer attitude towards (statutory or code) interpretation was acceptable and how this was to be handled. In fact, the issue had already been raised in Germany before the BGB was finally enacted in 1900. The more liberal attitude never meant a free-for-all and it only advocated greater flexibility, particularly to meet social needs, yet it sharply divided the followers of von Savigny, who were likely to be more systematic in their approach, on the one hand, and those of von Jhering, who were likely to be freer and more practical, on the other.

The twentieth-century development shows the ebbs and flows of these two approaches. By mid-century there appeared to be more freedom in this respect in legal writing than at the beginning and the end. Courts felt at first more constrained, but towards the end of the century there seemed to be greater flexibility in case law than there was in academic writing, where typical codification thinking still puts the system first, especially in Germany as we have seen, and interpretation is then rather seen as a way to elevate and complete it.[221] This is strongly supported by legal positivism, that remained prevalent in much academic discourse in Europe, see also the discussion in section 1.4.15 below.

The more extrovert, freer, socially oriented approach, one finds earlier reflected in France in the (later) writings of François Geny, in those of Saleilles and of Léon Duguit (who in its extreme form only recognised social, not private rights) at the turn of the nineteenth century, later in that of Demogue, and in the Netherlands in the writings of Paul Scholten. It had a direct effect on interpretation techniques. Philosophically, this is the field of *hermeneutics*. In a more *methodological* sense, it concerns the explanation of texts and application of rules in the manner as just discussed. In a more *ontological* sense, it concerns the intellectual power over this process but also the more conserving impact of culture, tradition, and habits or practices on the one hand and the expanding ideas of justice, social peace and efficiency on the other.[222]

Whatever the approach, a more ontological view readily leads to the insight that the purpose of the law is always extra-legal in that it serves practical, social, ethical, or even economic or political objectives, and that the law therefore never stands alone or is an end in itself. Except in areas where the law is clearly settled and becomes largely mechanical, as perhaps still in the conveyancing of real estate and the following of traffic laws, rules become more like guidelines, in their application largely dependent on the configuration of the facts and on the ends the law is meant to serve. Its objectives, whatever they may be and however determined, thus become important tools in the law's interpretation, also in private law. This may also be seen or expressed as 'policies'.

---

[221] See s 1.1.4 above for the notion of good faith and how its freedom may be recaptured in system-thinking by academia, even for the operation of the good faith notion; see in particular n 65 above.

[222] In this connection reference may also be made to H-G Gadamer, *Wahrheit und Methode* (JCB Mohr, Tubingen, 1972, English trans *Truth and Method* (Seabury Press, New York, 1975)), see also references to other modern German thinkers of a similar disposition in n 185 above.

What a reasonable person may have thought (differently for professionals and consumers), or what is fair in the circumstances, what good faith requires, or what is socially acceptable and practiced, or what is efficient or makes sense may thus become equally normative. One sees here a clear connection with American 'realism' and its law in action and search for better law which will be further discussed in section 1.3.4. below.[223] Legalism, positivism and formalism[224] are then abandoned. This may be supported by widespread redistributory ideas in respect of risk, particularly in consumer dealings.

Nevertheless, civil law judges in particular will remain concerned in their reasoning how to fit their decision into the system, even when forced to go beyond it in substance. This has also to do with their institutional powers which, especially on the European Continent, do not formally include law formation. In private law, there is certainly a tendency also in the judiciary to remain and to be seen as remaining in conformity with the system. In Germany, this attitude is the one still favoured in the leading work on legal methodology of Karl Larenz, as we have seen, who, although aware of the law's dynamics, captures it in interpretation of the national system only.[225] Again, the hope is that this contributes to certainty in the legal outcome, even though new cases multiply all the time, rules become antiquated, and factual situations diverse or ever more unusual in terms of old rules. Indeed, in this book, the accent shifts to finality in transactional matters and in payments and otherwise to predictability as a dynamic rather than a static concept. See section 1.1.5 above.

More importantly, the daily practice of the law outside litigation, which is much more crucial than the latter, may not be properly served in this manner; see further section 1.4.16 below for the law in action and law in litigation.

1.3 The Origin and Evolution of the Common Law. Its Approach to Law Formation and to the Operation of Private Law

1.3.1 Common Law and Equity

It is now time to come to the other great original legal system in Western Europe, that of the English common law.

It is impossible to thoroughly understand its beginnings without forming some mental picture of the England of the late thirteenth and early fourteenth centuries, when in the

---

[223] This connection seems obvious but was ultimately not accepted by Kantorowicz himself, who saw the difference in the attitude towards the rule as a major intellectual divide, see 'Some Rationalism about Realism' (1934) 43 *Yale Law Journal* 1240. In short, Kantorowicz saw legal rules as abstract structures whilst he assumed that the common law lawyers could never consider them separate from facts.
One cannot escape the impression that Kantorowicz's emphasis had changed since his first book of 1906 and that he had become more interested in systematic thinking and abstraction in the meantime. See for a fuller discussion VG Curran, 'Rethinking Hermann Kantorowicz: Free Law, American Legal Realism and the Legacy of Anti-Formalism' in A Riles (ed), *Rethinking the Masters of Comparative Law* (Oxford, Hart Publishing, 2001) 66.
[224] See more particularly the discussion in s 1.4.15 below.
[225] See n 2 and further n 185 above.

time immediately following the death of Bracton,[226] it had become clear that no general reception was to be accorded to Roman law and that English law was to be an independent development. It meant that, even where English law followed Roman law, it was following that law by choice and not by necessity.[227]

Nevertheless, the common law developed in a manner very similar to Roman law, that is, action-based, originating in the law of procedure.[228] This was favoured by the centralisation of the legal protection under the King almost from the beginning of the Norman conquest of England after 1066 AD. This centralisation was in turn a natural consequence of the feudal system, with the Crown at its pinnacle. In this system of essentially landholding, royal protection was demanded and given in land and criminal matters, but was eventually extended to civil matters also, especially tort. The original idea was that if the King agreed with the request for protection, he would issue the relevant order or *writ* to his sheriffs to take the necessary action.

This intervention was soon assumed by the royal *curia* with more regular procedures under which standardised writs or remedies (or indeed procedural relief) would be given provided the claimant could prove the basic facts on which the remedy was based. This function of issuing writs was later centralised in the office of the Lord Chancellor whilst the *curia* in the thirteenth century expanded into three royal courts in London (Common Pleas for normal private suits and supervision of the lower sheriff courts, King's Bench for politically-oriented matters or appeals, and Exchequer for taxes) supplemented by travelling or 'itinerant justices' operating on the King's behalf. Writs then became commands to the relevant judges to call the defendants into their courts to resolve disputes of fact in connection with the relief provided under the writ.

There were still specialised mercantile or commercial courts, as we have seen in section 1.1.1 above, which administered their own laws. Moreover, there was still some old Anglo-Saxon and also newer feudal law on the basis of which disputes were resolved in the ancient communal and newer private (and feudal) seigniorial or palatine courts for local tenants, but the issuing of writs leading to proceedings in the King's courts became popular. At first, they largely depended on favour, but they soon developed into the formulation of certain, but still in fact quite narrow, standard types of relief, which would be granted as of right, however, and lead to redress if the judges found that the factual conditions for the relief existed, whilst leaving the determination of these facts to a jury. These writs were subsequently written up and became accessible in the *register brevium* (a *breve* being another word for writ).

As the royal courts became the normal venue for these suits, they would by no means hear all types of complaints; it all depended on the writ. Thus, the claimant had to find the right form of action, without which he would fail, and there were no broader substantive rights. The King, through his Chancellor, at first retained freedom to develop new writs, but this power to make in fact new law was questioned after the basic English charter of *Magna Carta* was agreed in 1215, and it was curtailed in the Second Statute of Westminster in 1285. The facility to expand became limited to actions in similar cases

---

[226] See n 240 below.

[227] Hanbury, *Modern Equity* (1935) 1.

[228] For a full history of the English law, see WS Holdsworth, *History of English Law*, 16 vols (1922–56). The last four volumes were edited by AL Goodhart and HG Hanbury.

only (the writ *in consimili casu*). If there was doubt, the matter was to be referred to Parliament for statutory intervention. Thus even in common law, statutory intervention was not alien to its progression although it remained unusual.

The writ system itself still allowed a nucleus of more predictable law to develop whilst the writs evolved somewhat further and older ones were abandoned. It early brought *one national* law, although centralisation was at that stage a more outstanding feature than nationalism. This law was original, therefore not Roman, although of Anglo-Saxon or Germanic and feudal origin. It is interesting that no external law was used to achieve this unity in the laws of England. The result was a true English development, which led to a distinctive legal system and culture that was largely procedural, basically practical, and evolved over a long time in a peaceful, constant, but also haphazard manner.

Eventually under this law, the royal courts started to judge the 'fairness' of the older Anglo-Saxon and feudal laws surviving outside this system, as was at the time also done on the European Continent (see section 1.2.5 above); subsequently they suppressed them or brought them within the common law. In the process, they also subsumed the commercial law or law merchant into the common law (see section 1.1.1 above), which had until the sixteenth century been developed largely in trade with foreigners and had obtained some continental flavour. This also happened to Church law, as we have seen. As a consequence, from the seventeenth century onwards, the merchant and ecclesiastical courts were merged into the royal courts as the ancient Anglo-Saxon and feudal courts had been earlier.

Although the common law was, and is often presented as customary law of 'general immemorial usage', it originated rather in the writs and forms of action, resulting in constantly evolving judge-made law. Decisions were published from the thirteenth century in so-called Yearbooks, although judges would often invoke precedent on the basis of their memory and of what they had seen earlier in cases before them or remembered colleagues saying. The creation of the Inns of Court in which the practising lawyers—judges as well as advocates or barristers—would assemble and be educated, was favourable to this development. Four of these Inns still exist today, and all judges and barristers must be members. However, the rule under which these precedents had to be followed only developed much later.

As after 1285 the King or his Chancellor was no longer free to formulate new writs, common law was slowed in its further development. It acquired a rigidity that eventually necessitated a supplementary approach, statutory help remaining exceptional. This new approach emanated also (like the writs) from the King through the Lord Chancellor, but in a different system of law with its own courts. They acted not on the basis of writs but rather of *subpoenas* and sat without a jury whilst their practitioners were solicitors, although barristers later took over much of the court activity. This was the law of *equity*, administered by the Courts of Chancery.[229]

---

[229] For this development, it may be of interest to quote from the first edition of Hanbury, *Modern Equity* (1935):

In the mediaeval period, the Chancellor was the most important personage in the country next to the King ... A very important function of the Chancery was the issuing of writs ... A setback to the too rapid increase in its powers was provided by the growth of Parliament ... but this had its defects ... unadaptability ... [W]hile the certainty and rigidity of the law was a good thing, it was equally a matter of satisfaction, at any rate to the poorer class of litigants, that there should be some source ... whose justice should ... be able to grant relief in hard cases ... The law ... in that period presented somewhat the appearance of a young infant ... [L]ike most

At first, the Chancellor was given discretion to decide in pressing cases according to his own conscience, but after the Chancellors became secular persons (starting with Thomas Moore in 1529), the discretion faded.[230] As from the later eighteenth century, the further development of equity became increasingly embedded in precedent, as the (common) law also was, and equity thus acquired a rigidity of its own.[231] As a consequence, it became clear that equity was to remain incidental, and it never developed into a full system of more natural or equitable justice, but, importantly it went as far as to issue injunctions when fair and equitable. Although an independent system of rules, it could not ignore the common law and was meant to follow, not to obstruct it, and was as such only a reflection of the common law's imperfections.

It managed to fill a number of important gaps or shortcomings, however, and developed the trust whilst also recognising conditional and temporary ownership rights in movable property. In contract, it created the rescission remedies and also the notion of specific performance. More recently, it allowed notions of reliance or promissory estoppel to be substituted for consideration to back up the binding force of contract. Fiduciary duties were introduced to protect inequality of the parties, especially in situations of dependency. Most importantly, equity would combat many other forms of abuse directly. In all, it generally infused the old law with some more ethical notions, a more up-to-date set of values perhaps, and a greater sense of fairness, which even now can lead to new forms of relief. Thus important new vistas for original development are still open on occasion. In England, that concerned the law of assignment[232] and early in the twentieth century the development of

things that are both young and strong, obstinate and unbending. The mediaeval Chancellors were peculiarly well fitted to relieve hard cases; they were ecclesiastics and learned in the civil and canon law … They would give or withhold relief not according to any precedent, but according to … the merits of the particular case before them … [and] their innate ideas, prompted by morality, honesty, conscience, or knowledge of good or evil. From these abstract virtues springs equity … Maitland points out that in the thirteenth and fourteenth centuries the Chancellor very probably did not regard himself as administering new law. In many cases we see him working hand in hand with the common law judges … The great [new] weapons of the Chancery procedure were the writs of *subpoena* and *quibusdam certis de causis*, whereby the Chancellor could summon a defendant before him to answer certain *unspecified* charges. The very vagueness of these writs made it impossible for a plaintiff to fail … on a mere technicality.'

[230] The facility was believed to have become more or less mature by the time of Lord Eldon as Lord Chancellor at the beginning of the nineteenth century. Until the fusion of the administration of law and equity in England in 1873–75, the equity judges continued to operate separately (Court of Chancery). Even now, technically, law and equity have not merged, only their administration. The equitable powers still reside in a special branch of the ordinary courts, but other judges may also exercise this jurisdiction concurrently.

[231] In *Keppell v Bailey* [1834] ER 1042, 1049, the Chancery Court famously held that 'incidents of a novel kind cannot be devised and attached to property at the fancy and caprice of any owner'. In *Hill v Tupper* [1863] 2 Hurlst 7 C 121, it was further said that: 'A new species of incorporeal heriditament cannot be created at the will and pleasure of an individual owner of an estate and he must be content to take the sort of estate and the right to dispose of it as he finds the law settled by decisions, or controlled by act of parliament.'

In the US where there appears to be even greater flexibility and more recently statutory law has helped especially in respect of floating charges (Art 9 UCC), there are nevertheless also limits, especially in testamentary grants and grants of servitudes, see *Johnson v Whiton* 34 NE 543 (1893) and *Werner v Graham* (1919) 183 P 945, 947. Indeed there is a traditional resistance in the US, eg to recognise equitable servitudes in chattels and they are in any event cut off by the bona fide purchaser protection principle: see for a rare discussion, Z Chaffee, 'Equitable Servitudes on Chattels' (1928) 41 *Harvard Law Review* 945 and 'The Music Goes Round and Round: Equitable Servitudes and Chattels' (1956) 69 *Harvard Law Review* 1250.

[232] See *Dearle v Hall* (1828) 3 Russ 1, allowing the first collecting assignee if in good faith to retain the collections.

the floating charge[233] and much later the Mareva injunction.[234] It is thus fair to say that the equity judge still assumes at times broad law formation power and creates or develops new legal structures. In modern times, in England, Lord Denning in particular proved an activist equity judge.[235]

This shows some similarity with the development of the praetorian law or *Ius Honorarium* in ancient Rome, although there had already been some similar element in the original creation and expansion of the writs.[236] Equity remained more incidental in its relief but early on was particularly active in the area of fraud and breach of confidence;[237] in the development of the equity of redemption when forfeiture was threatened under a real estate mortgage; and later especially in the transformation of the use into the modern trust as already mentioned, where equity got its real chance. It was a facility the civil law missed. For more ethical considerations, on the European Continent, there had originally been the Canon law although it had a limited reach and later there was the natural law school, but both proved in a number of areas less creative than equity was in England.

As has already been said, the greatest practical differences between common and civil law today (apart from the former's more procedural attitude and feudal land law, and the latter's more systematic, codified and intellectual approach) are, in so far as the law of property and obligations is concerned, precisely in the products of equity, and in the more activist attitudes of judges under it, especially in combating abuse.[238] These differences are notably in the future proprietary interests in personal property, equitable mortgages and (floating) charges, trusts, constructive trusts, tracing, unjust enrichment, agency, equitable assignments, set-off and netting. Then there are the fiduciary duties in cases of dependency. In contract there are the rescission facilities. Most importantly, in the area of remedies, equity developed *injunctions* as (chancery) court orders to *prevent* rather than to indemnify harm after the fact. These court orders have no true equivalent in civil law and are issued when it is 'just and equitable' to do so, which implies considerable judicial discretion.

---

[233] The technique has generally been upheld in English case law since the end of the nineteenth century: see *Salomon v A Salomon & Co Ltd* [1897] AC 22; *Government Stock v Manila Rail Co* [1897] AC 81; *Re Yorkshire Woolcombers Associations Ltd* [1903] 2 Chap 284; and *Illingworth v Houldsworth* [1904] AC 355.

[234] *Mareva Compania Navietra SA v International Bulk Carriers SA* [1975] 2 Lloyds Rep 509.

[235] 'Equity is not beyond the age of childbearing' in *Eves v Eves* [1975] 1 WLR 1338, 1341, but recent case law appears more cautious, see 16(2) *Halsbury's Law of England*, 4th edn, reissue (2003) 149.

[236] See also WW Buckland and AD McNair, *Roman Law and Common Law*, 2nd edn (1952). See for the praetorian law, s 1.2.2 above.

[237] In fact, in this area the powers of the equity judge have never been questioned, see the old rhyme: 'These three give place in court of conscience: fraud, accident and breach of conscience.' It still suggests original power and no need for precedent or statute in these areas, *cf* also Lord Bingham in *Interfoto Picture Library Ltd v Stiletto Visual Programmes Ltd* [1989] 1QB 433.

[238] Although equity judges would at times rely on Canon law and Roman law texts and in particular on seventeenth-century Roman–Dutch legal scholarship and its fusion with natural law in the secular natural law school since Grotius, this was as supporting arguments and they were not directed thereby. In the areas mentioned, the law of equity managed to move much further and ultimately retained comparatively more flexibility as we shall see throughout, especially after Continental private law was set in concrete in national codifications in the nineteenth century, even if equity itself became more restrained as we have seen. Legislation took over, also in England, but never completely.

Greater judicial discretion coupled with judicial activism is more generally found in all equitable matters and explains much of the judicial activity in the law of trust and in company and bankruptcy law. Closely related to injunctions, is the order for *specific performance,* which is also an equitable relief measure. It remains more incidental and dependent on the facts of the case; see particularly Volume II, chapter 1, section 1.4.1. But the development of the law of equity remained limited to certain areas and is even there patchy. As in the cases of trusts, companies and insolvency, there only developed a more systematic approach through legislation.

Equity further used a number of *maxims,* which tended to broaden its reach somewhat further. Important ones are: 'equity looks to intent rather than to form', 'equity will not permit a statute to be made an instrument of fraud' or 'equity does not act in vain', 'where there are equal equities the first in time shall prevail', and so on. Others, however, rather limited it: 'he who comes to equity must come with clean hands', 'he who seeks equity must do equity', 'delay defeats equity' (laches), and 'equity follows the law' which suggest at least in principle (although certainly not always) a subordinate role.

The greater problems with equity resulted, however, from the duality in the courts. Points of law had to be dealt with in the King's courts, points of equity in the Court of Chancery. If points of law and equity were raised in the same case, the result was that the case would go backwards and forwards between both sets of courts causing endless delays and costs, as vividly recounted by Charles Dickens in his novel *Bleak House.*

In the nineteenth century, this led to the fusion of the courts of law and equity (in the Judicature Acts of 1871, 1873 and 1875). The result was one court system, although not strictly speaking the merger of the two sets of courts or laws. The Court of Chancery is still competent in typical equity matters, like trusts, company and bankruptcy cases, and grants injunctions if such is just and equitable. The main importance of the reform was that points of equity could now also be raised before the courts of law and vice versa.

Of the old law courts, the King's (Queen's) Bench (which since 1970 has included an Admiralty and Commercial Court Division) and the Court of Chancery became Divisions (together with the Family Court) of what is now called the High Court of Justice in London, to which the itinerant justices, who normally come from the Queen's Bench, also belong.

The above history explains a number of important aspects of English law and its legal system. As it is not intellectual or systematic but rather practical and the result of gradual development, no great need was traditionally felt for complete clarity in the authorities and competencies of the courts and in the type of laws they administer. There was always some overlap of functions, which gradually separated but also came together again. Thus originally the King was supreme but delegated authority to the Lord Chancellor, appointed and discharged by him, first to issue writs upon which his courts would act and later to give equitable relief. Subsequently, the courts acquired virtual independence from the King, whilst the Lord Chancellor as issuer of writs and later as equity judge also became independent (but could be dismissed) in these functions, which were not merged, whilst the King could still issue amnesties or commute sentences.

The Lord Chancellor could thus streamline the procedures in the King's courts through the writs; later he could in equity also derogate from their powers. Although he could not do so officially, as it was still said that 'equity followed the law', he could create a string of exceptions, for example fiduciary ownership-types giving beneficiaries proprietary protection whilst respecting the ownership position at law. He could also impose injunctions to order litigants to do certain things or refrain from doing them or he could issue an order or decree to comply with the law pending full litigation.[239]

The 1873–75 Act established that in the case of a conflict between law and equity, the latter prevailed (section 25(11)), but it should be realised in this connection that equity had by then lost its function of appealing to the judge's conscience and was largely formalised in a set of incidental rules. Inconsistencies remain, notably in set-offs, tracing, compound interest, illegal contracts, limitation of actions, and monetary remedies for wrongs. However, there seems no great urgency, at least not in England, to sort these inconsistencies out.

Through the existence of equity as distinguished from common law, common law may be referred to in the narrow sense of being the private law different from equity and statutory law, but the term is also commonly used for all private law in the Anglo-American world to distinguish it from the civil law. It then includes the other sources of English law, especially equity. It is a confusing terminology of which the novice should be aware.

1.3.2 The Common Law Approach to Scholarship

It has already been noted (in section 1.1.2) that Roman law never meant much in England, even though common law developed in similar ways. In the first four centuries AD, when England was part of the Roman Empire, Roman law must have been in force, but there were hardly any traces left of it when the common law started to develop. Henri Bracton tried to show the seeming similarities between the early common law and Roman law in the thirteenth century,[240] but this proved an idle, although spectacular effort. In the previous section, it was mentioned that in equity Roman law concepts were sometimes invoked but that was by choice, not by necessity.

In fact, although both Roman and Common Law were procedural in nature and developed in not dissimilar ways, Roman law was particularly incompatible with the Germanic or Anglo-Saxon notion of seisin or physical possession, which dominated the law of chattels in England, and with the feudal law that dominated the law of real estate and put all ownership of land in the Crown subject to individual estates or tenure in land, again based on the notion of seisin or physical possession.

The feudal system in respect of land and the physical notion of possession or bailment in respect of chattels still prevail in the common law to this day. Feudal law therefore still covers the traditionally most valuable class of assets. This law had also much influence on the law of chattels, as in equity the proprietary interests in land are often considered

---

[239] Thus the Court of Chancery was a prerogative court set up by the King to achieve greater justice against the common law. When, however, he tried to set up another prerogative court to protect *himself* against the common law, which also covers public law writs to protect citizens (*habeas corpus*) or to give orders to officials (*mandamus*), the result, the so-called Star Chamber, became an important issue in the Civil War that ended in 1640, when it was removed and the principle (since Magna Carta of 1215) that the King operated under the common law and its courts was firmly re-established. In this struggle, the King at one time even considered adopting the Roman law and ousting the common law altogether.

[240] H Bracton, *De Legibus et Consuetudinibus Regni Angliae* (see also the edition by T Twiss with a nineteenth-century English translation).

extended to them, which is of particular interest for beneficial and future interests in these assets. It primarily concerned here trusts and conditional or temporary ownership forms. It resulted in a flexible and open system of proprietary rights in chattels and intangible assets (see section 1.1.4 above and Volume II, chapter 2, sections 1.3.6 and 1.10.2) of which there is no real equivalent in civil law.

The practical nature of the common law never combined very well with the much more intellectual approach of the *Ius Commune*. In fact, in England, there was not much academic interest in the law at all. Legal teaching at first took place in the Inns of Court but rapidly declined and this decline continued well into the eighteenth century. Besides law reports, there were hardly authoritative legal texts. All depended on what lawyers picked up in practice and on their 'feel'. Only towards the latter part of the eighteenth century, Blackstone (since 1758 the first Professor of Common Law in the newly created Vinerian Chair at Oxford) was able to write down the first commentary on *both* private and public law (including criminal law), as common law never developed or set much store by distinctions in this regard.[241] The Downing Chair of Law was founded in Cambridge in 1800, but like the Vinerian Chair in Oxford was unsuccessful in creating a proper law school as there were no degrees in Common Law. Until that time, only Civil (in fact Roman or Roman-related) Law was taught (by Regius Professors of Civil Law) in both Oxford and Cambridge supported by a degree, but hardly attracted students. Modern law schools were first established at University College in London in 1826 and at King's College in London in 1831.

Only after a 1846 Select Committee of the House of Commons demanded a systematic instruction in the 'scientific and philosophical aspects' of the law, and called for proper academic degrees in the (common) law, did things change, but by 1900 there were still few law graduates and only about ten law schools. This number had risen by the 1970s to about 30 and is now around 75. Treatises and academic writings have also multiplied.

They became significant much earlier in the USA, as we shall see (in section 1.3.4 below). In England, well into the 1960s, much that was taught in law schools was taught by way of preparation for the solicitors' exam, and most law teaching remained part-time. Eminent law scholars (like Pollock, Anson, and Dicey at Oxford or Maitland at Cambridge) were few. Thus the status of legal scholarship remained subdued. In fact, in England for a long time the informal rule obtained that only the opinions of dead scholars could be cited as authority in court.[242] Opinions of the Bar (from whose ranks judges still largely come) were much more important than scholarly findings. Members of the Bar mostly held no university degree in law at all.

It may thus be seen that only in the last 35 years have English law schools developed more broadly, and English judges and the Bar have become more receptive of legal scholarship, which itself has become more imaginative and ultimately also showed some interest in sociology, economics and psychology, but it still retains a broadly formal (or doctrinal) bias,[243] intent largely on making some sense out of disparate cases and statutory texts. As such it remains essentially reactive and even system seeking.

---

[241] W Blackstone, *Commentaries on the Laws of England* 4 vols (1773).

[242] See *Donoghue v Stevenson* [1932] AC 562, 567.

[243] Note that in England and the US (in fact in the entire common law world) the term 'doctrinal' stands for the positive law and often for the more formal approach. That may be different in civil law, where it more generally refers back to legal doctrine or the results of academic thinking, which suggests a more jurisprudential attitude.

1.3.3 The Common Law Approach to Precedent, Legislation or Codification, and Statutory Interpretation

It was mentioned before that the common law eventually accepted the binding force of *precedent*, also referred to as the *stare decisis* (*et quieta non movere*) rule. It is often considered one of its basic traits, very different from the civil law approach,[244] but has been adhered to formally only since the end of the nineteenth century.[245] It ties a judge to his own decisions as well as to those of all his colleagues at the same or higher level, although only to the *ratio decidendi* of the decision, that is, to the legal principle involved. Observations on the law with no particular relevance to the case (*obiter dicta*) have no such force and effect.

The *stare decisis* rule was never so rigorously followed in the USA, where there are far too many cases and the Federal Supreme Court and lower *federal* courts are under the Constitution at times highly political bodies that must respond to quickly changing circumstances so that they could hardly be so bound. Still, they respect precedent in principle although the Supreme Court will overrule itself if it considers it necessary. Within a State of the Union, in matters of state law, the lower state courts still follow their own precedents, subject to the decisions of the higher courts, but the Supreme Court of each state will also overrule itself if necessary. Federal courts will apply the law of the state in which they sit, except in federal questions.

At least in England, the precedent rule also applies in equity,[246] which became as a consequence just as rigid as the law, and strictly speaking it applied even to findings on customs and their existence.[247] As already mentioned (in sections 1.1.2 and 1.1.7 above), this created rigidity even in the application of customary (commercial) law and risked depriving it of the flexibility and movement that are inherent in it. Particularly in this commercial law area, in England, custom now thrives perhaps less than one would expect, although it might still do better in this area than in the rest of private law.

In civil law, there was strictly speaking no similar need to follow precedent because of the codification of the law and its specific rules, which often pretended to contain the whole system of the law. Civil law traditionally is not dispute-resolution-oriented, as we have seen, but was meant to provide a system to regulate daily life as a whole and make it easier for all. Litigation is here the exception. In common law, the emphasis was different precisely because the law could only be known in the context of litigation.

---

[244] The Latin expression of the principle might suggest a Roman law origin but nothing would be further from the truth. Justinian law in C.7.45.13 had expressly rejected the principle: judges must judge only on the basis of the laws, not precedents (*exampla*); see also Baldus at C.7.45.13 pr. That remains the attitude in civil law till this day. It is also the attitude of international courts; see Art 59 Statute of the International Court of Justice (ICJ), and of arbitrators. The *Ius Commune* would allow, however, an interpretation to become customary when it acquired the same legal status as custom. This became generally accepted; see Baldus at D.1.1.37 under 2 and at C.9.1.4 under 4.

[245] In fact, it was only formally recognised by the House of Lords in 1898 in *London Tramways v LCC* [1898] AC 375.

[246] For equity, ossification in this manner dates at least from the early nineteenth century, see n 231 above.

[247] It set customary law in concrete, see also n 21 above and accompanying text. Custom thus lost much of its dynamic character; some believe that this was done to prevent courts from getting confused, see JH Baker, *An Introduction to English Legal History*, 3rd edn (1990) 418; see also RW Aske, *The Law Relating to Custom and the Usages of Trade* (1909) 23, and HJ Berman and C Kaufman, 'The Law of International Transactions (*Lex Mercatoria*)' (1978) 19 *Harvard International Law Journal*, 221, 227.

There is convergence here as aging civil law has become much more dependent on interpretation which manifests itself especially in case law. Civil law judges normally also try to stick to a line and do not want to be erratic. Nor do they want to be inefficient. In that sense, civil law judges also accept the persuasive force of precedents, whilst in the absence of clear codified rules, or in the case of old ones, they may rely even more firmly on reforming precedent within their interpretational freedom. Scotland, even if often considered a civil law country, accepted the binding force of precedent more generally, again explicable in the absence of a codification of its Roman-oriented laws.

Given the *stare decisis* rule in much of the common law, and barring correcting statutory law, it became more difficult to react to changing moral and social attitudes or to what was clearly wrong or had been superseded in the law and as a consequence the *stare decisis* rule came under pressure. Although it officially still prevails in England, in 1966 the Lord Chancellor announced that the House of Lords could henceforth overrule itself,[248] but that was not to apply to lower courts.[249] The system in England is therefore now much as in the US and always left considerable room for artful interpretation and the *stare decisis* rule probably never was what it is often reputed to be.[250] In fact, in England Lord Bingham, one of the most important modern judges and ultimately the (last) Senior Law Lord, said: 'I do not think any of us aims to be consistent. I actually regard consistency in a judge as a vice.'[251] This reflects individual attitudes but also confirms that English judges remain pragmatic, solution-, not system- oriented. Precedent is here only a guide. The greatest judges would not have it otherwise.

The idea is, nevertheless, that by following precedent in the absence of any general codification, the common law sustains itself in a similar rule-based manner, even though these rules are unwritten. It seeks in this way to promote predictability. Hence the frequent references to the rule in such and such a case. The crucial difference is, however, that these rules are not set in a coherent framework or applied systematically. There is no comprehensive effort to relate them to each other except in more academic writing, which has a tendency, at least in England, to become doctrinal, but law application remains fact based. Statutory law in the private law area, with the notable modern exception of the USA, as shown in the Uniform Laws and in the US Bankruptcy Code, and perhaps also with the exception of nineteenth-century commercial law statutes in England, does not have coherence as a primary aim either and remains therefore often a collection of incidental and disparate rules written for particular situations or covering particular concerns. In essence, it is still considered remedial and there definitely remains a lesser urge to conceptualise in common law, although this is no longer so in the US.

At the beginning of the nineteenth century, therefore at the same time that the *stare decisis* rule became more firmly established, Jeremy Bentham started to argue in England in

---

[248] *House of Lords Practice Declaration* [1966] 3 All ER 77.

[249] Notwithstanding Lord Denning's dissenting opinion in *Gallie v Lee* [1969] 1 All ER 1072.

[250] There is much confusion about this rule of precedent. It is submitted that the rule should only concern the way law is applied to fact situations, and not abstractly determine what is 'law' and therefore operate in isolation on the norm side: see for various views of precedent in common law countries, M Eisenberg, *The Nature of the Common Law* (1988) 50, 55.

Thinking in terms of precedent should also not be confused with analogical reasoning, which is rule-based and therefore more developed in civil law although even then it remains a narrow concept in the expansion of the system.

[251] Obituary *Daily Telegraph* 13 September 2010.

favour of codification, not on the basis of natural law as developed in the school of Grotius, but rather on the basis of his well-known utilitarian principle that the legal system should also contribute to the greatest happiness of the greatest possible number of people. [252] In his view, this primarily required a comprehensive body of laws, but this principle was also to be applied to each individual rule. Some of this has returned in the modern 'law and economics' movement in the USA, as we shall see. Although Bentham was principally opposed to the natural law school, in the practical elaboration of codes his approach would have led to some similar rational deductive manner of rule formulation. It would also have been normal to expect some *universal* law to emerge from this utilitarian approach but it was eliminated through his surprising requirement of codification at the *national* level.

Opposition to the codification idea, which in England never got much further, came in particular from Edmund Burke,[253] who did not believe that through legislation or otherwise one could or should overturn the fruits of the past. Bentham's disciple, John Austin[254] although a utilitarian, subsequently formulated the law, also private law, as pure command of the sovereign leading to a strong form of national positivism, which in England has deep roots until today and is probably reflective of a nationalistic attitude that might have preceded Burke, Bentham and Austin, but which was typical of the nineteenth century and the common core in the teachings of them all.[255] Thus law, even private law, only issues from sovereigns.

In Burke's approach, there was here an early vision of a *Volksgeist* in the development of the law, much as von Savigny would later propound in Germany (see section 1.2.9 above) and one still finds it in the US as well. But there was no preference for statutory law and none of the theoretical systematic attitude to rule formulation, which von Savigny wanted as a first step to, and a precondition for, codification at national level and which, in typical nineteenth-century scientific fashion, was ultimately favoured in Germany as we have seen. In fact, it led in the civil law codifications to a revolutionary break with the past—with Roman *as well as* local laws or custom, no matter how much lip service was still paid to them. Burke was here more consistent in leaving the development of the law to natural (but national) forces.

---

[252] 'Codification Proposals' in J Bentham, *Complete Works* (1854) 4. See also P Schofield and J Harris (eds), Jeremy Bentham, *'Legislator of the World': Writings on Codification, Law and Education* (Clarendon Press, 1998) 5.

As recently as 1974, Scarman LJ thought that the common law system had reached the end of the road, saw judges on the one hand as being duty bound to sometimes resist the will of Parliament, but argued on the other hand for the common law itself to move to a statutory basis as an exclusive source of law, see *English Law, the New Dimension* (Hamlyn Lecture, London, Sweet & Maxwell, 1974) 77. He wanted here also general principles, rather than detailed rules. The Law Commission set up in 1965 was seen as the centre of this codification activity but it soon downgraded its ambitions to more piecemeal proposals for law reform.

[253] *Reflections on the Revolution in France* (1790, reprint Oxford, Oxford University Press, 1993).

[254] See R Campbell (ed), J Austin, *Lectures on Jurisprudence*, vol 2, (James Cockroft & Co, 1875) c XXXVII.

[255] The nationalistic or perhaps more cultural historical element was first articulated in England by E Burke, *Reflections on the Revolution in France* (1793). Burke and Bentham thus came together in this nationalistic sentiment (although not in the codification idea), which in the teachings of J Austin culminated in the view that all law depended on the command of the sovereign, see Austin, n 254 above, vol 2, 91–103.

There is also an American version of nationalism that focuses on American values as the basis of the law as we shall see. See amongst those who see American law embedded in typical American values eg R Post, 'The Challenge of Globalisation to American Public Scholarship' (2001) 2 *Theoretical Inquiries in Law* 323, but in the 'realist' sense law may be validated in ways other than by state command or legislation alone. In the US, this type of nationalism has therefore not led to the idea that all law is necessarily statist and immanent law is not as such suspect, at least to the extent that it may be considered part of the American way of life.

It meant that, after the Napoleonic wars, English law was not overtaken by the codification ethos, even though now also becoming more nationalistic in the modern nineteenth-century statist sense. However, streamlining also came to be necessary in England, and even there, statutory law proved the only efficient way of doing so, overtaking the equity jurisdiction in this respect, but in England statutory law never claimed to cover the whole field as the civil law codes tended to do and remained essentially remedial or an expression of policy geared to particular situations or objectives (such as consolidation or simplification and later also social objectives). It remained in England only one source of law besides the old (common) law, equity and customary laws and only prevailed if it explicitly amended or abolished the earlier rules. Statutory law, at least in England, remains in that sense subsidiary, corrective and incidental even today.

In England, the court system was substantially modified and simplified by statute, first in the Common Law Procedure Act of 1854 and more fully in the Judicature Acts of 1871, 1873 and 1875 as already mentioned. They also unified the procedural laws. These acts made it possible to invoke law and equity in all courts (section 25(11) of the Act of 1873). Moreover, they abolished the forms of action (or old writs) and allowed all lawsuits to start with a simple (writ of) summons which did not need to articulate a specific type of claim or cause of action but only its substance. However, in practice, the relief that could be obtained in this manner still corresponded to that available under the former forms of action. This was particularly clear in tort cases where the old forms became the modern intentional torts. A more analytical approach became possible, however, and in case law eventually a broader tort of negligence was developed.

At the same time, important legislation was introduced in other areas of substantive private law, also in the commercial area, including the Bills of Sales Acts 1854, 1866, 1882, 1890 and 1891; the Bills of Lading Act 1855 (supplemented by the Carriage of Goods by Sea Act (COGSA) 1971 and 1992); the Bills of Exchange Act 1882, the Factors Acts 1823, 1842, 1877 and 1889; the Partnership Act 1890, the Sale of Goods Act of 1893 (replaced in 1979 by an amended version); the Maritime Insurance Act 1906; the Companies Acts, including the winding-up of companies, 1844, 1856, 1862, 1948, 1967, 1986, 1989, 2004 and 2006; and the Bankruptcy or (now) Insolvency Acts 1824, 1849, 1861, 1869, 1883, 1914, 1985 and 1986, 1994, and 2000, supplemented by the 2002 Enterprise Act. In 1925, the whole law of real property was restated by statute in the Law of Property Act. Also in the area of torts and consumer protection, there is now much legislation.

There is no doubt that even in private law, legislation has also become more policy oriented, as indeed modern civil law statutes are also. On the other hand, conceptualisation remains rare, it was already said that the English are not given to generalisations and mistrust general concepts and system thinking. This is still very clear in the company, insolvency, and financial services legislation. However, the English Bills of Exchange Act 1882 and Sales of Goods Act 1893, drafted by Sir Mackenzie Chalmers, have been lauded as great pieces of English conceptual (commercial) legislation. So is the 1996 English Arbitration Act, much inspired in the connection by the UNCITRAL Model Act.

In the US, the private law is still a matter for the different states of the Union, although they have obtained some uniformity in uniform laws prepared by the Commission for Uniform State Laws, of which the Uniform Commercial Code (UCC), co-authored by the American Law Institute (ALI), is the broadest and by far the most important one, accepted in all states as we have seen.

The UCC was substantially the product of the efforts of Professor Karl Llewellyn, who showed strong conceptual thinking, reflected at least in the original set-up. The result was an important reforming statute that did much more than restate the old law and was to some extent a reminder of the codification approach in Europe, very different therefore from the modern English approach to statutory law and its draftsmanship, which, except for the nineteenth-century commercial law statutes just mentioned, often still remains directed towards special situations and is casuistic in that sense. However, whilst not claiming sole authority and respecting other sources of law, especially the common law, equity, and custom unless overruled, the UCC remains very different from civil law codifications and, as already observed, is not a true codification in that sense.[256]

In the US, at individual state level, there had since long been some civil codes (the so-called Field Codes, inspired by Benthamite thinking), for example in California, in which much of the old common law was written up. However, their nature was always substantially different from that of the European Codes in that they did not overrule the common law either. In essence, they served only to facilitate access to that law.[257]

In the US, there are further the modern Restatements in which various areas of the law are summarised (like contract, trust and agency) by the ALI, a private institution created in 1923 by the American Bar Association, which also co-operated in the drafting of the UCC as just mentioned. The uniform laws as well as the Restatements are regularly updated. Although the Restatements are not legislation and may not even have persuasive force, their unifying impact is considerable. Like the method in the UCC, the one in these Restatements is more directly intellectual, and, again, reminds one in this aspect of the European codification approach. There is no equivalent in England, even though it has the Law Commission that suggests from time legislative improvements in the law, but rather on more specific issues as we have seen.

Also in common law countries, legislation raises the question of *statutory interpretation*. In most of them, particularly in England, statutory law of this nature is essentially still seen as a foreign element in the development of private law, mainly correctional and therefore *restrictively* interpreted, much as criminal laws are in civil law, and there remains therefore as much room as possible for law and equity. In any event, if the statutes do not clearly abolish older law, the relevant case law can still be pleaded. In that sense, all statutes in the area of the common law are considered only a restatement, elaboration or correction of what went before, unless specifically stated otherwise.[258]

---

[256] As mentioned in n 25 above, it also misses the typical nationalistic element and is practical: see further RM Buxbaum, 'Is the Uniform Commercial Code a Code?' in U Drobnig and M Rehbinder (eds), *Rechtsrealismus, multikulturelle Gesellschaft und Handelsrecht* (Berlin, 1994), 197; and J Gordley, 'European Codes and American Restatements: Some Difficulties' (1981) 81 *Columbia Law Review* 140.

[257] In fact, in 1888 the Californian Supreme Court in *Sharon v Sharon* (1888) 75 Cal 1, 13 declared that in instances where the Code was so confused and uncertain that it could be given no intelligible meaning, it could not be considered to have changed the common law. Already under its s 5, it was stated that the Code was substantially the same as prior law.

[258] More boldly, it was held in *Dr Bonham's Case* (1610) 77 ER 646, 652 that if an Act of Parliament was against common law right and reason, common law would control it and adjudge it void. At least in England, that is not the practice. As Parliament cannot act *ultra vires*, the courts cannot annul statutes. However, in the US the judiciary can hold statutes unconstitutional ever since the famous case of *Marbury v Madison* 1 Cranch 137, 2 L Ed (1803) 60. For civil law in respect of private law formation, see the situation under the French CC (Art 5) which expressly withholds that right from the courts and is here illustrative for much of the rest of civil law (see also s 1.2.5 above *in fine*).

In this connection, it is well known that English judges remain particularly wary of teleological interpretation of statutes, more so than their modern American counterparts,[259] and will commonly also not consider the preparatory instruments as a guide to (historical) interpretation.[260] This also excludes the consideration of the statutory history and parliamentary commentary in the drafting stage, the so-called *exclusionary rule* which finds its counterpart in contract in the *parol evidence* rule, see Volume II, chapter 1, section 1.2.4. Although the exclusionary rule has now been abandoned in England and the parole evidence rule much softened, the courts still remain reluctant to move too far from the texts.[261]

Again, this may be different in the US, especially in the so-called *realist* approach or legal realism as we shall see shortly.[262] In that approach, the Americans clearly allow room in appropriate cases for other considerations including pressing ethical, social and efficiency considerations. Even in their so-called codes like the UCC, which calls for liberal interpretation they do not follow literal or even systematic reasoning either or at least do not see it as a bar to achieve social adjustments or to evolving economic, utilitarian and efficiency considerations.

This difference with the English attitude is borne out by the English Interpretation Act of 1978, which was largely a restatement of the Interpretation Act of 1889, often considered a little precious and pedantic, even in England. The restrictive interpretation technique means in practice that the English legislator is required to be much more specific and precise than its civil law counterpart and that as a consequence the drafting of statutes is often cumbersome and unduly detailed, geared to particular situations and problems. But it is also an attitude and contracts in common law tend to be equally verbose and elaborate reflecting no less specific situations and worries whilst in this manner risking leaving other eventualities uncovered. It has already been said that the English legal mind is uncomfortable with and remains wary of generalisation. In short, in traditional common law practice, contractual drafting is not conceptual either, rather more practical and often long. This can have advantages but particularly poor examples of this type of *statutory* drafting appeared between 1985 and 1987 in the English Insolvency, Companies and Financial Services Acts.

For the reason stated, the technique of drafting lucid legislation seems to have eluded the English, although the nineteenth-century commercial statutes were sometimes more conceptual as noted before. So is the Uniform Commercial Code in the USA. Even in England, there are more modern exceptions such as the new English Arbitration Act of 1996 also already mentioned (which had, however, the UNCITRAL Model Law for an example). They also had largely single draftsmen. Clearly, it does not always need to be this way.

In statutory interpretation, there is in any event in England a gradual change in favour of a more 'purposive approach' 'to promote the general legislative purpose of enactments',

---

[259] See for the US s 1.3.4 below.

[260] See Lord Denning, *The Discipline of the Law* (1979) 11ff and his comments in *Bulmer v Bollinger* [1974] Ch 401, see text below.

[261] Legal certainty was often invoked as a conclusive argument, but Lord Denning in *Denis v Johnson* [1979] AC 264, 276 proved sceptical: 'Some may say—and indeed have said—that judges should not pay attention to what is said in Parliament. They should grope about in the dark ... I do not accede to this view. In some cases Parliament is assured [by the Government] in the most explicit terms what the effect of a statute will be ... In such cases, the court should be able to look at the proceedings.' See also the House of Lords in *Pepper v Hart* [1993] 1 All ER 42.

[262] See for a discussion RS Summers, 'Interpreting Statutes: Legislative History' in *Essays in Legal Theory* (2000) 251.

which eventually may also affect the drafting technique and there is a more flexible approach in contract interpretation as well.[263] Nevertheless, Lord Denning set the tone in the *Bulmer* case as follows:

> [T]he draftsmen of our statutes have striven to express themselves with the utmost exactness. They have tried to foresee all possible circumstances that may arise and provide for them. They have sacrificed style and simplicity. They have foregone brevity. They have become long and involved. In consequence the judges have followed suit. They interpret a statute as applying to the circumstances covered by the very words. They give them a literal interpretation. If the words of the statute do not cover a new situation—which was not foreseen—the judges hold that they have no power to fill the gap. To do so would be naked usurpation of the legislative function ... [T]he gap must remain open until Parliament finds the time to fill it.

One may perceive some irony in this statement, particularly by this judge who did not shrink from exercising considerable discretion, but statutes continue to be strictly interpreted in England, a rule, in fact, of long-standing validity (at least since 1343).[264] It allows more room for the old common law but there is clearly also a modern concern that the judiciary gets too close to legislative activity under the guise of interpretation.[265]

Under the influence of EU law, which, in the civil law tradition, is much more conceptual in its legislative approach, English judges will now also consider the preparatory work, however. EU law is further used to and perhaps even based on the expectation of teleological interpretation, which also affects the attitude in the UK, as was already discussed in the *Bulmer* case. It is unavoidable in the interpretation of EU Directives. It is nevertheless undeniable that, in common law for the time being, a restrictive attitude is still taken to the interpretation of statutes. This means that there is at least in private law ample room for the operation of law, equity and custom *besides* statute (as section 1–103 UCC also recognises). As we have seen, this is, besides the lack of system thinking, the fundamental difference with the civil law codification approach.

1.3.4 Intellectualisation and Conceptualisation in Common Law. Modern American Academic Attitudes towards the Law and its Development: Legal Formalism and Realism

In the foregoing, it was repeatedly pointed out that traditional common law tends to be practical and is not intellectual. It certainly never went through an intellectual phase as the *Ius Commune* had already done in the time of Bartolus and Baldus, and again but more markedly in the natural law school of Grotius and Pufendorf, and in the nineteenth-century German Pandektist School. Even if modern civil law became

---

[263] See for a number of recent House of Lord cases, Lord Hoffmann in *Investors Compensation Scheme Ltd v West Bromwich Building Society* [1998] 1 WLR 896, 913 and *BCCI v Ali* [2001] 2 WLR 749, in which in contract interpretation a reasonable-man approach was adopted. Yet at least as a starting point, the literal attitude towards statutory enactments remains largely intact.

[264] See also TFT Plucknett, *A Concise History of the Common Law* (1956) 333.

[265] See Lord Simonds in *Magor & St Mellons RDC v Newport Corp* [1952] AC 189, rebuffing Lord Denning on appeal.

ultimately dependent on positive state law or at least on *national* law (which could also be case law), all codification thinking was and remains basically intellectual and conceptual as we have seen. It found as such no clear counterpart in common law, also not when statutory law started to become more prevalent, although in the US through the Uniform Laws and Restatements, intellectualisation and conceptualisation became more prominent than elsewhere in the English-speaking world.

Indeed, in the US in the twentieth century, a need came to be felt to study the law in a more academic and abstract fashion. It was promoted at first by the coming into being of major national law schools like those at Harvard, Yale, Columbia, Chicago and Berkeley[266] and the requirement that all lawyers obtain an academic qualification in the law. At least in private law, this American legal scholarship was at first closely connected with the traditional search for *legal consistency* in rule patterns (whether derived from case law or legislation), which as we have seen continues to be the drift of the English academic approach .

This so-called *legal formalism* (an American term only invented later) was thus primarily intent on finding a more coherent system of rules especially in case law. Indeed, it remains the direction of present English scholarship, which is closely connected with legal positivism,[267] as such a reminder to some extent of the rule-based codification approach with its emphasis on intellectual coherence. Indeed, this scholarship particularly looks for the logical thread in disparate case law and often also in statutory enactments and means to articulate the underlying consistency of the rules and to incorporate or distinguish (new) cases on that basis. However, it never elevated this system to the highest pinnacle or believed it complete and self-sufficient as civil law was more likely to do, although this kind of legal formalism often also led in England to an academic predilection for black-letter law and automaticity in its application. For the applications of the rules so found or recast, common law like civil law, emphasised at first literal interpretation supported by logical reasoning through syllogism and subsequently analogy and inductive reasoning; see also section 1.2.13 above.

Unlike in England, in the US this more formal attitude—for case law articulated especially by Langdell at Harvard in the late nineteenth century—did not last long. There was also the attitude derived from the natural sciences and their mathematical models, much as there was in Germany at the time as already noted before, but the Americans soon became sceptical of a mechanical approach and they were more willing early to draw their conclusions and abandon it altogether.[268] There, the openly accepted political role of the US Supreme Court and of the federal circuit courts in particular, helped to create a greater interest in extra-legal or policy objectives or considerations behind the law and eventually in legal concepts and values rather than in their black-letter manifestations.

It means that law, even private law, including judicial decisions came to be seen primarily as policy instruments to promote welfare in particular and that such law and such decisions were no longer considered neutral or objective per se. Decisions were seen as 'rationally indeterminate' which means that they were not causally to result from rules. There is at most a special legal causality in this regard that is not mathematical. The behaviour of judges and juries and what motivated them is then of particular interest and acquires a

---

[266] See also LI Applebaum, 'The Rise of the Modern American Law School: How Professionalisation, German Scholarship, and Legal Reform Shaped our System of Legal Education' (2005) 39 *New England Law Review*, 251.

[267] See also s 1.4.15 below.

[268] See also R Feldman, *The Role of Science in Law* (2009).

special support in 'law and psychology', but altogether the study of the impact of the law in terms of welfare promotion but also of utility and efficiency became the more likely priority, hence at the academic level the connection with sociology, economics, the political sciences and the interdisciplinary approach that follows. It also explains the renewed respect for philosophy. In its most pronounced form, in academia the search may be on for an altogether newer model that lifts all positive law up to a higher level of enquiry and insight. What the Germans sought in the nineteenth century in system thinking acquires here another impetus: a search for a greater truth behind the law and its operation that will explain more. The expectation is then that there is a better academic model in the making and that we can reach for a better world in this manner.

This then becomes the real heart of the modern study of the law and starts in law school but is primarily an academic exercise that poses many problems in terms of reliability of outcome. Not only are the paradigms of this process and the process of their identification often unclear but the results of, for example, empirical research which must test the results, may also be superficial. Yet the effort itself is credible and, at least from an academic perspective, very necessary. European law schools are far removed from this world and in their practice orientation are usually still mechanical and hardly academic or innovative in that sense. American academia at the top rather seeks to test the practice for its continued validity according to newer academic insights developed in the above manner. It is in fact given over to critique of this nature, no more, no less and to the innovation that follows.

Dissenting opinions make it possible to follow the debates within the judiciary. Where such dissenting opinions are sometimes also given in Europe, it is indeed clear that there is not the some leeway in the alternatives. Whether in England or on the Continent, the judiciary does not have a similarly strong constitutional position vis-à-vis the legislature in law formation. Judges have therefore fewer alternatives and like to be more circumspect and perceive on the Continent system thinking and reasoning of that nature as their protection. English judges stay or profess the appearance of staying within precedent for much the same reasons. It has already been noted several times that, in this aspect, current thinking in England (at least at the academic level) may be closer to that of the European Continent than to that in the US.[269] It shows that the common law tradition is not uniform and is in fact subject to a considerable divide (between the US and the rest).

In the more open American approach, the search for *consistency* and *legal certainty* thus acquires another dimension. It is not the system or the existing black-letter rules that are believed to guarantee them in a useful manner. Rather, in all decisions, the outcome is ultimately deemed to be determined by what in society or in the relevant community is considered right or otherwise normative, articulated in each case. This becomes then the idea of 'policy'. Particularly in areas where the law remains unsettled, rules, even if derived from statute, largely acquire here the character of *guidelines*. This is reminiscent of the approach of the free law movement in Germany (see section 1.2.13 above), but probably goes well beyond it.

In the US, at the top, the Constitution is often considered complete in its arrangements and therefore always requires a flexible approach to interpretation to be able to cover rapid

---

[269] See PS Atiyah and RS Summers, *Form and Substance in Anglo-American Law: A Comparative Study of Legal Reasoning, Legal Theory, and Legal Institutions* (Oxford, Clarendon Press, 1987).

changes in society. This permeates the whole legal system and the approach to it. For private law, this is reminiscent of code interpretation in civil law, but without its systemic reasoning and the connected inherent limitation on innovation and dynamism. New circumstances and new factual patterns show the way. Law derives from fact: *ex facto ius creatur* is the leading principle so that there can be a living law. Rather than to a systematic approach (on the norm side), it confirms a policy oriented attitude (on the fact side), although in the US the extent of the freedom of the courts in this connection, and especially of the Federal Supreme Court in respect of the Constitution, remains a hotly debated political issue.

In this connection, the US Constitution is often said to have in itself ample resources for the changing needs of successive generations.[270] Thus from early on, constitutional law was meant to define 'the whole American fabric',[271] in which connection the courts were thought to speak for the whole experience as a nation and to reinterpret the Constitution on the basis of the prevailing American value system.[272] It helped that, in its general norms, like the due process, interstate commerce, and full faith and credit clauses, and in its bill of rights, a special overlay of fundamental principle was included in the text itself. It constitutes a system of higher norms or values that are constantly re-balanced in the ongoing construction of a collective entity, which is intended to be—in the language of the Constitution—an 'ever more perfect Union'.

To this should be added the already mentioned American facility of the federal courts to overrule statutes if deemed unconstitutional. State courts may also do so in respect of state statutes. They will be tested against the relevant state constitution which is likely to contain similar principled language as the US Constitution, in appropriate cases subject ultimately to the control of the Federal Supreme Court.

This attitude has had an important impact on all legal interpretation in the US, also on that of state (private) laws and even of contracts, which tends to be no less 'policy'— oriented. In the US, a liberal interpretation technique of statutes in this manner is now explicitly accepted in many fields of the law, in private law expressed particularly in section 1–103(a) UCC, as we have seen.[273] Similarly, in contract interpretation, mere deductive approaches or other forms of legal or logical formalism were increasingly rejected.[274] Legal sophistry is here particularly suspect. This is supported by academia in its search for newer ways through its improved models.

This more sociological approach in law-application and interpretation became apparent early on in the works of Oliver Wendell Holmes, the later Supreme Court Justice, and of Roscoe Pound at Harvard. Social needs would thus be considered in determining legal

---

[270] See notably PB Kirkland (ed), Felix Frankfurther, *Of Law and Life* (1965) 59.

[271] See John Marshall in *Marbury v Madison* n 258 above.

[272] See Oliver Wendell Holmes in *Missouri v Holland* 252 US 416, 433 (1920).

[273] 'To promote its underlying purposes and policies', which was explained as to simplify, clarify and modernise the law governing commercial transactions, to achieve uniformity amongst the various states and to permit the continued expansion of commercial practices through custom, usage and agreement of the parties; see also s 1.1.2 above. Here we see custom appear as an *alternative* and favoured source of law, as good faith (more timidly) is now also under the UCC, see vol II, ch 1, s 1.3.7.

[274] See MA Eisenberg, 'The Emergence of Dynamic Contract Law', (2000) 88 *California Law Review* 174. Here all axiomatic/deductive reasoning is abandoned and normative reasoning adopted, in which non-legal arguments will be considered and brought within the law. Where they conflict, such a conflict will be resolved in the context of deciding the case.

issues. The new approach itself was further elaborated by Karl Llewellyn in what, since the 1930s has been called the American School of *legal realism*.[275]

Indeed, legal *formalism* is then usually associated with the notion that law is rationality, to the point of forming a mathematical/logical model, and that its rules are pre-set and make the administration of justice a mechanical activity of application: law as technique, much of which can be found in the civil law codification ethos as we have seen. In this approach, law and fact are fundamentally separated, the law being considered as a system of rules and deemed self-contained, whether or not encapsulated in codification notions, and there is no outside goal. It assumes an order of its own, which, if properly applied, leads to the right answers.

The realists on the other hand[276] had more difficulty in precisely defining their method, but basically looked at the law as it functioned in society (law in action) and at its *operational sufficiency*.[277] Here the idea emerges that the law automatically changes in its application to newer situations whilst law and fact are thus not fundamentally separated. Again, in this approach, extra-legal objectives and policy considerations became important in the interpretation of the law.[278] The modern study of the law in the US attempts to guide this process better.

[275] See for the many other supporters at the time, MJ Horwitz, *The Transformation of American Law 1870–1960; The Crisis of Legal Orthodoxy* (1992) 171. The term itself appears to have first been used by J Frank, *Law and the Modern Mind* (1930).

[276] See for the modern views of formalism, B Leiter, 'Positivism, Formalism, Realism' (1999) 99 *Columbia Law Review* 1138. See for the classical texts on legal realism, K Llewellyn, 'The Effect of Legal Institutions Upon Economics' (1925) 15 *American Economic Review* 665; 'A realistic Jurisprudence—The Next Step' (1930) 30 *Columbia Law Review* 431; 'Some Realism about Realism' (1931) 44 *Harvard Law Review* 1222; 'The Normative, the Legal and The Law-Jobs: "The Problem of Juristic Method"', (1940) 49 *Yale Law Journal* 1355; and *The Bramble Bush: On our Law and its Study* (New York, 1951).

Most of the leading ideas were already contained in OW Holmes, *Path of the Law* (1897) and were authoritively restated by F Cohen, 'The Problems of a Functional Jurisprudence' (1937) 1 *Modern Law Review* 5.

[277] See L Alexander, 'With Me, It's All er Nuthin'—Formalism in Law and Morality' (1999) 66 *University of Chicago Law Review* 530, 531. Thus the essence of legal formalism becomes the systematic application of a rational system leading to mechanical decision taking and autonomous reasoning. It then stands for positivism, see B Leitner, n 276 above at 1145; see also B Neuborne, 'Of Sausage Factories and Syllogism Machines: Formalism, Realism, and Exclusionary Selection Techniques' (1992) 67 *New York University Law Review* 419, 421 (claiming that 'pure formalists view the judicial process as if it were a giant syllogism machine ...'); see further N Duxbury, *Patterns of American Jurisprudence* (1995) 10, putting emphasis in this connection on 'the endeavour to treat particular fields of knowledge as if governed by interrelated, fundamental and logical demonstrable principles of science'.

[278] There is a more sophisticated critique of legal formalism, especially in the US, which challenges more generally the law's claim to immanent moral rationality and inherent coherence: see R Unger, 'The Critical Studies Movement' (1983) 96 *Harvard Law Review* 561, 571, objecting to legal reasoning built on it as a pretentious and self-centred method of legal justification in dispute resolution concerning matters that are in truth often social and therefore ideological, philosophical or visionary in nature.

Here the critique especially concerns unjustified claims to impersonal or objective purposes, policies, and objective principles as tools of legal reasoning. The law's claims to objectivity and rationality are then altogether denied. See in support of this kind of formalism, however, EJ Weinrib, 'Legal Formalism: On the Immanent Rationality of Law' (1988) 97 *Yale Law Journal* 949; 'Jurisprudence of Legal Formalism' (1993) *Harvard Journal of Law & Public Policy* 583.

The discussion is not then about automatic application of black-letter law but the prime purpose is rather to separate law from politics whilst maintaining its autonomy. Religion, morality and considerations of social peace and of efficiency are not excluded but seen as immanently embedded in this type of legal reasoning, especially in terms of distributive justice. In that sense, there is nothing formal about this concept of law and legal method, which is not then statist or static either although it sustains itself from within.

Legal realism[279] here assumes a general awareness of what is ethically, socially, and perhaps even from the point of view of utility and efficiency, desirable, although legal studies may still not be able to claim a distinctive insight into evolving values and political preferences. In its studies, the realist movement tended to be empirical, whilst wanting to be scientific and objective at least in this manner, but it had to accept that mere behaviourism in the end did not provide all answers and could not fully explain law's normative (rather than descriptive) nature; see also the discussion in section 1.3.7 below. Yet it brought to an end the prevalence of literal and logical interpretation techniques.

Although it favoured conceptual thinking in law-formation, for which in private law there was German influence as may be shown in the UCC and also in the Restatements already mentioned, it can only be repeated that the existence of these texts was not to thwart other more urgent considerations whatever they were. It follows that in the US, the difference between *legal formalism* and a more policy-oriented approach to the law and its application has long been understood. A lesser need was henceforth felt to apply rules in a logical and intrinsically consistent manner and black-letter law as such lost much of its lustre in academia and was henceforth often deprecated as 'doctrinal'.[280]

In some writings,[281] a particular search was made, however, for the fundamental legal principles common to all civilised legal systems to arrive at a more objective and universal notion of fairness and justice in a modern redistributive social environment. This suggests natural law undercurrents at the same time.[282] In the US they are never far beneath the surface as may also be seen in the earlier work of Lon Fuller. The basic arbitrariness in rule making by the competent authorities is here identified and questioned.

In England, on the other hand, private law thinking remains largely dominated by the writings of Austin and later Hart,[283] based on a vivid statist positivism. Legal formalism

---

[279] There was also here an implicit reaction against 'laissez-faire' which was even associated with legal formalism and then deemed its accomplice. Soon there was emphasis on the makeability of society in which the law and its progression were actively to function. As such, legal realism became in the American mind closely connected with social pragmatism, see also TRS Summers, *Instrumentalism and American Legal Theory* (1982). In this approach, there was no reality beyond human experience, or, if there was, it was not relevant. It was always in flux and could be fashioned. There were no absolute answers but what was useful was true or at least true enough. That was, at least, the answer in American pragmatism, see also n 315 below. All law is here considered experimental and provisional. Determinism was rejected and optimism prevailed, see further the discussion in ss 1.3.6–1.3.7 below.

[280] As shown in n 278 above, the concept of formalism has not been completely abandoned. A plea for greater formalism at least in the interpretation of contracts between *professionals* is still heard (not unlike the approach of this book, see s 1.1.8 above), see, eg RE Scott, 'The Case for Formalism in Relational Contracts' (2000) 94 *North Western University Law Review* 847.

[281] J Rawls, *A Theory of Justice* (1971) and *Political Liberalism* (1996). As far as natural law undercurrents go, the work of Lon Fuller is also clearly inspired by secular natural law or fundamental legal principle, see *The Law in Quest of Itself* (1940). It laid much stress on the inherent morality of the law (rather than rationality). The approach of Rawls in search of public policy justifications in the law is very different but no less naturalistic.

[282] Notwithstanding the nationalistic tenor, also in American law, importantly in criminal law, references to international standards of human rights have been made by Justice Kennedy in the Supreme Court cases outlawing anti-sodomy laws and the death penalty for minors, see *Lawrence v Texas* 539 US 588 (2003) and *Roper v Simmons* 125 S Ct 1183 (2005).

[283] *The Concept of Law* (1961, 2nd unchanged edn 1994). Here we also find an intellectual justification for the *national* character of that law which leaves Parliament absolutely sovereign in law formation, although, as we saw, that does not rule out the further autonomous development of common law and equity unless specifically overruled. Other competent organisms of a national character (like judges on the basis of their professional practices) may contribute in the application of the law, but there is no true place for non-national sources of law, nor in

thrives in such an environment and is, as we have seen, still largely the adopted method of legal scholarship in the UK. However, the approach of Hart was fundamentally questioned by the American Ronald Dworkin,[284] his successor in Oxford, in whose view social and policy considerations play an important role and figure in legal principles. Again, this is in the tradition of American realism. Nevertheless, in as far as legal theory is at all of interest in the development of English law, which remains largely practitioner dominated (especially by the Bar), the approach of Hart remains still the prevalent one and appears unavoidably nationalistic, insular and formalistic.

1.3.5 Post-realism or Legal Functionalism in the US: The 'Law and ...' Movements

Legal realism is a development which became ever more pronounced in American legal scholarship towards the end of the twentieth century, where courses in law and ethics, law and religion, law and sociology (law and society), law and economics, law and psychology, law and aesthetics, law and politics, law and culture (or critical legal studies) and so on are now common. It is also referred to as post-realism or functionalism resulting in the '*law and ...*' movements which have become popular, with the result that black-letter (or so-called doctrinal) law is ever less favoured, at least in legal scholarship and in law teaching in the top American law schools. It is taught as an unavoidable minimum in the first year, often as a demonstration of how the law should be or should not be, or should be no longer. Legal scholarship has thus become ever more jurisprudential and less practice-oriented in nature. Again, its objective is rather the development of views that engender renewal and improvement of the law through intellectual analysis, academic critique, and a forward-looking attitude.

Especially in 'law and sociology',[285] 'law and economics',[286] and now also in 'law and psychology',[287] there is an ever greater shift to more *empirical* research to prepare legislation and monitor its effects. Proponents unite in wanting to fill a perceived vacuum in which law making and application are mostly considered matters of opinion, experience,

---

truth for public international law either, and in this view within England not even much for custom (which in this approach is seen as primitive or regressive law) or legal principle, let alone for a transnational law merchant.

[284] R Dworkin, *Taking Rights Seriously* (1977).

[285] At first, much associated with the work of Philip Selznick at Berkeley, see, eg P Nonet and P Selznick, *Law and Society in Transition: Towards Responsive Law*, 2nd edn (2001); and P Selznick, *The Communautarian Persuasion* (2002) and earlier *The Moral Commonwealth* (1992).

[286] The 'law and economics' movement tries to rationalise the legal rules and their effect from the perspective of economic efficiency and distribution. It is a more recent phenomenon, particularly derived from the economic thinking of von Hayek and the legal thinking of RA Posner, *Economic Analysis and the Law* (1973); see also WM Landes and RA Posner, 'The Influence of Economics on Law: A Quantitative Study', (1993) 36 *Journal of Law and Economics* 385, but it can be dated back to RH Coase, 'The Problem of Social Cost' (1960) 3 *Journal of Law and Economics* 1, and to G Calabresi, 'Some Thoughts on Risk Distribution and the Law of Torts' (1961) 70 *Yale Law Journal* 499.

[287] See for the uncertain and uneven progress of this approach, JRP Ogloff, *Taking Psychology and Law into the Twenty First Century* (2002). Earlier efforts had centred on the impact of psychoanalysis on the law see, eg J Frank, *Law and the Modern Mind* (1930); see also CG Schoenfeld, *Psychoanalysis and the Law* (1973), but it failed fully to convince.

intuition or perhaps (political) wishful thinking. Even if the law and its application are not neutral or objective, but rather policy oriented, the newer directions mean to bring a more academic flavour and in that sense objectivity to the discussion, although there was serious criticism from the beginning.[288] Excessive focus on dispute resolution is here also avoided.[289] There is genuine interest in how the law comes about and functions more generally. The effects of legal change are measured, in 'law and economics' especially for its efficiency and effect on distribution.

On the other hand, environmental justice and critical race theories (or critical or political legal studies more generally)[290] have added an ever stronger *political* dimension to legal theory. The critique now tends to go well beyond mere legal analysis of policy and action and there is also room for cultural considerations, national and other values or Burkean and *Volksgeist* notions, but also for (minority) group demands and for the notion that the law as it is cannot promote justice (or equality in a practical sense) without deep (political) reform.

In the wake of these developments, in the US more traditional jurisprudential concerns about 'law as justice', 'law as order' and natural or positive law approaches have receded into the background or are recast in a different mould. Where the positivist or black-letter law approach has been substantially weakened, the search for the true justification behind the law has intensified. It was already noted that there was always an idealistic undercurrent in American legal thinking probably connected with the strong idealistic flavour of constitutional principle.

It means that law in the US is hardly considered any longer a product of the command of the state, although it may still be seen as embedded in a national recognition and acceptance process, therefore in *American* values and culture rather than in more universal principle.[291] It may well be that a naturalism of American dimension is here impliedly assumed. Indeed, there is often little consideration of internationalism, universalism, or an acknowledgement that this American experience is part of a broader Western culture which is democratic and decentralist, subject to the rule of law, and mindful of basic human rights, even if in the twentieth century in the shaping of this more universal culture, the Americans have largely taken over from Europe as we shall see in section 1.5.4 below.[292] It is

---

[288] See RS Summers, *Instrumentalism and American Legal Theory* (1982) 115 with reference to the 'deadly bog of behaviorism'. See further also the classic retort of AA Leff, 'Economic Analysis of Law: Some Realism about Nominalism' (1974) 60 *Virginia Law Review* 451.

[289] As for dispute resolution, empirical answers may be sought to the question of when and how non-legal considerations enter into the judicial decision-making process thereby becoming legally normative and enforceable. What are the costs and benefits?

[290] The openly left-wing aspirations of this movement, see eg AC Hutchinson (ed), *Critical Legal Studies* (1989), have contributed to an old fashioned rhetoric, seemingly leading to unnecessary isolation. It has tended to cloud its innovative approaches and to conceal the much broader relevance of many of its ideas. It can be seen as the politicised branch of modern legal thought in which rationality and a unitary approach to justice are particularly questioned; see especially the work of RM Unger at Harvard, eg his 'Liberal Political Theory' in AC Hutchinson (ed), *Critical Legal Studies* (1989) 15.

[291] Others only advocate a *national* value system to underpin the law, which is not necessarily a conflicting proposition. It is sometimes even believed to be one of the great insights of legal realism; see R Post, 'The Challenge of Globalization to American Public Law Scholarship' (2001) 2 *Theoretical Inquiries in Law* 323; see also n 255 above.

[292] But see also *Roper v Simmons* 125 S Ct 1183 (2005) and *Lawrence v Texas* 539 US 558 (2003) and Justice Kennedy's references therein to international normativity of a human rights nature in the US.

Except for some comment in these cases, the idea here is that the legally relevant culture and values remain primarily national and do not therefore have an anchor in the broader modern Western world, even if that produced

probably the reason why the Americans are here less aware of the experiences of others. In its application, it may well be that, at least at the academic level, the law as a rational system is increasingly mistrusted in the US. In the manner of Hume's scepticism and of some of the twentieth-century Scandinavian scholars, contradictions and irrationalities in the law's aims are noted but accepted as unavoidable, even if the 'law and economics' movement tries to be more rational and in that sense also more scientific.

It is clear that the (a) lack of a unitary view of what justice is or of what the law needs to achieve in terms of social ordering; the (b) questioning of established value systems in favour of national or group cultures, race or gender; but also the (c) influence of market forces and what are considered utilitarian preferences or rational choices, have had a considerable effect on modern legal studies in the US. They may in so far have combined that ultimately the more extreme view is being heard that the law does not present an own normativity or system of values at all and therefore lacks autonomy[293] although it is not denied that in its daily application purely doctrinal thinking cannot be avoided.

It is submitted, however, that the law, being the prime vehicle for establishing order and balancing conflicting interests in that context, can hardly be entirely identified with some extralegal category, be it morality, sociology or economics and follows here its own line, although it will discount them all if sufficiently pressing, but always in its own manner. It follows that greater respect for the doctrinal aspects in the study of the law may be overdue. Finding structure (not system) in the law, especially private law, as it moves forward is then also a legitimate academic task.[294] That is not the approach, however, of much of the present-day American academia.

In the US since the 1970s, the result of the newer approaches has been a considerable further *intellectualisation* of legal studies particularly in the leading US law schools resulting in an immense flood of literature and debate that has produced some valuable new insights. Not all movements have retained their popularity, however, and 'law and society'

---

the idea of the modern state, of democracy, rule of law, and protection of basic values in the first place. None relies, however, on mere positivism or the state's command to validate the law.

Only in the American 'law and economics' movement does there seem to be some greater understanding of the international dimensions and validity of the basic legal concepts, at least in commerce and finance, see, eg RD Cooter, 'Structural Adjudication and the New Law Merchant: A Model of Decentralised Law' (1994) 14 *International Review of Law and Economics* 215, but it remains rarer and has barely affected trade law or transnational law formation more generally, see also text at n 312 below.

[293] RA Posner, 'The Decline of Law as an Autonomous Discipline: 1962–1987' (1987) 100 *Harvard Law Review* 761. Some care is appropriate here and semantics enter easily into the picture. Considering the law as an own (philosophical) category, therefore subject to its own structure and normativity, never meant isolation and absolute separation from other categories, like the ethical, social and economic ones, very clear, eg in the formulation of statutory law and regulation but now also in the normative interpretation technique. They are closely connected and influence each other, how much so and in what manner is an obvious area of jurisprudential studies. It is clear that in times of greater social and political movement and lack of consensus, there is greater tension but also a greater need (at least in an academic sense) for these categories to sustain and enlighten each other. That may well explain much of the 'law and ...' movements in the US at present.

That there is less use for them in Europe at this time might be explained by a greater social consensus or cohesion there (at present). This may also be relevant in international commercial and financial law, where, it could be argued, there is also a greater consensus and therefore less need for political, moral or social adjustments to the evolving new law merchant. On the other hand, the emergence and autonomy of the international commercial and financial legal order—it will be posited in s 1.5 below—is itself a social phenomenon whilst utilitarian considerations will naturally also be of great importance in what is largely the elaboration of commercial and financial exigencies and realities in the formation and application of this new *lex mercatoria* in which market principle plays an important role.

[294] *Cf* for this discussion n 207 above and accompanying text.

and 'critical legal studies' are perhaps less favoured now than they once were. The 'law and economics' school remains popular as the more rational and scientific branch of modern legal thought[295] that has attempted to translate and explain many legal structures in micro-economic terms,[296] whilst valuing predictability[297] and measuring the law's (economic) effects.[298]

[295] This school has different strands but the one associated with *neo-classical economics* is the more prevalent. Individual actors are here at the centre of economic activity. They are assumed (at least in the aggregate and in terms of a method of critique) to act as rational beings who maximise their own benefit or self-interest and respond to prices and pay-offs, including legal sanctions, rationally. The aggregation of their choices is assumed to result in a variety of standards and institutional frameworks that the law will (or must) sanction. Why we nevertheless maximise some preferences and not others is less clear and depends on values which economists on the whole do not seek to explain. They are a matter of internalisation.

The basic assumption is thus that all human behaviour is predictable and can be set out in a coherent intellectual framework. The notion of maximisation itself allows for calculation if one assumes that it is achieved where at the margin the cost and benefits become equal. If a utility function can be established which ranks the alternatives mathematically, maximisation results where the derivative is zero. It suggests an equilibrium when all participants have achieved this point. When utility is maximised in this manner, it suggests that the greatest good for the greatest number of people is achieved. This is therefore a powerful micro economic tool.

One important aspect of 'law and economics' is then to predict the effect of rule or sanction change on this equilibrium. From an economic point of view, considerations of efficiency and distribution of wealth and income promote change. Economics may suggest here the better rule, especially from the efficiency perspective, measured by the change in equilibrium.

What happens here is that the pursuit of justice is cast foremost in terms of the pursuit of economic efficiency (or public good effect). In this approach, economic ordering on the basis of efficiency in this sense is considered to be at the heart of the legal system. What is efficient is objectively the maximum that can be produced from the same amount of input, but there are other definitions, eg of Pareto and Kaldor-Hicks. In practice, what is efficient may primarily depend on an investigation of the behaviour of individuals and *how they respond to various incentives to maximise their self-interest* but it complicates matters and may, in terms of rule change, defy a priori analysis.

[296] One way to approach the subject has been to see legal sanctions as cost and apply conventional micro-economic price theory. In this way, it can be measured how people react and change attitudes. The idea is that people respond to higher sanctions as they do to higher prices and adjust their behaviour. Manufacturers may in this way minimise their risk and go for better quality if poor quality is punished. How much they do will depend on the level of the fine. This is capable of calculation by using supply and demand curves (assuming there is full competition).

[297] Cost, on the other hand, may also include social costs or *externalities* that may not be properly charged to those carrying out that activity such as (often) pollution of the atmosphere. Competing interests, such as the need for clean air as against industrial activity, determine the acceptance and extent of these social costs.

This implies a trade-off which, in 'law and economics', is cast foremost in *market* terms or as competition for scarce resources. It concerns here aggregated individual (rational) choices in which fault does not figure. Even if subsequently the law asks who is at fault, eg in pollution matters, or what legal justifications or excuses there may be, the efficiency question should first be posed as (in this view) the legal rule or result can (often) be explained in terms of a contribution to (or even being the product of) what was most efficient.

[298] For the legal allocation of social cost, the most important tool was produced by the Coase theorem; see Coase, 'The Problem of Social Cost', n 286 above. It works basically as follows. Intuitively we assume that a polluter should not externalise the cost of pollution and therefore be subject to claims of damages by victims of its pollution. However, this could be subject to more careful analysis. If a factory causes smoke damage to laundry hanging out to dry, the five most affected neighbours may each suffer damage of $75, giving a total of $375. A way to avoid this is for the factory to install a smoke screen at $150 or for each neighbour to buy an electric dryer at $50 each giving a total of $250. The question is, who pays, which depends on whether a right to clean air is assigned to the neighbours.

In the latter case, the factory can either pay the neighbours $375, build a smoke screen for $150 or buy the neighbours dryers for $250. The smoke screen will be most efficient. However, if the factory were given the right to externalise the pollution, rational neighbours would join together to purchase the smokescreen for the factory assuming that they do not have transaction cost that would increase the amount of $150. The conclusion is that *if there are no transaction costs*, the most efficient result will always obtain *regardless* of the choice of legal rule. However, it still affects the distribution of income, about which the theorem says nothing.

Nevertheless, it is widely understood and admitted that 'law and economics' provides little guide to legal reasoning or to the law's application and remains therefore limited as a legal tool. It has also not much advice to give on (re)distributive issues with which the law is often concerned.[299] Between economics and law, the shift is rather from the rational to the reasonable man. It has already been suggested that perhaps the true significance of 'law and economics' is as (yet another) model for academic critique of the legal rules we have.[300]

A lack of clear direction is indeed noticeable, and there is so far less impact on the positive law in the US than one might think, although attention is sometimes paid to these newer approaches and ideas in modern case law, especially in antitrust matters, in (draft)

If there were transaction costs (meetings of neighbours to arrange, transportation costs, etc) that might increase the cost of the smokescreen to $260. Dryers would then be preferred, whether the factory pays or the neighbours. It is then better that the rule puts the burden on the factory, which will save $110 overall and is clearly the most efficient rule. It minimises the transaction cost. Thus the rule depends on the minimalisation of the transaction cost; it is not principally a question of blame, although a fairer distribution of the cost may also come in (as a matter of wealth or distribution).

These theorems maybe too utopian or clever, as such not a true reflection of reality and present abstractions that never truly occur and may therefore be of limited value; see DA Faber, 'The Case against Brilliance' (1986) *Minnesota Law Review* 917, 918. More importantly, in terms of modern game theory, what is identified here as transaction cost, is in truth a price negotiation between strategic players who have different information, not therefore a given price like in price theory. Game theory should therefore be applied.

Attempts have been made nevertheless to explain more generally the law and the choices to be made in this connection in this manner; see in particular, AM Polinski, *An Introduction to Law and Economics*, 2nd edn (1989). It concerns here nuisance laws, contract breach, car accidents, product liability, and litigation. Legal rights and markets are thus believed to interact in the sense that legal rights may be understood through the contribution they make to an efficient trade-off in the above sense. The law of torts can so be explained as a tool to contribute to the optimum level of accidents (Calabresi), in terms therefore of its contribution to efficiency (Coase). In contract law, the contribution to efficiency (and reduction of transaction costs) may be even more obvious legally to explain its operation.

Although the focus of the law shifts here from justice to efficiency considerations, it is also shown that the latter need not conflict as much with the former as might be assumed. Clearly, as a (re)distributive concept, justice as a balancing of interests is not an economic concept. It is, however, argued that people are in fact worse off if distribution prevails over efficiency; see L Kaplow and S Shavell, 'Should Legal Rules Favour the Poor?' (2000) 29 *Journal of Legal Studies* 821, questioned by J Waldron, 'Locating Distribution' (2003) 32 *Journal of Legal Studies* 277. It is true, for example, that if we provide free housing to one poor person, it must be paid for by others; the other poor may suffer most, eg in a higher cost of their accommodation.

[299] The neo-classical strand lately focuses not only on the (aggregate) behaviour of individuals in the market, but also on what makes this behaviour more predictable, and on the development or evolution of the law in this connection and its contribution. This is sometimes also referred to as the second generation of 'law and economics' and suggests a close connection with social psychology. See for a good summary, R Nobles, 'Economic Analysis of Law' in J Penner, D Schiff and R Nobles (eds), *Jurisprudence and Legal Theory* (2002) 855.

What is self-interest; what are the preferences of people; are they always economic; how does this work in a group? The second generation is more interested in the internalisation of values in this connection, the motives for doing so, and the application of economic modeling techniques to this process, see esp R Cooter, 'Law and Unified Social Theory' (1995) 22 *Journal of Law and Society* 50; 'Three Effects of Social Norms on Law: Expression, Deterrence, and Internalisation' (2000) 79 *Oregon Law Review* 1; see also R Cooter and D Ulen, *Law and Economics*, 6th edn (2011).

[300] There is another more political strand in 'law and economics' which concentrates on how law is made in the legislative process, therefore as a political tool. This is the area of *public choice theory* and political economics. It comes down to analysing the personal interests and preferences of policy makers, who are assumed to act much like other individuals and rationalise their preferences and also maximise their self-interests. The state is here not the subject of study (like in political science) but rather the politicians, civil servants, pressure group officials and the like.

This strand of thought originates in L Jaffee, 'Law Making by Private Groups' (1937) 51 *Harvard Law Review* 201; and later in JM Buchanon and G Tullock, *The Calculus of Consent* (1962). Its offspring is part of the Chicago School which is largely empirical. Another variant is that of 'analytical politics', the idea being to build formal (mathematical) models of collective decision making, see eg A Schwartz and RE Scott, 'The Political Economy of Private Legislatures' (1994) 143 *University of Pennsylvania Law Review* 595.

statutory law, and in newer Restatements. It can be argued that the intellectualisation of legal studies in the US in this manner has contributed to a growing divide between academic legal thinking and legal practice in an environment in which the practical orientation of the living common law itself has hardly changed.

In private law, one may see this lack of theoretical input in particular in the regular amendments and revisions of the UCC, where pragmatism prevails. Even the further elaboration of the important federal bankruptcy statutes seems in the end not to have been greatly affected by newer thought.[301]

1.3.6 The Progress So Far

In evaluating the progress so far, particularly in private law, there is a further complication in that the emphasis on policy in modern legal realism, particularly in the US, may have shifted attention unduly to law making through legislators or to the courts in terms of *public* ordering. The essence of *private* law as a facilitating rather than mandatory force to balance conflicting interests may thus become misunderstood, distorted or ignored.[302] Also in the modern functional movements, policy remains the major area of concern, not only in the formulation but also interpretation of the law.[303] All is then perceived as *public* policy, even private law formulation and operation. This may be a misconception and it was explained in section 1.2.13 above that *social* policy is as important and may manifest itself autonomously through different sources of law and the judiciary.[304] But not all is social policy either.

If we finally reconsider legal *formalism* in the sense of textual coherence or systemic logic, it should not be entirely discounted and the following observations may be pertinent also for the US:

(a)   At the *legislative level*, absence of clear views on what private law is and how it operates, may have to be accepted. Here, policy considerations will prevail and determine what ought to be done. Lawyers have to accept the legislative outcome in respect of activities or transactions properly covered by it and are likely to be neutral except if fundamental principles of a modern open society are ignored, or the legislative result makes no sense or is practically unmanageable. The role of lawyers at the legislative level will mainly be in the drafting of statutes in such a way that they can apply them. Notably contradictions must be minimised. To that extent, not only some common sense but also a measure of systemic formalism is necessary and may be expected.

---

[301] See Elizabeth Warren, 'Bankruptcy policy making in an imperfect world' (1993) 92 *Michigan Law Review* 336; but *cf* also T Jackson, 'Bankruptcy, Non-bankruptcy Entitlements, and the Creditors' Bargain' (1982) 91 *Yale Law Journal* 857; see further GE Brunstad, 'Bankruptcy and the Problems of Economic Futility: A Theory of the Unique Role of Bankruptcy Law' (2000) 55 *The Business Lawyer* 499.

[302] This was noted before when the democratic legitimacy of private law was considered, see ss 1.1.6 and 1.2.13 above. In this manner, governmental interests and their validity became early on also an overriding theme in conflicts of laws in the US, see s 2.2.2 below.

[303] See, for a critique, A Katz, 'Taking Private Ordering Seriously' (1996) 144 *University of Pennsylvania Law Review* 1745.

[304] See text at n 211 above.

The perspective is here black-letter law, although in the interpretation and gap filling provisions (if any) a broader picture may still have to be assumed.

(b) For the *interpretation* of these statutes or subsequent case law, the absence of a unitary view on what private law is or should strive for may present greater problems.

As we have seen, at least in dispute resolution, American lawyers may now generally take a normative approach to interpretation and accept in that context extra-legal or policy considerations more freely in terms primarily of ethics, social needs, economic efficiency, or environmental requirements. Hence the idea here is also that all is policy. At least in contract, civil law lawyers may not be far behind notwithstanding their general inclination to system thinking. In fact, all lawyers will in normal cases still be constrained in the application of these extra-legal considerations if they are not in accordance with the drift of the positive law derived either from statute or precedent, therefore from black-letter law; this is also the case in the US. It would seem that only in *pressing cases* could that be different and would other, extra-legal considerations enter.[305]

Even in the US, in comprehensive statutory law, such as the UCC or Bankruptcy Code, tax laws, company laws and federal procedure, a more coherent and systemic approach to interpretation follows from the statutory example. More technical considerations may thus still be valid, but practical considerations also come in especially when a rule is ambiguous, increasingly out of date, or when it is unclear that it can apply to the facts of the case at all or leads to ethically, socially, or economically unacceptable results.

Lawyers of all eras whilst applying the law, will show respect for the positive law, whether statutory or case law, therefore for all black-letter law. To that extent, they will accept its autonomy and articulate its values even if the extra-legal purposes that the law serves and moral, social and/or economic values cannot be ignored and may in pressing cases motivate judges to reformulate existing legal rules at least for that occasion. Resort to immanent legal sources (such as fundamental and general principle or practices and custom) or public and social value considerations may then also come in.

The positive law is thus no longer merely black-letter and is constantly reformulated, not only in the USA—it is unavoidable everywhere, especially in periods of rapid social change—but the black-letter nature of much law cannot largely be ignored if legal texts are to have any meaning at all, and finding the law in newer situations remains, therefore, a cautious, searching process everywhere that is likely to lag behind, even if the American legal scholarship appears at present much keener to close the gap or lead the way.

(c) In the *transactional practice*, the task of practising lawyers is again different. They will have to write down in a comprehensive and coherent manner the deal reached by their clients and the risk distribution inherent in it. There is logic and coherence or formalism in that sense whilst taking into account the minefield (for them and their clients) of public policy and public order requirements, therefore, of regulation, taxation and more fundamental considerations, often in different countries. They will have a special role in assessing and distributing the *legal risk*, in international

---

[305] As could be expected, in the US the discussion on interpretation itself is lively; see for a balanced view, M Stone, 'Focusing the Law: What Legal Interpretation is Not' in A Marmor (ed), *Essays in Legal Philosophy* (Oxford, 1995).

cases particularly in terms of the applicable law and jurisdiction of the courts or arbitrators. As for the applicable law, this will also involve an assessment of context, policy and extralegal considerations that may become relevant in the application of the contract and of the law that governs it.

In international cases, that will be all the more challenging as these lawyers will often have to navigate or structure around atavistic and parochial laws and will in this connection also have to assess the possibilities and impact or effect of a contractual choice of law or jurisdiction. This requires a further assessment of what, for example, a contractual choice of law clause may mean in international cases in areas of the law that are not at the free disposition of the parties, usually those that have to do with third party rights, like property, collateral and bankruptcy issues, or with governmental or regulatory policies of the states most directly concerned, or with public order issues.[306]

A further assessment may also be necessary in respect of the applicability of the transnational *lex mercatoria* and its meaning and content, including considering the hierarchy of legal sources it represents, but also of notions of international public order or comity especially in respect of foreign regulatory laws that may have a sufficient relationship with the case, as we shall see more fully in section 1.5.6 below. It is submitted that the international practice, in particular in its structuring activity, is creating law, probably more than legislatures, judges and arbitrators. One may think of the eurobonds and the entire operation of the eurobond market and of the ISDA swap master agreement. International law firms are at least important spokespersons for the new transnational order, even if they do not (yet) realise it.

As far as dispute resolution goes, the feasibility of the jurisdiction of the ordinary courts in whatever countries, arbitration, and other dispute solution techniques will then also have to be considered, see section 1.1.9 above, and especially the role of bankruptcy courts in international finance which remain domestic. It is clear that legal formalism cannot be here much of a guide. Much will depend on good judgment.

(d)   In *legal scholarship* all is free. Here legal formalism or thinking in terms of black-letter law, systems and their application suggest a fixation with yesterday's law. Yet it is not always useless, especially not in statutory interpretation. Clearly, modern American academia goes beyond this, and concentrates on the transforming forces and processes in all law. In fact, it stimulates them and tries to guide them with endless new ideas. It also takes a vivid interest in why and how rules are better accepted (or internalised) and voluntarily complied with. Indeed, in the major American law schools, legal scholarship is deemed to be nothing if it is not innovative or fails to explore new ways in a (more) scientific manner.

American legal scholarship looks therefore for new paradigms all the time[307] and reflects their impact on legal principles and rules and their formulation and operation on a continuous basis. To repeat, innovation is the key to newer academic models to guide the law into the future

---

[306]   See JH Dalhuisen, 'What could the Selection by Parties of English Law in a Civil Law Contract in Commerce and Finance Truly Mean' in M Andenas and D Fairgrieve, *Tom Bingham and the Transformation of the Law* (2009) 619, and also the discussion in s 1.4.13 below.

[307]   See on paradigms text at n 208 above and s 1.3.7 below.

and to critique the existing positive law or find more structure or purpose in it. The newer functional approaches—especially law and economics—may play that role more particularly.

Empirical research becomes here a key issue testing these newer models and then leads to the study particularly of rules that respond to new situations and demonstrate their validity and effectiveness.[308] There is no less an interest in more epistemological issues like the meaning of fundamental principle, systematic thinking, and its relation to and effect on social realities, whatever they may be, the conditions for legal knowledge, and the use made of it. Cognitive psychology is not then far behind.

Legal education, at least in the best American law schools, follows and is conceptual but also free thinking and not doctrinaire, thus allowing for flexibility or pragmatism. It promotes a more modern outlook, vocabulary, and articulation of the law that is problem-solving oriented and does not find the solutions merely in past experiences. Each professor will espouse here its own views and students will be exposed from the beginning to great differences in approach. This is considered healthy and to reflect real life. It also allows flexibility in advocacy depending on client needs.

In the meantime a more activist *judicial* approach seems to have become apparent everywhere, not only in the US. It is obviously motivated by the enormous social, cultural, scientific, demographic and ecological changes we see pressing upon us all the time. It is a matter of perception and study whether this is affecting the very nature of the law itself and its operation in society. Even if as a result the law itself were in modern times in essence seen as an empty shell depending on other sciences to fill it, the next question would still be what should fill it on occasion and how? If extralegal norms or demands must increasingly be taken into account as legally normative and thus binding, it still has to be asked which ones, when and to what extent? Or to put it another way, when do these norms become legally enforceable (thereby entering into the law) and who decides or fulfills here the function of spokesman? What if they conflict?

That is, it is submitted, the true cause of the probing attitude of much modern American legal scholarship. Thus presented, this search is a function of the acceleration in social evolution. It has unavoidably led to disorientation, certainly also in the application of the law. American legal scholarship reflects this and has accepted it as a challenge rather than an embarrassment.

Outside the US (except for Canada), these modern American ideas have not so far played an important role, even though they have been noted,[309] not the 'law and economics' school,[310] not even in *international* relationships of a private law nature and in the reformulation of substantive rules at that level, notably in international commercial and financial or business law. As a consequence, it has hardly figured in the development of the new transnational law merchant or modern *lex mercatoria*, although one would assume that it is in principle friendly to it as would all legal currents that see group cultures and values as a determining factor in (bottom up) law formation.[311]

---

[308] But empirical research has its problems, see also s 1.3.7 below. It demonstrates one other point being that this type of interdisciplinary research is only worth doing at the top level. Much of it remains pure amateurism.

[309] See, eg Penner, Schiff and Nobles (eds), n 299 above.

[310] See exceptionally Cooter, n 292 above.

[311] Subject, of course, always to governmental interests, the extraterritorial validity of which would, however, still have to be determined on their relevancy from case to case (barring treaty law or accepted international law concepts): see s 2.2.6 below.

In international trade regulation or liberalisation, even many American commentators, looking mainly at trade restrictions, invoke here simply a liberal, market-oriented spirit aimed at the free movement of goods, services and capital.[312] Where a form of re-regulation is necessary, they are then likely to deprecate the notion of sovereignty so as to achieve a more proper balance between international and national legal orders or lower local or cultural organisms through notions similar to that of subsidiarity.

That the American ideas have not so far found great resonance, even in other parts of the common law world, let alone in civil law countries, especially in private law, is not entirely surprising in view of their already noted modest effect on the positive law in the USA itself,[313] whilst they tend in any event to be oriented more towards governmental interests and intervention, their policy, manner and desired or real impact, than towards the law between private parties.

The conclusion of the foregoing is that notwithstanding innovative thinking especially in the US, only modest progress has been made so far in terms of the functioning of other than formal national legal orders and the sources of law in such orders—which is the prime concern of practitioners of the transnational law merchant and of this book. In civil law countries, an old-fashioned positivism centred on formal system thinking founded in past experiences and formulated by states continues to prevail and is attempted to be recast in this imperative manner, now even at the level of the EU, *viz* also the DCFR effort. Although in common law countries, academic support for transnationalisation is at the moment more likely to come from American than from English academic thought, it has no great priority in most of these countries. As the international commercial arbitration practice may show, so far progress in terms of legal transnationalisation has probably been greater at the practical than at the intellectual level.

Nevertheless in focusing on the cultural, sociological and economic undercurrents in the operation of communities, including the international economic community of merchants and financiers, increasingly this community may be seen to exercise autonomous law-making powers within its own area, leading to the development of the new transnational *lex mercatoria* as the law for that community. It presupposes the end of legal formalism and the self-sufficiency of state imposed domestic legal systems and accepts the increasing prevalence of social and economic considerations in the formation and operation of the law amongst its participants as a bottom up process unless public policy or public order intervenes.

---

[312] See, eg John H Jackson, 'International Economic Law: Reflections on the "Boilerroom of International Relations"' (1995) 10 *American University Journal of International Law and Policy* 595 and for a discussion D Kennedy, 'The International Style in Postwar Law and Policy' (1995) 10 *American University Journal of International Law and Policy* 671. They focus in that context mainly on the removal of tariffs and quantitative restrictions without a cost analysis per se and present in essence a pragmatic rather than a theoretical approach, especially in the issue of re-regulation at international level (primarily in WTO/GATT/GATS).

This approach is not concerned with methodology or deeper theoretical insights. See for a criticism on this point, JP Trachtman, 'John Jackson and the Founding of the World Trade Organisation: Empiricism, Theory and Institutional Imagination' (1999) 20 *Michigan Journal of International Law* 175 and earlier, RA Posner, 'The Decline of Law as an Autonomous Discipline: 1962–1987' (1987) 100 *Harvard Law Review* 761 also touching on the lack of interdisciplinary work in the area of international economic law and on the dominance of positivism and utopian ideals in that area. See for a more recent comment on this discussion, M Koskennieni, 'Letter to the Editors of the Symposium' (1999) 93 *American Journal of International Law* 351, suggesting that lawyers employ the tools of any method they find useful in a particular case and should not be guided by any one in particular.

[313] See n 292 above.

1.3.7 The Quest for Modernity, the Problems in the Post Modern Era and the Effects on Law Formation and Operation

The modern world is marked by a search for the extension of its horizons in order to reach ever deeper realities that we cannot clearly perceive with our senses. We do this in order better to control daily life and to take advantage of its opportunities. This is the special preoccupation of academia, first in the world of the natural sciences, and of the academic model that, through a better insight into nature, has allowed us not only to discover and harness, for example, electricity but also to make use of many other facilities that we have found in nature. We can now put someone on the moon and get him/her back.

In the social sciences, it is allowing for the development of economic models that may better guide our economy so as to promote more and better growth, and for the development of social models or insights that give as us a better idea of social forces so as to guide and promote human relationships, social peace, and welfare. In modern times, states in particular seek out these models to advance society and use the law to enforce them. That is one aspect of modernity which assumes therefore the makeability and remodeling of society on this basis for the greater benefit of all. The resulting measures are then supposed to be objective and ultimately self-evident.

In private law, the codification system may thus be perceived as a similarly abstract and artificial model that may be equally considered scientific, as such contributing to a better world beyond a minimum of order. Hence also the increasing accent on private law legislation in common law countries. In that approach, all law tends to be seen as policy to whose ideals it is made subservient. One recognises here the struggle and progress of legal realism in the US. The law then seeks to promote justice, social peace, efficiency and growth in this newer environment. Private law is not exempt and may thus also be seen as foremost a policy tool. According to some, as we have seen, it is losing its independence or autonomy as a consequence. Again, this is much behind the discussion on legal realism and the modern functional approaches in the US. The idea is that the law in its evolution depends on deeper insights in which academia has a significant role to play. One notices here also an older German root in the discussion. Whether this can still be presented as an objective process is another matter.

There are here also issues of morality as well as religion. The main question is in this connection in how far states helped by their academies and laws should get involved in the shaping of a more modern moral order and even regulate religion. This was and is certainly the aim of totalitarian regimes, either to the left or the right. In a secular democratic society, on the other hand, religion is left well alone except for fanatical excess, but a question may still be asked about morality. Is it more like religion, where states within the limits of public order will respect it for what it is? It is a major issue and favourite debating point in the ethical aspects of modernity.[314] It should be realised that this goes beyond mere fairness in society of which politicians already consider themselves the ultimate arbiters.

Can we and should we devise better ethical standards to promote morality and make them stick? Is the law also subservient to this objective and what is to be the model? Is there statist morality as there is statist law? Could the state have a similar role to play in its

---

[314] These important issues can here only be flagged but not further discussed, but see MJ Lacey and MO Furner (eds), *The State and Social Investigation in Britand and the United States* (New York, 1993), especially their first chapter on the rise and role of modern government 'Social Investigation, Social Knowledge and the State'.

formation? Here the redistributive nature of modern society is in recent times in particular met by the ethic of social responsibility or loss thereof. What should the state do? Or is the modern state itself a moral problem, demonstrated in the Western world by its financial bankruptcy which may well entail a moral bankruptcy at the same time. The lack of discipline all around would then be the manifestation, which would at the same time imply the failure of the state's own more contrived, variable or 'new' concept of social order and moral discipline.

It is obvious that states and their powers are a key factor in the promotion of a modern and highly artificial world of which they are the central organisers hopefully for the greater benefit of all. It suggests a top-down world in which other forces are subdued or controlled. This may apply not only to market forces and the environment but also to other bottom-up or more natural processes, including more participatory forms of private law formation, such as in practices or custom. Religion, probably morality, and hopefully academia, remain here free, at least in democracies. It implies nevertheless a substantial redistribution of initiative, costs and risks.

Again this assumes the better insights at the level of the state. It presupposes at the same time the substantial reliability of academic models, an insight in their effects, and the absence of unintended consequences. A first observation to make here is that all academic insights so far developed are tentative at best and there can be no certainty that they work fully or better. Even the laws of Newton have not remained uncontested but it affects particularly the social sciences, including the law. It is obvious for economics which cannot show clear ways to prosperity for all nor predict its crises, but it is true everywhere. The new facilities created for example, paper currencies, remain poorly understood in their effect and management. So is the modern function of banks in that kind of environment. Academia is far away from any definitive insights into reality and how this new world truly works and there is therefore nothing compelling about the academic framework in as far as we have been able to develop it and experimentation and innovation remain more than necessary.[315]

Additionally, layer upon layer of laudable governmental regulation, however 'scientific', may stifle society because the effects of this layering itself are not properly understood and seldom adequately considered. Cost/benefit analysis is supposed to help but the tools and insights to make this work are largely missing. That may result in serious threats to growth or in a type of growth that proves to be unsustainable or misguided.

In fact, it must be considered that all is here potentially manipulated or artificial in search of a better world without a clear view of the results beyond much hope and wishful thinking or political expediency. In this void, the modern state is itself easily hijacked by self-serving insider groups that largely live by their own political survival instincts in the measures they order to which the public interest becomes subservient. In practice, there is little that is objective in this activity and, if convenient, it puts academic insights (in as far as we have them) often to the side or they become easy subjects of compromise or manipulation.

This has in particular allowed the middle classes, where the vote is, to use the welfare state—originally meant to help the poor—for their own advantage. They want free healthcare, free

---

[315] There is a determinism implicit in the scientific approaches to life which has long been spotted. Philosophers such as Berlin and Popper coming from the German scientific tradition, which they mistrusted, used their lives' work to warn against the enemies of an open society and of freedom limited in this sense. Earlier, the Kantian tradition had equally sought to preserve the maximum freedom outside the natural sciences out of similar concerns.

education, free (but unfunded) pensions (for people who want to retire earlier and live longer) and full protection of employment. For them it is convenient that the state provides all of this and that all its endeavours are made subject to these needs. In the meantime, 15 per cent of the population remains below the poverty line for all kind of intractable reasons, whilst the lower middle classes appear not to be able to maintain themselves financially and fall back into the poverty trap. This puts enormous pressure on the modern state and its laws. Redistribution of the cost through the tax system, public borrowing, printing money if deemed necessary, and devaluations are considered viable tools to deal with these matters. So are banks that are—through poorly focused or unenforced regulation—willing, encouraged, or forced to lend to everybody as a kind of human right of the multitude (then considered banks' 'social' function), and also to states, at low interest rates that are manipulated down by Central Banks. This is then considered to result in a fairer society, whether or not stable or sustainable and becomes an issue of tortured morality.

Rather, bankruptcy looms for the modern state which is apt to surrender here to irrationality. Yet it is clear that in the West this approach has promoted welfare enormously, although this significant achievement is recent. It dates from the period after WW II, may at least in part be credited to modernity in the above sense, therefore state intervention of this sort, but it is fragile. It is the thesis of this book that progress in this sense was achieved primarily because of a vivid competition between the state and other forces, mainly the markets, states being guided here by their own models and political instincts, the other forces by their own rationalities and by the invisible hand, although the market will also use scientific models of its own. In fact, market forces remain more than necessary to correct political culture and expediency and to sort out imbalances. This proves painful at times and a reversion to the laws of the strongest, but is the consequence of the modern state having a tendency to overreach and in this way losing control. It means that the autonomous forces in the markets, in society, but also in the law and in morality, which modernity had sought to diffuse or redirect, reassert themselves.

Post-modernism, as here understood—and there are many definitions—postulates the full achievement of a society that operates altogether on scientific models although they need not be entirely state driven and may also be used by markets or other forces to understand their own workings better. Such a society is considered to be entirely steerable, therefore mainly from above and more truly by states, also in law formation. As is well known, according to Weber, this could ultimately lead to an iron prison of rationality and bureaucracy. The continuing competition between states and market and other forces continues to suggest, however, that this process is by no means complete and that there remain important bottom-up energies that are not fully controlled or controllable in this manner and more than necessary to avoid excess. So post-modernity must and does also consider modernity's collapse and becomes again comfortable with the lack of structure that results. It is forced to live with many contradictions and unsatisfactory explanations.

Probably part of it is the realisation that existing models and processes are not objective and that there is nothing in this artificial world that can lay claim to it. What are the paradigms behind them; in particular how much room is left in the social sciences including the law for other ideas and forces, and what provokes change? It is clear that these paradigms are important and underlie much of our thinking and action, therefore also the way a fully operative modernist society would work and how it could be compatible with a modern democracy. These paradigms are not themselves state controlled, are to some extent generational, moved also by societal shocks or changes or newer needs and expectations. One consequence is that societal models that so emerge are likely to be disparate and may even severely conflict. Each presents no more than one particular view of or take on reality that can lay no great claim to 'truth' whether or not in academic packaging.

As to the relative virtue of the evolving models for action, empirical research should help but is often a poor check. This is at least in part because they invoke fact, but in a scientific environment, it may be very unclear what facts are. They can best be captured naively or intuitively; once we start to describe or define them, they tend to fall apart and become abstractions and contextual, often pure opinion.[316] First, there is the perspective we take: if we contemplate a work of art, for example, we may take a historical point of view and shall then be interested in the author and when it was made; the lawyer on the other hand would be concerned with the question who owns it; and from an aesthetic point of view, we are concerned with its quality. It may thus be clear, that we talk about different things from the start, often without realising it. More importantly, all would seem objective, but none is: if the painting is not signed and dated, there will be different opinions, while even if it is signed and dated there may be the matter of authenticity; the legal title may be obscure; and as to quality, which should be objective fact, it is in truth pure opinion. But the most important conclusion must be that from the perspective of the different disciplines, people are not talking about the same facts in the first place. Upon a proper analysis, most discussion breaks down in this way.[317] Unrealised, there are different perspectives.

Even within the same discipline, it can still be asked whether civil law codification works well. How could it be empirically established that other ways of law formation, for example, immanent law formation through practice and custom, does not work better even if it is much less 'scientific'? That could also be asked of the common law that has here also a different tradition. This is very relevant if we should now be moving into the direction of some kind of codification of private law in the EU, as the DCFR would want it; see section 1.4.19 below. These more fundamental questions are seldom asked by its protagonists, however, one reason being a lack of thinking about method, but the other probably being the problem with empirical research and with the determination of what is fact in this connection or what, indeed, works better.

---

[316] In American pragmatism, there is a belief in empiricism, where what seems useful or works best is the criterion for (greater) truth. This proves to be no less a subjective judgment, although it is mostly not perceived as such, or at least it is felt that it can be objectively stated what works better and is therefore more true in that sense. It is interesting that its protagonists maintain here the more instinctive or 'naïve' approach to facts and see these as objective. At least the result is an outward-looking attitude instead of the earlier German approach in which no empirical research was needed to test the model which was deemed correct per se until a newer model came along. Some have maintained in this regard that only that which can be expressed in language is real but we understand much more than we can say and it is probably not the true test either. In the meantime, it cannot be denied there is a considerable problem with empirical research and its methodology and reliability. Much of it is very primitive and does not go beyond basic statistics.

[317] In politics, the modernist approach divides more than anything else progressives and conservatives. The former have greater confidence in newer models and trust them better, never mind the occasional hiccup and potential straight jacketing of society. Societal forces, like market forces that are not yet fully controlled in this manner, should then be increasingly regulated in order to achieve a better world. Conservatives are more sceptical and also have confidence in more parochial concepts like religion, culture and nationality. They also are more comfortable with original market forces. Both invoke 'facts' to support their case, but they are likely to use here very different perceptions of reality: the conservatives the 'naïve' version, the progressives intellectualised versions. The key is to understand that by invoking facts, they are not talking about the same thing and will therefore never convince each other.

We are here scientifically on less solid ground than is often assumed and there is little certainty in the artificial modernist world. The approach in this book is one of modernity supported by the scientific cult. We have no other option than to move forward in more scientific ways; that is through ever newer scientific models if we wish to provide for the multitude, but we should also understand the limitations. We know far too little to be able to be confident. Competing forces, notably market forces, cannot be fully controlled. As long as we do not quite understand how to reshape them in more propitious ways, it may be better to leave them alone unless they offend public order. An abundance of unintended consequences is likely to be the result. With present insights, we need both government and the markets, whilst the balance is ever shifting and cannot be objectively determined.

In such a world, the law as pure expression of the statist principle is not all powerful. The law's autonomy reasserts itself all the time and it has structures that cannot be easily discarded or perverted without considerable lateral damage, for example, the whole notion of contract and property. Thus private law is not exclusively guided by statist principle or any other, and there also remains room for immanent or spontaneous law formation, especially (but not only) where the reach of governments is practically limited, such as in the transnational sphere or international market place, or patently confused: much regulatory law can never work. In a modern world, private law even as a political force, thus remains eclectic and experimental. It moves autonomously but may go nowhere in particular and has no natural compass except to follow society, although not necessarily or exclusively its statist superstructure and theoretical models. In a free society, this may be perceived as a good and necessary thing. The positive, state produced-law is not perfect and needs competition. It is not all powerful.

It is true that the new Millennium, being generally indulgent, had become bored with these major issues which in particular did not fit the modernist agenda, but the student must understand some of this in order to follow the discussions better as they have a major impact on how we look at the law, its formation, operation and interpretation, be it in private law (as a kind of scientific statist codified system or not) or in regulatory matters such as in financial or environmental regulation or in any other part of the law, not in the least within the EU. In any event, the financial crisis that erupted after 2008 and ultimately became a crisis of government debt, posed the question once more what the true role of modern government is and how it could best be activated.

1.4 The Sources of Law in the Civil and Common Law Tradition. The Approach in Transnational Private Law and the Hierarchy of Sources of Law and their Norms in the Modern *Lex Mercatoria*

1.4.1 Statutory and Other Sources of Law. Nationalism and System Thinking in Civil and Common Law

The practical significance of the discussion so far is as follows.

By the end of the eighteenth century, in Europe, Continental *private* law (which was substantially the only law there was) had largely developed spontaneously to the point where legal scholarship was able to formulate a large number of substantive legal rules on which individuals could base and claim their most important individual or subjective rights. They were no longer forced to rely on more narrowly defined causes or forms of action or enforcement rights. In formulating substantive legal rules in this manner, it proved possible to connect them intellectually into a system that was internally coherent, or could at least pretend to be so. That happened in civil law countries. Common law on the other hand, had not developed in this manner and remained in essence action-based, still developing from case to case. It was not intellectual and the urge to define subjective rights more abstractly and subsequently to find system in private law came much later, if at all.

In legal scholarship, which was here the driving force on the European Continent, the rules themselves were progressively drawn not only from Roman law casuistry but also from Canon and local laws or from more fundamental or general principles seen as part of the directly applicable natural law, which itself had become secularised. Indeed this was the achievement of the natural law school after the seventeenth century. In finding structure in this manner, the emphasis thus shifted from an inductive to a deductive approach of rule finding and application in the elaboration of which rationality took centre stage. Roman law was no longer believed to be its sole expression whilst religious and other cultural overtones were increasingly subdued.

In what was to become the civil law, it was in this way possible to formulate general rules of contracts (which became binding as such) in terms of offer and acceptance, consensus and its defects, enforcement and excuses. It also became possible to arrive at a unified concept of negligence, and to develop a single system of property law based on internally connecting notions of ownership, possession and holdership in respect of each proprietary right which were clearly defined but small in number (this is the *numerus clausus* notion). It allowed for some more limited, derivative proprietary rights to develop, like income and enjoyment rights through usufructs, easements and some types of long leases, and even security interests, but no others.

These proprietary rights became systematically distinguishable from obligatory rights. The difference could be illustrated in relation to rights and duties of third parties in respect of the assets concerned, particularly in terms of the recovery rights of owners or of secured creditors of a bankrupt debtor in (constructive) possession of the assets, in the sense that those with proprietary rights in it could set the asset aside or segregate it and take it whilst those with obligatory rights could not but became common creditors who could recover only pro rata from the proceeds of unencumbered assets of the debtor. Another aspect was the free alienability of these *proprietary* rights (therefore even without consent of the owner of the underlying asset if these rights were limited, such as usufructs or certain type of leases, and operated in the property of others).[318]

The codification drive, in which on the European Continent legislation moved to centre stage was a later, nineteenth-century, development. It needed the substantive rule formulation and subjective rights approach which were largely the achievement of the earlier secularised and de-romanised natural law school, but was itself mainly inspired and promoted by the evolution of the modern state in which the concept of a *national*

---

[318] This alienability did not strictly speaking apply to security interests (although they could be transferred with the debts they insured), the proprietary nature of which was illustrated primarily by their priority status in the secured asset and their ranking amongst each other according to the time of the creation of these rights.

law became a priority. At first, this was intended to promote uniformity, equality, and predictability in the exercise of the citizens' rights at the national level whilst doing away with antiquated, diverse and often regional rules, but subsequently also to help consolidate these states and to support and confirm their central organising power and view of society.

In the former objectives, one recognises the older ideals of the Enlightenment. It required a legislative drive, which in due course also became an important vehicle perceived to support and even enhance the national social order and its economy in a rational and more efficient manner. Thus legislation was considered to provide a ready and natural vehicle for reform, adaptation and greater efficiency, eventually even to support social engineering. Here the emphasis shifts to the role of the state per se and one may note the German Romantic tradition in which codification takes on a life of its own and private law soon lost its autonomy. Here the state, its insights and its organisational powers, became all.

This idea was subsequently joined by the German academic ideal that abstract rational models could be devised, for social intercourse too, that were sufficiently reflective of reality to steer and guide it better. These were formulated by the academies or law schools the state itself had organised and law formation at the national level was then their primary and early objective. One could say that in such an environment the true legitimacy of private law was considered to come from a form of self-evident systemic coherence that academia thought it was able to demonstrate and that their governments would underwrite. Society would conform and could thus be guided. One sees here three nineteenth-century paradigm shifts on the European Continent, already indentified, and which led to what we now perceive as the civil law and which set it fundamentally apart from earlier Roman and also from the common law: a) all law became national, b) even private law was nationalised in its creation at the level of the state through legislation and c) it was subject to intellectualisation and system thinking. Other sources of law became suspect or even anathema. In the process, the idea of individualism under the protection of an autonomous natural law or under fundamental principle weakened seriously, unless these concepts or values were more narrowly defined by statute as inalienable (human) rights or public order requirements. Internationalism and universalism came to an end and an overarching notion of statehood, national communities, national economies and social policies took over. Eventually, in commerce and finance, it was reinforced by all nations adopting their own currencies, and monetary and trade policies, which could be equally manipulated and cut off from (international) market forces.

On the European Continent, positive law of a *nationalistic* nature thus became dominant even in private and commercial law, whilst increasingly the only recognised true source of the law was the statute (or code), even for law of a private nature that was not meant to be mandatory but rather directory (or default rule). Another aspect of this development was that all legal structures like contracts and property rights were believed to be dependent on such law, therefore on state *fiat*. That also applied to party autonomy as source of law. In this approach, the impact of custom and practices on the law was there also by state authorisation alone. At least that became the codification ethos. Private law was no longer believed anchored in human civilisation, therefore in fundamental or general principle or in more informal participatory forms of law formation through practices and custom or party autonomy, but rather in a state's expression thereof and in the coherence of the model so presented.

In *civil law*, the inclination of state law became indeed to neutralise or push out all other sources of private law. Again, private law was *nationalised* and was considered henceforth to issue from states alone and national legislation took centre stage, also in private law formation. This affected first the old customary laws, but natural law notions became also increasingly discredited, which affected in particular the respect for fundamental and general principle unless they underlay the particular codification itself or were specifically recognised and admitted by it. So it was for party autonomy. Thus henceforth all had to be expressed or supported by domestic legislation and were perceived as being national. It followed that communities if not statist or state-recognised were in their law-making capabilities increasingly ignored. Even the international law merchant could not survive in that climate and public international law also risked being reduced to treaty law only that was enacted by states.

On the European Continent, private law codes thus started to exude the pretence of being all-embracing in the areas they meant to cover. The existence of gaps was even denied, and all were considered complete on the basis of a proper interpretation of these codes themselves, related statutes, or the system underlying them whilst case law acquired importance merely in that context. This became the attitude in the major civil law codifications, even if the idea was particularly stretched in interpretation: see section 1.2.13 above and also section 1.4.3 below. Although in civil law countries large areas of private law remained technically the subject of separate statutes, that did not make a difference as they were deemed to have the same status and approach as the codes and were all considered integrated in one system. This also included therefore commercial law.

Judges were then seen as administrators applying the applicable law as they found it in the codes and related statutes in a mechanical manner (*bouches de la loi*). The fiction was that solutions for all legal conflict would automatically follow the logical interpretation of this kind of law. Equality, consistency, and legal certainty were in this manner considered guaranteed. The result was just, socially balanced, and efficient per se. Being the law, its outcome could not be questioned, although it could of course still be academically critiqued but the tendency was increasingly to accept the result unquestioningly. But these truths held only per country and all law was considered territorial as a consequence of the statist idea. Natural cultures were said to support it. There was no law beyond it. Civil law thus fell apart.

For all its limitations and nationalistic confinement, the Continental civil law approach constituted nevertheless a major intellectual achievement and provided a clearer basis for interpretation, which was increasingly sustained by deduction or otherwise induction or analogy helped by systemic reasoning. It reduced the law's more subjective and historical elements: at least that was the aspiration. But whatever liberal interpretation was thus allowed, see section 1.2.13 above, the price overall was statism and a static view of the law based on the extrapolation of past experiences, assuming that life was in essence repetitive and that its operation could be mathematically mapped out and logically explained in an intellectual system that could also satisfactorily guide human behaviour and properly solve its problems in the future.[319]

---

[319] For the basic intellectual criticisms, see n 208 above.

1.4.2 Fact- and Law-finding in Civil and Common Law

Whether or not other sources of private law survived or can be revived, at least transnationally, it follows from the foregoing that the sources of law that are here of particular
interest are: (a) fundamental principle; (b) custom or industry practices which are not then
distinguished; (c) general principle; and (d) party autonomy. In a transnational context,
treaty law may also be important. Again, this is similar to Article 38(1) of the Statute of the
International Court of Justice for public international law. There is no clear reason why
things should be different in private law formation at least at the transnational level. Even
local law may still play a residual role, as we shall see, but is then part of the transnational
law and accordingly explained. In international commerce and finance, these sources are
indeed the pillars of the modern *lex mercatoria* and promote its autonomous revival, if not
also affecting and changing domestic laws.

In domestic law, especially of the civil law type, the revival of these sources of law takes
the form particularly of: (a) a more factual approach to law finding; and more especially
(b) a liberal interpretation technique in respect of statutory texts. In common law, it is
rather the restrictive interpretation of statutes and the continuing fact-oriented pragmatism of the courts which allows resort to various sources of law. In these aspects, common
and civil law may be separately considered and compared before we go to the subject of
transnationalisation itself.

It was noted before that the fundamental technical difference between civil and common
law is not in the statutory nature of the private law or in its codification as such, not even in
nationalism. In common law countries, there is now also much statutory private law, especially in the area of equity, *viz* tax, company, bankruptcy and trust law. Moreover, at least in
England, the idea became also that the sovereign was the ultimate source of law, although it
did not need to be expressed in statute. Even in the US, there is a strong sentiment that the
law is based in the own traditions and national experiences as we have seen, even though
this idea is less sovereignty infested as in the American sensibilities, sovereignty rests with
the people.

The basic differences between common and civil law are rather in: (a) the civil law's
monopolisation of the sources of the law by legislation; (b) its claim to completeness; and,
especially; (c) its systemic thinking. It follows that the law of the codification is in essence
norm- not fact-oriented. In its application, it seeks out the facts according to previously
established intellectual concepts, which are expansively applied. Norms are a given; facts
must fall into place; real life must conform. Legal dynamism thus suffers and many facts
may fall off the plate as being legally irrelevant.[320] In truth, civil law in its intellectual system
building has problems with facts and therefore with reality.

Common law jurisdictions on the other hand, never accepted the exclusivity of statutory
law and always retained two other basic sources: (common) law and equity, and in fact also
custom, the law merchant and party autonomy, as further sources of law, see also the key

---

[320] Before the notion of good faith was substantially stretched, this applied, eg to failure to disclose relevant
information in pre-contractual situations, to conduct and reliance in contract formation, and to fundamental
changes of circumstances in post-contractual situations. See for the modern approaches to contract, s 1.1.4
above.

sections 1-103(a)(2) and (b) UCC in the USA, already referred to several times, even if they may not or no longer fully reflect the modern English attitude.

Moving from case to case, even in statutory interpretation as we have seen, common law attitudes also did not succumb to system thinking. In fact, these deeper differences with civil law have long been spotted.[321] It concerns here mainly the common law's greater reliance on facts and it is more *casuistic and inductive* but also more pragmatic approach to law-finding.

By putting less emphasis on the positive law as a set of rules, and even less on a system, it means that the common law does not have the civil law's constraints as to the recognition of other sources of law. Even where, as in England, it has at least in legal scholarship probably become no less black-letter law-oriented through the academic deduction of rules from disparate cases and statutory texts, this system is still less closed, even if the role of custom as an independent legal source is now also often questioned in England (although less so in commercial law as noted before) and the English do not on the whole like generalities in terms of fundamental or general principle.

In the US, this is all less problematic, as there is also the political role of the courts which allows more easily for alternatives motivated, for example, by ethical, social, cultural or economic considerations or more generally by policies and values, as was discussed more extensively in section 1.3.4 above in the context of the discussion of 'legal realism'. Here the more ethical and human rights related philosophies in the Constitution also make a difference as to the acceptance of more fundamental and general principle.

As to the method of fact- and law-finding itself, there thus remain some important differences between civil and common law, which again go back to system thinking and also has an effect on the approach to rules and their interpretation. This may be explored somewhat further. The civil law lawyer faced with a legal problem normally starts from a point where there is some given system of rules and principles and attempts to deduce further rules and principles from them and from the system itself to apply to the case before him. He will spot the relevant facts in the light of these rules and principles, which provide for him a guide from the outset and which he received from education and practice.

The system plays an important role here. Other sources of law that are more dynamic would disturb the outlook. The common law lawyer, on the other hand, will first look at the facts and will then ask what the nearest case or statutory provision is, therefore whether a relevant rule can be found in precedents or in legislation that may be closest or otherwise relevant and have application to the particular case. It follows that systematic thinking and suspicion of other sources of law beyond legislation are here lesser issues.[322]

---

[321] See for important comments on the differences between common and civil law legal thinking, W Fikentscher, *Methoden des Rechts*, vol 2 (1975). See for an incisive comment on the nature of the common law, MA Eisenberg, *The Nature of the Common Law* (1988).

[322] In all rule formulation and certainly in statutory law, the traditional common law lawyer thus takes an ad hoc attitude and wants precise, fairly narrow rules and in statutes clear definitions, an attitude which the civil law lawyer is likely to adopt only in criminal cases. The civil law lawyer lives happily with greater abstractions and more general ideas. They quickly stake out the field for him, whilst the detail is left for later on in the proceedings; that is for more precise interpretation later on the basis of the facts. For the civil law lawyer, too precise a rule is often seen as an unnecessary limitation giving rise to distorted interpretation, to incongruous results, and extra litigation costs.

Much more might be made of this, and of the common law's emphasis on the facts closely tied to its trial practice. This trial practice is indeed geared to fact-finding and discovery to get all information first. In common law proceedings, it is as a procedural matter necessary to prevent any surprise in court (still considered to include

Indeed, common law is often thought to be primarily inductive on the basis of the facts, and civil law deductive on the basis of its rules,[323] although modern common and civil law are often less far apart than may appear. In first instance, the difference may be one of procedure, not always one of substance, connected with the operation of the common law with its greater and sometimes excessive emphasis on fact finding (for example, in discovery), not shared to the same extent in civil law.

The civil law lawyer, on the basis of his more abstract rules, seems to be able to distinguish sooner between facts that are or may become legally relevant, and facts that are not. As a consequence, the civil law fact-finding operation tends to be quicker and less expensive and this is certainly an important reason why going to court in civil law countries is often much cheaper.[324] There is the important point, however, that there may be intellectual prejudice implied in this codification attitude when it comes to selecting the relevant (new) facts.[325] The consequence may be a narrowing attitude in the search for them. It has already been said that much may fall off the plate. Again, other sources of law need not be considered. Thus, as has already been said, pre-contractual duties went at first unnoticed, until this became factually untenable and good faith notions introduced them.

This approach never took root in common law, nor in the more intellectually minded modern attitudes in the US, although in all law formation, at least that by legislators, some plan or model would seem to be appropriate.[326] In any event, the differences should not be exaggerated, especially not since the pre-ordained system of rules resulting in civil law from codification is often patchy, out of date, and in any event frequently too unfocussed to be of immediate help so that the facts also play an ever greater role in civil law (like in good faith situations and now also in much of the law of negligence). It has already been pointed out that in contract and tort, codification thinking is now often so old or abstract that case law also moves from situation to situation or from fact to fact so that both approaches become more similar. In fact, amongst the most prominent civil lawyers[327] it has been questioned

---

a jury, although in private law cases they are very rare outside the USA, where there is a constitutional right to a jury in all cases although it can be and is often waived for cost reasons). In this system, the court sits in only one session (which may, however, go on for days). In civil law, further particulars may be sought and dealt with in subsequent meetings of the courts as and when they become necessary.

[323] See for a classic essay in legal reasoning in respect of case law, statutory law and constitutional law in the US, which has retained its value until this day, EH Levi, *An Introduction to Legal Reasoning* (University of Chicago Press, 1949, reprinted 1962). Here a sharp distinction between a deductive and inductive approach is (rightly) questioned within the common law itself.

[324] As is sometimes said: 'opinion is cheap, fact is expensive'. The considerable difference in litigation cost is the more glaring, practical, and immediately visible consequence of this difference in attitude between civil and common law. This is aggravated in England by the multiplication of lawyers' functions and fees: those of solicitors, barristers and QCs in larger cases, whilst much of the rules of procedure and evidence is still determined by the jury tradition even if in private cases they are (in England) now hardly ever present. Thus at least in litigation, there clearly continues to be a different attitude to fact finding in civil and common law and to the guidance of the applicable law in finding the relevant facts early on.

[325] See J Vranken, *Exploring the Jurist's Mind* (2006) 99ff; see for the role of tradition and its limiting effect, JT Onnti, 'Law, Tradition and Interpretation' (1998) 11 *International Journal for the Semiotics of Law* 26, 36.

[326] The Dutch Civil Code of 1992 is here indicative of what codification does: confirm the status quo and legal rigidity especially in the law of personal property. It constrained in particular asset-backed funding which goes far beyond secured transactions and also includes leasing, repo-financing, and factoring of receivables, all forms of temporary or conditional ownership rights in finance sales, *viz* legal structures with which the common law deals in equity. See in particular s 1.1.4 above and vol III, ch 1.

[327] HCF Schoordijk, 'Enkele opmerkingen over de bronnen van verbintenis en "European law in the making"' ['Some observations on the sources of the law of obligations and European Law in the making'] (2006) *Emeritaal Werk* 137.

whether codification in the traditional civil law tradition still makes sense in the law of obligations, which may have become too factual or fact-driven to allow for one intellectual system to control all.[328]

The different approach to fact and norm between common and civil law nevertheless remains important. It is an issue that should be well *distinguished* from liberal interpretation of the rules themselves (see the next section) although in the practice of the civil law they often come together. In fact, the search for norm and fact cannot be truly separated. What is legally relevant in the facts depends on the norm but the properly applicable norm can only be found through an appreciation of the facts. They are irretrievably linked. That presents a conundrum that cannot be here further unraveled, except to say that the positivist sharp separation between them is also from this point of view unsustainable. In practice, it is the emphasis and where one starts that count. Common law starts with the facts and puts the emphasis there; civil law with the norms or the system.

1.4.3 The Revival of the Traditional Sources of Law through Liberal Interpretation Techniques

It has already been pointed out several times that in civil law the exclusive civil law *legislative* attitude based on system thinking presents a uniquely nationalistic nineteenth-century phenomenon, now often considered the ultimate democratic ideal, although, at first, this legislation was by no means always the result of a democratic process in the modern sense: the Prussian, French and Austrian Codes were hardly so enacted: see section 1.2.11 above. In any event, this legislative process is often overly formal and amounts mostly to rubber-stamping academic proposals which claim here qualitative superiority. It has already been noted that new values must come into this law in many other ways: see in particular section 1.2.13 above.

Thus the democratic legislative process is not the only way through which more fundamental notions or newer social and public order considerations or values progress through the law. Indeed, they can generally not wait for legislation. Legislative activity of this nature is further subject to the law of unintended consequences, sometimes fatally so; the result might not even work or might be simply wishful thinking, more especially in regulation, but this may no less apply to private law legislation. The new Dutch civil code showed many examples in personal property law especially in respect of assignments, finance

---

[328] There are, of course, other differences between common and civil law, already referred to. It is clear, for example, that the common law was itself much more of a long historical accident. Especially in England, it is still largely casuistic and even statutory law tends to be directed towards special situations, is remedial and incidental, which also affects its interpretation which is literal and restrictive, see s 1.3.3 above.

Furthermore, common law abandoned its action-oriented approach much later than civil law as we have seen and was much slower in the formulation of substantive rules and subjective rights. Although, through the *stare decisis* rule and statutory law, substantive rules are also more actively formulated in common law, again, they tend to be narrowly construed. It means that in common law individual decisions cannot always be so easily reconciled with the rest and amongst the judges there is certainly no primary concern with doing so, although again academic writing often gives a different impression and by its very nature looks for more coherence.

sales and security interests. Corrective activity in the courts then becomes necessary when fundamental and general principle revive.

The pretence of exclusivity and systemic completeness and the claim that the system can provide for all eventualities makes these Codes in any event dependent for their credibility on *liberal interpretation powers or techniques* of judges and therefore often on considerable judicial freedom and inventiveness. It puts the judge at the centre, which was not the original idea in civil law at all but also reintroduces the force of other sources of law, especially legal principle and therefore natural law overtones, which the codes had thought to expunge. Objectivity may then become a less absolute goal as ethical, social, economic and other considerations also enter the decision making process and therefore the law, although it may be repeated that they should only do so in more *pressing* cases where one may assume substantial community support. Otherwise, these considerations could easily lead to conflicting results and more controversy.

Common law did not have similar constraints in terms of the acceptance of other sources of law, as we have seen, even if it does not like principle but moves and progresses from case to case on the basis of the facts and practical needs. The differences are thus fairly obvious. Statutes are literally interpreted to leave as much room for the old methods, which are the further development of common law and equity on the basis of changing factual patterns and needs. Civil law, on the other hand, in order to progress, uses its system, in contract now supported by notions of good faith, to give it flexibility and the facility to reintroduce principle (of fairness or equality and social values) and it now also pays more attention to the facts, even domestically. Analogy is here another forceful facility.[329]

Other sources of law or legal considerations of a different nature revive here informally. How much room that may also create for new proprietary structures to develop may be more uncertain, but it is not impossible either; see section 1.1.4 above. In any event, a liberal interpretation technique is not necessarily limited to contract. In a codified system, unlike in equity in common law jurisdictions, there is a limited number of proprietary rights, the *numerus clauses*, as was noted before.[330] Only a freer, more practical and less systematic interpretation method could then allow for the development of newer proprietary interests if so demanded by commerce and the financial practice. Indeed, to some

---

[329] Thus if a new type of contract became fashionable, its rules, if not determined by the parties in the contract, would technically speaking somehow still have to be deduced from the general provisions concerning contracts in the applicable codes. Guidance would additionally be sought in the statutory provisions concerning special contract types that could be considered related when an exercise in making proper distinctions would follow but also in systemic and analogical interpretation.

In this manner, one could ask whether directors of companies had an agreement with the company in the nature of employment contract or a contract for the provision of services or rather a contract of a *sui generis* type that had nevertheless some features of both but that would still need to be defined further. Nevertheless, this could allow case law to produce over a period of time a new set of rules for that particular contract.

Another example may be found in the modern brokerage contract as an elaboration of the contract of agency. It takes longer to reach the appropriate level of modern investor protection against the broker and his practices and be less comprehensive than new legislation, but it is often the only way in the absence of much interest or a clear view from legislators. Thus it was unavoidable that in many civil law countries, much of the law of companies, partnerships, and employment was at first developed in case law and legal practice on the basis of rudimentary code provisions in this manner, and was only subsequently aided by legislation.

[330] See also JH Dalhuisen, 'European Private Law: Moving from a Closed to an Open System of Proprietary Rights' (2001) 5 *Edinburgh Law Review* 1, see further vol II, ch 2, s 1.3.7.

limited extent, this happened in Germany in the late nineteenth century.[331] There are also signs of it in recent case law under the new Dutch civil code (see Volume III, chapter 1, section 1.2).

Here more fundamental principle and practical need take over. Constructive trust, tracing rights, and liens shifting into future assets could then also appear,[332] subject to the protection of the ordinary commercial and financial flows, all in aid of practical commercial and financial needs or, perhaps on a higher note, to prevent a windfall for others, like creditors of an agent, who without this redress might become unjustly enriched in their own recovery possibilities. Conditional or temporary ownership rights may equally become more acceptable to underpin the safety of modern financial products, like finance leases and repurchase agreements. Although in civil law countries, domestic laws are still largely unbending, in section 1.1.4 above, these developments were noted and greater dynamism in professional law identified as necessary, at least in international transactions, and it centred on greater party autonomy also in proprietary matters as a matter of modern risk management.

Acceptance of the concept of the more formal trust in civil law may then not be far away either, but again it should be realised that it goes against the grain and system thinking of civil law, which, however, presents no legal unity, and different civil law countries may here take very different attitudes.[333] Indeed, it may be seen that non-statutory sources of law that go beyond its system are used all the time, also in civil law. As will be argued, this acquires a particular importance in the revival of transnational private law.

On the other hand, it may exactly be the benefit of a more limited systemic interpretation that no Pandora's box is opened, and that at least in property some room for the traditional bankruptcy law principles and considerations is preserved, thus favouring the common creditors of a debtor over those who claim all kinds of proprietary interests and retrieval rights in the assets, even though the former normally receive very little in whatever approach and any restriction on preferential rights usually means the reshuffling of these interests amongst professional creditors; common creditors are unlikely to benefit from the room so created, see again the discussion in section 1.1.4 above.

---

[331] Note in this connection the early creation of the non-possessory security interest or the *Sicherungsübereignung* in chattels and much later in the twentieth century the development of the proprietary conditional ownership expectation in the reservation of title, ultimately leading to the concept of the *dingliche Anwartschaft*: see for these legal structures more particularly vol III, ch 1, s 1.4.1. These were major case-law developments, upon a proper analysis going against the (closed proprietary) system of proprietary rights of the BGB, even if often explained as developments *praeter legem*, therefore as being parallel to, and not truly in conflict with, the existing system. In fact, it can be argued that established practices took over and were accepted by the courts.

In a similar manner, a more liberal interpretation approach, the concept of good faith or acceptable morals (*gute Sitten*) has been used in Germany in bankruptcy, here to deny proprietary execution rights or to readjust seniority and priorities against the rules laid down for them, at least in Germany.

In the civil law of agency, the direct proprietary rights of principals in assets (goods or proceeds) the (undisclosed) agent buys or receives for them in his own name also became more firmly established against the system, again on the basis of practicalities.

[332] Indeed, one of the major draftsmen of the Dutch Civil Code of 1992, now noting its practical insufficiencies, especially in property law, has proposed exactly aggressive case-law, but it may be doubted whether that is the general attitude in Dutch legal scholarship: see W Snijders, 'Ongeregeldheden in het Vermogensrecht' [Irregularities in the Law of Property and Obligations] (2005) *Weekblad voor Privaatrecht, Notariaat en Registratie* (*WPNR*) 6607/8. The statutory insufficiencies are not necessarily seen here as a disadvantage and it is suggested that they give judges greater flexibility.

[333] See also JH Dalhuisen, 'Conditional Sales and Modern Financial Products' in A Hartkamp et al (eds), *Towards a European Civil Code*, 2nd edn (1998) 525.

In any event, the civil law idea remains that, short of legislation, all is extrapolation from the existing system; the inveterate Germanic desire for re-systematisation, even in good faith case law, was noted earlier. Again, the common law is not so confined and is here more comfortable with case law that develops on the basis of the facts and practical needs rather than of deductive reasoning or analogy in the application of existing rules. In this connection, it was also noted before that at least in England, statutory law is largely remedial and seldom conceptual and that the way of drafting statutes normally remains geared only to special fact situations and not to stating principle: see section 1.3.3 above.[334] This statutory law is literally interpreted so that there remains ample room for law and equity to operate besides it unless specifically overruled. Statutory interpretation accepts this and does not go beyond it. There is no teleological or normative interpretation, at least not in commercial matters, where contracts are often also literally interpreted. As already mentioned, principle is disliked.[335] Yet, here again, the differences with civil law may appear sometimes greater than they are: even in civil law, good faith may require a similar restrictive and literal attitude to contract interpretation if the contract is a road map and risk-allocation instrument amongst professionals, see again section 1.1.4 above. Similar attitudes may be expected in the interpretation of bills of lading and letters of credit. However, the distinction between professional and other dealings is less vivid in civil law. It still aspires to a unitary system, which may be a considerable drawback. Consumer notions thus easily enter into the determination of the precise relationships between professionals; see further also Volume II, chapter 1, section 1.1.1.

In contract interpretation, modern Continental and American attitudes may more readily converge here, even to the point of the Americans becoming comfortable with the good faith concept, see also Volume II, chapter 1, section 1.3.7, but again it may be more restrictively handled in professional dealings than it often is in civil law countries. It still has less meaning in pre-contractual and post-contractual situations.

Especially in civil and commercial matters, it should never be forgotten, however, that the *practical* differences between the various advanced legal systems are not always great, all the more so in Western culture where there is everywhere a similar combination of the rule of law with a neo-capitalist economic and social system.

---

[334] In this way the common law and equity still develop further. Thus in modern times, promissory estoppel or reliance notions were accepted to substitute for the consideration notion, see vol II, ch 1, s 1.2.3. In common law, the movement to accept the binding nature of offers between merchants, therefore regardless of the consideration requirement that made them logically (on pure syllogism) unenforceable, may also be strengthened by case law on business grounds (as was eventually confirmed in the UCC). Here we see extralegal or economic considerations leading to legal adjustment in which an expansive interpretation of a rule may allow for the evolution of alternative legal structures. In equity, floating charges were also developed through case law, as was in England more recently the important Mareva injunction see s 1.3.1 above and vol III, ch 1, s 1.5.2.

[335] In England, there is now at least the *purposive* approach of statute (see more particularly s 1.3.3 above) but it does not amount, as yet, to a more fully normative approach. It is often distinguished from teleological interpretation, which is then considered to take into account extra contractual/legal considerations derived from pressing moral, sociological or efficiency considerations.

EU legislation and its interpretation force English judges more generally into teleological interpretation of European scripts.

In interpretation, there may also be detected a stronger normative element in modern contract law, even in England, such as in the notion of reliance, implied terms, or distinctions on the basis of the character and nature of legal relationships as between professional and non-professional dealings. See also n 61 above and more particularly vol II, ch 1, s 1.3.7.

But the remaining differences are not irrelevant, and may also acquire a competitive aspect in international dealings. As has already been observed, the greatest *practical* differences between common and civil law, as far as commerce and finance are concerned, are in equity. This may be clearly seen in the development of fiduciary duties in trust, agency and company law. It may no less be seen in the laws of tracing, equitable interests and similar restitutionary claims, shifting liens and floating charges, conditional and temporary ownership rights in chattels, and equitable assignments of intangibles, or the set-off.

At least in business, the common law would appear to have the advantage here in terms of a more dynamic and responsive law, further supported by a more pragmatic judiciary.

1.4.4 Survival of Transnational Legal Sources in Commercial Law. EU and Public International Law Attitudes

Strong nationalism is still inherent in both modern civil and common law. This is also so in professional dealing even if international. It means that there is in either system in principle little room for transnationalisation as overarching law derived from different legal sources in cross-border private law activities. On this view, (national) judges will apply only a national law (although it could be that of other states, but they would allow it only under their own rules of private international law or comity) and ignore all others.[336] Here the common law of the English variety and Continental law increasingly combined.

It was noted that they often combine in the positivist and formal approach, in which, in England, principles are considered too vague (even when fundamental) and custom generally atavistic (although with some greater respect for it in commercial law) and in which, on the Continent, both are considered extra-statutory and do not therefore count, unless they underlie and support the system itself or are specifically mentioned and authorised in the texts, like custom in contract interpretation.[337] Here emerges further communality between both legal systems, which was earlier identified as having to do with academic rationalisations of statutory and case law in England and a desire for legislation in the Law Commission, which supports experiments like the Principles of European Contract Law (PECL) and the Draft Common Frame of Reference (DCFR) in the EU, and therefore the push for codification in the traditional civil law sense at EU level, even including England. This is, however, not supported by the commercial practice in England and most likely also not by its courts.

In the previous section, it was also pointed out that in modern times in civil law, even domestically the different sources of law may hide behind the facade of good faith, at least in contract law. In a generally more liberal interpretation approach, even in the law of movable

---

[336] See, eg M Mustill, 'Contemporary Problems in International Commercial Arbitration' (1989) 17 *International Business Law* 161ff, who even considered as absolutely void a contract in which transnational law is chosen as controlling. These views are not unknown in the US either, see s 1.3.5 above, especially not in the more critical legal studies or sociological approaches.

[337] See also K Zweigert and H Kötz, *An Introduction to Comparative Law*, 3rd edn (Oxford, Oxford University Press, 1997) 265. See for the perceived approximation of the English and Continental law, PS Atiyah and RS Summers, *Form and Substance in Anglo-American Law*, n 269 above.

property, there was also some flexibility. This may even support transnationalisation by expanding in a first stage domestic notions. This is, however, not the way of current civil law thinking.

However, it was also noted in this connection that the transnational sources of private law were never completely extinguished in commerce and finance, and continued to contribute to the infrastructure for the international marketplace. One may think here of the law concerning bills of lading,[338] negotiable instruments, especially eurobonds and euromarket practices including clearing and settlement,[339] the law of international assignment,[340] of set-off and netting,[341] and of letters of credit (UCP) and trade terms

---

[338] See W Haak, 'Internationalism above Freedom of Contract' in *Essays on International and Comparative Law in Honour of Judge Erades* (1983) 69. It is sometimes also suggested that international mandatory customary law overrides the jurisdiction of the *forum actoris* (of the plaintiff therefore), see P Verheul, 'The Forum Actoris and International Law' in the same *Essays in Honour of Judge Erades* (1983) 196.

[339] It is often said that the negotiability of eurobonds derives from the force of market custom: see the older English cases on international bonds law *Goodwin v Roberts* [1876] 1 AC 476 and *Picker v London and County Banking Co* [1887] 18 QBD 512 (CA), which relate to Russian and Prussian bonds and emphasised that the financial community treated these instruments as negotiable regardless of domestic laws.

See further P Wood, *Law and Practice of International Finance* (London, 1980) 184. See also *Bechuanaland Exploration Co v London Trading Bank* [1898] 2 QBD 658, in which it was accepted in connection with the negotiability of bearer bonds that 'the existence of usage has so often been proved and its convenience is so obvious that it might be taken now to be part of the law'. Modern case law does not, however, exist confirming the point but in England these cases are still considered good law. See for the explicit reference in this connection to the custom of the mercantile world which may expressly be of recent origin, *Dicey, Morris and Collins on the Conflict of Laws*, 14th edn (2006) r 222, 1800. This general part was deleted in the 15th edn of 2012 but reappeared in part on p 2099 where in the text, but no longer in the rule, a reference to custom was maintained

The transnational status of eurobonds is probably not affected, even now that in most cases they have become mere book-entry entitlements in a paperless environment, see s 3.2.3 below. It also affects the way these instruments are repossessed or given in security, cleared and settled.

[340] Important issues of notification and documentation arise especially in respect of the use of receivables in modern financing, where local law impediments to bulk assignments are increasingly removed and a reasonable description and immediate transfer upon the conclusion of the assignment agreement is becoming normative. Future (replacement) receivables are increasingly likely to be able to be included so that questions of identification and sufficient disposition rights do no longer arise either. Exceptions derived from the underlying agreements out of which these receivables arise are increasingly ignored, especially any third party effect of contractual assignment restriction whilst others are limited to situations in which the assignment gives rise to unreasonable burdens, see also ss 2-210 and 9-404 UCC and for a comparative summary vol III, ch 1, s 2.2.4.

The promissory note as negotiable instrument with its independence from the underlying transaction out of which it arises becomes here the better transnational analogy, perhaps aided by the UNCITRAL 2001 Convention on the Assignment of Receivables in International Trade, although it has not received any ratifications and is certainly not as clear and advanced as it could have been, see vol III, ch 1 ss 2.2.4 and 2.4.8.

[341] In this connection, in the swap and repo markets, the ISDA Swap Master Agreements and the PSA/ISMA Global Master Repurchase Agreement may acquire the status of custom in the areas they cover, at least in the London and the New York markets where they operate. This may be particularly relevant for their close-out and netting provisions in an event of default. The status of contractual bilateral netting with its enhancements of the set-off principle and its inclusion of all swaps between the same parties, leading to a netting out of all positions in the case of default at the option of the non-defaulting party and *ipso facto* in the case of bankruptcy, could otherwise still remain in doubt under local bankruptcy laws if not properly amended.

In the 1996 Amendments to the 1988 Basel Accord on Capital Adequacy, the netting principle was internationally accepted; see also vol III, ch 2, s 2.5. It concerns here so-called soft law but nevertheless a most important international acknowledgement of the concept of netting, although still subject to the condition that the law of the country of the residence of the counterparty (or his place of incorporation) and of the branch through which the bank acted as well as the law applicable to the swap must accept the netting concept (which had required changes or clarifications in domestic law of several countries).

(Incoterms).[342] It may also concern the important and connected issue of finality of title transfers and payments.[343]

Also in an EU context, the question of the proper *sources* of the private law has come up, notably in the interpretation of private law conventions, such as the Brussels Convention on Jurisdiction and the Enforcement of Judgments in Civil and Commercial Matters (the 1968 Brussels Convention),[344] since 1 March 2002 succeeded by Regulation and the proper implementation of the Directives touching on private law harmonisation, such as those operating in the consumer area.

The distinctive interpretation technique of the European Court of Justice (ECJ), for example, as to what is contractual or not, what is a consumer contract or an employment contract or not, what is a bankruptcy matter or not, and how requirements of good faith should be defined, is *not* based on national laws or on principles deduced from them: see also section 2.3.2 below. The ECJ maintains here its own normativity, which it finds in European *principles* and not necessarily in national laws,[345] see also sections 1.4.5 and 1.4.6 below for its use of fundamental and general principle, and Volume II, chapter 1, section 1.3.8 for the notion of good faith. This attitude necessarily also filters through into the

---

[342] The idea of the UCP being transnational customary law is associated with the views of the Austrian Frederic Eisemann, Director of the Legal Department of the ICC at the time, and was first proposed by him at a 1962 King's College London Colloquium, see *Le Credit Documentaire dans le Droit et dans la Pratique* (Paris, 1963) 4. This approach was followed in England by Clive Schmitthoff, although in his views always in the context of some national law which had to validate it.

See for France, Y Loussouarn and JD Bredin, *Droit du Commerce International* (1969) 48. In France, their status as international custom is now well established: see also J Puech, *Modes de paiement*, in Lamy, *Transport Tome II*, No 324 (2000); see also B Goldman, '*Lex Mercatoria*', in *Forum Internationale*, No 3 (November 1983); *Trib De Commerce de Paris*, 8 March 1976; 28 Le Droit Maritime Francais 558 (1976) (Fr); *Cour de Cass*, 14 October 1981, Semaine Juridique II 19815 (1982), note Gavalda and Stoufflet; *Cour de Cass*, 5 November 1991, Bull Civ IV, no 328 (1992).

In Belgium their status as international custom was accepted by the *Tribunal de Commerce of Brussels*, 16 November 1978, reprinted in 44 *Rev de la Banque* (1980) 249. In Germany, see N Horn, *Die Entwicklung des internationalen Wirtschaftechts durch Verhaltungsrichtlinie* 44 *Rabels Zeitschrift* (1980) 423, but German doctrine remains uncertain, especially because of the written nature of the UCP and its regular adjustments which is seen there as contrary to the notion of custom, see CW Canaris, *Bankvertragsrecht*, 3rd edn (1988) Pt I, 926.

In the Netherlands, the Supreme Court has not so far fully accepted the UCP as objective law. See *Hoge Raad, 22 May 1984* (1985) NJ 607. The lower courts are divided. So are the writers, with PL Wery, *De Autonomie van het Eenvormige Privaatrecht* (1971) 11, and this author in favour, see JH Dalhuisen, 'Bank Guarantees in International Trade' (1992) 6033 *WPNR* 52.

English law does not require any incorporation in the documentation. See *Harlow and Jones Ltd v American Express Ban Ltd & Creditanstalt-Bankverein* [1990] 2 Lloyd's Rep 343 (concerning the applicability of the ICC Uniform Rules for Collection (URC) which are less well known, but nevertheless subscribed to by all banks in England); *Power Curber International Ltd v National Bank of Kuwait SAK* [1981] 2 Lloyd's Rep 394 (Denning, L considering the UCP as such, also with reference to the fact that all or practically all banks in the world subscribe to them, which seems the true criterion in England).

For the US, see *Oriental Pac (USA) Inc v Toronto Dominion Bank* 357 NYS 2d 957 (NY 1974), in which the force of law of the UCP was accepted 'to effect orderly and efficient banking procedures and the international commerce amongst nations': ibid at 959. In the US the Incoterms and UCP are matched by similar rules in Arts 2 and 5 UCC, which may leave open the question of them operating as international custom in the US, but they would likely have that status in international cases and then supersede any conflicts of law rules in this area.

[343] See nn 72 and 73 above.

[344] See, eg the line of cases starting with Case 12/76 *Tessili v Dunlop AG* [1976] ECR 1473. See for the EU good faith notion, vol II, ch 1, s 1.3.8.

[345] Here again, as in statutory interpretation, exposure to European law may make a difference in English law: see K Schiemann, 'The Application of General Principles of Community Law by English Courts' in M Andenas and F Jacobs (eds), *European Community Law in the English Courts* (1998) 136.

national courts of Member States in the areas of private law subject to European law, which these national courts must uphold.

It has already been pointed out several times before that public international law always recognised a wide variety of legal sources culminating in Article 38(1) of the Statute of the International Court of Justice, which refers to fundamental and general principle, contract and custom as independent sources of law.[346]

1.4.5 Autonomous Legal Sources: Fundamental Principle

In sections 1.2 and 1.3 above, it was discussed how modern civil and common law came about, became both nationalistic, and gradually pushed out other non-nationalistic sources of law, at least at the domestic level, although always less, or at least less fundamentally, in commercial law in common law countries. These sources themselves and their progressive limitation in the civil law and their handling in the common law of the English variety will now be more broadly considered and summarised, as well as their reappearance, first in interpretation everywhere but now more particularly also in commerce and finance at the transnational level. Indeed it has already been posited that these notions always come back in times of renewal, now particularly because statutory law of the domestic kind is no longer able adequately to cover international transactions. As such, at this moment, domestic law, especially that of the black-letter type is challenged in particular by the progressive globalisation of commerce and finance.

We are concerned here above all with the force of law of fundamental and general principle, custom or industry practices, and party autonomy, the latter two being the expression of more participatory non-statist immanent law. These will each be discussed further in the next sections. This discussion will be concluded by revisiting the question of legal positivism versus legal principle at the transnational level.

It has been said before that a key issue is the role of fundamental principle, earlier often cast (together with general principle) in terms of natural law as the basis of the whole system. The idea of fundamental principle operating in this sense could already be found in Grotius in terms of secular natural law[347] and remains a pillar of public international law: see Article 38(1) Statute International Court of Justice. As we shall see, in international commerce and finance, these rights or principles may not be many but they are the foundation of the whole system of the modern *lex mercatoria* as transnational law.

In recent times, even domestically, at least the impact of human rights on private law formation has been noted. This is now often referred to as the *constitutionalisation* of private law.[348] It operates at several levels and may primarily impact on the power of states

---

[346] See also Roy Goode on this divergence in attitude between public and (civil law) private law in the acceptance of different sources of law, in 'Usage and its Reception in Transnational Commercial Law' (1997) *ICLQ* 1 and JH Dalhuisen, 'International Law Aspects of Modern Financial Products' (1998) *European Business Law Review* 281.

[347] See more particularly s 1.2.7 above.

[348] See for this concept in Germany CW Canaris, *Grundrechte und Privatrecht, eine Zwischenbilanz* ['Human rights and private law, an interim evaluation'] (Berlin, 1998) and in England, D Friedmann and D Barak-Erez (eds), *Human Rights in Private Law* (2001), and H Collins, 'Utility and Rights in Common Law Reasoning:

to intervene in private law through mandatory rules. Respect for the freedom to contract and to own property are here especially important for business. Then there are procedural protections, especially in state courts. It may on the other hand also be considered to what extent the so-called horizontal effect (sometimes) of human rights, therefore their effect between private parties, is in truth no less a revival of secular natural law notions, now in the form of fundamental and general legal principle. Analogy presents itself. It may amount to a redistribution of risk especially in consumer dealings and labour contracts in favour of weaker parties. Stronger parties, on the other hand, may be less protected but the imposition of unconscionable reparation duties or damage provisions could be in the same category and still offend fundamental principle, also for professionals. The introduction of overriding social values or public order notions in the law's application is of a similar nature.[349]

Other fundamental principles include the duty to repair damage improperly caused, the duty to give back what is not owned, and the duty to respect reliance of others on one's own conduct. They represent other key notions of private law, which are not new but rather the foundation of its entire system. One recognises here in particular the basics of contract, tort, property and unjust enrichment law. Again, this is pure Grotius. Property could then also be seen as a fundamental right. All these principles remained relevant in public international law and now also in foreign investment law as a form of transnationalised administrative law,[350] but they are also regaining their role in the transnationalisation of private law, thus escaping the grip of nineteenth-century legal nationalism and statist thinking.

It was said before that fundamental principle also re-appeared in interpretation, even domestically. The notion of good faith shows that very clearly in contract law and is then often believed itself a fundamental principle and thus mandatory.[351] There is here overlap with the normative or liberal interpretation technique of statutory law which may reintroduce fundamental notions of fairness, proportionality or balance. It is true that there is still an argument that invoking good faith itself is acceptable only when it is especially authorised by prevailing codified contract law (see ss 157 and 242 BGB in Germany and Articles 1134 and 1135 CC in France for the interpretation and supplementation of contracts), but, at least in Germany, it became clear that good faith was a source of law that could also impact on company and proprietary law or, as good morals (*bonnes mœurs*) or *gute Sitten*, even in the law of secured transactions that had no special provisions for it. The new Dutch law (Article 3.12 CC) refers in this connection to generally-recognised legal principles, the convictions living in the (Netherlands) population at large and the social and personal interests involved.

Rebalancing Private Law through Constitutionalization', LSE Law Dept, Law and Society Working Paper Series, 2nd issue, September 2007.

[349] See also the discussion in s 1.2.13 above.

[350] See, eg HP Loose, 'Administrative Law and International Law' in P Bekker, R Dolzer and M Waibel (eds), *Making Transnational Law Work in a Global Economy, Essays in Honour of Detlev Vagts* (2010) 380. *Cf* also R Dolzer, 'The Impact of International Investment Treaties on Domestic Administrative Law', (2005) 37 *International Law and Politics* 953–72.

[351] See Art I-1:102 DCFR and vol II, ch 1, s 1.3.10, but truly it is not always so; at least in the US professional parties may set standards under s 1-302 UCC as we saw. In fact, good faith is a multifaceted concept, see also n 58 above and vol II, ch 1, s 1.3.4, in many instances not mandatory at all. It also has another more institutional facet in relating the norm better to the facts, see also vol II, s 1.3.4.

In Europe, the Draft Common Frame of Reference (DCFR 2008/9) which now figures as some model for a European private law codification, see Volume II, chapter 1, section 1.6 and chapter 2, section 1.11, pays in this connection some lip service to (the horizontal effect of) human rights notions in Article I-1:102(b). This may be the reflection of the modern notion of constitutionalisation,[352] but only as a matter of interpretation of the text. The DCFR does not seem to be aware of other fundamental principles and of their status as an autonomous source of law except for the prohibition of discrimination, expressly mentioned in Article II-2:101ff. In fact, it is clear from the Introduction, re-written in 2009, that it does not know quite what to do with fundamental principles, except to point out that many provisions of the DCFR are related to them or expressions of them. Beyond (the horizontal effect of) human rights and the discrimination prohibition, which are closely related, they are not given a mention in the text, however, let alone an autonomous status, although good faith is (wrongly in its generality) given mandatory force and thus considered fundamental in a substantive sense.[353] It is, however, often simply liberal interpretation technique.

There is further a curious section (Article II-7:301ff) which talks about "infringement of fundamental principle or mandatory law" and voids contracts if infringing a principle recognised as fundamental in the laws of the Member States. This seems to suggest a EU public order principle derived from the laws of Member States in the nature of general principle. It would still appear to admit that there are no common EU values per se, but that nevertheless we can have a common EU private law.

However this may be, the DCFR conforms to the traditional codification ethos and its formal and positivist attitudes and beliefs in black-letter rule to be systematically applied as a matter of logic which does not allow for extraneous considerations, see further sections 1.4.14 to 1.4.15 below. Private law is in this view not a carrier of values except to the extent expressly formulated and can as such serve any regime or political system.

The DCFR thus becomes the paradise of the black letter specialist and rule fetishist. In that world all principle, even fundamental principle is at best soft law unless it finds clear expression in the text. This is in vivid contrast, however, to what EU case law itself has been doing, of which the DCFR seems wholly unaware. Culminating for the time being in *Mangold*[354]

---

[352] This goes back to the discussion above at n 348. The EU Human Rights Charter is not supposed to be here directly relevant unless specific and distinguishes in this connection sharply between rules and principles (Art 52). This was politics, but the distinction may prove to be hardly sustainable. It was earlier submitted that there is in law no fundamental difference between principle and rule. In fact, many rules are never much more than principles; it depends on the level of abstraction and intellectualisation which may be found in all rules of general application. As far as the EU Charter is concerned, exception is in any event made for principles that are further developed by ECJ case law or in legislation.

Other instances of horizontal effect may ensue when, on the basis of EU and implementing legislation, private rights and obligation are newly created, varied, or extinguished, but this is less likely to be based on fundamental or general principle directly although they may surface in the interpretation of the relevant laws, *cf* Case 36/74 *Walrave v Wielerbonden* [1974] ECR 1405, 12 December 1974; Case13/76 *Dona v Mantero* [1976] ECR 1333 14 July 1976; and Case 94/07 *Raccanelli v Max Planck Gesellschaft* [2008] ECR I-5939 (at N 50), 17 July 2008.

[353] See also n 351 above.

[354] Case C-144/04 *Werner Mangold v Rüdiger Helm* [2005] ECR I-19981, upholding as fundamental principle the concept of non-discrimination on the basis of age. This has become a check on private law legislation, although it may not (yet) be invoked directly between private parties. Non-discrimination according to nationality is no less fundamental, see Case 115/08 *Land Oberoestereich v Cez* [2009] ECR I-10265 and also applies in private dealings under EU laws, in this case directly.

This case law may also be seen in the light of the extension of the Court's jurisprudence following Case C-33/76 *Rewe v Landswirtschaftskammer fur das Saarland*, [1976] ECR 1989, disallowing, even in the absence of precise EU

in 2005 and in *Audiolux* in 2009,[355] the ECJ has made it very clear that there are overarching fundamental principles that operate and are enforceable at the same level as the Founding Treaties and need *not* be written. In *Audiolux*, the Advocate General called them 'deeply rooted principles without which a civilised society would not exist'.[356] They are generally effective and therefore also underlie private law.[357] They also introduced private law notions, not only of damages, in the determination and enforcement of public law obligations.[358]

These principles have had an immediate effect on the interpretation (and supplementation for those who make here a distinction) of all legal EU texts and their implementation in Member States. There may even be a corrective function if such superior principle is invoked which may also affect the legality of these instruments at EU and Member State level and will then often be related to the effective operation of EU law or to public order at that level. They may even affect the Treaty texts if conflicting with them. New causes of action may follow[359] whilst procedurally there may also be further immanent protections of this nature.

This may put the whole process of the formation of private law at EU level in a different light and its statist form is then no longer axiomatic. That would also affect the DCFR if it ever became operational. It is surprising that the drafters did not seem to be aware of these developments but the DCFR cannot ignore these principles even where not restated in the text. That also applies to its sales carve out in the Common European Sales Law or CESL; see Volume II, chapter 1, section 1.6. In the US, under the due process and similar clauses in the federal Constitution, the impact of fundamental principle has long been clearer, in private law as well, at least in the elaboration and application of procedural and conflict of laws rules. There is also the all pervading reach of the Bill of Rights as positive law, not as mere principle.

Fundamental principles of this nature are indeed the foundation of the whole structure of private law, now reviving particularly in the modern *lex mercatoria* where it may be seen by all who wish to see it. Other sources like general principle, custom and party autonomy are no less autonomous but not fully independent as they can elaborate on but not avoid, confine or overrule these fundamental principles. They cannot, for example, abolish contract and property altogether, but they can formulate structure and fill in the details.

---

rules, restrictive rules of national laws if affecting private law aspects such as damage calculations, statutes of limitation, interest charges, res judicata effect, etc when these national laws obstruct the effectiveness of EU principle, enforcing notably the basic EU freedoms of movement of goods, services, capital, information and persons.

[355] *Audiolux a.o v Gruope Bruxelles Lambert SA a.o, n Case* C-101/08, [2009] ECR I-9823.

[356] See para 40 of the Opinion of AG Trstenjak.

[357] See also D Kraus, '*Die Anwendung allgemeiner Grundsaetze des Gemeinschaftsrecht in Privatrechtsbeziehungen*' in K Riesenhuber (ed), *Entwicklungen nicht-legislatorischere Rechtsangleichung), in Europaeischen Privatrecht* (2008) 54, and A Metzger, 'Allgemeine Rechtsgrundsaetze in Europa' (2011) 75 *RabelsZ* 845.

[358] Notably in instances of failure of Member States timely to incorporate EU Directives at the expense of private parties, see Cases C-6/90 and 9/90 *Francovich and Others v Italy* [1991] ECR I-5357. These types of cases respond to the need to make EU law fully operative or effective, sometimes believed to be another fundamental principle by itself. In Case C-47/07 *Masdar v Commission* [2008] ECR I-9761, an action for unjust enrichment against the EU was created on the basis of similar reasoning.

[359] This may be relevant especially if the EU gives rights without a clear enforcement mechanism. The principle of effective judicial protection is then believed to give access to the local courts, see Case 222/84 *Johnson v Chief Constable of the Royal Ulster Constabulary* [1986] ECR 1651. This right to access to the local courts in these circumstances is now enshrined in Art 47(1) of the EU Human Rights Charter. Local rules of procedure may be adapted accordingly.

The drafters of the DCFR should have understood this, but never considered their method. Old fashioned codification technique was unquestionably and uncritically adopted. A proper consideration of methodology should have come first and would have required the authors better to understand, appreciate and evaluate other sources of immanent law formation, above all fundamental principle.

1.4.6 Autonomous Legal Sources: General Principle

General principle should be distinguished from fundamental principle. General principle is based foremost on an analysis of the answers or alternatives modern domestic legal systems may present. It highlights in particular what may be found in more advanced legal systems,[360] but also relates to rationality, utility and common sense. Grotius referred to it as part of the *Ius Gentium*, or the changeable law. It is as such a vital part of the modern transnational private law or new *lex mercatoria*.

Common law, always having been wary of generalisations, especially in England, is not much given to general principle as has already been noted. One may recall is William Blake's well-known view that 'to generalise is to be an idiot'. Civil law codifications only accepted general principles if they underlay its system even if others could never be entirely ignored. Quite apart from the notion of good faith in contract, the rules of which are at least in part a reflection of general principle (if not also referring to fundamental values), the law of tort and its development were in civil law countries always a reflection of what was considered anti-social, as such in many civil law countries still an extra-statutory norm which has nevertheless legal status. Bad behaviour may then also become legally relevant, for example, in environmental law. So are (often) the notion of good government and the administrative law protection of citizens against government that derives from it. Although often firmly based in fundamental principle as we have seen, their elaboration is r subject to more general notions and perceptions.

Again, the general principle is better known in public international law and mentioned in Article 38(1) of the Statute of the International Court of Justice as those principles recognised by civilised nations. In foreign investment law, general principle also tended to be referred to in these terms.[361] The reference to and meaning of 'civilized nations' is in

---

[360] See for the aims of comparative law more particularly the discussion in s 1.5.7 below. *cf* in this connection also the collection of the Center for Transnational Law Cologne: Trans-Lex.org Principles with Commentary, March 2012, which contains 130 principles and rules of transnational law with commentary. There is no clear distinction between fundamental and general principle and no hierarchy. Also, there is no distinction between consumer and other dealings and a fundamental difference is not maintained, but the collection is nevertheless of interest.

[361] See Lord Asquith of Bishopstone, who appears to have been the first one (in 1951) to refer in this connection to 'the application of principles rooted in the good sense and common practice of the generality of civilised nations—a sort of 'modern law of nature', see Award in the Matter of an Arbitration between *Petroleum Development (Trucial Coast) Ltd and the Sheikh of Abu Dhabi*, reported in (1952) 1 *ICLQ* 247, and (1951) 18 *International Law Reports* 144.

That formula was taken up in oil concessions later, therefore as a matter of contractual choice of law. Thus, in oil concessions references to the law of all civilised nations used not to be uncommon, although now probably considered offensive to the oil producing country in question.

this connection entirely transformed but in commercial and financial law we probably still mean here the more advanced countries.

It may be of interest in this connection that the construction contract of the Channel Tunnel provided that it was to be governed by 'the principles common to both English law and French law, and in the absence of such common principles by such general principles of international trade law as have been applied by national and international tribunals'.[362]

In the international commercial and financial legal order as a newly emerging order, one would expect here an attitude to problem solving that is less encumbered by the past, first by borrowing concepts from domestic law in a comparative search. The key is then better solutions from more highly developed law or more up to date legal sources. In this book, comparative legal studies are indeed not used for their own sake, but foremost to search for a new normativity that enlightens at the transnational level unless public order requirements militate against it, which requirements, however, may themselves be trans-nationalised.

In this connection, it must also be considered what makes better sense or works better in the particular legal order it concerns. In international commerce and finance, this concerns the international commercial and financial legal order. Here the search for principle leaves the domestic scene and comparative law behind, and acquires a more universal utilitarian impetus. Importantly and as already been mentioned in section 1.4.4 above, in the case law of the ECJ there are also 'borrowings' of private law concepts in the nature of general principle,[363] like the notion of good faith, the notion of contract, the notion of tort and causality in that context, of property, of abuse of rights, of force majeure and change of circumstances, see further also the notion that interest may have to be paid as damages, although it is likely that these concepts acquire special features in a public of administrative law context, where the ECJ often develops them, such as, for example, in the administrative contract, the administrative tort and so on. Guidance may then be sought from administrative law principle as much as from private law, but

---

Under ad hoc exploration agreements with Libya, the arbitrations that eventually also decided on the nationalisation issues were to be governed by the 'principles of the law of Libya common to the principles of international law and in the absence of such common principles then by and in accordance with the general principles of law, including such of these principles as may have been applied by international tribunals'. *Texaco Overseas Petroleum Co & Cal Asiatic Oil Co v The Government of the Libyan Arab Republic* (1979) 4 *Yearbook Commercial Arbitration* 177, 181.

Especially in the oil and gas industry there were many similar clauses. Thus, the Aminoil Concession Agreement of 1979 made reference to the law of the Parties 'determined by the Tribunal, having regard to the quality of the parties, the transnational character of their relations and the principles of law and practice prevailing in the modern world'. *Kuwait v Aminoil*, reprinted in (1982) 21 *International Legal Materials* 976, 980.

[362] *Channel Tunnel Group v Balfour Beatty Construction Ltd* [1995] AC 334, 347.

[363] For the interaction in comparative law especially at EU level, see K Lenaerts, 'Interlocking Legal Orders in the European Union and Comparative Law' (2003) 52 *ICLQ* 873, in which the nature of legal order itself was not further explored and was in essence perceived as statist, but the emphasis was put on common denominators in the law of Member States as normative guidance for the ECJ, in which connection the reference in Art 288(2) of the Treaty (now Art 340(2) TFEU) referring to 'general principles common to the laws of the Member States' for contractual liability of the Union was noted, not so far elaborated in a clear body of law, but it reinforced also notions of non-contractual liability under EU law in respect of national and Community public authorities; see eg joined Cases 83/76 and 94/76, 4/77, 15/77 and 40/77 *HNL and Others v Council and Commission* [1978] ECR 1209. A common vision of Member States may also underlie state liability for non-implementation of community law; see joined Cases C-6/90 and C-9/90 *Francovitch and Others* [1991] ECR I-5357.

the method of 'borrowing' in this sense based on general principles of private law is well established.

Again, it is submitted that this would also affect the DCFR if it were ever to become law. It may still pretend to be one system, but following present ECJ case law, general principle would likely operate besides it as an autonomous other source of law which it could not ignore or declare irrelevant.[364]

1.4.7 Autonomous Legal Sources: Custom and Practices

In the context of searching for autonomous sources of law in the transnational business sphere, the notion of custom and practices[365] also needs to be considered more properly. From the outset it should be emphasised that there is a difference between: (a) custom operating as a separate, autonomous source of law; (b) custom referred to in codifications or statutes when it does not operate autonomously; and (c) custom (or usages/practices) operating as an implied contractual term, when it operates by virtue of the parties' intent,[366] (which in codification countries itself may not be independent either). In the latter case, the rules are basically contractual and would have no meaning outside it.[367] This is hardly custom in the proper sense.

---

[364] In s 1.4.5 above, reference was also made to Art II.-7:301ff DCFR which appears to maintain a notion of public order distilled from the laws of the Member States. Thus general principle is sometimes also relied upon in the text of the DCFR itself.

[365] The idea that customs are old-fashioned, atavistic and representative of primitive law is here utterly rejected, see also n 372 below, as well as the notion that the force of custom depends on long-serving usage. They may change overnight if the course of business changes, are as such a prime expression of legal dynamism, and basic to the operation of all legal systems, see JH Dalhuisen, 'Custom and its Revival in Transnational Private Law' (2008) 18 *Duke Journal of Comparative and International Law* 339.

[366] This concept is fluid, however. It is not uncommon for custom as an implied condition of a contract to move from party intent to objective law. This has happened, for example, to the concept of good faith, which in England remains largely an implied condition, whilst in Germany and the Netherlands it now constitutes an objective norm. Conflict rules in contract law were for a long time also considered implied conditions until it was found no longer appropriate that their status, and thereby the applicable law, was dependent on the parties' intent, whereupon these rules became also accepted as objective norms.

The reverse also happens: confidentiality has long been considered an essential feature of arbitrations, so much so that it was often not even mentioned in arbitration statutes or rules, but its status as an objective norm to be respected by all is increasingly reduced to at best an implied condition and it is possibly now necessary to insert an express term in the arbitration clause for parties still to be able to rely on it. Thus arbitrations remain private but not necessarily confidential. It might yet be different in alternative dispute resolution (ADR) proceedings, like mediation, see also s 3.2.4 below.

[367] It should be clear from the above that not all custom is legally the same. It should, in particular, be considered that some customs are no more than behavioural patterns, habits without legal significance, for example the canons of politeness and social intercourse. Others may acquire some legal effect but can be unilaterally abandoned by giving notice to the other party.

If, for example, a broker normally gives certain commission discounts, clients may come to expect them, but they prevail only until the broker unilaterally (but explicitly) amends his terms unless the habit became an industry practice when a legally enforceable rule may be the result. If in the particular instance the concession was specially relied upon, it becomes a matter of *contract* law, not custom or practice.

This may apply more generally to most habits and routines in the sense that participants may signal their withdrawal when the otherwise applicable law would start to prevail.

The working definition often used in this connection for *custom proper* is a practice which is universal in the trade or a relevant segment thereof and can as such *not* be unilaterally withdrawn or changed except if it is in its very nature, but would rather require an industry shift or the other party's consent to be set aside in an individual case (unless the custom is mandatory as it might be in property matters including negotiable instruments and some other situations as we shall see).

Such custom is traditionally perceived as an independent and autonomous source of law. They are not to be distinguished from usages or practices, although it is not uncommon to reserve the latter terms for implied contractual conditions, which is notably also the approach of the Vienna Convention on the International Sale of Goods (CISG) and the DCFR as we shall see, but it is misleading. Although immanent law, custom as an autonomous source of law is not contractual but *hard law* as such, no different from other sources of law including legislation and case law. It means that it must be applied by judges or arbitrators if its other conditions of applicability are met. That was indeed the position in civil law at least until the nineteenth century, but it was also the original position in the common law. It did not therefore depend on special government or state sanction, either in statute or treaty, or on contract, but spoke for itself.[368] Article 4 CISG still seems to leave room for this; at least it does not detract from it.

As we have seen, the nineteenth-century civil law of the codification became in principle hostile to custom as an independent source of law. Caught up in the codification ethos and sovereignty notion, custom started to suffer as all other sources of law (except statute) did. This affected the status of international custom all the more as it was not even national. Similar considerations started to affect the status and legitimacy of custom as source of public international law.

It may be recalled here that the earlier *Ius Commune* had been friendly following the Justinian Digest, but it had been concerned with priority in the case of conflict, see section 1.2.5 above, where in Northern France (the area of the *droit coutumier*) precedence was given to local laws, but notably not in Germany and Italy, except for city laws in trade and commerce, which remained, however, narrowly interpreted. The codifications of the French and German variety both gravitated towards and were ultimately expression of exclusive statism, and monopolised, as such, law formation.[369]

Custom was thus affected, and at least in private law it became ignored unless statutes specifically referred to it.[370] That was done mainly in matters of contract interpretation

---

[368] If we still wish to talk about a rule of recognition, that rule is not then statist either, but will be another kind of rule in the legal order in which the custom operates and may in the transnational commercial and financial legal order itself be customary or an expression of its public order.

[369] Indeed the main author of the French Civil Code, Portalis, considered the abolition of local custom to be one of the great achievements of the Code, see FA Fenet, *Receuil complet des travaux préparatoires du Code Civil* (1827) xcii–xciii.

In Roman law, custom functioned as source of law at the same level as legislation, Inst 1.1.2 and D 1.3.31. It could even overrule the written law, the idea being that custom was rational law, D 1.3.39, C 8.52.1.2 but it had to be demonstrated by a form of consensus and was as such considered participatory. In the *Ius Commune*, some believed custom to be the unexpressed will of the sovereign, but most, like Bartolus, saw it as a creation of the community, see text at n 161 above.

[370] The former Dutch Civil Code (in force until 1992) in Art 3 of its General Provisions was specific in this policy and expressed it clearly, but even then it was sometimes still thought that the force of custom was ultimately decided by a higher rule, as indeed the validity of the code was, see P Scholten, *Asser Algemeen deel*, 2nd edn (1934) 131. One source of law could not itself wipe out another.

where custom normally figured besides good faith notions in this respect; see French *Code Civil* Article 1135; and the German Civil Code (BGB) section 157.[371] Custom's role was in fact hardly discussed any further and its status in the rest of the private law, especially in property law, unclear, but particularly since legal positivism started to catch the eye towards the middle of the nineteenth century, the struggle concerning custom's status as an independent source of law came more into the open.

Common law remained friendlier towards custom, at least in commerce, as we have seen. In fact, even the common law itself was often explained as law of immemorial usage. Similarly, Roman law had been considered a higher form of custom in the *Ius Commune*, as we have also seen, but in England the status of custom in a narrower sense also became uncertain, caught up as it was in sovereignty ideas but it was also rubbished as being primitive and atavistic.[372] In the meantime, commercial law and practice as well as its courts had already been subsumed in the common law and its judicial system, see section 1.1.2 above, whilst its impact at least in England was further reduced by applying the rule of precedent to it, so that a finding of custom tended to deprive this law at the same time of the flexibility and adjusting facility that is its very essence.[373] Common law judges may thus be forced to distinguish cases more aggressively in commercial disputes in order to overcome the restraints of binding precedent, and some greater dynamism in the development of commercial customary law in this manner appears to have been accepted.

In these circumstances, in Europe, both domestically and transnationally, it proved easier to accept the force of custom, at least in contract, on the basis of an implied term (especially in England)[374] or otherwise (in civil law) only when codes or statutes made a specific reference to it. At least in civil law, that preserved the idea that the statute or code always remained superior and the ultimate source of the law and that domestic law remained superior in this area too.

Instances of a special statutory reference to custom could be found in the French Law of 13 June 1866 concerning commercial usages, and the Law of 19 July 1928 concerning the relevance of usages in the settlement of employment disputes, see Y Loussouarn, 'The Relative Importance of Legislation, Custom, Doctrine, and Precedent in French Law' (1958) 18 *Louisiana Law Review* 235.

In Germany, s 346 HGB, which refers to custom in commercial transactions, is also such a provision but is often viewed as no more than an elaboration of s 157 of the German Civil Code or BGB, which allows references to good faith and custom in contractual interpretation.

[371] As it is now mostly accepted that such good faith notions may in pressing cases also be used to adapt the contract, when they become absolutely mandatory, eg to protect weaker parties, it is conceivable that in the normative interpretation method custom may sometimes play a similar corrective role as s 157 BGB in Germany clearly suggests. Although parties may normally deviate from it when the clear provisions of the agreement prevail, this may not then be effective, custom in this instance also having become absolutely mandatory.

The new Dutch Civil Code in Art 6(2) always gives good faith a leading role and allows it to overrule not only the wording of the contract but also the effect of custom and equally of statutes impacting on a contract. This is a unique approach, so far not followed elsewhere. It confirms that notions of good faith can be absolutely mandatory, certainly when they appeal to more fundamental principles of protection, but so may be custom that could similarly protect.

[372] This remains in more modern times even the view of HLA Hart, *The Concept of the Law*, 2nd edn (1994) 95, 106.

[373] See s 1.3.1 above.

[374] See *Product Brokers Co Ltd v Olympia Oil & Cake Co Ltd* [1916] 1 AC 314, 324. *cf* also *General Insurance Corp v Forsakringaktiebolaget Fennia Patria* [1983] QB 856.

As in practice, custom is in England thus often seen as an implied contractual condition,[375] this poses, as already mentioned, the question whether it can also operate outside contract law. Although the ambivalence towards custom in England leaves more room for it in commerce, it is in fact not certain how much.[376] It was already said that custom figuring as implied contractual condition is in fact not custom proper at all.

Only the UCC in the US makes it clear in its section 1-103 that custom, particularly if also law merchant, is favoured whilst providing that the Code is to be interpreted liberally in order 'to permit the continued expansion of commercial practice through custom, usage, and agreement between the parties' whilst 'unless displaced by the particular provisions of the Code, the principles of law and equity including the law merchant .... supplement its provisions'.

Custom is here not defined but its overriding importance in commercial law is made plain and accepted. Implicitly the notion of one single systematic body of national law is here abandoned. The UCC otherwise avoids the term 'custom', and refers to the 'course of business' or 'usage of trade', at least in the context of the interpretation and supplementation of agreements for the sale of goods, therefore in contractual matters, see sections 2-202(a) and 2-208 UCC. They may not be invoked to contradict the express terms and would therefore appear never to be mandatory, even when they concern the contractual infrastructure or issues of contractual validity. It may be asked whether that could be correct. Perhaps another form of custom operates here.

Section 1-303 defines the usage of trade in this connection, and also contains a statement as to the role of the course of dealing. The usage of trade is 'any practice or method of dealing having such regularity of observance in a place, vocation or trade as to justify an expectation that it will be observed with respect to the transaction in question'. A course of dealing 'is a sequence of previous conduct between parties to a particular transaction which is fairly regarded as establishing a common basis of understanding for interpreting their expressions and other conduct'. It is further stated that:

> a course of dealing between the parties and any usage of trade in the vocation or trade in which they are engaged or of which they are or should be aware give particular meaning to and supplement or qualify terms of an agreement.[377]

---

[375] See for custom as implied term in England, generally *Custom and Usage*, in 12(1) *Halsbury's Laws of England*, 4th edn (1973) 601.

[376] See in England for the notion that practice is not law, and therefore international practice also not international law, R Goode, 'Rule, Practice, and Pragmatism in International Commercial Law' (2005) 54 *ICLQ* 539, 549. This is in the positivist tradition. Legal rules in this view always national or must at least be sanctioned by some national legal system to become effective. Although usages are here distinguished and their normative force accepted, it is less clear why and whether they can be international and autonomous in that sense.

[377] There is a more recent view in the US that the UCC was mistaken in its reliance on custom, course of dealing, course of performance and trade usages and their unifying force, see L Bernstein, 'Private Commercial Law in the Cotton Industry: Creating Cooperation through Rules, Norms and Institutions' (2001) 99 *Michigan Law Review* 1724; L Bernstein, 'The Questionable Empirical Basis of Article 2's Incorporation Strategy: A Preliminary Study' (1999) 66 *University of Chicago Law Review* 710; L Bernstein, 'Merchant Law in a Merchant Court: Rethinking the Code's Search for Immanent Business Norms' (1996) 144 *University of Pennsylvania Law Review* 1765.

Here the view is presented that custom, course of dealing, trade usages and so on, are first often replaced by trade organisation rules that are more precise and dispute-avoiding and may therefore play a more fundamental role than the UCC and its reference to customs when a dispute arises. It is further argued that usages have validity mainly outside the area of litigation, therefore only in an environment in which co-operation is productive. In litigation, it is believed that parties want to rely on state law as end game. Intriguingly, it suggests that there are different legal standards when it comes to litigation, see also s 1.4.16 below.

Sensitivity to accepted practices and custom is particularly important in international trade. The CISG avoids a reference to custom, however. In the English tradition, it uses the terms 'usages' and 'practices' instead and follows the implied term approach, in the context of contract law with which the Convention only deals.[378] As a consequence, custom of this nature is subjective and has to be proven, but must still be more than a course of action habitually followed, has to have consistency and regularity, and must be recognised as binding by the parties. All the same, it is not, strictly speaking, possible for the Vienna Convention or any other to be conclusive in this matter as the force of international usages and practices may derive autonomously, as indeed the force of fundamental legal principle also does and even more basically. So much seems still to be recognised in Article 4 of the Convention, which leaves custom as such well alone.

The DCFR is also ambivalent on the subject. In Article II.-1:104 it deals with usages and practices as implied contractual conditions much like the CISG. There is a particularity in so far as in its the application these usages must be reasonable. What is reasonable is itself defined in Article I.-1:103 as being dependent on any relevant usage and practice, so that the regime becomes circular. In the interpretation sections, again, there is only a reference to usages and practices, Article II.-8:102(1) (c) and (f); *cf* also Article II.-9: 101(1). More important is that any other forms of custom are ignored and Article 4 CISG language is not repeated. This confirms the codification ethos, but is defective at least where custom cannot be reduced to contract as in property, now also covered by the DCFR. It also considers custom irrelevant, in that context. That tallies with its notion of a closed regime of proprietary rights and suspicion of market forces. See further Volume II, chapter 2, sections 1.10ff.

In its essence, custom is an expression of what is understood as normal or best practice in the group or community that it concerns and of what is in that group perceived to be the most desirable in terms of rationality, utility, common sense and experience, also when situations change. As such, resort to custom is engrained in all law and its application. Normality is the true legal default rule and custom is one of its major expressions. Being immanent law, it is in business not likely to be political, censorious, or society changing,

---

Rules are needed in all areas where the emphasis is on finality as in payments and property transfers, see also nn 72 and 73 above. But custom and practices will support this too and may even go further and be more precise. It should be noted in this connection that custom and practices have important effects outside the area of contract, which in the above criticism seems to be the area primarily considered. In international transactions that may be their major importance. In any event, to obtain in this manner greater legal clarity in certain areas of international business through statist laws or trade association rules, would not seem to condemn the use of custom and similar practices in others and affect its autonomous status.

A main area of confusion appears to arise from the fact that custom can be further elaborated by trade associations for example, internationally by the ICC. It is submitted that that does not detract the resulting rules from customary status, which could thus change overnight. These trade associations are merely spokesmen of transnational law in this sense, see also text below at n 381.

In modern American literature notions of custom and industry practices and their meaning are receiving renewed attention. See RA Epstein, 'Confusion About Custom: Disentangling Informal Custom from Standard Contractual Provisions' (1999) 66 *University of Chicago Law Review* 821; TJ Hooper, 'The Theory of Custom in the Law of Tort' (1992) 21 *Journal of Legal Studies* 1; D Charney, 'The New Formalism in Contract' (1999) 66 *University of Chicago Law Review* 842.

[378] Thus according to Art 9(1), the parties are bound by 'any usage to which they have agreed and by any practices that they have established between themselves'. This is simply an extension of the contract and intent principles. It implies a subjective approach to custom. Art 9(2) tries to undo some of the impact by accepting as an implied condition 'all usages of which the parties knew or ought to have known and which in international trade are widely known to or regularly observed (but not merely widely operative) between the parties to contracts of the type involved in the particular trade concerned'.

its only objective being best to facilitate and support the needs of that community given its own perceptions of reality. It concerns its routines and is as such dynamic in concept. It can never be fully captured, therefore neither can the *lex mercatoria* of which it is an important component, nor in fact, can any other living law.

In the elaboration of the rules of contract, property, set-off, and procedure (in international arbitrations), *mandatory* rules of custom may also develop, even in contract, especially in the areas of legal capacity and contractual validity and no less in personal property, more particularly in demands for a re-transfer of ownership upon default or upon an invalid contract of sale. Concepts of *finality* on the other hand may demand here extra rules in terms of the independence of the transfer, protection of bona fide purchasers or purchasers in the ordinary course of business (for commoditised products) and reliance notions, also in the case of payments, and international custom may increasingly oblige.[379]

In this connection, it should further be noted that custom or practice as an independent source of law, may still surface in various ways, for example as presumptions, such as, amongst professionals, the presumption of the capacity of the parties. At least in the international commercial sphere, typical legal capacity limitations derived from domestic law, even that of the residence of the party concerned, are increasingly ignored especially in the case of legal entities, although purely domestically they may still remain of the greatest importance.[380] In international commercial matters, local aspects of capacity, but also of illegality, nullity and collapse of title or voidable title, might thus well become less relevant. International trade and its flows may be considered here a more overriding concept, at least between professionals in the business sphere. Again, this goes to the issue of finality.

Custom or trade or industry practices may also be found in industry standard terms and may then even be reflected in *written* compilations, often of private bodies like the ICC (in Incoterms and UCP).[381] The International Capital Markets Association (ICMA) has already been mentioned for its role in the eurobond market. These codes may be regularly updated by these bodies and therefore abruptly changed without undermining their basic status of custom or objective law. Thus these industry bodies, if recognised as *proper spokesmen* for the relevant immanent legal order, may further elaborate on them without detracting from their customary status.

Custom should be distinguished from *standard contract* terms. The latter are contractual, in essence an organisation technique of a dominant operator covering all its customers or clients and they are therefore specific to it. As contracts of adhesion, they must be reasonable in content although this may have less of a meaning and impact in professional dealings. That does not make them custom, however, and only when they become standardised for an industry, either informally or through the operation of trade associations, may they acquire the form of custom, although they normally do not.

Another point must also be made. Most authorities suggest a longer process for custom to emerge out of practice. This has already been questioned. The business community itself should grasp the nettle and simply insist on its rules or law merchant to be applied and enforced regardless of other criteria. As we have seen, trade organisations may here be of considerable help. A key modern insight is then that the formation of custom in this sense may not be a

---

[379] See nn 72 and 73 above.

[380] This was shown in the cases concerning swaps entered into with municipal authorities in the UK in *Hazell v London Borough of Hammersmith and Fulham and Others* [1991] 1 All ER 545 (Lord Ackner).

[381] See also n 342 above.

long process; custom of this nature is dynamic and may change overnight.[382] That is the simple consequence of it following and sustaining the commercial and financial practice and flows.

In this connection, it should be considered that custom may in particular develop and provide guidance in terms of what reasonably needs to be done or is efficient or otherwise clearly desirable. Again, trade associations come into play more specifically. Rules are likely to exist merely because they work, are accepted, and can be identified.[383] Trade associations as, for example, the ICMA in the eurobond market and the ICC for the Incoterms and UCP may play an important role in moving these rules further forward.[384]

These are key aspects of the operation of the international markets and it is somewhat hard to understand why, this being the case, in modern writing the operation of legal custom and of custom creating forces is sometimes still flatly denied.[385] It has already been noted that they may even be mandatory especially where the infrastructure of the law of contract and property is concerned. These rules are not then at the free disposition of the parties. They may as such be closely related to, be supported by or an elaboration of fundamental principle or in other cases of (the transnational) public order.[386]

1.4.8 The Competition between Custom and Statutory or Treaty Law

As far as the effect of the autonomy of custom is concerned, this customary law will first overrule directory private law, even if statutory, unless parties wish it to be otherwise. But it

---

[382] See their fluid character, n 366 above. See for the notion of 'instant customary law' as a source of public international law, B Cheng, 'United Nations Resolutions on Outer Space: "Instant" International Customary Law?' (1964–65) *Indian Journal of International Law* 4–5.
  Modern game theory also shows that, in so-called information cascades, when the benefit of predecessors' actions is compelling, widespread imitation will follow immediately: see D Hirschleifer: 'Social influence, fads and information cascades' in M Tommasi and KI Ieruli (eds), *The New Economics of Human Behaviour* (1995) 188.

[383] That was Hart's view of international law, see Hart, n 372 above at 227, 231 which, it would seem, could then also apply to private law custom, either domestically or transnationally, but see for Hart's deprecating attitude to custom also text at n 372 above, a remnant of Bentham and Austin.

[384] Private codification but also case law and arbitral awards are ways through which we can know this law and it has already been said that judges and arbitrators also fulfil here a spokesman function, as does legal scholarship, but their formulations are only persuasive and cannot stultify this law, especially not in terms of precedent. Their findings are primarily declaratory of the law so found and applied. Private codifiers may move on more quickly. It may even be said that formulation of custom in this manner is not always an advantage and may deprive it of some of its nimbleness. This law, as any other, is in its nature not an 'is' but can be and often is an expression of fast moving realities, especially in commerce and finance.

[385] See for public international law, JL Goldsmith and EA Posner, 'A Theory of Customary International Law' (1999) 66 *University of Chicago Law Review* 1113, but *cf* for support in private law, HJ Berman and FJ Dasser, 'The "New" Law and the "Old" Sources, Content and Legitimacy' in TE Carbonneau (ed), *Lex Mercatoria and Arbitration* (1990) 21, 28.

[386] Traditional theories on custom like the one of von Hayek, see FA Hayek, *1 Law, Legislation and Liberty: Rules and Order*, vol 1 (1973) 35–54, 74–90, go largely as follows: effective custom evolves through the natural selection of rules and practices but may be guided by deliberate improvements on the part of the participants, legislatures (especially if called upon to help), courts and others like arbitrators.
  In modern law and economics, this discussion acquires a broader flavour as it goes to the existence and operation of immanent legal orders more generally and that may well be the better context in which now to consider custom. It concerns a more fact-finding approach. RD Cooter, 'Structural Adjudication and the New Law Merchant' (1994) 14 *International Review of Law and Economics* 215; 'Decentralised Law for a Complex Economy: The Structural Approach to Adjudicating the New Law Merchant' (1996) 144 *University of Pennsylvania Law Review* 1643, see also the discussion in s 1.5.5 below. It poses the key question of the tipping point: when does habit or routine become legally enforceable. This is not only so because of justified reliance although it has much to do with it.

is in the nature of custom that both parties would have to agree. Without such an agreement, custom is the default rule[387] and no single party can opt out on its own and insist on the default rule of the otherwise applicable law, unless this is in the nature of the relevant custom itself. Thus unless custom is in the nature of a concession, like a price reduction, even if habitually given, no party can unilaterally withdraw. It would not be possible either if the other party relied on the discount in ongoing transactions. That is then a matter of contract proper rather than of custom as explained in the previous section.[388]

But even mandatory statutory or case law may become ineffective if the practice will not conform and other custom develops. This is the issue of *non-usus*, especially relevant for regulation, therefore in situations where governments intent to guide.[389] It usually means that the mandatory measure is too far removed from reality to be capable of being or remaining effective, or was wishful political thinking in the first place. In other words, a rule that cannot (or no longer) or will not stick becomes ineffective even if it was meant to be mandatory. There is a lot of this in regulatory law but also in criminal reform legislation. It is obviously a delicate issue but also relevant in private law formation and may then be conducive also to the operation of new proprietary rights or set-off facilities. The law as mandatory statutory system may thus be overturned by practices that move forwards in more realistic ways. Also here, public policy expressed in terms of support for such systems is not immune.

Another issue already mentioned in the previous section was whether mandatory good faith notions can prevail over custom, which is doubtful if the custom itself is mandatory also unless good faith in the particular instance reflects higher fundamental principle. A particular problem arises in respect of custom as an autonomous source of law in respect of judges' and arbitrators' powers to invoke it upon their own motion. It may follow from custom being such a source of law that judges and arbitrators would have to accept and could invoke custom of this nature *ex officio*: *ius curia novit* is a well-known civil law maxim. Arbitrators might still require elucidation by the party invoking it, but it is not mere fact (but law) even though parties may be wise still to treat it so and prove it, whilst the question how far judges and arbitrators may invoke it, especially in respect of international or transnational custom, may still be the subject of justified enquiry.[390] They would in any event be unwise to do so without inviting further argument by the parties. There should be no surprises on this point in the award. This important aspect will not be discussed here any further.[391]

---

[387] A competing statutory default rule or such a rule formulated in case law would be of inferior status. However, it may be that the customary default rule in its interpretation would be subject to notions of good faith, especially in contract, like any other default rule but again there might be less room for it in professional dealings.

[388] Yet it might be wise all the same to introduce an anti-waiver provision in the contract, see also Omri Ben-Shahar, 'The Tentative Case Against Flexibility in Commercial Law' 66 *University of Chicago Law Review* 781.

[389] A famous example has presented itself in the US where the Aliens Tort Statute of 1789 was entirely forgotten but was revived by the federal courts in respect of foreign human rights violation in *Filartiga v Pena-Irala* 630 F2d 876 (2nd Circ 1980) followed by the Supreme Court in *Sosa v Alvarez-Machain* 542 US 692 (2004). The revival in this manner of an old statute whose objective was never entirely clear is problematic.

[390] It was queried especially in *BP v Lybian Arab Republic* 53 ILR 279, 359 (1977), see also the discussion in vol III, ch 1, ss 1.1.14ff concerning arbitrators' status and powers in this connection in financial arbitrations.

[391] It is possible to argue in this connection that as custom derives from factual behavioural patterns, it must as such be proven like any other fact except when generally known. On the other hand, especially if the arbitrator is selected as expert out of the peer group, his knowledge of the customs of the trade may be depended on and

In conclusion, it would seem that there are several questions that merit special attention in connection with custom: (a) is custom subjective in the sense that it only applies if implicitly made part of a contract and is therefore merely an implied term? (b) can it also be objective and an independent or autonomous source of law in contractual and non-contractual matters? (c) can it supersede statutory or even treaty law as a demonstration of *non-usus* of those laws? (d) is it subject in international transactions to any domestic or international public order constraints, including notions of good faith? (e) is it based on regularity or is it a dynamic concept allowing change overnight in view of rapidly changing trade or financial patterns and practices or taxation rules? (f) can it be propelled by trade organisations?; and (g) can it be invoked and applied by judges and arbitrator upon their own motion?

1.4.9 Autonomous Legal Sources: Party Autonomy

Party autonomy as an autonomous source of law in contract is based on the idea that the single word binds and forms the contract as a matter of fundamental principle, to be recognised (not created) by the positive law unless public order forbids it.

In a strong metaphor in France, Loysel, as early as 1607, had observed in this connection: '*On lie les boeufs par les cornes et les hommes par les mots*' ['One ties cattle by their horns and people by their words'].[392] That was the traditional French view. The text of Article 1354 of the French Code Civil still reflects this: '*Les Conventions legalement formées tiennent lieu de loi a ceux qui les ont faites*' ['Agreements legally entered into are the law for those who have made them'] and suggests the autonomy of the law that parties create.[393]

However, codification thinking also intruded here, and in France too freedom to contract is now often believed to depend on code authorisation, see also Article II.-1:102 DCFR. However, party autonomy as some autonomous source of law revived in France for international contracts. This became particularly relevant for the validity of gold clauses that were upheld in international contracts (but not in domestic French contracts) in the 1930s.[394] Indeed, the long-standing relative popularity of the modern *lex mercatoria* in France may be seen in the light of the development in that country of the notion of the 'international contract' operating under its own transnationalised rules.

The concept of the party autonomy as autonomous source of law, at least at the transnational level, was in recent French case law also dramatically underlined, in that international arbitration clauses were considered autonomous and not anchored in any domestic

---

arguably nothing needs to be pleaded or proven. This is, however, a dangerous position to take in international commercial arbitrations and would suggest leaving facts to the autonomous determination of arbitrators.

It may be recalled in this connection that where arbitrations depend entirely on knowledge of the peer group eg concerning quality, resulting decisions are not based on law and are not normally considered arbitral awards in the more traditional sense, even though of great importance in commodity business. They are often not reasoned either and, if international, may not be covered by the New York Convention.

[392] A Loysel, *Institutions coutumieres* (1607).

[393] In modern times, this basic principle has continued to find important support, see notably P Scholten, *Convenances vainquent loi*, Report Royal Netherlands Academy of Arts and Sciences (1930) 187, 3 *Assembled Works* 196, but party autonomy is now mostly explained as government licence.

[394] See GR Delaume, *Transnational Contracts* (1989) 119.

law, reason why an award being set aside in the country of the seat of the arbitration or origin of the award need not have an effect on recognition in France. This is a matter of French law.[395] Here the existence of an autonomous international arbitral order was accepted and the award was considered to be a judicial decision in that order, albeit still subject to recognition in the relevant domestic legal orders.

It is submitted that this international arbitral order is the same as the international commercial and financial legal order, see sections 1.5.1 and 1.5.4 below. It means, however, that strictly speaking, party autonomy does not entirely stand alone but is embedded in the legal order in which it operates and the fundamental principles of that order. It is also subject to its requirements of public order, but they are not, or not necessarily, of a statist nature. It is clear that not everything goes, but this does not distract from the principle of contract being transnationally an autonomous source of law.[396]

It was also explained before that party autonomy in this sense may even enter proprietary laws concerning movable assets operating in the transnational legal order, see section 1.1.4 above. The special role of party autonomy in choosing the applicable law and its meaning within the modern *lex mercatoria* will be discussed in section 1.4.13 below.

1.4.10 Autonomous Legal Sources: Treaty Law

Treaty law is another source of law in an international context but remains territorial, applicable therefore only in the territories of Member States and is as such not truly transnational, although it was earlier suggested that if a large number of states participate, it may become general principle and acquire meaning also outside the group of Member States.

Nevertheless, amongst legal positivists, there is still the opinion that only treaty law can truly be a source of transnational law.[397] It builds on the notion that only states can make law, even private law, and that there are no other sources. The CISG is the most important example of this type of uniform substantive treaty law in the area of private law.[398] It is then perceived as covering the field within its scope to the exclusion of other sources of law notwithstanding its Articles 4, 7 and 9 which would appear to leave its relationship to these other sources of law open. In the absence of a higher norm, the CISG misses the authority to determine its own rank.

---

[395] See *Cour de Cass. Civ* 1, 29 June 2007 in *Ste PT Putrabali Adyamulia* available at www.courdecassation.fr/ jurisprudence and n 11 above. See further P Pinsolle, 'The Status of Vacated Awards in France: the Cour de Cassation Decision in Putrabali' (2008) 24 *Arbitration International* 277.

[396] See for this discussion also what was said about delocalised arbitration in n 90 above and about the formation of legal orders in s.1.5.3 below.

[397] See, eg Goode, n 9 above.

[398] The original idea of uniform sales laws dates from 1928 and came from UNIDROIT. They are associated with the name of the German Professor Ernst Rabel. The Diplomatic Conference concerning the uniform sales laws immediately followed the 7th Session of the Hague Conference in 1951, which had the conflicts Convention in the area of sales as one of its main topics. Many of the same persons became involved in both projects notwithstanding the considerable difference in approach. The *Uniform Sales Laws* were finally agreed in the Diplomatic Conference of 1964 which immediately preceded the 10th Session of the Hague Conference, see further also the discussion in s 1.4.18 below on the agents of international convergence in private law.

As previously mentioned, at EU level, treaty law translates into Regulations or Directives, even though the latter do not achieve unity in the strict sense. They still allow for different implementations in Member States; see further section 1.4.19 below. In this connection, there are in private law several important company law and consumer law Directives and in area of finance, the Settlement Finality and Collateral Directives. As we shall see in section 1.4.18 below, UNCITRAL and UNIDROIT have proposed more of such texts in specific commercial and financial areas, but they have on the whole met with little success.

In private law, in the EU, Regulations have been used particularly in the area of conflicts of law; compare the Brussels I and II Regulation and Rome I and II in the areas respectively of the Recognition and Enforcement of Judgments in Civil and Commercial Matters and the Law Applicable to Contractual Obligations. So far Regulations have not been used to create substantive uniform private law and we are a long way from the DCFR ever being so adopted,[399] although since October 2011, there is a draft Regulation on a European Sales Law (CESL) for cross-border transactions. Regulations are sometimes also used to implement Directives in the financial area, such as the Markets in Financial Instruments Directive (MiFID) and the Prospectus Directives (see Volume III, chapter 2, section 3.5) and may in such cases also have (some) private law effect.

In the EU, the uniform law so created might only cover interstate or cross-border (therefore international) transactions like in the case of CESL, but it will often be broader and then be intended to affect all transactions, see further section 2.3.2 below, although this raises even more urgently the question of EU legislative authority, see the discussion in section 1.4.19 below. That is, nevertheless, also the ideal of the DCFR. These EU efforts are not then transnationalisation of private law proper, but they are statist interventions to create private law top-down for the EU area as a whole, it being considered one jurisdiction at least for this purpose and treated as if the EU were one country. Unlike for transnational transactions under the modern *lex mercatoria*, other sources of private law would then be eliminated in the nature of all civil law codification. There would be nothing transnational about this law. Although the proposal for an EU sales law in CESL is limited to cross-border transactions only, as just mentioned, it still eliminates the other sources of law—at least that is the attempt but it may again be asked whether the EU has that authority under its own founding treaties.

As we have seen, within the USA, there has long been *uniform* private law amongst the various states—of which the UCC is the most important example. This uniformity is adopted for *all* transactions the subject matter of which is covered by these uniform laws, like within the US all sales of goods.

This American uniform law, prepared by private groups in the American Law Institute, is neither federal law nor is it agreed between the various states of the USA: see section 1.4.18 below. It is, incorporated in state law, but in the absence of an agreement amongst the states, this incorporation remains unilateral to each state and allows for variations in the text per state, of which there are some even in respect of the UCC. That is the difference with EU Regulations. As far as suggested amendments are concerned, some states may also move more quickly than others so that further disparities emerge, even if only temporarily.

---

[399] It also raises important issues of EU jurisdiction in these matters, see s 1.4.19 below. Where the EU has no jurisdiction, Member States may still operate through treaty law as was indeed the original approach in the Brussels and Rome Conventions concerning respectively the Recognition and Enforcement of Judgments in Civil and Commercial Matters and the Law Applicable to Contractual Obligations, now both replaced by Regulations.

There may be further differences in interpretation. Hence the continued importance of conflicts of law notions in the US regardless of uniform law. Nevertheless, in the USA there is on the whole a positive attitude towards uniform state law, particularly towards the UCC, and judges seek uniformity in its interpretation even though the UCC itself does not demand it.

These two uniform law approaches, either through treaty/Regulation or as parallel laws are in principle also open to Member States of the EU. Both are to be distinguished from transnationalisation which would, at least for cross-border transactions even within the EU, consider texts of this nature amongst the other sources of law, it being noteworthy, however, and only to be repeated, that the UCC in the US explicitly recognises and favours these alternative sources of law even for purely infra-state transactions (see its section 1-103).

In this book, treaty law in the area of private law is accepted as part of the *lex mercatoria* even though it remains territorial and as such does not fit very well, but especially in respect of those treaties that have broad international following, of which there are few so far, it is more practical and also more intuitive to include them as one source of transnational law.

1.4.11 Uniform Law and Private International Law

Where substantive uniform law is developed to cover international transactions or other international legal relationships, there follows an approach to the applicable legal regime which is *fundamentally* different from the private international law or conflicts of law approach. It is often presented as a divide between uniform treaty law and private international law, although it would be better to see it as a divide between the transnationalisation or *lex mercatoria* and private international law approach. The uniform treaty law versus private international law debate dates from the time that all private law formation was still considered statist, hence for this uniform law the emphasis was also on treaty law.

This uniform substantive private law to the extent (sometimes also called 'international private law') tries to formulate a *joint* set of norms, therefore equal norms, between different countries for a particular subject, as UNCITRAL (partially) did in the 1980 CISG and UNIDROIT has also done in other areas as we shall see. Again, if other sources of transnational law are also accepted as here proposed, the uniform or transnational private law may also emerge from these other sources and treaty law would only be one of them and would have to find its place amongst them.

The private international law approach, on the other hand, relies on conflicts of law rules under which ultimately a *national* law results as the most appropriate law to govern the case. These rules are in fact not international at all but are usually considered particular to each state which in this way decides which foreign (domestic or national) rules its courts may recognise and these private international law rules may, as such, differ considerably from country to country and from case to case. They will be discussed in Part II of this book.

These conflict rules or rules of private international law may themselves, however, be made uniform internationally, normally also through treaty law. This is very much the remit of the Hague Conference: see section 1.4.18 below. This Conference drafts uniform conflict rules to be incorporated in treaties, which should therefore be clearly distinguished from the just-mentioned uniform substantive (treaty) rules. In this connection, reference is sometimes also made to the '*voie directe*' as against the '*voie indirecte*' uniform approach in respect of treaty law applicable to international legal relationships of a private law nature.

The *voie directe* approach leads to the formulation of substantive transnational rules of private law by way of treaty, to be incorporated in the domestic laws of the treaty states. As just mentioned, the 1980 CISG is its most important example. It can still be said that at least theoretically only national law results in this manner, although alternatively at EU level it might also be introduced through a system of Directives or Regulations and would then be European law. This technique does not normally contemplate uniform parallel laws, although in UNCITRAL model laws are developed for international arbitration and insolvency which have proved successful and have been followed by many countries, all in their own ways.

The *voie indirecte* approach, on the other hand, only leads to the formulation of some uniform conflict rules as a conduit to reach the most appropriate *domestic or national* substantive rule. Uniform laws as part of the *voie indirecte*, notably the private international law conventions of the Hague Conference, have been successful, especially in the area of family law, but also in trusts and agency, although often with few ratifications. There is also one for sales.[400] Note that these rules may still lead to the application of domestic law that is itself uniform law under applicable treaty law.[401]

Beyond the efforts of the Hague Conference in this respect, the 1980 EU Rome Convention on the Law Applicable to Contractual Obligations was one of the more successful conflicts conventions in modern times, now succeeded (in amended form) by the 2008 EU Regulation in the same area. It also covered sales but went beyond it.[402]

The uniform substantive and conflict of laws approaches are conceptually mutually exclusive, and to the extent that both were embodied in treaty law from the 1950s onwards, they openly clashed when the Hague Conference at its seventh Session in 1951 and at its eighth Session in 1955 ultimately completed a private international law Convention on the Law Governing the International Sales of Goods at the same time as in a separate Hague

---

[400] The original idea for the project of uniform *conflicts* rules in the area of sales dated from the 6th Session of the Hague Conference in 1928 and is associated with the name of the French Professor Julliot de la Morandière. It led to a first draft in 1931. The Hague Conference produced a final text on the *Law Governing the International Sale of Goods* in 1955.

[401] In fact, conflicts of law specialists prefer uniform law to come in only in this manner and not be applied directly to transnational transactions, see for further discussion s 2.3 below.

[402] As will be discussed more extensively in s 2.2.4 below, the evolution of the conflicts approach towards more substantive rules and principles of fairness and common sense *itself* suggests a development towards *substantive* transnational standards which are result-oriented, at least in the professional sphere. It was earlier said that expanding domestic concepts through liberal interpretation techniques to reach foreign situations in this manner would have been possible as a method of transnationalisation, not favoured, however, at present in civil law countries, nor indeed, in England.

However, it is exactly such a development within the modern *lex mercatoria* that is becoming significant, now that the globalisation of the international marketplace increasingly demands it. It is particularly relevant for international sales regardless of what Arts 7 or 9 of the Vienna Convention provide, as they cannot rule on the effectiveness of other sources of law.

In fact, it is becoming more obvious that the law of international sales should be considered from the perspective of the *lex mercatoria* and its hierarchy first, in which the Vienna Convention plays a role as a partial codification only (if applicable under its own terms or otherwise perhaps as an expression of general principles), rather than that any *lex mercatoria* notions must be fitted into the Vienna Convention and its methods of interpretation and supplementation under its Art 7.

(diplomatic) Conference, the Hague Uniform Sales Laws were agreed which were the pre-decessors of the CISG.[403] The discussions continued thereafter, in the sense that the Hague Conventions on the uniform law of sales were succeeded in 1980 by the CISG. The 1955 Hague private international law Convention on the Law Governing the International Sale of Goods was updated by a new text in 1986.

1.4.12 Domestic Laws as Autonomous Source of Transnational Law

It will be argued in section 1.4.13 below[404] that in the formative era of transnational private law, domestic law retains residual importance if the other sources of law do not provide the necessary solutions. It may be found through the traditional conflicts of law rules. However, such law then operates in the transnational sphere, must find its place and meaning therein, and will be adjusted accordingly. It means that domestic law applied in a domestic case may be different from its application in an international case even if there are no higher transnational laws available in the circumstances.

1.4.13 The Hierarchy of the Sources of Law in Modern International Commercial and Financial Law

If one assumes an independent international legal order in which international commercial and financial transactions or perhaps all professional dealings are or may be operating, see section 1.1.8 above, and which is increasingly detached from domestic legal orders, see section 1.5.1 below, the question becomes what law prevails in that order and how it must or can be found.

It has been submitted that this new law or modern *lex mercatoria* is essentially built on the traditional legal sources, therefore on fundamental and general principles, on custom

---

[403] Some of the animosity against uniform substantive law at the time transpired in an important contribu-tion of Professor Kurt H Nadelmann, 'The Uniform Law on the International Sale of Goods: A Conflict of Laws Imbroglio' (1965) 74 *Yale Law Journal* 449, which also reproduces the negative opening statement on the uni-form substantive law approach by the President of the Hague Conference at the time Professor J Offerhaus from Amsterdam (at the 10th Session of 1964).

In the Vienna Convention, there was an attempt at reconciling both approaches which resulted in a substantial step backwards from an internationalist perspective. Whilst the Hague Sales Convention in the areas it covered more logically only relied on its general principles (Art 17) for its interpretation and supplementation, the later Vienna Convention retreated from the transnational uniform approach and allowed in areas not expressly settled by it (but always within its scope, see Art 4), the applicability of private international law rules (Art 7(2)).

The result is therefore ultimately the application of a domestic law in these areas which the Convention gen-erally covers, although only after consideration of the general principles on which it is based (which are largely unclear, as we shall see, and there is no longer any pretence at completeness of the uniform law in areas it covers), apparently without further consideration of the international context of the sale, which is only mentioned in Art 7(1) in the context of interpretation, see for a discussion and critique more particularly vol II, ch 1, ss 2.3.6–7.

[404] See also JH Dalhuisen, 'What could the Selection by Parties of English Law in a Civil Law Contract in Commerce and Finance Truly Mean' in M Andenas and D Fairgrieve (eds), *Tom Bingham and the Transformation of the Law* (2009) 619.

or industry practices, on party autonomy and in some areas on uniform treaty laws. As mentioned in the previous section, this new law may residually still use private international law rules pointing to a domestic legal system if no transnational rule can be found, local law remaining in this approach the residual rule but it will then become part of transnational law itself and will be transformed accordingly.

When different sources of law potentially apply, the key is to determine the *hierarchy* between them, which in this book is considered the essence of the modern *lex mercatoria*. These sources although autonomous often build on each other and subsequently allow substantive rules to develop further. Details of these will be discussed more extensively in Part III of this Volume.

First, at the top there are a number of fundamental basic principles already mentioned in section 1.4.5 above and further discussed in section 3.1.1 below. Foremost there is the notion of *pacta sunt servanda*, establishing the binding force of promises. Closely connected are the detrimental reliance and apparent authority notions.

There is also the notion of ownership, establishing the principle of exclusivity of property rights subject to the protection of the appearance of ownership, particularly in the possession of movables, the need for third parties in principle to respect these rights and their transferability as well as the issue of the finality of these transfers. There is further liability for the consequences of one's own actions, especially if wrongful or leading to unjust enrichment; and finally there is the notion of fair dealing guarding in particular against fraud, market manipulation including insider dealing, and anticompetitive behaviour. There may here also be fundamental principles of environmental, safety and health protection.

There are more of these fundamental principles—human rights and European law also tell us so, see also section 1.4.5 above—but they are not many in international commerce and finance. All are in essence mandatory or *ius cogens* and form the basis of the whole system. They contain the essence of contract, agency, property, tort (negligence), and restitution law.

Second, in the details, one should *first* look for custom or practices of a *mandatory* nature, including proprietary protections. They are still rare but conceivable, especially in the area of financial products. That was already clear from the development of negotiable instruments. It was, in more modern times, reconfirmed in the status of the eurobond.[405] Mandatory rules have undoubtedly developed internationally amongst the participants in the financial services industry, where it is often a matter of evolution of the law of movable property, at least in asset-backed funding of all sorts, including security interests and temporary or conditional ownership rights. Importantly, one may also think of the rules of set-off and netting and the priority or preferences they create. The views of the more sophisticated modern financial regulators may provide here a further lead.[406]

Third, one should subsequently look for uniform substantive *treaty* law of a *mandatory* nature, at least to the extent that transactions are covered by them. Mandatory treaty provisions of a private law nature are still rare[407] but could in the area of financial regulation and market behaviour increasingly derive from standards set by the EU as they already do in the

---

[405] See n 339 above.
[406] See for the rules between the international capital markets participant, s 3.2.3 below.
[407] An example is Art 12 of the 1980 Vienna Convention on the International Sale of Goods.

Settlement and Collateral Directives. They could also derive from the BIS, even though they operate so far only through so-called soft law that could, however, still acquire the form of (mandatory) custom for example in the area of set-off and netting, or other international organisations such as the WTO. In the proprietary aspects, UNCITRAL's work on assignments of receivables could prove to be increasingly important, although its 2001 treaty on receivable financing proved a failure, see also Volume III, chapter 1, sections 2.4.5ff. The UNIDROIT Mobile Equipment Convention may be more successful, at least in the Aircraft Protocol, see Volume III, chapter 1, section 2.1.8.

Fourth, there may also be *mandatory* general principles, although also still likely to be few, but where good faith notions are considered mandatory, for example as elaboration of the fundamental principles of dependency, trust, and confidence, they may fall in this category. In movable property, if it is true that new financial structures are developing transnationally, we may also see further progress under this heading, here likely as further elaboration and support of mandatory industry custom and practices. Again, set-off and netting spring to mind.

Fifth, in contractual matters, one should subsequently look for the precise *contractual* terms, the force of which derives in this approach directly from the fundamental notion of *pacta sunt servanda*, therefore from the principle of party autonomy as an autonomous source of law: see section 1.4.9 above. Into this bracket also fit incorporated standard terms like, in finance, the ISDA swap master and the PSA/ISMA Global Master Repurchase Agreement, if not also customary.

Although in property law, the power of the parties to create new proprietary rights is generally limited, it has already been pointed out in section 1.1.4 above that one may expect here greater dynamism in transnational law subject to the protection of the ordinary flows of business. That is the approach in equity in common law countries and is likely to also prove increasingly relevant in international finance, where many products and facilities, including expanded notions of set-off and netting, are equitable in that sense and may be activated on the basis of party autonomy.

The selection of a local law is also part of this power of the parties and would operate at this level of the hierarchy but local law so chosen then functions in the international legal order as part of the *lex mercatoria* and must make sense in that context.[408] In particular, such a chosen local law cannot be meant to undermine the essentials of the deal itself, for example on the basis of purely domestic notions like 'consideration', 'statute of fraud' (in respect of the required documentation) or 'parol evidence' (in respect of the content of the contract) when, say, English law is chosen in a transaction that has nothing to do with England, unless of course the parties expressly mean to domesticate their transaction. That would appear unusual.

A similar situation obtains for eurobonds as negotiable instruments when, for example, English law is made applicable. Strictly speaking a eurobond might not be a bearer negotiable instrument in English terms, see section 3.1 below, because of multiple terms and conditions it often incorporates (which goes against its nature), but it is generally assumed that it is so according to international practice, making a choice of English or New York law irrelevant at the same time in proprietary issues of this nature, although it may still be different if these bonds are held in a book-entry system. Again, the likely result is that a

---

[408] See Dalhuisen, n 306 above.

local law functions differently locally than in an international setting or in the international marketplace.

There would seem to be nothing against parties choosing the *lex mercatoria* itself as the applicable law if in issues at their free disposition it does not operate already (as mandatory law); see also the observation on the *lex situs* in 'Ninth' below. That such a choice is possible is now also confirmed in Preamble 13 of the 2008 EU Regulation on the Law Applicable to Contractual Obligations, replacing the earlier 1980 Rome Convention, which did not contain such a reference. It is best understood in terms of the hierarchy of norms here proposed. Again, in international transactions, the higher mandatory laws, mentioned above, in any event prevail over local laws and their application is therefore not dependent on a clause opting for the application of the *lex mercatoria*. It leaves the question whether judges or arbitrators may apply the *lex mercatoria* in its totality if parties have not chosen a law at all. Judges may still hesitate; it was already said that arbitrators are more likely to feel free to do so, see section 1.1.9 above.

Sixth, thereafter one should look for directory customs or practices, like those for example that may prevail in the contractual aspects of underwriting, trading and settlement of eurobonds, partly to be found under ICMA rules or recommendations obtaining in that market, and one may similarly search for them in respect of other financial products. In this layer, we also find the UCP for letters of credit and the Incoterms, issued by the ICC if we may assume that they are now customary: see section 1.4.18 below.

Seventh, subsequently one should look for uniform *treaty* rules of a *directory* or default nature like those of the CISG if and when applicable to the legal relationship in question. Again, there are not many of these rules, and their force may be limited to transactions between ratifying states or only bind courts in such states; it depends on these texts.

Eighth, one should further look for directory *general principles* of the particular legal structures or relationships that may be considered common to leading developed legal systems. Many of the more precise rules concerning contracts and personal property may be found here. In this layer, one may also look for the intrinsic logic of the transaction and for what good faith and common sense may require beyond the dictates of the fundamental principles or public order requirements as *ius cogens*. As mentioned before, uniform treaty law may be of further guidance as expression of general principle even if under its own terms it is *not* applicable to the transaction in question for lack of an association with a Contracting State in the particular instance. Master Agreements or ICC rules, even if not incorporated in the contract, may also come in under this heading of general principle (if not already as custom). Even draft treaties may have here some meaning.

Ninth, by now most of the missing parts of the *lex mercatoria* should have been filled out, but *ultimately*, if there is no solution, one could still apply a national law found through the most appropriate conflicts of law rules. Thus particularly in property matters including secured transactions, conflicts of law rules may still prove relevant in the formative period of the transnational *lex mercatoria* in the professional sphere.[409] Here the *lex situs* traditionally prevails and is then mandatory. Again, traditionally, party autonomy and the directory

---

[409] Transnationalisation may arise sooner when these proprietary structures are created in assets that move transborder or are intangible or if they are created in internationalised assets, like aircraft and ships, but no less in eurobonds or other types of negotiable instruments or documents of title if used internationally. There are particular problems here with domestic rules governing non-possessory security interests including floating charges or shifting liens. This concerns *their type, coverage and ranking*, see vol II, ch 2, ss 1.8 and 1.9.

sources of law have no meaning except if the analogy with equity could be accepted at the transnational level and in that way a measure of party autonomy, subject to the better right of bona fide purchasers or purchasers in the ordinary course of business of commoditised products, see section 1.1.4 above.

Indeed the *lex mercatoria* as mandatory law at the transnational level could take over; see also the comment under '*Fifth*' above. Even now, the classic *lex situs* rule creates serious\ problems for assets that move transborder and for intangible claims of which the location is much more difficult to establish.[410] This may also leave more room for party autonomy, here sometimes defended in respect of the choice of the applicable national laws concerning assignments of portfolios of receivables with debtors in different countries.[411]

In the hierarchy of norms as here explained, there is in this application of domestic law through conflict of laws rules in any event a *discretionary* element; these rules are too *residual* in the hierarchy of norms to be binding without adjustment to allow for the internationality of the transaction so that the local laws so found applicable makes sense in the context of the international transaction. Again local law then operates as part of the transnational *lex mercatoria*. As regards what conflict rules would be applicable, the Hague Conventions could give some leads, as could, in the EU, the 2008 Regulation in contractual matters even though not binding on arbitrators.

The significance of a law selection clause in favour of a domestic law is that such an election moves the domestic law higher, to fifth place, and therefore eclipses the directory customary law, treaty law, and general principle. That is the difference, see also the comment made above (under '*Fifth*') in connection with a contractual choice of domestic law and its significance.

The introduction of domestic law as the residual rule makes the *lex mercatoria* a system of law that is at least as complete as any other and overcomes the argument, frequently heard, that the new *lex mercatoria* cannot operate because it is not a fully operative system for those who seek it. That is in any event a misconception. What is happening is, however, that the domestic law so applied will increasingly be preceded by ever more industry practices, customs, general principles and the demands of party autonomy and is itself transnationalised.

Finally, as an example, it may be of interest briefly to consider at this stage the discussion of the impact of this hierarchy approach within the *lex mercatoria* for letters of credit. Naturally, we have here the trade practices embodied in the UCP. It is of course possible that the UCP do not fully incorporate them or that new practices develop before the UCP text

---

In a substantive transnationalised law sense, as to type and coverage, common law notions may increasingly show the way, see s 1.1.3 above. As regards ranking, since it concerns here the world of professionals whilst small creditors are mostly out of it and bona fide purchasers of chattels in any event mostly protected against these charges, the substantive transnational rules could be fairly basic: the older go before the younger, the specific before the general, the contractual before those arising from the operation of the law, and purchase money security before loan security.

At the international level, secured loan financing is increasingly eclipsed by the use of other techniques, especially the sale and repurchase or conditional/finance sale (repos), as a funding alternative in finance leases, repos and factoring, see more particularly vol III, ch 1. One of the reasons for this development must be that domestic notions and formalities, including publication requirements in connection with the creation of secured interests are avoided in this manner, although other problems arise, especially in the proprietary position and protection of the prospective owner of the assets and its creditors.

[410] See vol II, ch 2, ss 1.8.2 and 1.9.2.
[411] See n 41 above.

itself is adjusted, in which case these additional or newer practices obtain. Incorporation in the contract is not necessary as the UCP are now mostly considered customary,[412] but if they are incorporated they achieve a higher ranking in the hierarchy of norms as just explained, and may well continue to prevail in that manner also over newer directory custom and practices. That could be the true meaning and effect of incorporation in the contract terms, which might then be less desirable.

As the UCP concern only a partial codification, often they need supplementation. Again, one way is to go immediately to conflicts of law rules. Another is to explain the UCP rules first from the point of view of their own logic, look at general principles commonly applied to them in the most important commercial countries, and only as a last resort apply a national law via conflicts rules, in the manner as here explained, therefore always with some discretion. That would seem to be the better approach.[413]

In any event, any domestic laws still applied becomes part of the transnational *lex mercatoria* and figure therein, therefore no longer as domestic laws. This is here a key insight.

1.4.14 The Concept of Natural Law and the Legal Status and Force of Fundamental and General Principle in the Modern *Lex Mercatoria*

To conclude, it may be of interest to return briefly to the issue of the autonomous force of fundamental and general principle and therefore to its self-executing status and direct applicability in international transactions. This needs to be contrasted with the claims of modern legal positivism and formalism. Fundamental and general principle in this sense now stand for the more modern version of natural law, a term that would probably not have been invented to-day. It may be backed up by what becomes customary. Whatever the terminology, the basic issue is the existence and status of law outside the positive, mostly statist order, often unwritten and in the case of fundamental principle of an overarching nature or *ius cogens*.

As we have seen in section 1.2.6, the Romans knew the notion of natural law.[414] In Europe, it acquired a religious connotation after the twelfth century AD, when it was given

---

[412] See n 342 above.

[413] One may see an incipient recognition of this in Lord Denning's remarks in *Power Curber International Ltd v National Bank of Kuwait SAK* [1981] 3 All ER 607, in which it was said in connection with bank guarantees that courts should not interfere with them at the behest of the underlying parties nor recognise such interference by the courts of other countries. This would appear an expression of a more fundamental underlying international principle.

[414] See text at n 139 above. Ever since, natural law has had many different meanings and explanations. They all have in common that it is a law that for its force it is not, or at least not entirely, dependent on human intervention, as positive law is. It is not believed therefore to need for its validity or recognition the support of any public authority, whether of a national/statist or supra-national character, or the support of an ultimate rule of recognition in the sense of Hart, or an apex norm or *Grundnorm* in the sense of Kelsen.

In terms of 'fundamental principle' as basis of this law, there is clearly an idealistic element and notion of pre-existing values. This law is not necessarily equated with the demands of morality, however, although there is often a close affinity. It is not necessarily immutable either, although many consider it so. Rather, in its secular form, it became in its method closely related to rationality and in its value system more recently to human rights considerations, which both claim a more universal reach. See for an important reflection on natural law, positive law and historicity, J Berman, 'Faith and Order' in *Emory University Studies in Law and Religion* (1993) 289.

a particular meaning and status in Christian teaching as first reflected in Canon law. This natural law was secularised in the more modern natural law school of Grotius and his successors. It has been an important source of law ever since, although its status, even in its secularised form, became much contested in particular by those who subsequently adopted a statist view of law formation and no longer accepted the legal force and effect of broader more fundamental principles or of principles that may be found in all developed laws or in rationality or common sense. We are then on nineteenth-century civil law codification territory.

The point has been made particularly by modern positivists like Hans Kelsen that it is not possible to have natural law and positive law operating side by side in the same areas. They believe them to be mutually exclusive, but this depends on definitions and the issue would in any event only arise if there was genuine conflict. That is not necessarily the case. It is, for example, quite clear that in private law fundamental principles such as those of *pacta sunt servanda* or party autonomy, the notion of ownership, of contract, unjust enrichment, and detrimental reliance or fiduciary duties in the case of dependency, may easily lend themselves to further elaboration without creating any conflict.

On the other hand, where there may be conflict between fundamental principle and the written positive law, for example when the latter becomes irrational or disrespectful of changing social values, or its rules contradictory amongst themselves, interpretation of the fundamental principles operating behind the positive law may alleviate these problems and tensions, and usually does so in order to make the law function at all. There is much of this in all legal interpretation although it often remains hidden in the reasoning.

Indeed, the more basic truth is that the positive law is riddled with contradictions and lack of clarity and needs constant sorting out in individual cases, quite apart from new and unfamiliar fact situations arising all the time. Thus principle is commonly used to meet shortcomings and contradictions in the positive law itself. *Non-usus* of black-letter laws may even become the consequence as a matter of customary law, see also the discussion in section 1.4.8 above, and may figure in the positive law, even if statutory and/or mandatory, becoming legally irrelevant. In fact, many rules and their original meanings are quickly forgotten. Case law is soon forgotten too. This is a continuous process that has nothing to do with a perceived natural law/positive law divide, which is in any event not caused by the operation of fundamental or any other principle.[415]

Positive private law is not then merely black and mostly statist law but should be defined in a different manner, not simply therefore to create a contradiction. Rather, it is the continuing progression and expression of these fundamental concepts, either directly or more

---

In modern times, natural law often became an effort to find structure in the law and its progression (not a fixed system therefore). It is comfortable with private law being immanent and as such an original source of law. In that sense, custom could even be considered part of it, except that to the extent the idea is to find more universal principle, custom is usually being set apart, although it may no less be used to identify more general concepts.

In constructing a new *lex mercatoria*, these attitudes return, as we shall see, and they remain therefore most relevant in terms of this book.

[415] Human rights and environmental protection notions may here increasingly figure as fundamental principles as well, therefore even in private law, although they might still be contentious when corrective of more positive, especially statist rules, see also the discussion on constitutionalisation in s 1.4.5 above. Overriding fundamental notions of justice, social peace and efficiency also operate and it is increasingly accepted, as we have seen, that they may supplement and, if sufficiently pressing, even correct, the positive law in its interpretation. In fact, this now happens all the time, especially in private law, and is associated with the *normative* interpretation technique or more modern notions of social policy, social values and public order, see also s.1.2.13 above.

likely through the other autonomous sources of law, in which connection custom and practices, party autonomy and general principle but also treaty law, national legislation and even its system, may acquire considerable significance. Especially in academia, although also in case law, this reference frame is constantly developed and explained further or should be.

In fact, in practice there is no clear distinction or borderline between principle and positive law at all, and modern private law is in its formulation and application full of (implicit) references to more fundamental and other principles or concepts, a situation that even the DCFR in its introduction recognises. This is also clear in teleological and normative interpretation, where a re-definition of a rule's purpose or pressing demands of justice, social peace, and efficiency ever more liberally enter the equation. There is therefore no sharp distinction either between the demands of morality and law, the demands of social peace and law, or between the demands of efficiency and law, which demands when becoming sufficiently pressing all enter into the law and its applications. This is a continuing process that keeps the law living and responsive to legitimate needs, which are all needs that are not barred by public order considerations.

Much law emerges in this manner or becomes in this way part of the positive law. In modern contract law, the notion of *good faith* and its use are here particularly indicative and in truth a cover. It has already been said that other sources of law, including fundamental principle often hide behind the notion of good faith in this sense. As we have seen, it is itself mostly considered a higher norm or principle although it need not always to be so. A liberal interpretation technique more broadly fulfills a similar function and also discounts all sources of law; see section 1.4.3 above. Consequently, in this book no fundamental distinction is made between rules and principles; it is all a matter of degree. In any event, even specific black-letter rules are often very broad and in any event no more than guidance in new or incongruous fact situations.

Law, even positive law in this sense is then not, or not necessarily, national or domestic either, or even territorial; only the legislative variant will be. If conflicts still arise between the various norms that are emerging from different legal sources, especially when they claim mandatory application, as for example in movable property law, the hierarchy of norms of the modern *lex mercatoria* as explained in the previous section will take care of them at the transnational level.

The independence of the modern *lex mercatoria* is here particularly sustained by the operation of an international or *transnational commercial and financial legal order* which can be equally identified. One could also call it the international market place itself, but it is better to refer here to an own distinct legal order. This at least is the view and approach in this book and will be more extensively discussed below in section 1.5. It highlights one other particular aspect of modern developments: the emergence and operation of distinct *legal orders*, like states, but also international legal orders as the ones between states, like confederate and federal legal orders, as in the EU and US respectively, see further section 1.5.9 below. There are others such as traditionally the legal order of churches which may equally operate transborder, and now the transnational commercial and financial legal order. It is submitted that all law in all its sources acquires its force and effect ultimately from and in these legal orders and is characterised by them. Hence the difference between church and commercial law, or typical state or regulatory law.

The concept of legal order is thus crucially relevant, and institutionally particularly supports the notion of fundamental principle as the basis of its legal system and is likely also to suggest some *institutional infrastructure* through which the law in such orders can better develop and be known. As we shall see in section 1.5.5, in international commerce and finance, this order finds its origin and motivation in distinctive *social and economic* forces, now often connected with globalisation and the international flows of goods, services, information and technology, and capital, if not also of people.

Again, this approach to the modern *lex mercatoria* implies a return to pre-codification times in attitude and method. It is the reason why in the foregoing so much attention was paid to them, its emergence and operation. It could hardly be a return to the *Ius Commune* variant of the Roman law itself, however, which the secular natural law school had already abandoned,[416] or to the approach of the German nineteenth-century Pandectists. It could also not mean a return to the nineteenth-century codification practice and its intellectual model building or system thinking, which in Europe would suggest a reconstituted BGB now at European level. This is nevertheless what the DCFR is proposing for the EU. It would seem unfeasible and undesirable if only because it is unlikely to be able to accommodate the common law tradition on the one hand and the requirements of the modern *lex mercatoria* in terms of business practices and risk management in a larger world on the other.

In the meantime, it may well be asked whether there is at present a sufficient number of lawyers who have the insight, vision and education legally to underpin international business in Europe and elsewhere in this manner. It means awareness but also the ability to help build a transnational professional law out of fundamental legal principle and general principles derived from the diversity of national laws (civil and commercial) and particularly of industry practices, and party autonomy, in business supplemented by the demands of efficiency and rationality or common sense. Is there a methodology and is there a sufficient unity in view to articulate the new transnational law on a more than incidental basis? In particular, is there in the legal profession and in legal scholarship a sufficient understanding of the *dynamics* of modern commerce and finance and of the different perspectives of civil and common law and of their more fundamental differences to make some fusion possible or to reach beyond either? Is there a sufficient understanding of international law and its operation, whether of the public or private law variety?

If one looks at the efforts in UNCITRAL and UNIDROIT, one must doubt that there is at the moment any *consensus on method and content* at all. Implicit in them is the civil law codification approach and ethos with their narrowing perspective of written rules only. At EU level, it is also mostly lacking, even in connection with the DCFR and there is no proper discussion on the methodology and objectives. At present, unity or uniformity is largely seen as a question of compromise between national legal rules and concepts in the context

---

[416] One sees a different tenor in the work of H Coing, *Europäisches Privatrecht* (1985–89), and of R Zimmermann, *The Law of Obligations: The Roman Foundations of the Civilian Tradition* (1990/1993). These authors look for a revival or at least continuation of the *Ius Commune*. They follow in this respect in the steps of Koschacker and Wieacker, n 1 above, who wrote, however, for a different time. Their approach was rejected, rightly so it is suggested, by R Feenstra, 'The Development of European Private Law' in Miller and Zimmermann (eds), *The Civilian Tradition and Scots Law* (Berlin, Duncker and Humblot, 1997).

Scotland and South Africa are often held up as an example in this connection, but they have systems of law that substantially developed beyond their Roman and *Ius Commune* pasts. At least in commerce and finance, they may be some model in so far as they show a fusion between modern common and civil law notions and point to a future law in which commercial law is less systemic, more flexible and above all dependent on legal sources other than mere legislation, but that would be all.

of treaty law. At least von Savigny had a method based on the analysis of a fairly neutral set of outside norms (the Roman law). That may now not be much more than the BGB.

The developers of the new *lex mercatoria* miss such a neutral model, and need to be guided by the ever-changing dynamics and requirements of modern commerce and finance. Mere borrowing from existing civil or common law countries, or finding some kind of compromise between their laws, is unlikely to prove to be sufficient or an appropriate and adequate response. It reduces the effort to amateurism.

1.4.15 An End to the Confining Views of Legal Positivism, Formalism, and Nationalism in the Professional Sphere

The now more traditional *notion of positive law* in terms of black-letter law, statist rule and doctrinal thinking, which is often contrasted with the natural law approach, may require here some further clarification and is in modern times closely connected with the notion of legal *formalism*, statutory law or similar written texts, logic and system thinking, and then mostly also with nationalism and territorialism. As we have seen, it is often unclear, however, what it truly stands for as any liberal interpretation technique fatally undermines the concept. When contrasted with legal realism, especially in the US, its limitations become clearer. This type of statist legal positivism was an important contributory factor to the final demise of the old *lex mercatoria* and probably remains the main strand in legal thought in Europe, both on the Continent and in England, although in the latter country the judiciary remains pragmatic.

It is of interest in this connection to note the evolution of the term 'positivism' in legal terminology. The term came into common use in the middle of the nineteenth century following the writings of Auguste Comte in France.[417] In its origin, positivism denoted the scientific study of human behaviour and the identification of rules or regularities therein as the basis for the studies of the social sciences. In this sense it was *factual, not normative*; it did not aspire to a better rule or result.

The study of the law in this way became therefore a study of natural phenomena based on the observation of human (or state) behaviour in an *inductive* manner. As such legal positivism could indeed be seen as the opposite of natural law which adhered to a more theoretical deductive approach and logical process of rule formulation on the basis of some larger ideas. It was an acceptance of Hume's scepticism in this respect. In this approach, custom was important and originally highly respected as a source of law. But there was always a problem for more academically-oriented observers how to bring these inductive results together in one system. This still required some pre-existing notions of logic whilst in subsequent interpretation a more deductive or analogical approach could also not be avoided.

More importantly, in law, the concept of positivism soon became sovereignty infested and as a consequence the notion of 'positivism' underwent a sea change. Not least because of the just mentioned problems and doubts with the original concept, in legal positivism,

---

[417] A Comte, *Cours de philosophie positive* (1830–42).

law became a state construct, at best based on empirical knowledge but often inspired by political ideas of what was best in terms of transforming society. That was then used to distinguish it from morality, sociology and economics. In *private* law, positivism thus came to stand for black letter law, legal formalism, nationalism, and doctrinal system thinking. Indeed, we may in particular identify the following characteristics:

(a) a state's central role in all law formation (even if it is through its courts) and certainly in all law enforcement which suggests that no law can exist outside its authority; this is statist thinking;

(b) law given in this manner, being domestic and therefore nationalistic and territorial in nature, captured in texts and in time, as such valid and static until its next formal amendment or adaptation in case law; this is black letter law thinking;

(c) this law being possessed of some comprehensiveness in terms of an intellectual system, as such considered effectively to capture reality and being capable of ordering human relationships for the present and the future; this is doctrinal thinking;

(d) this law being dependent on logic and automaticity in its application with a sharp distinction between norm and fact, and a connected formal or technical approach to the interpretation of legal texts; there is then also a sharp separation from morality, social needs and values, and efficiency considerations; this is legal formalism;

(e) application of domestic law in this sense to all international dealings (through a system of conflicts rules or rules of private international law, itself considered part of the domestic law of the forum); this is nationalism run wild and becoming irrational; and

(f) the science of the law becoming an effort to avoid all speculation, to clarify only the most necessary concepts, and for the rest to simplify and describe the intellectually found rules and their application whilst ironing out in as much as possible all contradictions.

In this world, the law is what is on the table and there are no concepts beyond it. Critical analysis becomes irrelevant or impossible because there are no criteria on the basis of which such an analysis can be conducted. There is empiricism only in determining which formal rules there are, but they are not tested for their responsiveness to social needs or their efficiency.

Again, other sources of law are here ignored or reduced to the rank of soft law, which is the usual positivist fall-back position.[418] Law becomes technique and is assumed by

---

[418] Soft law means rules that do not emerge from an authorised source of law, such as in international commerce and finance proposals or sets of principles from UNIDROIT, UNCITRAL or other such organisations or from think tanks that aspire to reflect the living law particularly at the transnational level. In regulatory law, the concept of soft law also exists; the capital adequacy rules of Basel I, II, and III for example, have been so identified, see for the BIS and its activities, n 438 below. Custom and academic opinion may then also be considered part of it. So, in fact, may be custom and practices and general principle. It may even apply to fundamental principle. They denote some guidance, some persuasive authority but no legal status.

It was posited, however, that pressing moral, social and efficiency considerations enter the law, especially in its interpretation and application. They are not soft law. If soft law attains the level of custom or general principle, it must also be considered good law at least within the modern *lex mercatoria*, as we have seen. The work of the ICC is here an important example: the Incoterms and UCP have been exceedingly successful and although normally incorporated by contract and then operating as contract law, they may well operate as custom if not so incorporated and are indeed now usually so considered and applied, see n 341 above. The same goes for general principle and especially for fundamental principle. That is not soft law at all.

definition to come up with the correct answers. Whatever results, it is the law, is right, and can as such not be questioned.

All modern legal authors present here some view, although it remains often implicit. Natural law tendencies are the traditional antidote. Much of present day discussion, at least in the context of transnationalisation, centres here on the role of fundamental and general principle as law, whether or not directly applicable as such. It should be clear that the *lex mercatoria* approach as here explained, therefore with its reliance on fundamental and general principle as basis for the whole system, is comfortable with and relies heavily on this direct applicability. In fact, reliance on such principle usually stands at the beginning of any new development in the law that goes beyond the detail. So it is in transnationalisation, but it was also said that even domestically, principle, often fundamental, is no less necessary to iron out local contradictions in the positive law, update it and move it forward.

Legal positivism can be much more easily explained and accepted in public law, notably regulation, which is substantially formulated by government, subject to political expediency, and to goverments' immediate enforcement power, either through the courts or more directly through governmental agencies (by withdrawing licences and so on). It is much harder to defend and understand in private law as it develops and moves forward. It is important to note in this connection, that modern positivist scholars and philosophers often have little knowledge of private law and its functions and hardly understand its subtlety and sophistication.

The development of the modern *lex mercatoria* through the process of transnationalisation of private law in the transnational commercial and financial legal order may here be perceived as the clearest demonstration of spontaneous non-statist law formation in modern times. Again, this approach is not new and was more generally promoted by Grotius and his followers. On the European Continent, it was superseded by nationalism and the monopoly of legislation in private law in the nineteenth century, but it is still intact in public international law (although also much infested and weakened by sovereignty notions) and still finds there powerful recognition and expression in Article 38(1) of the Statute of the International Court of Justice (ICJ) as we have seen.

Thus transnationalisation breaks with the positivist attitude in many ways and leaves legal formalism and doctrinal thinking behind. First, it does not see private law any longer as a statist phenomenon, bases itself on fundamental legal principle, accepts many sources of law to clarify and implement it further, and maintains a dynamic concept of law that moves with the facts unless contained by public policy and public order. The traditional and fundamental Kantian divide between fact and norm is here also abandoned. Rules may be found in fact, like in custom, and the ever evolving factual situations change the rules. Law

---

For those who deny the status of an autonomous source of law to custom, general principle and even fundamental principle, soft law is often an option to give them some meaning, but it would be wholly unclear what it could be. Nevertheless, especially for legal positivists, soft law has often been a way to deal with a more dynamic concept of law and newer ideas. It may explain the increasing popularity of the notion, but it cannot stand in for legal dynamism itself.

Indeed, legal dynamism is of a different nature and, in the view here presented, produces hard law of which market practice and general principle are important manifestations.

In fact, norms are either law or they are not. There is not truly a medium category. It means that they either must apply or they do not. If through interpretation soft law is incorporated, it is law and strictly speaking this could only happen if it were an expression of principle or custom. The same may go for academic opinion. It must as a minimum be recognised in the relevant community as responsive in order to count as law. If it is, it is no longer soft law either, if it is not, it truly has no legal significance at all and is mere opinion.

finds its true meaning and expression in its application. A-aprioristic norms or black-letter rules are only guidance (unless there is pure repetition and the law is absolutely settled).

In concluding, it may also be noted that in philosophical discourse on the subject, the term 'positivism' often remains closer to the original idea of Comte and especially when we talk about legal positivism in the way of Kelsen and Hart, that remains largely the case. Law is then social fact and can be anything or nothing. The essence is that it is what it is, cannot be defined, and could be an empty shell. It is then sharply distinguished notably from morality but in fact also from all other normative rule systems, therefore also from social rules or rules derived from efficiency considerations.

The view presented in this book is that law, private law in particular, always has an extra-legal meaning and finds its purpose in the support of morality, social peace and safety, or efficiency and possibly growth. Those are the basic needs it serves and it is qualified thereby even though these objectives may often be contradictory and do not by themselves present a legal normativity. Law, private law in particular, operates here through a multitude of sources (fundamental and general legal principle, custom and practices, party autonomy and legislation) and has many spokesmen (legislators, judges, arbitrators and practitioners). It is not nationalistic or territorial per se but serves every particular legal order in ways typical for that order. These orders may be national or transnational. Law in whatever order always moves with it and is dynamic, often uncertain, even contradictory and confusing, and is in its formulation and application heavily dependent on the facts of the case. Private law must be found in each instance and it cannot always be said with certainty what it is. It can never be fully known. That is why we have lawyers. Legal positivism suggests greater clarity, at least at the national level, but it is very doubtful whether it can make that true. There would be less strife and litigation if it was so.

Positivism and its nationalistic undercurrents remain nevertheless the prevailing tendency in Europe, in England supported by the followers of Hart, on the European Continent by the followers of Kelsen. It may be different in the US, where legal scholarship and the courts are more used to experimentation, the tenets of legal formalism having been left far behind whilst the UCC remains explicitly receptive to custom and other non-statutory sources and promotes them as we have seen. In Europe, legal positivism explains the widespread European academic hostility towards the modern *lex mercatoria* and its revival, which attitude is also strongly presented in teaching and from there also in the legal practice. But it cannot satisfactorily explain how new values and perceptions constantly enter the law, even domestically, and why international transactions must always be covered by this type of national law. This is dogma, of nineteenth-century vintage, while only 50 years earlier people had generally held exactly the opposite view when natural law tendencies were still strong.

Law is formed in many ways and immanent law formation in the international commercial and financial legal order is a fact and, it is submitted, a normal function in any market place, and was never fully eradicated; see also the comments in section 1.4.4 above. The hierarchy of norm in the modern *lex mercatoria* as explained above in section 1.4.13 further suggests a complete and wholly operative legal system for those who still think in terms of systems. It is in this context rejected, at least as a general proposition, that the modern *lex mercatoria* serves merely to supplement contracts, especially duration contracts operating under local laws,[419] or to exert a new form of social control (as arbitrators may

---

[419] Even the power to supplement was originally controversial in international arbitrations, arbitrators' task being characterised earlier mainly as procedural, see W Craig, W Park and I Paulsson, *International Chamber of*

deem fit under notions of good faith or otherwise),[420] or to impose a new sense of morality or fairness on business, or to introduce equitable considerations.[421] This misses the
point, which is the operation of a new law in a new legal order with an own hierarchy of
norms that must be followed and implemented in international commercial and financial
dealings. But it is accepted that arbitrators may act in appropriate cases as equity judges in
the way English judges have been able to do,[422] that is to say remedially in individual cases
which may, however, also contribute to the formation of new law and could in this manner even develop new proprietary and set-off structures at the transnational level.[423] This
denotes a special role and specialised function for arbitrators, institutionally rooted in the
transnational legal order itself and not merely in the arbitration clause which only activates
this power but does not create it.[424]

This is highly important as an insight and is not an issue of redistributing the risks
between professional parties, for which, under the cover of good faith or otherwise, there
may be room and sometimes a need in consumer but not in professional dealings, except in
extreme cases. It also does not allow international arbitrators generally to base themselves
on notions of fairness or make them *amiable compositeurs*.[425] That is notably *not* the role
of the modern *lex mercatoria*, which is law, although it is sometimes so confused.[426] In any
event, considerations of efficiency may be just as important as notions of fairness, especially in the business community, where fair dealing is an unclear concept unless it means
the prevention of abuse, deceit or fraud.

Another important aspect is that in international cases this law (or any equitable relief
sought under it) must be pleaded; it is not for arbitrators to apply it autonomously. It has
already been said that the civil law maxim '*ius curia novit*' ['the court knows the law'] does
not apply to international arbitrators who have no law of their own on the basis of which
to state or it would have to be the *lex mercatoria* itself. Even then, application of such law
without giving parties the opportunity of a proper hearing on it should be anathema to
international arbitrators.

Not only judges, but also international arbitrators state on the basis of the law as they
find it. In a modern international setting, this will increasingly be the modern *lex mercatoria*, which should not then be confused with or be characterised as a semi- or quasi-legal

---

Commerce Arbitration, 2nd edn (1990) 143. This view has now been abandoned and supplementation and adjustment may be part of international arbitrators' ordinary interpretation facility in which they have not necessarily
more power than ordinary judges. Their power to adjust for change of circumstances in particular must be considered very limited in professional dealings, see further Vol II, ch 1, s 1.4.7ff, unless there is a hardship clause in
the contract itself.

[420] Wrongly, it is submitted, proclaimed by AE Farnsworth, G Bonell and A Hartkamp in *Tulane Journal of
International and Comparative Law* (1994) as basic tenets of good faith and fair dealing in the professional area.
[421] J Covo, 'Commodities, Arbitrations and Equitable Considerations' (1993) 9 *Arbitration International* 61.
[422] See JH Dalhuisen, 'International Arbitrators as Equity Judges' in PH Bekker, R Dolzer and M Waibel,
Making Transnational Law Work in the Global Economy, Essays in Honour of Detlev Vagts (2010) 510.
[423] It may be recalled that this was the medieval idea of the operation of precedent, see n 244 above.
[424] It was explained more extensively in s 1.1.4 above what the special (equitable) arbitral powers may amount
to in international professional dealings in terms of finding and operating a dynamic transnational contract and
movable property law in the context of the development and application of the modern *lex mercatoria*, which is
more fully covered in vol II and put there in its comparative and historical context.
[425] Even if modern international commercial arbitration under the *lex mercatoria* may get closer to an *amiable
composition*, it is by no means the same and should remain well distinguished, notably because it is based on the
law, see Dalhuisen, n 422 above.
[426] See, eg WW Park, 'Judicial Controls in the Arbitral Process' (1989) 5 *Arbitration International* 230.

regime. Although arguably arbitrators may have special (equitable) powers in this regard, they do not amount to a general licence to change the rules. In fact, it was pointed out before and will be discussed in Volume II, chapter 1 more extensively, that good faith in particular may well require a literal interpretation of commercial contracts, especially if they are meant as road maps or risk management tools, which they usually are. It leaves also little room for the excuses of mistake, *force majeure*, or change of circumstances in professional dealings unless the situation becomes clearly untenable. That is not soon the case amongst professionals and requires in any event taking into account the overall position of the suffering party and not only its position under the particular contract complained of, unless of course the contract itself specifically provides otherwise, for example, in a hardship clause; see further Volume II, chapter 1, section 1.4.

1.4.16 Dispute Prevention or Dispute Resolution? Law in Action or Law in Litigation

A last thought may complete the picture. Both in civil and in common law academia, it has become normal to look at the law through the judges' eyes, although this was not the original civil law attitude, which was policy oriented and meant to make daily life easier for all; dispute resolution was secondary and an imperfect art. But older codes and ever newer fact situations also required adjustment in civil law, and this had to come increasingly from the courts especially through the vehicle of interpretation. Thus in both systems, dispute resolution is or has become the major perspective of legal education and legal scholarship, at least in private law. In common law, that was nothing new. It is traditionally based on case law and emerges from it; indeed originally the law could only be known through it.

Legal scholarship quite naturally then tried to draw some further rules from cases. Even the common law could thus acquire some coherence or could appear a system, although, as we have seen, systemic considerations never achieved in common law the dominance it has in civil law. The common law courts' activity remained, and remains, fact-based and pragmatic, still moving from situation to situation, even when there is statutory law. On the other hand, civil law is rule- and system-based, but in practice, civil law judges have also often started moving from fact situation to fact situation much like the common law judge does, at least in the law of obligations. In contract, that is demonstrated by the use of the good faith notion. In tort, the norm became anti-social behaviour, which was so broad that for its meaning it also started to depend on the facts.

This is an important approximation but there remains a difference. First, civil lawyers are less comfortable with handling facts, and continue to view them from the perspective of their system, which, it has been submitted, could amount to intellectual prejudice and arbitrariness whilst considering and selecting the relevant facts in new situations.[427] The norm or system, whatever it was or is, still comes first. It was also noted that even in good

---

[427] See n 325 above.

faith case law, in Germany, academia strives to find renewed system and continues the pretence that it can solve all problems.[428]

American realism was able to move altogether to a more dynamic concept of private law and more fundamentally accepted that a rule acquired its ultimate meaning only in its application to facts, which application changed it at the same time. It is in truth not far removed from the old Digest maxim: *ius in causa positum* which expressed the same idea. In the more modern 'law and …' movements, there is more attention for the rule itself, its origin, operation, sufficiency and meaning, but it moves beyond litigation. Litigation is then only a mopping-up exercise in respect of the past. Rather, law is then seen as a *macro event*, as a way foremost to guide society, provide some basic order, and make it work better for the future. It is dispute prevention and much more. How the population can know these rules and obey them (voluntarism and internalisation) became here another important field of study.

Dispute resolution remains best seen as exceptional, exercised at the *micro level*, and indeed perhaps the most imperfect part of the law. In the one world, we are concerned about the law of tomorrow, the better rule to propel society forward; in the other about the law of yesterday, a cleaning-up operation. These two worlds and two concepts of the law are perhaps not easy to combine. In disputes, people need to be judged according to some existing standards that crystallise at the moment of their action. That is the law in litigation that needs to be fixed in time; in the law in action it is rather adaptation and movement.[429]

In the meantime, it could be noted, that this American approach has some affinity with the original civil law codification idea before system thinking took over.[430] which was also to make life easier for all, clean the slate of a myriad of inconsistent, and antiquated local rules, and to simplify human relationships. Order came here first, but it was obviously better if it was also just, promoted social peace and safety, and was efficient, to be realised in a dynamic continuous process of legal evolution that remained as much daily life as litigation-oriented.

1.4.17 The Role of National Courts and of International Commercial Arbitration

In the previous sections, it was argued that domestic courts should and could directly apply the hierarchy of norms inherent in the *lex mercatoria* to professional disputes as international commercial arbitrators may do. If that remains problematic for national courts, an international commercial court system might be considered. As already suggested in

---

[428] See n 65 above.

[429] In n 377 above, the view was noted that informal custom, course of dealing, trade usages and so on are often replaced by trade organisation rules that are more precise *especially when disputes arise*. It follows that, whilst participants may accept custom in their dealings as long as co-operation is productive, when disputes arise, they prefer these more precise rules by way of endgame. This suggests that these (black-letter) rules are absolutely mandatory in litigation judging behaviour that was earlier prescribed by *other* rules. It was said before that this is an interesting twist in the operation of private law that may need further thought.

[430] See s 1.2.14 above.

section 1.1.9 above, *national* courts could function in international commercial cases as international commercial courts in the international commercial and financial legal order.[431] It would provide a more appropriate alternative to international arbitrations. Their judgments would then also be international and they should become universally enforceable as such, much like international arbitration awards are now under the New York Convention and as ordinary civil and commercial judgments resulting from forum selection clauses are now proposed to be recognised under the Hague Convention of 2005 on Choice of Court Agreements. The main difference with international arbitrations would be the potentially greater stability in the system and a facility for appeal, reasons why such an international commercial court system might still function as a true alternative for the parties.

Such a new international dispute resolution facility, which would appear to require some treaty support, might include lay judges, and could have a central highest court to deal with appeals and from which binding *preliminary opinions* could also be sought, especially in matters of the application of the *lex mercatoria* and the reach of domestic regulation in international cases or even in procedural matters. This was also suggested in section 1.1.9 above. Importantly, a highest international commercial court in this sense could, as a special function, also supervise the recognition and execution (or setting aside) of international arbitral awards. It is then also conceivable that arbitrators could seek preliminary opinions from this court. The facility to ask preliminary opinions in this manner could thus become an important aid to the development of transnational commercial and financial law.

At one time in the 1970s, the English commercial courts thought that they could operate as ordinary international commercial courts.[432] In view of what has just been said, this is not as strange as it may sound. All courts applying commercial law in international cases could thus be seen to be operating in the international commercial and financial legal order, just as all courts in the EU are competent and obliged to apply EU law when appropriate and they operate then as EU courts in the EU legal order subject to a facility to ask preliminary opinions from the ECJ.

Not only international arbitrators but also courts in such a system should have the freedom to find the applicable *lex mercatoria*, and where necessary balance its outcome or result against governmental interests of the forum, or of other states. Under a proper understanding of the rule of law, the resulting decisions should indeed be enforceable wherever parties require them to be, and all civilised nations and their courts should co-operate in the enforcement effort assuming minimum standards of procedural protection and public order are met.[433]

Indeed, this situation predominantly prevails for international commercial arbitrators in international arbitrations. These may be conducted ad hoc or under existing arbitration rules. The most important of these rules are the UNCITRAL Rules, the ICC Arbitration Rules of the International Chamber of Commerce in Paris and the LCIA Rules of the London Court of International Arbitration. Under the latter two sets of rules, a whole organisation and administration of international arbitrations is provided. These sets are

---

[431] JH Dalhuisen, 'The Case for an International Commercial Court', in KP Berger et al (eds) *Festschrift Norbert Horn* (2006) 893, see further the authors cited in n 99 above.

[432] *Amin Rasheed Shipping Corporation v Kuwait Insurance Company* [1983] 1 WLR 228, 241; see more particularly n 100 above.

[433] The English attempt to consider the English courts international commercial courts, was rejected by the House of Lords, however: see *Amin Rasheed Shipping Corp v Kuwait Insurance Co* [1984] AC 50; see also n 432.

regularly updated; the LCIA rules the last time in 1998 and the ICC Rules in 2012. As far as the applicable law is concerned, they leave great flexibility to the arbitrators, see section 14(2) of the LCIA Rules, which allows arbitrators to apply whatever rules of law they consider appropriate.

This leaves ample room for the application of the *lex mercatoria* and its hierarchy of norms. French arbitration law (Article1496 CCP of 1981, now replaced by Article 1511 as part of the new French international arbitration law in 2011) and amended Dutch arbitration law (Article 1054 CCP) already allowed this earlier. The English Arbitration Act of 1996 continues to refer here rather to conflicts of law rules even if the arbitrators are free to determine what the appropriate conflict rule is (section 46(3)). It followed in this respect the UNCITRAL Model Law (Article 28 (2)), which was also reflected in the UNCITRAL Rules of 1977 (Article 33), and thus remained more restrictive.[434] In the meantime, the UNCITRAL Rules themselves were replaced in 2010 leaving the determination of the applicable law to arbitrators (Article 35).

The fact that the UK (unlike, for example, France and Switzerland) did not opt for a legislative split between domestic and international arbitrations may have retarded the development in this regard. The lack of distinction tends to limit the space for international commercial arbitration and to ignore its transnational character.

Most importantly, international commercial arbitration is supported by the New York Convention on the Recognition and Enforcement of Foreign Arbitral Awards of 1958 which (under certain minimum conditions) makes them enforceable in all participating states. They include all substantial trading nations. Such wide treaty support has notably been lacking for the international recognition and enforcement of ordinary judgments. Bilateral treaty law still remains here the most normal response but is still rare. In the USA amongst the states, the Full Faith and Credit Clause of the Constitution at least guarantees the recognition of sister state judgments. In the EU, since 1968 there has been the important Brussels Convention on Jurisdiction and the Enforcement of Judgments in Civil and Commercial Matters, now superseded (since 2002) by a Regulation in this area, followed by the very similar Lugano Convention which ties in most other Western European Countries.

---

[434] Nevertheless even English case law upheld the application of 'internationally accepted principles of law governing contractual relations' in an award rendered pursuant to an arbitration governed by Swiss law, *Deutsche Schachtbau- und Tiefbohrgesellschaft mbH v Ras al-Khaimah National Oil Co* [1987] 3 WLR 1023. There was no contractual conflict of laws clause and Art 13(3) of the old ICC Rules, which still required settlement of the dispute through conflict of laws rules, was applicable. Such a requirement thus seems no longer to exclude the application of general principles or of the law merchant (*lex mercatoria*), see also the Austrian Supreme Court (18 November 1982, (1984) 34 *ICLQ* 727) and the French Cour de Cassation (XXIV ILOM 360, 1984)), in cases upholding the award in Case 3131 *Norsolor (Pabalk Ticaret Sirketi) (Turkey) v Ugilor/Norsolor SA*, (1979), one of the first awards making a direct reference to the *lex mercatoria* under Art 13(3) of the old ICC Rules.

An award that is altogether detached from a *national arbitration* law may have greater difficulty in being recognised under the New York Convention, although upheld in the US: *Ministry of Defense of the Islamic Republic v Gould, Inc* 887 F 2d 1357 (9th Circ, 1989), see more particularly also J Lew, 'Achieving the Dream: Autonomous Arbitration' (2005 Freshfields lecture) (2006) 22 *Arbitration International* 179, see also n 89 above.

In England there is in particular the problem that the 1996 Arbitration Act does not distinguish between domestic and international arbitrations which tends to suggest greater court control in (all) arbitrations with a seat in London than may be desirable. In *Occidental Exploration Production Corp v Republic of Ecuador* [2005] EWCA Civ 1116, it was even held (by the English Court of Appeal) that all arbitrations with a seat in London result in *English* awards. Implicitly, the existence of *international* arbitration awards was here denied. This must be a mistake.

In any event, it does not directly affect awards rendered on the basis of other than a national substantive law, see also AJ van den Berg, *The New York Arbitration Convention of 1958: Towards a Uniform Interpretation* (1981) 33.

1.4.18 Agents of International Convergence and Harmonisation: The Role of UNIDROIT, UNCITRAL, the ICC, The Hague Conference, the EU, and the American Law Institute and Commissioners on Uniform State Laws in the USA

In the previous sections, reference was made several times to organisations such as UNCITRAL and UNIDROIT as agents of international convergence and harmonisation of commercial and financial laws.

UNCITRAL is the United Nations Commission on International Trade Law. It was created in December 1966 and has operated from Vienna since 1969. It has been particularly active in the area of the international sale of goods and prepared the 1980 Vienna Convention on the International Sale of Goods (ICSG). The UNCITRAL Model Arbitration Law has also already been mentioned. UNCITRAL operates in many other areas generally through conventions, model laws, legal guides, and, in the area of arbitration, also through Rules and Notes.

Thus there are UNCITRAL Conventions on the International Sale of Goods, on the Limitation Periods in the International Sale of Goods, on International Bills of Exchange and International Promissory Notes, on the Carriage of Goods by Sea, and on Independent Guarantees and Standby Letters of Credit and on Receivables in International Trade (to be discussed more extensively in Volume II, chapter 2, section 1.9.3 and Volume III, chapter 1, section 2.4). There are Model Laws on International Commercial Arbitration, Cross-border Insolvency, Electronic Commerce, the Procurement of Goods and International Credit Transfers. There are Legal Guides on International Counter-trade Transactions, Electronic Funds Transfers and Drawing up International Contracts for the Construction of Industrial Works. Rules have been issued on Arbitration and Conciliation. There are, finally, also Notes, such as those on Organising Arbitral Proceedings.

UNCITRAL is directly run by the UN, and operates under the General Assembly. UNIDROIT is the older organisation and is a left-over from the old League of Nations. It was not converted into a UN agency but re-established in Rome after World War II as an independent organisation.[435] It is funded by Italy and other participating countries. There is a healthy competition with UNCITRAL, even some overlap, but the UNCITRAL remit is narrower and limited to trade law.[436] Important newer UNIDROIT Conventions are the ones on International Financial Leasing, on Factoring, on Agency in the International Sale of Goods, on Stolen or Illegally Exported Cultural Objects, on Mobile Equipment (also known as the 2001 Cape Town Convention), and on Intermediated Securities (also known as the 2009

---

[435] It has 56 Member States and operates under a Governing Council consisting of 25 members appointed by its General Assembly for five years. This General Assembly meets once every year to vote the budget. It also votes on the Work Programme proposed by the Governing Council, which is in charge of policy, implemented by the Secretariat headed by the Secretary General. The President is appointed by the Italian Government and an *ex officio* member of the Governing Council.

[436] The main UNIDROIT project was originally the International Sales of Goods Convention, a project started in 1928 at the initiative of Professor Ernst Rabel from Germany, later at the University of Michigan at Ann Arbor. Because of the non-functioning of UNIDROIT during and after World War II, the Dutch Government was asked by the United Nations to provide a venue for the continuation of this work, which was completed in two diplomatic conferences in The Hague in 1951 and 1964. They resulted in the Hague Conventions on Uniform Law in the International Sale of Goods. The project was subsequently taken over by UNCITRAL resulting in the successor Vienna Convention of 1980.

Geneva Convention). The first two and the Cape Town Convention will be discussed more extensively in Volume III, chapter 1, the Geneva Convention in Volume II, chapter 1

As was shown, UNCITRAL has produced more results although in a narrower field but, with the exception of the CISG, has, like UNIDROIT, suffered from little ratification. On an international scale, the International Chamber of Commerce in Paris (ICC) has also been operative in the area of international trade. The Uniform Customs and Practice for Documentary Credits (UCP) have been in existence for letters of credit since 1933. Since 1956 there have also been Uniform Rules for Collections (URC). For guarantees, the ICC compiled two sets of uniform rules, the first being the Uniform Rules for Contract Guarantees of 1978 (URCG) and the second the Uniform Rules for Demand Guarantees of 1992 (URDG).

The ICC Incoterms have since 1936 covered the basic trade terms like FOB and CIF and now also cover many others. In the area of international sales, the ICC produced a Model International Sales Contract. There is also the UCP. These various rules and practices, which are important, are deemed applicable by virtue of contractual incorporation or on the basis of custom only. They are not promulgated in any way. The significance of the ICC and its various committees in this respect is that these texts are very regularly updated and have acquired full industry acceptance. Outside organisations such as UNCITRAL sometimes co-operate, as in the revisions of the UCP for letters of credit. These revisions do not always promote conceptual clarity and academic input is often missing, but they are at least up to date and work as they have obtained the industry's confidence and support. As such they have proved more important than the work in both UNCITRAL and UNIDROIT so far.

Besides the UNCITRAL and UNIDROIT, the WTO should now also be considered as a modern organisation, which, in the area it covers, equally moves forward on the legal front amongst its Members.[437] The Bank of International Settlement (BIS)' efforts[438] in the area

---

[437] The WTO dates from 1996 and was product of the Uruguay Round. It is the successor of the former GATT (which was reconstituted under it) and it acquired some broader powers also in the area of services (through GATS): see vol III, ch 2, s 2.1. In particular, it established (a) a new legal pattern of conduct, integrating all previous GATT agreements into one system including the trade-related movement of persons and investments. It also instituted (b) a new infrastructure for trade relations, with its own Ministerial Conference, General Council, Council for Trade in Goods, Council for Trade in Services, Council for Trips, Committee on Trade and Development and its own Secretariat. The WTO further provides (c) a forum for further negotiations; and also (d) a dispute settlement procedure; (e) a policy review procedure; and (f) some special trade agreements, such as those on civil aircraft and government procurement.

The basic tools of the most favoured nation clause and of national treatment, which may also cover legal and regulatory issues, are conducive to legal harmonisation, even though national policies must be respected. See further AT Guzman and JHB Pauwelyn, *International Trade Law* (2009).

[438] The BIS itself is the bank of Central Banks, originally created in 1930 to manage German reparation payments, and is directed by the Central Bank governors of the Group of Ten (G-10), which are (or were) economically speaking the most prominent nations, see vol III, ch 2, s 2.5.1. It also serves as a think tank to Central Banks for banking regulation through the important Committee on Banking Supervision. This was extended to a much broader membership and is now called the Basel Committee

This co-ordination is motivated by the internationalisation of the banking industry. It concerns here primarily the business and regulation of *commercial* banks. The most important result has been in the area of capital adequacy for these banks, through the 1988 *Capital or Basle Accord, cf* the BIS Document on Convergence of Capital Measurement and Capital Standards, not to be confused with the just-mentioned 1983 Concordat concerning international banking supervision, as amended after 1992. The *Basle Accord* was based largely on a joint 1986 UK/US initiative which adopted the risk–assets methodology. Following the Accord of 1988, the BIS produced a number of further communications in the capital adequacy area, leading to a formal amendment in January 1996, whilst in 1999 it proposed a complete overhaul of the 1988 document which was followed by further proposals in 2001, leading to what is now commonly referred to as Basel II, effective since 1 January 2008, although it has no

of banking supervision, especially in respect of capital adequacy requirements, are relevant too although not amounting to binding texts. The work of IOSCO[439] should then also be mentioned. Related are the IMF efforts in the area of financial stability. By the end of 2008 the G-20 had stepped forward to review financial regulation at world level where earlier the Financial Stability Forum (FSF since 1999) had also been operative.[440] The OECD has also been active in certain areas.[441]

In the USA, the work of the National Conference of Commissioners on Uniform State Laws and of the American Law Institute on Restatements has already been mentioned many times before. It resulted from private initiatives, not supported by any agreement amongst the various states. The National Conference has drafted a number of Uniform Laws for adoption. The most important one is the UCC, which was (exceptionally) a joint project with the American Law Institute. Normally this Institute prepares only Restatements, which are non-binding, are not meant to achieve the force of legislation, but have nevertheless had a considerable impact on the further development of the law in the relevant areas. They also serve as guidelines for the courts and have a strong persuasive force.

The Uniform Commercial Code is now accepted (with some minor modifications) in all 50 States of the Union. It was substantially conceived by Professor Karl Llewellyn (1893–1962) of Columbia University (later of University of Chicago) as Chief Reporter with the particular help of Soia Mentschikoff as Associate Chief Reporter. Others also had a substantial input, like Professor Grant Gilmore of Yale on Article 9, concerning secured transactions. The UCC is regularly updated and a number of new chapters have also been added, notably Article 2A on equipment leases and Article 4A on electronic payments.

The above institutes and organisations mainly aim at producing uniform substantive laws, either through treaty law, as parallel laws (in the USA), as models, or through guidance. As we have seen, there has also been an attempt at drafting uniform conflict rules.

---

treaty status and operates more as uniform general principle or international standard for financial regulation. It proved an immediate failure and was followed by an amended version in 2010, called Basel III. In the EU, the Basel Accords acquired official status (albeit with some modification) through Directives.

The BIS is also active in other areas and issued amongst its many communications a Declaration of Principle on Money Laundering in 1988, a Code of Conduct on Large Risks in 1991, and Core Principles for Effective Banking Supervision in 1997. In 1998 there was a paper on Enhancing Bank Transparency and another one on Sound Practices for Loan Accounting, Credit Risk Disclosure and Related Matters. In the same year, the BIS (together with IOSCO, see n 439 below) published Recommendations for Public Disclosure of Trading and Derivatives Activities of Banks and Securities Firms. In 1999 there followed a Core Principles Methodology supplementing the 1997 Core Principles, both of which were reviewed in a consultative document of April 2006.

[439] The securities business missed a similar organisation like the BIS for the international and co-ordination aspects of modern regulation. In the Americas there existed, however, IOSCO, the International Organisation of Securities Commissions as a voluntary organisation of securities regulators based in Montreal. During the 1980s many other securities regulators joined, and this organisation now provides, through its regular meetings and various committees, a focus for international securities regulation, although not yet of the same standing as the BIS. It co-operates with the latter particularly in the area of capital adequacy for universal banks. It is most important achievement is probably the 1998 IOSCO Principles and Objectives of Securities Regulation, which contain a statement of best practices. It particularly seeks to prevent abuses connected with multi-jurisdiction securities activities.

In the insurance business, there was even less international co-ordination between supervisors. The International Association of Insurance Supervisors (IAIS) is meant to fill this gap. Like the BIS, it is based in Basle. Its main achievements are in its 1995 Recommendation Concerning Mutual Assistance, Cooperation and Sharing Information and in its 1997 Model Principles for Insurance Supervision.

[440] The IBRD or World Bank is also involved and the IMF particularly in connection with financial crisis management (for instance during the last decade in Mexico, Russia, Asia and Argentina).

[441] See notably its (failed) project for a Multilateral Agreement on Investment (MAI 1998).

This has long been the objective of the Hague Conference on Private International Law, set up in 1893 under the leadership of Professor TMC Asser (1838–1913) from Amsterdam, who was later given the Nobel Peace Prize for his efforts (1912). This Conference produces draft treaties on private international law topics. It meets every few years on an irregular basis.

Its approach is therefore notably *not* one of formulating uniform substantive laws. On the contrary, it is a proponent of the private international law approach to international transactions, looking for the application of a national law to apply to international transactions. It only seeks to formulate, through treaty law, common conflict principles in specific areas. In the business area, such conventions are not frequent, but an important recent example is the Hague Convention on the Law Applicable to Dispositions of Securities held through Indirect Holding Systems (see more particularly Volume II, chapter 2, section 3.2.2). Others are in the field of trust and agency.

The Conventions prepared by the Hague Conference are commonly referred to as Hague Conventions, but should be clearly distinguished from the Hague Uniform Sales Conventions, which produced uniform substantive sales law for goods. These were prepared at Diplomatic Conferences in The Hague in 1951 and 1964, as we have seen in section 1.4.11 above, and the Hague Conference was not involved in them.

1.4.19 EU Attempts at Harmonising Private Law

Within the EU, efforts have been made in the area of unification of *private international law* rules of which the 1968 Brussels Convention on the Recognition and Enforcement of Judgments in Civil and Commercial Matters and 1980 Rome Convention on the Law Applicable to Contractual Obligations were at first the most important, both now replaced (since 2002 and 2008 respectively, in amended form) by Regulations, commonly referred to as Brussels I and Rome I.

So-called soft law, through principles defined and formulated per topic, is often considered a first step, and we have seen them arising in contract, trusts and even in secured transactions and insolvency.[442] This activity may be worthwhile provided the need for professionals and others, like consumers, are clearly distinguished and reflected. Such

---

[442] In the EU, in contract, a private informal group financially (but not otherwise) supported by the EU (the Lando group) drafted *European Principles of Contract Law* (PECL), published between 1995 and 1998, largely as an amalgam or common denominator of domestic consumer laws, which will be more extensively discussed in vol II, ch 1, s 1.6. They were very similar to the UNIDROIT Contract Principles, already mentioned in the previous section, which, however, did not apply to consumer dealings, although they were hardly less consumer-oriented in their approach. Neither set proved convincing as they missed the connection with modern needs and thinking in this area: see also s 1.1.4 above.

At the academic level other principles were also being developed. The Principles of Trust Law, see vol II, ch 2, s 1.4.6, are perhaps the most important and were formulated in a working group at the University of Nymwegen in 1998. They were short and of considerable interest.

More incidental projects also emerged especially within the so-called *Ius Commune* Programme such as the Tort Law project at the University of Maastricht in 1998 (under Professor Walter van Gerven), followed (together with the University of Leuven), by Contract Law, Unjust Enrichment and Civil Procedure Law projects resulting in books with cases covering similar fact situations under different national laws.

principles depend for their effectiveness on clarity, inspiration and guidance rather than on detailed compilations of minuscule rules derived from often consumer-oriented domestic laws, which at least in contract and now even in movable property seems to have been the preferred approach of many so far.

In the mean time, beyond merely soft law of this nature, especially for *consumers*, many incidental harmonisation measures have been implemented at the EU level through Directives,[443]

The *Trento Project* concerned itself since 1995 with the Common Core of European Private Law, which it primarily means to find in the study of case law in specific areas. It does not mean to produce Restatements. Both groups therefore explore case law rather than expounding new ideas.

There followed the *Study Group on a European Civil Code Project* (Von Bar Group), which as a first step wanted to formulate Restatements in the various areas of private law. Younger academics in various Universities were allotted special projects, likes sales, service and duration contracts at Utrecht/Tilburg and Amsterdam. A Co-ordinating Committee emerged, under which projects were spread locally.

Although of interest and a good way to spread knowledge on different approaches in different European legal systems, one may well ask what the purpose of these projects was with practitioners' input and interest largely lacking. The excitement clearly arose from the prospect of future codification, which remained unquestioned as concept and method.

Again, the ultimate test for the validity of these exercises in the professional sphere is not the academic quality but whether the practice of the law recognises itself in the result in the light of its needs. If so, these studies could obtain an international normativity and become persuasive of general principle. Without it, they are no more than academic exercises, mainly about what the law used to be in strict black-letter terms in different countries, generally with an insufficient distinction between professional and consumer law.

[443] This is so notably in the protection of consumers through consumer contract law. The ECJ has defined 'consumers' as natural persons acting outside the range of professional activity: see Case C-361/89 *De Pinto* [1991] ECR I-1189. Problems may arise where individuals also act professionally, raising the question whether such activities may still benefit from consumer protection: protection is not afforded unless the professional activity was insubstantial: see Case C-464/01 *Gruber* [2005] ECR I-439. However, the counterparty may here still rely on his good faith when an individual contracts for his business. It is also relevant whether the goods are or could be used for professional purposes, require delivery at a business address, or there is VAT registration. This suggests that the (consumer) buyer may have raised wrong expectations and accordingly bears the risk, but in internet transactions it may be simply the nature of the goods and the likelihood of professional use that will determine the issue.

See for the relevant Directives notably Council Directive 85/374/EEC [1985] OJ L210 on the approximation of the law of the Member States concerning liability for defective products; Council Directive 85/577/EEC [1985] OJ L372 to protect the consumer in respect of contracts negotiated away from business premises; Council Directive 87/102/EEC [1987] OJ L42 later amended, for the approximation of the laws, regulations and administrative provisions of the Member States concerning consumer credit, now superseded by Directive 2008/48/EC of the European Parliament and of the Council on credit agreements for consumers [2008] OJ L133/66; Council Directive 90/314/EEC [1990] OJ L158 on package travel, package holidays and package tours; Council Regulation 295/91 [1991] OJ L36/5 establishing common rules for a denied-boarding compensation system in scheduled air transport; Council Directive 93/13/EEC [1993] OJ L95/29 on unfair terms in consumer contracts; Council Directive 97/9/EC [1997] OJ L144/19 on the protection of purchasers in respect of certain aspects of contracts relating to the purchase on a time share basis; Council Directive 97/5/EC [1997] OJ L43/25 on cross-border credit transfers; Council Directive 97/7/EC [1997] OJ L144/19 on the protection of consumers in respect of distance contracts; Council Regulation of 9 October 1997 [1997] OJ L285/1 on air carrier liability in the case of accidents; Directive 98/27/EC [1998] OJ L166/51 on injunctions for the protection of consumers' interests; Directive 00/31/EC [2000] OJ L178 on Certain Legal Aspects of Electronic Commerce in the Internal Market; Directive 2002/65/EC [2002] OJ L271 concerning the distance marketing of consumer financial services. The E-Commerce Directive 2002/87/EC [2003] OJ L35/1 contains in its Art 3(4) some special rules for consumer protection and allows host country measures in very narrowly defined circumstances.

A new EU Consumer Rights Directive, 2011/83/EU was issued in October 2011 and is foreseen to become effective by 2014. It replaces Directives 85/577/EEC (contracts negotiated away from business premises) and 97/7/EC (long distance selling) and amends Directives 93/13/EEC and 99/7/44/EC a number of the above. The new Directive is a maximum Directive and cannot therefore be exceeded in protection by better local provisions.

One of the keys of the protection continues to be the facility to cancel the contract on receipt of the goods for which there is now a period of 14 days starting on the date of receipt of the goods. The problem remains that not all countries can afford as yet the same type and level of consumer protection. This required the Directive to be watered down substantially and again poses the question of the feasibility of one type of protection for

which can, however, only be issued in areas where the EU has authority. Furthermore, as Directives, they present harmonisation efforts that still need implementation at national levels, which allows for variation in the end result by Member State, although much less so in so-called maximum directives which may not be topped up in terms of protection. In the private law area, EU Directives have also been popular in respect of *employment* contracts[444] and to achieve some harmonisation of *company* law.[445] Financial Directives may also have a private law impact.[446] In the professional sector, such Directives touching upon private law are otherwise rare.

consumers EU wide, especially now that we have a maximum Directive which does not allow richer countries to offer more.

The other point is that the EU jurisdiction is here normally based on the promotion of the internal market, see text below. It is a connected issue. This effectively subordinates consumer protection which must fit in with it. This issue and the friction it produces has started to surface in case law, see Case C-205/07 *Gysbrecht/Santurel* [2008] Jur.I-9947 16 December 2008, here in respect of a domestic protection going beyond the standard set in the long distance selling Directive (which extra protection was condoned in the circumstances of the case) but it applies to all consumer protections, which cannot obstruct the internal market. The issue is here often the extra cost of sending and returning the goods.

[444] See especially Council Directive 76/207/EEC on the implementation of the principle of equal treatment for men and women as regards access to employment, vocational training and promotion, and working conditions [1976] OJ L39; Council Directive 2000/78/EC establishing a general framework for equal treatment in employment and occupation [2000] OJ L3003/16.

[445] See First Council Directive 68/151/EEC on co-ordination of safeguards which, for the protection of the interests of members and others, are required by Member States of companies within the meaning of the second para of Art 58 of the Treaty, with a view to making such safeguards equivalent throughout the Community [1968] OJ L65/08; Second Council Directive 77/91/EEC on coordination of safeguards which, for the protection of the interests of members and others, are required by Member States of companies within the meaning of the second paragraph of Art 58 of the Treaty, in respect of the formation of public limited liability companies and the maintenance and alteration of their capital, with a view to making such safeguards equivalent [1977] OJ L26/1; Third Council Directive 78/855/EEC concerning mergers of public limited liability companies [1978] OJ L295/36; Fourth Council Directive 78/660/EEC on the annual accounts of certain types of companies [1978] OJ L222/11; Sixth Council Directive 82/891/EEC on the division of public limited liability companies [1982] OJ L378/47; Seventh Council Directive 83/349/EEC on consolidated accounts [1983] OJ L193/1; Eighth Council Directive 84/253/EEC on the approval of persons responsible for carrying out the statutory audits of accounting documents [1984] OJ L126/20; Eleventh Council Directive 89/666/EEC concerning disclosure requirements in respect of branches opened in a Member State by certain types of company governed by the law of another State [1989] OJ L395/36; Twelfth Council Company Law Directive 89/667/EEC [1989] on single-member private limited-liability companies OJ L395/40; Directive 2003/58/EC amending Council Directive 68/151/EEC as regards disclosure requirements in respect of certain types of companies [2003] OJ L221/13; Directive 2004/25/EC on takeover bids (text with EEA relevance) [2004] OJ L142/12; Directive 2005/56/EC on cross-border mergers of limited liability companies [2005] OJ L310/1; Directive 2006/68/EC amending Council Directive 77/91/EEC as regards the formation of public limited liability companies and the maintenance and alteration of their capital [2006] OJ L264/32; Directive 2007/36/EC on the exercise of certain rights of shareholders in listed companies [2007] OJ L184/17.

The EU has used the legal form of a Regulation to create new types of associations or companies at EU level, see Council Regulation (EEC) 2137/85 on the European Economic Interest Grouping (EEIG) [1985] OJ L199/1; Regulation (EC) 2157/2001 [2001] OJ L294/1 on the Statute for a European Company (SE) supplemented by Directive 2001/86/EC of the same date [2001] OJ L294/22 on employee participation; and Regulation (EC) 1435/2003 on the statute for a European co-operative society (SCE) [2003] OJ L207/1, supplemented by Directive 2003/72/EC of the same date on employee participation [2003] OJ L207/25.

[446] See as part of the 1998 EU Financial Services Action Plan especially Directive 2004/39/EC on Markets in Financial Instruments (MiFID) [2004] OJ L145/1; Directive 2003/6/EC on Market Abuse [2003] OJ L96/16; Directive 2003/71/EC as regards information contained in prospectuses (the Prospectus Directive) [2003] OJ L345; and Directive 2004/109/EC on the harmonisation of transparency requirements [2004] OJ L390/38 (Transparency Directive). The rules on conduct of business in MiFID and its implementation instruments are here especially important as they concern issued of agency in brokerage relationships and mean to protect (smaller) investors.

In the financial area, in matters of private law, the Settlement Finality Directive 98/26/EC [1998] OJ L166/45 and the Collateral Directive 2002/47/EC [2002] OJ L168 are especially relevant. They aim largely at private law harmonisation and within it at uniformity in much narrower specialised fields.

Through Regulations, the EU could impose uniform law directly, but in the private law area it has not so far done so, except in the areas of recognition of civil and commercial judgments, bankruptcy and in the implementation of some financial directives. The former Regulations concern private international law subjects and not the substance of private law itself.

More significant is that beyond these incidental measures, there is increasingly a call for uniform or at least harmonised texts in all *substantive parts of private* law to be produced at EU level. The essence of these projects is that the EU is then seen as one market that is considered domestic, legally subject to only one text per subject, if not full codification in the civil law manner. This is the idea behind the DCFR, mentioned several times before.

In this market covering the whole EU, no special regime is then envisaged any longer for cross-border transactions in the sense that they are considered to operate in the transnational legal order. That would—in the approach of this book—mean the emergence of different sources of law of which legislative (treaty or similar) texts would only be one, which was perceived to be the essence of the modern *lex mercatoria*. It follows that these EU efforts, whilst domesticating all transactions within the EU, seek to ignore the modern *lex mercatoria*. In fact, the idea is here that the nineteenth-century nationalisation of private law at the level of the state continues unabated in statist texts that claim a monopoly in law formation, now at the level of the EU. The aim is then full codification in this traditional narrow civil law sense. It should be noted that the method is not truly considered: the traditional civil law codification ethos that eliminates all other sources of law is uncritically accepted here as being correct.

Beyond method, there is the important issue, however, of whether the EU has sufficient standing to legislate in the private law area, whether through Directive or Regulation. The competency of the EU in these matters must derive from the EU Founding Treaties. Articles 81, 114, 169(2) and 352 TFEU are relevant here. It is clear that they do not present sufficient original authority for full codification of private law within the EU, not even in the consumer area (Article 169(2)) and could hardly be so interpreted. Full unification of private law, including for consumers, would be a prime policy issue that would have to be decided at the level of the Founding Treaties themselves and Member States have not so far chosen to do so.

Even in commercial and financial law, it could be asked how far this power goes. Payments, bills of exchange and cheques, letters of credit, bills of lading and trade terms may be directly connected. So may be the important issue of transactional and payment finality and the question of the treatment of collateral in cross-border finance to which the EU Settlement Finality and Collateral Directives testified, but what about contract and the law of movable property more generally, even sales in their contractual and proprietary aspects? In any event, cross-border and other sales would then have to be distinguished and for local sales at best some uniform law between the different Member States could be created with their consent; importantly, this would not be an EU jurisdiction.

In the professional sector, EU Directives touching on private law issues are otherwise much rarer but there is concern over late payments in commercial transactions, see Directive 2000/35/EC [2000] OJ L35. See for another area where the EU has acted in the commercial sphere, Council Directive 86/653/EEC on the co-ordination of the Member States relating to self-employed commercial agents [1986] OJ L382.

It may be recalled in this connection that constitutions tend to be specific on the point of codification and this for very good reasons.[447] No Member State would want to be deprived of its own law without it, especially England of its common law. Revolutions have started for less. It means that Member States if they want to proceed in this manner must take the lead and change the Founding Treaties first. In other words, there must be clarity up front at the political level, in particular on whether an effort of this nature should result in a tool box as a set of uniform definitions, restatement, set of principles, opt-in document, full codification or whatever. This cannot be decided through the back door of an expansive treaty interpretation in which all is brought under the promotion of the internal market.

Thus generally the EU has insufficient power,[448] even in the consumer area, except where the issue can be closely connected with the free movement of persons, goods, services and capital under Article 114 TFEU, traditionally a flexible concept, however, in the eyes of the

---

[447] For the moment, Art 114 TFEU is the only pertinent article and allows unification of this nature to be undertaken only in the context of the completion of the internal market, to which Art 169(2) also makes reference for consumers. This is a narrow base. It means that unification of the rules must be considered from the perspective of trans-border business activity that would demonstrably be promoted if rules were uniform. That could especially apply to mandatory rules (as they cannot be set aside by the parties), relevant more in particular in terms of consumer protection (although it would also have a meaning in movable property law).

It is, therefore, not surprising that these matters are often largely considered from the perspective of consumer protection, but that cannot be the principal objective as under Art 114 TFEU the promotion of trans-border business rather than of consumer protection would have to be the goal. This creates little room for the extension of such protection itself beyond the policies already pursued by Member States to which Art 169(2) also testifies, although there might still be harmonisation, but, again, only to the extent that the promotion of the single market demonstrably requires it and always subject to the principles of subsidiarity and proportionality. See for the tension here also the ECJ case law cited in n 443 above. A more immediate tension is the one that results when consumer protection and the promotion of the internal market conflict. Under Art 114 TFEU as basis for EU legislative jurisdiction, the requirements of the internal market would have to prevail.

The issue has arisen in long-distance selling, in the right of the buyer to cancel the contract and the matter of state and cost of the return of the goods, see Case C-205/07 *Gijsbrecht/Santurel* [2008] *Jur* I-9947 16 December 2008. The promotion of the internal market on which consumer directives are normally based requires consideration of this basic principle, if necessary against the protection of the consumer, and a balance will be struck. Cancellation without cost may therefore not always be the proper remedy. In particular, further-going local rules in this respect in the country of the consumer under minimum directives may not square with the operation of the internal market, but neither may be the protection of the directives themselves. At least in the interpretation of them, the higher principle of the promotion of the internal market on which they are based will be considered.

It is clear that full codification of all aspects of consumer or any other law could hardly fit under Art 114 TFEU. This would be all the more true for professional dealings in general (B2B). Moreover, whatever uniform rules of private law would emerge, there would be a continuing requirement to interpret them in accordance with the limited objective of promoting the internal market. This creates a layer of interpretation in private law that is unusual but would be continuously confining. Again, it could not be guided by the interest of consumers, easily the contrary.

[448] See also S Vogenauer and S Weatherill (eds), *The Harmonisation of European Contract* Law (Oxford, Hart Publishing, 2006); G Alpa and M Andenas, *Fundamenti del diritto private europeo* (Milan, 2005); and J Mance, 'Is Europe Aiming to Civilise the Common Law' (2007) 18 *European Business Law Review* 77.

It could further be argued that at least in real estate and the consumer areas, domestic laws should remain dominant as a matter of subsidiarity, although, as just mentioned, the EU was given some authority in the consumer area in the Treaty of Maastricht in 1992. The ideas concerning one European private law emanated indeed from the Health and Consumer Directorate within the EU, but the EU has no general and original jurisdiction to create uniform private law, in this area either.

The DCFR, see below, accepted that at least real estate law should remain domestic. Here it may be asked whether it can be separated from the rest of the private law if one believes in a system. In its Green Paper of July 2010, COM (2010) 348 final, the EU Commision sought to split out contract law but similarly it may be asked whether it could stand sufficiently alone. Especially in civil law countries that may be problematic in view of its system thinking approach.

European Court of Justice,[449] but it would not appear to allow for a full codification of European private law. Private law would therefore normally still operate in the domestic spheres and remain domestic.

Nevertheless, increasing EU interest in private law harmonisation, especially in the European Parliament, led in February 2003 to an EU Action Plan on a 'more coherent European contract law'. It introduced the idea of a Common Framework of Reference (CFR), following an earlier EU Commission publication in 2001, and was itself followed by a later one in 2004 ('The Way Forward'), which widened the scope. It instituted a group of researchers that was to deliver a final report in 2007. It was hoped that by 2009 the CFR would be ready for adoption. The European Principles of Contract Law (PECL)—earlier drafted in an anthropomorphic and consumer mode, see Volume II, chapter 1, section 1.6—appeared to be the basis in contract. In the meantime, another group (the Acquis group) which had tried to deduce common contract principles from existing EU private law and operated mainly at the level of consumers, came together with the first group in the production of what became the Draft Common Frame of Reference (DCFR) in 2008–2009 as an unofficial academic proposal for full codification in the EU in the traditional civil law manner. It also covered the law of movable property including claims.

Subsequently, in a Green Paper of 1 July 2010, the EU Commission mentioned a number of options. It seemed to be heading for an opt-in model in the area of contract law, but that still would assume that it had power to legislate such a model, short of which such a text would risk to be declared invalid or, in Member States that have constitutional courts, unconstitutional. This by itself would make such an option unviable as participants would (retroactively) risk that their chosen law had no legal base and therefore no validity.

Nevertheless, in 2011, there appeared a first more official EU project from a so-called Expert Group on EU Contract law, instituted by the EU Commission (in 2010). It called itself a European contract law for consumers and business, but was limited to the sale of goods both for consumer as well as professional dealings with distinctions mainly in the area of pre-contractual duties. It followed the work in this area of DCFR closely, itself inspired on the 1980 CISG (now extended to consumer dealings), and substantially also adopted the DCFR general part of contract so as to form a full text. It did not deal with property aspects, however, although transfer of title is the principle objective of a sale, except to require the seller to transfer the property but left open how that was to be done. There is thus no full coverage of sales at all and in the way title is transferred, especially transborder, there remain considerable problems and uncertainties.

Ultimately, in October 2011, the EU published a draft Regulation on the European Law of Sales (CESL or Common European Sales Law) that was substantially based on the proposals of the Expert Group. It still tries to cover both consumer and professional dealings in a unitary approach and mixed in this connection—fatally, it is submitted—consumer and professional protection needs, see further Volume II, chapter 1, section 1.6, even though professional sales are only covered if including one SME (small and medium seized enterprise)

---

[449] Another problem with the ECJ may be that it is hardly equipped for private law issues. It would probably require a new chamber with experts in private law. Its working language in French is another impediment which marginalises most judges and may give excessive power to the few who write French or otherwise to their referendars who do so and are educated in it. This could suggest a preponderance of French interpretation techniques to prevail rather than an original EU technique that could also deal with common law perspectives, especially in professional dealings where the common law is generally better developed and more practical and flexible.

party (as defined). Importantly, the project, being based on Article 114 TFEU, is limited to cross-border dealings. It would thus seem that it has limited scope but the adoption of CESL would still introduce and legitimise a general part of contract law that is wholly unsuitable for professional dealings, including long-term supply agreements with large service elements, see again the discussion, especially on this unitary approach, in Volume II, chapter 1, section 1.6. That is the true danger.

The question of proper jurisdiction under Article 114 TFEU is buttressed by the suggestion that such a uniform sales law promotes the internal market in protecting small businesses and consumer cross-border dealings in particular. Great expansion of cross-border business was claimed, but this remains very much to be seen.[450] The impediments of cross-border activity are mostly of a very different nature. At the practical level, this sales project suffers from the main flaws already shown in the 1980 CISG: the concept of fundamental breach is too subjective, so is the concept of force majeure, and the unilateral right of the buyer to reduce the price is unmanageable.

These are the principal reasons why the commercial practice has rejected the CISG. Small and medium sized companies may be even more vulnerable through lack of leverage and organisational acumen. Moreover, they will have to face an extra layer of consumer protection. The project is meant as an opt-in facility and one must wonder who would want to be covered by it under the circumstances, except supposedly consumers as buyers, but the consent to the opt-in must also come from their suppliers.

Again, methodology and objectives were never clearly considered, nor indeed the practicalities.[451] Stakeholders that were originally to accompany the DCFR project with their

---

[450] It is relevant that the claims that are made by the Commission in CESL in this connection border on the delusional. This undermines the entire projects and its credibility. CESL is claimed to be conducive to overcome the present financial crisis. It is further said that billions of business would be added to cross-border trade, especially by SMEs, and that consumers would also more actively engage in buying products elsewhere in the EU. However, SMEs are usually very successful because they are small, want to remain so, and have no interest whatever in foreign adventure where they would meet risks that are many times greater than some differences in the applicable sales laws. As far as consumers are concerned, in an open market they buy petrol in another country if, taking into account the distance and cost to get there, the price is still lower. Consumers never have an idea of the applicable law. Moreover, in all cases, buying elsewhere detracts from local business and the net result in terms of activity may be neutral at best and is not by definition an increase in overall activity.

The idea that transaction costs will be limited must also be in doubt. For SMEs they would be increased if cross-border business now became their objective. In any event, in the key issue in sales, the transfer of title, CESL has no answer and provides no uniformity. Thus legal differences and impediments remain. More importantly, most people and businesses can live with that and we know from the US, which has a market that is far more integrated but where private law has remained state law, that diversity of the law is no true barrier. Even the UCC remains state law; an attempt to make it federal law was abandoned early on.

[451] A critique of this nature operates at least at three levels, which should be distinguished although they cannot be fully separated. In the above, some general, although fundamental, observations were made on the nature and ambitions of the DCFR, which carry over into CESL, but it is also necessary to go deeper into the approach of the DCFR and CESL itself to gain an idea of their sufficiency or insufficiency. The third level is the very detail of the text, which as for the DCFR is at this stage perhaps less relevant, although ultimately determining. That would be the case even now for CESL.

In s 1.1.4 above, I set out what I believe a modern professional private law should look like in contract and movable property and identified in that connection as the most substantial differences between common and civil law (of contract and movable property) which may be summarised as follows.

(a)   in the area of contract, the anthropomorphic attitude in civil law, its emphasis on the will of the parties, its parochial concepts of offer and acceptance, the position of the parties in the case of non-performance (and the attitude to force majeure), and in the pre- and post- contractual phases;

(b)   in the area of movable property, the operation of trusts, including constructive and resulting trusts, tracing and tracking, floating charges, conditional and temporary ownership rights (including finance leases,

comments were soon elbowed out. This is normal in academic projects designed by system thinkers. The DCFR itself proved to be largely an update of the German BGB (including its amendments of 2002), although the Germans themselves complained that it was not German enough to pass muster. Reactions to the DCFR were not favourable, even in Germany. For more extensive comment and critique, including on the 2011 project of the Expert Group and the Draft Regulation (CESL), which nobody seems to like either, see Volume II, chapter 1, section 1.6.and for property law chapter 2, section 1.11.[452]

repurchase agreements and certain forms of receivable financing), agency and fiduciary duties, assignments, set-off and netting. This is in common law countries typically the area of equity and of an open system of proprietary rights, charges and preferences, where there is a substantial degree of party autonomy between professionals, proprietary rights being here cut off at the level of their operation (in respect of buyers in the ordinary course of business) rather than at the level of their creation; and

(c)   in transactional law, the issue of transactional and payment finality leading to an abstract system of title transfer and an extended protection of bona fides and reliance in equity, all in order to present transactional and payment stability and clear in this connection also the ordinary commercial flows from all kind of proprietary interests that may have been created, confining their effect to the insiders such as banks and suppliers who can or should know of them, but not to others (the ordinary flows).

These are all matters substantially ignored in or not central to the DCFR. Whilst opting for the causal system of title transfer, it even undermines the vital notion of finality. It is of interest in this connection and telling that the DCFR does not manage or attempt to integrate the important EU Collateral Directive. This again follows the German codification which did not manage to do so either, but it shows more than anything the insufficiency of system thinking in the German manner when it comes to modern financial or other practices and needs, to which it is inimicable. It may have to do with the fact that Germany is an industrial rather than a commercial or (financial) services nation.

(d)   The concept of good faith in contract should also be considered. Its place is very different in common and civil law. Civil law makes much of its modern advance in this area but it remains in essence a concept that needs much further development and clarification. Common law traditionally has more refined tools to achieve smooth operation in contract and supplement or adjust basic protections.

First, common law primarily distinguishes between parties according to their nature. In this approach, notably in contract, the emphasis is indeed on the nature of the parties rather than on the type of contract. In civil law, it has always been the other way around. Thus a rental agreement in England is considered to be a quite different type of agreement if entered into between a real estate company and a hotel, between a community and its residents in the social sector, or between a parent and a child.

Although in civil law, the good faith concept may now start doing something similar, it is here only in its infancy. It is more likely that good faith protection meted out in the social sector is also transferred to the professional sector as a rental agreement, in essence the same for all. Again this also remains the approach in the DCFR.

Further refinement exists in common law through the notion of implied conditions, fiduciary duties (especially in situations of dependency), reliance and sometimes natural justice. Altogether this provides a number of concepts that makes the common law of contract much more flexible but always adjusted for the nature of the relationship between the parties, notably distinguishing between consumer and professional dealings.

Again, the DCFR is far away from this thinking. The common law has better tools and is here probably also more sophisticated and often more precise. Nevertheless, German scholarship frequently believes the common law of contract primitive because it has not developed the civil law concept of good faith but this is less than perceptive. The common law of contract needs it much less.

The DCFR's other problem is that it sees good faith in principle as absolutely mandatory and prescriptive in a consumer protection sense. It may be mandatory where it refers to fundamental principle, on the overriding nature of which the DCFR is on the whole not keen, but often it does not and in any event has very different functions, which are still poorly distinguished in civil law thinking and it is in any event very different in consumer and business dealings.

In common law, parties can always set standards by themselves which are enforced unless this becomes manifestly unreasonable (cf s 1-302 UCC) which in professional dealings is not likely to happen soon. Here again, the key is the nature of the relationship of the parties, which in the unitary approach of the DCFR is not given its proper place.

[452]   On the effort as a whole, an early critical article appeared in Germany, see W Ernst, 'Der "Common Frame of Reference" aus juristischer Sicht' (2008) 208 Archiv fur die civilistische Praxis 248, followed by two more technically critical contributions, first of the work of the Acquis group, N Jansen and R Zimmermann, 'Restating the Acquis Communautaire? A Critical Examination of the "Principles of the Existing EC Contract Law"' (2008)

All these efforts raise fundamental issues. Was this to be the more academic and abstract, intellectual and rule-based system approach of civil law codification, or the more pragmatic fact and needs-based common law approach? A lexicon or tool box of common terms appeared to have been an earlier preference, but even a common lexicon could here assume or even require underlying systemic coherence as it suggests a definitional approach. Could such an approach based on some compromise between domestic notions ever make sense? Ideally, codification, if still thought desirable at EU level, for example, to provide greater unity more quickly (assuming a true need could be established also for professional dealings), should be the end of a process rather than the beginning, as indeed it was in nineteenth-century Germany.

In fact, it has already been said that the true aims and methodology were never clear nor properly discussed—the project is political and not a matter of method or quality—but they should logically have been established first. In this connection one should ask in particular whether the professional and consumer rules should be distinguished, as is much more a common law approach, where, for example, contract and movable property law developed in commercial law first. Clearly, professional law can often be rougher and less detailed; more can be left to party autonomy as has already been demonstrated in the foregoing several times, even in the area of movable property, see section 1.1.4 above. At least in the professional sphere, and quite apart of competences, legislation at EU level seems premature, and consumer law in order to be truly effective and affordable may still need to remain largely domestic too. That leaves little room for the project.

It would seem that the project as it now stands in the form of the DCFR and more in particular CESL, is too intellectual and devoid of both practitioners input and empirical testing. But in its extreme formalistic approach and its rejection of overriding values except if expressed in the text, it also lacks sensitivity to fundamental principles—this against the gist of EU law itself, see the discussion in section 1.4.5 above. It thus remains wedded to private law as technique in the form of applying written texts which are supposed to present a system which can deal with all eventualities and per definition achieves justice, social peace, efficiency and growth. This is assumed and is the typical civil law codification tradition in the German manner, as we have seen, and is indeed the nineteenth-century concept of codification as product of German romanticism and idealism which led to the state supremacy ideas of those days.

Whether that still makes sense in transnational professional dealings with their forward moving needs and requirements is here no valid concern. It was already said that the EU perspective is to domesticate the entire internal market and legislate it accordingly. Codification EU wide thus becomes a technical, internal affair, whether or not the relevant transactions are cross-border in the EU or not. The modern *lex mercatoria* and its operation is then ignored for all transactions in the EU, even for cross-border professional dealings.

Yet it may still be asked whether, even if Article 114 gives the EU sufficient authority to legislate in this manner as an aspect of the promotion of the internal market, it also gives

71 *MLR* 505; and subsequently of the DFCR, H Eidenmuller, F Faust, HC Grigoleit, N Jansen, G Wagner and R Zimmermann, 'Der Gemeinsamen Referenzrahmen fur das Europaische Privatrecht' (2008) 63 *Juristenzeitung* 529, translation The Common Frame of Reference for European Private Law, available at papers.ssrn.com/so13/papers.cfm?abstract_id=1269270. See for a more favourable comment from a member of the Acquis group, T Pfeiffer, 'Methodik der Privatrechtsangleichung in de EU' (2008) 208 *Archiv fur die civilistische Praxis* 227.

the authority to eliminate in projects of this nature all other sources of law in cross-border dealings to which these projects would then have to be confined. In the absence of a general codification authorisation civil law style, there is nothing in the Founding Treaties and in Article 114 TFEU in particular, that would suggest so. ECJ case law itself, it was demonstrated above in sections 1.4.5 and 1.4.6, maintains at least fundamental and general principle as independent sources of private law.

Rather, a text such as CESL would still have to find its place amongst them and could not regulate them. This is a very important conclusion so far generally overlooked. These projects are therefore not codifications in the traditional civil law sense, whatever their intent. As things stand, there is no authority for that whatever. It may be recalled in this connection that the UCC in the US, in Article I, section 1-103, clearly promotes other sources of law besides it, especially the common law, equity, custom and the law merchant. That was indeed submitted as the correct approach. Whatever its name, it is no codification in the civil law tradition at all and neither can CESL be. In other words, it becomes part of the modern *lex mercatoria* and cannot avoid it.

In conclusion:

(a)   there are serious issues of proper EU authority in the formation of private law whilst the need for such projects, at least outside the consumer sphere, has never been convincingly demonstrated; there is no cost benefit analysis either, except in the most primitive and speculative manner;

(b)   there are serious problems with the democratic nature of the project, especially with bottom up or other participatory law formation, market custom and practices, and diversity in the sources of law;

(c)   the top-down statist attitude presents a danger to an open society and difficulty in dealing with new needs and in remaining socially and economically responsive; and

(d)   there is an even more serious danger of consumer law protection notions spilling over into professional dealings and a censorious regulatory approach being applied to all activity.

It is questionable whether commerce and finance can prosper in such an (statist and prescriptive) environment, especially now that they are substantially globalised. As a minimum, consumer and professional dealings must be substantially separated and consumer protections should never spill over into the professional sphere. Especially the good faith notion in contract, which tends to be regulatory in consumer dealings, has a different role to play in professional dealings and may itself have to be perceived there as being increasingly transnationalised.

The hierarchy of norms within the modern *lex mercatoria* as proposed in this book for professional dealings is at present more likely to respond to true needs, at least in international business, including within the EU and its structure, role and operation should be recognised for what it is or tries to achieve. Importantly, it also aims at a broader worldwide coverage. Indeed, this new *lex mercatoria* develops for the entire international professional community whose own separate legal order should be recognised and accepted, see the discussion in section 1.5 below. It then naturally transcends a national attitude, but should also transcend a regional, even EU-based approach, at least in professional dealings. It challenges the statist attitude and also allows for bottom-up law formation as the UCC in the US does and which is mainly professional law too. In practice, the American approach has been highly successful especially because of its innovative nature and quality. The EU effort has nothing of this and—it has already been said—recommends itself only in political terms.

If an effort of this nature, therefore having written texts, also needs to be made for professionals at this moment, it should indeed be considered whether the Americas and the Far East should become involved as well. Such an approach should be practitioner-oriented and internationalist, and there should never be an exclusively statutory attitude until the commercial community wishes it and asks for it. For professional activity, the typical civil law top down codification ethos should thus be left behind. It was earlier noted that in the law of obligations it has already had its day. Even domestically, contract and tort are now too factual for codification in a civil law manner and all of this needs to be re-thought.[453] That has not happened and—it is submitted—has led to the low credibility and quality of the present efforts and must lead to their inevitable failure.

1.5 Cultural, Sociological and Economic Undercurrents in the Formation of Transnational Commercial and Financial Law (Modern *Lex Mercatoria*). Different Legal Orders, their Manifestation, and the Competition between Them

1.5.1 The Concept of Legal Orders

It is posited that international commercial and financial law as an autonomous phenomenon and force presumes some legal environment or order in which it can emerge and operate. Alternatively, it could be said that law is what it is, and therefore also transnational law, but all law would seem to require some institutional context or environment in which it is created and operates. It may also make it easier to find the relevant law and detect more structure. In this connection, the notion of legal orders may be useful and represent some reality. It is not new. States were always prime examples, but they are not the only ones. There is, for example, also a legal order between states, namely the (public) international legal order. The notion of legal order is particularly used within the EU, where it denotes a (confederate) legal order separate from that of the Member States.

Other non-statist legal orders may also be identified, as will be shown in section 1.5.9 below. Traditionally it was often assumed, for instance, that the major churches had their own legal order, of which church law was the result. Ecclesiastical courts could then exist and adjudicate this law or it could be adjudicated in the ordinary courts but always on the basis of church law. Even now ecclesiastical law may still take different views on gender and life issues, which may affect the opportunities of appointment to the clergy and on church membership more generally.

---

[453] See text at n 328 above.

If we assume that a church internal legal order has validity, these rules would be enforceable in state courts unless seriously offensive to that particular state's public order. A case can be and is here usually made for (some form of) autonomy. It means that such (church) rules are effective by themselves and do not depend for their effect on state recognition. This is a key insight. It follows that under the rule of law, properly understood, state courts have no option but to apply them in appropriate cases unless they become grossly offensive to the community at large.

As we have seen, in England in the eighteenth century, church law was subsumed in the common law and the ecclesiastical courts were absorbed by the common law courts. This posed the question of the continuing autonomy of this law. The same thing happened to the commercial law and commercial courts. Until that time, this commercial law or law merchant had also been independent as the expression of the legal order of the commercial and financial community of those days. Although even later, there continued to be an own place for this type of law within the common law as there also is for church law, it posed no less the question of the continuing autonomy of this law which was dented, see more particularly section 1.1.1 above.

It may be asked whether this integration into the national law presented the correct perspective or whether it is an anomalous situation waiting for correction. That is the view maintained in this book, at least for international, commercial and financial dealings. Naturally, a state can use its sovereign powers to prevent any other rules from being followed on its territory (at least in respect of any conduct and effect on that territory) but the question is whether that is in accordance with the modern rule of law, its notion of diversity, and the justified rights of different communities as long as they do not seriously offend the public order of the state in question, assuming further that this public order concept itself is reasonably enlightened and proportionally applied. The true issue here is the monopolisation (for good reasons) of *enforcement power* in states, which act in these matters commonly upon the instruction of their own courts; the true issue is *not* therefore the monopolisation of *law formation* by states, which at least in international dealings presents a situation of overreach and concerns the issue of legal plurality.[454]

In discussions concerning the nature and operation of commercial law, these matters tend to be neglected. It has been said by legal philosophers that 'We do not like commerce (because we are largely ignorant of it) and we would prefer not to write about it.'[455] For the few modern writers who have shown interest in the subject,[456] bottom-up law formation

---

[454] This issue is not new but has only acquired urgency in more recent times, see, eg J Griffith, 'What is Legal Pluralism' (1986) *Journal of Legal Pluralism and Unofficial Law*, 1, suggesting even in those early days that legal pluralism was a fact, legal centralism a myth, an ideal, a claim, an illusion, with such power nevertheless over legal practitioners and theorists that it became the foundation stone of all legal and social theory as from the nineteenth century. See more recently, also P Berman, 'Global Legal Pluralism', (2007) 80 *Southern California Law Review* 1177, and C Scott, 'Transnational Law as Proto-Concept', (2009) 10 *German Law Journal* 866. These discussions operate at the level of legal theory. This book is particularly concerned with and sees it as its task to demonstrate the translation of these ideas into positive law in international commerce and finance, where they can now best be tested.

[455] J Waldron, 'Cosmopolitan Norms' in S Benhabib (ed), (2006) *Another Cosmopolitanism* 83. See also Hall Scott, 'The Risk Flyers', (1978) 91 *Harv L Rev* 737: 'There is no real jurisprudence of commercial law.'

[456] J Linarelli, 'Analytical Jurisprudence and the Concept of Commercial Law' (2009) 114 *Penn State Law Review* 119, 195, maintains here a cosmopolitan concept of legal positivism—that is a concept that describes what this law is and how it comes into operation and functions. This approach abstains from any critique of content.

is important. Indeed it is not difficult to maintain that all communities form own sets of rules.[457] For the current discussion, a key factor is to determine which of them have sufficient standing and autonomy to have their rules recognised and accepted as legal rules in the ordinary courts or may even create their own courts in the manner as just mentioned (like international arbitration panels), the decisions of which would then have to be enforced by states either with or without a review of these decisions by the courts of such states (basically in terms of any offence to public policy or order). Only such communities could be considered proper legal orders. It means that rules do not operate and emerge in a void, but are tied to the operation of legal orders which come first.

The evolution of legal orders in this sense might be seen as a predominantly *cultural* phenomenon, but it may also have its base more properly in *sociological* and, at least in trade and commerce, in *economic* realities, globalisation being here a closely related issue for international commerce and finance. All seem to play a role, but the criteria that actually distinguish communities in this sense, that is communities with rule-making powers amongst their members, from mere communes that cannot be considered to have a similar standing (and are therefore not legal orders) are not clear-cut. As to competition with states, statist ambitions in this field, and states' desire for monopolies in legislation have since the nineteenth century obscured the underlying realities and tensions. These questions only now resurface and get their chance mainly through globalisation, as state powers recede and the force of the international flows in people, goods, services, money and knowledge becomes prevalent and no longer manifests itself incidentally. The modern communication revolution supports and amplifies this.

In England, this friction between national and international commercial law already developed earlier in the eighteenth century, as we have seen, followed on the European Continent in the nineteenth century, when all private law formation was ultimately nationalised. In the process, much of the modern idea of legal diversity was lost at least within each country. However, particularly in an international setting, freed therefore from direct state intervention and benefiting from legislative competition between states, internationally organised communities may re-emerge as independent legal orders and re-assert their standing whilst more effectively challenging state monopolies in their law-making or law-sanctioning activities. Political philosophy that demanded in the nineteenth century nationalist domination and the monopoly for states in law formation may then adopt again a more universalist and diversified approach as it did earlier.

Removed from states, five conditions are identified for a transnational legal system of this nature being valid, binding and authentic. The concept of 'legal order' and 'participant' is not further elaborated:

(a)   acceptance by its participants as legally binding;
(b)   the rules being intelligible or comprehensive to the participants;
(c)   the existence of secondary rules (of recognition) and secondary rule officials who may operate across different states or other legal orders;
(d)   shared agency between secondary rule officials demonstrating sufficient mutual responsiveness and commitment to the legal system; and
(e)   primary rules that deal with the major private law topics like contract, property and dispute resolution.

See for the 'law and economic' approach, in particular the work of RD Cooter, 'Structural Adjudication and the New Law Merchant: A Model for Decentralisation' (1994) 14 *International Review of Law and Economics* 215.

[457] JH Dalhuisen, 'Legal Orders and their Manifestation: The Operation of the International Commercial and Financial Legal Order and its *Lex Mercatoria*' (2006) 24 *Berkeley Journal of International Law* 129.

In this connection, it is submitted that the international business community is a prime example of these communities and that the re-emergence of a new and autonomous international *lex mercatoria* as transnational law for that community and its dealings is the natural result. This theme will be explored in the next few sections. The nineteenth-century nationalisation and territorialisation of private law come to an end here, especially in the professional sphere. It has already been observed that there is here a return to some of the environment that obtained at the time of the *Ius Commune*, therefore to the Continental European approach that obtained in the seventeenth and eighteenth centuries, or even before. This being said, it should, of course, be realised that the content of the new *lex mercatoria* can hardly bear comparison with the *Ius Commune* or the older *lex mercatoria* as developed quite separately from it in those days, and there is no revival of that old law as to its substance.

The component parts of this new law merchant were discussed in section 1.4 above, and will be revisited at the more concrete level in section 3.3 below and revolve around the more traditional sources of law: fundamental and general legal principles; industry practices; customs and party autonomy, not only in the law of obligations but also in the proprietary rights that are particularly propelled by the modern laws of international finance. A hierarchy in these norms (or legal sources) is here assumed and is considered the essence of the modern *lex mercatoria* as discussed in section 1.4.13 above.

In this part of the book, the prime objective is first to investigate: (a) the notion of legal orders; (b) the manner of their modern manifestation; (c) the role of cultural, sociological and economic forces in this connection; (d) when immanent rules become legally enforceable; and (e) the nature and outcome of the competition with state laws.

1.5.2 Law as Cultural Phenomenon

In section 1.2.9 above, reference was made to the people's spirit, or *Volksgeist*, in the formation of the law. It became an important consideration in Germany in the early nineteenth century in the formation of a new German private law that was meant to replace the more universal (Roman law-related) *Ius Commune* and the also more universal (ethics, rationality, and efficiency-related) natural law tendencies that had also spread in Germany until that time. In the end, it also replaced the more local commercial laws.

In the law, the *Volksgeist* notion is associated with von Savigny and von Puchta, but was more properly an early expression of the age of Romanticism[458] that followed the age of Enlightenment or Rationality. As was discussed before, it can be seen as an irrational element that led to (extreme) nationalism even before Germany was unified in 1870, and received strong support in the work of Hegel, which only recognised national laws (see section 1.2.9 above).

As such it had an early equivalent in England in the works of Edmund Burke: see section 1.3.3 above. In England, it subsequently translated into the Austinian view that all law emanated from the sovereign's command and was therefore statist even if not statutory. This Burkean view also had a sequence in the US, where American values are now often

---

[458] See also n 191 above.

considered to be the basis of the US legal system, see more particularly the discussion in section 1.3.5 above. Here we have a nationalism that is not necessarily statist in the sense that it does not require all law to emanate from a sovereign—sovereignty in the US being in any event seen as vested in the people—but it still considers all law a typical domestic product or a *national* cultural manifestation. This then also applied to the common law operating in the US regardless of its roots in England.

In this manner, an important *cultural* dimension in the formation of the law is noted.[459] Although this is often conveniently associated with nationality,[460] *culture*—whatever its precise meaning—may just as easily, or perhaps more convincingly, be associated with other important notions, such as religion (for example, Christian, Islamic, or Buddhist cultures); region (for example, Asian, European, American or Western cultures); language (for example, Anglo-American, French-speaking, or Russian cultures); political/economic systems (for example, Western democratic/capitalistic/decentralised, or other more totalitarian cultures); or (more commonly in the German approaches) with aesthetic or intellectual endeavours (for example, Aztec, Maya, Roman, Greek, Hellenistic, Renaissance or Baroque cultures). In fact, culture itself is all that mankind achieves, although usually captured in a positive sense (defying therefore anarchy and other destructive human tendencies) and is as such what it is. It is not nationalistic by definition and *only* obtains a more distinctive meaning when used in a clearly marked *narrower* sense (like in a religious, ethnic, linguistic, nationalistic, political, or artistic sense), particularly when it denotes some communal *mindset*.

But as far as rule making or law formation is concerned, that requires at least two further building blocks. First, to provide a distinctive basis for the formation of legal normativity, culture as mindset must not only be *strong* but also needs *group cohesion* (amongst those of a similar mindset). Secondly (although not unrelated), there must also be some strong sense of order and some common values. In terms of law formation, culture should therefore be cast foremost in *sociological* terms, that is to say, in terms of community and its behaviour or operation as a group.

---

[459] Whilst discussing the effect of culture on the law, some idea or assumption of what law proper is would seem useful even if it has largely defied definition. As a mere *working hypothesis* it has been said that it concerns rules of action or conduct prescribed by controlling authority and having binding force, see *United States and Guarantee Company v Guenther* 281 US 34 (1929). This begs the question, however, what 'controlling authority' and 'binding force' are and when they arise. Another way of defining law is as a body of *social* rules prescribing external conduct and considered justiciable, see H Kantorowicz, *The Definition of the Law* (trans E Campbell 1958) 79.

This puts emphasis on the close association between law and sociological forces discussed in detail in the next section, but still begs the question what 'justiciable' is (as distinguished from moral dictates and social conventions). Briefer is the simple observation in 'law and economics' that law is that set of rules that states sanction. It all suggests some state coercive power but does not explain when this must back up the rules of other (private) groups or associations (therefore when these rules reach the status of legal enforceability) or allows other (group) sanctions if the rules are not voluntarily complied with.

Another important question is why law in this sense is usually complied with voluntarily without which it would collapse. What is the role of group culture in this connection and what is the connecting factor in terms of internalisation of its rules?

[460] In the writings of many, this seems to be axiomatic and often leads to a narrow nationalism in the law on the basis of cultural arguments, then seen as deep underlying national currents, perhaps in a mystical, irrational sense. This view tends to be highly romantic, see in this vein particularly P Legrand, 'Europeanisation and Convergence' in P Beaumont et al (eds), *Convergence and Divergence in European Public Law* (Oxford, Hart Publishing, 2002) 225, and more soberly C Harlow, 'Voices of Difference in a Plural Community', *ibid* at 199, but *cf* also N Walker, 'Culture, Democracy and the Convergence of Public Law: Some Scepticism about Scepticism' *ibid* at 257.

That suggests as a minimum a close connection between cultural and sociological currents or forces when it comes to the law and its formation.[461] It would allow us to deduce from such a group mindset some *predictability of behaviour*, and therefore some ways of doing that may be considered more deeply rooted, likely to recur within the group, may be relied upon as to be adhered to and forthcoming, capable therefore of producing behavioural standards that become norm setting and thereby controlling for its members. Indeed there is here a strong reliance element.

As just mentioned, *national* culture is only one expression of culture in this sense and often springs to mind first in terms of support for autonomous law formation. It should be realised, however, that nationality may produce or be based on a rather weak kind of mindset in the above sense. Other cultural strands may be much stronger in terms of group formation and might from this perspective have a much greater claim to and potential impact on the formation of law.

It is the group aspect that in modern times makes us look primarily at *national* cultures, however, and therefore at states in terms of law formation, even if we can see that group cohesion along cultural lines needs not be associated with a state per se, and may in fact much better be seen in other types of communities—reference may in this respect be made, for example to churches at one end of the spectrum or to the international business community at the other.

Thus even if for culture to count in this connection, it cannot be merely a personal or individualistic experience but must show a close association with group trends so as to become relevant in the law-making process, that group need not be a state. It could even be argued that it was rather *unexpected* that modern states came out on top here. On the European Continent that was certainly not so in the times of the earlier *Ius Commune*, but it did later lead to its demise. This had to do with the fact that power ultimately became aggregated at state level. In other words, the state ultimately proved to be the more natural level at which power was to be monopolised (and secularised). That is in Western Europe a typical nineteenth-century development, in England perhaps a little earlier. It is true of course that there had been dominant regimes before but they never had the physical means of communication and control to dominate society as a whole for any period of time. Rulers could at best send an army or police force around from time to time or try to rule through a kind of feudal or similarly layered system.

In fact, in connection with the cultural impact of group formation on its rules and the position of states in this connection, another development should be noted. It is likely that, whatever the cultural base, group cultures of whatever type have become *less* strong in Western society. This is so, first because Western society is itself likely to promote *cultural diversity*. As a consequence, there may be different cultures of various sorts at work on the same territory which may easily compete within states with other groupings or even the state itself. Especially where cultural diversity is promoted, national culture may thus be weakened. But perhaps more importantly, Western culture itself suggests *individualism* and an open, thriving, forward-looking personal attitude based on experience and investigation, therefore on *experimentation* at the more personal level.

---

[461] The notion of culture and its definitions have perplexed many: see for a discussion GH Hartman, *The Fateful Question of Culture* (1997).

That is likely to make people less conformist, perhaps more tolerant and in any event more changeable but also harder to identify with group authenticity, especially at the state or national level and perhaps with culture of any sort. It may be another reason why it may cause surprise that states came out on top in the power game only in modern times and that law formation subsequently became a state preserve and in the mind of many continues to be so. On the other hand, one could say in this connection that it was precisely the *lessening effect* of group cultures that left room for the modern state and gave its growing power a chance to impose its own laws on all within its territory even though it constitutes itself hardly any community at all (except amongst hardened nationalists). It confirms at the same time that the true basis for modern law formation at the state level is *not*, or not chiefly, cultural but mere power. It raises serious questions about the legitimacy of the ensuing laws, at least in a cultural sense, and may then also cause problems in terms of identification, internalisation and voluntary compliance.[462]

In other words, some introspectiveness would seem inherent in all types of cultures, but with greater individual mobility and more external information, all cultures are likely to lose at least some of their singularity, and as a consequence also some of their particular mindset, behavioural predictability and group cohesion, not least in terms of values. Modern Western civilisation could be called *a-cultural* in this sense (not necessarily anti-cultural because it allows a variety of cultures to operate in terms of diversity, but not as monopolies) and is rather the result of this type of development in which greater individualism has emerged and is cultivated after group culture first moved away from a more tribal to a family environment, now often also abandoned.

This has led to a typical Western culture trait in which individuals are now primarily bound together in an *organisational* rather than in a cultural sense. That organisation became the modern state,[463] shorn therefore of much cultural ballast. It could thus be said that it does not derive, or no longer derives, its impetus from culture, but rather from the absence of it. Even if we still speak here of Western culture, it should be repeated that this is primarily a practical development that rather shows the *weakening* of any particular cultural drive. Even if the result can be characterised as another culture (Western culture), it should be considered that in that kind of culture the identification with the group and therefore the group element is often weak.

---

[462] Strands of culture that are or have remained more traditional are likely on the other hand to have a much more doctrinaire and unchangeable attitude. They may produce much closer-knit communities showing much more coherence, but they may at the same time lack adaptability because of the dictates of tradition or scripture. It may be easier, however, to find a much greater group sense and group normativity in such communities which are often of a religious nature representing religious values. Thus in a theocracy, law is likely to be primarily seen as part of a religious *all life* experience which dominates everything, also the rules of the group and of the nation.

We may think this atavistic, but it is not so very far removed from some Scandinavian legal philosophers, who, in the last century, thought modern law hardly different from witchcraft: see the theories of A Hagerstrom, *Der roemische Obligationsbegriff*, vol I (1927) 17 and of V Lundstedt, *Die Unwissenschaftlichkeit der Rechtswissrenschaft*, vol I (1936) 21. In any event, religious, especially Christian values or overtones, were, until quite recently, a most obvious feature of Western values and laws as well.

It is of interest in this connection, that even the fundamentalist (universalist) Islam concept of the law of the shari'a could not avoid the influence of the state and its *raison d'etat*, see for this development in the West in respect of the universalist natural law s 1.2.6 above. It substantially diluted it even if law formation by (Islamic) states was meant to be left only to god fearing rulers or Caliphs, aware of the divine commands, see, eg NJ Coulson, *A History of Islamic Law* (Edinburgh, 1964) 129.

[463] See also T Burger (trans), J Habermas, *The Structural Transformation of the Public Sphere* (1991).

Its effect on the substance of the law is therefore also weakened as that law, like the group it serves, becomes *organisational*, dependent on conceivably more rational choices but also more subject to political expediencies and to the law of the unintended consequences. It is thus *opportunistic, political, or co-incidental* in nature.

1.5.3 Law as a Political Organisational Tool. The Importance of Diversity, Group Autonomy, Democracy, Rule of Law, and Human Rights

For Western society, its a-cultural or culturally diverse nature underscores the need for and existence of a more sophisticated organisational infrastructure to hold modern societies together and make them functional. Culture alone can no longer do this at that level and loses here at least an irrational or more romantic grip. Culture, to the extent it survives as a real force, then becomes more orderly, more modern and less forceful at the same time. This may also apply to the law that modern states produce. The political process may on the other hand also acquire irrational political features of its own and may as such no longer be an expression of common values, not even of increased and better informed rationality, but rather political expediency. It may also seek to alter or correct the common values or even more rational patterns.

It follows first that, in Western society, states and law as a purely organisational tool are likely to be closely connected and figure larger than in more traditional or static cultures, and that the law that is produced in this way is more variable, rather policy, and may become in principle a mechanism for remedial action, social and cultural change, and economic development. Indeed through legislation, law became in Western society an important instrument of public policy or the ever-expanding notion of the *raison d'etat*, in which particularly *public* law, as the law that concerns itself with a state's organisation and objectives, acquires an enhanced status. Indeed, in its more practical aspects, the operation of states may change *overnight*, depending on the prevailing political currents. Thus social and budgetary law will vary with each government and the impact of deep cultural under-currents in this process or of pure nationalism becomes an exaggeration. This is modernity in which nationalism itself ultimately also flounders, never mind how much invoked as justification, see further for modernity, its meaning and impact section 1.3.7 above.

Modern states may then also intervene in private law formation. State intervention in private law and its formulation becomes here primarily intent on streamlining, greater efficiency and lower transaction costs in which connection the state is likely to provide in legislation private law models as directory law (with its default rules) but sometimes also (such as in property rights) mandatory law to protect against interfering outsiders. That at least was the Enlightenment or French version of codification, as we have seen.

That is so, not only in codification countries of the civil law, but also in common law countries, of which, in the US, the Uniform Commercial Code is an important example. In civil law countries, this kind of statist private law is now often given a higher status, how-ever, than more traditional customary or other law, as states were increasingly seen as the ultimate organisational force and as deriving a legitimacy from this state of affairs, so that their laws assumed a semblance of exclusivity, supplemented by strong intellectualisation expressed through system thinking. That was earlier identified as the Romantic or German idealist tradition in codification thinking, where states start claiming deeper insights. Here they may claim further legitimacy by using and supporting their academies to provide the necessary models even if this may lead to pure abstraction, see for the codification ethos and its modern justifications and draw backs, section 1.2.12 above. It is notably not the attitude of the UCC in the US: see its section 1-103 but it was demonstrated that it is still the one of the DCFR in Europe.

In the latter more Romantic version of codification, which also highlights the state's transformation powers in private law, codification may also assume new meaning under which, for example, the concept of property itself acquires a more political dimension and the social function of private property may then become more dominant. That is policy.

In an organisational and political environment like that of the US, there may appear another strand in thinking. It is in fact sometimes thought that respect for the law is the only thing that holds this country together, and is as such the only real bond amongst great cultural and ethnic diversity where national culture plays a role only in the very broadest sense of the word. It suggests a survival instinct rather than any common underlying values, on very much of which there is unlikely to be any consensus at all. No wonder the vehemence of the American political debate and the great interest in America in the law; how it can be known and still be accepted by all or most; how it constantly transforms itself; and why it must do so to remain living law able to continue to fulfill its function of holding society together and forming an ever closer Union.

If we still speak of a common culture, here primarily a Western culture, therefore culture in a broad (a-cultural) sense, it is indeed particular in that, without a strong group sentiment and regardless of its intrinsic individualism, it still manages to produce a set-up in which states and their governments can operate and provide added value to society as a whole without becoming all dominant and suffocating, although that risk is always there. As such, these modern states appear primarily the expression of *societal energy* rather than of a communal mindset or culture, an energy which does not allow itself to be fully exhausted by and entirely absorbed in the modern state, however, but also competes with it, for example in the market place, to the likely advantage and the greater stability of both, even though at times of economic or financial crisis it may seem otherwise.

Although such a state has moved into law formation in a major way, it would still have to allow room for communities and cultures that are able to maintain themselves in a rule-creating function within or beyond its territory in a kind of competition in which the lines of competency are never clearly drawn. There is in truth no higher rule that governs this process except the rule of law itself, if it is to mean anything at all. Indeed, other legal orders operate in this margin, in a modern way especially the *international commercial and financial legal order*, as will be the subject of the following sections. This may be expressed (to some extent) in Constitutions or similar organisational instruments, which provide a legal framework guaranteeing some order and continuity for various groups, but more important is probably that modern Western states remain de facto (therefore regardless of the constitutional framework) subject to a constant *redistribution of organisational power* (and wealth) between different individuals or groups, in which different cultures may still play important roles but do not determine the outcome any longer. Nor does the modern state itself, now particularly because it cannot isolate itself from the world scene, but it was always subject to internal competing forces as well, which it could never fully dominate or in any event not forever. Again, especially in commerce and finance, the power of the market place springs to mind.

It follows, and has been stated before that, whilst operating in this manner, modern states (have to) accept and promote the rule of *all* law, whatever its legal source, unless it offends their public policy and order (in a modern sense). Especially in private law formation and operation, modern states should as a consequence be decentralist, therefore foremost facilitators that respect individual and group autonomy, unless internal peace is challenged, efficiency is substantially threatened, or a need for a redistribution of risks and reward is indicated. In such cases, major public policy issues are likely to be at stake, which are, however, likely to be balanced by popular feelings and human rights considerations, and now also by the forces of globalisation and much stronger international competition.

In the private sphere, this type of decentralist, organisational, individualistic and rather a-cultural or culturally neutral Western 'culture' allows as a minimum for organisational autonomy of parties, partnership and groups or communities, at least as long as others are not unduly affected and the public good is not unduly threatened in the territory in question. It will then also allow or even encourage cultural diversity in a religious, ethnic, linguistic or aesthetic sense, as long as these cultures prove tolerant. Totalitarian tendencies are likely to be alien to this 'culture' which at its best invites others into it, whilst the rule of law and the concept of human rights underline basic respect for the private sphere and individual or group endeavour.

It follows that, even where the modern state assumes a central role in the formulation of private law through legislation, it should still consider itself limited, whatever its pretence. In business, for example, its action will be mainly directed at anti-competitive behaviour and other market abuses, or interference in other people's affairs, or taking undue advantage. In other private areas, such as families, churches, and similar associations, or in partnerships and companies, state intervention will also be directed primarily against excess, like intolerance and fanaticism, subjugation of gender, or abuse of minorities or children. Again, only if a major public policy issue arises should modern states intervene in these communities or in private relationships through mandatory laws. Even then, they are subject to rule-of-law and human-rights limitations. Where states devise rules for communities beyond these public concerns, they are likely to be merely directory or guidance and can thus be set aside by these parties, groups or individuals concerned. There will then also be the force of fundamental and general principle as well as of custom and practice, as we have seen in section 1.4.

Whatever the claims of nationalism in this connection, it is here also important and of prime interest to note that these key notions of diversity, group autonomy, democracy, rule of law, and human rights are *neither* themselves nationalistic in nature nor do they belong to any national culture. At most, they belong to the much broader notion of Western culture (or a-culture) in which they are embedded and of which they are the expression, suggesting a broader attitude that is also concerned with efficiency and impatient with monopolies of whatever kind (except in respect of state enforcement power, itself considered subject, however, to the rule of law). The function of the modern state as promoter and engine of modernity here reaches its limits.

In its progress, Western culture in this sense relies heavily on individual exertion but no less on self-restraint, tolerance, civic sense, and participation at that individual level; on rationality and efficiency in an economic sense; and on flexibility and experimentation in an intellectual sense. Again, none of these is a typical national cultural trait or preserve, even though they may reflect them; they derive from a *broader* set of human experiences.

To repeat, in a modern world, culture, to the extent the term is properly used, is likely to lose much of its more mystical, idiosyncratic and nationalistic features. Cultural aspects of the older type are likely in modern states to be preserved only in the manner of folklore unless they retain a community form. It must be admitted that as such they may be *regressive* (such as nationalistic sports fanaticism), in the form of rigid social structures not seldom used, however, by the establishment to maintain itself.[464]

1.5.4 The Revival of Legal Universalism in Professional Private Law

It must be accepted that what has propelled this broader Western culture is particularly the *American experience*, which became prevalent in the West in the twentieth century, when Europe lost its grip through its internecine wars, its experimentation with totalitarian ideas, its ultimate promotion of both fascism and communism, only demised through American intervention. The American experience to the extent here relevant would appear to be marked by at least *five basic characteristics* that confirm the perception of modern Western culture mainly as an *organisational philosophy* for a dynamic modern society or indeed of modernity itself.

First, it is *secular*. This does not mean that it is anti-religious, but religion is considered a private matter and the US Constitution makes sure that it remains so, so that its divisive nature is not allowed to dominate public debate or enter the public domain unduly (unless prefaced by a reference to tolerance). In fact, in this environment, fanaticism of whatever kind is not accepted, but is perceived as undemocratic and in that sense as culturally 'un-Western'.

Secondly, it reaches out and it is *outward looking*, meaning that more extreme forms of nationalism and culturalism or similar introspections are not encouraged but considered regressive. Even if more conservative political forces, in the US as elsewhere, play with nationalism and culturalism from time to time, whilst local establishments may hide behind them, they do not carry the day.

Thirdly, the American experience has a long *democratic and market tradition*, which continuously separates, breaks down and fractures power and has close connections with the rule of law and human rights. It appreciates diversity and cultural competition and also understands the notion of community and party autonomy. *Decentralisation* in an organisational sense is an important feature, which also means that the state represents a fairly low percentage of GDP. It steers particularly clear of the idea that modern wealth and well-being is largely due to a socio-economic infrastructure in which only the contribution of the state counts which would therefore be entitled to dominate all, at least within its own territory, and could take as much as it thinks it is entitled to or can get away with (notably in terms of taxation). It is the balance between the state and the market that makes here the difference.

Fourthly, the American experience is determined by an all-absorbing and self-propelling inquiry into nature and mankind, its motive being the discovery of truth guided by

---

[464] See for this view in particular, Foucault and other French deconstructionalists.

experience and investigation, therefore to uncover reality beyond what we can observe and know through our senses (which may be very little). This was always the professed objective of academia, but may well have lost its compelling message in Europe and may have acquired an altogether different dimension in the US. It leads to a broader demand and respect for research and learning centred on the great American universities and research institutions (with their related strong philanthropic support). This search transcends the cults of Washington, Wall Street, Hollywood, or Silicon Valley which nevertheless become close second, third, fourth, and fifth elements, and are in their own ways all part of the same process of discovery and revelation. By looking for truth or what is real (rather than fantasy, myth or mystique) in nature and its processes, the American experience thus lives in the hope of greater understanding and greater control, therefore of a better or at least a more interesting world and of progress in that more objective sense although it guarantees nothing.

There is a *fifth* feature of the American experience, in which it may be more truly unique, even within the West: *it does not seek to dominate*, although it will forcefully defend itself against any physical assaults. Instead, it desires to be emulated, to convince, and to involve all others to join the process. This is very different from many other cultures that have more often sought domination and find it natural to do so. That may still be the basic attitude in Western Europe, where the reflex is often to see the American experience not as an example but as a form of intrusion, imposition, or threat.

The question is how modern law, its formation and further evolution and operation, is caught up in the dynamics of our present situation, this voyage of discovery, this openness, and cultural demystification. Of course we have here first the day-to-day practice of the law to consider. Much of it does not go beyond a 'practitioners' manual' or 'lawyers' toolbox' that can hardly be more than black-letter law. That is what in essence is now taught in European law schools, whether of civil or common law. As discussed earlier, this shows an unhelpful concern with the past and how it should be remedied, and is intellectually only of modest interest and value.[465]

Although traditionally, finding some order and structure in the law may have been enough, more important and more truly a subject of academic investigation is now where the law is going, what the alternatives are, what the law may or should achieve in an ever evolving environment, society or civilisation, when and why it finds acceptance at group, national and international level, how it can be known and how its focus may change in this respect over time. This is the gist of much modern American research in its major law schools which have in this respect divided in the various 'law and …', directions discussed in section 1.3.5 above. Thus the law moves with society and can never be fully known.

There is a search here for new paradigms or models that are closer to reality, explain it better, simplify, and therefore hold the prospect of greater steering and predictive value. In a newer generation, they may even substantially be grounded in pop culture or other

---

[465] It may be illustrative to cite in this connection the important dissenting opinion of Lord Bingham in *JD v East Berkshire Community Health NHS Trust* [2005] UKHL 23: 'The question does arise whether the law … should evolve analogically and incrementally so as to fashion appropriate remedies to contemporary problems or whether it should remain essentially static, making any such changes as are forced upon it leaving difficult and in human terms very important problems, to be swept up by the convention. I prefer evolution.' So does this author who considers that this evolution may be quite abrupt and is not always merely incremental in a smooth and gradual development.

popular perceptions. In business, they are likely to result from technical progress and efficiency considerations which may change rapidly. These new paradigms may at the same time allow for a more rational evaluation or critique of existing legal structures. The positive law is then explained merely as example of how the law should be, or should not be, or should be no longer. Positive law is what it is and not therefore itself any great subject for academic study or intellectual analysis, although finding structure (rather than system and its inclination to staticism) in it remains a legitimate academic pursuit; this was discussed in section 1.1.5 above, but is not its true vocation. That at least is the approach in the best American law schools, where as a consequence professors refuse to write practitioners' handbooks. Practitioners must do this themselves. It is hardly intellectually challenging but time-consuming for academia whilst tending to be destructive of deeper analysis and newer thought. Law is not perceived here merely as technique in which only the written up version of it counts.

If in Western society the law is now steeped in secular principle, therefore in some basic values of which the rule of law, human rights, and respect for individualand group autonomy are indicative,[466] or even in some new rationality or utilitarian principle as more in particular identified by the 'law and economics' school, this alone would suggest that local, national, or statist cultural content in the law will ultimately yield to more *universal* notions at least in international professional dealings. Much centres here around the idea of an open society, not merely as a sign of civilisation. It is also economic necessity that demands that all contribute according to capacity and no one is held back, excluded by insiders, or assigned their roles. Even the emergence of women and other minority rights can be so explained. Again, as a minimum, this suggests that in modern Western society the basic tenets of the legal system have a foundation that is considerably broader than mere nationalism or statist activity and leaves room for other sources of law at the same time. This would certainly be so in business and then concerns especially the law of professional dealings and its transantionalisation into a new legal order, here called the 'transnational commercial and financial legal order' with authority and dynamism of its own.

In other words, if it is true that the modern democratic state, like the modern decentralised social and economic structures through which individuals and groups or communities may exert their autonomy, has a foundation in a broader Western culture which is *not* itself statist or nationalistic and as such hardly cultural in that sense, it would suggest that, even if the law, its development and application have at the level of the positive law at present still an important anchor in the nation state and its organisation, that cannot be the whole story and need not be so per se or forever. It should never be forgotten that it was not even so in Western Europe till the nineteenth century. The territorial limitation of law, especially of commercial private law, is a recent phenomenon.

It follows that in our part of the world, the law, especially private law, is (like the modern state) primarily Western and *only subsequently* national or cultural in any other sense and law formation should be considered by group, community. It is not all left to states. At least that would seem a perfectly valid proposition to make. Some of this group or community law might be regressive but that need not be so. The new *lex mercatoria*, for example,

---

[466] Note also in this connection the Preamble to the EU Treaty which refers to the Member States' 'attachment to the principles of liberty, democracy and respect for human rights and fundamental freedoms and of the rule of law'.

emanating from the new transnational commercial and financial legal order, is sustained by modern sociological and economic forces and is therefore likely to be forward looking and reforming. Its dynamics were demonstrated in section 1.1.4 above for modern contract and movable property law. In terms of sophistication, it goes well beyond most state laws.

Finally, in considering whether or not nationalism and national culture still have a decisive meaning, at least as far as professional private law is concerned, it should also be considered that much of it, at least in the law of property and contract, was seldom of a purely national (cultural) origin, even in the nineteenth century when nationalism started to prevail. Indeed, private law always had much broader historical roots (Roman or Germanic) in virtually all its major aspects in whatever civil law country. In the nineteenth century, whole private law systems were transferred from France and later from Germany to other countries. In the common law world, the law came from England, whether in the US, Canada, Australia or wherever.

In its newer aspects, this law, at least in business, is likely to be primarily technical, utilitarian, and meant to solve present day societal, commercial or financial problems which in professional dealings are now seldom of a typical national character. In private law, it may thus be asked, for example, what the cultural or typical national aspect is of the notification requirement for a valid assignment in some countries, not demanded in others, whilst in 1992 the Dutch started to require it and in the same year the neighbouring Belgians abolished it. It might look like a little thing but it has major consequences in the structure of the law of receivables. There is much like this in modern private law in which practicalities decide these issues rather than deeper considerations, which are better left behind. Perhaps they never entered much into it.

This may well be so increasingly for the entirety of commercial and financial law or for most of the law concerning professional dealings, based as it is in the rationality of commerce and finance. In any event, at least in international commerce and finance, it never found its cultural support in typical national considerations. Even within modern states and their organisational structures, there is hardly any true national principle or value in this type of law. Even if there was, there is ever less reason for there to be. One could still say (in civil law terms) that being part of the intellectual national system of private law presents some national value, but this system itself is largely contrived, often outdated, seldom capable of covering all realities, and, like most intellectual endeavour, in any event hardly culturally specific. At best, these systems present models that are still close enough to national reality to steer it better; at worst they are counterproductive and they have little to say about or hardly capture modern international realities (and cannot then steer them very effectively either).

To conclude: the new law merchant or *lex mercatoria* is more likely to provide such a model and be able to do so. In fact, it was pointed out in section 1.4.4. above, that it was never entirely forgotten in the international market place. At least the renewed search for it is legitimate and necessary. It finds its reason in its own international environment and in the exigencies of its own legal order. As an expression of the needs and logic that prevail in that transnational community, it is likely also to provide a better steering tool for that community to manage its business and to progress. But the mechanism of the modern state is here not dysfunctional and must continue to provide the regulatory balance that market power requires to avoid excess. In an international setting, in the absence of international regulators, this is an imperfect art which for financial regulation will be discussed in Volume III.

If it is true, as is maintained in this book, that the Western model has been successful mainly because of this balance between the international marketplace and domestic political forces, which will hopefully continue albeit constantly redrawn, it means that the transnational commercial and financial legal order must remain respectful of the modern state and deferential to it, but it is no less true that transnationalisation guides here against excess in state powers and may thus be seen as helping to maintain a better equilibrium, which in dispute resolution international arbitrators in particular are meant to enforce.

1.5.5 Sociological and Economic Considerations in the Law

In the previous sections, for Western society, modern private law as a typical statist or national cultural phenomenon (or both) was de-emphasised. This may be especially clear in the case of commercial and financial law. Instead, the more pragmatic organisational aspect of modern law formation was noted, whilst the sociological background of other sources of law was emphasised, in particular law's association with groups or communities and their functioning. The possibility of competition between legal systems on the same territory was also mentioned.[467]

At least in the communitarian view, in which, in the opinion of some,[468] the notion of community may claim moral primacy over the notion of states, it is only logical to question whether states or nations can remain the only true sources of law and of its values. No less important is a modern strand in 'law and economics' that posits that the decentralisation of the law is a modern necessity.[469]

---

[467] See further JH Dalhuisen, 'Legal Orders and their Manifestation: the Operation of the International Commercial and Financial Legal Order and its *Lex Mercatoria*' (2006) 24 *Berkeley Journal of International Law* 129 and BZ Tamanaha, 'Understanding Legal Pluralism: Past to Present, Local to Global', (2008) 30 *Sydney Law Review* 375.

The competition between different legal orders in the same territory is by no means a modern issue and was squarely faced in colonial times, particularly in the Dutch East Indies, where the Dutch had never been intent on bringing their own language, religion or legal system, which only operated in parallel. Legally, the local population continued to deal under local *adat* law that was in the law of property and obligations only amended in minor detail.

Where conflicts arose, the so-called intergentile laws of those days tried to achieve equivalence of the system and the European (Dutch) law was not considered to be overriding or superior per se (which had been much the approach in the French colonial world). See for some important studies on this subject, RD Kollewijn, 'Inter-racial Private Law' in BOJ Schrieke (ed), *The Effect of Western Influence on Native Civilisations in the Malay Archipelago* (1930) 204; and 'Conflicts of Western and Non-Western Law' in *The International Law Quarterly* (1951) 307, showing also the different French, German and English attitudes.

In modern times, in a similar manner, Nigerian courts have struggled with the recognition of tribal decisions based on tribal and also sharia law; see MM Akanbi, *Domestic Commercial Arbitration in Nigeria: Problems and Challenges* (2006 unpublished PhD Thesis King's College London).

[468] See P Selznick, *The Communitarian Persuasion* (2002) 64. Some French legal scholarship insisted on the internal sovereignty of all social groupings much earlier, see G Gurvitch, *L'idee du Droit Social* (1932) 84; G Gurvitch, *Sociology of Law* (1942). They were even within nations considered to create their own law, which limited that of states and was, in principle, superior to it. For a similar approach in the Netherlands, see HJ van Eikema Hommes, *Hoofdlijnen der Rechtssociologie en de Materiele Indeling van Publiek en Privaatrecht* [Main Principles of the Sociology of Law and the Material Distinction between Public and Private Law] (1983).

[469] RD Cooter, 'Structural Adjudication and the New Law Merchant: A Model for Decentralisation' (1994) 14 *International Review of Law and Economics* 215.

It was earlier posited that all law emanates from or within *legal orders*, which are community related and of which states are only one particular example, even if at present the most important and powerful, although not the most culturally driven. If, as suggested in the previous sections, societal energy is at the heart of all modern state formation, it will also sustain other communities within and beyond such states. Indeed, that could be seen as the essence of all civil societies and their evolution. It is also at the heart of the recognition of the importance of diversity and gives it meaning, even though modern states were able to grab most power and monopolise it in their legislative process and enforcement facilities sometimes for the better, at other times for the worse.

As a minimum, it gives states a strong hand on their territories when there is competition with the rules of other orders and when it comes to enforcement, but it does not rule out the law-creating power of other communities, even if for enforcement of their rules they may ultimately be dependent on (the same) states as the sole enforcement agencies in the modern world. Again, the key is that in a modern society, under the rule of law, law enforcement but *not* the law creating function is monopolised by states. It means that states have to recognise *all* law and enforce the decisions legitimately based on it, unless there are overriding public policy issues at stake.

The question then is which communities function as legal orders, are therefore likely to produce their own law, and are entitled to have their laws recognised and respected by other legal systems or orders, therefore also by states, which will have to give their sanction to it, much as they do to sister state laws and judgments (subject to a number of conditions which should then be clarified). It was already put in a different way: not every commune is a community in this sense and not all make law, but some do. Who counts in this connection? Who may compete with states in the law formation function and under what circumstances? Where must we draw the line? And what are the rules of the game?

The notion of community in this sense could not be left to state recognition alone as that would deny all autonomy of other legal orders and could not explain international legal orders. In this connection, it could be intellectually attractive to attribute autonomy to them *all*, therefore to any grouping no matter how ephemeral and transient, at least to the extent that *participation* could be considered to have been *consented*. Party autonomy would then by itself present a legal order, in fact be at the heart of it. It is not that simple, however, not merely because it would make the setting aside of, or at least the challenge to state rules a seemingly casual affair, but more fundamentally because the notion of participation itself presupposes other (*external*) rules which determine when it counts, which rules are not necessarily of a consensual nature but concern the group or order (and its functioning) as a whole. These rules are thus likely to have a more objective status and a more independent origin which as such are or should be identifiable. Even contracts are embedded in and depend for their binding force on a broader legal set up that is not necessarily voluntary in all its aspects or depends on consent and participation alone.

Participation and consent are therefore *not* the sole determining factors for the autonomy of these legal orders and the law that results in them. Other more objective criteria must be found to delineate the various legal orders and mark out the law that they produce.

(a)   This would appear to concern the identification of the relevant circle of participants in a given range of activities or with a particular purpose.

(b)   There also has to be some sustaining force or motive, as in international commerce and finance there are the modern international flows of professionals, goods, services, technology and money, and the need for encouragement and adequate protection of the commercial or financial interests involved in these flows.

(c)   This force must be capable of not only delineating the group but also of producing and maintaining some infrastructure for it.

(d)   At least in (international) business, one would also expect some economic component in terms of efficiency, rationality, common sense, consistency and predictability, if not also some kind of morality in terms of honesty, transparency and accountability.

(e)   It then also requires some consensus on the basic economic system which suggests a market approach in which states may nevertheless figure as important balancing or facilitating actors.

(f)   Finally there is the spokesmen function, that means the institutional aspect which allows for articulation of the rules in which, for example, the ICC and especially international arbitrators may play an important role.[470]

This raises many fundamental issues. If we limit ourselves to international commerce and finance, the relevant circle of participants in a given range of activities are likely to be the professionals in those trades and dealings.[471] A more specific feature of the international and commercial legal order may indeed be found in its foundation in the modern *flow* of professionals, goods, services, knowledge, capital and payments, the freeing of which has been the main motive in the creation of the economic legal order of the EU and its internal market and in the creation of the WTO as GATT successor. These flows suggest a *connected* way of dealing or operating and an own pattern of rules which have no origin in domestic laws, can often not be satisfactorily explained by them but must be attributed to the operation of the international commercial and financial legal order itself.

As a practical matter, in these international flows, the dynamics are likely to be wholly different from the local ones. Local law, whether statist or not, is unlikely to have been developed for them, and may be deficient, parochial and atavistic or make no sense in international commercial transactions. This may show for example, in the limitations local laws may place on the protection of bona fide purchasers or in the type of proprietary and similar rights (such as trust structures, assignment possibilities, security interests and floating charges, set-off facilities, agency relationships, and book-entry entitlements in respect of investment scurrilities) which local laws may allow to operate against third parties: see also section 1.1.4 above.

In this connection, the view has authoritatively been expressed that new law is constantly formed through the sectarian separation of communities. In this view, each legal order perceives itself as emerging out of something that itself is unlawful.[472] *Separation* is here identified as a crucial constitutive element of new legal orders, which may require in each case a normative mitosis or radical transformation of the perspective of a group or a new total life experience for a new legal order to emerge and qualify.

---

[470] See further also JH Dalhuisen, 'International Arbitrators as Equity Judges' in P Bekker, R Dolzer and M Waibel (eds), *Making Transnational Law Work in the Global Economy, Essays in Honour of Detlev Vagts Harvard* (2010) 510. See for the operation of a specialised international commercial court in this process, JH Dalhuisen, 'The Case for an International Commercial Court', in KP Berger et al (eds), *Private Law and Commercial Law in a European and Global Context*, Festschrift Norbert Horn, (2006) 931 and s 1.1.9 above.

[471] See s 1.1.8 above.

[472] See R Cover, 'Nomos and Narrative' (1980) 97 *Harvard Law Review* 4, 31.

There follows the emphasis on *separateness, sustainability* and *prospectiveness* as group, on a *rule producing willingness and capacity,* and on *a capability* to hold the group as group together or at least to make it function better on the basis of their own rules. Mere communion is not enough and some (incipient) organisational structure will be required.

The emphasis moves here to struggle and triumph, therefore to a revolutionary element in the creation of new legal orders, which essentially compete with the older ones. In line with this approach, in commerce and finance, the freeing of the international flows could then be seen as the fuse for the change of perspective in its participants and the establishment and operation of new (international and commercial) legal order between them.

Others[473] have put emphasis rather on how the new law can be found and identified, and they have suggested that, for international commercial law to arise and to count legally, in the sense that states must accept it and back it up by coercive power (unless it has major public policy reasons not to do so): (a) the norms that arise in this specialised business community should be empirically identifiable; (b) the incentive structure that produces or internalises these norms should be capable of being analysed (by using game theory and the notion of equilibrium) in order to determine whether the norms empirically found are more than social convention or moral dictates and are experienced as binding; whilst (c) the *efficiency* (or public good effect) of the incentive structure should be measurable using analytical tools from economics to avoid harmful laws (such as monopolistic practices, which will therefore not be enforced). Here the emphasis shifts from struggle to *rationality, consistency* and *predictability.*

In 'law and sociology' other (supporting) insights have emerged.[474] It is submitted in this connection that 'modernity' and the 'advanced nature' of the new legal system might

---

[473] RD Cooter, 'Structural Adjudication and the New Law Merchant: A Model for Decentralisation' (1994) 14 *International Review of Law and Economics*, 215.

A law-making community is here assumed to have a minimum level of control over the behaviour of its members. Group internalisation is the key but ultimately a question of maximising self interest. The starting point is that members will not invest unless others follow. If upon proper signaling some co-operate and others appropriate, it means that some will make money every time, others sometimes more but other times none at all. In equilibrium, both earn the same overall, but those who co-operate have also a public good on offer, which may induce the appropriators increasingly to co-operate. Thus in this approach, the rule forms in a community when private incentives for signaling co-operation in the group align with a public good in that group. It creates momentum which shifts the equilibrium towards general acceptance. The suggestion is that when this happens the rule becomes legally enforceable.

One problem is that much private law does not operate at the level of internalisation as it is technical and must be learnt by the participants and their lawyers. Trade-offs hardly work in much of private law as it has developed and probably apply only to the bigger concepts. Once some such structures become a given, it is the innate sense, requirement of order and need to avoid contradictions that propel this law further. Businessmen learn rather than internalise and their lawyers may internalise but only after a long learning process. Conceivably, academia has here also an important role to play. External forces like those of states may facilitate (if asked to do so), eg through treaty law (or similar interstate structures in organisations like the EU), or, in regulation, impose themselves, even through the infusion of mandatory private law, which in particular also raises the problem of proper jurisdiction to prescribe in international cases, see also ss 2.2.6ff below.

[474] See G Teubner, 'Breaking Frames: The Golden Interplay of Legal and Social Systems' (1997) 45 *American Journal of Comparative Law* 149, for a somewhat different slant on the positive new law merchant and its origin. It is seen in the 'close structural coupling with non-legal rule production' (in terms of a paradox not of a dialectical process between fact and norm) in an evolutionary progression that, in this view, in its origin relies on an imaginary or fictitious legal environment in which there is mostly a pretence of legal rights and obligations fed by expectation. This is ultimately believed to lead to ready acceptance of the binding nature of the new law, even though non-political and factual, but also to a concern about the supposed destructive role of practising lawyers and their distortion of business realities in their alleged reference for a static (statist) system of rights and obligations.

themselves become supporting elements in the context of their international validity and force.[475]

Similar objective criteria may also emerge from a rule of law test itself. It has already been said that it assumes threshold standards of a more universal nature and not mere state recognition. It is possible to refer here to the rule of law both in an institutional ('law of rules') and substantive ('set of values') sense. It is the common yardstick by which the exercise of power in Western society is now more generally channeled, constrained and informed, not only at the national but also at the international level.[476] It could also play a significant role in the allocation of competencies between legal orders or in the acceptance by states of laws and decisions based on these competencies when rendered in other legal orders. The fact that there are here concepts at work that are more universal does *not* need to mean that they are also static, immutably pre-determined by rationality, unchangeable values, or (metaphysical) truths (as natural law concepts are sometimes considered to be). In fact, especially in the area of the rule of law and human rights, perceptions have greatly changed over the last century.

These concepts are unlikely to go as far as to require high-minded moral standards for legal orders to operate and be recognised even if in an ideal world this might be better. At least international business and its requirements present a more mundane environment. Legal orders, in order to function, need not necessarily be democratic or be supported by more advanced values either; it has never been a precondition for their operating at national levels.[477] However, international (or other) legal orders are not necessarily indifferent to such values either.[478] It was shown that fundamental principle is at the core of the modern *lex mercatoria* and this being so it must also be considered that this law is likely to operate much better if it also fights abuse and excess and extols virtue in its participants.

1.5.6 The Formation of Non-Statist Law in Modern Social and Economic Theory

In the previous section, reference was already made to law and society and law and economic theory supporting a bottom up approach to law formation especially in private

---

[475] Hence sometimes also the reference to the law of all civilised nations, see n 361 above. The concept of what was civilised in this context underwent a sea change in the meantime.

[476] See M Krygier, 'Rule of Law' in NJ Smelser and PB Bates (eds), (2001) 20 *International Encyclopedia of the Social and Behavioral Sciences*, 13403; and P Selznick, 'Legal Cultures and the Rule of Law' in M Krygier and A Czarnota (eds), *The Rule of Law after Communism* (1999).

[477] J Habermas, *The Structural Transformation of the Public Sphere* (trans Thomas Burger, 1991) 76, notes that the great codes in Europe were never democratically sanctioned but were subject all the same to some participation process which might have made them reflective of their times. See for the discussion of democratic legitimisation of private law formation and operation, also s 1.1.6 above.

[478] In a Western sense, it suggests the existence of more universal values that affect the legitimacy of all legal orders, of their operation, and the legal force of their rules (even internally). In the twentieth century, the well-known example was the legal effectiveness of the Nazi laws within the German legal order or their voidness per se even within that order after WWII.

It has already been noted that in commerce and finance, amongst professional operators who deal in risk, short of abuse and fraud, there may be few higher overriding rules governing or values operating amongst them.

law.[479] In business this is more closely related to market efficiency considerations and can be more clearly demonstrated in relation to the operation of the international market place upon globalisation where states and state law, especially of a private law nature, cannot or no longer be considered always to have an adequate response to the problems that may arise in international transactions. This is seen here at the heart of the demise of the traditional conflicts of law doctrines in commerce and finance which remained predicated on the premise that all law including that applying to international transactions had to emanate from a state and was therefore territorial. This will be the subject of the discussion in the next Part of this chapter.

A basic more modern idea is that self-interest promotes cooperation in inter-human affairs or relationships and is the essence at least of contract compliance, which is normally voluntary; no legal system could survive without it. It is therefore not force or the threat thereof but self-interest and the survival instinct that propel this system. Both parties benefit from complying. But this concept or need is not confined to contract. In a state of anarchy, it will soon become clear for example, that everyone benefits by driving in the same direction on one side of the road, leaving the other side to the opposing traffic. This will create a self-enforcing system of traffic control. Soon further rules will emerge: side street traffic must give priority to main street traffic before joining in and so on. It is likely that some busybody will emerge as policeman and introduce further specific rules, sustaining the equilibrium that was already achieved. This busybody is now the state devising traffic rules. This type of rule formation could also happen in the further development of contract and tort law. The busybody might here be the state but also agencies like the International Chamber of Commerce or similar think tanks.

But there are situations where one party may attempt to appropriate more than others and where defecting from this system may be the smarter move from a self-interest point of view. It presents a big problem where there is no third party enforcement mechanism. This situation is theoretically clarified in the so-called *prisoners' dilemma* and works as follows. Two persons are suspected of having committed a crime together. They have been caught and are separated in prison without the possibility of communication. The law is that if neither one confesses, each will be sentenced to one year in prison. If A confesses, but not B, the former goes free and the latter gets 10 years; the reverse when B confesses and not A. If both confess, they get five years each.

In this scenario, confessing is in aggregate the best strategy; at least it cuts the exposure by half. It is not dependent on the other party except if the first party expects that the latter does not confess when it would go free. This would be the hope of either whilst confessing. Thus each will get five years in the hope of better. It is true that if both stayed mum, each would get one year, but that would require some trust and may depend on them wanting ongoing co-operation as the incentive. This is indeed often considered the solution to the conundrum. Each will say nothing and both will get one year. This is also referred to as the *iterated game* which achieves a new equilibrium. Short-term hope is exchanged for long-term co-operative gain and prevents defection.

Transferred to commerce and finance, we may thus exchange a short term gain of 500 for repeated gains of 100. Hence the maxim: 'one-shot encounters encourage defection, frequent encounters cooperation'. Innate compliance is strengthened in such cases and

---

[479] See for a discussion of the modern functional approaches in the US, section 1.3.5 above.

rules develop. It may be followed by legal institutions being created within such groups to sustain cooperation, but it is accepted that in larger groups there may be a greater need for third party intervention and enforcement, notably through states.[480]Also it may become too unclear what everyone wants and the result may become disorderly and contradictory. However, this is not much of an option in international dealings and the transnational commercial and financial legal order must create its own agencies or spokespersons, including international arbitrators to articulate its rules.

At the business level contracts are often seen as creating smaller groups or merely one counterparty where repeat business will give a good incentive for performance. So may standardisation which supports business because of the efficiency built into it, and legal orders (through its practitioners and their lawyers) will self-standardise for that reason and create common perceptions. This is clear in contract, where standard terms are frequent and recur, but it may also happen in tort in the formulation of (traffic) offences and even in property. These are important areas for customary law formation, which can also ensue in contract, concerning particularly its infrastructure in terms of capacity and validity and affect much larger groups. Law evolves here without states as happened before the modern state emerged in the nineteenth century and it still happens—it is submitted—in the international commercial and financial legal order operating around a globalised market mechanism. The value of such law grows as the number of participants increases.

But standardisation has its limits and is not all-controlling, even if routines and standardisation are key to all societies (language being the foremost example).[481] Specialisation and the need for tailor-made products or specific risk management tools disturb this order[482] as does the need for innovation. In fact, there is never one standard, although certain standards may last longer than others, such as languages and legal systems, but even they evolve, sometimes quite rapidly in order to remain up to date and functional. Modern life is not and cannot be fully commoditised or remain mainly repetitive. It has been said before that the future is not captured by the past and its experiences. Efficiency ever requires us to move on. In our time, that results, it is submitted and is demonstrable, in particular in immanent law formation in this newer legal order of a commercial and financial nature. Top law firms, not judges or even arbitrators, are especially important as spokespeople for the new order navigating the pitfalls of public order and public policy and using a combination of principle, custom and party autonomy in the course of action they advise, especially for international professional dealings. The eurobond and the operation of the euro markets were early examples, but the same applies to the ISDA and similar master agreements that now operate for swaps and repos transnationally.

---

[480] In particular in R Ellickson, *Order without Law* (1991), there is this emphasis on smaller groups.

[481] See for these routines in particular, the discussion in section 1.4.7 above.

[482] See for the problems in this connection with standardisation of proprietary rights, the discussion in vol II, ch 2, s 1.3.9.

1.5.7 The Competition between Transnational Law and Mandatory State Laws or National Public Policies and Public Order Requirements

The premise in this book is that states and their courts have to recognise law from wherever it comes as a basic tenet of the rule of law and must enforce it through their courts or other facilities unless their public order is offended. It is quite obvious that in the recognition by states and their organs (including their judiciaries) of other legal orders and their laws and decisions, and in any subsequent competition between the transnational *lex mercatoria* and statist laws, the accepted set of values (or the absence thereof) in non-statist legal orders may play a role in this recognition process, also in a more tolerant and secular Western environment, imbued by notions of the rule of law. There are clearly limits in any established legal order (certainly that of states)—expressed as public order limitations—to what can be recognised and accepted as law from whatever other (immanent or statist) legal order or source. That is firmly established, although there may well have to be a large margin for any legal order to operate in its own way, also upon the territory of nation states, where the local laws should be increasingly accommodating except in more extreme cases. In commerce and finance, this process is well underway and is a trade off. If a state wants to have its citizens and businesses operate internationally and have that benefit, it must itself also contribute in supporting the transnational order unless its rules are manifestly objectionable.

Internationally, it has, for example, in private international law always been clear that the toleration of rogue states may ultimately also lead to the acceptance externally of their internal domestic legal order whatever its values and laws in transactions considered subject to their laws[483] and the same may go for other legal orders. Nevertheless,

---

[483] The operation of competing international legal orders may be instrumental, at least on occasion, in containing local cabals, even in democracies, or indeed expose them to openness and better practices or in an economic sense to more rational decentralised approaches or privatisation when more efficient. Globalisation has contributed in this way to the demise of inefficient governmental controls, to more choice and competition, lower cost, perhaps lower inflation, more openness and diversity, a better informed public, less jingoism, more co-operation (whether in G-7/8, G-20, IMF or WTO). Nobody claims perfection, but what may be a-statist or a-nationalistic in the transnational order is not per definition anti-democratic, democracy-offensive, or devoid of modern Western values at the same time.

In the meantime much has been written on the democratic deficit of these organisations and also of the EU both in Europe and the US. The traditional view is here that democratic control is best exercised at the level of the participating governments, therefore nationally. That was also the EU's original stance and is still the reason for the limited powers of the European Parliament.

There is another problem, however. The highly technical nature of much of the discussions at the international level escapes the public and it is difficult therefore for international parliaments to profile themselves, acquire credibility and inspire the masses. For the WTO, similar arrangements are suggested but unlikely to work better.

The alternative is greater openness in the negotiation processes and more reliance on public opinion and non-governmental organisations' input, besides that of local politicians. This raises the question of who may legitimately talk, whilst it is not clear whether the results would be any better. In all these organisations there appears to be a bureaucratic phase that precedes further democratisation and seems to be necessary to get things off the ground. The EU is the best example, but it is no different in the WTO.

Of course if the international community was truly serious and willing in the matter, the democratisation process could easily be taken a step further. It is not beyond present-day technical means to call an international 'constituante', in the election of which all citizens of the world could participate and which would devise a framework that at an institutional level could deal with globalisation issues democratically. But it would be a serious inroad into the remit of the nation state, may undermine non-Western cultures, and also mean the *de iure* end of the influence of NGOs, reasons why this option may not gain much ground for the moment.

it was noticed before and it is fundamental that modern states may still continue to counterbalance for example, international market forces if driven to excess and that there is here an equilibrium to be achieved under which the transnational legal order supporting these forces in principle (subject to its own public order requirements) remains deferential to legitimate governmental interests of a domestic nature especially in respect of all activity or conduct in or having an effect on the territory of the state in question.

The limits to what will be accepted by states as valid law from other legal orders operating within it, are here discussed in terms of democracy, rule of law, human rights, social policies, transparency, market abuse and corruption and proportionality, all of which will probably be affected by public order requirements in the recognising country. Nevertheless, within Western society, this allows for a broader discussion of the values of other legal orders (or the absence of such values in them), of the redistributive powers in or the fairness or unfairness of their systems (as may become clearer through, but also be compounded by globalisation), and of any rightful or erroneous claims of the law in the transnational commercial and financial legal order to objectivity and formal effectiveness in supporting trade, commerce and finance internationally.[484]

In subscribing to this approach, we should be helped by the fact that, at least for the economic benefits it brings, the present more or less decentralised, more or less democratic, more or less market supported socio-economic system finds some broad international support, at least throughout the Western world and also in large parts of Asia. In the international commercial and financial legal order, the daily business of trade, commerce and finance is in any event less politically and culturally sensitive than larger labour and environmental issues or the much broader political issues concerning growth and stability with which G-8, G-20, WTO and IMF must grapple and which might then also have an effect in the international commercial and financial legal order, assuming some legal expression can be given to any ensuing political intervention in it.[485]

At the micro level, these broader considerations seldom play a major role in business transactions. What, for example, is the value content of set-offs, floating charges, constructive trusts, book entry systems for investment securities and their operation, and the different rules that have developed in different countries in this regard? As has already been mentioned, (important) details of these legal structures would often seem to be matters of historical developments, coincidence, and especially of practical needs as perceived from time to time in different locations. Even where legislators have spoken, the result is seldom more fundamental and the results normally limited to past experiences or the insights and exigencies of the day.

Nevertheless, the minimum-required communality of values assumes a more immediate material meaning, when decisions reached in other legal orders, like the transnational commercial and financial legal order, are asked to be enforced in a state legal order by inviting

---

[484] Critical Legal Studies have, eg always been sceptical of the objectivity and effectiveness of black-letter law in pursuing social ordering in whatever form, therefore also when emanating from states: see for some in depth studies the anthology of AC Hutchinson (ed), *Critical Legal Studies* (Totowa, NJ, Rowman and Littlefield, 1989).

[485] The rules of foreign investment and their protection against governmental (host state) intervention under public international law, especially through BITs is another aspect of these international business dealings, which, protection against states being the issue, go beyond the mere tenets of private law.

its coercive sanction. Assuming for the moment that the relevant legal order can be found and its laws determined, we therefore still have the questions:

(a)   when precisely a transaction may be deemed to arise in the international legal order;
(b)   how the matter of competition with state legal orders is to be handled; and
(c)   what to do with enforcement?

As to the first issue, there has to be some definition of *what is international* and then there have to be some ground rules as to whether or not a transaction takes place in the international legal order. Here modern conflicts of law rules may still be of help in determining when a transaction is international, and what the most appropriate order is in which international professional activity is to take place. Traditionally the conflict rules had the handicap that they were meant to indicate a *state* order only. That was the consequence of von Savigny's approach to these rules, which date from the nineteenth-century era of state positivism and nationalism, (see more particularly section 2.1.1 below,[486] in which only national law had validity.

Conflicts rules pointing to the application of state law may therefore still be helpful and necessary in a broader context and may show the way in terms of centre of gravity of an activity or closest connection. A more advanced view favoured in section 1.1.8 above is that *all professional* business dealings are increasingly likely to operate in the international legal order even if they have no international connection on occasion, as it is ultimately unlikely that they retain different dynamics locally. In other words, they will increasingly aspire to similar legal standards, even if on occasion these transactions are purely local.

Such an evolution in thought would greatly simplify the issue of finding the appropriate legal order. Of course, if all the contacts were local, the impact of the pertinent national or statist regulatory and public order requirements in respect of the transaction would more readily have to be accepted.

As to the second question of the interaction between legal orders and the *competition* between them, this is a question of attributing competences. At the practical level, we have to consider in particular *governmental interests*, or public policies, or public order requirements of the recognising state, which, as suggested before, may be the case particularly in respect of international actions or transactions with conduct and effect in the territory of the concerned state and it then often concerns the effect of local regulation. This may, for example, concern domestic *competition* and *environmental* issues or policies and the effect of domestic regulation (or governmental interests) in all that happens on the territory of the particular state, even if the action or transaction is itself international: see for greater detail sections 2.2.6, 2.2.7 and 2.2.8 below.

In this connection, we have to consider the issue of the *attribution of competences* between the various legal orders in what is in essence a *decentralist* or pluralist view of law making which encourages this competition and limits the facility of states to frustrate it. But it also means that the transnational legal order and its laws are not per se higher. Again, in respect of legal pluralism or diversity, the proper concern is *not* here to find some *super* or *world* laws per se, but rather the identification of the *more competent or pertinent* legal order in respect of the particular actors or actions internationally, the law of which would then prevail.

---

[486] There was probably never much wrong with the idea that all legal relationships have a seat in a legal order, as long as that could also be the international legal order or others that were not territorially defined and confined.

A key point here, already mentioned, is that the new *lex mercatoria* is deferential to governmental policies and local public policy and public order considerations, at least to the extent that they have a reasonable connection with the case and the relevant government has a reasonable interest in it, does not intend to overreach, and there is proportionality. It is therefore not true that the modern *lex mercatoria* seeks to circumvent these legitimate domestic interests. This is very clear in tax laws that apply regardless of what law the parties may have chosen or operate under, but with present insights, these issues can often only be considered from case to case on the basis of a balancing of interests between international and domestic requirements and interests, also taking into account, however, developing international minimum standards. These international minimum standards may increasingly suggest a more objective transnational or international regime even in regulation. This could affect competition or the environmental restrictions on international business activity or the regulatory constraints on international banks.

Thus, at least if there is sufficient urgency and balance in the approach, specific domestic policies remain relevant and legitimate in international transactions, as such to be respected, even if not in accordance with the international trade practices which may, for example, have a more liberal bias. This balancing itself is more properly a matter of comity, in the manner of the US tradition of conflicts of laws (Restatement (Second) of Conflict of Laws section 6) and Foreign Relation Laws (Restatement (Third) of Foreign Relations sections 402–03) or, in the EU, in the manner of Article 9 of the 2008 EU Regulation on the Law Applicable to Contractual Obligations (Rome I), when not all elements of the case are connected with one country, see more particularly the discussion in sections 2.2.6, 2.2.7 and 2.2.8 below. It follows, however, that the reach of policy-oriented *domestic* rules may either become too remote or be *excessive* in international transactions and that they therefore do not apply or do not apply without modification.[487]

This leaves the last question of enforcement. The assumption was that under a proper understanding of the rule of law in an integrating world, decisions rendered in one legal order are accepted in others subject to minimum requirements of due process and public policy only. Indeed, at least in Western culture, it would appear incumbent on all states to enforce decisions rendered on the basis of the law of other legal orders operating within Western cultural confines subject to procedural fairness standards. There should be restraint, which, as already submitted, is needed and derives from the willingness of states to have their people and businesses operating internationally. That is a two-way street. If states do not want to cooperate in this manner, they should ask their citizens and business to stay at home. All will probably be poorer but that is a policy choice to make.

This attitude to international enforcement is the underlying theme in the 1958 New York Convention on the Recognition and Enforcement of Foreign Arbitral Awards. It is indeed still wedded to national considerations in terms of public policy constraints on the recognition and enforcement of international arbitral awards, in a more modern interpretation of

---

[487] Of course, when all aspects of a transaction are in a particular country, the public policy rules of this state legal order will prevail and no other. That may be so even if the transaction is international in nature as long as all its contacts are with one country only. That was clearly expressed in Art 2 of the 1980 EU Rome Convention on the Law Applicable to Contractual Obligations, now replaced by Art 3 of the 2008 EU Regulation. If they are not, there arises a discretionary element as reflected in Art 9 of the Regulation (in the context, however, of applying only domestic laws), even if it remains rule- rather than interest-oriented. In Europe the problem is usually identified as one of *règles d'application immediate* (see also s 2.2.6 below).

the Convention increasingly limited, however, to narrower notions of international public policy,[488] therefore to international (minimum) standards. But it is also very much the philosophy in the EU in its 2002 Regulation and in its earlier Brussels Convention on the Recognition and Enforcement of Judgments in Civil and Commercial Matters.

To repeat, this means that even if an effect on public policy or order in the recognising state cannot be denied, any overriding public policy interest or public order consideration of the recognising state is only accepted when it is overwhelming and might increasingly be tested on the basis of *international* minimum standards as an expression of *international* public order.

1.5.8 The Twentieth-Century Dominance of Statist Legal Orders and the Effect of Globalisation

In the previous sections, reference was made to social pressures and great social changes forcing adaptation of the prevailing legal norms including domestic norms, even in private law whether of the common or civil law type, either formally though legislation, or through principle and, in business, ever-changing custom. The effects of globalisation and transnationalisation with their own values and demands, which may be supporting or conflicting, have also been mentioned. In particular, in section 1.3.7 it was submitted that the law as an autonomous force retains its place in this manner, room being created for it at the transnational level particularly for cross-border activity. To some extent, states recede here in law formation, at least in private law, but they will still pursue their own public policies and public order requirements in respect of conduct under, and effect of, such transactions on their own territories as already mentioned.

In either system of private law, therefore both in common or civil law, domestically the outstanding feature of twentieth-century legislation has indeed been that the law was not only streamlined or adapted by states but became more generally imbued by policy considerations per country and was, in what became the modern welfare state, especially after World War II, increasingly used as a public policy tool, therefore even in areas traditionally considered the preserve of private law. This was done in order to achieve what was perceived as a better social balance. There also appeared to be a more active economic

---

[488] International public order requirements proper are well known from the international arbitration practice in the context of determining *arbitrability* issues and in connection with the recognition and enforcement of arbitral awards under the NY Convention. The Paris Court of Appeal dealt with the issue of arbitrability of public policy related issues (which were normally not considered arbitrable) in a judgment of 29 March 1991, *Ste Ganz, Rev Arb* (1991) 478, 480 and held that, while international arbitrators determine their own jurisdiction including the matter of arbitrability, they may use an internationalised concept of public order, see J-P Ancel, 'French Judicial Attitudes Toward International Arbitration' (1993) 9 *Arbitration International* 121; see also V Lazic, *Insolvency Proceedings and Commercial Arbitration* (1998) 149, 278.

See for the public policy bar to recognition of arbitral awards under the NY Convention, also P Lalive, 'Transnational (or Truly International) Public Policy and International Arbitration' in P Sanders (ed), *Comparative Arbitration Practice and Public Policy in Arbitration* (ICCA Congress Series no 3) (1987) 257. These are only two instances in which public policy plaid a role at the international level and may itself be international. It may also in other instances and it would appear that there may be also transnational mandatory competition rules operating that may void contracts in the international legal order as a matter of public policy in that order, see JH Dalhuisen, 'The Arbitrability of Competition Issues' (1995) 11 *Arbitration International* 151.

policy and infrastructure-building activity on the part of states and a much greater need for government supervision, often expressed in regulation. One may think of finance and of the environment. Everywhere, this elevated the importance of statutory law further which did not leave private law formation behind, in common law jurisdictions either. The statist legal orders thus became ever more dominant in law formation, even including the formation of private law.

As a consequence, private law acquired many more mandatory features than before. It was perhaps an unavoidable consequence of: (a) the further consolidation of central government and national administrations in the nineteenth century; (b) the legitimate policy objectives of modern states even in capitalist, decentralist, systems; and (c) the acknowledgement that both government and capitalism had to come together to make the modern highly developed economies feasible after a long period in which, during the nineteenth and early twentieth centuries the statist approach had mostly been balanced by a liberal or laissez faire economic and social outlook. This disappeared under the pressures of economic shocks and, at least in Europe, of disastrous wars in the first half of the twentieth century.

Subsequently, technical developments strengthened governments' idea that they were perhaps better than autonomous market forces at creating the optimum environmental, economic and social conditions for a modern society in building and restructuring its infrastructure, actively redistributing wealth, and engaging in what came to be called more broadly 'social engineering' and the operation of the 'welfare state', which included substantially also the nationalisation of health and education. This is the idea of the make-ability of society under newer technical models supported by academic insights. In section 1.3.7 above, the effects of modernity were already mentioned. It did not eclipse private law, but it had a considerable influence on it. One needs to think only of workers protection of all ages and both sexes, rent protection, and later of consumer law protection. Modern investors' protection is another such area.

In the economic crisis of the 1930s, there followed the introduction of protectionist measures more generally. Governmental intervention of this nature was always easier behind state borders, cut off from the international marketplace and its management of resources. Unsurprisingly therefore, (domestic) governmental intervention was facilitated by a simultaneous and intentional control of the international flows of persons, goods, services and money. This had a deep impact and stifling effect on these flows, which at the beginning of the twentieth century had still been largely free worldwide. It led to an increased division of markets along national lines and, after the abandonment of the gold standard, to paper currencies that could also be easily manipulated per country, for example through competitive devaluations, resulting in ever more extreme forms of nationalism. It resulted in a large number of import and foreign exchange restrictions everywhere, but it left private law, which had already been nationalised in the nineteenth century as we have seen, largely unaffected, although the severe currency devaluation in Germany in the early 1920s had an impact especially in the concept of 'changed circumstances' in contract law.

After World War II, the economic dangers inherent in this kind of nationalism were better understood but budgetary requirements and fiscal policies in strongly socialised market economies gave rise to new layers of state intervention at domestic level; again, this was all the easier behind national barriers where paper currencies continued to remain isolated subject to national interest rate and foreign exchange policies and were, often as a matter of policy, not made freely convertible and transferable in order further to allow for a more *dirigiste* nationalistic approach in economic and social affairs.

In many European countries, more governmental intervention resulted in this connection also from national industrialisation policies or nationalisations and central planning objectives, which left whole areas of activity exclusively to state enterprises. Immediately after World War II, this was especially so in the areas of public utilities, but was in countries like France and the UK soon extended to other industries. In the meantime, modern welfare states required mutual insurance and support systems, especially in respect of unemployment and old age to be organised at the national level. In other sectors, price controls had emerged because of chronic shortages, particularly in the rental of real estate. The organisation of a modern society with the need for an adequate infrastructure itself exerted many new pressures.

Thus, inner city and transportation policies and other infrastructure concerns, including health and education, created new areas where public or semi-public law started to impact on the rights and duties of private citizens and companies to operate. Yet the intervention on the basis of a perceived public interest could sharply differ by activity and by country. It meant that even in the Western World, governmental intervention was by no means uniform, although it was increasingly understood that a modern society that aims at feeding the multitude and at providing something extra for personal advancement depended on a more positive interaction (and competition) between an advanced state infrastructure and a vibrant market economy.

It is indeed the proposition of this book that the combination (and competition) of the market and the state have created and made possible a modern society that has proven to be the first one able to push back large scale poverty. The market still operates here but is checked by regulation at the level of the state. This has proven a key successful combination, but it has already been said that this success depends largely on states having adequate insight. In finance and the environment, this may often be seriously doubted, hence unexpected chocks and crises. On the part of states much remains here political guesswork and wishful thinking that may not be supported by sufficient rationalisation.

It is clear that in this strongly interventionist climate private property was not as unassailable as it once seemed. Contractual freedom in many areas proved now more limited than had once been believed, and the freedom of movement of goods, services and money became more supervised than it had ever been. Undoubtedly, modern society as a whole became more centralised and controlled, which had its effect both on civil and common law through wave upon wave of new legislation which also impacted on private law. As the private law had essentially been nationalised in the nineteenth century, the interventionist effect on it became evident particularly in the twentieth century.[489]

---

[489] From a legal point of view, *regulation* is here no more than governmental intervention through the law to achieve certain policy objectives. In discussing governmental policies and their implementation, this regulation is usually considered to be environmental, economic or social, therefore with an environmental, economic or social objective.

Although this sounds like an administrative law intervention in terms of licensing and supervision, it may take other forms. Thus competition policy may also figure and affect the status of contracts in private law. Other areas of private law intervention are through the formulation of mandatory law in the area of workers' and consumers' protection (like in new laws concerning unfair contract terms) or in the area of investors' protection (under the laws of agency or through issuers' disclosure and prospectus liability), the result in such cases being private law suits for damages or other redress rather than administrative action. But the fact that policy intervention is now

The role of modern states in providing a strong economic and social infrastructure internally and in promoting some order in international economic affairs thus became well established and at least to some extent trusted and expected. But this expanded role ultimately also showed that the more traditional liberal, democratic and economically decentralist outlook needed not be fundamentally impaired and that such an interventionist approach could remain credible by putting emphasis on the essentially still limited nature of this intervention. Although coming at a high regulatory and tax cost, this type of state action became in fact associated with and was typical for the richest countries that commonly identified with this type of (democratic) evolution of the notion of the modern state and of the markets, especially in Western Europe.

Where the precise balance was between market and government remained largely unclear, however, and could not be determined once and for all, although it was obvious that too much of the one or the other would lead to decline. In any event, although the movement initially was into the direction of ever more state intervention, developments never move in one direction only. Layer upon layer of laudable regulation spelled considerable danger in terms of unintended side effects and social and economic sclerosis. Initiative and the innovative spirit were likely to suffer. This led to some reaction, at least in Western Europe that seemed to be held back most. Healthy doubts in terms of efficiency of governmental management and capital use, suspicion that such a centralised system could lead to stagnation, higher inflation and unemployment, and resentment of the tax consequences started to weigh on it and contributed to a mood of government re-evaluation and retrenchment. Thus already by the 1980s in Europe domestically, privatisation and de-regulation became political alternatives that could again be discussed and put into practice. Regulation, for example, in privatised public utilities such as rail, electricity and water, became no less the subject of discussions about its objectives and effectiveness and as a consequence less overbearing. Negotiation with affected parties on the details, reliance on forms of self-regulation (in whole or in part), no-action letters, and plea-bargaining facilities became more common.

But there was also the idea that domestic markets at least in the smaller countries were too small to support their social systems. The layering of production and the provision of services, including financial services internationally became for them much of a need whilst the communication revolution had made globalisation possible. That had a further effect on the powers of local governments and gave markets an extra push. The early emergence of the GATT and the EEC in Europe may have reflected the beginning of this process after World War II, but it is now much more evident in the development of the successor organisations which thus became possible: the WTO and EU. Indeed, they only succeeded in the late 1980s when globalisation began in earnest.[490]

---

also endemic in private law does not make all private law public law. The difference is in the cause of action and remedies: see also the discussion at n 209 above.

[490] It may even have led to a more fundamental reconsideration of concepts of national sovereignty. In Europe, within the EU, it made the completion of the Single Market and the Monetary Union, both early EEC objectives, possible. Eventually, even domestic currencies gave way to the EURO as an international currency. The EU itself, being the early product of this evolution and reformed for its next phase in this development in 1992 at Maastricht, thus proved not immune to further modern worldwide influences and continues to be no less subject to these strong opening-up undercurrents (leading potentially also to further concessions in WTO), which, at least in the short term, seem to have been greatly beneficial to all.

The result was that further to this opening-up effect of the EU in Europe[491] and the consequences of trade and services liberalisation in the GATT/GATS/WTO, by the turn of the twenty-first century, in all modern societies, there remained a widely-accepted role for the modern state (apart from its traditional role in internal and external security), but there also was a greater consensus that it had to concentrate on health, education and social services, and to some extent on road and rail infrastructure but even the continued acceptance of these roles became more dependent on showing better results and there followed a call for accountability from this perspective with some cost/benefit analysis also. In other areas, state intervention became still stronger, however, as in environmental and financial supervision, although perhaps not strong enough, misfocused or poorly enforced. What also became clear was that much of this could no longer be handled at the purely national level. But building an international consensus proved not easy. At least within the EU there was a framework, although the exercise of considerable power at that level, its legitimacy and efficiency were not uncontested either.

Indeed, the proper insight into what exactly was needed often failed as the 2007/2009 financial crisis and the lack of consensus in environmental research dramatically showed. This was followed by a crisis in government debt. The social welfare state and its sustainability became severely tested when it appeared that the demands of healthcare and the need of pensions over a long period for a large older generation, the cost of a better environment, the possibility of redistribution through the tax system, and ever greater dependence on easy bank financing had reached their limits and destabilised society in a situation where growth itself had become substantially curtailed not in the least through an excess of regulation which could hardly be undone. But especially in Europe there were also problems with a lack of innovative spirit and perhaps energy. The system became paralysed and the concept of the modern welfare state and its leadership a central issue. Soon there was talk of a fundamental crisis in Western government.

The key point is here that public action in these and other areas is no longer perceived as being a given based on a pre-conceived (dogmatic) model of governmental intervention and powers at the national level. Public concerns change fundamentally over a generation constantly shifting the face of government and its intervention in the process. This is now better understood and policy thus becomes less doctrinaire and more pragmatic. This may be reversed after the 2007–2009 financial crisis but this is unlikely to be permanent and all government intervention is increasingly tested for its nimbleness,

On the other hand, the problems with the EURO which came down to lack of discipline in several member countries was conducive to giving the EU more power over the budgetary policies of these members.

[491] Whilst the immediate restrictive effects of World War II and the earlier economic depression abated, the emergence of the EEC (later EU) in Europe in 1958 meant to reopen the borders, but it made at first only a modest impact. In reality, the 1970s and 1980s showed the high tides of governmental *domestic* intervention in peace time in Europe (the further cause being the 1970s oil shocks) behind national borders.

In the EU, it took until 1989 before the capital and money flows started to be fully liberated. Only the implementation of the Single European Act in 1992 liberated the goods and services sectors, although some services, like financial ones, had to be re-regulated, partly through harmonisation at European level. This will be dealt with extensively in vol III, ch 2.

The monetary union (like the single market foreseen and demanded from the beginning to be created by 1970) was only completed after 1992, culminating in the Single Currency in 1999 in which not all Member States participated, however. In practice, there still continue some important restrictions on the free movement of persons and labour and also in the area of regulated services like finance.

responsiveness, cost, effectiveness and sustainability. It also means, that, whilst regulation and full public ownership or management must justify themselves continuously, they cannot a priori be excluded from any particular field either, as the 2007–2009 financial crisis also showed.

But the more discerning public will also be concerned about power broking in public services, about their monopolies, about any resulting inefficiencies and stagnation, and in particular about entrenched or immutable bureaucracies and the abuse of little dictatorships created in them. On the other hand, there will also be room for re-nationalisation or re-regulation if private alternatives or deregulation do not work. At least until the 2007–2009 financial crisis, the result of international market forces appeared to be lower inflation, greater diversity, more competition, more choice, better quality and lower prices at national levels. It did not prevent government becoming even more over-extended, however. In the crisis it appeared to have lost most of its levers, not least because of its overreach and own over-indebtedness. It risked giving the market place the last word – the right of the strongest to destroy the social balance.

The renewed interest in more liberal social and economic values on the other hand led to protests of minority groups, at first especially focused on international agencies like the IMF, World Bank (IBRD) and WTO. There was a successor in 2011 in the Occupy Wall Street movement, concerned mainly with the after-effect of the 2008 banking crisis but the lack of focus in these sentiments also became clearer. Abuse of the system was rightly decried, but how growth could be restarted beyond governments printing money or devaluing currencies, and how to deal with the negative consequences thereof especially in terms of the savings of an aging population, remained unclear.

Clearly, the advance of international market forces and their reforming, rebalancing or cleansing dynamics in the above manner are not welcome to all and in any event they are no panacea and may become too powerful when government weakens, albeit its own fault. They are sometimes thought not to square with democratic accountability either, which in this view is seen to be (best) exercised at national levels within complete state control. Any other autonomous and countervailing forces, especially those of the markets, are in this view always suspect. That the statist approach often proved to have favoured local cabals, reduced openness, promoted manipulative practices, and tolerated corruption, all at the expense of the people, and was ultimately bankrupted, is in this view readily discounted. But, it can be compellingly argued that many countries of the world (and all the poorer ones) are primarily held back by their own governments, incapable or unwilling to slot properly into an international economic order that seems to provide greater hope to adjust and balance their own powers accordingly.

In private law, creating a more robust legal environment amongst professionals that is dynamic and can better deal with risk and change at a global level is then another important issue. That leads into the operation of a new transnational legal order and transnationalisation of its law, the modern *lex mercatoria*, the major subject of this book, which in its own way may contribute to better risk management in international business dealings, see for a summary section 1.1.4 above, again unless public policy or public order intervene for example in financial and environmental aspects of international transactions, as already discussed.

This is to show that globalisation need not mean less supervision and protection but it will redirect it. The hope must then be that it is less geared to local sectarian interests and works better for the common good.

1.5.9 The Operation of Different Legal Orders in Private Law: Evolution of a US Federal Commercial Law, of Transnational Private Law Concepts in the EU, and of International Human Rights Law in the Council of Europe (European Court of Human Rights)

Ultimately it may be of interest to look more carefully at the spontaneous evolution of commercial or other forms of private law in some easily identifiable different legal orders like the federal legal order in the US (where private law is normally a state matter), the confederate legal order of the EU, and the international order which the Council of Europe represents, if only to show that nothing of the above in terms of the operation of different and competing legal orders beyond domestic ones, even in private law, is far-fetched.

It has already been mentioned several times before that, in the US, private law remains in essence a matter of state law and that goes also for commercial law. As a consequence, the Uniform Commercial Code (UCC) is state law, based on unification of the law between States without any federal involvement (even though at an early stage in its preparation it was considered to make commercial law federal law but this idea was not pursued). There is no agreement between the States either and the UCC was adapted in each state separately and autonomously, often with some differences. That was the case from the beginning. Further differences may arise where some states adopt amendments and others do not or only do so later, although the unity that the Code has brought is impressive and treasured. No state lightly goes its own way and the courts, both federal and state, the former especially in bankruptcy cases, in which Article 9 (on Secured Transaction in movable property) is often tested, support this uniformity in the interpretation process.

The foregoing would suggest that there is no room in the US for federal commercial law, therefore for commercial law in the federal legal order but that is not strictly speaking so. First, specific provisions in the US Constitution may lead to it. Foremost there is original federal power to legislate in the area of interstate commerce (Article II, section 8, clause 3). It forms the basis for the legislation in admiralty or maritime transport (like the Pomerene Act for bills of lading issued for transportation between the various states of the US, to foreign countries, US territories or the district of Columbia, see also Volume II, chapter 2, section 2.1.5. Treaty law may provide another base, like the adoption of the Brussels Convention incorporating the Hague Rules in the US Cogsa in 1936 (see also Volume II, chapter 2, section 2.1.10). The ratification of the Vienna Convention on the International Sale of Goods (CISG) may provide another example in the area of international sales, although here there may primarily be reliance on any direct effect under state law.

At one stage, there was a broader, more general attempt made to create federal commercial law for all *interstate* commercial transactions. It was not unlike the creation of federal *jurisdiction* in cases where there was diversity of citizenship. It would not have been unlike the de-nationalising process, as we now see globally. In the US it took indeed (some) commercial law outside the States' sphere proper, in which connection developing custom or the broader law merchant was instrumental. The important role of all commercial custom was acknowledged in the UCC itself, in section 1-103(a)(2) to which reference has also already been made several times, even though here still by virtue of state law recognition and incorporation. However, this attempt at federalising commercial law failed in its generality; yet there remain some areas or pockets where federal commercial law is still important, even beyond specific federal statutes in this area or treaty law adopted by the US.

To better understand this broader movement towards federalisation of commercial law within the US and its ultimate defeat, although never entirely, one has to take a step back and consider first the picture of the applicable law in *interstate* cases, either because of diversity of citizenship or because of the interstate nature of the subject matter. Such cases arise in interstate commerce when, for example, contracts are concluded between persons from different States of the Union or the object of a sale must move from one state to another as part of the delivery process. They arise for similar reasons also outside the commercial areas in an environment where there was under the Constitution (Article III, section 1) always a dual court system (state and federal), so that both types of courts (therefore also federal courts) could potentially deal with commercial issues.

Under the US Constitution, federal and diversity (of citizenship) cases are assigned to the federal courts but *not* technically cases with other interstate aspects. A difference may be made here further between procedural and substantive issues. As for the former, even in federal and diversity cases, it left the possibility of federal courts still applying the procedural rules of the states in which they sat. This did not happen. Although at first, federal courts only applied federal procedural rules in equity cases, they now do so in all diversity cases pursuant to the Federal Rules Enabling Act of 1934 and the Federal Rules of Civil Procedure that resulted from it (subsequently also used as the most important model for state procedural law reform leading to an important measure of harmonisation).

In diversity of citizenship cases, the issue similarly arose whether federal or state law applied to the substantive issues or merits (in terms of statutory, regulatory or case law). If federal law was to apply that would have called for the development of a federal common and commercial law if these cases were civil cases. However, in the important *Erie* case of 1938,[492] the applicable law was considered always to be the law of the state in which the federal court sat (if necessary varied through state conflict of laws rules, see, for example, section 1-131 UCC, which refers in this connection to the law of the state that bears an appropriate relationship to the case).

For this restrictive attitude, there had always been a strong foundation in the Judiciary or Rules of Decision Act 1789 (section 34) even though the US Supreme Court had at first tried to construe some substantive federal common law in areas not already covered by federal statutes. Since 1938, however, it has been accepted that there is *no* federal common law as such (including federal commercial law). Yet as already mentioned, there are still some pockets of federal private law, especially in federal statutes and case law pursuant to it, but also in some areas of commercial law and custom. Thus in marine insurance and the interpretation of the relevant policies, federal law was applied by the federal courts from early on, followed later by the law concerning negotiable instruments and interstate common carriers, even in diversity cases and this continues.[493]

---

[492] *Erie v Tompkins* 304 US 64 (1938). See in this connection especially WA Fletcher, 'The General Common Law and Section 34 of the Judiciary Act of 1789: The Example of Marine Insurance' (1984) 97 *Harv L Rev* 1513.

[493] *Robinson v Commonwealth Ins Co* (1838) 20 Fed Cas 1002. A diversity case involving a bill of exchange in respect of the sale of land, title in which was subsequently disputed, was also held to be covered by federal law; *Swift v Tyson* (1842) 41 US 1, in which s 34 of the 1789 Act was not held to apply to questions of commercial law but only to the interpretation of local statutes and customs. With reference to Lord Mansfield in *Luke v Lyde* 2 Burr R 883, 887, it was stated that the law of negotiable instruments was not the law of a single country. In *Western Union Telegraph Co v Call Publishing Co* (1901) 181 US 92, the use of common information carriers was not

There is an emphasis here on the interstate nature of commerce and the need to follow its ways and thus provide certainty, especially in terms of transactional and payment finality, therefore beyond the confines of individual states. This may indeed shift the law creating force to another more efficient legal order, in the case of the US to the federal order always to the extent the commerce clause can support it. That is a most important conclusion. Whilst in *Erie* the further development of a federal common law was halted in principle, it did not strictly speaking exclude the further development of federal commercial law under the commerce clause or pursuant to interstate custom or the law merchant, especially where the formal diversity notion did not strictly cover all interstate activity, which could be broader.

On the other hand, it cannot be overlooked that the UCC firmly re-established an efficient state law regime in much of the traditional areas of commercial law including negotiable instruments and letters of credit. Yet at least in specialised areas, a federal commercial law still applies, such as for cheques drawn on the US Treasurer or in notes issued by the US. In this connection, reference is indeed still made to a *federal law merchant*, which continues to develop separately from state law.[494] Similarly special federal statutes may concern bills of lading as we have seen, but there may still be scope for more under the commerce clause. It is suggested that this law would be built on diverse sources of which custom, and fundamental and general principle would be important manifestations. Party autonomy would follow. Again, it is reminiscent of the modern *lex mercatoria* development transnationally as described in this book, in which connection it is again important to note that the UCC in its section 1-103 accepts and favours the multiplicity of legal sources and their further development.

It is even argued that there is in the US effectively a *national* private law that transcends both the federal and state legal orders and finds its legal force in the recognition and invocation of its rules by the American legal profession.[495] Such a transcendent law would suggest the existence of a *national* legal order in private law in the US with a momentum and inner structure of its own.

It will be interesting to see whether within the EU similar common notions will be allowed to develop, especially in intercommunity trade, in that case also better considered in the context of the modern development of the international law merchant or *lex mercatoria* and its multiplicity of legal sources. Article 114 TFEU would then provide the legal basis,

---

believed subject to any state law either, but in the absence of any federal statute rather to federal general common law, containing the general rules and principles deduced from the common law enforced in the different States.

[494] *Clearfield Trust Co v US* (1943) 318 US 363. An important instance is thus the further development of the law merchant as such in interstate trade, more generally beyond diversity of citizenship, where it is now normally excluded, see further *Southern Pacific Transportation Co v Commercial Metals Co* (1982) 456 US 336. It shows clearly that there is room for such interstate commercial law in the US.

Typically federal matters are also lifted out off state law like a claim in respect of injuries caused to a federal soldier, *US v Standard Oil of California* (1947) 332 US 301. The key is here the protection of uniquely federal interests and situations in which Congress has given the power to develop substantive law, see *Texas Industries v Radcliff Materials Inc* (1981) 451 US 630.

[495] See MA Eisenberg, 'The Concept of National Law and the Rule of Recognition' (2002) 29 *Florida State University Law Review 1229*. In this view, an economic and convenience argument may be invoked but also a common tradition fostered by national law schools and a large 'national' slice in the bar examinations of each state. The informal creation of this law is stressed and its flexibility noted. The rules do not then figure as black-letter law and their binding force may depend on the situations in and the purposes for which they are invoked. They may as such provide the framework for much legal argument and the central core of much of the living (private law) in the US, much more and more fundamentally than is normally acknowledged.

but it is a narrow one, see section 1.4.19 above, and it would still have to be considered what it covers, not unlike the commerce clause in the US. But there is here room for further development at the EU level, although, it was submitted before, not without at the same time recognising the force of different sources of law, of which custom and party autonomy would be important manifestations besides statutory texts in the nature of the DCFR or CESL, or any other, see below. Again, this is also suggested by the American example.

It was noted in sections 1.4.5 and 1.4.6, that fundamental and general principles are also used by the European Court of Justice. As already mentioned in section 1.4.4 above, in the case law of the ECJ there are in this connection often 'borrowings' of private law concepts for all kind of purposes, therefore often not connected with the promotion of the internal market. They are then mostly identified as general principle, like the notion of good faith, the notion of contract, the notion of tort and causality in that context, of property, of abuse of rights, of force majeure and change of circumstances, and also the notion that interest may have to be paid as damages.

In these instances, these concepts often acquire special features in a public or administrative law context, where the ECJ often develops them, such as, for example, in the administrative contract, the administrative tort and so on. This may explain the lack of a reference to the promotion of the internal market. Where EU levies or taxes must be reimbursed, some special EU rules of tort and unjust enrichment have also been developed.[496] Guidance may be sought here from administrative law principle as much as from private law, but the method of 'borrowing' in this sense based on general principles of private law is well established.

This movement is supplemented or potentially superseded by the efforts producing the DCFR, including the 2011 Draft Regulation on a European Sales Law (CESL), see again section 1.4.19 above as EU codifications in the traditional civil law manner, excluding therefore any other sources of law, in the case of the DCFR (not CESL) for all activity in the EU, whether cross-border or not. This law is then to supersede all local laws and is meant to form a statist codification at EU level unaware that for cross-border professional dealings, the modern *lex mercatoria* may lay better claim to application as a matter of the operation of the transnational commercial and financial legal order itself. For the DCFR and its progeny there is no other law or legal source but their own and they operate here like state law, now at EU level, and mean to monopolise the field also in respect of professional dealings trans-border within the EU. But it has already been said that the ECJ itself operates quite differently and is well aware of overriding fundamental principle and also of general principle being operative outside legislation, see sections 1.4.5 and 1.4.6 above.

Finally, in Europe, the European Court of Human Rights, established by the Council of Europe (which needs to be distinguished from the EU European Court of Justice or ECJ), in its jurisdiction under the European Convention on Human Rights of 1950 and its Protocols, and therefore in the legal order it represents, has developed a notion of ownership independent from national laws in the context of ownership protection as a human right (pursuant to Article 1 of the First Protocol). This case law is important and original as it seeks to develop amongst others an internationalised ownership concept.[497]

---

[496] See also T Tridimas, *The General Principles of EU Law* (Oxford University Press, 1999) 313.
[497] See also Jan-Peter Loof et al (eds), *The Right to Property, The Influence of Article 1 Protocol No 1 ECHR for Several Fields of Domestic Law* (Maastricht, Shaker Publishing, 2000).

Its main features are that no-one may be deprived of his possessions except in the public interest, but always subject to the conditions provided for by the general principles of international law (except that the payment of taxes or other contributions or penalties is not affected). There is therefore a need to define possession, interference and any justification thereof. The Court gives to the notion of possession in this context an *autonomous meaning* which is ownership-connected[498] but notably not limited to physical goods. There is here an emphasis on economic realities covering also beneficial rights.[499] From a jurisprudential point of view, the importance is indeed that possession, ownership or property need *not* be connected with a *national* legal order but may acquire an *internationalised* meaning in the international legal order the European Court of Human Rights represents and defends. The evolution of *international* property rights will be further explored in section 3.2.2 below.

The conclusion is that European students in particular must learn to think in terms of the operation of different legal orders side by side in the same territory; American students are used to this from the beginning of their studies. There will be the statist legal order, the legal order between states, in Europe for EU Members the EU legal order, and now in business also the transnational commercial and financial legal order, all with their own laws. One might even discern an international sports legal order, probably closer to many students' hearts and imagination. They may all come onshore at different times in different countries, which would have to accept their rules and rulings unless offensive to the domestic public order of such states, if not itself declared irrelevant as a bar to the effect of these rules, like in the EU if it purports to limit the operation of the internal market disproportionally or unnecessarily.

1.5.10 The International Commercial and Financial Legal Order and its Relevance: The Role of Legal Theory, Legal History and Comparative Law

International flows of goods, services, technology and capital go in all kinds of directions. In an open society, it is not unlike water finding various ways towards the seas. There are here inherent forces at work, whether or not considered organised by the invisible hand

---

[498] See *Marckx v Belgium* ECHR 13 June 1979, Series A, vol 31, para 63.

[499] See *Gasus Dosier und Foerderintechnik v Netherlands* ECHR 23 February 1995, Series A, vol 306B, para 53. It can as such cover security interests of the tax authorities and others, reservation of title and other conditional ownership interests or limited proprietary rights. It also includes intellectual property rights and claims based on contract and tort. This is clear from the reference to '*valeur patrimoniale*' or asset, which suggests at the same time that the essence is right with a commercial value that can be sufficiently ascertained.

It may as such cover goodwill or an existing clientele, see *Van Marle v Netherlands* (1986) Series A, vol 101, para 41, and later in *Iatridis v Greece* 25 March 1999, no 31107/96, §54, ECHR 1999-II, but not a mere expectancy (of an inheritance) or a right to receive property, see *Marckx v Belgium* cited in the previous footnote. Yet a right to an inheritance of a deceased person may be claimable even if non-partitioned, *Inze v Austria* Series A, vol 126, para 38, 9 December 1987, and *Mazurek v France* ECHR 1 February 2000.

A disputed claim is not sufficiently established, but once adjudicated it is and a state against which the claim was awarded can no longer annul the claim through legislation, see *Stran Greek Refineries v Greece* Series A, vol 301B, para 61, 9 December 1994. Even a claim in a prima facie case might be so protected, see *Pressos Compania Naviera v Belgium* Series A, vol 332, para 31, 20 November 1995.

of market behaviour. They produce their own rules, which are connected with the risk patterns and natural needs for protection of the parties concerned. For them they are primarily dictated by common sense and rationality in the relevant trade. This implies a strong reliance on principle, closely connected with emerging custom and practices which may have an important risk management aspect and may then even become mandatory, especially in terms of property rights or transactional *finality*, as we have seen. Professional parties will elaborate in their contracts or otherwise impliedly rely on them. They form the basis for the rules in the transnational commercial and financial legal order as discussed more extensively in the preceding sections. Reasonable reliance is itself here a strong argument and condition for giving these rules or rule-patterns binding or legal force unless there are overriding public policy or public order requirements against it.

International sales are a case in point as we shall see in Volume II, chapter 1, Part II. There are obvious extra risks attached to the sale and transfer of assets internationally in terms of their transportation, proper delivery, quality and title for the buyer and payment for the seller. Without some clear rules in these regards it would require an excess of optimism to sell and send goods across the world. At the practical level handling agents are here a great help. They may be warehouse operators or carriers of the goods and will take the goods from the seller with the sole purpose of delivering them to the buyer. They have no own interest in the transaction except for their agreed reward and the goods are therefore in independent, safe and professional hands whilst having left the seller, who has lost control and can no longer interfere with them. That is an important safeguard for the buyer.

On the other hand, the seller will be concerned about the latter's payment and will not want the handling agents to deliver the goods to the buyer without such payment. These agents, when warehousing or transporting the goods, may issue warehouse receipts or bills of lading, without which the goods could not then be reclaimed. Possession of these documents therefore allows the buyer to claim the goods, but, for the protection of the seller, they may and will often be given to a bank, as another independent agent in this circuit, with the instruction not to release them to the buyer except against payment. That is the concept of (documentary) collection. It may even be that the bank (upon instructions of the buyer) will pay upon receipt of the bill of lading and becomes as such a guarantor of payment. That is the concept of the (documentary) letter of credit.

These structures never derived from great legal thought but suggest themselves in the practicalities of international trade and are only further perfected to enhance that trade. Bills of exchange had a similar origin and motivation. So had the protection of bona fide purchasers, who may claim a better title to the goods (or documents) than the seller could. These rules develop all the time and are not restrained in their application by pre-existing black-letter laws. It is true that much nineteenth- and twentieth-century codification in this area left that impression but it is not a correct reflection of the applicable commercial law and the way it evolves.

Here the importance of custom or industry practices can be clearly demonstrated and properly understood. By referring to them and their importance in this connection, we in fact underline more than anything else the dynamic nature of this law itself. It means that these customs and practices are not static and do not require for their validity longstanding usage. As has been shown before, they can change overnight with the nature and logic of the business and so the law changes with them.

It suggests that in this area, perhaps more than in any other, *both* the *relevant* law and the *relevant* facts must always be found and articulated *together* in each case. They are most closely connected. The one cannot be found without the other and there can be no question here of a sharp separation between norm and fact, either in the origin of the rule or in its application, or in the collection of the facts that may be considered legally relevant under it. It follows that at least in international cases both must be proven.

Even if commercial law remains in the perception of many still largely in the clutches of domestic legal systems—on the European Continent often in nineteenth-century codified form—whilst even in England it lost its independence in the eighteenth century as we have seen, it now reasserts its own nature at the international level, through the internationalisation and liberalisation of the commercial flows. However, it needs the help of legal theory, of legal history, and comparative law to regain its proper place.[500]

---

[500] The most important early advocate of the new *lex mercatoria* was B Goldman, see B Goldman, 'La lex mercatoria dans les contrats et arbitrage internationaux: realite et perspectives' (1979) 106 *Journal du Droit Internationale* 475; B Goldman, 'Lex Mercatoria' in (1983) 3 *Forum Internationale* 1; TE Carbonneau (ed), B Goldman *Lex Mercatoria and Arbitration: Discussion of the New Law Merchant* (Transnational Juris Publications Inc, 1990); B Goldman, 'Nouvelles reflexions sur la Lex Mercatoria' in *Etudes de droit international en l'honneur de Pierre Lalive* (1993) 241.

The long-standing relative popularity of the *lex mercatoria* in France may be seen in the light of the earlier development in that country of the notion of the 'international contract' operating under its own internationalised rules. It was particularly relevant for the validity of gold clauses that were upheld in these international contracts (but not in domestic French contracts) in the 1930s. See GR Delaume, *Transnational Contracts* (1989) 119.

See for the early interest in notion of the new *lex mercatoria* in England, C Schmitthoff, 'International Business Law: A New Law Merchant' (1961) *Current Law and Social Problems* 129; C Schmitthoff, 'International Trade Law and Private International Law' in *Vom deutschen zum europaischen Recht Festschrift Hans Doelle*, vol 2 (1963) 261; C Schmitthoff, *The Unification of the Law of International Trade* (1968) *Journal of Business Law* 109. See for a compilation of his most important writings on the subject, Chia-Jui Cheng (ed), C Schmitthoff, *Select Essays on International Trade Law* (1988).

In the UK, Mustill LJ has been particularly critical of the *lex mercatoria* as a trans-national legal system and wonders where this new law could come from. See LJ Mustill, 'The New Lex Mercatoria' in M Bos and I Brownlie (eds), *Liber Amicorum Lord Wilberforce* (1987) 149; LJ Mustill, 'Contemporary Problems in International Commercial Arbitration' (1989) 17 *International Business Law* 161.

The *lex mercatoria* found early support in Germany. See N Horn, *Das Recht der internationalen Anleihen* (1972); N Horn, 'A Uniform Approach to Eurobond Agreements' (1977) 9 *Law and Policy in International Business* 753; N Horn, 'Uniformity and Diversity in the Law of International Commercial Contracts' in N Horn and C Schmitthoff (eds), *The Transnational Law of International Commercial Transactions* (1982) 3.

In Denmark, see O Lando, 'The *Lex Mercatoria* in International Commercial Arbitration' (1985) 34 *ICLQ* 747.

There is a fair amount of other early literature reflecting on the topic. See E Langen, *Studien zum internationalen Wirtschaftsrecht* (1963); P Kahn, *La Vente Commerciale Internationale* (1961); 'Lex mercatoria et euro-obligation' in F Fabritius (ed), *Law and International Trade* (1973) 215.

See, more recently, AF Lowenfeld, 'Lex Mercatoria: an Arbitrator's View' (1990) 6 *Arbitration International* 133. See also R Goode, 'Usage and its Reception in Transnational Commercial Law' (1997) 46 *International & Comparative Law Quarterly* 1; LY Fortier, 'The New, New Lex Mercatoria, or, Back to the Future' (2001) 17 *Arbitration International* 121; ME Basile et al, *Lex mercatoria and Legal Pluralism: A Late Thirteenth Century Treatise and its Afterlife* (1998); H Mertens, 'Lex Mercatoria: A Self-applying System Beyond National Law?' in G Teubner (ed), *Global Law Without a State* (1997) 31; Emmanuel Gaillard, 'Transnational Law: A Legal System or a Method of Decision Making?' (2001) 17 *Arbitration International* 59. But *cf* Pierre Mayer, 'Reflections on the International Arbitrator's Duty to Apply the Law' (2001) 17 *Arbitration International* 235.

For a more comprehensive recent elaboration in France, see the work of P Fouchard, in particular P Fouchard et al, *Traite de l'Arbitrage Commercial International* (1996). See also P Fouchard, *L'Arbitrage Commercial International* (1965); Gaillard and Savage (eds), *Fouchard, Gaillard and Goldman on International Commercial Arbitration* (1999). For a recent overview, see KP Berger, *The Creeping Codification of the Lex Mercatoria* (1999). For an earlier sceptical analysis, see F De Ly, *International Business Law and Lex Mercatoria* (1992).

For a fuller elaboration and academic discussion of the subject and in particular of the development of a hierarchy of sources of law within the modern *lex mercatoria*, see JH Dalhuisen, n 467 above, and for a more sociological approach, see G Teubner, 'Global Bukowina: Legal Pluralism in the World Society' in G Teubner (ed), *Global Law*

Legal theory proves its importance in all periods of great change and must provide a vision. That is the traditional task of jurisprudence in the US. It does not necessarily provide instant clarity. The American modern 'law and …' movements such as 'law and morality', 'law and sociology', 'law and economics', 'law and psychology', 'law and aesthetics' and so on, show great differences in emphasis, although they also demonstrate that, in the evolution, explanation and application of the law, external or non-legal considerations play an important role. When and how they do remain a matter of study, and how they can all be distinguished and connected is an *epistemological* question that has to do with the nature of our perceptions and the acquisition and meaning of our knowledge. These questions have received renewed attention, especially in the major law schools in the US, where the need for a better understanding of what is going on is acutely felt. It has also led to more empirical research. Again it must be admitted, however, that this American jurisprudential interest has not yet been greatly extended to the study of the law-creating forces in international legal orders (see further section 1.3.6 above), but it may well show its true importance in that connection.

It is clear that legal theory has a particular contribution to make to our subject of globalisation of commerce and finance and of the effect this has on the applicable law. More particularly, this contribution may concern the concept and operation of distinct legal orders[501] that may be separated from or transcend national legal orders.

As we saw in the preceding sections, legal orders are not necessarily territorially defined, but may operate by class of activities or of persons, for example, amongst professionals in their business dealings. It suggests a more or less consistent set of rules by order, closely connected with its dynamics. They may be self-created in that order, based, in the case of commerce and finance, on innate or commercial logic and on common sense, whilst the rules could change very quickly, depending on the change in the nature of the business. These rules are likely to be articulated in many ways, through practitioners, think tanks, academics, the ICC, UNCITRAL, UNIDROIT (in treaty or model laws or through general

---

Without a State, (1997) 3. See also G Teubner, 'Breaking Frames: The Golden Interplay of Legal and Social Systems' (1997) 45 *American Journal Comparative Law* 149; G Teubner (ed), *Autopoietic Law: A New Approach to Law and Society* (1988).

The matter has received relatively little attention in the US. But see FK Juenger, 'Private International Law or International Private Law?' (1994–95) *King's College Law Journal* 5; FK Juenger, *The UNIDROIT Principles of Commercial Contracts and Inter-American Contract Choice of Law*, (Universidad Nacional Autonoma de Mexico—Universidad Panamericana 1998) 229–36; FK Juenger, 'Conflict of Laws, Comparative Law and Civil Law: The Lex Mercatoria and Private International Law' (2000) 60 *Lousiana Law Review* 1133. It is also largely neglected in the more functional approaches to the law. But see R Cooter, 'Structural Adjudication and the New Law Merchant: A Model for Decentralisation' (1994) 14 *International Review of Law and Economics* 215; R Cooter, 'Decentralized Law for a Complex Economy: The Structural Approach to Adjudicating the New Law Merchant' (1996) 144 *University of Pennsylvania Law Review* 1643. See further also JE Rauch, 'Business and Social Networks in International Trade Law' (2001) 34 *Journal of Economic Literature* 1177; Y Dezalay and B Garth, 'Merchants of Law as Moral Entrepreneurs: Constructing International Justice from the Competition for Transnational Business Disputes' (1995) 29 *Law & Society Review* 27.

[501] Julius Stone, although a positivist in the Hart tradition, was concerned with legal orders, but since he concluded that law could not be defined, it was also impossible in his view to define legal orders but both could be described to some extent; see *Legal Systems and Lawyers' Reasoning* (1964) 178ff.

Other modern writers mention legal orders or systems, but it is as such not a major area of study in modern legal thought. The concept has received some more attention in public international law, see N MacCormick, *Questioning Sovereignty* (Oxford, 1999), especially chs 1 and 5, and certainly also in EU law; see the seminal Case 26/62, *Van Gend & Loos* [1963] ECR 3 Case 6/64 *Costa v ENEL* [1964] ECR 1203 Case 14/68, *Walt Wilhelm* [1969] ECR 1, and any current EU law handbook on the subject.

principles that may be deduced from them even if they are not incorporated in domestic laws).

Legal theory may thus help in the identification of the international commercial and financial legal order (as of any other), the various sources of the law in that order, and their relationship and use. Practices and custom may in this manner be given their proper place whilst the impact of extralegal considerations in the formation and application of the law may be better assessed and understood. It may give a more coherent insight in the formulation and operation of the ensuing rules and in their ranking amongst each other. It is likely to show that, in an ever-changing environment, black-letter rules can often hardly be more than guidance, no matter from which legal source they come.

Legal theory may then also be able to reconsider the status and impact of private international law or conflicts of law doctrine and determine the proper residual role of domestic laws. It will also show that, although the necessary means of enforcement may still be through national courts, they may and should apply these new transnational rules in professional dealings. Alternatively, compliance could be through international arbitrations or other international fora (yet to be created), the rulings of which should be supported by all courts of modern commercial nations. It would be of prime self-interest to such nations (assuming they would want to continue to participate in the international flows of goods, services, capital and payments) that such support should be quickly and efficiently forthcoming, again unless domestic public order concepts are manifestly intruded but they may themselves be increasingly transnationalised.

Legal history is here also a help in showing that various sources of private law always operated side by side, and that the attempted monopolisation of private law creation by modern states, particularly in civil law countries through legislation, is a recent phenomenon, was never entirely successful, and is probably an aberration.[502] It may also show that much in the law developed in a haphazard manner, was coincidental or transplanted from other legal systems. Indeed in many countries much of private law has no national root at all.

Comparative law, finally, gives us a feel for our legal environment, provides us with a mirror and ideas at the practical level, and gives us an inventory of common problems and solutions. It may also give us an insight into the general or core principles that could suggest an international normativity, as such in private law potentially of great relevance in the hierarchy of norms within the modern *lex mercatoria*. But that could only be so if the commercial practice recognises itself in the result. That is the limit of comparative law in international trade and finance and also of the relevance of the sets of contract and other principles, like the European (PECL) and UNIDROIT Principles of Contract Law, which are now proffered at the more academic level. The same goes for the DCFR and the proposals for a CESL in the EU.

The comparison may be all the more subtle and valuable if the different legal orders from which the various rules hail are more fully understood and their own dynamics by order (and their limitations) better articulated. Traditional comparative law had little eye for these aspects and remained wedded largely to black-letter laws and statist notions of the

---

[502] See, for a reconsideration of legal history and its role at least in common law research in the twentieth century, KJM Smith, 'History's living legacy: an outline of "modern" historiography of the common law' (2001) 21 *Legal Studies* 251.

sources of law. This has come in for some important criticism[503] but it does not altogether do away with the usefulness and need for comparative law studies in a functional sense.[504] This will show that, especially in the West, mythical or more mysterious origins of the law in a national psyche are largely unsupported, at least in commerce and finance, and are replaced there by greater openness and rationality.

It can only be repeated in this connection that much present property and contract law is in its origin not nationalistic but rather Roman, Germanic or feudal, whilst, at least in commerce and finance, much modern law is practical, technical, and problem-solving in ways that do not differ a great deal from country to country, except sometimes in the detail, where the differences seem often more coincidental than fundamental. Whereas in other areas of the law, diversity may be of value and could be cherished, in international commerce and finance this is only disruptive and costly. There it operates more properly at the level of different sources of law subject to a clear hierarchy. The conclusion must further be that, in commerce and finance, modern public policy considerations of a domestic nature also play a lesser role in a globalised world to the extent that all want to participate. Finally, where other cultures are involved that cannot accept Western standards in terms of the prevailing economic system and its flows, in international commerce and finance their own practices are so far hardly a model for anyone else.

In international commerce and finance, the emphasis in this connection may therefore still be usefully limited to the study of the living laws of the main modern trading nations (in this book limited mainly to the laws of England, France, Germany and the US) whilst, as just mentioned, the comparative results must always be tested for their usefulness in the light of the dynamics of the international flows of goods, services, information, capital and payments, the risks participants incur and the protections they need in that connection to the extent they cannot be negotiated. Comparative law beyond these limits may still have some academic value but no great practical meaning or authority.[505]

---

[503] See, for a discussion of the critiques and a re-evaluation, A Peters and H Schwenke, 'Comparative Law beyond Post Modernism' (2000) 49 *ICLQ* 800. See further also G Samuel, 'Comparative law as a core subject' (2001) 21 *Legal Studies* 444.

[504] A more structuralist approach assumes on the other hand an immanent legal model against which national laws or even transnational law can be tested. This gives another important meaning to comparative law, which is not, however, directly relevant in the context of this book. Whilst in this book a mere black-letter approach is generally avoided in the search for substantive transnational law, this search is perceived in terms of a probing attitude, in which domestic laws are tested for their usefulness in an international context as they may be an expression of a potentially broader normativity in the dynamics and further development of modern international commerce and finance.

In this connection, domestic laws may also usefully show the legal *issues* that need to be dealt with in the formulation of the new *lex mercatoria* and for which the traditional solutions need also not a priori be rejected. Rather, they must be retested for their validity in an internationalised context.

[505] Not much further attention can be given here to the aims of comparative law and its objectives. Some look for a common core in the law (whilst rejecting any mythical search) like RB Schlesinger, 'The Common Core of Legal Systems, An Emerging Subject of Comparative Law Study' in KA Nadelmann, AT von Mehren and JN Hazard (eds), *XXth Century Comparative and Conflicts Laws. Legal Essays in Honor of Hessel E Yntema* (1961) 65ff. It leads to a search for universal, non-structural principles common to all legal systems. This may most certainly be of some use in international commerce and finance.

See also for a discussion about Germany J Esser, *Grundsatz und Norm in der richterlichen Fortbildung des Privatrechts. Rechtsvergleichenden Beitraege zur Rechtsquellen- und Interpretationslehere*, 4th edn (1990), where the emphasis is particularly on the role of principles common to all legal systems in the further development of national laws, so also E Rabel, 'International Tribunals for Private Matters' (1948) *The Arbitration Journal* 209.

In T Weir (trans), Zweigert-Kötz, *An Introduction to Comparative Law*, 3rd edn (Oxford, 1998) 40, there is even a presumption of similarity (*praesumptio simultudinis*), at least in the less politically driven areas of private law

Above this was demonstrated for *international commerce* with international sales as an example. It may be useful to also mention in this connection a number of structures that require particular attention *in international finance* and where there is traditionally little communality. Again one may refer here to set-off and netting, assignments of receivables (or of contractual rights more generally, especially important in securitisations), floating charges, finance or conditional sales and reservations of title, trusts and constructive trusts, and to book-entry systems concerning investment securities entitlements. They will all receive a great deal of attention in the rest of this book and the succeeding volumes with a view to the transnationalisation of the evolving legal structures and practices concerning them.

because the needs are very similar everywhere. However, it remains a fact that, even in commerce and finance, there are great differences especially in the law of property but also in equity concepts, such as trusts, beneficial ownership interest, conditional ownership rights, or security interests and floating charges where any common core becomes so general or superficial that it has hardly any distinctive or guiding meaning.

It should be noted that much of the search for common principles by these authors took place in a somewhat different context and tended to be directed towards showing that the differences between common and civil law are not as great as sometimes assumed. In this book, the emphasis is primarily on legal *issues* that commonly arise in different legal systems, therefore on an inventory of problems that normally arise in more advanced economies in respect of certain commercial legal structures, such as, for example, security interest, conditional and beneficial ownership, or investment securities entitlements, rather than on common solutions, as these solutions are more likely to be dictated by the evolving needs of international commerce and finance itself than by examples in existing national laws.

Part II   The Nature, Status and Function of Private International Law

2.1 Modern Private International Law

2.1.1 The Underlying Concept of Modern Private International Law

For the reasons already explained in section 1.4.13 above, in this book, private international or conflicts law is relegated to a back seat in the hierarchy of norms of the *lex mercatoria*, although that does not make it irrelevant in areas where transnational law has not yet developed or is slow to do so. This means that in the modern *lex mercatoria* domestic law remains the residual rule and allows it in this way to operate as a full system for those who still look for this in order for private law to be fully functional. It then also allows for the continuing operation of conflict rules to find the proper domestic law but only residually.

However, even in those areas where transnational law does not yet present a clear normativity, the residual role of private international law would have to be tested for its results in international cases. Thus the application of a domestic rule and the result thereunder would still need to be evaluated in the light of business realities and the dynamics of international trade, commerce and finance. In fact, it was argued that in this manner the domestic law so applied becomes part of the transnational law merchant itself and loses its domestic status. The conclusion was that domestic law applied domestically is therefore likely to be different from it being applied in international cases.

In the last generation, a more widespread unease with the traditional methods and results of private international law or conflicts of law doctrine had already become evident.[506] It centres on the resulting applicability of (only) domestic law in international situations for which it is seldom written. For one thing, the dynamics are likely to be quite different: see also section 1.1.4 above. It nevertheless remains important to see what the traditional private international law is, what it meant to achieve, and how it operates.

The fundamental underlying concept of modern private international law remains that all legal relationships have a basis or seat (*Sitz*) in a *national* law or national legal system and are thus all domestic in nature. This was a new insight at the time but it became axiomatic; there is no longer any concept of international legal orders. This view is associated with the teachings of F von Savigny (1779–1861) in the German Historical School of the

---

[506] See for a discussion, eg FK Juenger, 'Private International Law or International Private Law?' (1994–95) 5 *King's College Law Journal* 1; FK Juenger, 'The UNIDROIT Principles of Commercial Contracts and Inter-American Contract Choice of Law' (1998) *Universidad Nacional Autonoma de Mexico—Universidad Panamericana* 229–36; FK Juenger, 'Conflict of Laws, Comparative Law and Civil Law: The Lex Mercatoria and Private International Law' (2000) 60 *Louisiana Law Review* 1133.

early nineteenth century,[507] who saw all law as national and therefore territorial, which followed from his view that law was culturally bound: see section 1.2.9 above. Within this approach, Savigny proceeded to formulate a set of (in his view) objective conflicts rules aimed at reaching *automatically* the applicable national law in cases with international aspects, therefore in cases that could conceivably be covered by more than one domestic law. Such law would then have to be applied by any court wherever, in preference to its own law (*lex fori*).

The original objective of this approach was that the application of foreign law was no longer dependent on the co-operation of or recognition by states (in terms of comity or otherwise) and could therefore be applied without bias in favour or against any of them. In this original view, the applicable law was thus considered neutral and not dependent on the outcome, but it was always domestic, and private international law had no longer any transnational substantive law element in it. Again, this new approach was an important and logical by-product of the nineteenth-century notion that all law was national per se and that there were no longer universal legal concepts, principles or rules.

In this approach, the conflict rules were originally considered simple in essence and few in number, the most important ones being the *lex rei sitae* or *lex situs* for proprietary issues, the *lex (loci) contractus* for contractual issues, and the *lex loci delicti* for tort issues. These rules were not in themselves new, as we shall see in the next section. However, used in this manner, they replaced earlier notions of: (a) *acquired* rights, which had been more interest- or fact- rather than rule-oriented; and (b) *comitas*, which had been more concerned with the extraterritoriality of local rule patterns and the validity of their application to cases with foreign elements, in which connection the *lex situs, lex contractus,* and *lex loci delicti* had served as *sub-rules* or guidelines but not as a set of hard and fast rules to determine conflicts of (domestic) laws, see also s 2.1.2 below.

The older approach left ample room for the consideration of state interests, but also for overriding notions of a more substantive uniform nature derived directly from rationality, logic or fairness and therefore from a more universal system of (often received Roman) law as prevailed on the European Continent at that time. In view of a perceived substantial subjective element in this approach, this was what von Savigny sought to eliminate, but the real problem was nationalism, especially in commercial law, coupled with the fact that domestic private law had become much more diverse after the civil law codifications. There was no longer much of a common denominator, as Roman law had once been or the natural law had provided, even though in Savigny's approach, illogically, these conflict rules themselves claimed a more universal status.[508] As we shall see, they later became pure national law too and varied therefore from state to state. The consequence was that the application of a foreign law became an issue of the domestic *lex fori* which had to authorise it.

The modern proponents of transnational substantive law (which could but, like international custom, need not be treaty law) and more recently the supporters of the modern *lex mercatoria* approach in trade and finance are more likely to insist that, in the international

---

[507] F von Savigny, *System des heutigen römischen Rechts* VIII, no 360, 108 (Berlin, 1849). See for this School, s 1.2.8 above. The term 'seat' was first used in this context in the US in the Supreme Court decision of *Pritchard v Norton*, 106 US 124, 131 (1881). It is unusual now to use this terminology but there is an important remnant in international arbitration which in the minds of many is still controlled by the *lex arbitri* as law of the *seat*. It is in fact a strange concept that stands for a political choice.

[508] See Savigny n 507 above, 27.

sphere, legal relationships are by their very nature *denationalised* and that application of a national law, even if the most proper one could be found, could be potentially distorting, if only because domestic laws were seldom made for them. On this view, a set of (often considered rough, automatic and neutral) hard and fast conflicts rules, like those just mentioned (*lex rei sitae, lex contractus, lex loci delicti* and so on) pointing to a particular domestic legal system as a whole is unlikely to deal satisfactorily with the problems arising from the international setting itself and therefore unlikely to take properly into account the particular nature of the relationship between the parties as developing in that context and to balance properly the parties' legitimate interests at that level.

In its more radical form, in this sceptical view, application of domestic private law could be seen as the truly alien and disturbing element in international transactions and the private law applicable to it. Rather, these transactions should always be governed by their own transnationalised law unless all the elements of a transaction could be attributed to one country, in which case the transaction would hardly be international any longer.[509] One may think of the sale of a piece of real estate between persons from different countries.

In any event, serious problems arose even in conflicts law of this more modern type. First, in its further development, it led to such detail and intellectual refinement in rules and sub-rules that the rationality of the whole exercise became severely stressed. Confusion, therefore uncertainty in the applicable domestic law, and lack of credibility were the result. Even more important perhaps is that private international law of this sort is unlikely to be able properly to take into account the ever-increasing legitimate interests of the parties' own states or those of any other that might be directly concerned with the transaction and have some valid governmental interest in the implementation and enforcement of their own rules to the extent that the international transaction plays out on their own territory. This as a matter of their own public policy, usually regulation and is so, for example, in the area of foreign exchange or in trade restrictions (still important in the arms trade and in the trade of forbidden substances), in environmental or in competition matters.

Such regulatory laws could even affect the validity of a contract (at least in the country of the prohibition and in its *fora*), which according to the applicable *lex contractus* (if of another country) could otherwise be perfectly valid. Whether that validity would be upheld could thus still depend on the place where the case (for example, for delivery or payment) arose or was brought. In international cases, the court of such a place could not then avoid balancing the various interests of the parties and of the governments involved, especially if they were their own, for which there was no preset rule in private international law. It would seem therefore that the older comity approach which had left courts discretion in the application of foreign laws was dispensed with too soon, or at least too radically, especially where rules had a regulatory content or public policy or public order flavour.

As far as such public interests were concerned, which could even be meant to prevent the transaction, as in the case of boycotts or tariff and foreign exchange restrictions, it was clear that in such instances—which increased dramatically through the rise of governmental intervention, even in aspects of private law—the Savigny model was hardly adequate, thus quite apart from the more fundamental sceptical view presented in this book that domestic

---

[509] See JH Dalhuisen, *Wat is vreemd recht* ['What is Foreign Law?'], Inaugural Address Utrecht (Deventer, Kluwer, 1991) 27.

private law was unlikely to be meant or to have been written for international cases, which may have a different dynamic.

There are now also public policy rules showing particular governmental concerns with the protection of certain classes of interested *private* parties, such as consumers, workers, or small investors, the effectiveness of which could not solely depend on the contacts approach of private international law either, such as the place of the contract or tort. We enter here the modern mandatory protection aspects of private law itself, for which in the case of conflicts the traditional private international law rules also had no real answer. In short, in these areas of extra private law protection too, expressed in terms of private law remedies (like prospectus liability in the placement of new securities and worker or consumer law protections), there could be a problem in the search for the most appropriate rule in the case of conflict or in the impact of modern mandatory, public law-related domestic rules of private law.

Again, the *lex contractus* could result in the application of a domestic law (for example, that of a foreign issuer of securities) which from the perspective of the law of the residence of an investor (the buyer) was wholly inadequate to protect it in terms of prospectus liability of the issuer and could create injustice for the investor. Similar problems could arise where foreign sellers sold goods to consumers in other countries that had a stricter regime of consumer protection but the law of which was unlikely to prevail on the basis of the *lex contractus* rule, which would be more likely to make the law of the seller applicable.

In the traditional conflicts of laws or private international law approach, it was thus difficult to take into account the special but nevertheless justified interests of the harmed parties as recognised by their states. In fact it was difficult in such cases to weigh the foreign element per case, as comity had once tried to do, not least to consider the different *social* or *political* setting in which the parties operated, and to honour the requirements of justice, which could be very differently perceived. It must be said that Savigny had noted these issues but had not been greatly concerned in an era of limited government intervention beyond tariffs.

On the other hand, it must also be admitted that, even whilst applying transnational law or the modern *lex mercatoria*, courts or arbitrators still have to consider these special governmental interests or social concerns as well, and must also decide on their relevance in the light of the nature and dynamics of the international transaction. This transnational law (that derives from fundamental principle, custom or general principle, in the manner discussed in section 1.4 above) whilst being applied (by the courts or in arbitrations), must thus also consider and no less take into account these special interests to the extent they may be considered justified. It has already been said that the modern *lex mercatoria* is deferential to these policy issues to the extent that conduct and effect of an international transaction play out in the territory of a particular state that is concerned. This may indeed be an issue of the international public order itself, sometimes still referred to as (international) comity. In such cases, the relevance of these policies depends on the circumstances and ultimately remains a matter of appreciation by case, in which connection the degree of conduct and/or effect of the international transaction in the territory of the relevant state plays an important role: see further the discussion in section 1.4.13 above and sections 2.2.6ff below.

Even in purely contractual interpretation, extra-legal elements of an ethical, social or efficiency nature could create similar problems when the *lex contractus* and the law of the persons most directly involved differed greatly. In the private international law approach, it was not possible to use here internationalised concepts either, so that altogether justified expectations risked being ignored. On the other hand, as we have seen, in international *professional* dealings less good faith, fewer pre-contractual disclosure duties and fewer post-contractual renegotiation duties may emerge than domestic *leges contractus* more generally dictate.

In this context, the role of *party autonomy* also needs to be clarified: see more particularly section 2.2.9 below. That is, the right to spell out the applicable legal regime or to choose a national system that appears more appropriate than the one resulting from the applicable conflict rules (or even the *lex mercatoria*, which in the view of many could now also be chosen to confirm its applicability). It is often considered a basic rule of private international law that parties may choose any other domestic law they prefer as being applicable, but such a choice is certainly not absolute in its reach.

As we shall see, this freedom generally exists *only* in matters at the *free disposition* of the parties, which are in essence those matters that raise no public interest or do not affect third parties. That excludes proprietary rights or the contractual infrastructure, such as issues of contractual validity, legality or capacity. They can hardly be determined by the parties themselves. Where a public policy matter of a particular state may be involved, such a choice may still be possible in favour of the law of the country which has the more obvious interest in the case, but even then this may not avoid the need to weigh any conflicting governmental policies or interests of this and other states to precede the acceptance of party autonomy.

When party autonomy is exerted to choose an applicable law, there is therefore always a question of how far parties by common consent can *opt out* of the laws of the legal system or policy rules otherwise more properly applicable. Consumer protection presents a good case, showing the limits. If a consumer is protected against unfair contract terms in his own country but buys products in a country that has no such rules or has other rules in this respect which might be less favourable to consumers, parties choosing the law of the latter country or of a third country might not find it to be controlling in the matter, and a more objective balancing of the policy issue may precede the application of the rule so chosen. It can only be repeated in this connection that, in the absence of such a contractual choice, the application of the traditional conflicts rule, like the *lex contractus* in the sense of the law of the place where the contract was concluded or had its centre of gravity or closest connection, might not (or no longer) decide the issue either.

Thus, whilst opting for the law of a particular state, there remains the question of how far party autonomy goes, and of how far parties may in this manner avoid the application of laws (especially of a public or semi-public regulatory or mandatory nature) normally applicable in the given territory for any conduct and effect in it of an international transactions, but less suitable to them. Tax laws may present another vivid example. Obviously, parties cannot opt out of tax laws and create their own tax regime in this manner.

On the other hand, a contractual choice of law may not mean the application of the mandatory or regulatory rules of the law so chosen either, especially if the case has no real contacts with the country of that law. Choosing the law of England to apply to a contract does not mean also adopting the UK taxation regime or the English regulatory regime if the transaction has no contact with England in terms of conduct and effect. Thus there is not only the question which law parties have opted out of, but there is also the question as to the coverage of the law parties have opted into. The public or semi-public law rules of that country are in such cases hardly likely to apply.

Assume, for example, an English and a French resident agree to sell jute on the international market and apply the law of India which (let us assume) declares the selling of jute in the international markets outside its foreign exchange controls illegal. It is a prohibition unlikely to be upheld in respect of jute already outside India and not destined for it. Another example is in the choice of English law in a contract concerning the sale of mineral water from France to Germany. Mandatory English water quality standards are unlikely to apply. The German rules in this connection will claim priority in order to protect the German mineral water-drinking public, regardless therefore of the contractual choice of law, although the choice of English law could still have a meaning in terms of conform delivery. It is a matter of interpretation which then also goes into the issue of damages.

Nor may a contractual choice of law even mean the application of the more eccentric provisions in the private law so chosen, as for example the application of the doctrine of consideration in a contract between a German and a Swiss made subject to English law.[510] As has been mentioned before, it could be seen as a structural or mandatory rule not applying to contracts not having any contact with England at all. Perhaps in that context parties could opt for English law, yet exclude at the same time its consideration doctrine. Should they not have done so (and it is most uncommon), the doctrine may still not be upheld in respect of them as they may not be deemed to have contemplated its application if leading to the non-existence of an agreement they clearly wanted. English lawyers asked to advise generally on the contract under English law may not flag the problem because they will not understand where the Continental lawyers come from. Here a comparative law background in several legal systems becomes urgent for counsel.

These are important issues already briefly discussed above in section 1.5.6 and more fully to be covered in sections 2.2.6 to 2.2.8.below, whilst the concept of party autonomy in matters of choice of law will be revisited in section 2.2.9 below.

2.1.2 Earlier Approaches

The earlier comity approach referred to in the previous section which von Savigny sought to replace had resulted from Dutch seventeenth-century scholarship (Huber and Voet) and prevailed until the nineteenth century as a refinement of the even earlier *statutist* approach.

To prevent local court always applying their *lex fori*, the statutist approach developed in the Middle Ages, first between the city states in Northern Italy. It became relevant where Roman law or natural law did not apply as universal standard but purely local (commercial) laws developed. The statutist approach was mainly concerned with the sphere of

---

[510] In this connection, it may also be relevant that the Vienna Convention on the International Sale of Goods abandoned the consideration doctrine. So did the European and UNIDROIT Contract Principles and the DCFR. Indeed, it may well be the demonstration of a general principle in modern transnational contract law that has done away with the doctrine in international cases. It is a vivid expression of domestic law being applied differently in domestic and international situations, see further in particular JH Dalhuisen, 'What could the Selection by Parties of English Law in a Civil Law Contract in Commerce and Finance Truly Mean?' in M Andenas and D Fairgrieve (eds), *Tom Bingham and the Transformation of the Law* (2009) 619.

application of these special laws or complexes of rules meant to govern certain situations or relationships only: hence the personal statute for the law concerning the person and its capacity and the property statute concerning real property and its status and so on. In such cases, under the personal statute, for example, a person would take his own personal laws with him wherever he went. The applicable property law on the other hand would be that of the place where the assets could be found.

The personal statute determined in particular the legal and marital status of persons, where as a consequence *extraterritoriality* came in. Real estate, on the other hand, would be governed solely by the law of its location as the property statute, which was therefore not personal (or extraterritorial) but remained purely territorial. Contract was governed by the law of the place of its formation, and not as such considered extraterritorial either, even if parties came from different countries and moved about, and so on.

It sounds simple but it required a distinction to be made in each case between *personal or extra-territorial* and *territorial* statutes, which did not always prove easy, for example, where the law concerning movable property was concerned when it was transferred abroad. The trend was nevertheless in the direction of ever greater territoriality, exercised in state courts always with a prevalence of the *lex fori* covering everything that happened in the territory of the court. Foreign law was thus little considered except in personal matters concerning foreigners.

In order to avoid the constraints of this model, *acquired rights* and *comitas* notions later concentrated on the recognition of the ensuing rights elsewhere, but, as we have already seen in the previous section, they introduced here a substantial *discretionary* element as to the applicable law (as no state was considered to be bound by the laws of any other state) and were *fact-* or *issue-oriented*. Under it, in an international sale and transfer of goods, rights acquired in a movable asset created at its place of origin could thus be recognised at the place of destination, at least to the extent there was some kind of equivalent in that place. Another way was to recognise the foreign law as a matter of comity in which notions of *lex situs* and *lex contractus* or *lex locus delicti* were used as subrules. It followed, however, that there was no automaticity in the application (or refusal) of foreign law (except for the personal statute). This was very much the seventeenth-century approach as developed in the Netherlands by Voet and Huber, largely followed by Story in the US as late as the nineteenth century. Transnational law or the *lex mercatoria* of those days and the exigencies of international commerce themselves were then often invoked to resolve the conflicts and to reduce the discretionary element.

All the same, it resulted in a lack of certainty. That was meant to be cured in the new approach advocated by von Savigny. Although it still used statutist and *comity* language in referring to the *lex rei sitae*, *lex contractus*, *lex locus delicti*, and later to the *lex societatis* in company law matters, the issue was no longer the question of personal or territorial statutes or the determination of the extraterritorial effect of certain laws (or acquired rights thereunder) depending on the situation, but rather the automatic application of a domestic law with reference to the *seat* of each legal relationship, which was on all occasions to be found in a particular country. The new approach was thus more rational but also fundamentally *nationalistic*. To identify objectively the relevant country (of the seat of the legal relationship) became its objective. So the perspective moved from the nature of the laws to the nature of connection between a transaction or other legal relationship and a country, later widened to a contacts' approach.

2.1.3 Drawbacks of the Modern Conflicts Rules

As we have seen, the approach of von Savigny, especially as later elaborated by his student Ludwig von Bar,[511] nationalised all international legal relationships (of private law) with reference to their seat in a certain jurisdiction. As such, it was a typical product of nineteenth-century nationalistic thinking in the German Historical School and supplemented the codification approach, although it was at first balanced by a liberal market sentiment and the free movement of (most) goods, services and money, so that at least the disturbing factor of governmental interest derived from regulation or trade and currency policies was not so likely to arise (except in tariffs). Thus the presumed neutrality of the new conflict rules could be fairly convincingly sustained.

In the absence of much other mandatory (or regulatory) law at the time, it also left ample room for the parties to determine their own legal regime, supplemented by any national law of their choice, although there were always problems with the law of property, which, whilst affecting third parties, could not be truly chosen by the parties. Here the *lex situs* dominated, although it created problems of its own with intangible assets and assets meant to move internationally like ships and aircraft as there was hardly a clear *situs* in respect of them.

As already mentioned, the principal aim of the new method was to produce some *objective* clear-cut conflict rules from which the applicable law would automatically follow, regardless of any outside interests in the outcome, notably of states. For this purpose, legal relationships were primarily understood in terms of their underlying legal *characterisation* as proprietary, contractual, delictual, corporate or procedural. Importantly, like the basic rules themselves, these characterisations were also perceived as *essentially universal*, intrinsically unchangeable and, even in the Historical School, probably independent of a state.

The rules applicable to these legal relationships could obviously still vary, depending on the expression of them in local law, especially in the details. This gave rise to the conflicts in the first place, but that was originally not thought a great problem as the differences were in essence expected to be in the detail only, not in the essential structures, and therefore relatively few.

The new approach was therefore intended for a situation in which the international flows were limited and the perceived conflicts were considered fairly *insubstantial*. The conflict rules and the adjustments they required to the application of the *lex fori* were thus believed to be *incidental* and minor. Indeed, the conflict rules developed in this approach were few, the most important of which have already been mentioned: the *lex rei sitae or lex situs* for property issues; the *lex locus delicti commissi* for tort issues; the *lex locus contractus* for contract issues; the *lex societatis* for company issues; the *lex fori* or *locus actus* for procedural issues. As such the new approach was a *rule-* rather than an interest or fact-oriented method of conflict resolution.

Yet this new approach soon proved naïve and started to face a number of more fundamental problems. First, the notion of the seat of legal relationships proved too narrow and could be difficult to pin down. So even in the Savignian approach, the notion of the *seat* of the legal relationship in a structural sense eventually shifted to the notion of the

---

[511] L von Bar, *Das internationale Privat-und Strafrecht* (Hannover, 1862).

centre of gravity of the legal relationship in a non-structural sense,[512] whilst the automatic link between the applicable law and this presumed centre became the *closest connection*. However, all three (centre of gravity, relevant legal relationship and closest connection) were *poly-interpretable* and subject to an appreciation by case resulting de facto in a measure of *discretion* for the courts, thus also in renewed uncertainty.

Another problem was that in practice, the basic structures themselves could not always be so easily defined in terms of, for example, property, contract, tort, restitution, company or procedure. Characterisation problems thus moved to the centre. In tripartite relationships with contractual and proprietary aspects, like agency and trusts, but also in documents of title and negotiable instruments with their element of abstraction and independence and the own rights and obligations of the holders, there was often no obvious and certainly no single conflict rule that could point to a solution in a domestic law. So it was for letters of credit or in assignments of monetary and other claims (see for assignments Volume II, chapter 2, section 1.9.2). Through so-called *dépeçage*, different conflicts rules had then to be devised for different aspects of a transaction.

Indeed, a complicated conflict of law structure is now often invoked in these instances, even in Hague treaties, which seek uniformity in conflict rules between ratifying states through treaty law, like in agency and trust, see also section 1.4.18 above, in practice often subjected to further (public policy) corrections of the end result by the forum, which are then often explained as yet other facets of conflict rules. The result thus proved often not transparent or predictable, although the true problem always was that the private international law or conflicts of laws approach did not take the underlying objective or logic and dynamics of the particular legal structure in its international context into account and refused to make them ultimately decisive.

There was also the poly-interpretable aspect of the basic notions. Thus the principle of the *lex contractus* had left open the important question whether it was the law of the place where the contract was *concluded* (in any event problematic when parties came from different countries) or where it had to be *performed*. The reference to the *lex locus delicti commissi* left open the question whether the applicable law was the law of the place where the wrongful act was *committed* or where it had its *effects*. Under it, both French and Dutch law could be applicable in the case of the pollution of the river Rhine in France, causing serious damage downstream to horticulture in the Netherlands.

The *lex societatis*, which later became the basic conflicts rule concerning company law, could mean the law of the country of *incorporation* (*siège social*), generally the view in common law countries, Switzerland and the Netherlands, or the law of the country of the *main activity* of the company (*siège reel*), generally the German and French approach. As for the *lex situs* rule, in proprietary matters concerning movables, it was likely to resolve nothing, as problems arose mainly when, in an international sale, these assets had to move across borders, leaving a choice between the law of the country of *origin* and of *destination* in respect of the transfer of title; both could lead to impractical results.

In proprietary matters, when assets moved between countries, the answer could much sooner be in the reasonable acceptance of the proprietary rights acquired at the original *situs*, subject to a measure of adjustment to the equivalent interests (if any) in the country of destination to fit these rights into the latter's proprietary and, in the case of security

---

[512] H Batiffol, *Les conflits de lois en matière de contrats* (1938) 3.

interests, priority regime (see more particularly Volume II, chapter 2, section 1.8). But this merely re-introduced a variation on the old *acquired rights* theme and allowed an unavoidable measure of discretion, which was precisely what the conflicts system, built upon von Savigny's ideas, had sought to avoid, as we have seen.

In other areas of property law, it was even less clear how any one *national* law could deal with the differing complications that derived from the international setting of the case itself, such as in bulk transfers of assets located in different countries, when it was unlikely that one domestic legal system could satisfactorily cover this legal structure even in a contractual sense, unless one assumed that all assets were always located at the place of the owner. The protection of debtors in various countries under bulk assignments equally did not appear to be capable of a solution by application of one single domestic rule (except for each debtor their own).

Subsequently, and equally importantly, the environment in which these conflict rules were meant to operate changed dramatically in the twentieth century as a result of much greater governmental intervention in private law, see sections 1.5.7 and 2.1.1 above. As noted therein, this highlighted the difficulty of using the new conflicts approach to contend with a rapidly increasing number of different mandatory national policy rules particularly those protecting weaker parties (for example, workers), but also those protecting consumers and smaller investors providing services or buying products or investments in other countries. As also already mentioned, Savigny had noted this problem and allowed exceptions on the basis of public policy but thought that the problems would diminish over time. The opposite proved to be the case.

To repeat, in these cases, a *discretionary* element (instead of an automatic conflicts rule) must of necessity be maintained when mandatory rules are invoked before the courts of other countries, as recognised in Article 9 of the 2008 EU Regulation on the Law Applicable to Contractual Obligation (Rome I). The notion of directly applicable unilateral public policy rules in respect of all that takes place in the territory of a state or *règles d'application immédiate* in French or *Eingriffsnormen* in German,[513] is an area of the law covered in the US by section 6 of the Restatement (Second) Conflict of Laws (1971) for interstate conflicts and by sections 402 and 403 of the Restatement (Third) Foreign Relations Law (1986) for international conflicts (see more particularly sections 2.2.6 and 2.2.8 below).

Again, this is reminiscent of the old *comity approach* (here limited, however, to rules with a clear public interest element to them), the approach which von Savigny had so carefully sought to avoid. As we shall see in section 2.2.2 below, much of the American conflicts revolution has revolved around it, and can indeed be seen as a retreat into the older approach, but also as a basis for internationalisation of the conflicts of law rules through the formulation of substantive transnational rules (from which in trade and commerce the modern *lex mercatoria* is then an important progression). Thus for governmental interests *balancing guidelines* and *comity* rules re-emerge. They may be relevant also in the more traditional approach in the area of statutory penalties and statutes of limitations, which

---

[513] In Europe, the direct application of mandatory rules (without reference to conflicts rules), especially those with a social or public policy objective, was noted in modern times, primarily by Ph Francescakis, 'Quelques précisions sur les lois d'application immédiate et leurs rapports avec les règles de conflits de lois' (1966) *Rev Critique de Droit International Privé* 17. Earlier, Pillet, *Principes de droit international privé* (1903) 265, had distinguished between laws protecting private and social interests; the former protect the individual against the state, the latter the state against the individual. He considered these respectively extraterritorial and territorial in nature.

also have some clear public order overtones, in the case of conflict not satisfactorily to be resolved through mere conflict rules either.

In any event, even in the approach of von Savigny, the end result under the application of the standard conflict rules (such as the *lex situs*, *lex contractus* and so on) was always considered on its suitability and, if necessary, corrected on so-called *public order* grounds. This was especially important where different ethical and social standards prevailed. The discretionary element was thus never entirely lost with the consequence that less progress was made through modern conflict rules than at first expected.

So we see that: (a) at least in movable property matters, the old acquired rights theory was revived; while (b) in public policy connected issues the old comity approach survived; and (c) domestic public order was always allowed to function as a correction of the result of any conflicts of law rules on the basis of local values. Whatever the objectives of the new approach, from the beginning the new conflicts rules thus proved less clear-cut and less automatic than was suggested on their face.

Where terms became poly-interpretable, where characterisation issues arose, or where discretion resurfaced, the unavoidable result was that the selection of the country assuming jurisdiction to resolve the issue began to make a difference also. This raised the important matter of *adjudicatory* jurisdiction where, at least in the English version, a measure of *discretion* also lurked, including *forum (non) conveniens* notions.

A further complicating factor was that the resulting conflict rules were increasingly viewed as rules of *domestic* law, notwithstanding the fact that von Savigny had considered them universal. Again this made forum shopping an important issue. As such, these conflict rules frequently failed to cover common ground and could in fact differ greatly, as became evident especially in areas where the method itself proved less clear, as in the definition of the closest relationship or connection. This presented a particular problem in international arbitrations where there is no natural *lex fori* and therefore also no naturally applicable set of conflict rules, and raised the question whether there were at least some common principles or standards of conflicts of law resolution to preserve the pretence of certainty, objectivity and unity of the system.

An obvious need to develop common conflicts rules consequently arose. However, even the development and formulation of these common rules, since 1893 promoted by the Hague Conference (see also section 1.4.18 above), although also in bilateral or (more recently) EU contexts, remained marred by differences in view. The criteria used or proposed were often uncertain. Thus the Benelux Convention on Private International Law of 1951 (never ratified, and withdrawn in 1976) referred, in relation to sales, to the law of the country with the 'closest connection'. The Hague Convention of 1955 on the Law governing the International Sale of Goods (not to be confused with the Hague Conventions concerning the Uniform Laws on the International Sale of Goods of 1964) referred to the law of the residence of the seller as the basic conflict rule in sales. The EU 1980 (Rome) Convention on the Law Applicable to Contractual Obligations returned to the notion of the 'closest connection', but presumed this to be the place of the residence of the party that must effect the most characteristic performance (Article 4(2)). It left substantial flexibility in the interpretation of this term with the additional facility to ignore the resulting law if it proved inappropriate (Article 4(5)).

This is followed in the succeeding EU Regulation of 2008, which, however, uses a list approach first (Article 4(1)) as a consequence of which the law of the residence of the party that must perform the most characteristic obligation became the residual rule

(Article 4(2)), even though the list itself does not normally point in a different direction. In any event, under Article 4(3), a different law may still result if the contract is manifestly more closely connected with another country. In the meantime, Article 8 of the Hague Conference text of 1986, superseding the one of 1955, also uses the notion of the most characteristic performance for international sales. It leads mostly to the applicability of the law of the residence of the seller, but with a number of specific exceptions in favour of the law of the residence of the buyer.

It should perhaps also be noted that, notwithstanding von Savigny's emphasis on the independent nature of each legal relationship and regardless of some modern day relaxation, private international law still tends to use the legal relationship principally in terms of classification or qualification (as proprietary, contractual and tortuous and even then it may run into serious problems),[514] therefore as *formal* structures and *not* in terms of the *specific needs and interests* to be protected (including governmental interests) and the special requirements and dynamics of the situation. Lesser responsiveness to practical needs and objectives is therefore implied in this approach.

That also concerns the *social* aspects of a case, which may require a more incidental solution. This was already mentioned in section 2.2.1 above, but may need some further elucidation. Locally, the solution is often provided, at least in contractual matters, by the application of good faith notions, or through common sense and established practices in the commercial sphere. In an international professional context, however, these practical considerations and social needs may acquire an independent meaning which local laws can hardly discount. They may have a substantive law impact with which private international law cannot always adequately deal. For example, in international professional dealings, there may be much less need for good faith adjustments than local laws may assume, but it is not clear how choice of law rules aimed at finding the appropriate local law can deal with such an independent international requirement.

Some of this is acknowledged, and modern developments in Europe have led to some considerable amendment of the traditional conflicts approach. As we shall see, the changes have been even more fundamental in the US. For example, the newer European approach allows consumers and workers the protection of their own law as a matter of non-choice (of law), compare Articles 5 and 6 of the EU Rome Convention 1980 on the Law Applicable to Contractual Obligations, now Articles 6 and 8 of the EU Regulation of 2008 (see also section 2.2.1 below), and gives maintenance creditors the benefit of the best rule for them, compare Articles 5 and 6 of the Hague Convention on Maintenance Obligations (see also section 2.2.1 below).

However, more universal substantive principles of fairness and reasonableness are increasingly applied *directly* and the need for a sensible outcome is increasingly acknowledged. This is particularly so in the USA in interstate conflicts, see more particularly section 2.2.2 below. It may lead to new and uniform *substantive rules* at the international level, which therefore apply before the more traditional choice of law rules. The substantive law approach through uniform treaty law may be seen as another consequence of this insight,

---

[514] Eg, when determining whether particular aspects of a case are contractual, tortious, or proprietary—as in the formalities and validity of bulk assignments, including transborder receivables. See for the difficulties in this respect under Art 13 of the EU Regulation of 2008 (Rome I), vol II, ch 2, s 1.9.3 and vol III, ch 1, s 2.4.5.

even if the result may still be only partial coverage and even then be unsatisfactory (see more particularly section 1.4.10 above).

It is the position of this book that in the end in international trade, commerce and finance, the *lex mercatoria* approach provides the more satisfactory alternative. It is particularly inspired by the freeing of the commercial flows or globalisation of the markets in the professional sphere and the independent legal order there created. Under it, the traditional conflict rules play only a residual role (see sections 1.4.12 and 2.1.1 above and section 3.2.5 below). What happens here is that the number of *substantive rules* have ballooned before conflicts' rules become necessary, thus reducing them to a lesser place, although in areas where transnational law is not yet developing, they may still have a substantial impact assuming that the result makes sense in terms of the needs and dynamics of international commerce and finance.

Within the *lex mercatoria* approach, fundamental principle, custom, general or common rules thus take precedence over private international law or conflict of laws rules in the hierarchy of norms which allows different sources of law to operate side by side. This approach of 'conflict removal' was early on identified as unavoidable, even by conflict specialists, and is the essence of the modern development in conflicts resolution, at least in the law of property and obligations.[515] It still requires, however, a view on the treatment of governmental interests, a matter more broadly discussed in section 2.2.6 below.

2.2 The Modern European and US Approaches to Conflicts of Law

2.2.1 Refinement of the European Model

As we have seen, private international law or conflicts law as it developed in the nineteenth century tended to be rule-, not fact- or interest- or protection-oriented, and automatically assumed the appropriateness of the application of a national law to international transactions and a satisfactory outcome to the international dispute under the domestic law whose applicability was derived in this manner from the application of its conflict principles. However, further refinement proved necessary and even in the traditional European mould, there is now everywhere an increasing search for a more refined private international law approach allowing for:

(a) separation of the various aspects of a legal relationship (*dépeçage*) so that for different aspects different domestic laws may be appointed: see Article 3 of the EU Regulation of 2008 on the Law Applicable to Contractual Obligations (Rome I);

(b) reliance on concepts such as the centre of gravity, closest connection and most characteristic obligation with the flexibility they provide, compare Article 4 of the EU Regulation;

---

[515] *Cf* KH Nadelmann, 'Marginal Remarks on the New Trends in American Conflicts Law' (1963) 28 *Law and Contemporary Problems* 860; and G Kegel, 'The Crisis of Conflict of Laws' (1964) 112 *Recueil des Cours* 260.

(c)   open or exception clauses allowing for the application of a different (domestic) law altogether if another law in the circumstances as a whole is manifestly more closely connected, Article 4(3) of the EU Regulation;

(d)   more substantive rules, especially in the area of the protection of consumers and workers, see Articles 6 and 8 of the EU Regulation, often allowing them the protection of their own law, even though still fashioned as a conflicts' rule,[516] whilst sometimes the most favourable rule may apply as in the case of maintenance creditors under the Hague Convention on Maintenance Obligations;

(e)   adjustments of the results, for example, in the case of the recognition of foreign proprietary rights and security interests in assets that move to other countries or figure in a bankruptcy elsewhere;

(f)   abandonment of conflict rules altogether and the (discretionary) acceptance of (a degree of) extraterritoriality in the case of foreign public policy and similar mandatory rules (or *règles d'application immédiate*), see Article 9 of the EU Regulation; and finally

(g)   the result obtained under the conflicts rule generally being tested on its appropriateness; compare Article 8 of the previous 1992 Dutch draft of the Introductory Statute Law concerning Private International Law amended in 2002, discussed in section 2.2.4 below, allowing for adjustment within or even outside the concept of public order (or local values); and

(h)   the possibility of the choice of a non-statist law, such as in commerce and finance the modern *lex mercatoria*, see the Preamble (13) of the EU Regulation.

The end result has been a substantial (further) refinement of the method of von Savigny and his successors. Even if the system remains based on a number of hard and fast rules, they are more flexible. Yet in essence, the idea of the applicability of (an appropriate) *domestic* law to *international* dealings is fundamentally maintained.

It marks nevertheless the increased unease with the traditional conflicts notions, even in Europe, although not necessarily the acceptance of transnational law, even for the international professional sphere. Many still see the law, even commercial law, as anchored in sovereignty rather than in social and economic realities. In such an atmosphere, even transnational notions of good faith cannot develop in international contracts. Social policies and values also remain nationalistic. Another consequence of this approach is that it remains in essence rule-based rather than interest- or fact-oriented. Even though (surprisingly) also greatly popular in England, it shows its nature as corollary to the civil law codification approach.

2.2.2 Developments in the USA

In the USA, since the 1930s, unease with the nineteenth-century conflict rules led to a substantially different approach, at least to interstate conflicts. This example later also tended

---

[516] See also CGJ Morse, 'Consumer Contracts, Employment Contracts and the Rome Convention' (1992) 41 *ICLQ* 1, and TM de Boer, 'The EEC Contracts Convention and the Dutch Courts, A Methodological Perspective' (1990) 54 *RabelsZ* 24.

to liberate the European attitude to some extent, as was shown in the previous section, but the flexibility it brought remained more limited in Europe. The new European attitude remains basically cast along the lines of the propositions enumerated in the previous section, which were substantially embodied in the 1980 EU Rome Convention, succeeded by the 2008 EU Regulation on the Law Applicable to Contractual Obligations.

In the US, conflicts law has lost its hard and fast, rule-oriented character altogether and has become no more than an aid to what is believed to achieve a more rational and acceptable result. That does not strictly speaking require the application of a particular state law. It could be an adaptation or mixture or rather an application of a more fundamental legal or rational principle. It could even suggest an adaptation of local rules (*lex fori*) to the nature of transborder transactions, the result of which could in fact be the application of a transnational rather than a national rule as a matter of expansive interpretation of the *lex fori* in international cases.

It is important in this connection to appreciate that the earlier developments in the USA towards flexibility took place against a somewhat different background, to wit in interstate rather than in international cases. It should be understood that other influences were here at work. First, in the USA interstate, the area for conflicts of law is reduced through the existence of the common law, which, with the exception of Louisiana and some nineteenth-century Spanish influence via Mexico in the southern and western states, essentially led to a fairly homogeneous system of civil and commercial law throughout the USA. Although the common law is unavoidably fractured by state intervention through statutory, policy-oriented laws, for example in the area of product liability, this diversion may in modern times in other areas be counterbalanced, particularly in commerce by the UCC.

Yet some divergence remains unavoidable, particularly because of the mandatory, protection- or own interest-inspired policy enactments (leading to specific governmental or regulatory interests) of the various states. States may thus have differing and outspoken policies on insurance protections, on liability for passengers (guest statutes), in product liability and in environmental matters. On the other hand, much policy is exerted at the federal level so that policy issues are more likely to figure as an issue in *international* conflict cases than in interstate conflict cases, as for example, in competition matters, boycotts, embargoes and so on.

Secondly, in the common law tradition, *no* sharp distinction is made between the public and private law aspects of such intervention. Putting the emphasis on government intervention itself or more generally on policy (whether in public or private law), this tends to reduce the area for true private conflicts of law even further. They are often ignored, unless they can be reduced to *a mere difference in policy*. In this manner, in the US in interstate conflicts, *all* conflicts of law enter the ambit of what in Europe are called the *règles d'application immédiate* (see section 2.2.1(f) above), where for governmental action or mandatory laws a form of *comity* or judicial discretion also continues to rule in civil law countries. All is (considered) policy.

It is less surprising if one realises that in the nineteenth century, Story had maintained the Dutch comity approach to all private law conflicts in the US. This tended to result in an interest-oriented approach across the board, even in the more traditional areas of private conflicts of law, as in contract, tort and property. The American approach thus remained more comfortable with judicial discretion all round, highlighted at the same time the importance of (adjudicatory) jurisdiction (rules) and ultimately put particular emphasis on the *lex fori* and its interpretation techniques in accommodating foreign (sister state) interests, both of a public *and* private nature, which, as just mentioned, are in common law in any event not so clearly distinguished, whilst the effect and impact of the latter are much reduced through the operation of the common law in most states and of uniform law as we saw.

Section 6 of the *Restatement (Second) Conflict of Laws* (1971) reflects this attitude and introduces a flexible conflicts rule which explicitly rejects any rigidity or automaticity. It allows a court to apply its own *mandatory* rules on choice of law in the absence of which a number of factors are provided for consideration. They centre on the needs of the inter-state system, the relevant policies of the forum, the relevant policies and interests of other states in the determination of the issue, the basic policies underlying the particular field of law, the certainty, predictability and uniformity of the result, and the ease in the determina-tion of the law to be applied.

Again, it should be kept in mind that in the USA, this approach to interstate conflicts is often distinguished from the approach to international conflicts and the domestic attitude may not automatically be extended to the latter field, although it is unavoidable that the approach to international conflicts is becoming similar.[517]

In interstate conflicts, the accent is in fact primarily on a satisfactory solution with regard to the interests to be protected in the particular case in the light of all rules poten-tially applicable in order to achieve the application of 'the better law'.[518] Again it may mean a more *direct* and *substantive law* approach. One of the early leaders of this new movement (regardless of its many variants), Professor Brainerd Currie from Chicago,[519] who adopted an interest analysis, saw in it essentially a return to the true method of the common law and a denial of the Continental European approach of von Savigny (although this German approach acquired and still has particularly deep roots in England). In more modern ter-minology, it may perhaps be said that facts and needs rather than rules dominate. That is indeed the common law inheritance.

The idea of clear conflicts rules as essential conduits to reach a *domestic* law is here abandoned. In interstate conflicts in the USA, the applicable law may be reached by other means, either through a re-interpretation of the *lex fori* in the light of the foreign elements of the case or more directly through reliance on general principles, especially of due process and fairness under the relevant provisions of the US Constitution. It is thus possible to weigh the various opposing interests independently of any particular conflicts law or even domestic law. The search for objective, rule-oriented elements of conflict laws, so prevalent in the traditional European conflicts approach, is here abandoned.[520]

Even though the Americans often continue to use private international law terminology, compare for example the reference to *the most significant relationship*, both in section 188 of the *Restatement (Second) Conflict of Laws* for *contracts* and in section 145 for *torts* (both subject to the already-mentioned section 6, however), they appear to gravitate ultimately to directly applied *substantive* principles of *reasonableness* and *fairness*. Domestic laws are mere guidance. In this connection, the constitutional due process and full faith and credit

---

[517] See AA Ehrenzweig, *Private International Law, A Comparative Treatise on American International Conflicts Law, including the Law of Admiralty, General Part*, (Leyden, 1974).

[518] A term particularly used by R Leflar, *American Conflicts of Law* (1977) 205.

[519] B Currie, 'The Verdict of Quiescent Years' in *Selected Essays on the Conflict of Laws* (1963) 627.

[520] See for an up-to-date case book DP Currie, HH Kay, L Kramer and K Roosevelt, *Conflict of Laws, Cases-Comments-Questions*, 7th edn (2006). It sets the tone in the Preface: 'Law comes from many sources. In an ideal world, the authority of these sources would be clearly defined and neatly demarcated ... but such is not our world.'

clauses, as just mentioned, may provide a more specific base for these higher principles in certain cases. Under them, the arbitrary application of own state law and the automatic rejection of the law of other states is unacceptable but a system of pure conflicts rules is discouraged at the same time.   .

This attitude is further buttressed by the important facility to litigate in the federal courts in disputes where there is a diversity of citizenship (and a certain minimum amount at stake), even if state law remains in principle applicable. To the extent conflicts of law arise in bankruptcy cases, these are also handled in federal courts under the federal Bankruptcy Code.

European criticism of the American approach centres on the high level of judicial discretion allowed and the supposed lack of predictability in that approach. It is also considered too dependent on the forum and its own laws, in turn leading to considerable dependence on the rules of (adjudicatory) jurisdiction.[521] The lack of rules is clearly felt. This is somewhat strange in countries which now often use a very flexible good faith approach, also in interpretational matters. Nevertheless, in practice, there is l approximation between the European and American approaches, of which, as was shown, in Europe the earlier EU Rome Convention and now the EU Regulation are the clearest examples and of which Article 8 of the previous Dutch proposals for a new private international law statute (to complete its new 1992 codification) were the culmination, allowing the applicable law derived from the conflicts rules to be set aside if the result was inappropriate, unreasonable or unfair (see section 2.2.4 below).

There is in any event no doubt that the European conflicts approach—as indeed the general approaches under national laws, especially where imbued with the good faith ethos—is becoming gradually more sensitive to the nature of the parties' relationship, the interests to be protected and the nature and objectives of their deal in its (international) context, to the application of general principles of fairness, market and business requirements and practices, and of directly applicable substantive rules either of a mandatory or protection nature, although in this context use is often still made of pseudo-conflict language, allowing the fairest or most favourable domestic rule to prevail. Given this gradual change in attitude, however, one may also expect a greater receptiveness to substantive transnational rules, therefore in commerce and finance to the modern *lex mercatoria* for professional cross border dealings.

2.2.3 The Various Modern US Conflict Theories

As we have seen in the previous section, in US interstate conflicts the accent has been increasingly on the evaluation, acceptance or rejection of so-called *governmental interests or policies*, understandable because most differences in the applicable law derive in the USA from

---

[521] See notably G Kegel, 'The Crisis of Conflict of Laws' 112 *Recueil des Cours* 95 (Hague Lectures, 1966), and 'Paternal Home and Dream Home: Traditional Conflict of Laws and the American Reformers', (1979) 27 *American Journal of Comparative Law* 615; R De Nova, 'Historical and Comparative Introduction to Conflict of Laws' 118 *Recueil des Cours* 443 (Hague Lectures, 1966); P Lalive, 'Tendances et méthodes en droit international privé' 155 *Recueil des Cours* 1 (Hague Lectures, 1977); E Vitta, 'Cours general de droit international privé' 162 *Recueil des Cours* 9 (Hague Lectures, 1979).

the legislative governmental intervention of the various states with clear policy objectives. This approach leads on its own to a predominance of the *lex fori* if the forum state has a particular interest in the application of its law in respect of everything that happens on its territory. If not, the law of the other interested state is applied and if there are more states with an interest, the court may revert to its own law or apply the, in its view, superior law. Whether or not this leads to a balancing of these interests proper is contested. It would seem unavoidable but courts have sometimes been thought to be ill-suited for it.

This at least was the view of Professor Brainerd Currie of Chicago, who started the new thinking, in which courts were never to apply another law but their own, except where there was a good reason for doing so under the rules just mentioned.[522] This rigidity is not generally followed,[523] but there is here a strong element of a *lex fori* (or *homeward trend*), which returned in the USA in all the newer theories, most generally so in that of Professor Albert A Ehrenzweig of the University of California at Berkeley,[524] unless there were settled rules of choice that had worked satisfactorily, like the application of the *lex situs* in the proprietary aspects of physical assets that do not move.

As already noted in the previous section, in this *lex fori* approach, the accent is not merely on governmental interests (and certainly not on the prevalence of rules), but the application of the *lex fori* in this sense becomes principally a matter of *interpretation* of the forum's laws, including its private laws, aiming at the accommodation of *all* foreign elements of each case within it. In this *lex fori* approach, the attention naturally shifts to the proper forum applying the proper (own) law of the forum, as may be adjusted (*lex propria in foro proprio*), with the resulting emphasis on proper jurisdiction rules based on substantial contacts, which itself also suggest a discretionary element or at least some flexibility. Conflicts of law in the traditional sense do not arise here. *All* foreign rules (even of private law) then operate like *règles d'application immédiate* in a European sense, in their application subject to the evaluation of their relevance by the forum as an expression of its own social policy.[525] In this way, we seem to be back entirely in the comity approach, although with a more conscious effort to develop some rules (see also section 2.2.6 below). On this view, there is, however, only one applicable law possible, which is the law found in this manner and tailored to the case. It is strongly fact-oriented.

---

[522] See B Currie, 'A Critique of the Choice of Law Problem', (1933) 47 *Harvard Law Review* 173 and also his *Selected Essays*, n 519 above, 119, 621. A governmental interest is here defined as a governmental policy and the concurrent existence of an appropriate relationship between the state having the policy and the transaction, the parties, or the litigation.

[523] Besides aversion to balancing and the consequential preference for the *lex fori* in the case of conflict, there are two other important aspects to the interest analysis in the manner of Prof Currie. It is in this approach first necessary to determine the governmental interests as it may appear from numerous statutory texts and case law. This requires *purposive* interpretation and may introduce a considerable degree of uncertainty whilst the attribution of a purpose may become fictitious or unrealistic and may also lead to a special protection of forum residents, see eg L Brilmayer, 'Interest Analysis and the Myth of Legislative Intent' (1980) 78 *Michigan Law Review* 392. In the process, other than state interests may easily be ignored. Closely related is the question whether there is a *true* or *false* conflict. The latter arises foremost when both 'conflicting' laws would yield the same result; see on this issue D Cavers, *The Choice of Law Process* (1965) 89.

[524] AA Ehrenzweig, 'The lex fori—Basic Rule of the Conflicts of Laws' (1960) 58 *Michigan Law Review* 637. The local law theory can be traced to Judge Learned Hand in *Guinness v Miller*, 291 Fed 768 (SDNY 1923) and to WW Cook, 'The logical and legal Basis of the Conflict of Laws' (1924) 33 *Yale Law Journal* 457. Here the idea is that instead of foreign vested rights, there are only rights created in the forum state even though often in the form of recognition of foreign rights which then may be adjusted.

[525] See Ehrenzweig, n 517 above, 92ff.

In contract, it results in the application of the law that best supports its true meaning given the situation in which it is to operate, but it could still mean respect for performance and foreign exchange or investment restrictions in the country where the performance should take place, especially if that is the country of the forum, assuming the contract still made sense. If not, it could be at an end. In the case of a tort, it could mean respect for foreign limitations on liability, but the *lex fori*'s own views on a reasonable protection of victims and equitable distribution of unavoidable loss in the circumstances would ultimately prevail.

Under the influence of Professor Willis Reese of Columbia University, the *Restatement (Second) Conflict of Laws* (1971) adheres more to the 'centre of gravity' approach.[526] Earlier, Professor David Cavers of Harvard had proposed a method with outright emphasis on the most satisfactory result through the interpretation of rules and policies,[527] but he still allowed some principles of preference to develop and be taken into account, notably protecting weaker parties and party autonomy in contract.[528] The theory of Professor Leflar (Choice-influencing Considerations or Factors) came close to an elaboration of this approach, although seemingly more receptive to foreign interests.[529] His choice of influencing factors were predictability of result, maintenance of the interstat international order, simplification of the judicial task, advancement of the (own) st .nmental interests, and the application of the better rule of law requiring court. .ake some more objective evaluation. Von Mehren and Trautman in their 'fi .pproach'[530] finally sought a balance or accommodation between the domesti . and those individual and state interests which became relevant in multi-state .. If such an accommodation failed, promotion of interstate activity, the parti .or judicial economy and simplicity was to prevail.[531]

One could criticise all these th. .i indeed no less the traditional approach of von Savigny to the conflicts of laws, o. .ie basis that they do not define any clear objective, except that in the American approach the forum's support of the own system and especially policy, whatever their merit, is often unashamedly clear, at least if there is some relevance in the case. Only in the approach of Leflar was this somewhat different but it lacked the elements of evaluation.

Ultimately, these elements emerge in the application of *better or more just laws*, which implies a *substantive* law approach around a difficult *value judgment* that often leads to the application of the forum law. That is the *homeward trend*, but it need not be so. At least the forum law could be recast to take care of the foreign elements in the case. In that event, for commercial transactions there could also be an element of efficiency and cost to consider, which is perhaps easier to evaluate. This substantive law approach may also be the more receptive to *lex mercatoria* considerations, and therefore to broader considerations of

---

[526] See also W Reece, 'Conflict of Laws and the Restatement Second' (1963) 27 *Law and Contemporary Problems* 679.

[527] See D Havers, 'Critique of the Choice of Law Problem' (1933) 47 *Harvard Law Review* 173.

[528] See D Havers, *The Choice of Law Process* (1965).

[529] See R Leflar, *American Conflicts of Law* (1977).

[530] A Von Mehren and D Trautman, *The Law of Multistate Problems* (1965) 304.

[531] See for a more recent discussion and evaluation of the American approaches in particular E Vitta of Florence, 'The Impact in Europe of the American "Conflicts Revolution"' (1982) 30 *American Journal of Comparative Law* 1 and the important contributions of other authors in the same issue of that journal.

uniform law.[532] It has already been said that law and economics are also likely to support such an approach, although this is not so far its focus in the US.

The American approach to conflict of law is clearly more sensitive to substantive law considerations than the European approach, but it is true that the legal criteria often remain elusive, although there is a large body of case law. All the same, the notion that domestic laws may altogether be inappropriate to deal with international legal relationships remains here also under-explored.

Special problems with this homeward approach, to the extent existing in the US, result in *international commercial arbitrations* that have no natural forum law and are therefore forced into balancing policies more acutely, whether they like it or not. Here the Restatement (Second) Conflict of Laws and the Restatement (Third) Foreign Relations Laws may provide at least some guidance: see more particularly section 2.2.6 below.

2.2.4 The European Approach of Exception Clauses: Reasonable and Fair Solutions in the Dutch Proposals

In Europe, more particularly in civil law countries, the American approach has not gone unnoticed, and, as we have seen in section 2.2.1, its flexibility has elicited a response of which there was some tangible evidence in the 1980 Rome Convention on the Law Applicable to Contractual Obligations now succeeded by the 2008 Regulation (Rome I). Thus it referred in Article 4 to the applicability of the law of the country with the closest connection with the contract, and presumed this to be the country in which the most characteristic performance took place. Subject to a list approach, that system has been maintained in the 2008 Regulation. It left room for another law, if the circumstances as a whole suggested that the contract is more closely connected with another country, maintained in the present Article 4(3).[533] This approach remains, however, principally wedded to the application of domestic laws only.

In this connection, problems often arise when delivery and assembly of goods take place (by the seller) in the country of the buyer, whilst the seller's most characteristic performance is presumed to take place at its residence, pointing to its own law as the most appropriate. The problem can be particularly pressing in the construction industry, where all kinds of local rules at the site may in any event prevail as semi-public or mandatory law.

---

[532] *Cf* also F Juenger who, in *Choice of Law and Multi-State Justice* (1993) 45, 190, notes the type of transaction and its requirements. Note also the approach of the UCC in s 1-301 to the extent that the uniform law still creates conflicts of law. It relies on a 'reasonable relationship' and allows parties to elect the law assuming that that relationship exists.

In other areas, the contractual choice of law is explicitly limited or excluded like in s 1-301(f) and (g). It concerns here more in particular the rights of creditors in sold goods (s 2-402), leases (ss 2A-105 and 2A-106), bank deposits and collections (s 4-102), funds transfers (s 4A-507), letters of credit (s 5-116), investment securities (s 8-110), and the perfection provisions of Art 9, ss 9-301–9-307. One may recognise here proprietary issues that are not usually at the free disposition of the parties in view of their third-party effect.

[533] See for the first English application, *Bank of Baroda v Vysya Bank* [1994] 2 Lloyd's Rep 87 in a letter of credit case.

Use of selling agents in the other country may also complicate the picture, but does not necessarily shift the balance of the contract towards the other party.[534]

The problem of the place of the most characteristic performance or closest connection also aroses in connection with Article 5(1) of the 1968 Brussels Convention on Jurisdiction and the Enforcement of Judgments in Civil and Commercial Matters, which ties jurisdiction in contractual matters to the place of performance of the contract rather than the residence of the performer, now replaced by Article 5(1) of the EU Regulation on Jurisdiction and the Recognition and Enforcement of Judgments in Civil and Commercial Matters of 2000, effective 1 March 2002, which is more specific in Article 5(1)(b) for the sale of goods and the rendering of services by opting for the place of delivery in the first instance and the place where the services are or should be rendered in the second.[535]

Thus the place of performance rather than the residence of the performer may sometimes be more relevant. Exceptions may thus be made, hence this technique of the so-called *exception clauses*, as a further modification to the traditional conflicts approach in Europe. In statutory conflicts law, in tort, one sometimes sees similar corrections to the *lex locus delicti*, in that case in favour of the law of the forum (usually that of the tortfeasor as defendant) if both parties to an accident, which took place elsewhere, are resident in the same country, see for example Article 45(3) of the Portuguese General Private International Law Statute of 1965 and Article 31(2) of the Polish Private International Law statute of the same year. This may also result under the guise of the law of the forum (of the defendant) being always considered more closely connected, such as under the open adjustment possibility of Article 15(1) of the Swiss Statute of 1987, not applicable, however, if the tortfeasor could have foreseen that the result of his action would be produced in another country (see Article 133(2)).

As mentioned above, social considerations such as the protection of consumers and workers have given rise to the setting aside of traditional conflict rules altogether, in such cases in favour of their own laws (Articles 6 and 8 of the EU Regulation). It may still be seen as a conflicts approach of sorts, but only in the sense that it ultimately points to a domestic law. In truth, it is an exception clause and there is really no choice of law here. As pointed out before, the Hague Convention on Maintenance Obligations gives maintenance creditors the benefit of the best rule for them. They thus have a choice. This is not a proper choice of law or conflicts rule either but again an exception clause.

Dutch law in its 1992 draft Introduction Statute to Private International Law (Article 8) extended the common public order exception to the application of a conflicts rule, and allowed considerations of reasonableness and fairness *always* to affect the result. In this connection, it did not suggest the application of the law of any other country (with a closer connection), although according to some this was still implied. The rule was more properly a sequel to Article 6.2(2) of the new Dutch CC, which submits all applicable private law, be it statutory or customary, to the requirements of reasonableness and fairness, and allows at least in the law of obligations the necessary corrections in the result as an *autonomous*

---

[534] See in the Netherlands, HR 25 September 1992 [1992] NJ 750, which interprets Art 4(5) restrictively and in case of doubt finds for the presumption of Art 4(2). The Court of Appeal of Versailles was much more forthcoming in favour of a rebuttal of this presumption, see its decision of 6 February 1991 [1991] *Rev Crit de Dr Intern Privé* 745.

[535] See the Dutch case cited in n 534, and further also *Dicey and Morris on the Conflict of Laws*, 14th edn (2012) r 223, 1820 and r 35, 478.

function of the forum. In the area of conflicts laws proper, this is closer to the modern American approach than may be found anywhere else in Europe, and was to be welcomed. Arguably, this autonomy was still an aspect of the *lex fori*, although it could also be seen as an aspect of the international public order.

For conflicts, this approach received little support, however, in Dutch private international law scholarship, which is still on the lookout for clarity and certainty under some domestic rule. A new draft of 2002 was therefore more modest, and removed the references to reasonableness and fairness from the public order exception (Article 12). The notion of public order remained, however, undefined in this connection and could therefore still cover some fundamental legal principles maintained by the forum regardless of conflicts law or theory. They may (but need not) derive from international agreements or from EU legislation concerning, for example, market manipulation, money laundering and the protection of the environment or cultural objects.

Thus it would appear that, within the public order exceptions, compelling Dutch notions of fairness and reasonableness may still be used to test the result of the application of conflict rules, even though this is no longer expressly stated. Of course, this may also be done elsewhere, but in the Netherlands it would be supported by the general approach of Article 6.2(2) Dutch CC. The discussion of a draft bill of 2009, codifying the conflicts of law rules in the last book (10) of the new Dutch Civil Code, since adopted, did not provide much further clarification.

Notably, the German Statute of 1986 and the Italian Statute of 1995 did not introduce similar flexibility. Also, Article 15 of the Swiss law does not go so far, and remains well within the proximity approach and traditional conflict of laws solutions. Again, the ultimate question remains whether the application of any domestic law continues to be appropriate in international cases, especially if playing themselves out in the international professional sphere in manners and forms that have no domestic equivalent.

The corrections to the applicable (domestic) law through exception clauses may not apply to situations where the parties have made a contractual choice of law, but there are even then exceptions in the case of consumer and workers contracts in order to protect the weaker party under Articles 6 and 8 of the EU Regulation (Rome I) as we saw. Moreover, it can only be repeated that a contractual choice of law is not always fully effective, certainly not in matters which are not at the free disposition of the parties to regulate amongst themselves, as in private law is often thought to be the case in proprietary matters, therefore in respect of any third-party effect. In contractual matters, mandatory rules of a country with which all elements relevant to the situation are connected (at the time of the choice) cannot be set aside either (Article 3 of the EU Regulation). Also in tort matters the freedom to choose an applicable law is not always unrestricted: it is limited to the *lex fori* in Switzerland (Article 132).

Finally, corrections to the conflicts rules and applicable laws thereunder may also result indirectly from *forum non conveniens* considerations to the applicable jurisdiction. However, this concept, which is of Scottish origin, now generally adopted in common law countries, remains alien to Continental European thinking and does not figure in the Brussels and Lugano Conventions on Jurisdiction and Enforcement of Judgments in Civil and Commercial Matters either, nor in the 2002 EU Regulation replacing the Brussels Convention (Brussels I).

In domestic law, the *forum non conveniens* notion, where known, is sometimes restricted to a correction of the choice of jurisdiction by the parties only, see Article 5(3) of the Swiss law of 1987, which allows rejection of the choice of Switzerland if neither party has a domicile, residence or establishment in that country. Article 429 of the (old) Dutch CCP rejected the election if neither party had a sufficient contact with Dutch public order, whilst case law required an interest (which could exist if Dutch law was applicable, the Dutch language was used, or a specialty of Dutch courts such as shipping matters in Rotterdam, was involved).[536] It could be seen as an expression of the *forum (non) conveniens* doctrine in continental terms. New Dutch legislation concerning international jurisdiction confine themselves to the criterion of foreign parties being able to show an interest: Article 8(1) CCP.

The European response to the modern American theories is significant, but, as shown above, remains incidental, and is thus often expressed in terms of corrections to the prevailing proximity rules by substituting another conflicts principle. A more open system based on the acceptability of the results remains exceptional, and is not even now the law in the Netherlands or likely to be accepted without much further discussion.[537]

2.2.5 The Role of Practitioners. Emphasis on the Facts rather than on the Rules: The Nature of the Relationship of the Parties and the Nature of the Transaction Distinguished. The Effects of Transnationalisation

The difference between the classical and more modern approaches to conflicts of laws is often dictated by temperament and practical experience. This difference pervades the approach to all law, its formation and application generally, but is of particular interest in attitudes to conflicts of law and no less to the new law merchant or *lex mercatoria*. In fact, it may also be seen in modern foreign investment law as part of public international law, which—with its dependence on customary law, general principle and treaty law—has much the same structure as the modern *lex mercatoria*. What we are talking about in the more modern approaches is:

(a)   a search for predictability in the behavioural patterns of the participants and peer group (and their transactional structuring) rather than in a set of hard and fast superimposed rules of whatever nature supposed to bring ultimate clarity;

(b)   a degree of suspicion towards artful rules that provide an appearance of certainty but solve nothing;[538]

---

[536] See also HR 1 February 1985, NJ 698 (*Piscator*, 1985).

[537] See also for the subject of the exception clauses and *forum non conveniens*, the reports to the 14th International Congress of Comparative Law in Athens, and especially the general report of D Kokkini-Iatridou, *Les Clauses d' Exception en Matière de Conflits de Lois et de Conflits de Jurisdiction* [Exception Clauses in Conflicts of Laws and Conflicts of Jurisdictions—or the Principle of Proximity] (Dordrecht, 1994) 3.
    The author proposes—with reference to JG Castel, 'Commentaire sur certaines dispositions du Code civil du Québec se rapportant au droit international privé' ['Commentary on certain rules of the civil code of Quebec concerning private international law'] (1992) *Journal du Droit International* 630-2—a second phase in the openness debate and, whilst criticising Art 8 of the Dutch proposals of 1992, suggests that, exceptionally, the traditional conflicts rules should not be applied if in all the circumstances it would be better to apply the law of another state, thus returning to the application of a particular domestic law with an emphasis on rules rather than on interests and results, the proximity notion being exceptionally abandoned, however. It is unlikely to be more satisfactory than the other exception clauses looking for better *domestic* laws to apply in international cases.

[538] See for the more convoluted results, even by conflict of laws standards, particularly the approach in tri-partite situations such as agency, vol II, ch 1, s 3.2; bills of lading, vol II, ch 2, s 2.1.9; bills of exchange, vol II, ch 2, s 2.2.10; and assignments, vol II, ch 2, s 1.9.

(c)   a level of comfort with and acceptance of a measure of flexibility in respect of the applicable (black-letter) law in order to facilitate

(d)   a search for better, fairer or more sensible and practical results, thus substituting a normativity of a different sort which accepts in appropriate cases transnational law to apply in which reliance on legitimate expectations figure high;

(e)   allowance, including in international cases, for ethical, social, economic and environmental considerations to be taken into account which are not necessarily of a national character either but respond to international values and transnational law (in which connection reference may also be made to the international public order or international minimum standards).

There is always tension in these aspects in view of the facts of the case, the interests to be protected, the needs of the parties in this respect and the impact of public policy, and thus between more positivist and teleological or normative approaches, aggravated where the conflict rules themselves are contrived or remain uncertain and contested as in the proprietary aspects of many modern financial transactions and set-off facilities.

It is true that practising lawyers often continue to rely on a domestic law (preferably their own) in a mistaken search for certainty and clarity in this manner. In this connection, they are often also oblivious of the limited or adverse impact of a contractual choice of domestic law (even their own) which might prove entirely unsuitable in the circumstances. For example, domestic good faith considerations may play out very differently in international transactions as has already been demonstrated. In a highly regulated environment, a choice of law by the parties may in any event cover much less ground than is often believed and it must then be established how far these contractual choice of law clauses reach. It has already been said that they can only affect issues that are truly at the free disposition of the parties to settle the way they chose. They cannot therefore easily concern proprietary issues that by their very nature involve third parties as competing interest holders or creditors of the transferor. They cannot avoid consumer and small investor protections. They cannot circumvent tax and regulatory law.

This was discussed in section 2.1.1 above, and will be further discussed in section 2.2.9 below. Many practitioners do not like to consider these issues at the time of the formation of the contract. It is against their instinct and it could also mean that the contract might have to be handled by lawyers of other jurisdictions. More generally, the suitability of the chosen law is difficult to judge by lawyers who are mainly educated in one legal system (their own).[539] Of course, the more the concept of transnational law or the modern *lex mercatoria* starts to prevail, the quicker the monopoly of the lawyers who like to hide behind their own law would disappear. The legal profession itself would then be opened up in the handling of international cases, which would no longer be exclusively subject to any party's domestic legal regime and rules.

It is increasingly clear that the better result is likely to be obtained under the evolving rules of the legal order in which the transactions take place, such as, in trade and finance, the international commercial and financial legal order and its new law merchant or *lex mercatoria* as will be shown more in detail in Part III below. This realisation alone may more readily produce corrections to the prima facie applicable domestic law in international

---

[539] See also text following n 510 above.

cases, at least in the professional sphere, where parties are used to some uncertainty whilst often taking greater risks. That does not mean that they will not try to unbundle legal risks and seek better to protect against these risks in the structuring of their transactions. In fact, it has already been said that transnationally the major law firms may prove to be the foremost spokespersons for the new order. They created the legal frame work for the eurobonds and helped formulate the market practices concerning them. They drafted the swap and repo master agreements, broadened the notion of set-off in the process, and may well also find new ways in the clearing and settlement of non-standardised products. That is what transaction lawyers do and they use a combination of developing market practices, general principles and party autonomy to move things forward and stabilise the legal environment. Although obviously more difficult in international transnactions, there is nothing to prove that the present legal flux, especially at the transnational level, is largely unmanageable, certainly if the approaches suggested in section 1.1.4 above for contract and movable property are better understood, but it takes imagination both of structuring lawyers and adjudicators to reduce legal risk at this level through transnationalisation.

It is clear that in the case of disputes, a more sensible solution for professionals is ultimately always more valuable than the pretence of legal certainty, based on old concepts, potentially leading to low quality law. Again, it can hardly be produced on the basis of the application of domestic laws that were never meant for international transactions and are often entirely out of date. Indeed, in the professional sphere, corrections to any prima facie applicable domestic law (on the basis of the traditional conflicts rules) or its disapplication in the circumstances are likely to be based principally on what makes better sense and was as such expected or even relied upon by all. Transnational law or the modern *lex mercatoria* in the manner as here explained has the advantage of being predictable in that sense and then also of being in fact more precise.

It has already been pointed out in this connection that for professionals this basic approach might mean rougher justice, with less, rather than more, refinement in the legal concepts or protections used, compared to whatever domestic law may otherwise be deemed applicable. A more literal interpretation of the text may result especially if the contract was meant as a roadmap and risk management tool. This was demonstrated especially in connection with good faith protection. At this level, there may be an extra reliance on the precise wording of an agreement or letter of credit, and therefore on a more literal interpretation, compared to in the civil law tradition that otherwise may depend on a more teleological or good faith approach. On the other hand, a lesser acceptance of specific performance than in civil law countries may follow at the transnational level, because it is less disruptive of the commercial flows. The return of title in the goods upon default, even if the contract provides for it, may then be deemed also to go against these flows; so, under modern law, may be any contractual restrictions on assignments of receivables. Transactional and payment finality is here always favoured. Thus for professional participants there is here emphasis on certainty but rather as industry practice geared to specific situations and then reinforced, not then as a general expectation, irrationally expected from rule conformity. In fact, a more teleological and normative interpretation may itself lead to this result.

The emphasis is thus on the identification and (teleological and normative) interpretation of all legal rules and principles that are in varying degrees connected with the case and on the determination of their relevance in the circumstances. No rule or principle, whether or not purely domestic, has in that approach any absolute value or force whilst even the fundamental principles (or the *ius cogens*) are always subject to interpretation in the light of the circumstances of the case. Yet there are situations, as just demonstrated, where for professionals the law will cut out argument and especially sophistry in legal reasoning. The *facts of the case* especially in terms of: (a) the nature of the relationship of the parties; (b) the interests to be protected therein; and (c) the particular dynamics and logic of each transaction, are then likely to play a preponderant and potentially the decisive role barring overriding public policy or order requirements. This is here seen as the inheritance of the traditional common law approach and technique to finding and applying the applicable law. Internationality and professionality may thus acquire a special meaning, and may indeed suggest a different legal order, here called the transnational commercial and financial legal order, with its own laws (*lex mercatoria*), which was largely the gist of the discussions in the first Part of this volume.

To put it in a more extreme form: if a rule of whatever nature does not fit the facts, it will not apply, as it cannot have been meant for them. Again, this may be more apparent where the reach of domestic rules through private international law rules is attempted to be extended also to cover international situations for which they were never made and which hardly fit. In modern times, we think in any event less in terms of grand designs or systems of law—like that of the civil law or any other—but are forced to become more pragmatic which means paying more attention to the configuration of the facts by case. This is even so at the national level, but more apparent transnationally.

Emphasis on the nature or type of the relationship of the parties and their own requirements is now more prevalent and has also become an aspect of the notion of good faith in civil law countries, but it still remains undervalued in civil law, see the discussion in Volume II, chapter 1, section 1.1.1. As will be shown there, this was always an aspect of the common law, at least in contract. It points the way, even domestically, but more so transnationally and suggests different legal rules that might apply per relationship or existing rules that will need to be adapted to allow for any differences.

That is indeed the essence of the developing transnational law merchant or modern *lex mercatoria*, which was earlier perceived as a hierarchy of norms amongst different sources of law that are all conceivably applicable, and amongst which domestic norms continue to figure but only as the residual rule with different degrees of prominence depending on the facts of each case, whilst higher transnational law will increasingly emerge on the basis of fundamental legal principle, custom, to some extent uniform treaty law (or EU directives or regulations), and otherwise common legal principles or party autonomy, see more particularly sections 1.4.13 above and 3.1.1 below. Domestic law found residually through the traditional conflicts' rules will still figure here but only as part of this transnational law itself, must find its role therein, and will be adjusted accordingly.

2.2.6 The Issue of Public Policy or Governmental Interests and its Impact. The Notion of Comity and its Application. Competition between Transnational and State Laws Revisited

There can be little doubt that national governmental policies have had an enormous impact on the development of the law in the twentieth century, when the law became the state's special vehicle to effect change. This has not left private law untouched. The issue was raised in more general terms in section 1.5.7 above. It led to many forms of regulation, which can take the form of public or private law intervention. In the first, governments will tell citizens directly what to do. In the second, they may amend private law to give citizens better protections against each other. That may be clear in company law and bankruptcy. But it is also at the heart of consumer and investor protection law.

An example may serve as clarification. Governments may directly license and supervise financial intermediaries such as banks and investment brokers and advisors. Governments may withdraw these licences or impose further conditions in case of bad behaviour. It is a matter of administrative law which does not normally give individuals a private action. Individuals cannot force governments to act; we mostly accept that governments may have their own reasons (within the law). But governments may give private parties a direct action against misbehaving intermediaries, against brokers, for example, through tightening agency laws and fiduciary duties. That results in private remedies under private law which gives private parties direct recourse. These protections are then likely to result in mandatory law which affected parties cannot waive by choosing another system of law. This is to avoid undue pressure.

Mandatory private law may thus increase as governments often use private law to achieve their policy objectives, for example in the protection of consumers and smaller investors, the first often through good faith notions, the latter through the extension or amplification of agency and fiduciary duty notions as just mentioned.

However, it should be realised and never forgotten that, by using notions of fairness and good faith, in contract, for example, in terms of pre-contractual and post-contractual duties, courts themselves have often introduced mechanisms to initiate or broaden similar policies. Here one sees instances where newer social values are not only imposed by governments but may enter private law in other ways, notably through the court system, often in terms of public order or policy considerations. There is here not necessarily a government monopoly, as was already discussed in section 1.2.13 above where it was said that it would be a sad day indeed if citizens had to wait solely for government to take action in these matters.

New values or policies thus enter the law all the time, including in private law, often in a mandatory fashion, either directly through government intervention or more indirectly through the courts. They are likely not only to further the demands for justice, social peace and perhaps also the utilitarian and efficiency principle or common sense notions, in this way updating the living law, but may also reinforce governmental policies. Although normally governmental policies are likely to regulate and prescribe social and economic behaviour more directly, even this public and regulatory or administrative law may spill over into the application and interpretation of private laws, for example when under competition or securities laws or under export restrictions contracts are invalidated. Again, the difference will be in the cause of action and type of recourse: see further the discussion in section 1.2.13 above.

As we have already seen, in international cases, such domestic governmental interests or policies, or domestic public order requirements or values, as expressed in local laws, present special problems in the operation of other legal orders, in international transactions, in particular of the transnational commercial and financial legal order, to the extent an international transaction has an effect on the territories of states that are or may be affected or if there is conduct in such territories. A purely private *lex mercatoria* approach cannot ignore these local concerns or interests, is in fact deferential of them, and must take them into account to the extent justified, the determination of which then becomes a key issue with which we shall be most particularly concerned below.

It is clear that domestic laws of this nature do not become part of the hierarchy of the *lex mercatoria*, as other domestic rules of private law may still do residually, as we have seen, but these rules *compete* with the *lex mercatoria* and, even if public order-based, should in principle be *well distinguished* from fundamental legal principle as *ius cogens* or human rights or similar public order considerations which operate in the *lex mercatoria*, and therefore into private law itself, and are for international transactions, it was submitted, of a transnational nature.[540] The impact of governmental interests on the *lex mercatoria* can also be considered a competition between different legal orders on the same territory, that is competition between the transnational commercial and financial legal order and domestic legal orders which remain territorial.

Again, this is especially relevant in respect of international trade conducted in whole or in part upon the territory of the state or government concerned or having an effect there. In American terms, it becomes a question of competent *jurisdiction to prescribe the applicable public policy rules*. Governments are sovereign on their own territory. On the other hand, they cannot in principle reach beyond their own legal order nor, it was submitted, can they interfere under proper notions of the rule of law within their own borders in other legal orders operating in their territory without showing proper respect and in a globalising world willingness to co-operate in principle; but the other side of this coin is that their own public policy or order rules cannot always be ignored in other orders either, especially if operating on their territory.

The fact that governmental interests of a national character cannot be ignored in the operation of the transnational commercial and financial legal order arises first because in the case of disputes, their own courts may be asked to pass on situations that, although originating abroad (or in other domestic legal orders), depended on *conduct* or had an *effect* in the forum state, so that the forum government's policies could legitimately impact on them. International arbitrators are not able to avoid these issues either. These situations arise in many different ways, and to determine whether there was sufficient local conduct and effect to invite the application of the regulatory laws of the country in question will depend on the facts that will normally prove decisive. This is likely to affect private parties in their international dealings and governmental interests of this nature may, in appropriate cases, thus interject their force in the operation of the *lex mercatoria*, disturbing or suspending its effect, but only if the relevant governmental interest can be considered sufficiently dominant in the particular international case. Arbitrators are likely here to be more sensitive to this state of affairs than local courts, which is the reason why parties may prefer an international arbitration.

Competition policy has been tested more extensively in this context and has always shed a particular light. Can it be effective and applied extraterritorially, for example when non-residents organise a cartel elsewhere, which affects prices in the forum state such as in the US or in the EU? In practice, this raises a number of important sub-questions, first whether under the American or European competition laws, these laws extend under their own terms to activities abroad. This is often referred to as the issue of extraterritoriality, or as the question of *subject matter jurisdiction*. At least in the US, there is a presumption against

---

[540] See for fundamental principle, s 1.4.5 above.

extraterritoriality of national laws, but it depends, first, on the intent of the legislator, and subsequently, in the application to foreign situations, also on the court's considerable discretion in these matters. American and EU competition laws are now considered to have that effect.

In fact, discretion in balancing the interests if there are other competing (competition) laws is assumed by the (American) courts to be quite separate from the legislator's (presumed) intent and is based on *comity*, which has fairness at its centre. It is in such cases still mostly seen as a *national* rather than an international concept, in which connection reference is now often made to moderation.[541] Awareness of the interests of other states is assumed, in which context at least some attention is now commonly paid to international law.[542] In this regard, sections 402 and 403 of the Restatement (Third) Foreign Relations Law of the US (1987) refer to reasonableness and set guidelines. They are of great interest, need to be carefully considered, and may also be indicative of a more international trend.

In Europe, as we have seen, reference in this connection is often made to *règles d'application immediate*: see Article 9 of the 2008 EU Regulation on the Law Applicable to Contractual Obligations (replacing the earlier 1980 Rome Convention on the same subject, Article 7). Here the formulation of a conflict or private international law rule is preferred, even though it does not concern a private law matter. Reference is sometimes also made to a so-called *unilateral* conflicts rule giving effect to public policy of forum states in such circumstances.[543] Under it, precedence is indeed given to governmental policies when they are more obviously relevant, notably therefore when there is (significant) conduct or effect on the territory of the state concerned, although the courts may always apply the policies and public order requirements of their own forum state. As already noted, since international arbitrators do not have an own forum state and are in any event not covered by the EU Regulation, it is likely that in international arbitrations these various domestic laws or claims to jurisdiction to prescribe will be more objectively weighed and considered.

As long as the same public policy and public order standards are not used everywhere, it may be shown that in this manner the outcome in terms of the applicable mandatory domestic laws and respect for the relevant domestic governmental interest or policies in international cases may at least to some extent still depend on the location or nature of the forum (or on forum selection by the parties or on international arbitration being agreed, see below). This raises at the same time important issues of *adjudicatory jurisdiction* (as distinct from the jurisdiction to prescribe), the question therefore whether the forum in the offended state has sufficient jurisdiction over the international transaction.

---

[541] See for this international law principle the *Barcelona Traction, Light and Water Company, Ltd (Belgium v Spain)* (1970) ICJ Rep 3.

[542] See for the extraterritorial application of competition laws in the US the line of cases starting with *United States v Aluminium Company of America (Alcoa)* (1945) 148 Fed 2d 416 and *United States v Imperial Chemical Industries (ICI)* (1952) 105 F Supp 215. The creation of a (potentially fraudulent) worldwide patent network and its effect on the US may in this connection also be considered under American tort and competition rules if restricting American plaintiffs activities, see *Mannington Mills Inc v Congoleum Corp* (1979) 595 F2d 1287. What will be considered in this connection is whether the ties with the foreign country are strong enough whilst ultimately the reasonableness may also be tested, see *Timberlane Lumber Co v Bank of America* (1976) 549 F 2d 597, in which the relative effect on the US as compared to the effect on others was thought to be an issue and also whether there is another court readily available, see for a fuller discussion, and for the move from comity to legal guidelines or principles, also *Hartford Fire Insurance Co v California* (1993) 509 US 764.

[543] See for a comparative study also GA Bermann, 'Public Law in the Conflict of Laws' (1986) 34 (Supplement) *American Journal of Comparative Law* 157.

Here, at least in the US, constitutional considerations of due process, therefore of fairness, are additionally invoked to avoid excessive jurisdiction of the plaintiffs' chosen courts (preferably their own) even if this has not led to a set of rules of adjudicatory jurisdiction over foreigners that is always entirely clear.[544] Generally, the type of activities is considered and the situation carefully explored for adequate contacts with the forum, but in the US a hard and fast set of adjudicatory jurisdiction rules in respect of absent defendants has been increasingly abandoned as unworkable and is in any event not considered in accordance with due process.[545]

In England,[546] the courts assume broader discretion in a reflection of a more obvious comity approach which is in this area of international adjudicatory jurisdiction (on its face still) mostly avoided in the US. In Continental Europe, more traditional hard and fast rules attaching jurisdiction to the place of the tortuous effect or to other connecting factors are being used.[547] That is also the approach in the 2002 EU Regulation on the Recognition and Enforcement of Judgments in Civil and Commercial Matters.

---

[544] See the line of cases starting with *International Shoe Co v Washington* (1945) 326 US 310 and *Helicopteros Nacionales de Colombia, SA v Hall* (1984) 446 US 408.

[545] The approach used in interstate cases, where there is no true discretion, is by extension also used in international cases where it could be asked whether the discretion that comes with comity plays a more fundamental role or is perhaps the chief consideration (rather than constitutional due process).

For example, exporting goods or services *from* the US is unlikely to result in jurisdiction of the American courts, no matter how large the transaction is, and it may even have some service element attached to it within the US. Obviously it is against the interest of US commerce to act otherwise and the State Department will seek to protect foreign buyers from American jurisdiction through *amicus curiae* briefs in the respective courts. Keeping a bank account in the US, taking out a loan there, or organising a letter of credit or other type of bank guarantee is likely to be similarly considered. The more important issue is the importation of goods or services *into* the US and the extent to which this may create a business in the US and therefore adjudicatory jurisdiction of the American courts.

That issue has been tested in numerous cases, particularly in product liability situations where various defending importers start cross claims for contribution against each other in the US (even through foreign themselves) on the basis of the original jurisdiction asserted by harmed American plaintiffs, see eg *Asahi Metal Industry Co Ltd v Superior Court* (1987) 480 US 102, *cf* also *Deutsch v West Coast Machinery Co* (1972) 80 Wash 2d 707. Cross claims of this nature are, however, unlikely to succeed for lack of sufficient presence in the US, certainly in respect of component suppliers to the importers outside the US.

The issue of jurisdiction over importers into the US has also come up where foreign manufacturers like Volkswagen AG from Germany have tried to organise themselves in such a way that they do not come on-shore in the US for jurisdictional purposes, their policy being that if there is to be litigation, they wish to be sued in their own courts (for Volkswagen in Germany).

Here concepts of agency, control or de facto amalgamation with the US sales organisations have been tried to establish jurisdiction of the American courts but generally not very successfully. Agency requires the American sales network to be able to legally bind the foreign manufacturer, a situation that is therefore frequently avoided. Full control can be alleged between a foreign parent and American subsidiary, making the former subject to American jurisdiction, but must be proven, a situation also much avoided in this type of scheme, see *Delagi v Volkswagenwerk AF of Wolfsburg* (1972) 29 NY 2d 426, but amalgamation may be considered to exist when foreign subsidiaries are newly set up and are not yet able to organise themselves, see *BulovaWatch Co Inc v K Hattori & Co Ltd* (1981) 508 F Supp 1322.

A forum selection clause in favour of a foreign court may also be sufficient to avoid jurisdiction of the American courts, see *Volkswagenwerk AG v Klippan, GmbH* (1980) 611 P2d 498.

Whether the situation is different in respect of services and whether in that case, at least when unsolicited, jurisdiction of the American Courts is less likely to result, came up in *Landoil Resources Corp v Alexander & Alexander Services Inc* (1990) 918 NYS 2d 739, in which the American insurance broker unsuccessfully sued a Lloyds of London syndicate in New York in a cross claim for contribution.

[546] UK Civil Procedure (Amendment) Rules 2000 r 6.20.

[547] See as main example Art 5 of the EU Regulation No 44/2001 on Jurisdiction and the Recognition and Enforcement of Judgments in Civil and Commercial Matters entered into force on 1 March 2002 replacing the similar Brussels Convention of 1968.

The acceptance of this approach under common international law standards is often emphasised.[548] It suggests a preference for a more certain, less discretionary approach in which potential unfairness may be less of a concern or a concern that is considered to be adequately dealt with in the prevailing hard and fast jurisdiction and conflicts-of-law rules (the latter always subject, however, to public order considerations).[549]

The key issue is everywhere whether the application of domestic policy rules in international cases may be *tested and balanced under international standards*, that is to say in the own courts under comity notions or in international arbitrations rather under notions of the international public order. This may ultimately also lead to the application of *international minimum standards* against which these domestic objectives are being tested for their validity and application in international transactions. That could mean that transnational public order requirements or fundamental principle take over. This is quite conceivable, for example, in competition cases or for workers protection issues or in determining the environmental standards for international operations.

2.2.7 States as Counterparties de *Iure Imperii*

Where states operate as *counterparties* with international companies, they are likely to operate themselves in the international legal order, especially when engaging in *ordinary international commercial or financial transactions (de jure gestionis)*. The rules obtaining in that order (the modern *lex mercatoria*) would then also apply to them, although enforcement against and recovery from states may still be difficult and, if sought in other countries, potentially subject to claims of sovereign immunity. This remains a problematic area and it is still difficult to recover large arbitral awards against governments, probably even more so in their own territory. As a practical matter their own courts may not co-operate or find exceptions, not even if required to do so under treaty law, for example the 1958 New York Convention on the Recognition and Enforcement of Foreign Arbitral Awards, or under the Washington (ICSID) Convention of 1965 in respect of foreign investments disputes and awards, which under the latter Convention are supposed to be self-executing.

In any event, as just mentioned, attachment and execution in other countries is often still limited under sovereign immunity statutes. They may allow only commercial property of a state to be attached, and often only to the extent that this property has itself been the subject of, or has been closely connected with, the litigation.[550] Where, like under the ICSID or Washington Convention, awards are directly enforceable against Contracting States, under Article 54 they are still treated as no better than ordinary judgments. It means that they are still subject to sovereign immunity restrictions on enforcement in other than the state involved in the dispute.

---

[548] See Case 89/85 *Alstrom v Commission (Woodpulp case)* [1988] ECR 5193. In the EU, it does not yet give rise to a balancing of competing interests.

[549] There is much increased awareness of the need for rules in the US as well, see, eg the concurring opinion of Judge Adams in *Mannington Mills* n 542 above, but they are not necessarily the old rules.

[550] On the other hand, in the US under its Foreign Sovereign Immunity Statute, claims against foreign state entities (like central banks or governmental trading agencies) may be more easily enforceable, even against bank accounts (in the US) that were not an issue in the litigation.

A more important issue is that states, whilst engaging in business, may contend to be doing so solely or substantially in the exercise of a public or semi-public function (*de jure imperii*). They may, for example, grant oil and gas or other mining or lumbering concessions to foreign enterprises in that capacity. Whilst doing so, however, they may concede at the same time a related foreign investment protection regime, which will usually include a stabilisation of the investment and taxation terms, guarantee the repatriation of the investment and its profits (in hard currency) and of the extracted substances or manufactured goods with the opportunity to retain the sales proceeds abroad. There may also be protection against expropriation or more indirect government (regulatory) takings. Moreover, a foreign legal regime may be made applicable to substantive legal issues or otherwise probably to general principles of law and an international arbitration facility may then normally also be added to decide any disputes.

Whilst entering in such agreements, states may be considered to surrender their absolute monopoly of the rules governing investments on their territory and may no longer be able to claim full autonomy but become subject to the rules of the transnational commercial and financial legal order also, in which they themselves then chose to operate. Regardless of the nature of the activity (be it mineral substances extraction, the lumbering of wood, or the selling of local lands or cows), in terms of the thesis of this book, that would imply that they bind themselves by contract under the modern *lex mercatoria*, therefore under *private* transnational law. But it is also the approach of this book that this still leaves room for their own domestic public policies in the manner as explained in the previous section for conduct and effect in their own territories. A state cannot bind its sovereignty by private agreement. It would require customary international law or treaty law, but traditionally that is not directed towards the protection of private parties who have no standing (in principle) under public international law. That would strictly speaking require the development of an *international administrative law* and it is a legitimate question how far such law already exists.

It may thus be seen that a state may give under transnational private law but take back under its own domestic public policy (especially where there is appreciable conduct and effect in respect of the international transaction on its own territory, which in the extracting or manufacturing business will normally be the case), as perhaps balanced (in international dealings) by more objective considerations of fairness and subject to at least some minimum international tests or standards of protection. There is here a traditional *conflict of interests* but increasingly also some protection under international (administrative) law or otherwise perhaps under the administrative domestic law of the host country. The fair and equitable treatment clauses in BITs spring to mind.

This may raise important *characterisation* issues. Part of the concession may indeed be merely *private contract law*, where states are bound as any other private party. Breach of contract then gives rise to an ordinary damage action (under domestic or rather transnational private law). On the other hand, in other aspects, parties may be considered to have entered an *administrative* agreement, which may give the state more scope unilaterally to vary the terms subject always to proper indemnification under the applicable *administrative law* (its own or perhaps even transnationalised in terms of international public order or minimum requirement as just mentioned).[551]

---

[551] The notion of the international administrative contract, although regularly re-emerging as a concept, remains underdeveloped in international law: see, for an important early contribution, A Fatouros, 'The

More likely, states may now also be bound and restrained under *treaty law*, in which connection bilateral investment treaties (BITs) have become of special interest. These treaties may also be multilateral, as in North America under the 1992 NAFTA Treaty (Chapter 11), other multilateral efforts having failed so far.[552] They suggest that under such treaties states indeed owe investors some duties under public international law.[553]

On closer analysis, what may be happening is that states bind their regulatory or public policy powers, *not* vis à vis the investor directly, as they do under stabilisation clauses, but vis à vis the other Contracting State. As we have seen, stabilisation clauses may not prove strong enough to overcome claims by a host state to overriding full sovereignty or public order imperatives. But the regulatory power of the host state may be restrained under a treaty with the home state of the investor. Arguably, investors are not, therefore, capable of directly exercising and waiving their rights under these treaties because they are not directly vested in investors. They can only do so in the context of any special arbitration facility offered them (under such treaties) when disputes have arisen. That is now common and gives investors at least derivative rights under public international law.[554]

Such treaties are likely to include special provisions for equal treatment with other domestic or foreign investors, a fair and equitable standard of treatment, a formula for awarding damages in the case of creeping or direct expropriation, and an international arbitration regime to which the host state binds itself and of which the investor may take advantage in the case of a dispute. Such a dispute would not be an interstate dispute (although there may also be a separate arbitration procedure for the Contracting States in matters of interpretation of these BITs).[555]

Administrative Contract in Transnational Transactions' in Festschrift *Max Rheinstein* vol 1 (1969) 259. See for an important more recent contribution, HP Loose, 'Administrative Law and International Law' in P Bekker, R Dolzer and M Waible (eds), *Making Transnationakl Law Work in a Global Economy, Essays in Honour of Detlev Vagts* (2010) 380. Some of these problems were also discussed by Z Douglas, 'Nothing if Not Critical for Investment Treaty Arbitration: *Occidental, Eureko* and *Methanex*' (2006) 22 *Arbitration International* 27.

[552] See for an overview and much respect for sovereignty notions at the expense of the further development of public international law in this area, M Sornarajah, *The International Law on Foreign Investment*, 3nd edn (Cambridge, 2010) but *cf* also R Dolzer and C Schreuer, *Principles of International Investment Law* (Oxford, 2008), who are more investor protection oriented.

[553] So also the English Court of Appeal in *Occidental Exploration and Production Co v Republic of Ecuador* [2005] EWCA Civ 1116, [18] and [2005] 2 Lloyd's Rep 707.

[554] Earlier, in s 1.4.10 above, it was suggested that treaty law may figure in the hierarchy of the transnational *lex mercatoria*. That was in connection with harmonised *private* law, such as the 1980 Vienna Convention on the International Sale of Goods. It should be appreciated that BITs are not the same and only concern (and restrain) the exercise of domestic public or regulatory policies in international investment transactions of an otherwise private law nature.

[555] BITs may reinforce concessions, or other types of investment or establishment agreements in so called *umbrella clauses*, which aim at ensuring each party 'the observance at all times of any undertakings it may have given in relation to investments made by nationals of the other party'; *cf* Art 2(2) of the UK standard text, which states that 'each Contracting Party shall observe any obligation it may have entered into with regard to investments of nationals or companies of the other Contracting Parties', and Art 16 of the US standard agreement, which expresses, more negatively, the idea that the treaty shall not detract from 'any obligations assumed by a Party, including those contained in an investment authorisation or an investment agreement'. This may be especially relevant for stabilisation and arbitration clauses.

The meaning of these umbrella clauses has been the subject of much discussion and important case law: see TW Waelde, 'The "Umbrella" Clause in Investment Arbitration' (2006) 6 *Journal of World Investment and Trade* 183, and *SGS v Pakistan* (2003) 42 ILM 1290, and *SGS v Philippines* (2003) 42 ILM 1285, both ICSID cases.

Clearly, these umbrella clauses give extra protection only in the manner envisaged by the relevant investment treaty and need in the view of many to be precise and well directed in order to be effective. They do not normally cover any purely private law aspects of any concession or similar arrangement. It would appear that these aspects

2.2.8 Practical Issues Concerning Conflicting Public Policies: Effect on the *Lex Mercatoria* and the Importance of the Notion of *Forum non Conveniens*

As we have seen in section 2.2.6 above, in practice conflicts of public policies arise most particularly when, for example, anti-competitive activity is perfectly legal in the countries where it has been organised but not in the countries where it may have an effect. The courts in the countries of the alleged perpetrators may in such cases not wish to consider the offensive effect of the conduct elsewhere (under statutes of the place of the effect, for example in the US) and may in any event not apply the foreign competition rules. It may be very different in courts of the offended country. This may be a particular reason for parties to choose in their contract a neutral court or international arbitration in the interests of achieving a better balance,[556] the decisions of which might then still be recognised in the offended country; it will be a question of its public policy.

Similar issues have arisen in the enforcement of (American) securities legislation in respect of offensive acts abroad that affect American investors based in the US, for example in securities fraud (according to American standards) on a foreign exchange or in a foreign issue of new securities.[557] Naturally, American courts would apply their statutes in the matter, at least in respect of American investors, if called upon to decide these issues. Courts in other countries may not, but even if an American court found itself competent in these matters, *remoteness* is still an issue. Not all American investors in foreign markets can expect to be protected by the American securities laws in their own courts, assuming these courts accept adjudicatory jurisdiction. There comes a moment that even American investors are on their own or must sue in the place of the wrong under the laws of that place, although in situations of patent fraud, the American courts might still be more indulgent.

More traditional situations are questions of tariffs, import restrictions and boycotts and their effects on foreign contracts and on the delivery of goods thereunder if offensive to the forum state or any other. There is ample case law on these matters in the US and also some in the UK.[558] Cases typically arise where a contract is asked to be enforced in another country—the *forum country* (for example, delivery or payment is requested therein)—but concerns a trade that goes against tariffs (smuggling) or export restrictions (boycotts) in the original country (the export country) and may as such be void under the law of that country, which is likely to be the one most directly concerned. Its laws may then be upheld in the forum country as a matter of international public order or comity.

Yet, especially if a boycott is directed against the forum country, it might not be enforced by that forum and the contract is then more likely to be upheld (which may still give rise, however, to a *force majeure* excuse on the part of the exporter). Other instances may be

---

still have to be litigated under the concession or similar agreement itself and the ordinary court or arbitration dispute facility agreed therein, unless these facilities were themselves abused. At least to that extent, there is no need nor indeed much justification, to create within the treaty set up (therefore under public international law) a special contract law besides the transnational *lex mercatoria*.

[556] *Cf* House of Lords in *British Airways Board v Laker Airways Ltd* [1985] 3 WLR 413.

[557] See *Leasco Data Processing Equipment Corp v Maxwell* (1972) 468 F2d 1326.

[558] The base case is often still thought to be *Holman v Johnson* (1775) 98 ER 1120 (Lord Mansfield), formulating the so-called Revenue Rule. See for a more recent approach House of Lords in *Regazzione v KC Sethia (1944) Ltd* [1958] AC 301 and in the US *Banco do Brazil, SA v AC Israel Commodity Comp Inc* (1963) 12 NY 2d 371 239.

where foreigners deal in real estate in another country which they are not entitled to do under the laws of their home state or for which they need a licence under its laws. In such cases, the courts in the countries where the property is located are unlikely to declare the ensuing contracts and property transfers void. They will consider the undisturbed functioning of their own real estate market and transactional finality in that sense a superior interest.

A classic example arises also where a spouse under the law of her home country cannot give valid surety undertakings in respect of the business of her husband, but is prevailed upon to do so in another country whilst that guarantee is subsequently sought to be enforced in the home country. There is an indication in all these protection cases that the domiciliary principle replaces notions of territoriality (therefore notions of the spatial effect of the law with which conflicts of law rules are more traditionally concerned) in the name of fairness as a substantive law requirement.

Another instance arises when, under so-called guest statutes, the liability in respect of the transport of passengers may be limited or extended in some countries. Conflicts of law may result when an accident occurs in such a state but the passengers and driver are both from other states or when the car is insured somewhere else. At least in case law in the US, the more traditional approach pointing to the law of the place of the wrong may no longer be upheld in such cases[559] and any defence on the basis of a limitation of liability in the place of the wrong is no longer accepted either, at least not when the passenger and driver are both from the same (other) state where the insurance policy is held and the suit is brought.

Here again, one could see an overriding *substantive* law element of fairness and justice. As we have seen, in the US, it is more often expressed in a weighing of different policies in which the forum state policy tends to prevail or, under sections 6, 145 and 188 of the Restatement (Second) Conflict of Laws (1971), the law of the most significant relationship. It allows for a broad range of policies to be considered, but may no less result in the application of forum law (see also sections 2.2.2 and 2.2.3 above). Hence again the importance of adjudicatory jurisdiction and the possibility of so-called forum shopping by plaintiffs to find the (for them) most convenient forum, unless restrained from doing so under forum selection or arbitration clauses. The *forum non conveniens* doctrine is here also relevant. As we have already seen, the US is long used to an interest analysis in interstate conflicts and within that approach a weighing of policies of other nations can be easily accommodated. One could see sections 402 and 403 of the Restatement (Third) Foreign Relations Law of the US (1987) as a logical sequel to it in cases where public policy or regulatory considerations are more pronounced.

It means that in the US, prescriptive jurisdiction (and also act of state notions) are carved out of the more traditional conflicts of law approach and a different treatment is given here to governmental interests which easily fits into the interest analysis which in the US has now become common in all private law conflicts (as public and private law issues are not as fundamentally distinguished as in civil law, see more particularly section 2.2.2 above. As noted before, it fits much less easily in the more conventional European conflicts of law approach, which has been largely abandoned in the US, first in interstate cases but later also in international cases exactly because of the weight of these governmental

---

[559] See *Babcock v Jackson* (1963) 240 NYS 2d 743, and *Tooker v Lopez* (1969) 301 NYS 2d 519.

or policy interests, which have also long become evident in private law cases, see more particularly section 2.2.4 above.

To repeat, in the 2008 EU Regulation on the Law Applicable to Contractual Obligations, Article 9 covers this type of situation or at least the more traditional and more incidental ones associated with tariffs, boycotts and foreign exchange restrictions.

As has been stated several times before, the *lex mercatoria*, whilst operating in its own international legal order cannot be insensitive in its application to governmental or similar interests deriving from other, notably statist legal orders and it will have to be considered from case-to-case to what extent the *lex mercatoria* and its application are to be overruled or adjusted on the basis of such interests when *sufficiently connected* with the case in terms of conduct or effect in the relevant state territory so that the consideration of such governmental interests may be justified.

As we have seen, in courts in the US, the *comity approach* is used and remains important in such cases. It concerns the relative relevance of these governmental interests in international cases. It is still considered a domestic American facility although for comity to be more credible, it should become a concept of international and not domestic law, in which connection the balancing factors developed, for example, in American case law as summarised in the Restatement (Third) Law of Foreign Relations 1987, may still be of exemplary interest. Again, in the absence of a uniform approach, the issue of adjudicatory jurisdiction remains important as it will determine which courts (or arbitration panels) will be called upon to identify and, as the case may be, weigh the relevant interests and thus determine the meaning of comity.

The impact of forum selection and arbitration clauses must then also be considered. Three American Supreme Court Cases are here of fundamental importance.[560] They broadly upheld forum selection and arbitration clauses in international cases even if bearing on American *public policy* issues, notably securities and anti-trust laws, although always subject to *forum non-conveniens* considerations in which the applicable substantive and procedural law normally do not figure,[561] but in which (the balance of) public policies may still play a role if these policies are *sufficiently strong.*[562]

It is then for the party wanting to sue in an American forum to show that the selected foreign forum or arbitration proceedings are improper. The obvious advantage of a more neutral forum to consider the relevance of public policies is recognised in this regard, however, and in *Scherk* it was specifically accepted that an arbitration clause 'obviates the danger that a dispute under the agreement might be submitted to a forum hostile to the interests of one of the parties or unfamiliar with the problem area involved'.

The advantage of avoiding in this way the jurisdiction of multiple competing *fora* was also noted. The risk that such proceedings may affect the application of public policy, as embodied in securities laws of the US, was clearly accepted. But it was pointed out in *Mitsubishi* (see note 580 below) that the combination of a forum selection with the selection by the parties of a foreign law should not be intended simply to block strong (American)

---

[560] *The Bremen et al v Zapata Off-shore Co* (1972) 407 US 1; *Scherk v Alberto-Culver Co* (1974) 417 US 506; and *Mitsubishi Motors Corp v Soler Chrysler-Plymouth, Inc* (1985) 473 US 614.

[561] See *Piper Aircraft Co v Reyno* (1981) 454 US 235 and *Re Union Carbide Corp* (1987) 809 F2d 195.

[562] See for a similar approach in England, *Unterweser Reederei GmbH v Zapata Off-shore Company*, CA [1968] 2 Lloyd's Rep 158.

public policy claims. Recognition of the ensuing decisions under the New York Convention may not then pass the public policy test, at least not in the US.

Here also enters the idea that an arbitration panel *itself* should adopt a *forum non conveniens* approach in respect of public policy related issues and, depending on their nature, decide to leave them to the ordinary courts to be decided in *parallel* proceedings. The phenomenology of the issue may also play a role. What antitrust violation is alleged; is it sufficiently incidental to the case even if not to the particular issue to be decided (such as contract validity)? Are the alleged perpetrators all subject to the arbitration clause and so on? In an intervening bankruptcy of one of the parties to an arbitration, similar issues may arise, for example in terms of proof of claim, suspension of enforcement rights.[563]

It is therefore *not* so that these public policy issues have become irrelevant in international cases, but the assumption, at least of the American courts, is that they may be competently handled elsewhere. This assumes that the foreign courts or international arbitrators will give these issues sufficient weight on the basis of the connection with the country concerned whilst more ordinary choice of law and conflict rules will *only* become relevant to point to the appropriate law *after* the issues of reasonableness and remoteness have been separately considered in respect of these governmental interests.[564]

In regulatory matters, the key may be increasingly to develop more *substantive* international rules to restrain the effects of domestic *public* policies and to determine when they must be given weight. This is the question of international minimum standards accompanied by issues of fairness, legitimate contact (through conduct or effect) or remoteness, proportionality and legitimacy of the policy. Domestic case law and standards such as those found in the US foreign relations laws and in similar laws of other countries may serve as examples in this regard and show the way and may then lead to such international minimum standards,[565] whilst in the *private* law aspects proper, including its own mandatory rules and values, substantive international or transnationalised rules may also derive from the *lex mercatoria*.

The important consequence of the American cases also accepting forum selection and arbitration clauses in respect of public policy issues—which were motivated by the recognition that international trade had started to require these forum selection and arbitration clauses to be upheld—is that, in so far as international arbitration is concerned, the

---

[563] This may also affect bankruptcy issues: see V Lazics, *Insolvency Proceedings and Commercial Arbitration* (1998); see also vol III, ch 1, s 1.1.14ff.

[564] Yet the law resulting as applicable under contractual choice of law clauses may still be allowed to settle the issue when it is one of a public policy *protection* that may be deemed contractually waived by the protected parties, see *Simula, Inc v Autoliv* 175 F3d 716 (9th Circ, 1999) and the earlier Lloyd's cases; see, eg *Bonny v Lloyd's of London* 3 F3d 156 (7th Circ, 1993).

It would not appear helpful to see this development as an instance of privatisation of public policy, the issues arising thereunder subsequently to be decided under the standard rules of private international law (which have in any event little to say on the law applicable in respect of public policy as they were never developed for this complication either). The ultimate consequence would then be that private parties could opt in and out of any public policy they wanted or disliked. They are unlikely to succeed.

[565] It should be repeated that in civil law, this type of discretion in the jurisdiction to prescribe and also *forum non-conveniens* considerations do not apply and that relevant arbitration and forum selection clauses are normally upheld as a matter of law except that national courts may not wish to put the resources necessary to hear cases that have no conceivable contact with the forum (see also s 2.2.4 *in fine* above).

As far as the applicable law is concerned, in the traditional civil law approach, the tension between public policy and private international law rules has proved less easy to resolve probably also because of the ingrained tendency to bring all under traditional conflict of laws rules, therefore within the purview of private law.

arbitrability notion has been greatly expanded. Was it formerly possible to say that public policy issues were not normally arbitrable and therefore had to be moved to the ordinary courts in duplicate or parallel proceedings, even in minor cases (so that arbitration panels would not enter into the consideration of governmental interests and their balancing if conflicting), this is now, at least from an American perspective, no longer the position. It signalled a profound change in the nature of international commercial arbitration which has also had a resonance elsewhere,[566] even in the ECJ.[567]

Although arbitration tribunals at the beginning of the case may in such instances still be ousted by appropriate state courts (for example, if a major antitrust case arises which may hardly be considered incidental to the litigated contract) at least on the basis of *forum non conveniens* notions (in the US, and probably also the UK, where this doctrine is known), awards may still ensue if the panel does not believe the state courts to be the proper venue and does not consider its task finished by their intervention. As things now stand, such an award might still be challenged, however, on the basis of public policy in the place where it was rendered (the seat). Under the New York Convention, it would in any event be subject to a public policy test in the country where recognition is asked. This may still entail an important limitation on such issues being determined by arbitration tribunals. An important question in this regard is whether the public policy test itself may be subject to trans-nationalisation, presenting therefore an objective international substantive (minimum) standard. One must assume that the trend is in that direction.[568]

2.2.9 Party Autonomy and Contractual Choice of Law

In the foregoing paragraphs, especially at the end of section 2.1.1, the parties' ability to choose the applicable law was mentioned.[569] In that connection, it was pointed out that such a choice itself, which normally means the choice of a domestic law (but might now also mean the choice of the *lex mercatoria* or even sharia law or European Principles, a facility since 2008 recognised in the Preamble of the EU Regulation that replaced the 1980

---

[566] See in Switzerland *GSA v SpA* 118 Arrets du Tribunal Federal [AFT] II, 193 (28 April 1992), in which the Swiss courts held that an arbitration panel wrongly refused to apply the EU competition laws whilst determining the validity of the contract. See for a further discussion JH Dalhuisen, 'The Arbitrability of Competition Issues' (1995) 11 *Arbitration International* 151.

[567] See Case C-126/97 *Eco Swiss v Benetton* [1998] ECR I-3055, in which it was held that the antitrust provisions of the EC Treaty (Art 81) were matters of public order that could first be raised in setting-aside proceedings (the original agreement had not been properly notified to the EU antitrust authorities and was thus void). See further also Paris Court of Appeal 18 November 2004, Case no 2002/60932 (*Thalès*) JCP G 2005 II 10038. It rejected annulment on the grounds that there was no prima facie case and more complex investigation was believed to be beyond the court's statutory task.
The ECJ did not strictly speaking decide whether arbitrators may or must apply antitrust rules *ex-officio* but it seems implied and it would appear that arbitrators may at least raise the matter in oral argument (so as to prevent a later setting aside procedure) and are not then exceeding their mandate.

[568] See also s.1.1.10 above.

[569] In England, the Privy Council in *Vita Food Products Inc v Unus Shipping Co Ltd* [1939] AC 277 expressly accepted that parties are free to choose a legal system to govern their contractual relationship subject to that choice not being contrary to public policy and it being bona fide and legal. That is a general principle of contractual freedom now also embodied in the EU in Art 2 of the 1980 Rome Convention of the Law Applicable to Contractual Obligations and its successor the EU Regulation of 2002, always assuming, of course, that the legal issues are at the free disposition of the parties.

EU (Rome) Convention on the Law Applicable to Contractual Obligations) may still raise major questions, especially when public policy issues are involved in the particular country or case.

The first one is how far this choice goes, in which matters therefore such a choice may prevail. This issue was already briefly raised earlier. Obviously, it does not mean the application of the tax laws of the country whose laws have been chosen, nor its regulatory laws, eg those concerning the environment or finance which will be particular to that country. Nor does it mean the adaptation of the bankruptcy laws of the chosen country to determine the effect on the contract when either party is bankrupt. The competition laws of such a chosen legal system are not automatically activated in this manner either.[570]

It was also noted that there are obvious limits too as to proprietary issues in respect of assets located elsewhere. There is, for example, no way in which a mortgage can be created in real estate in England in the French or German manner, no matter how much parties might wish it (even if in an assignment of claims against foreign debtors, parties are sometimes thought to have more autonomy over the applicable law including in its proprietary consequences, which may also apply as to the applicable custodial regime or trusts).[571] Applicable public policy rules or mandatory provisions other than the ones already mentioned (in tax, bankruptcy and competition matters) can also not simply be discarded by party choice, unless they themselves allow it. Thus consumer protection will not cease simply by parties having selected a foreign law that does not provide any, *cf* in the EU Article 6(2) Rome I Regulation 2008. What may also play a role is that a particular mandatory law so chosen may not have extraterritorial effect under its *own* terms, but that is not always decisive as, for example, tax, bankruptcy and competition laws (which, from the perspective of the country of origin, are usually applied extraterritorially regardless) show.

Even in contractual matters, especially in respect of the contractual infrastructure, parties may only achieve limited success by choosing a foreign law, for example as to their own capacity and the legality of their actions. In addition, they cannot simply declare a contract valid even if the formation rules are disregarded. These are areas in which the objectively applicable law is likely to speak much louder and is unlikely to tolerate its removal by party autonomy. A contractual choice of law may then simply be ineffective. By choosing a foreign law, therefore, it still remains a question of interpretation what this choice entails,

---

[570] See JH Dalhuisen, 'What could the Selection by Parties of English Law in a Civil Law Contract in Commerce and Finance Truly Mean?' (n 86) 619.

There remain problems, however. If the law of a particular third country is chosen to cover the sale of goods, does that imply a choice of mandatory or regulatory quality standards? They might be entirely irrelevant in the country of importation or exportation, but they could still be relevant in determining whether there was a breach of contract in terms of delivery, assuming the contract itself does not specify the quality. It is a matter of interpretation.

Another issue is what regulatory quality requirements in the country of importation mean if the contract itself has defined other standards, assuming these importation restrictions are legal, which may not be so any longer in the EU, see Case 47/90 *Delhaize v Promalvin and AGE* [1992] ECR I-3669. May there be *force majeure*?

If these restrictions are legal, who would do the importation may still be relevant. If the importer was in charge of the transport, it would be buying in the exporter's country and could not invoke *force majeure*. Bringing the goods up to the required standard would be at its cost, assuming always that the contractual standard was met. If it was the exporter, it may be impeded from importing the goods and might claim to be excused, at least if the restriction had not been foreseen. Otherwise, the exporter may have to adjust the quality to the demanded regulatory standard to make importation possible, even if this standard is different from the standard defined in the contract, but there may still be a claim for damages in respect of the extra cost.

[571] See also n 41 above.

whilst the objectively applicable law is not necessarily avoided, nor is the law which the parties have opted into necessarily effective in its entirety. Courts and arbitrators will thus have to assess what a contractual choice of law means and in how far it must be ignored.

Other issues already mentioned arise when the effect of the contractual choice cannot have been reasonably intended by the parties, for example, French and German contracting parties opting for the law of England under which their contract would have been void for lack of consideration, a concept probably not properly understood and considered by either party, let alone its consequences for the validity of their contract (which they obviously wanted).[572] Here the chosen law may give the wrong answer, but it could also not give any answer at all—not unlikely in respect of the more advanced modern financial instruments—or answers that are so antiquated as to be useless, for example in the areas of set-off and netting.

Of course, one could say that parties should have been wiser at the outset, and it is true that choices of a legal regime are often made without much thought of the consequences.[573] But that also suggests that they may not be intended to apply in all their effects and such a lack of considered intent may matter. In private law matters, the more natural answer in such cases would be to compare the result with that which would obtain under a *lex mercatoria* approach and see what makes more sense or is more just and reflective of the true needs of participants in the particular trade unless international public order requirements are directed against such an approach or even a domestic public policy if it can be shown to be more relevant in the case. At least gaps in the applicable law are then likely to be filled by transnational law. It is a variation on the earlier rejection (in this book) of the (formal legal) notion that domestic laws are always complete in themselves. This may in some fashion still work at the domestic level but is unlikely to do so in international cases for which these local laws were seldom made.

In the *lex mercatoria* approach with the hierarchy of norms as advocated in this book, see sections 1.4.13 above and 3.1.2 below, party autonomy including the choice of a domestic law would in the transnational commercial and financial legal order still be subject to the higher norms derived from the fundamental legal principles (including international public order requirements in terms of ethical, social, economic and environmental considerations as internationalised values, even if the details may have to be left to lower norms), mandatory customary law or industry practices (particularly relevant in the proprietary aspects of these transactions to the extent their emerging), and mandatory treaty law in as far as existing (including in the EU its Regulations and Directives), even if it must be admitted that what is mandatory in this connection may still be a matter of interpretation,

---

[572] See also O Lando, 'The *Lex Mercatoria* in International Commercial Arbitration' (1985) 34 *ICLQ* 747.

[573] See for the link between the choice of law by the parties and economic realities, G Cordero-Moss, *International Commercial Law* (Oslo, 2010) 81 and the often entirely irrational motivations in such choices. See further also A Briggs, *Agreements on Jurisdiction and Choice of Law* (Oxford, Oxford University Press, 2008) 383, who goes into the parties' power, the problem of mandatory law in this connection and their direct effect under Art 9 Rome I; and G Ruehl, 'Party Autonomy in the Private International Law of Contracts' in E Gottschalk et al (eds), *Conflict of Laws in a Globalized World* (New York, Cambridge University Press, 2007) ch 9, who illustrates the attitude of evaluation of overall effect and the issues of fairness and due process as overarching notions in choice of law doctrine in the US, particularly in areas of law not at the free disposition of the parties (where different governmental interests may operate) and suggest here a closeness to the European approach which may not yet exist.

which in the transnational legal order would, however, be primarily a matter to be determined under the rules of that order.

Directory customs or practices, even of an international nature, could, on the other hand, still be overtaken by a contractual choice of law, assuming it is clear what parties intended. So would be any resort to directory general principles, again unless there are clear gaps in the applicable law so chosen or if the result of such a choice of law would clearly be absurd in terms of the dynamics of international commerce and finance. The general principles may also acquire a higher status if they implement fundamental principle or mandatory custom or treaty law.[574]

It has already been said that the choice may now also be in favour of a non-state law, for example, in appropriate cases the *lex mercatoria* or sharia law.[575] Where parties have not provided for any choice of law clause at all, in international commercial and financial matters their application could still appear appropriate and international arbitrators in particular may be willing in such cases to directly apply transnational law or even sharia law rather than resort to choice of law considerations leading to the application of a domestic law. At least under the EU Regulation, that may still be more difficult for ordinary judges, but it would appear an undesirable difference. It was argued before that domestic courts could be considered to sit as international commercial courts in the transnational legal order, see section 1.1.9 above, and should apply the modern *lex mercatoria* no differently than international arbitrators.

---

[574] In the *Pyramids* case, *SPP (Middle East Ltd) and South Pacific Projects v Egypt and EGOTRH* [1988] LAR 309, 330, the ICC Tribunal held that even though Egyptian law was the proper law of the contract, it had to be construed so as to include principles of international law and the domestic law could only be relied upon in as much as it did not contravene international principle.

The LCIA Arbitration Rules (Art 22(3), the ICC Arbitration Rules (Art 17(1)), and the ICSID Convention (Art 42(1)) make it perfectly clear that general principles may be considered in international arbitrations.

Art 28(1) of the UNCITRAL Model Law is also usually interpreted in such a way that general principle may apply, especially where it refers to 'rules of law'. That would also cover the *lex mercatoria*. Only where the reference is to 'law' it is now thought that a national law is being meant, see further also M Heidemann, *Does International Trade Need a Doctrine of Transnational Law? Some thoughts at the Launch of a European Contract Law* (2012) 2.4.2.

French Arbitration law (formerly Art 1496 CCP of 1981 now replaced by Art 1511 CCP as part of a new international arbitration law in France in 2011) sanctions the application of the *lex mercatoria*, and there is little doubt that arbitrators may apply it. The new law refers here to 'rules of law' which are considered to cover the point. International arbitrators also may have greater freedom when determining the relevance of domestic public policy considerations per case as we have seen.

[575] Earlier, on the basis of Arts 1, 3 and 7 of the 1980 Rome Convention on the Law Applicable to Contractual Obligations, it was sometimes argued in Europe that a choice of law in respect of the *lex mercatoria* was not possible, in other words that the freedom to choose the applicable law had to result in the choice of a domestic law. The text of Arts 2 and 3(2) appeared to go in another direction, however. The point was in truth not considered at all by the Convention. The underlying idea was here that only statist laws could count as laws whilst other legal sources could not be considered, a view which must be considered out of date. The 2008 EU Regulation succeeding the Rome Convention conceded the point, at least in Preamble 13, but the relevant language was ultimately removed from the text, mainly under pressure from the Germans.

It should be realised that the earlier Convention and present Regulation did not and does not speak to international arbitrators. Yet the dichotomy that is here suggested between the application of the law by arbitrators and ordinary judges is not welcome or convincing. In truth, ordinary judges should take a similar approach in international business cases and are now allowed to do so but only if parties have opted for the *lex mercatoria* and not otherwise. That remains a substantial restriction in proceedings in the ordinary courts in the EU.

2.3 Interaction of Private International Law and Uniform Law

2.3.1 Private International Law and the Application of Uniform Law

Uniform law in the traditional sense is treaty law like the 1980 UNCITRAL Convention on the International Sale of Goods (CISG), and when properly incorporated by the Contracting States in their own law, it is usually applied automatically and directly by their judges as part of the national *lex fori*, assuming, of course, that the uniform law under its own terms applies to the transaction or situation in question. They may only cover international transactions (or situations) but need not be so limited. The relevant convention may include in this connection a definition of what is considered international. Thus, depending on the subject, it may limit the uniform law to international dealings, but the relevant convention may also apply under its own terms to (similar) purely domestic situations or transactions. This raises several issues, one of which was identified above as the re-emergence of other autonomous sources of law besides these texts at the transnational level when the transaction is cross-border.

If only international dealings are covered, conflicts specialists may further argue that there is always a preliminary question of the applicable law to be determined first under the private international law rules of the courts of Contracting States so seized. They would in that manner first decide which country's laws apply, which could but need not be their own, and only if those are of a country that is party to the relevant convention, would the application of the relevant uniform treaty law follow.

This is, however, *not* generally the approach of the uniform treaty laws themselves, which tend to unilaterally determine the field of their application. This is also the approach in the 2011 draft Regulation concerning a Common European Sales Law (CESL). If they cover international transactions, they then prevail over otherwise applicable domestic private international law rules, *at least* in cases brought before the courts of Contracting States. In other words, such uniform law is then mostly considered to have *direct effect* at least in Contracting States (even if on the whole still objected to by organisations such as the Hague Conference on Private International Law).

Thus the Vienna Convention on the International Sales of Goods (CISG) applies automatically in Contracting States if both parties to the sale come from different Contracting States (unless they have excluded the application of the Convention (Article 1(1)(a)). Only in *non-Contracting* States would the applicable private international law first have to point to the application of the law of a Contracting State for the uniform law to apply, assuming that the other application (or scope) criteria of this uniform law are also met.

Another issue arises when such directly effective uniform laws allow for differences in incorporation of that law. In that case, discrepancies between the incorporation texts may still give rise to the question of which state laws prevail in the circumstances, even amongst Contracting States. This may easily arise under EU Directives in the area of private law; see the next section. Such questions might also arise in the US, where the Vienna Convention was ratified by Congress but the proper incorporation and interpretation remains a question of state law (which determines commercial law) unless considered self-executing. In this context, the question of the appropriate relationship will still acquire relevance to determine which state law is applicable. That is also an issue under the UCC if differently adopted among the various US states: see section 1-301 UCC.

In the EU financial Directives following its Action Plan of 1999, see Volume III, chapter 2, section 3, we see on the other hand that the (uniform harmonisation) rules apply to domestic as well as cross-border financial activity, and no distinction is made between them. There is yet another issue, however, as the division of labour between a home and host regulator does not apply if there is no cross-border trade proper,[576] whilst the issue of passporting, meaning the possibility of offering products and services in other Member States under home country supervision, does not then arise either. The law of the place where the service is rendered would in that case apply to the transaction. There is no cross-border complication.

2.3.2 The Situation with Regard to EU Directives of a Private Law Nature

In the EU under Directives affecting private law (for example consumer law, product liability, and conduct of business and segregation issues in investment services), incorporation in domestic laws leaves much scope for differences as no uniform law but only harmonisation is the objective. Questions of applicable law may thus still arise in these areas between Member States regardless of the harmonisation effort, even if in the EU, as we shall see, the implementation and interpretation by each country needs to conform to the wording and purpose of the relevant Directive. There is therefore a *direct* harmonising effect under these Directives under the ultimate supervision of the ECJ, but in the case of conflict in the details of the implementation, it is still necessary to establish which domestic law applies. Again, under conventional private international law rules, this is likely to be a (closest) relationship issue in matters of private law.

Following the discussion in the previous section, it raises first the preliminary question whether the relevant Directive under its own terms directly applies to cross-border transactions or situations. The Directive may itself clearly determine the applicability or reach of the law formulated therein. That would, in principle, pre-empt the operation of private international law. CESL if it became law, would thus only apply to cross-border dealings, although in the nature of a Regulation as proposed, there would be no differences in implementation. As in the case of uniform treaty law, a Directive may also apply to all transactions or situations. That is indeed the case for the consumer law Directives and also in principle for the banking and investment services Directives, although, as we have seen, there is still a distinction when it comes to passporting and the issue of home and host regulation arises which may also affect private law protection aspects in the conduct of business by intermediaries affecting investors.

Again, often the relevant Directives are not specific on their field of application and do not therefore consider the issue at all. It then becomes a matter of interpretation what their field of application is and whether they also *directly* cover the situation or transaction if they are cross-border or even crossing into non-Member States.[577] It follows that

---

[576] See for the definition, vol III, ch 2, s 1.1.8.

[577] The scope may be even more difficult to determine in respect of transactions or situations with possible contacts in *third* countries, again especially where the Directive does not go into its scope at all. Is it applicable at all? A field of application must be assumed to be inherent in all of them. If not all elements of the case are

only if they do *not* apply directly to cross-border transactions, the normal rules of private international law would apply to cross-border transactions and they would *not* be pre-empted by the Directive.

If the Directive does apply or is deemed to (also) apply to cross-border transactions, this must then be considered a form of *direct* application and harmonisation, which as just mentioned, generally pre-empts the application of domestic conflict rules (again, as in the case of uniform treaty law, discussed in the previous section, unless there are still implementation differences). The 2008 EU Regulation on the Law Applicable to Contractual Obligations is in that case postponed under its own terms (Article 23 Rome I).

It should be realised that, if there are differences in implementation in the various Member States, this would still have a consequence in terms of the applicable law if the Directives were directly applicable to cross-border traffic, but these conflicts would then primarily have to be resolved with reference to the Directive itself (the 'Directive-conform Implementation')[578] and its interpretation at EU level as a matter of uniform European law, rather than through a conflicts of law approach. At least that would most likely be the position of courts within the EU, who could in the case of doubt ask for an opinion of the ECJ in Luxembourg under Article 267 TFEU.

If the matter arose in the courts of non-Member States, however, but still involved the choice of law between two Member States, the normal conflicts rules of those non-Member States would more likely be applied in order to determine the applicable regime in the traditional conflicts of law manner. If the result was subsequently the choice of the one or the other law, the Directive's text itself would then be less likely to be considered in interpretational questions. Of course, the European Court would in such cases not supervise the uniform interpretation either.

If mandatory private law was involved in the Directives (as in consumer law), the courts in Member States may be particularly sensitive to its uniform interpretation. The courts in non-Member States, on the other hand, may again stick to the implementation text of the country which laws it deems applicable under the more traditional conflicts of law

---

connected with the EU, the field of application, eg in respect of consumer law Directives, might then have to be determined with reference to the domicile of the consumer being within the EU. Alternatively, as for the product liability Directive, the true issue may then be whether the product is being marketed in the EU.

[578] An important question remains: which law applies in the case of a different implementation of EU Directives when it is clear that the Directive in principle covers the subject matter and is applicable in cross-border transactions? That remains strictly speaking relevant even if subsequently the competent court must seek a *Directive-conform interpretation* of the local implementation, as it remains to be determined which implementation would in litigation be the *starting point* for the interpretation of the Directive itself.

Assuming that the case is brought in a court in the EU, it raises the question whether that court always starts with its own implementation as a matter of the application of its *lex fori*, or whether the better starting law might be the implementation in another Member State, eg the one of the State whose laws under prevailing private international law rules are more likely to be otherwise applicable in the case. That would still raise conflict of laws problems at that stage of enquiry.

It is indeed mostly assumed that the *lex fori* applies and that there is therefore no need for courts in EU countries to probe whether another implementation of the relevant Directive needs to be considered first. It would seem to be the most efficient approach as the result ultimately should be the same. The implementation law of other countries will then only be relevant as a matter of interpretation, and may especially be considered if there is a reasonable connection with the case.

In international commercial arbitrations, the situation would be different as there is no *lex fori* per se and arbitrators would most likely start with the implementation law of the country most directly concerned or otherwise perhaps the one of the country of the Respondent (if in a Member State).

approach, subject to their own overriding public policy in particular if residents of their own country were affected.[579] It follows from the foregoing that the determination (directly or indirectly) that the scope of EU Directives also covers cross-border transactions within the EU would make them also prevail over uniform conflicts rules derived from EU texts: compare again Article 23 of the EU Regulation (Rome I).

Adjudicatory jurisdiction issues remain here important as well. The House of Lords, now the UK Supreme Court, had, for example, a much more literal interpretation technique in respect of domestic laws than, say, the Dutch Supreme Court, and therefore also had more difficulties in referring to the purpose and hence the scope of Directives, although it did find comfort in this regard in the case law of the European Court[580] or, if necessary when the issue had not yet been clarified at EU level, in the facility to refer the issue to it for a preliminary ruling.

Finally, there are a number of more specific points to make. First there is the approach of the ECJ itself which has, since 1984, demanded a *Directive-conform interpretation* of national implementation legislation, as already mentioned. This is simply a result of the legal order of the EU, which in the areas in which it operates is superior to domestic legal orders.[581] Domestic courts have here a support function in the system and operate therefore in relevant cases as European courts.

An important issue remains, however, the relevance of domestic procedural limitations in the interpretation and the acceptance or rejection of these limitations by the European Court. The accepted objective here is an efficient and real protection which is non-discriminatory and allows the EU objectives to prevail. Local procedural restrictions, although in principal respected may therefore not frustrate this process, for example, in disallowing the testing of Directives in some specialised (provisional) procedures or in rejecting punitive damages where the Directive's implementation would require it.[582]

---

[579] If the transaction is in the international professional sphere, under the approach advocated in this book, the applicable law, if of a private law nature, would be subject to the hierarchy of norms of the *lex mercatoria*, amongst which these harmonised (domestic) rules (if meant to cover international transactions) would figure like treaty law, assuming they were applicable under their own scope provisions. The EU in its DCFR and progeny is not aware of these trends or does not want to consider them. Fundamental principles and mandatory custom and practices particularly would then still prevail over the rules of the Directive even if they were mandatory. Conflicting governmental interests of individual states would have to be separately considered, especially if the transaction stretched into third countries; see also the discussion in ss 1.4.5, 1.4.6 and 1.4.19 above. As far as Member State implementation of the Directive is concerned, international arbitrators might be more readily inclined to go for a Directive conform interpretation; they generally are now less inclined to be convinced by rules of private international law pointing to a domestic law in cross-border transactions. Within their discretion to determine the applicable law, they may also look at the text of the Directive rather than at the implementation statutes.

[580] So indeed in *Lister and Others v Forth Dry Dock and Engineering Co Ltd and Another* [1989] 1 All ER 1134, in which accordingly a purposive interpretation technique was adopted.

[581] See the seminal Cases 26/62 *Van Gend & Loos* [1963] ECR 3; 6/64 *Costa v ENEL* [1964] ECR 1203; 14/68 *Walt Wilhelm* [1969] ECR 1. A prerequisite is that the relevant rule of community law is meant to have direct effect in Member States.

Even though Directives are not directly effective in Member States without domestic implementation, this general precedence of EU law provides the facility of direct application of Directives in the interpretation of domestic implementation laws: see Case 14/83 *Von Colsen and Kamann* [1984] ECR 1891, 10 April 1984. It leaves, however, a question whether this type of interpretation may in fact lead to the de facto adjustment of the implementation legislation if considered defective.

[582] See Case C-261/95 *Palmisani* [1997] ECR I-4025, and W van Gerven, 'Of Rights, Remedies and Procedures' (2000) *Common Market Law Review* 501.

Secondly, there is the untimely or faulty implementation which is strictly speaking not a mere interpretation issue. Normally, *direct effect* of Directives may here be assumed provided the Directive is itself sufficiently precise. In this manner, it may still operate vertically against the defaulting state, not vice versa, and also not between citizens horizontally.[583] The Directive conform interpretation is there partly to remedy this latter problem, however, and may be effective especially in the case of incomplete or defective implementation when it will acquire a correcting function.

Another more draconian remedy, admitted in case law since 1991, is state liability of the defaulting Member States that may thus become *directly* liable for any adverse consequences for citizens when the other two methods fail, which may happen if a State is not otherwise directly liable under the relevant Directive. Domestic courts will thus be able to impose penalties on the defaulting State if a citizen misses a chance or a protection against other citizens as a consequence.[584]

There is here also the question of the power of domestic judges to invoke the relevant Directive autonomously, therefore without any of the parties having invoked it. This is, in principle, admitted if the EU rules are absolutely mandatory, assuming always that the local judge has the power to apply mandatory rules *sua sponte* or on its own motion under its own laws.[585]

A last point is that in interpreting EU Directives, the European Court is likely to use Europeanised concepts, even in private law. These are therefore concepts that could be quite different from those which are known to local judges under domestic laws and that are used in the implementation legislation; see also the discussion in sections 1.4.4 and 1.4.6 above. The notion of good faith, especially relevant for the interpretation of the Consumer Directive, may be a case in point; see Volume II, chapter 1, section 1.3.8. No less dramatic could be the interpretation of the client asset segregation requirement and agency duties in the field of investors' protection originally under the 1993 Investment Services Directive, succeeded in 2007 by MiFID.

So far, they may have received inadequate implementation in several civil law countries in private law, especially in the agency protection aspects (see further Volume III, chapter 2, section 3.2.6). It concerns here issues of tracing and constructive trust and of relative rights of principals after the disclosure of their interests in a bankruptcy of their broker/agent: see also Volume II, chapter 1, section 3.1.6 and chapter 2, section 1.4.3 and Volume III, chapter 2, section 1.3.10. The reasons for the discrepancies is that domestic laws in Member States are here far apart and systemic considerations do not allow for easy incorporation, which has affected more particularly the EU Collateral Directive. It may well be that in these types of cases, at EU level, the interpretation that will achieve the *best* customer or investor protection overall will be chosen.

---

[583] Case C-91/92 *Faccini Dor* [1994] ECR I-3325.
[584] Cases C-6/90 and C-9/90 *Francovich* [1991] ECR I-5357.
[585] Cases C-430/93 and C-431/93 *Van Schijndel* [1995] ECR I-4705, 15 December 1995. See for the *Eco Swiss v Benetton* case, n 567 above.

Part III The Operation and Substance of Transnational Commercial and Financial Law or the Modern *Lex Mercatoria*

3.1 The *Lex Mercatoria*, Interrelation with Private International Law, Legitimation

3.1.1 The Background to the Revival of the *Lex Mercatoria*

In the foregoing, it was explained that the transnational *lex mercatoria* disappeared as a consequence of the nationalisation in Europe of all law formation from the early nineteenth century onwards. In this climate, even private law, not excluding commercial law, became purely national and territorial. It was posited, however, that the idea that modern law, especially private law, is always statist and therefore territorial was only a nineteenth-century theory and political objective connected with the emergence of the modern state as organisational superstructure and motor of modernity. At least in private law, only 50 years earlier, political philosophy had held exactly the opposite view. It was never more than opinion and to assume henceforth that there could be no other law was always surprising. Here the tide is turning.

At the outset, it should be repeated that at least on the European Continent, the statist idea of law formation was never greater democratic legitimacy. Rather, it concerned state absolutist ideas. In Germany, nineteenth-century Romantic notions of nationality and of the modern state as the true expression of the human condition and the only legitimate actor in the march of history had seen to that. The French and Austrian Codes of 1804 and 1811 had still been more the product of the age of Enlightenment, meant to clean the law of a myriad of local or regional rules whilst at the same time providing greater clarity and transparency. Whatever the original idea, henceforth the law, even private law, could only be national and issued from a legislature, never mind whether it was public or private law and meant to apply to a national or international/transborder fact situation, or whether or not that legislature was itself democratic.

Moving national legislation to the centre of law formation in this manner had the advantage, however, of providing a ready vehicle for legal change and adaptation. Assuming the proper insights, it allowed rapid progress and further adjustments and rationalisation, although in practice, at least in private law, updating became often patchy and increasingly late. The price was doing away with all alternative laws even where they were community-based and potentially more participatory, responsive and efficient in terms of practical needs, such as, conceivably, customary law at least in trade and commerce or finance. The idea was rather one national and super-imposed unitary system for all, regardless of the nature of the relationships, therefore in modern terms in principle the same even for consumer transactions and professional dealings. In the EU, the 2008–2009 Draft Common

Frame of Reference (DCFR), as an unofficial academic text, remains wedded to this basic idea and concept, as we saw in section 1.4.19 above. So does the 2011 Draft Regulation for a Common European Sales Law (CESL) (see Volume II, chapter 1, section 1.6), which is in essence an anthropomorphic consumer law text.

In this approach, fundamental or general legal principle, earlier captured in natural law notions, were rejected as autonomous sources of law. In contract, party autonomy took a back seat and operated only by legislative authorisation, whilst customs and industry practices became suspect and at most relevant in interpretation. They were often seen as regressive legal elements, pushing the modern law back into a cultural environment that was thought to be parochial or atavistic, although especially in modern commerce and finance that may be greatly contested. Particularly after World War II, this statist attitude became intertwined with the modern notion of regulation and the idea of the welfare state, under which states not only tried to provide a better infrastructure but also attempted to remake society according to the prevailing political views, often with a strong redistribution element. That became clear in consumer law, earlier in employment law, but, because of the unitary approach, it easily spilled over into professional dealings as well.

In private law formation in codification countries, a more particular feature of this movement was that, at least in Germany, private law became an intellectual construct that was supposed to have unity in itself and was then believed to represent by definition the reality of human relationships and their best balance. That became the idea behind all later codifications, whose texts were then considered self-sufficient, in the sense that they were thought to have the answer in them to all legal questions, either directly or otherwise through correct interpretation techniques which had the intellectual system as its base, even more than the text. It was thus assumed that pure intellectual abstraction could satisfactorily capture the reality of all human relationships and, where needed, govern them properly.

But even this intellectual system was considered territorial per se, only meant to meet domestic needs, and therefore no longer intellectual and rational in a universal sense like the secular natural law had been. Not even in international commercial transactions thereafter was there room for a more universal normativity, even if greater rationality or efficiency would have supported or dictated it.

As we have seen, in England, although not accepting the intellectualisation of private law and its centralisation at the level of the legislature in this manner, the idea also took hold that all law in whatever form must emanate from a sovereign (which could be through the court system). So there was no less nationalism in law formation, including in private law, although it did not lead to a similar emphasis on legislation or the state as its only legitimate source. There were no overriding systematic considerations either. The common law itself was rather of 'immemorable usage', gradually formed in the King's courts and first only corrected in equity, later mainly by the state through legislation, which is still believed to be exceptional in private law. However, in the eighteenth century, it had already absorbed the commercial law, which as a consequence also became largely territorial, even if it retained some independence and there was still some respect for commercial custom, but it could then hardly be international whilst it also became subject to the law of precedent, further limiting the flexibility it had once brought. That also happened to equity.

At least in England, custom is now generally considered an implied condition only and admitted mainly as such, thus limiting its force to the law of contract. It is then no longer an autonomous dynamic source of law either, unless specifically so authorised, although there may be some more room for it in commerce as just mentioned—it is unclear what its true status is then—whilst it was also noted that the UCC in the US in section 1-103 takes a different view and leaves ample room for other sources of law (as had the Justinian codification in D.1.1.1.6ff) such as equity but also custom, whether national or international. Thus the UCC is not a codification in the European sense, as it does not aspire to be laying down an inherently coherent intellectual system that is complete and has all the answers.

The consequence was that, both in the civil law and common law at least of the English variety, even commercial law became national and territorial, on the European Continent contained in national commercial codes that served as supplements to the civil codes and their intellectual systems and provided only some special additional rules for commercial transactions (as defined). In particular it left international commercial transactions and the laws applicable to them exposed, as the old *lex mercatoria* as substantive transnational law was at least in Europe soon abandoned, although still referred to in the first (1893) English Sale of Goods Act. It is true that it had never been universal, but where it was still territorial, it was not confined to a national territory. Thus one law of admiralty had developed on both sides of the English Channel, one law of transport by land between the provinces of Eastern France and Northern Italy.

However, henceforth the conclusion was drawn, as already by von Savigny as we have seen, that all legal relationships, no matter how international, always had a seat in a domestic law and that this seat and therefore the applicable law could be identified through the conflict rules of private international law. They were, therefore, no more than conduits through which the properly applicable domestic law could be found in international transactions. It seemed the inescapable result once all law had been nationalised and became only domestic, but it was no less an intellectual presumption and in truth a mystical nineteenth- and twentieth-century pretence which made little sense as these domestic laws were seldom made for international transactions and could be wholly inadequate or inappropriate for them. The further irony was that these conflict rules were at first seldom statutory but depended on some principles that were at first often considered universal.

The subsequent denial of the force of international commercial custom, of party autonomy (which was also thought to operate only by domestic legislative authorisation or licence as we have seen), and of general principles (unless underlying the purely domestic system), although not to the same extent in the US, was an important consequence. No less destructive was the idea in civil law countries that the applicable domestic laws were self-contained and intellectually complete, for international transactions as well. Certainty was often cited, but in the circumstances could be of such a low quality that it unsettled international transactions. This may now be better shown in modern international financial dealings.

It is the thesis of this book that there is no rational argument against, rather a strong sociological and economic argument in favour of, a *transnational substantive* law for professional dealings, therefore an independent transnational law obtaining between professionals in their international business transactions, as indeed there was before the time of the great European codifications. It is the issue of different legal orders and of legal plurality, which allows for different sources of law to operate side by side of which statist texts are only one. We still have this between states in public international law, to which Article 38(1) of the Statute of the International Court of Justice testifies, and it mentions the different sources. It is somewhat perplexing that public international law presents here no intellectual problem for its functioning (although it was also infested with nineteenth-century sovereignty notions) whilst a substantive transnational private law operating along similar lines and in a similar manner in the minds of many still does.

In private law, the result of newer thinking in this area (which in civil law reverts to pre-codification days) is the new *lex mercatoria*, which is not statist, and is therefore not territorial either, but emanates—it was submitted—from the international commercial and financial legal order that businessmen maintain amongst themselves. At least in international business transactions, private international law or conflicts of law notions come here to their useful end. Although they may remain valid to the extent that domestic law retains a residual function in the *lex mercatoria* where transnational law has not yet developed, they will become ever less important now that in this order fundamental legal principle, custom and industry practices, party autonomy, and international general principle retake their place, all as autonomous sources of transnational law, although combined in and still subject to the pubic order requirements of the international commercial and financial legal order itself. Even where in the ensuing hierarchy of norms at the transnational level domestic law still retains a residual function, it operates—it was posited—as part of the transnational law, must make sense therein, allow for the demands of the transnational public order, and is in its application to be re-interpreted and adjusted accordingly.

It has also been said, however, that the international commercial and financial legal order must respect local statist legal orders to the extent that they may claim a justified interest in the international transaction, which is relevant especially in regulatory matters in respect of conduct and effect of the international transaction on the territory of the state concerned. Nobody can deny that a state is sovereign in respect of all that happens on its territory, even if non-statist legal orders now also ask room for their operation and a proper understanding of the rule of law encourages this. It was earlier identified as a question of competition between different legal orders on the same territory and a matter of balance, which is becoming an ever more important issue in commerce and finance; see sections 2.2.6ff above. As part of this balance, local statist legal orders in their enforcement function must recognise the transnational laws and the decisions based thereon (for example, in international commercial arbitrations) to the extent not offensive to their internal public order. In fact, this was identified above not only as a rule of law issue, but also as a quid pro quo: if a country wants its own people and businesses to operate internationally and receive reasonable protection internationally, it must also offer reasonable protection itself.

3.1.2 The Concept of the Modern *Lex Mercatoria* as a Hierarchy of Norms

To determine the private law applicable to international commercial and financial transactions, the key question is thus whether there may exist or may be developing a whole new pattern of substantive transnational law in the professional sphere within an *own, non-territorial non-statist legal order*. It is the contention of this book that there is now such a legal order operating in international trade and finance as a natural consequence of the globalisation of the international professional activities in these areas, and the freeing of the flows of persons, goods, services, capital and technology internationally; for the introduction of this theme, see section 1.5 above.

It was also submitted that this order has now acquired the capacity and energy to move itself forward, creating its own laws and even law-making institutions or facilities such as ICC committees for Incoterms and UCP and international commercial arbitrations for dispute resolution purposes. In international sports, there may also be an own legal order, operating with institutions like the Olympic Committee and FIFA that have even assumed a quasi-criminal jurisdiction over the behaviour of sportsmen and women in international competitions.

Originally, it might have been thought feasible and logical to build the new *lex mercatoria* around a nucleus of uniform treaty laws[586] as formulated, for example, in the area of international sale of goods by the 1964 Hague Conventions and subsequently in the 1980 Vienna Convention (CISG) and in the area of transportation by sea in the 1924 Brussels Convention (the so-called Hague Rules, later amended by the Hague-Visby Rules for bills of lading, especially in their transportation rather than proprietary aspects) or in the 1978 UNCITRAL Hamburg Rules, and in the area of bills of exchange and cheques by the 1930 and 1932 Geneva Conventions and later the 1988 UNCITRAL Convention for International Bills of Exchange (and in several other areas by other UNCITRAL efforts like the one on the statute of limitations), see for the efforts at uniform law of both UNCITRAL and UNIDROIT more particularly section 1.4.18 above.

However, once the operation of the international professional legal order is identified, these Conventions cannot remain the nucleus of the new law. They are at best only one source of it. More importantly, they remain in essence statist and territorial. Upon the incorporation into national laws, these treaties remain national and limited in reach. Under their own terms, there may be further limitations, for example they may apply only to residents of Contracting States, although they may also reflect more general principles and industry practices and could also be expressions of non-territorial law. There are other significant drawbacks of uniform treaty law, already spelt out above in section 1.4.10, connected with the often limited and partial coverage of the area of the law treaties seek to unify, and especially with the difficulty of amending them and keeping them up to date. There is also the point that they are too often the result of a myriad of compromises or a trade-offs in domestic legal concepts and may not reflect the dynamics and justified needs of international trade and commerce nor its rationality as it moves forward. There is mostly very limited industry input. In the civil law codification tradition which favours the intellectual model this is not truly considered necessary either.

As suggested above in sections 1.5.5 and 2.2.5, the new transnational law would in fact primarily result from: (a) the nature of the relationship between the (professional) parties;[587] (b) their special interests, needs and protection requirements; (c) the nature and logic of their transactions and of the legal structures used therein; and (d) common sense, rationality or utility, or what participants consider fair and reasonable amongst themselves or need in terms of risk management. Again, it is driven by the internationalisation or globalisation of the flows in goods, services, technology and money. The evolution of this law should be perceived as a macro- or institutional and not as a micro-event. It is geared to elevate business and avoid disputes rather than primarily to resolve them in individual

---

[586] This is still the attitude of Roy Goode, see n 9 above.
[587] See for this approach in the UK, Bingham LJ in *Interfoto v Stiletto* [1989] 1 QB 433, 439.

cases, which has always remained an imperfect art. The modern perspective of law as mainly a dispute resolution device here recedes into the background.

To properly assess each party's rights and duties, an analysis of the *facts and circumstances* of the transaction or the case is central, supported by: (a) the terms of the agreement in the areas of the law at the free disposition of the parties; (b) patterns of commerce already established between them and their ever developing usages in terms of industry practices or custom; (c) uniform treaty law to the extent formulated and applicable under its own terms; and (d) common legal notions (for example, of contract, tort or property) whether or not expressed in international conventions, like those just mentioned or in collections of principles (like those for contract law of the EU and UNIDROIT see Volume II, chapter 1, section 1.6) and now in the EU even in full codification proposals in the 2008–2009 Draft Common Frame of Reference (DCFR and its progeny, see Volume II, chapter 1, section 1.6 and chapter 2, section 1.11).

It has already been said that the application of these rules should always be *preceded* by the application of: (e) *fundamental legal principles* as the basis of the whole system; and (f) any *mandatory* custom as such usually closely connected with these fundamental principles; or (g) *mandatory* uniform treaty law (again if applicable under its own terms); and perhaps also (h) *mandatory* general principle as it may develop especially in movable property law and set-off/netting, or in matters of contractual validity and issues of legal capacity.

If upon a proper analysis of the facts in the light of the norms that thus become available, there is still no solution, these norms would be finally *supplemented* by: (i) the domestic law found under the traditional conflict of law rules. To repeat, this domestic law would then residually function in the transnational legal order itself and be subject to it so that its application would have a discretionary element as the result would have to be fitting as transnational law.[588]

Again, in this hierarchy, *public policy* or *public order* requirements of a domestic or transnational nature are not discounted. As has been explained before, they compete and cut through it in the manner as described in sections 2.2.6 to 2.2.8 above. It concerns here mostly *national* regulation or public order requirements or similar national values in respect of international transactions that have some (appreciable) effect or conduct on the territory of states that in this manner may claim a governmental interest. Again, this is truly a matter of *competing* legal orders and ultimately of balance. But public order requirements as fundamental mandatory legal principle in private law could also operate in the *lex mercatoria* itself, in commerce and finance notably to eliminate market abuse or anti-competitive behaviour or to counter other excess.

In section 1.4.13 above, the multiplicity of the sources of private law at the transnational level and the *hierarchy* of the norms flowing therefrom were identified as *the essence* of the modern *lex mercatoria* and its details will be further discussed in section 3.2 below.[589] In

---

[588] In WA Bewes, *The Romance of the Law Merchant: An Introduction to the Study of International and Commercial Law* (1923, reprinted in 1986) 13, there is an interesting comment where it is explained that the *lex mercatoria* had its origins in the law of nations as it grew to a great degree out of transactions that took place between different nations (but not necessarily by these nations). Thus private international law is here in its origin seen as a branch of the law of nations and closely connected with substantive international or transnational law.

[589] See originally, JH Dalhuisen, *Wat is Vreemd Recht?* [What is Foreign Law?], Inaugural Address, Utrecht (Kluwer, Deventer, 1991).

confirming domestic law as the residual rule, it affirms that this new transnational law or the modern *lex mercatoria* is not more incomplete than any domestic law and is thus fully operative as a complete system for those who seek this. The ranking was given as follows:

(a) fundamental legal principle;
(b) mandatory custom;
(c) mandatory uniform treaty law (to the extent applicable under its own scope rules);
(d) mandatory general principle;
(e) party autonomy;
(f) directory custom;
(g) directory uniform treaty law (to the extent applicable under its own scope rules);
(h) general principles largely derived from comparative law, uniform treaty law (even where not directly applicable or not sufficiently ratified), ICC Rules and the like;[590] and
(i) residually, domestic laws found through conflicts of law rules.[591]

As to the *fundamental* legal notions or principles of private or transactional law which come first and form the basis of the whole system, they have also already been briefly discussed, in section 1.4.5 above, and are particularly:

(a) *pacta sunt servanda* as the essence of contract law;
(b) the recognition, transferability and substantial protection of ownership to be respected by all as the essence of all property;[592]
(c) the liability for own action, especially:
  (i) if wrongful (certainly if the wrong is of a major nature) as the essence of tort law;
  (ii) if leading to detrimental reliance on such action by others as another fundamental source of contract law;
  (iii) if creating the appearance of authority in others as the essence of the law of (indirect) agency; or
  (iv) if resulting in owners creating an appearance of ownership in others as an additional fundamental principal in the law of property leading to the protection of the bona fide purchaser (setting aside the more traditional *nemo dat* principle).

There are other fundamental principles in terms of:

(d) apparent authority and fiduciary duties leading to special protections of counterparties, notably if weaker or in a position of dependence (including principals against agents, consumers against wholesalers, workers against employers, individuals against

---

[590] These are unlikely to be mandatory but should they be so, as they might in proprietary matters, they would move up above party autonomy (under (d)) but still be subject to mandatory custom or mandatory treaty law.

[591] Should domestic law be mandatory, as generally in property law, it then also moves above party autonomy (under (d)), but will still be subject to mandatory customary law or mandatory uniform treaty law, and therefore be firmly anchored in the transnational law itself.

[592] Traditionally, the *nemo dat* principle was considered to capture the essence of property law but property is now also a human rights' supported notion particularly in the context of protection against expropriation, see Protocol 1, Art 1 of the 1950 European Convention on Human Rights and s 1.5.8 above, to be respected by governments and (horizontally) by other citizens alike.

the state, smaller investors against brokers), and to duties of disclosure and faithful implementation of one's contractual and other obligations;

(e)   notions of unjust enrichment;

(f)   respect for acquired or similar rights, traditionally particularly relevant to outlaw retroactive government intervention, but also used to support owners of proprietary rights in assets that move to other countries; and

(g)   equality of treatment between creditors, shareholders and other classes of interested parties with similar rights unless they have acquired proprietary protection or have postponed themselves.

Then there are:

(h)   fundamental procedural protections in terms of impartiality, proper jurisdiction, proper hearings and the opportunity to mount an adequate defence, now often related to the more recent (and also internationalised) standards of human rights and basic protections (see Article 6 of the 1950 European Convention on Human Rights (ECHR));

(i)   fundamental protections against fraud, sharp practices, excessive power, cartels, bribery and insider dealings or other forms of manipulation in market-related assets (also in their civil and commercial aspects) and against money laundering; this concerns the *transnational public order*;

(j)   transaction and payment finality, equally demanded by the transnational public order itself; and finally

(k)   there are also increasingly fundamental principles of the protection of the environment, of labour and financial stability developing.

As many of these fundamental principles are public order or even human rights related, this underscores their absolutely mandatory nature. No doubt there are other fundamental principles, and the above list is not meant to be exhaustive. It is often a matter of basic values, which here acquire the force of law. Although in commercial and financial law, there may not be many, the essence is to show that fundamental legal principles are at the heart of all civilised modern legal systems,[593] and therefore also operate in trade and finance, when others, like the notion of contractual finality, are more closely related to utility and efficiency considerations, rather than to redistribution and social peace notions. In modern law, especially of the codified variety, these fundamental principles are often hidden, but they come into their own again in the international legal order. The idea is not new and it was a key feature of all secular natural law, see Grotius's principles discussed in section 1.2.7 above. It is also not strange, it is submitted, that public and private law formation come here together at the transnational level. There is at that level no fundamental difference in the nature and operation of the various sources of law, although of course the details may be very different. Again, in as far as method is concerned, reference may be made to Article 38(1) of the Statute of the ICJ.

Thus these fundamental principles might in international sales adjust the balance between the parties on the basis of social or public order considerations (of the international legal order itself), although again in the professional sphere this is less likely. They

---

[593] See for the EU and ECJ in particular, the cases cited in section 1.4.5 above, which were ignored by the DCFR.

may increasingly be considered to have a universal reach, as indeed they had in the natural law school. In contract, they could be considered partly incorporated in a transnational concept of *good faith* when called upon to adjust imbalances or prevent abuse. In this connection it should be noted that in the foregoing good faith itself was *not* elevated to the level of fundamental principle as it had been earlier identified as a multifaceted concept,[594] and is not always fundamental and mandatory. As we shall see, it often primarily denotes a liberal interpretation technique, in which older norms are restated to reach newer fact patterns or situations.

It is submitted that the fundamental principles identified above are not immutable per se and are in any event likely to acquire a special form and meaning depending on the legal order in which they operate. Another connected point is that the fundamental principle of protection between certain parties, like professionals in certain types of deals, even if mandatory, may not result in the same protection as enjoyed by other (less professional) types of parties in otherwise similar circumstances, for example in a sale of goods to consumers. As was observed before, lesser protection and refinement of the law may result between professionals in commercial and financial matters as an overriding requirement connected with the continuation of the normal commercial flows and the imperatives imposed on all participants in their order in this respect. Where the contract is a road map and risk management tool, adjustment is also far less appropriate and could only result in extreme circumstances which will not often occur between professionals.

In sales, this confining approach may indeed be expressed in a transnational concept of good faith in contract law (that distinguishes sharply between different types of parties) and in a transnationalised notion of finality in property law. In contract a more literal reading of the text may follow between professional participants. It is in any event natural for the law to be sensitive to these differences in requirements, which in contract may also emerge in the form of implied conditions or industry custom. This will be discussed in more detail in Volume II, chapter 1.1.4, and was mentioned in section 1.1.4 above in the context of the discussion of legal dynamism in modern professional dealings. As a consequence, the impact of overriding fundamental principle will quite naturally still vary depending on the type of relationship and nature of the transaction and will in any event limit itself to the basic legal structures and not extend to details. This is left to the other sources of law.

Fundamental principle may thus be further directed by established *practices or custom*, which in their supporting role are then likely also to be *mandatory*. For example, where these practices or customs are property-connected, they will prevail over a contractual choice of law. In negotiable instruments, contractual concepts of consideration did not prevail in common law countries either and could not therefore undermine finality, whilst bona fide purchaser protection was developed here early for similar reasons, whilst the notion of independence was favoured from the contract out of which the claim (incorporated in the instrument) arose.

This is now also relevant in the proprietary aspects of more modern international negotiable instruments, such as eurobonds, or increasingly even in all types of trade receivables and the manner in which they are being held and transferred; see also section 3.2.2 below. In section 1.1.4 above, the issue of a modern dynamic movable property law for professionals, especially in their financial dealings, has already been already discussed, in which

---

[594] See n 58 above.

connection party autonomy was found to acquire a special meaning in the creation of new proprietary structures, always subject to the protection of the ordinary commercial flows. Similarly, where an automatic return of title upon default is demanded in the contract, party autonomy may not prevail in practice. It would no less undermine the notion of finality of property transfers and may not prevail in the international legal order, except perhaps if couched in terms of a reservation of title.

Also, *specific performance* of sales agreements, normally available in civil law, might be deemed against the commercial flows and hence commercial practice or realities and common sense may rule out this possibility in international commerce unless it is the only realistic alternative. It does not rule out declaratory findings either, but suggests nevertheless a confining transnational custom.

International conventions with uniform law further supplement the fundamental principles and transnational custom, like those on sales, transportation and payment methods. They naturally supersede domestic laws in contracting states in the areas they cover, even if the domestic law was mandatory, which means that a mandatory domestic rule may be replaced by a directory treaty rule. Their incongruous status in the *lex mercatoria* has been noted several times before as they may still be considered expressions of national and territorial laws upon incorporation into domestic laws. These Conventions contain so far only occasionally mandatory law (see, for example, Article 12 of the Vienna Convention on the International Sale of Goods). This may become different if more progress is made through treaty law in receivable financing, factoring, leasing or mobile equipment where UNCITRAL and UNIDROIT have made some progress as we saw in section 1.4.18 above (see also Volume III, chapter 1, sections 2.3 and 2.4). Even then, it is unlikely that they will prevail over fundamental legal principle or mandatory custom in the international legal order.

In all of this, there are, of course, in contractual matters also the *wording of the contract* and the intrinsic logic of the transaction itself to be considered, if necessary under transnationalised standards of good faith, as already mentioned, although this is probably less relevant in the commercial sphere, which needs special protection only in more extreme situations. As just noted, even in movable property, the impact of party autonomy may have to be reconsidered as well, subject to an extended notion of bona fide purchaser protection. Only fundamental legal principle, and mandatory international custom or mandatory uniform treaty law, to the extent existing, and mandatory general principle would prevail over it, but at least mandatory custom and general principle increasingly support it.

If as part of the contractual terms, a domestic law is chosen as applicable to the transaction by the parties, domestic law then moves up to this rank, but no higher, as it would concern matters of private law not at the free disposition of the parties. Still such a domestic law cannot go beyond what makes sense in the international legal order, as we have seen, and the domestic law so chosen will be adapted to function properly as part of the transnational law: see further the discussion in section 2.2.9 above.

It was shown that such a choice of a domestic law does not normally cover the mandatory public policy or regulatory rules of the law so chosen, at least if they have no relevance in the transaction, especially therefore when that state's public interest is not engaged, for example if the law so chosen would contain an environmental constraint that has no meaning or relevance in the place or places where the transaction is likely to impact. The environmental laws of such places would then have to be considered first, regardless of what the contract says on the applicable law. In short, the chosen law cannot exclude relevant domestic public policy laws.

Common legal principles will have a further effect in defining (normally in a directory manner) international legal relationships where the contractual terms, fundamental principles, custom and treaty law fail or need further elaboration. They may be deduced from national laws if there is a wide consensus between them, and from rationality, efficiency and common sense notions. As was submitted before, especially in property they could even obtain a mandatory normativity in which case the rule moves above party autonomy but would still be subject to mandatory custom and treaty law.

If the applicable transnational private law is still not sufficiently established in this manner, *domestic private law* may still remain relevant (assuming it had not been chosen as the applicable law). Again, the important point here is that such a domestic law then operates in the international legal order and thus becomes part of the transnational law and may be adjusted accordingly to make it fit. The difference with the situation in which this law is chosen is that directory customary law and general principle take precedence.

The result is the hierarchy of norms within the modern *lex mercatoria* discussed in section 1.4.13 above, the details of which will be further explored in the following sections. This hierarchy is here considered the *essence* for the time being of the modern *lex mercatoria* and makes it workable as a fully-fledged system of law for those who still see the system as the essence of all private law.

3.1.3 The Major Protagonists of the *Lex Mercatoria* and their Views: Legitimation

It was posited that the search for a better law based on fundamental and general principles, custom or industry practices, and party autonomy, has culminated in the modern concept of *transnational professional* law or international civil, commercial and financial law, or the new law merchant or *lex mercatoria*. This is not viewed as merely desirable but as an historical trend that reverses the nineteenth-century nationalistic order under the pressure of globalisation and the needs of the international marketplace (subject to its own public order and values or limitations). In this book, the concept of the modern *lex mercatoria* as a hierarchy of norms is not advocated as an article of faith or yet another political theory, but rather as an academic *model* that better explains what is happening, simplifies the argument and makes it more transparent and coherent, and indicates more satisfactorily what is likely to work in an ever more globalised environment.

Indeed in commercial transactions, in the internationalised professional sphere or in the international commercial and financial legal order it represents, this law is now more often referred to as the (new) *lex mercatoria*, a term in modern times particularly associated with Professor Berthold Goldman from France (1913–93), who identified this new legal order based on industry custom and common legal notions, even if not using legal order terminology and the concept of an hierarchy of norms or even fundamental principle.[595]

---

[595] B Goldman, 'La lex mercatoria dans les contrats et l'arbitrage internationaux: realité et perspectives' *Clunet* (1979) 475; B Goldman, 'Lex Mercatoria' *Forum Internatiohale* no 3 (Kluwer, 1983); B Goldman, 'The Applicable Law: General Principles of Law—Lex Mercatoria' in J Lew (ed), *Contemporary Problems in International*

As was noted, the notion of the *lex mercatoria* or law merchant had existed between the Middle Ages and the eighteenth century, particularly in England, and was referred to in English case law well into the nineteenth century, especially in connection with documents of title and negotiable instruments. It was still mentioned in the English Sale of Goods Act of 1893, as it still is in section 1-103 UCC in the USA, where it remains good law, except if specifically overruled. Yet there is here an important difference: the new *lex mercatoria* is at this stage perceived in this book as being in essence a hierarchy of diverse sources of law that operate in a legal order of their own, whilst the old law merchant was a system of largely unwritten uniform customs and practices. Naturally the modern contents are also quite different from what they once were, in which connection it was observed earlier that the new law is likely to be driven as much by modern finance as by mercantile considerations.

Other authors, like Professor Clive Schmitthoff in the UK, were similarly sensitive to the new development but took a more restrictive view and saw the new *lex mercatoria* primarily as an elaboration of domestic law,[596] whilst early protagonists like Professor Norbert Horn from Cologne,[597] Professor Ole Lando in Denmark,[598] Professor AF Lowenfeld in the USA,[599] and more recently Professor Roy Goode in Oxford,[600] are largely pragmatic, but see for a more principled position in the USA in favour of this new law in particular the work of Professor FK Juenger.[601]

As in the field of conflicts law (*cf* section 2.1.1 above), from a more academic point of view, there are here, in essence, two schools of thought: the internationalist and domestic. Those who see a new legal order emerging are to be found in the internationalist camp.

Arbitration (Queen Mary College, London, 1986) 113; B Goldman, 'Lex Mercatoria and Arbitration: Discussion of the New Law Merchant' in TE Carbonneau (ed), (New York, Transnational Juris Publications, 1990).

See n 500 above for a more comprehensive list of major authors on the modern *lex mercatoria*. In France the work of P Fouchard should particularly be noted, see P Fouchard, *L'Arbitrage Commercial International* (1965); P Fouchard, E Gaillard and B Goldman, *Traite de l'Arbitrage Commercial International* (1996); and E Gaillard and J Savage, *Fouchard, Gaillard and Goldman on International Commercial Arbitration* (1999). See more recently in France also E Gaillard, 'Transnational Law: A Legal System or a Method of Decision Making?' (2001) 17 *Arbitration International* 59, but *cf* also P Mayer, 'Reflections on the International Arbitrator's Duty to Apply the Law' (2001) 17 *Arbitration International* 235.

[596] It forestalled local criticism: see C Schmitthoff, *International Business Law: A New Law Merchant, Current Law and Social Problems* (University of Western Ontario, 1961) 129; C Schmitthoff, 'International Trade Law and Private International Law' in *Vom deutschen zum europäischen Recht, Festschrift Hans Doelle* (Tübingen, 1963) vol 2, 261; C Schmitthoff, 'The Unification of the Law of International Trade' (1968) *Journal of Business Law* 109. See for a compilation of his most important writings on the subject Chia-Jui Cheng (ed), *Clive M Schmitthoff's Select Essays on International Trade Law* (Dordrecht, Kluwer, 1988).

[597] N Horn, *Das Recht der internationalen Anleihen* (1972); N Horn, 'A Uniform Approach to Eurobond Agreements' (1977) 9 *Law and Policy in International Business* 753; N Horn, 'Uniformity and Diversity in the Law of International Commercial Contracts' in N Horn and C Schmitthoff (eds), *The Transnational Law of International Commercial Transactions* (1982) 3ff.

[598] O Lando, 'The Lex Mercatoria in International Commercial Arbitration' (1985) 34 *ICLQ* 747. See also for earlier reflections on the phenomenon E Langen, *Studien zum internationalen Wirtschaftsrecht* (Munich, 1963) and P Kahn, *La Vente Commerciale Internationale* (Paris, Sirey, 1961) and 'Lex mercatoria et euro-obligation' in F Fabritius (ed), *Law and International Trade, Festschrift C Schmitthoff* (Frankfurt, 1973) 215.

[599] AF Lowenfeld, 'Lex Mercatoria: an Arbitrator's View' (1990) 6 *Arbitration International* 133.

[600] R Goode, 'Usage and its Reception in Transnational Commercial Law' (1997) 46 *ICLQ* 1. Here we see a dependence mainly on treaty law as the core of the newer developments, see n 9 above. The role of international custom and general principle then remains also largely unclear, see also n 376 above.

[601] FK Juenger, 'Conflict of Laws, Comparative Law and Civil Law: The Lex Mercatoria and Private International Law' (2000) 60 *Loyola Law Review* 1133. See for recent writers on the subject, and more theoretically, especially G Teubner and RD Cooter nn 473 and 474 above.

Others, mostly in the positivist tradition, cannot see any legal order outside the context of a state. This might not prevent international considerations from being taken more directly into account in the interpretation of substantive domestic law, much as in the *lex fori* approach to interstate conflicts in the USA: see section 2.2.3 above. The difference is, however, that, in the latter approach, each country will ultimately go its own way, and no true uniformity is likely to result, as the unity of the law in the international legal order is not more fundamentally recognised and neither is then its own law-creating force.[602]

As suggested throughout this book, the key is the acceptance (or rejection) of the own legal order of international trade, commerce and finance, and within that order of the formation of transnational commercial law, based on fundamental legal principles providing the basic core and major protections.[603] The second feature is the acceptance in that legal order of party autonomy and of international custom; and the third the development of general more practical principles of international commercial and financial law. The relegation of domestic laws to residual status automatically follows from the acceptance of the four prime sources of transnational private law identified earlier and to be further discussed in the next section. Again, the conflict between this law and domestic public policies and public order requirements is seen as a special complication, to be resolved outside the hierarchy of norms of the *lex mercatoria* itself. It concerns here the competition between legal orders and ultimately a balancing of affected public policies or governmental interests against each other and against those of the transnational public order requirements themselves.

3.2 The Hierarchy of Norms: Elaboration

3.2.1 Fundamental Legal Principle. Transnational Rules of Contract Formation and the Normative Interpretation Technique

In contract, the impact of fundamental legal principle appears transnationally first and foremost in formation and interpretation. The principle of *pacta sunt servanda* stands out here as the basic norm for all contract law and is supplemented by, but must be

---

[602] See further the analysis of F De Ly, *International Business Law and Lex Mercatoria* (Amsterdam, 1992). Mustill LJ in the UK has been particularly critical of the *lex mercatoria* as a transnational legal system on the basis of his nationalistic views, wondering where this new law could come from: see 'The New Lex Mercatoria' in M Bos and I Brownlie (eds), *Liber Amicorum Lord Wilberforce* (Oxford, 1987) 149, and 'Contemporary Problems in International Commercial Arbitration' (1989) 17 *International Business Law* 161, criticised by AF Lowenfeld, *Lex Mercatoria*, n 599 above, 123, who believes that the question where the law comes from could particularly be asked for all of the common law. It has already been noted above that this dismissive attitude in England is not necessarily to the advantage of London as international business centre.

See also for a more recent overview, KP Berger, *The Creeping Codification of the Lex Mercatoria*, 2nd edn (2010), who does not present a theory but looks for more black-letter law in the new *lex mercatoria* and collects these rules; see also Translex.org Law Research *Principles with Commentary* (2012) identifying 130 rules. There is here no distinguishing between fundamental and general principles nor between consumer and business rules.

[603] Goldman himself came to the realisation of the importance of fundamental principles in this respect relatively late, when he started to emphasise them besides his common legal notions (and industry practices), which were mainly derived from comparative law research into the different legal structures and terminologies: see 'Nouvelles réflexions sur la Lex Mercatoria' in *Etudes de droit international en l'honneur de Pierre Lalive* (Basle, 1993) 241.

distinguished from, the notion of party autonomy, which is based on it and as autonomous source of law elaborates on it (and is in a modern approach not merely a contractual concept but also operates in movable property law: see section 1.1.4 above).

Since the natural law school, the principle of *pacta sunt servanda* in its further elaboration has often been associated with the concept of consensus between parties, later on developed in offer and acceptance notions. It is unlikely, however, that professional contracts depend solely on consensus promise or intent for their validity and coverage, certainly not in a psychological sense, if only because, at least in business deals of some size, the person who signs the agreement is unlikely to know much of its detail, whilst no single person will have dealt with the various issues, and the end drafting is often left to outside lawyers.

Indeed, in modern law, there is a more objective concept of contract formation at work, that first and foremost depends on the notion of conduct and reliance. In appropriate cases it is supplemented by pre-contractual disclosure and negotiation duties, contractual cooperation duties, post-contractual pre-negotiation duties. Custom and industry practice will also be relevant and taken into account. Offer and acceptance as a kind of theoretical formal model here fade into the background and become at best a subcategory of conduct and reliance, whilst an anthropomorphic idea of contract promise and intent is abandoned; for modern contract theory see also section 1.1.4 above and Volume II, chapter 1, section 1.1.4.

Fundamental legal principle in terms of liability for the justified reliance by the other party on conduct of the first one, and the objective requirements of trade or the course of business, including a beginning of performance, may then become more important in establishing the binding force of an agreement and subsequently its coverage, and to provide explanations, additions and, in extreme cases, possibly even corrections, to the ultimate wording. General principle may offer further support. For sales, treaty law like the 1980 Vienna Convention on the International Sale of Goods (CISG) could also be relevant (at least in countries that accepted it if not excluded by the parties), but it is more likely to distract and will have problems to figure as general principle especially in its paragraphs on formation.

In civil law terminology, the more objective approach to contract formation may to some extent be expressed in the concept of good faith or in non-Member States, normative interpretation of the contractual meaning and content in which the other sources of law may be encapsulated: see further Volume II, chapter 1, section 1.2.1. It would seem a logical approach in transnational law too. Although in this law, domestic law may provide the residual law, as we have seen, it may be superseded by transnational notions earlier than the law in other areas, like movable property, as will be discussed in the next section. The transnational professional law is not personal but mainly directed towards the business sector. Its more objective approach also fills in contractual gaps, and requires a measure of diligence and fair play in its performance, but only in the manner as customary and anticipated or relied upon in that world.

In this connection, it has already been pointed out several times that, although this objective or normative approach to contract formation and interpretation may lead to more refinement, it may also lead to *less*, particularly in the professional sphere, therefore also in respect of defects in the consensus or to lack of clarity of the parties' intent carrying less weight. This will also have an effect on the defenses and excuses. Notions of mistake and excuses such as *force majeure* or change of circumstances or hardship are then likely to be less important. Professional parties are used to risk-taking, and often make that their business. If they have not dealt with something in their contract as a matter of risk management, they must in principle accept whatever comes, except in extreme situations which for professionals do not soon arise and would require consideration of the effect on their overall position, not only the one under the contract.

In other words, professional contracting parties take a lot of risk, excepting only extreme cases. Where contracts are primarily road maps and risk-management tools, they are likely to be *literally* interpreted; see further Volume II, chapter 1, section 1.1.4. It has already been mentioned that the objective approach itself may lead here to greater reliance on the text of the contract and may interpret the parties' duties strictly. Good faith in civil law terms may thus extend or restrict protection depending on the nature of the relationship.

Custom and industry practices will back this up, as general principle is also likely to do. It was always the approach of the specialised commercial courts, which also had quicker procedures and lay (or peer group) input, as they still have in France. As already suggested in section 3.1.2 above, it shows that even fundamental principle, like the binding force of agreements or of obligations resulting from detrimental reliance on someone else's action or conduct, is not insensitive to commercial needs and in any event functions differently in different relationships and transactions, as it does in different legal orders.

The particular (commercial) nature of business relationships may also curtail special duties or remedies such as disclosure and co-operation duties in the pre-contractual or formation phase; limit protest periods; and discourage transactions from being undone, especially in their proprietary aspects (although claims for damages may still be valid). This concerns the protection and continuity of the international flows and also the issue of transactional and payment finality. As was noted above, that type of finality may itself figure as a fundamental principle or transnational public order requirement.

Except in extreme cases such as fraud, the special professional nature of the relationship of the parties may also restrict negligence or other misbehaviour arguments to the more obvious cases. Even questions of capacity or ultra vires legal acts may not have the same importance and impact in the commercial sphere, and good faith reliance on the appearance of capacity is now normally enough. It may also mean that an agency may be assumed sooner than might otherwise have been the case. Apparent authority amongst professionals could even be assumed upon the mere declaration of the agent itself (for example, employees), if the principal has taken that risk, for example by allowing him to use a business card with the principal's name on it.

The attitude of rougher justice in the commercial sphere, even against the more traditional rules of contract law, in the interest of (a) the flow of commerce, or (b) greater certainties, may be also demonstrated with reference to the status of *letters of intent* which are normally preludes to a contract. As intent or the lack of it is not the sole determining factor in establishing a legal relationship and detrimental reliance may in any event be another fundamental principle, these letters may acquire some binding force between the parties if acted upon in good faith or even reasonably, which may imply a lesser requirement.

In the professional sphere, however, its also needs to be considered that parties are left to their own devices to a greater extent and so should not readily rely on these concepts; see also Volume II, chapter 1, sections 1.3.11 to 1.3.14. Thus, until there is a substantial degree of detrimental reliance or reasonable expectation fully justified in the circumstances, taking into account the normal perceptions and practices between the parties or similar parties in like circumstances, professional actors may not be bound in this manner.

Although no written documents indicating the state of the negotiations may exist, under the general law there may still be duties to continue the discussions in good faith and an action if these duties are broken. Yet at least amongst professionals, mere expectation of a favourable conclusion does not in itself give rise to legal rights.[604] Again, the key is that the justification may be less obvious in commercial cases. Once there is such justified reliance, however, the other party may be forced to negotiate the full contract in line with reasonable expectations, short of which there may be room for claiming damages against the party wrongfully terminating the negotiations. Whether this also covers expectation damages is another matter and they may be limited to situations where clear promises were made.

German and Dutch law particularly are now more categorical in the imposition of pre-contractual duties, and hold that late withdrawal from negotiations may impose heavy contractual liability, including damages for *lost profits* under the contract, but probably always in the context of substantial reliance or because of other improper reasons to withdraw. It again suggests a lesser concern in the commercial and professional sphere, although as yet German and Dutch law are seldom so analysed.[605]

It must be admitted, also, that in the UNIDROIT and European Contract Principles and in the DCFR, there is as yet little appreciation of other sources of contractual rights and duties, other than an old-fashioned idea of the parties' intent as further laid down and defined in these texts, which allow specifically for some pre-contractual and post-contractual duties: see for more detail Volume II, chapter 1, section 1.6. In the case of the European Principles and the DCFR, this may derive from the fact that they mean to cover both business and consumer dealings, the latter being increasingly subject to statutory policy requirements. Again, in international transactions that is not a happy combination. Consumer notions (and protections) are then likely to enter the professional sphere. An anthropomorphic or personalised idea of contract is here sustained in all relçationships.

Unlike the European Principles and the DCFR, the UNIDROIT Principles apply only to international commercial contracts (which remain undefined), but the rules are hardly different. Unfortunately, the closeness of all sets demonstrate that the UNIDROIT Principles are also imbued with consumer law thinking and old-fashioned anthropomorphic notions of contract, being considered principally as commitments between living natural persons. Most of the following comments therefore apply to all of them, but the UNIDROIT Principles will here be principally considered as they were perceived as being relevant for professional dealings only.[606]

---

[604] See also the generally more conservative attitude taken by Lord Ackner in the UK in *Walford v Miles* [1992] 2 WLR 174, in which, at least in commerce, a duty to negotiate in good faith was thought to be unworkable and inherently inconsistent with the position of a negotiating party, as long as there was no detrimental reliance justified by the circumstances of the case.

[605] But see also vol II, ch 1, n 4 for more recent Dutch case law.

[606] Thus for contract formation, Art 3.2 of the UNIDROIT Principles still seems to rely chiefly on a personalised consensus notion, although subject to reasonableness, established practices and fair dealing and the nature of the contract, but as implied terms only and not as more objective standards (Art 5.2), whilst Arts 1.6 and 4.1ff also maintain a narrow concept of interpretation and supplementation. The broad and abstract notion of mistake in Arts 3.4ff also testifies to a doctrinaire attitude still connected with a psychological understanding of the consensus. In a similar vein, the notion of avoidance of the contract for lack of this kind of intent is broadly upheld, Art 3.17.

It is true, on the other hand, that Art 1.7 generally requires each party to act in accordance with good faith and fair dealings in international trade. However, there are no guidelines on its meaning nor is there any apparent sensitivity towards the circumstances of the case in terms of the nature of the relationship, the type of transaction, and outside forces such as market conditions. Nevertheless, good faith is declared a mandatory requirement, Art 1.7(2), without any consideration of whether its requirements are truly fundamental in the circumstances or of lesser urgency in commercial transactions. That is also the attitude in the DCFR: see further vol II, ch 1, s 1.3.10.

In the USA, s 1-302 UCC is notably more circumspect and allows parties to set the standards of good faith, diligence, reasonableness and care unless they are manifestly unreasonable. That is the correct approach.

It has already been said that in the context of the modern *lex mercatoria* and its fundamental legal principles, pre-contractual duties, a duty to renegotiate or a duty to continue agreements beyond their termination date must not quickly be assumed and any damages payable upon discontinuation of such negotiations must be considered exceptional and limited to cases of obvious misbehaviour. The UNIDROIT Principles do not appear to reflect international commercial practice in their (generally strong) support of these duties. Neither does the DCFR.

The importance of modern contract theory in the development of transnational contract law has already been stressed in section 1.1.4 above and will be revisited in Volume II, chapter 1, section 1.1.4. Fundamental principle and modern notions of party autonomy supported by custom and general principle support it but the above sets of Principles seem little aware. The same applies to the DCFR and now also to CESL, see for further comment Vol II, chapter 1, section 1.6.

3.2.2 Fundamental Principle. The Notion of Transnational Ownership. A Dynamic System of Modern Movable Proprietary Rights

From the enumeration of the fundamental legal principle in section 3.1.2 above, there follows a notion of ownership which reaches across borders. At the more practical level, this has always been clear in the operation of negotiable instruments and documents of title, which depended in their development on a transnational concept of property rights. In modern times, the eurobond as a bearer instrument (and now a security entitlement of a similar nature) presents another important example, see also the discussion in sections 1.1.4 above and 3.2.3 below.

Negotiable instruments are documents of title representing money claims, such as bills of exchange or promissory notes (for example, bonds) and cheques. They developed in Europe as early as the fourteenth century under 'merchant law', mainly for use in the international payment circuit; see Volume II, chapter 2, section 2.2.1. They obtained their present form during the first phase of the industrial revolution at the end of the eighteenth century as did the bill of lading, which is a negotiable document of title representing goods (movable physical assets); see Volume II, chapter 2, section 2.1.1. This was closely connected with the evolution of the CIF contract, which was itself also considered covered by 'merchant law'.

It is also of interest in this connection that in the UNIDROIT Principles the impact of custom may be limited by unreasonableness (not good faith); Art 1.8, which precisely in the commercial sphere for which these Principles are collected may be less desirable. There is a separate and (very) broad notion of hardship in Art 6.2, whilst a subjective concept of *force majeure* is maintained in Art 7.1.7. Both may be a great deal more generous than business requires and depends on: see further the discussion in vol II, ch 1, s 1.3.14.

Attendant negotiation duties are determined by the need to avoid bad faith without any guidance on what that may be in business dealings, which may require a narrower concept, Art 2.14, whilst co-operation duties at the performance stage are expressed in terms of reasonableness: Art 5.3. They seem to be distinguished from the general duty of parties to act in good faith under Art 1.7 and are somewhat better described in Art 5.5. Parties appear able to deviate from them to the extent that these duties may be considered outside the good faith ambit of Art 1.7, but it remains unclear when this may be the case.

In England, modern writers still maintain this *lex mercatoria* approach in respect of them in the absence of statutory law.[607] International bonds as negotiable instruments have acquired a similar status, and were as such revived in the eurobond market, operating since the early 1960s.[608] Their replacement by securities entitlements in a book-entry system would not have appeared to change the internationality of these instruments and, even if local law of the register is now widely thought applicable, international practices must still be considered as preceding the application of such domestic law which appears clearer when adverse local case law is produced in respect of similar domestic instruments.[609]

These instruments or documents of title, especially if made negotiable (by the insertion 'to order' or 'bearer'), thus acquired an independent proprietary status largely demonstrated by an own manner of transfer normally achieved through *physical delivery* (with endorsement if issued to order). This was so regardless of domestic laws, even if these instruments were used between nationals or residents from the same country. In further recognition of these instruments or documents operating under a separate law, in common law countries the concept of consideration was never applied to their transfer either. There also followed an own protection of bona fide purchasers/holders notwithstanding *nemo dat* principles. This extra protection was often applicable even in the case of a bona fide purchase from a thief—in modern times evidenced particularly by stolen banknotes. This is an issue of finality.

It follows that there is also an independent system of limited proprietary rights in these assets, but only in their most simple form based on physical possession of the instrument (like a possessory pledge). Any more complicated or non-possessory interests in them, for example under a floating charge, are for the time being still likely to operate under an applicable domestic law, except increasingly modern financial structures based on party autonomy but then operating subject to the unhindered continuation of the international flows, as we have seen in section 1.1.4 above.

For the more traditional negotiable instruments, including eurobonds, there is also likely to exist an independent approach to the question of the causal or abstract system of title transfer, see Volume II, chapter 2, section 1.4.6, and therefore to the proprietary consequences of an invalid transfer of the document, particularly relevant for eurobonds when mistakes were made in the delivery. This then also becomes an issue of finality under which bona fide acquisition is protected and the flows in these instruments safeguarded.

Again, one is likely to see here at first the bare (and *fundamental*) principles of (personal or movable) property rights in which physical possession still figures large. This conforms to the development of common law in this area. In the international commercial and financial legal order, any further refinement then becomes a matter of international custom, uniform treaty law, or, failing these, of general principle and ultimately still of domestic laws. Here we have to start thinking in terms of the operation of the entire international market place, see also the discussion in section 1.4.4 above. The application of conflicts of law within the *lex mercatoria* is then limited to these domestic refinements. But again, this

---

[607] See, eg R Goode, *Commercial Law*, 4th edn (2010) 513.

[608] See for older English case law, *Goodwin v Roberts* [1876] 1 AC 476 and *Picker v London and County Banking Co* (1887) 18 QBD 512 (CA), with emphasis on the financial community treating these instruments as negotiable regardless of domestic laws.

[609] Adverse local case law was therefore ignored in Belgium in relation to the operations of Euroclear, see vol II, ch 2, n 494.

domestic law would have to play its role as part of the new transnational law of which it becomes the residual rule in such cases, as explained earlier. Thus in international situations where the basics of property law identified above now tend to reassert themselves at least in tradable assets including negotiable instruments, domestic refinements would be disregarded altogether if they concerned the core or contradicted the essence of the instrument or its proprietary structure.

Indeed, in other international assets, like bills of lading, we see the operation of similar principles of transfer through delivery, bona fide third party protection and possessory security operating, and these principles cannot be violated by domestic laws without rendering them ineffective as documents of title, even purely domestically. In bills of lading, the title transfer is commonly considered delayed until the actual handing over of the document, which represents the underlying goods; see more particularly Volume II, chapter 2, section 2.1.1. In countries like England and France where title in chattels normally transfers upon the mere conclusion of the sales agreement, this delay is still considered implicit in FOB and CIF terms, even domestically, and a form of delivery is then accepted as an additional requirement.

Again, one may view this as emanating from long-standing international practice or the operations of the international market place itself, meaning a reversion to a more basic form of transfer of ownership based on physical delivery. This practice is confirmed in countries such as Germany and the Netherlands, which still require delivery for title transfer in all movables. In these countries transfer of the document then substitutes for delivery of the underlying assets where there is a document of title. The difference is that this delivery is always physical and cannot be constructive. It would seem to be a further recognition of international practice, which local law cannot ignore in the creation of these documents without them losing their character. There are here clearly more fundamental principles at work supported by practical needs which may be confirmed by (international) custom that is mandatory in these aspects.

Indeed, one should ask whether the recognition and further development of an independent transnational proprietary regime in this manner, based on fundamental legal principle and mandatory trans-national custom, is also conceivable for assets *other than* negotiable instruments or documents of title like commodities, and ultimately also for intangible monetary claims like receivables. It is difficult to see why not, at least for the more common aspects of property rights and their transfer. Especially coming from the English and possibly French approach to title transfer in the sale of goods, it may be possible to let the parties decide. It then becomes an aspect of party autonomy, in transnational law operating as an autonomous source of law in its own right.

However, some form of publicity traditionally facilitated third-party or proprietary effect, like *physical holdership* and delivery for title transfer in sales. In terms of international custom, they may remain basic additional requirements or formalities for the international transfers of goods, as they are for negotiable instruments and documents of title. A strong bona fide purchaser protection would be the necessary sequel of such a system, as it is also for negotiable instruments and documents of title. In this manner, title transfer in oil installations on the high seas is often achieved only through transfer or delivery of certain documents, like completion certificates even if such installations may be considered immovable. Exclusive access may be another objective requirement and a sufficient outward sign of ownership in these situations. Clearly, the emphasis here is still on a form of physical control.

In countries like Germany and the Netherlands, which upon a sale require delivery for title transfer, this would indeed seem more normal (although delivery could still be constructive therefore not physical), but in international situations of this sort the delivery requirement is also found in English contract models. Again, it relates clearly to a *more basic model* of ownership and its transfer, which puts emphasis on physical possession, user and disposition rights and their *physical* transfer and protection (rather than on more theoretical concepts of ownership and legal or constructive possession). Protection of bona fide purchasers against *nemo dat* principles may then equally follow in internationalised assets, at least if these purchasers also acquired *physical control.*

As just mentioned, it is not to be excluded that more advanced proprietary notions may subsequently develop in transnational law. Thus conditional title transfers in the international commercial sphere may at the same time allow for the creation of beneficial ownership rights and limited proprietary interests in internationalised assets including (substitute) secured interests and floating charges. They could approximate the common law trust construction at the same time. In line with common law (in equity), it renders proprietary rights more contractual in nature, which may be a modern trend everywhere, although always subject to a strong protection of bona fide purchasers and could conceivably also become the approach of customary transnational law: see for these developments the discussion in section 1.1.4 above.

Indeed, an important *other* root of modern proprietary rights is in the protection of contractual rights in chattels against successors in interest who know of these rights. Potentially, this concept also operates at the transnational level, where it may be especially revealing and important. Traditionally it underlay the proprietary interests recognised in the law of equity in common law countries, as was mentioned in section 1.1.4 above and will be discussed more extensively in Volume II, chapter 2, section 1.10. It is another source—much more sophisticated and abstract—of modern proprietary rights and their third party effect. It follows that these newer rights may ultimately still be cut off in respect of bona fide purchasers or the purchaser in the ordinary course of business of the underlying assets. There will normally not be any search duty in registers or otherwise, meaning that all non-suspecting successors in interest take free and clear of such contractual claims unless they are professional insiders like banks and major suppliers who would therefore need to search for older charges if they demand newer ones for themselves in the same assets or asset classes.

Nevertheless, it follows from this line of thinking that more intricate property rights and especially non-possessory security interests may still be more difficult to develop in transnational customary law and may therefore longer remain the preserve of domestic laws, if only for lack of common features and easily understandable structures. Where common structures exist, however, which may well be in international finance (for example, in terms of set-off and netting and in finance sales), they may acquire international normativity also on the basis of *general principle* which in such cases is likely to be *mandatory* as well (and as such moves up in the hierarchy of norms above contract but below mandatory custom and treaty law, if any). International master agreements as drafted by ISDA for swaps and by PSA/ISMA for repos (see also section 3.2.5 below), may be a further expression of newer international practices or general principles, which may then also be considered transnational, supported by party autonomy which, however, in proprietary matters and in issues of set-off and netting appear to require more objective support, indeed in such practices and principles themselves.

Incipient transnational ownership rights have also been spotted in other areas such as fishing and mining or drilling rights, in broadcasting and telecommunications and in intellectual and industrial property rights. This evolution is of great importance as it often concerns large investments and major capital goods or productive assets.[610] They *confirm* the thesis concerning the operation of transnational property rights just propounded.

The development of transnational ownership rights under broader human rights notions was noted in section 1.5.8 *in fine* to at least protect against seizure and expropriation. No less interesting in this connection is the development of the notion of *international investments* under public international or private transnational law, now much promoted by the multitude of existing bilateral investment treaties or BITs. Here it is clear that 'international investment' itself becomes a kind of proprietary right protected under these treaties and earlier under customary public international law against expropriation or more informal forms of taking. The difference is that in treaty law the measure of compensation is normally better clarified, an area where customary public international law remained unsettled.

The notion of international investment as an international or transnational property right develops here regardless of the strong attachments with the host state where the investing companies may be incorporated (usually as subsidiaries of the foreign investor) and where its know-how and patents will require recognition and protection under the intellectual property laws of the host state, which will also determine the kind of authorisations or administrative licences required. Nevertheless, if the supporting capital comes from elsewhere, the investment will qualify as international and will be proprietarily protected accordingly.

This is likely to include an entitlement to a minimum standard of treatment and procedural protection. It is still possible in this connection to ask whether this regime is one of public international law or of administrative or private transnational law or whether there is a combination of these. This has not so far been decided, but, whatever the outcome, there is likely to be a strong transnational private law analogy. In other words, it is unlikely and unnecessary to build an entirely new property law within public international law, where the concept is likely to operate in the manner of an administrative licence, also increasingly transnationalised.

The development and recognition of an internationalised concept of ownership in this manner (based either on physical possession implying some form of publicity or even of purely contractual user, enjoyment and income rights in the property to the extent known by outsiders) may at the micro level also facilitate the process of characterisation, recognition and adaptation of proprietary interests when assets are transferred to, surface, or play a role in other countries with different legal systems, see for this recognition and adaptation process more particularly, Volume II, chapter 2, section 1.8.2.[611]

---

[610] Except to some extent in air and sea transport with the connected bills of lading and negotiable instruments, and now also in international finance, the notion of international property rights remains unexplored, but, again, it may be less unusual in the context of public international law and in intellectual property, see, eg R Churchill and AV Lowe, *The Law of the Sea*, 3rd edn (1999); M Roggenkamp et al, *Energy Law in Europe* (2001) paras 2.01ff; S McCaffrey, *The Law of International Watercourses* (2001) ch 5; P Birnie and A Boyle, *International Law and the Environment*, 2nd edn (2002) chs 1, 5, 6, 7 and 10; A Gillies and J Marshall, *Telecommunications*, 2nd edn (2003) ch 4; C Tritton, *Intellectual Property in Europe*, 2nd edn (2002) chs 2–6.

[611] In the meantime it is doubtful whether within the EU harmonisation of ownership concepts can be attempted in view of the text of Art 222 of the founding treaty (the Treaty of Rome of 1957), although in the area of security rights some early efforts were made, see vol III, ch 1, n 31, and in matters of patent law the EU has repeatedly been active sanctioned by the European Court in Luxembourg, see Case C-30/90 *The Commission v The*

3.2.3 Eurobonds and Analogous Transnational Proprietary Structures. Fundamental Principle and Custom Support

To demonstrate the transnationalisation of the fundamental ownership concepts further, it may be of some interest to return to the modern eurobond. They have become the standard instrument of the largest capital market in the world. Imperceptibly, transnational ownership notions were adopted for them in the last 50 years. For the most part, these bonds are subject to a contractual choice of law for the proprietary regime, which is often English law, marked as such on the back of the instrument. The question is what this choice of law means in the circumstances. It is clear that a bearer instrument is normally intended, but it is often unlikely that there was negotiability in the strict terms of section 83 of the English Bills of Exchange Act 1882 because the terms of the bond are not always sufficiently certain, especially the payment which may be subject to all kinds of variations and conditions. This is counter to the concept of negotiable instruments under English (and most other domestic) law and especially to the requirement of simplicity traditionally necessary for their operation.

However, in practice, the contractual choice of law in proprietary aspects is not decisive. This is so first because of the third-party proprietary effect which cannot be freely created or conferred by choosing foreign laws. In any event, it would have to be determined how domestic law would subsequently function in the international legal order, itself conceivably becoming thereby transnational law and adjusted accordingly as mentioned before. It would then be possible or even necessary to rely on more fundamental or common proprietary principles to determine the true international status of eurobonds as negotiable bearer paper. This is in fact what happened, as negotiability in these circumstances is always presumed, regardless of what English law said on the matter—in fact even English domestic case law is accommodating.[612]

As mentioned at the beginning of this section, modern book-entry systems for (intermediated) security holdings have changed the basic system of securities holding, and have had to do away with physical paper, as have the bearer eurobonds, at least at the level of the end investors, see Volume II, chapter 2, Part III. The question is whether this has changed the

---

UK [1992] ECR I-858. In these cases the Court held that Art 222 did not allow the Member States to legislate in the area of industrial and commercial property rights in ways which would impact the free movement of goods.

It seems that the Court is more favourably inclined towards extensions of these property rights in a transnational sense than to their limitation to purely domestic concepts. See further also the EU Settlement Finality Directive and Collateral Directive which touch on the status of payments and some security rights and finance sales such as repos, and on a number of bankruptcy aspects, also in connection with the netting principle, see vol III, ch 1, ss 3.2.5, 2.6.7 and 4.2.4.

The DCFR, see vol II, ch 2, s 1.11, presents a full text for a codification but is far from being adopted, one issue again being, besides its sense of confinement and its quality, whether the EU has the power to legislate in this area.

[612] It is often said that the negotiability of eurobonds derives from the force of market custom: see the older English cases on international bonds cited in n 608 above, which relate to Russian and Prussian bonds, and further P Wood, *Law and Practice of International Finance* (London, 1980) 184. See also *Bechuanaland Exploration Co v London Trading Bank* [1898] 2 QBD 658, in which it was accepted in connection with the negotiability of bearer bonds that 'the existence of usage has so often been proved and its convenience is so obvious that it might be taken now to be part of the law'. Modern case law does not, however, exist confirming the point but in England it is still considered good law. See for the explicit reference in this connection to the custom of the mercantile world which may expressly be of recent origin, *Dicey, Morris and Collins on the Conflict of Laws*, 14th edn (2006) r 222, 1800, deleted, however, in the 15th edn of 2012, see also n 339 above.

nature of the international eurobond investment and has reversed the role of transnational custom in favour of the law of the place of the custodial or brokerage security account (PRIMA). Contractual choice of law is supposed to play a greater role here as also recognised by the 2002 Hague Convention on the Law Applicable to Certain Rights in Respect of Securities held with an Intermediary, see Volume II, chapter 2, section 3.2.2. It favours domestic laws but there appears little enthusiasm left for the project.

Here again the force of international custom and practices should not be underestimated. They have been ignored in the discussions and a re-nationalisation of the law in this area seems to be the consequence, but may not succeed. In other words, where the Convention does not prove effective or is not adopted, international custom will continue to prevail. Furthermore, the idea that a custodian would work under a multitude of legal regimes depending on what his client wants is not manageable. In any event, in the *lex mercatoria* approach of this book (mandatory) international custom, practice and general principles would prevail over the application of any domestic law in this area resulting under the Convention.[613] Practices appear to be the decisive factor and are then likely to be *international* or transnational, as an internationalised instrument is concerned here. The mere crediting of the securities account is here the essential feature and full ownership results. The bona fide client receives the assets free and clear of any prior charges and need not fear that the bookings will be undone because of internal errors of the lack of sufficient asset back-up. Again this is the issue of finality.

As suggested in the previous section, this may indeed be based on the absence of knowledge of third parties with respect to pre-existing rights in the property. On the other hand, it may provide enough protection against them in such cases or simply their trading in the ordinary course of business. The commercial flows, here of investment securities, will then be protected against any such charges or defects which will only affect insiders such as banks or other brokers who may know or should find out. Others have no search duty.

---

[613] In this connection, it may also be of interest to look rather more closely at the operations of underwriters in the international bond markets (euromarket). The main concern here is to create a situation where the capital raising operation is as far as possible *detached* from local elements especially in terms of tax, foreign exchange, syndication, underwriting or placement rules.

To achieve this at least in the eurobond market, the issuing company (often through a fully guaranteed financing subsidiary) traditionally operates from a tax haven base so as to avoid withholding tax payments on interest. The foreign exchange restrictions on payment of interest and principal are likely to be minimised by the creation of paying agents in several countries providing a choice for the investor. Another measure to promote the detached nature of the instrument is the creation of an underwriting syndicate that operates from a country, such as England, that does not hinder or regulate the operation unduly and allows placement in other countries (although it may still limit the placement of eurobonds in the own currency in the own country). To have syndicate members in various countries promotes at the same time the international character of the syndication and placement.

These are practical measures an issuer can take to promote the internationality or transnationality of the negotiable instruments issued by him. The documentation surrounding the creation, nature and sale of these instruments like the subscription, underwriting and selling agreements, may as a consequence acquire a transnational flavour as well.

Here too, the choice of a domestic law in the documentation may not be controlling and could even be inappropriate as it may disturb the balance between all the elements of transnational law or the *lex mercatoria* to operate fully. In this connection, the Recommendations of the International Primary Market Association (IPMA) for the issuing activity and initial placement and the Rules of the International Security Market Association (ISMA, earlier the AIBD), since 2005 merged into the International Capital Market Association (ICMA), have a natural role to play within the hierarchy of the transnational law. They key here is that they may acquire a mandatory flavour as well, although the former are officially not even binding between the members but intended as guidance only.

In this vein, it is not inconceivable either, as also already suggested, that from a more fundamental ownership perspective, monetary claims, especially trade receivables, are increasingly considered much like negotiable instruments and thus become internationally transferable in similar ways through transfer to the assignee of the collection right and of the power to give notice to the debtor. Transfer restrictions and debtors' defences against payment would be de-emphasised. It is the approach that is increasingly favoured in the US; see sections 2-210 and 9-406(d) UCC and Volume II, chapter 2, section 1.5.3. It is likely, however, that at least the set-off right against the assignor would be kept intact (supplemented by one against the assignee).

As was noted in section 1.1.4 above, in asset-backed financing, modern financial law in particular emphasises the movement towards new proprietary rights in an international commercial (professional) context. The modern *lex mercatoria* serves here as a modern conduit to introduce them transnationally, especially relevant where domestic law cannot accommodate them, for example in respect of receivable portfolios with debtors in many countries.. It has already been said that the common law example in equity is likely to serve here as the better and more flexible model, including its approaches to bulk transfers or assignments and (constructive and resulting) trusts. That may be especially relevant in civil law countries which normally practice a closed system of proprietary rights and their creation, protection and transfer.

Thus beneficial, conditional, and temporary ownership rights in portfolios of present and future tangible or intangible movable assets may become more readily recognised in international commerce or professional dealings. Advanced types of floating charges, bulk assignments even of future claims, or bulk transfers of future goods, repos and leases as conditional sales and transfers may become accepted as well, whilst domestic bankruptcy laws will also learn to recognise these customary international financial facilities and structures and to respect them.

As just mentioned, in common law countries, they found their expression primarily in equity. Civil law never had that facility but in international finance transnational commercial law may now serve to further develop these structures. It is a most important development, inspired by the fact that traditional private international law has always had difficulties in dealing with intangible assets or in assets that habitually move across borders whilst its reliance on domestic laws is increasingly unlikely to lead to internationally acceptable solutions in the financial area. In fact, from a common law perspective, one could see these developments as the revival of equity now in a transnationalised context, therefore rationalised and freed from the domestic shackles in which it had become entangled.

As in equity (in common law countries), the new proprietary structures that will be so admitted or created may not immediately present a unitary coherent system of ownership, although the true underlying theme would be prior knowledge in the acquirer of any type of adverse interest in the asset (whether proprietary or contractual) for the interest to be maintainable against him, as just mentioned. Initially, modern transnational proprietary rights are more likely to be defined for each structure without regard to an underlying system, which can only develop later. Such a more open proprietary system needs fundamental balancing through the notion of protection of bona fide purchasers or the buyer in the ordinary course of business of commoditised products, as just explained. That is also the bottom line in common law countries (in equity) that have learnt to be comfortable with this state of affairs, elaborated in modern statutory law in the US notably under the UCC. Indeed, it uses different proprietary concepts and third party protections in Article 2 for the transfer of title in the sale of goods, in Article 2A for equipment leases, in Article 4A for payments, in Article 8 for investment securities, and in Article 9 for secured transactions.

This may be more difficult for civil law lawyers, but whatever their feelings and preoccupations may be, there is ample evidence from common law countries that a unitary systematic approach is not necessary, even in proprietary matters. In fact, it may be argued that the absence of it has always been an advantage in common law contracts, especially in the further development of new financial instruments and structures. The trust, constructive trust, resulting trust, tracing and set-off concepts, transfers in bulk, temporary and conditional transfers are here perhaps the best demonstration, concepts without which modern financial products and structures could hardly operate.

3.2.4 Fundamental Principle in Procedural Matters

Fundamental legal principle must also be considered in the context of procedure, certainly at the transnational level in international commercial arbitrations as the main dispute-resolution facility in the international commercial and financial legal order. We are concerned here in particular with the equality of all parties and the proper protection of respondents in the composition of the panel, their rights to a fair hearing, presentation of and search for documents, and adequate time for defence. Especially here, the operation of transnational fundamental legal principle or mandatory public order requirements can hardly be denied, but they may also go to the binding force of the arbitration clause, separate from the rest of the agreement, whilst the connected concept of severability of this clause, the status, powers and duties of arbitrators, their jurisdiction, and what is arbitrable may no less have their foundation in mandatory transnational principle or public order; see also section 1.1.9 above.

It can even be argued that institutionally the power of arbitrators derives from the transnational legal order itself, the arbitration clause merely activating it and that is held in this book to be the better view. In any event, the power of the *lex arbitri* of the seat in these matters is here increasingly eclipsed. The developing transnational arbitral practices strongly support this evolution; see further the discussion in section 1.4.17 above.

3.2.5 Mandatory Custom and Practices

In section 3.2.3 above, the supporting role of custom in eurobonds and similar transnational proprietary structures was noted. As further elaboration of fundamental principle in movable property, these customary rules are likely to be mandatory.

The phenomenon of the law-creating force of custom and practices has given rise to much academic discussion, see section 1.4.7 above, with the possibility itself sometimes being doubted. In modern civil law that has had to do with the denial of sources of law other than statute, as we have seen. Custom is then often believed atavistic and its recognition a sign of regression, a relapse into cultural particularity inimical to modern progress and the role therein of the modern state as ultimate social organiser and (therefore sole) source of law. It is the reason why a distinction between custom and trade practices is often made. In this view, custom is objective law, to be avoided, whilst trade practices are implied contractual terms and may as such be acceptable. This view still exists in common law countries, particularly in England. It is a sequel to the view that law can only issue from a sovereign, not therefore from industry custom and practice even though the common law leaves more room for them in commerce and finance but it is not quite clear how much.

This is not the approach of this book, and it seems particularly inappropriate in the international commercial and financial sphere, where proprietary structures rather than contractual arrangements are often the issue, particularly in asset backed financing. In the international sale of goods, we have the important issue of transactional finality, earlier also identified as proprietary. In fact, custom's role is of much greater importance outside contract, where new structures cannot be freely created by parties. It is in any event hardly perceptive to call the legal developments in that sphere regressive. In international commerce and finance, customs and practices are likely to be highly sophisticated, much more than state law can ever be on its own. They concern in essence all that is considered normal by participants and on which they commonly rely in their businesses and markets. It basically concerns their routines and perceptions in this regard.

In the modern *lex mercatoria* approach as a hierarchy of norms derived from different autonomous legal sources, after the fundamental principles which are the basis of the whole system, there follow indeed the customs generally prevailing in each trade if considered mandatory, which is still rare, although the Hague-Visby Rules are sometimes so defined where not incorporated by statute.[614] Their being mandatory means in this instance that they need not be incorporated in the bill of lading or in any domestic law to be effective. Parties may, however, still deviate from them, but they risk that the result is no longer a proper bill of lading. The more modern version of this customary law may be found in the Hamburg Rules prepared by UNCITRAL.

As already noted, true mandatory custom is more likely to be relevant and emerge in non-contractual aspects, especially in proprietary matters or also in contractual aspects that, like issues of validity and capacity, cannot be freely determined or changed by the parties either. It is for international arbitrators and the courts, when asked to rule on them, to acknowledge transnational customs and practices in these areas. In guidelines for foreign direct investment, there may even be a transnational public policy element to custom which might then also become mandatory.

Thus, in the elaboration of the rules of contract and property, further mandatory rules of custom may develop, especially in the areas of legal capacity and contractual validity and more particularly of the transfer of ownership (in whole or in part, conditionally or temporarily, as usufruct or security) or in the area of the return of title upon default, such as in a reservation of title, or in matters of bona fide purchaser protection or the protection of buyers in the ordinary course of business of commoditised products. Similar status may be conferred on the bona fide collecting assignee unaware of any other assignment of the same receivables for whatever purpose. This concerns the infrastructure of the law of contract

---

[614] See W Haak, 'Internationalism above Freedom of Contract' in *Essays on International and Comparative Law in Honour of Judge Erades* (The Hague, 1983) 69.

and property, and is as such unlikely to be at the free disposition of the parties. These rules are likely to be closely related to, or an elaboration of the fundamental principles embodied in transnational public order requirements. Custom builds on this.

Custom or practice may still here surface in different ways, for example in certain presumptions, such as, amongst professionals, the presumption of the capacity of the parties. At least in the international commercial sphere, typical legal capacity limitations derived from domestic law, even that of the residence of the party concerned, are increasingly ignored, however, especially in the case of legal entities, although purely domestically they may remain of the greatest importance. This was shown in the cases concerning swaps entered into with municipal authorities in the UK.[615] Mandatory transnational custom may also affect the rules of adjudicatory jurisdiction. It has been said in this connection that transnational custom is now averse to jurisdiction being exercised by the court of the plaintiff (*forum actoris*) without any other supporting grounds for such jurisdiction.[616] This would be a further incidence of customary law acquiring a mandatory or fundamental flavour at the transnational level.

In the swap and repo markets, the ISDA Swap Master Agreements of 1987/1992/2002 and the PSA/ISMA Global Master Repurchase Agreement of 1992/1995, already mentioned in section 3.2.2 above, might acquire a similar status of custom in the areas they cover, at least in the London and the New York markets where they operate. Again, this may be particularly relevant for their close-out and netting provisions. The status of contractual bilateral netting with its enhancements of the set-off principle and its inclusion of all swaps between the same parties, leading to a netting out of all positions in the case of default at the option of the non-defaulting party and *ipso facto* in the case of bankruptcy, could otherwise remain in doubt under local laws.

This is indeed particularly relevant in bankruptcy, because of the substantial impact of netting on the rights of other creditors whilst an important and broad indirect extended preference is created. Transnationally, the acceptance of the set-off principle in this manner may well become customary, if it is not already so, and may then also impose itself on domestic bankruptcy laws as a mandatory principle. It may help in this connection that international regulators favour this limitation of risk in the financial system, as demonstrated by the 1996 amendment to the Basle Accord; see more particularly Volume III, chapter 2, section 2.5.5.

In the area of *foreign direct investment*, international agencies have attempted to define certain principles and set certain standards which may also be reflective of international practices or initiate them.[617] Less developed countries saw here possibilities of abuse, whilst investors held out for more protection. The former sentiment held sway in the later 1960s and 1970s and gave rise to the OECD Guidelines of 1976 (following the 1969 Andean Investment Code for the Latin American Region). They were not legally binding and often thought still to represent the views of only the richer countries.

---

[615] *Hazell v London Borough of Hammersmith and Fulham and Others* [1991] 1 All ER 545 (Lord Ackner).

[616] See JP Verheul, 'The Forum Actoris and International Law' in *Essays on International and Comparative Law in Honour of Judge Erades* (The Hague, 1983) 196.

[617] Foreign direct investment is here commonly defined as a long-term interest with an active management role in an enterprise or utility operating in a country other than that of the investor; see also s 3.2.2 above.

In this climate, the World Bank (IBRD) tried to help, as it had earlier taken a leading role in the formulation of the 1965 Washington Convention on the Settlement of Investment Disputes between States and Nationals of Other States, presenting an institutional framework (through the International Centre for the Settlement of Investment Disputes or ICSID) for disputes between foreign investors and home states through arbitration. It also came up with Guidelines on the Treatment of Foreign Direct Investment in 1992.[618] They cover four areas, ranging from admission, treatment and expropriation of foreign investments to the settlement of disputes in respect of them, and consist of general principles to guide governmental behaviour towards foreign investment, and purport to reflect generally acceptable international standards for the promotion of foreign investment.[619] These Guidelines were based on a study of the then current practices as reflected in international investment treaties, national investment codes, writings of international law experts and a host of arbitral awards mainly emanating from the ICC, ICSID and the Iran–US Claims Tribunal.

These guidelines are extensive and, although no more than guidelines, their standard- and norm-creating effect has been noted, which suggests international custom.[620] Although it would be custom under public international law, not under the modern *lex mercatoria*, it shows the process. It is not impossible that whilst becoming customary law they become mandatory at the same time and could as such become serious compilations of compulsory international practices.

3.2.6 Mandatory Uniform Treaty Law, Contractual Provisions (Party Autonomy), Directory Trade Practices, Directory Uniform Treaty Law and Common or General Legal Principles

Following what was said in sections 1.4.13 and 3.1.2 above, in the context of the modern *lex mercatoria* and its hierarchy, after (a) the fundamental legal principles, and (b) the mandatory customs and practices, there follows (c) uniform treaty law to the extent applicable under its own rules and mandatory. Thereafter, there figure (d) general principle to the extent mandatory, and (e) party autonomy, or, in contractual matters, the contractual provisions themselves. They are supplemented in descending order by (f) directory trade practices, (g) directory uniform treaty law (if applicable under its own terms), (h) common legal notions and, if all else fails, finally by (i) domestic laws identified under the private international law rules of the forum if the issue is not yet decided under the higher rules.

It was said earlier that mandatory uniform treaty law is rare, but Article 12 of the Vienna Convention was mentioned as an example. It allows Contracting States to demand written

---

[618] The climate changed in the 1990s when Bilateral Investment Treaties (BITs) started to become popular, superseding to some extend the need for these Guidelines: see for these Treaties also s 2.2.7 above and for the protection of foreign investments (as defined thereunder), s 3.2.2 above.

[619] See also the Report to the Development Committee on the Legal Framework for the Treatment of Foreign Investment (1992) 31 ILM 1368.

[620] See I Brownlie, 'Legal Effects of Codes of Conduct for Multinational Enterprises; Commentary' in N Horn (ed), *Legal Problems of Codes of Conduct for Multinational Enterprises* (Deventer, 1980) 41 and N Horn, 'Codes of Conduct for Multinational Enterprises and Transnational Lex Mercatoria' in the same volume, 52.

international sales agreements. If the 2001 UNCITRAL Convention on the Assignment of Receivables in International Trade were to be widely adopted, there would be a great deal more of these mandatory provisions in Contracting States, particularly in the formalities and proprietary aspects of international bulk assignments of receivables. There are also some in the 2001 UNIDROIT Mobile Equipment Convention.

Mandatory general principle must equally be deemed rare for the moment, but may derive from conventions of this nature, if not themselves adopted, to the extent that they represent the international business consensus and are then likely to be closely connected with industry practice. They may also further implement or supplement fundamental principle and custom in transnational proprietary matters.

Subsequently, the contract itself may of course set important rules—that is the question of party autonomy—but as already pointed out several times, see section 2.2.9 above, these contractual rules can in principle only prevail in contractual matters, and even then only in matters that are at the free disposition of the parties, which may not be the case as to their own legal capacity, the binding force and legality of the agreement, and in the matter of remedies, especially in the case of error or fraud. Also parties would not be able to address in their contract matters regarding third parties, and therefore especially not proprietary issues, even if in matters of assignment of contractual rights there is a modern tendency to allow parties greater freedom transnationally (see more particularly Volume II, chapter 2, section 1.9.2). It was also pointed out above in connection with mandatory custom and general principle, that the civil law idea of a closed system of proprietary rights is increasingly under pressure and that a measure of party autonomy has entered the world of movable property structures, subject to a better bona fide purchaser protection.

After party autonomy, we have the directory customs and practices. Much has been said about them which needs no repetition. As to these directory customs and practices, the status of the UCP, URC and Incoterms may be of special interest. The latest version of the Incoterms date from 2012. The UCP are the Uniform Customs and Practice for Documentary Credits compiled by the International Chamber of Commerce since 1933, the latest version being from 2007. They are in the nature of a private codification of some of the most important rules concerning letters of credit, and have gained worldwide acceptance. Even in countries like the US, where state law deals through Article 5 UCC with letters of credit, the latest amendments of section 5-116(c) UCC assume derogation if the UCP is explicitly made applicable to a letter of credit. The UCC and UCP thus became complementary sources of law for letters of credit in the USA.[621]

Nevertheless the status in law of the UCP has remained in doubt where the letter of credit does not contain a reference to them and the subject matter is not dealt with by an applicable statute. Many see them as transnational custom,[622] subject to regular adjustments by the ICC, and as such part of the objective international or transnational commercial law, even though the ICC itself is not a legislative body but only a compiler of international customs and practice, in the process of compiling these it also develops them further. In the international commercial and financial legal order it may be considered an authentic spokesperson. The status of their rules as international custom means that for

---

[621] See also JF Dolan, *The Law of Letters of Credit, Commercial and Standby Credits* (1999) 4.06 [2] [l].
[622] See n 342 above.

their effectiveness they need no longer be incorporated in the text of the arrangements concerning the issuance of letters of credit or characterised as implied conditions.

It must be said, however, that the formulation of the UCP does not help here. In the 1974 version, Article 1 considered the UCP binding in all circumstances except if parties agreed otherwise. In 1983 the impression was created that the UCP were implied contract terms through the addition of a sentence requiring incorporation in the documentation. Since 1993, the UCP require incorporation in the documents and have deleted the earlier language of 1974, although there is a second sentence which suggests otherwise. ('They are binding on all parties thereto, unless otherwise expressly stipulated in the credit.') This suggests a contradictory sentiment in the drafting. In any event, their legal force as custom or other source of law cannot be pre-determined by the UCP themselves and is a matter of the objective law. The approach in case law has therefore not changed. The Incoterms are similarly treated and often considered custom, at least in the commodity trade in Europe.

The UCP, UCR and Incoterms are partial informal codifications only and, even if accepted as customary law, do not cover the whole field and are in any event subject to interpretation and supplementation, as is the partial uniform law contained in the Vienna Sales Convention. The first rule here must be that they are to be explained on the basis of their international character and the general principles of these compilations themselves, but probably more important is to place them properly in the hierarchy of principles and rules constituting the *lex mercatoria*, as here explained.

That is to say that they are to be interpreted, explained and even superseded by the fundamental principles of law and any mandatory custom or treaty law (if any, and applicable under its own terms). Thereafter there are to be considered the wording of the relevant contract itself, the notions of *good faith* in the application of these contract terms (which may refer back to more fundamental notions), the logic and nature of the transaction, other (directory) custom, uniform directory treaty law like that of the Vienna Convention (especially for the Incoterms), and common legal notions. Finally, if still no solution has been found, there remains to be considered the choice of law rules identifying a national law, but only on a result-oriented basis,[623] whilst these domestic laws themselves are thus transnationalised.[624]

Another elaboration of directory customs and practices might be found in the confidentiality of arbitrations. It was said above that, in international contractual matters, party autonomy determines in the first instance the applicable regime (unless there is other mandatory law or principle) supported by implied conditions and ultimately industry practices and uniform treaty law to the extent existing. One may see here a progression from explicit contractual term to industry custom. It was noted earlier, however, that the reverse may also happen, and established custom may lose its autonomous status and acquire at best the status of implied term to be proven by the party relying on it or even loses that status and

---

[623] See for this approach also MN Boon, *De Internationale Koop en het Documentair Accreditief ingevolge de UCP 1993* [The International Sale and the Documentary Letter of Credit under the UCP 1993] 7 and 425 (1998), and MN Boon, Book Review, RA Schuetze, *Das Dokumentenakkreditiv im Internationalen Handelsverkehr (1996)* in (1998) *European Business Law Review* 331.

[624] One should note here the difference with the language of Art 7(1) and (2) of the 1980 Vienna Convention on the International Sale of Goods, copied in much of the newer uniform treaty law, which uses some of these sources of law but does not manage to set them in a hierarchy; see further the discussion in vol II, ch 1, ss 2.3.5ff.

then requires for its continuous effect explicit agreement between the parties. The principle of confidentiality in arbitrations was given as an example.[625]

After directory (or default) customary rules and practices we have the directory (or default) rules of uniform treaty law but only in Contracting States and if applicable under their own terms. As we have seen for the Vienna Convention on the International Sale of Goods (CISG), which is the most important example, normally these Conventions only present partial codifications. Only the 2001 UNCITRAL Convention on the Assignment of Receivables in International Trade appeared to present a fuller regime of international bulk assignments, but is in its proprietary aspects mandatory and therefore, if it were sufficiently ratified, likely to be of higher rank within the *lex mercatoria*, as it would also be if followed as general principle: see the earlier discussion.

Subsequently we have the directory of general principles or common notions. These common notions may emerge, for example in the area of offer and acceptance, duress, misrepresentation, negligence, liability without fault, proprietary rights, damage mitigation and computation, *force majeure* and hardship,[626] *exceptio non adimpleti contractus*

---

[625] The discussion in this respect was initiated by a decision of the High Court of Australia in *Esso/BHP v Plowman*, see (1995) 11 *International Arbitration* 235. The question of confidentiality of arbitrations often arises in the context of the joining of different but connected arbitrations when one of the parties objects because it may violate the privacy of the proceedings, see *Oxford Shipping Co v Nippon Yusen Kaisha* [1984] 3 All ER 835, in which the confidentiality argument was upheld. It also arises where orders are issued to reveal particulars of other arbitrations, see *Dolling-Baker v Merret* [1990] 1 WLR 1205, in which such orders were set aside, or where particulars are disclosed to reinsurance companies likely to be sued for recovery of the amount lost in the arbitration, see *Hassneh Insurance v Mew* [1993] 2 Lloyds Rep 243, in which such disclosure was limited to the mere finding and the reasoning had to remain confidential.

In the 1995 Australian case *of Esso/BHP v Plowman* quoted above, it was the State of Victoria which wanted to find out certain information concerning cost, price, volume and revenue given to a gas utility by Esso in one arbitration, in order for the State to use it in another. The High Court of Australia found no confidentiality rule (or custom) or even an implied term requiring the protection of confidentiality. It only accepted the privacy of the hearings, whilst documents compulsorily produced could not be used for any other purpose than the arbitration. Short of a specific confidentiality undertaking in the arbitration clause itself, it found no obligation of confidentiality, and noted in this respect that the results of arbitrations are commonly divulged whilst witnesses could in any event not be held to secrecy.

It was probably always clear that where a public interest was involved, as in disputes concerning the use of public property or possibly in consumer arbitrations, awards could be disclosed. This may all the more be the case in foreign investment disputes, see the ICSID and NAFTA practices. However, it appears that the disclosure possibility now goes much further and may affect ordinary commercial arbitrations.

Thus, apart from exceptional cases, confidentiality seems no longer guaranteed in commercial arbitration, at least not if the Australian case reflects modern thinking. Of the original three main justifications of arbitration (*viz*, speed, confidentiality and expert handling) at least confidentiality appears to have lapsed for all but the privacy of the hearing itself and the protection of confidential information presented therein. This may be because arbitrations have increasingly become pseudo-judicial proceedings. They have also lost much of their informal character. The awards are now also often published, at least by the ICC and ICSID, or in the *Yearbook of Commercial Arbitration*, even if in a sanitised form to render them more anonymous. In such procedures confidentiality has clearly taken a back seat.

Alternative dispute resolution (ADR) may, on the other hand, have retained more informality and may as a consequence also enjoy greater secrecy protection.

[626] The problems concerning *force majeure* and hardship will be discussed more extensively in vol II, ch 1, ss 1.4.6–1.4.8. There is no consensus, and it may well be asked whether there is one unitary notion of *force majeure*, including hardship considerations. The defence of *force majeure* appears to depend much on the nature of the parties (professionals in their relationship to each other, consumers or states), on the time span of the contract (spot or duration), and on its very nature and objectives (therefore quite different in concession agreements, long-term supply or service agreements).

There are other problems: are we only concerned here with external events such as wars, earthquakes and the like, leading to absolute impossibility to perform, or also with more subjective considerations such as unconscionability, economic impossibility/hardship and how they need to be defined? Is there something like a contractual or anticipatory breach, set-off and other remedies including specific performance (*cf* also Article 28 of the Vienna Convention), statute of limitations, and the like, all forming the normal infrastructure of the law of contract. European and UNIDROIT Contract Principles would help here if less consumer-oriented and anthropomorphic. There are procedural questions, such as burden of proof, evidence and disclosure issues, to be considered as well. Contractual provisions in particular may also be supplemented by notions of intrinsic logic, common sense or efficiency at this level of general principle. Common notions may also be relevant outside the law of contract and procedure and may in fact concern the whole law of obligations and movable property and could even become mandatory as we have seen.

These common notions often derive from comparative law research, in the sense that, where similar rules are found in the domestic laws of the more advanced nations, they may enter into the *lex mercatoria* at this level, assuming that they capture the dynamics of modern business. Rules of uniform treaty law may also be considered in this connection even outside Contracting States. The UCP, UCR and Incoterms could also figure at this level, if not already included at higher levels like the contractual one (if incorporated in the contract) or as directory custom or practice.

3.2.7 Domestic Laws, Private International Law: Mandatory Provisions and Public Policy or Regulatory Issues

Finally, in the hierarchy of norms in the modern *lex mercatoria*, there is domestic law to consider, and there are the private international law rules of the forum in this regard to choose the proper law if the issue has not yet been decided under the higher rules as just described. The rules of private international law are even then unlikely to be applied as hard and fast conflict rules, if as such still practiced in the law of property and obligations.[627] As pointed out in sections 1.4.13 and 3.1.2 above, they are too residual in the whole hierarchy of norms here proposed to operate in that manner. However, they may indicate the closer contact and thus the domestic laws more particularly affected and to be considered. It is possible to think here in particular of the status of proprietary rights and the ranking of security interests in the country of destination of the goods in which they are vested, or in a bankruptcy initiated in a third country.

A hard-and-fast conflicts rule does not work here anyway, because the recognition of these rights elsewhere often entails adaptation if assets move to other countries, or if their status needs to be assessed in a foreign bankruptcy of the owner/debtor (see the discussion in section 2.1.2 above). A simple reference to the (new) *lex situs* is then inadequate, if at all

---

balance that is or should be maintained all along? May reasonably foreseeable events be included if giving rise to a severe imbalance? What are the consequences for the contract: suspension, termination, or adjustments/renegotiations? Whilst in supply agreements there is also the notion of the transfer of risk (asking which party bears the risk of *force majeure*), has this notion of risk allocation also a meaning outside supply agreements, especially where subjective considerations are invoked?

[627] See for the more flexible American approach, s 2.2.2 above. See for the direct application of considerations of cogency and moral data, even in conflict laws, either under the guise of public policy or natural law, Ehrenzweig, above n 517.

relevant. More fundamental overriding notions of acquired rights of beneficiaries or security interest holders may play an important role here besides the practical question of how the recognising country can incorporate the foreign proprietary right into its own system to give it adequate protection particularly in its own bankruptcies. As a consequence, the conflict rules and their application will have to take into account other relevant considerations, the evaluation of which is, not necessarily a matter of the application of one legal system alone.

It was also observed that, more generally, the application of a domestic law in an international transaction transnationalises that law, which may as a consequence be adapted. The crucial point to understand here is that English law even when elected by the parties may not function the same in an international transaction as it does in English transactions. That may particularly affect the consideration requirements in the case of nullity or amendment and the needs for documentation and other formalities;[628] see further the discussion in section 2.2.9 above. If parties choose a domestic law, the consequence would appear to be that it moves higher to the level of party autonomy, but it must no less function in the transnational law and may be adjusted accordingly to make sense therein. The effect is, however, that directory custom, treaty law and general principle do not then prevail over this domestic law.

In international cases, the adjudicating court or arbitration tribunal will also have to decide what force, if any, it must give to *domestic public policies or public order requirements*, as contained in local law. It was said earlier that this law is not part of the modern *lex mercatoria* and does not figure in its hierarchy; they are not private law at all, and compete. It is an important issue more developed in the US, often identified there as the jurisdiction to prescribe. It was more fully discussed in section 2.2.6 above.

These local *public policy* considerations or governmental interests and public order requirements may play an important role in international transactions when there is (appreciable) conduct and effect on the territory of the state in question. The modern *lex mercatoria* will in such instances be deferential of such policies, which may be even more readily accepted if they are connected with or an expression of overriding fundamental principle or of transnational public order and are then no longer purely domestic in nature (although the elaboration is still likely to be). In the transnational commercial and financial legal order they could find an echo in international minimum standards developing as a matter of the transnational public order itself, that may thus restrain domestic interference in international transactions, particularly if overbearing, arbitrary, discriminatory, disproportionate or vindictive. There is ample demonstration in investment dispute case law of these constraints.

Beyond this, domestic public policy bearing on international transactions may also be evaluated for reasonableness or rationality and weighed or balanced against the public policies of other governments that may also have a legitimate interest in the international transaction. It can only be repeated that conduct under and effect of the international transaction on the territory of a concerned state obviously gives its government a legitimate regulatory interest but the outcome will still depend on how much conduct and effect there is on its territory and on the nature of the measures it has taken and on its measured response under standards of governmental behaviour that must be considered increasingly international as well.

---

[628] O Lando, 'The *Lex Mercatoria* in International Commercial Arbitration' (1985) 34 *ICLQ* 747.

3.3 Operation of the *Lex Mercatoria.* Objections

3.3.1 Operation of the *Lex Mercatoria* and Direct References to It

It is submitted, and is the key message of this book, that in a globalising world in international business transactions, practitioners, courts and arbitrators may be better guided in matters of the applicable substantive private law by the hierarchy of norms of the modern *lex mercatoria* resulting in the application of transnational law than by application of private international law rules (even if it is clear which ones apply) which point to a domestic law that is unlikely to have been designed for international transactions and cover their dynamics, is often atavistic or parochial, likely to be fixed in time, and a given, in which context interpretive freedom was considered limited and unable to stretch to adjust and restate the applicable domestic law properly to discount the foreign elements in the case. Were this nevertheless to become the approach under local laws, it would likely introduce the *lex mercatoria* through interpretation, but each national legal system would still do it in its own way so that uniformity would remain elusive.

The stress that the application of local laws to international transactions causes has become particularly clear in modern international finance, but it was always unlikely that the ever larger international flows of goods, services and money could continue to be adequately guided and protected by some national law. The more fundamental question is why all private law must be domestic per se and find its origin solely in the modern state. It would seem an irrational and unnecessary presumption, and was never more than political philosophy. In the present day it can hardly be maintained at the practical level, if only because the internationality and professionality of the transaction necessarily introduces non-national considerations into the application of any law. The cause of the problem is the continuing modern predilection for legal positivism which was discussed more extensively in section 1.4.15 above and means that academia, at least in Western Europe, often remains unusually hostile to the revival of the modern *lex mercatoria* as non-statist law. It has even been argued that the positive (national) law is exactly there to prevent informal norm change and that that is one of its major functions. The principal function of law is then seen as a massive project of norm standardisation that does not favour change.[629]

However, in a post-modern outlook, where even in the field of the natural sciences time and place have become less absolute whilst the notion of causality has also suffered re-evaluation, territorial and temporal confines of the law and its static character or systematic nature may more confidently be questioned, whilst a functional, dynamic and self-propelling approach in law formation and application may regain an important place. Logic and automaticity in the application, predicated on the notion that all human activity, if properly understood, is repetitive and predictable, are then rightly also questioned and seen merely as a form of intellectual neo-classicism.

The search for certainty necessarily acquires here another dimension and urgency whilst issues of quality arise. It was said before that certainty of this type may be low quality and may have too high a cost. Globalisation with its ever larger movements in goods, services,

---

[629] For standardisation see also s 1.5.6 *in fine* above. See for a reference to state law squeezing out rival forms of social control, R Ellickson, *Order Without Law* (1991) 276.

technology, capital, investments and payments, needs a (new) legal framework that is more flexible and aware of and adaptive to newer and ever-evolving needs at least in professional dealings. In scientific terms, actions may be more random. As submitted before, certainty comes here not merely and automatically from pre-conceived rules, but from the self-discipline of the community in which they operate, although there are areas as in transactional and payment *finality* where it plays a special, elevated role. It was never otherwise but it is reinforced at the transnational level, as we have seen.[630] It also emphasises the important role of voluntarism in compliance (and the incentive structure to achieve it), on which a modern society is utterly dependent.[631] The idea that (private) law is there mainly to determine disputes is here abandoned in favour of the view that it is chiefly a facility to make life easier for all concerned, operates primarily at that level, and that such is its principal task.

The conclusion is that, also intellectually in the international commercial and financial legal order, there is now more room for transnational private law that is not territorial, pre-conceived, or static in the above sense. Nor can it be applied on the basis of logic only. It is dynamic in nature, as was demonstrated in section 1.1.4 above both for contract and movable property law. Nevertheless, because of the ambivalence on the subject and probably the lack of a clear idea what the modern *lex mercatoria* truly is and how it functions (as a hierarchy of norms from diverse autonomous legal sources), direct references to the *lex mercatoria* remain rare and are on the whole also still avoided in arbitration statutes or official commentary (except in the Netherlands)—it is sometimes deemed implied and fully contained in a reference to transnational custom[632]—whilst courts and arbitrators often prefer to use different terminology and (rightly) like to limit theoretical controversy.[633]

Equally, a contractual choice of law in favour of the *lex mercatoria* remains uncommon, and has even been thought to render the contract void.[634] This must now be considered an

---

[630] See the discussion in s 1.1.5 above and for finality n 72 above.

[631] See RD Cooter, 'Three Effects of Social Norms on Law: Expression, Deterrence and Internalisation' (2000) 79 *Oregon Law Review* 1.

[632] Art 28(4) of the UNCITRAL Model Law allows the arbitral tribunal in all cases to decide in accordance with the terms of the contract and to take into account the usages of the trade applicable to the transaction. This is not dependent on the parties' authorisation and precedes any application of conflicts rules, Art 28(2), but may not cover the whole of the *lex mercatoria* as here explained.

One must assume that in international cases, the fundamental legal principles will always be applied if considered *ius cogens*, that international custom and then most likely common legal principles will also be applied, whilst the interpretation and supplementation of the contract increasingly acquire the status of an autonomous function, confirmed in international sales by the Vienna Convention (Art 7).

In fact, in the absence of a clear view of what the modern *lex mercatoria* is, there is some ground to assume that a reference to international custom is in fact tantamount to a reference to the modern *lex mercatoria*.

The Dutch (Art 1054 CCP) follows the UNCITRAL Model Law in international cases without clearly describing what is meant by the usages of the trade. However, the Dutch official comment at the time referred to the *lex mercatoria* in this context and allowed its application without discussing exactly what it was.

The English 1996 Arbitration Act, in s 46, copies to a large extent the UNCITRAL Model Law, but notably deletes the reference to the usages of the trade applicable to the transaction. It may mean that the parties would still have to authorise any considerations to be taken into account other than the ones resulting from the applicable domestic law under the conflict of law rules the arbitrators deem applicable. In this sense, it could be concluded that the English Act, in particular, is unfriendly to the modern *lex mercatoria*. This is regressive.

[633] But *cf* ICC Case No 3131, 26 October 1979 (Bernardo Cremades, President) (1984) IX *Yearbook Commercial Arbitration* 109, which was probably the first major international arbitration in which the modern *lex mercatoria* was applied. See the main text below for more recent instances.

[634] See Mustill LJ, 'Contemporary Problems in International Commercial Arbitration' (1989) 17 *International Business Lawyer* 161ff.

extreme view, in any event likely to be limited to England, which remains more generally reluctant to accept what it considers extralegal standards, sometimes, it would seem, even in international arbitrations. It has been said before that this is not necessarily to the advantage of the legal profession in England, which stands to gain greatly from a more open attitude. The possibility of the application of the *lex mercatoria* is suggested in the UNIDROIT and European Contract Principles (PECL), which both make a reference to the modern *lex mercatoria*, although not expressing any views on what it is or how it works.[635] The DCFR omits any such references, as it is concerned with old fashioned codification, now at EU level which still means to exclude all other sources of law. The 2008 EU Regulation on the recognition and enforcement of judgments in civil and commercial matters, in its Preamble (13) makes an indirect reference, whilst clarifying that parties may choose a non-statist law, although the relevant text in the body of the regulation was ultimately omitted under German pressure.

Indeed, not choosing any (domestic) law may become here a viable option and the best alternative, although a contractual choice of law clause in favour of some domestic law is for many still an article of faith, never mind how little it may cover, especially in proprietary and public policy matters; see the discussion in section 2.2.9 above. Without such a clause in favour of a national law, courts or international arbitrators in particular may feel freer to decide the issues as they think fit on the basis of a multiplicity of norms, whether or not within the context of the hierarchy of norms of the modern *lex mercatoria*, although the latter would be better in the view of this book.

At a practical level, not choosing the applicable law may even now be the better option if there is a cluster of contracts involving performance in several countries, whilst problems may only arise years after the signature of the contracts in circumstances and places that could hardly be predicted. Choosing domestic laws is here not a good alternative. In any event, it should be clear from the above that a contractual choice of a domestic law in international cases may upset the hierarchy and balance between the various principles and rules implied in the *lex mercatoria* as explained before and could therefore prove a dangerous and unbalancing manoeuvre.

It appears now to be increasingly accepted that arbitrators may apply the modern *lex mercatoria* if the contract is silent on the applicable law. It is not deemed any longer against public order.[636] But even if there is a choice by the parties in favour of a domestic law, it was submitted that international arbitrators may or even must put this choice within the context of the operation of the *lex mercatoria* and its hierarchy of norms as here explained. It would mean in particular that mandatory transnational fundamental principle, custom and general principle, including transnational public order requirements and proprietary law, would prevail over such a choice of a domestic law, but directory transnational fundamental principle, custom and general principle would still be trumped by it, see also section 1.4.13 above.

As just mentioned, the 2008 EU Regulation now clarifies the issues in the sense that at least a non-statist law may be chosen, including therefore the *lex mercatoria*, although that

---

[635] See for early comments on the UNIDROIT Principles, the ICC Publication, *The UNIDROIT Principles for International Commercial Contracts: A New Lex Mercatoria?* (ICC Dossier of the Institute of International Business Law and Practice, 1995).

[636] *Fougerolle (France) v Banque de Proche Orient (Lebanon)*, Cour de Cass 9 December 1981 (1982) *Revue de l'Arbitrage* 183.

does not determine what it really is nor its reach. Under the Regulation, there remains also the question whether the *lex mercatoria* may be deemed impliedly applicable if no law is chosen by the parties or indeed whether the absence of such a choice (of a domestic law) may automatically mean application of the *lex mercatoria* in international cases. It would not appear problematic with regard to the application of fundamental legal principles as *ius cogens* and of mandatory customs. From this, the application of the rest of the *lex mercatoria* would logically appear to follow.

Ultimately, there remains the question of enforceability of any judgment or award based on the *lex mercatoria* notion. It still depends on the jurisdiction where enforcement is sought but many will now allow it.[637]

An arbitration clause allowing arbitrators to decide *ex aequo et bono* or as *amiables compositeurs* (which two forms of arbitrating are not here distinguished) does not necessarily mean a reference to the *lex mercatoria* (as is often suggested), although it may come close, see also the earlier discussion in section 1.4.15 above. The two types of arbitration may, however, be more similar than is often assumed.[638] On the one hand, international arbitrators state on the basis of law but under the modern *lex mercatoria* have considerable freedom in finding the applicable substantive (and procedural) law. On the other hand, arbitrators *ex aequo et bono* operating in the international commercial and financial legal order, are in principle not stating on the basis of any law although they are no less bound than ordinary international arbitrators by fundamental principles and international public order requirements obtaining in that order, although not necessarily by the other components of the *lex mercatoria*.

Indeed, the arbitration *ex aequo et bono* suggests beyond these fundamental principles greater discretion, although public policy rules of a national system that clearly affect the case may not be ignored either and still have to be given their due weight. It should also be considered whether property issues can be decided by them outside the mandatory framework of property law. At least there may not be third party effect of such proprietary or ranking findings. These are most important issues, particularly relevant and bound to

---

[637] The French Cour de Cassation allows it, see *Compania Valenciana de Cementos Portland SA v Primary Coal Inc* Cass Civ (1) 22 October 1991, 1991 Bull Civil I, no 275; and earlier *Pabalk Ticaret Ltd Sirketi (Turkey) v Norsolor SA (France)*, (1984) IX *Yearbook Commercial Arbitration* 109. So did the Austrian Supreme Court earlier and after much soul searching on 18 November 1982 in the ICC Case No 3131, (1984) IX *Yearbook Commercial Arbitration* 159; see also AJ van den Berg, *The New York Arbitration Convention of 1958* (Deventer, 1981) 29, who accepts the enforceability of a-national awards under the Convention provided the awards are themselves not detached from a national arbitration law. This is in itself increasingly contentious, see n 90 above.

The English courts, after having consistently rejected awards based on equity until 1978, see *Maritime Insurance Co Ltd v Assecuranz-Union Von 1865* [1935] 52 LILR 16 and *Orion v Belfort* [1962] 2 Lloyd's Rep 251 (QB Com Ct), changed their attitude thereafter: *Eagle Star v Yuval* [1978] 1 Lloyd's Rep 357. Application of general principles may now be acceptable in England: see *Deutsche Schachtbau- und Tiefbohrgesellschaft* [1987] 3 WLR 1023, in which the Court of Appeal under Sir John Donaldson held unanimously that *at least international arbitrators* could rely for the applicable law on internationally accepted principles, see also n 100 above, thus accepting not only general principle as a source of law but allowing *international* principles and customs to operate in that connection also.

In the US, US arbitrators have less trouble in applying the modern *lex mercatoria* in international commercial disputes and this is not normally challenged, see DW Rivkin, 'Enforceability of Arbitral Awards Based on Lex Mercatoria' (1993) 9 *Arbitration International* 67. It is also reflected in the UCC explicitly recognising the force of custom, see s 1-103 UCC.

[638] See JH Dalhuisen, 'International Arbitrators as Equity Judges' in PH Bekker, R Dolzer and M Waibel, *Making Transnational Law Work in the Global Economy, Essays in Honour of Detlev Vagts* (2010) 510.

come up in international finance disputes, see more particularly the discussion in Volume III, chapter 1, section 1.1.14ff.

In any event, it would appears incorrect to assume that arbitrators finding *ex aequo et bono* state entirely outside the law[639] but the difference with ordinary international commercial arbitrators is that they may not be strictly bound by the hierarchy of norms as they find them in the modern *lex mercatoria*.

In all cases, it is therefore still necessary to determine under applicable contract law what parties intended arbitrators to do, and what their role exactly becomes if they are allowed to decide *ex aequo et bono* or as *amiable compositeurs*, their powers under these facilities not being entirely settled.[640]

3.3.2 Objections to the *Lex Mercatoria* Approach

The objections to the transnational or *lex mercatoria* approach, also in the manner of a hierarchy of norms as here explained (in which domestic law remains the residual rule even if such law then starts to function as transnational law in the international legal order and must recognise in its application higher transnational rules), are both of a fundamental and practical nature. As we have seen, fundamentally it is sometimes still believed that no law can develop outside the framework of a state or that at least a state cannot provide a sanction for laws that are not essentially its own or are authorised by it. This is largely the nineteenth-century positivist framework and perspective. At the practical level, the new approach is usually considered to provide too little legal certainty, a reproach very similar to that affecting the newer attitudes to conflicts law as well, see section 2.2 above. Also here the objections are likely to come down to questions of temperament and practical experience.

It should never be forgotten that the dynamics of the law leading to its autonomous development at the transnational level are by no means new in their discovery, and remain recognised in public international law whilst the recognition of the independent status of the *lex mercatoria* in the manner here explained is particularly relevant where potentially applicable domestic laws result that are incomplete, old fashioned, fractured or wanting, and have nothing to contribute when seen from the perspective of the globalisation of international trade—which is now taking place on a scale never seen before.

Unavoidably, there is less certainty as a result, as always at the beginning of new developments. This issue has been discussed several times before. To repeat, the certainty that is here often praised as the ultimate objective and to which national laws are then supposed to contribute may be of a very low quality, especially in international transactions, prevent us moving forward and may in fact destroy everything. In any event, it must be weighed against the suitability of these laws, which are unlikely to be written or developed

---

[639] If it should be felt that this is different for *amiable compositeurs*, who (according to some) may be distinguished and are in this view under a greater duty than arbitrators *ex aequo et bono* to find a sensible solution in the manner they deem fit whilst working out some compromise, in doing so, even they are not able to ignore fundamental principle and duly applicable mandatory law.

[640] Art 28 of the 1985 UNCITRAL Model Law on International Commercial Arbitration allows the arbitrators to find *ex aequo et bono* or as *amiable compositeurs* (without definition of this concept), but only if the parties have expressly authorised them to do so. There is no reference to the *lex mercatoria* in this connection.

to co-ordinate and support new (now often internationalised) transactional (commercial and financial) patterns and needs, particularly amongst professionals, and against the ever greater uncertainty in the applicable conflict rules themselves.

The true issues were identified earlier as predictability and transactional finality which is a narrower but more important concept than that of certainty, see section 1.1.5 above. In a dynamic legal environment, legal certainty, also in the domestic variety, is always relative and can only be achieved when new ideas and notions sufficiently crystallise and are tested over time. This also means that we need time and more experience. Only then is it possible to consider to what extent the international community of states should more generally intervene through facilitating or correcting treaty law or codifications provided always that the international community feels that need or that public policy or order require it. The present urge to present all kinds of Principles, now even the DCFR in the EU, often as an academic exercise is as such undoubtedly of some interest, but vitally lacks industry backing and therefore credibility at least in the professional sphere. It still assumes that all law is imposed from above and does not require participatory frameworks and demonstrated need. This assumption is still behind the idea that these texts serve as a model for domestic or perhaps EU legislation. This applies in particular to the DCFR and its sales carve out in CESL.

There are also serious quality issues: all these efforts are in mentality consumer driven and do not wish to accept other sources of law, even in cross-border dealings. There is nothing forward-moving in them, quite unlike the drive behind the UCC in the US. The DCFR in particular is unaware of the operation and needs of a transnational commercial and financial legal order in international commerce and finance that operates besides statists legal orders including that of the EU itself. It was submitted that this is not the right approach and way forward, at least for professional dealings.

In the meantime, the development of new law in the transnational professional sphere is unavoidably haphazard. For the time being only a hierarchy of norms in the sense of the modern *lex mercatoria* can provide order, but, as was submitted, the residual role of domestic law means that the new *lex mercatoria* as here described is *not* incomplete and is a full legal system for those who seek this, although it is not systematic in the codification sense, finding structures (not system) having been identified earlier, in section 1.1.5 above, as the more important issue. The difference is that this domestic law is preceded by other transnationalised norms or sources of law, and residually functions as transnational law itself. Conceptually, that is all.

On the other hand, it should not be overlooked that much is settled law worldwide and not even now really contentious. Disputes are always exceptional; in commerce and finance, it is in the interest of all to minimise them. Yet, especially in the area of proprietary rights and security interests in movables and intangibles, there may be a need for more international action. The evolution through case law can be rapid, but may ultimately also result in confusion, as the development in the USA has shown, when notions of conditional sales developed under state law, giving rise to the later consolidation in the UCC, Article 9 (see Volume III, chapter 1, section 1.6.3). But by then, at least, the true needs had become apparent.

Particularly in contract, where most rules are in any event directory or default rules, the professional sphere used to risk taking is probably better able to deal with a degree of uncertainty associated with normal developments than with any certainty believed to result from inappropriate (domestic) rules. In proprietary law, local rules may even present a serious risk, such as those attempting the abolition of the *fiducia*, as in the new Dutch Civil Code (see Volume III, chapter 1, section 1.2.2), or the automatic conversion of conditional sales into security interests, as under Article 9 UCC in the USA in a serious and thoughtless challenge even to financial leases and repurchase agreements (see Volume III, chapter 1, section 1.6.2).

Similar arbitrary governmental interventions in domestic legal systems may create unexpected uncertainties and obstacles, only compounded transnationally by the application of inflexible conflicts rules for no obvious reason. Also in questions of finality of transactions and payments, national laws may be weak. This was also discussed in section 1.1.5 above. The concept of finality may in fact be considerably enhanced in transnational law, as it should be, where commercial needs may be taken into account more specifically and the old law of negotiable instruments (which was product of the old *lex mercatoria*) may serve as an example.

In the professional commercial sphere, modern legal thinking requires a greater degree of imagination and, at least in the private law aspects, a willingness to think more in terms of legal guidance and peer-group experiences than in terms of clear-cut academic rules and a corrective intellectual legal framework. Again, domestic public policies remain relevant and should be tested in a comity approach based on models as provided to some extent in Article 9 of the 2008 EU Regulation on the Law Applicable to Contractual Obligations (Rome I) and better in sections 402 and 403 of the Restatement (Third) Foreign Relations Laws in the US. That was discussed in sections 2.2.6ff above.

In such an environment, more precise legal concepts can and will develop within the modern *lex mercatoria*. As mentioned earlier, it may even include a more dynamic approach to movable property law in which party autonomy will have a role to play, subject to a better protection of the commercial flows, see section 1.1.4 above, and also a stronger concept of transaction and payment finality as mentioned.

Although the transnational law approach combined with a rejection of automatic conflicts rules is often believed novel since it was signaled particularly in France in the 1960s and 1970s by Professor Goldman (see section 3.1.3 above), it was in modern times in the Netherlands foreshadowed in the writings of Professor D Josephus Jitta (1854–1924),[641] the successor of Professor Asser as first Chairman of the Hague Conference. This approach has also become much more understandable through the critical attitude in the USA towards interstate conflict rules since the 1930s, see section 2.2.2 above, even if in the USA the modern developments in conflicts law are not analysed in terms of a newly emerging transnational law, but rather as interpretations of the own law (*lex fori*), although at least in interstate conflicts often fed by uniform overriding substantive notions of justice, whilst in the application of domestic public policy the trend is mostly liberal and also internationalist, see section 2.2.6 above.

3.3.3 Application and Enforcement of the *Lex Mercatoria*

Finally, not much more need be said on the application and actual enforcement of the *lex mercatoria*. This subject has been covered throughout. Its application will be a matter for

---

[641] DJ Jitta, *Internationaal Privaatrecht* (1916). It is an idea whose time has now come but had not in 1916, although it also found expression in France in the works of Pillet.

both the ordinary courts and international arbitrators. It is often assumed that the latter have broader powers in this connection, even if it is not quite clear why ordinary courts should assume a lesser role here. The rule of law, if properly understood, requires that they do the same and, it was submitted, the ensuing decisions or awards should be also similarly recognised elsewhere, either under treaty law or otherwise under the normal rules in each country, to be enforced therefore through the ordinary court system everywhere only upon a minimum of review that is geared to proper jurisdiction having been exercised to avoid obvious irregularities, and also to evaluating public policy and other confining public order requirements of the recognising country. Here again, the use by the courts of international minimum standards in weighing the different interests will help in the recognition and enforcement process, whilst the public policy bar to such recognition in each country could itself also be considered increasingly to be the subject of an international standard.

It was stated before, particularly in section 1.1.9 above, that state courts operating in international cases should be seen here as agents of the international commercial and financial legal order, therefore as international commercial courts in appropriate cases, no less than international commercial arbitration tribunals, and their decisions should then be seen as rendered in that order, subject to similar recognition if their enforcement in (other) state legal orders is necessary under the residual rules just mentioned. Standards set under the 1958 New York convention in respect of international arbitrations, under the 2002 EU Regulation on Jurisdiction and the Recognition and Enforcement of Judgments in Civil and Commercial Matters (Brussels I), under the Hague Convention of 2005 on Choice of Court Agreements, and under the (1998) Draft Hague Convention on Jurisdiction and the Recognition of Judgments, may provide here important guidance, even in situations where they do not directly apply. Indeed there is much to be said for international commercial law decisions in ordinary state courts in the above manner to be recognised elsewhere in the manner of the New York Convention.

It was further argued in section 1.1.9 above, that a *central highest international commercial court*[642] could usefully be set up to further (a) guide the development of the *lex mercatoria*; (b) develop the criteria for balancing governmental interests (or domestic public policies); (c) set the terms for or take over the challenges to international arbitrations at their seat, if still considered a useful facility; and (d) supervise the recognition and execution facilities under the New York Convention especially in respect of the public policy bar. This court could (e) even function as the normal appeal court in respect of decisions taken in the ordinary local (commercial) courts in the first instance. It would not otherwise be an appeals or review court, but would be limited to giving preliminary opinions on points of transnational law or public policy only when asked by commercial courts or arbitration tribunals or by the parties if in agreement on such a request to do so.

This may present a helpful and most significant development, not far-fetched at all, and at this moment probably more important than codifying or rather restating the new transnational law merchant itself, for which the necessary method is unlikely to be sufficiently agreed and a sufficient insight into what is needed is mostly still missing.

---

[642] See JH Dalhuisen, 'The Case for an International Commercial Court' in KP Berger et al (eds), *Festschrift Norbert Horn* (2006) 893.

Index

Introductory Note

References such as '178–9' indicate (not necessarily continuous) discussion of a topic across a range of pages. Wherever possible in the case of topics with many references, these have either been divided into sub-topics or only the most significant discussions of the topic are listed. Because the entire work is about 'transnational law' and 'commercial law', the use of these terms (and certain others which occur constantly throughout the book) as entry points has been minimised. Information will be found under the corresponding detailed topics.